Study Guide

Cornelius Rea

Study Guide

to accompany

DISCOVERING PSYCHOLOGY

SIXTH EDITION

Don H. Hockenbury
Sandra E. Hockenbury

With contributions by Loren L. Toussaint

WORTH PUBLISHERS

Study Guide
by Cornelius Rea
to accompany
Hockenbury and Hockenbury: **Discovering Psychology**, Sixth Edition

Printed in the United States of America

ISBN 10: 1-4641-0820-X
ISBN 13: 978-1-4641-0820-4

First printing

Worth Publishers
41 Madison Avenue
New York, NY 10010
www.worthpublishers.com

Contents

To the Student vii

CHAPTER 1
Introduction and Research Methods 1

CHAPTER 2
Neuroscience and Behavior 31

CHAPTER 3
Sensation and Perception 57

CHAPTER 4
Consciousness and Its Variations 87

CHAPTER 5
Learning 119

CHAPTER 6
Memory 145

CHAPTER 7
Thinking, Language, and Intelligence 169

CHAPTER 8
Motivation and Emotion 193

CHAPTER 9
Lifespan Development 227

CHAPTER 10
Personality 261

CHAPTER 11
Social Psychology 289

CHAPTER 12
Stress, Health, and Coping 315

CHAPTER 13
Psychological Disorders 341

CHAPTER 14
Therapies 369

APPENDIX A
Statistics: Understanding Data 401

APPENDIX B
Industrial/Organizational Psychology 413

To the Student

This Study Guide is designed to help you to study effectively and to learn the important concepts in *Discovering Psychology*, Sixth Edition, by Don and Sandra Hockenbury. Use this study guide in an active manner and as a complement to the textbook, not as a substitute for it. By actively interacting with the text material and this study guide, you will be able to master the chapter concepts in a straightforward and enjoyable manner. Our goal is to create independent, motivated students who enjoy learning for its own sake, who can think critically, and who have a deep conceptual understanding of the information presented in the text.

Your first course in psychology is both exciting and challenging. Besides the volume of new information you will be asked to learn, you are faced with learning new terminology, novel concepts, unfamiliar theories, and, most important, the scientific way of thinking. "How to Use This Guide" explains how best to use the study guide to learn all the new material. "Study Tips" (p. ix) provides some practical suggestions for improving your ability to learn, understand, and remember.

HOW TO USE THIS GUIDE

Scanning

Scanning is a useful strategy that can facilitate learning. When you scan a chapter, you get a better idea of what lies ahead. So survey the text chapter first. Spend some time looking at the graphics, and examine the special features, boxed inserts, and concept reviews; note the parts that look interesting to you. Pay attention to the diagrams, graphs, photographs, cartoons, and tables. This preview will give you a clearer impression of what is going to be covered in the chapter. Don't worry about the details at this point; just try to get the big picture.

Next read the chapter overview (Chapter . . . At a Glance) in the study guide. This will give you a general, but more detailed, summary of what you are about to encounter in the chapter. This type of previewing activity will help you to develop a conceptual framework (or cognitive map) that will allow you to more readily understand the details of what you are about to read and will make learning the material easier. For example, imagine trying to put together a large jigsaw puzzle without knowing what the finished picture looked like. Do you think it would be easier if you could see the finished picture? Of course it would! Likewise, when you scan the chapter and read the preview, you will have some idea of the big picture and of how the various pieces of the chapter fit together.

Advance Organizers and Preview Questions

The text authors have provided advance organizers at the beginning of each major section of a chapter in the form of key questions/key themes. These will help you to start thinking about the material and will give you an overview of what lies ahead. The preview questions at the beginning of each main section in the study guide are derived from these advance organizers. Read these preview questions before you read each section of the text chapter and before you start the exercises in the study guide. Both the advance organizers and the preview questions are directly linked to the concept checks, true/false tests, matching exercises, progress tests, and graphic organizers in the study guide. Successful completion of these activities will prepare you for tests, quizzes, exams, and other evaluation procedures.

Structured Note Taking

Good note taking is very important to learning, so we encourage you to take notes. The study guide structures your note taking by prompting you to write definitions, to paraphrase information, and to integrate concepts. Simply highlighting sentences in the textbook is not sufficient. Highlighting does not involve active cognitive processing of the information, whereas writing, especially using your own words, does.

Graphic Organizers

An important aid to better understanding text material is the use of visualization. Completing the graphs, charts, and flow diagrams will provide a visual synopsis that will help you understand and remember the material. So be sure to complete all these exercises, and practice making up your own graphic organizers.

Corrective Feedback: Concept Checks, Matching Exercises, True/False Tests, and Progress Tests

At the end of each major section in the study guide are learning checks in the form of conceptual questions, matching exercises, and true/false tests. These exercises provide you with feedback as you progress through the chapter. Be sure to complete each of these before going on to the next section. Three progress tests containing multiple-choice questions conclude each chapter. These are designed to help you assess your mastery of the material. If you don't know the answers to these questions, go back and study the parts of the text that you didn't understand.

If your instructor gives a quiz or test after each chapter, complete all three progress tests before the exam. Testing, and the corrective feedback it provides, will give you a more realistic idea of how well prepared you actually are and thus reduces the tendency for "overconfidence."

If your exam covers a number of chapters, it is a good idea to complete progress tests 1 and 2 after you have studied each chapter, then create a "comprehensive pretest" from progress test 3 in all the relevant chapters. Taking this larger test will give you a better idea of what the exam is going to be like. Also, be sure to ask your instructor if material other than that covered in the textbook (e.g., material from lectures, videos, lab demonstrations, and tutorials) will be on the exam.

One additional point: It is important not to confuse your recognition ability with your ability to recall and write about a topic. Multiple-choice questions tap your ability to recognize the correct answer, but do not assess your ability to express your ideas logically and coherently. You need to develop both types of skills.

Something to Think About

Each study guide chapter concludes with a special feature called "Something to Think About," which contains thought-provoking questions about the material. We encourage you to think actively about what you have read in the chapter. Discuss these topics with friends and family members. This will help you remember the concepts and make learning more enjoyable.

You can also use the ideas from these sections as a guide for writing short essays or papers, or for preparing for a presentation.

Answers The answers to all the questions are included at the end of each chapter. Check your answers as you work your way through the material: Getting immediate corrective feedback facilitates the learning process.

STUDY TIPS

What are the five or ten most effective ways to improve your ability to learn, comprehend, and remember the material in this course? The truth is that there is probably no single list of techniques, no matter who develops it, that will work for all learners all the time. Everyone has a different way or style of learning; becoming familiar with your own unique learning style is the first step in becoming a successful student. However, we can all improve our ability to learn and to remember what we have learned. On that optimistic note, here are some general strategies that can be of value and can benefit almost anyone who makes the effort to use them. So, when faced with the challenge of mastering a large amount of new material try some, or all, of the following (For additional information about how your memory works and how to improve it, look ahead to text Chapter 6; in particular, read the Application "Superpower Memory in Minutes per Day!"

Use Distributed Practice You know that you should not cram. Cramming, or what psychologists called massed practice, is not good for long-term retention of material. Spacing out your studying, or distributed practice, on the other hand, enhances your ability to remember. This is one of the most well-established principles in psychology—the spacing effect. Instead of studying for five straight hours at one time, you would be much better off studying one hour a day every day for five days. This technique also works at shorter intervals. For example, if you have to memorize a formula, you will probably repeat it over and over (say, ten times) until you feel confident you have it memorized. This, of course, is massed practice, and the sense of confidence that typically accompanies it is often misleading. A better way to maximize the benefits of those ten rehearsals is to space them over time, allowing a longer interval after each rehearsal than the one before.

Reduce Interference One reason we tend to forget new information is that other information (either previously learned or learned later) can interfere with the material we are trying to master. So, if you are studying for a number of courses at the same time, try to study subjects that are different from each other. The more similar they are, the greater the interference. Another source of interference comes from social activities, such as watching TV or interacting with friends. When you engage in these activities after studying, you increase the risk of interference. In addition, playing loud music, having the TV on, or listening to other people's conversations while you are studying can cause distraction and interfere with learning. The best advice? Go to sleep after studying. A good sleep is the best way to cut down on interference and it helps consolidate memories. The worst thing to do? Stay up all night cramming for an exam that is being given the next day.

Try Overlearning Overlearning is another very effective, and relatively simple, technique for preventing forgetting. When you feel you have mastered the material in a chapter, and you have just answered all the progress test questions correctly, you usually feel relieved and put away the books. It is at this point, however, that overlearning is useful. If you had spent, say, an hour and a half getting to this level, what you need to do now is spend another 10 to 15 minutes reviewing the material one more time.

These few extra minutes of studying are the most beneficial minutes you can spend in terms of consolidating your memory and preventing the forgetting of material you have just learned. Hermann Ebbinghaus showed, over a hundred years ago, that most of the information is lost very soon after it is learned. He was the first to demonstrate the powerful effect of overlearning as a way of dealing with this problem.

Get Corrective Feedback

If you studied hard and felt you really knew the material, it is a bit of a shock to find that you did poorly on the test. What could have happened? One possibility is that you only thought you knew the material and you were suffering from "the overconfidence effect." A simple way of preventing this is to get corrective feedback on what you know before taking the exam. For example, using the true/false tests and the matching tests, completing the graphic organizers, and, of course, taking the progress tests will give you the feedback you need.

Be aware, however, that this is not necessarily a perfect gauge of how you will do on the real exam. When you are testing yourself, you tend to be in a much more relaxed state: You have just studied the material and you are in no particular rush. If you make a mistake, it is no big deal; you can simply look up the answers at the end of the chapter (this is not something that you can do in the exam!). These factors often lead students to the false conclusion that the questions on the real exam were much harder than the ones in the progress tests, sample exams, and so forth. Try to make your self-testing as real as possible (get a little anxious); that way you will benefit most from corrective feedback.

Use Mnemonics

Use of memory aids, called mnemonics, can help in memorizing new material and in preventing forgetting. Visual imagery, in particular, is very effective with some material. Try to vividly imagine what it is you are attempting to memorize. A picture is worth a thousand words and is much more memorable. For other material, try making up a story that links elements together. Create acronyms for lists of terms or complex concept names, for example (it is easier to remember SCUBA than self-contained underwater breathing apparatus).

Develop Good Study Habits

Most top students get good grades because of effective study habits (not sheer brilliance). Evaluate your current study habits. Manage your time effectively. Remember, we are usually poor judges about how long things take to do (late papers are a typical example that is the result of our poor judgment). So, after you have made your plans, allow yourself some extra time.

Make studying a priority and firmly commit to doing well in school. Don't let other people interfere with your goal of mastering the material and getting good grades. Study by yourself (too much socializing takes place in study groups). Reward yourself with social activities, if that's what is important to you, AFTER you have successfully completed your study and have achieved an A+ on the progress tests. If you like music, play soft instrumental music. Take a short break after an hour or so of studying—walk around for a few minutes. Do some exercise. Don't study when you are sleep deprived, very tired, or stressed out. If you are getting nowhere and can't concentrate on the material, do something else for a while (a breath of fresh air, a brief nap, a little walk, a chat with a friend, a little meditation or exercise, can all be helpful).

Try Exercise Exercising before you study will help relieve stress and will induce a more relaxed state. This is because exercise causes the brain to release pain-killing chemicals called endorphins (you have your own little drug-producing factory). It is also a good idea to exercise before a major exam for the same reasons. If aerobic exercise is not your thing (if it makes you tired and unable to concentrate), try something less strenuous, like walking. Anxiety interferes with performance, so anything you can do to effectively control and reduce your anxiety will help. Have fun, good luck, and enjoy your introductory psychology course.

Comments are welcome at StudyGuide@DiscoveringPsychology.com.

Study Guide

CHAPTER 1

Introduction and Research Methods

PREVIEW

Reading the section below first will give you a general sense of the chapter's contents and an initial introduction to some of the major concepts and terms. This will prime you for what you are about to read and help you to develop a "cognitive map" that will guide your study of the material in this chapter. Likewise, reading the **preview questions** at the beginning of each major section will improve your ability to understand, learn, and retain the information.

CHAPTER 1 . . . AT A GLANCE

Chapter 1 first defines psychology, then gives a brief history of the people and events that influenced its development. Beginning with the contributions of philosophy and physiology, the chapter discusses the two early schools, structuralism and functionalism, as well as psychoanalysis, behaviorism, and humanistic psychology; the emergence of the major perspectives in contemporary psychology; and the major specialty areas.

The four goals of psychology are used to introduce the scientific method. The descriptive research methods are outlined, and some advantages are discussed. Important issues such as the need for representative sampling and random selection are raised. The section concludes with a discussion of the uses and limitations of correlational studies. The concepts of correlation, the correlation coefficient, and negative and positive correlations are described and explained.

The experimental method is explained in detail, using specific studies to illustrate important concepts such as dependent and independent variables, experimental and control groups, extraneous variables, the placebo effect, random assignment, the double-blind technique, demand characteristics, practice effects, and main effects. Also presented are limitations of the experiment and variations in experimental design, as well as a discussion of the increasing use of brain imaging techniques (PET, MRI, and fMRI) and their limitations.

The chapter concludes with a discussion of the ethical guidelines that regulate psychological research and the role played by the American Psychological Association. Enhancing Well-Being with Psychology provides important guidelines for evaluating information about psychology and psychological topics reported in the mass media.

Introduction: The Origins of Psychology

Preview Questions

Consider the following questions as you study this section of the chapter.

- How is *psychology* defined today?
- Which two disciplines influenced the emergence of psychology as a science?
- Who established psychology as a distinct scientific discipline?
- What were the first two schools of psychology called, who is associated with their founding, and how do they differ?
- Which four students were influenced by William James, and what were their accomplishments?
- Who founded psychoanalysis, and what was its main focus?
- What are the goals of behaviorism, and who were the three main proponents of this perspective?
- What is the emphasis of humanistic psychology, and what are the names of its two major advocates?

*Read the section "Introduction: The Origins of Psychology" and **write** your answers to the following:*

1. *Psychology* is defined as ____________________
____
2. The two disciplines that influenced the emergence of psychology were____________________
____
3. The person who established psychology as a distinct scientific discipline was ____________
____
4. The first two schools of psychology were
____________________,
and the people associated with their beginnings were ____________________
5. Structuralism emphasized ____________
____
____
Functionalism stressed the importance of
____
____
6. Four students (and their accomplishments) who were influenced by William James were
____
____
____
____
7. Psychoanalysis was founded by
____________________. This theory focused on ____________________
____
____
8. Behaviorism focused on ____________
____
____
and rejected ____________________
____
____
9. The main proponents of behaviorism were
____
10. Humanistic psychology emphasized __________
____
Its two major advocates were
____

After you have carefully studied the preceding section, complete the following exercises.

Concept Check 1

Read the following and write the correct term in the space provided.

1. A psychologist who stresses the importance of how behavior enables organisms to adapt to their environment would be classified as belonging to the ____________ school of psychology.
2. Dr. Levine adheres to the theory that emphasizes the role of unconscious conflicts in determining behavior and personality. This viewpoint is most consistent with the ____________ school of psychology.

3. Environmental influences and overt measurable behavior are to ______________ as conscious experience, psychological growth, and self-direction are to ______________________ .
4. While researching a paper on the history of psychology, John discovered that René Descartes, a seventeenth-century philosopher, promoted the idea that the mind and body are separate entities that interact to produce sensations, emotions, and other conscious experiences. Descartes's view is called ______________ ______________________ .
5. Dr. Brunac's research focuses on the question of the degree to which heredity and environment influence the development of human abilities such as intelligence and personality characteristics. Dr. Brunac is interested in the ______________________ issue.
6. Alvira believes that our most complex conscious experiences can be broken down into elemental structures, or basic components, of sensations and feelings through the research method of introspection. Alvira's view is most consistent with the school of thought in psychology called ______________________ .

Review of Terms, Concepts, and Names 1

Use the terms in this list to complete the Matching Exercise, then to help you answer the True/False items correctly.

psychology
interactive dualism
nature–nurture issue (heredity versus environment)
physiology
Wilhelm Wundt
Edward B. Titchener
structuralism
introspection
stimulus
William James
Charles Darwin
functionalism
G. Stanley Hall
Mary Whiton Calkins
Margaret Floy Washburn
Francis C. Sumner
Sigmund Freud
psychoanalysis
behaviorism
overt behavior
Ivan Pavlov
John B. Watson
learning
B. F. Skinner
humanistic psychology
Carl Rogers
Abraham Maslow

Matching Exercise

Match the appropriate term/name with its definition or description.

1. ______________ American psychologist who established the first psychology research laboratory in the United States and founded the American Psychological Association.
2. ______________ Looking inward in an attempt to reconstruct feelings and sensations experienced immediately after viewing a stimulus object.
3. ______________ School of psychology and theoretical viewpoint that emphasizes each person's unique potential for psychological growth and self-direction.
4. ______________ American psychologist who founded the school of behaviorism, emphasizing the study of observable behavior and rejecting the study of mental processes.
5. ______________ Early school of psychology that emphasized studying the purpose, or function, of behavior and mental experiences.
6. ______________ The scientific study of behavior and mental processes.
7. ______________ The idea that the mind and body are separate entities that interact to produce sensations, emotions, and other conscious experiences.
8. ______________ German physiologist who established psychology as a distinct scientific discipline and opened the first psychology research laboratory in 1879.
9. ______________ British-born American psychologist who founded structuralism, the first school of psychology.
10. ______________ School of psychology and theoretical viewpoint that emphasizes the study of observable behaviors, especially as they pertain to the process of learning.
11. ______________ American psychologist who was largely responsible for founding the school of humanistic psychology.
12. ______________ Anything perceptible to the senses, such as a sight, sound, smell, touch, or taste.
13. ______________ The acquisition and modification of behavior in response to environmental influences.
14. ______________ American psychologist who was the first African American to receive a doctorate in psychology in the United States.

True/False Test

Indicate whether each statement is true or false by placing T or F in the blank space next to each item.

1. ____ Margaret Floy Washburn was the American psychologist who conducted research on memory, personality, and dreams and was the first woman president of the American Psychological Association.
2. ____ Structuralism was an early school of psychology that emphasized studying the most basic components, or structures, of conscious experience.
3. ____ Physiology is a branch of biology that studies the functions and parts of living organisms, including human beings.
4. ____ William James was an American philosopher and psychologist who was instrumental in establishing psychology in the United States and established the psychological school called functionalism.
5. ____ The issue of heredity versus environment is the same as the nature–nurture issue and refers to the debate over which is more important, the inborn characteristics of the individual or the impact of the environment.
6. ____ Mary Whiton Calkins was an American psychologist who published research on mental processes in animals and was the first woman in the United States to earn a doctorate in psychology.
7. ____ Ivan Pavlov was an Austrian physician whose work focused on the unconscious causes of behavior and personality formation and who founded psychoanalysis.
8. ____ B. F. Skinner was the American psychologist and leading proponent of behaviorism who emphasized studying outwardly observable behaviors that could be measured and verified.
9. ____ Abraham Maslow was an American humanistic psychologist who developed a theory of motivation that emphasized psychological growth.
10. ____ Psychoanalysis is a personality theory and form of psychotherapy that emphasizes the role of unconscious factors in personality and behavior.
11. ____ Sigmund Freud was a Russian physiologist whose pioneering research on learning contributed to the development of behaviorism and who believed he had discovered the mechanism by which all behaviors were learned.
12. ____ Observable behavior that can be objectively measured and verified is called overt behavior.
13. ____ Charles Darwin was the English naturalist and scientist whose theory of evolution through natural selection was first published in *On the Origin of Species* in 1859.

Check your answers and review any areas of weakness before going on to the next section.

Contemporary Psychology

Preview Questions

Consider the following questions as you study this section of the chapter.

- What are the eight major perspectives in contemporary psychology, and how do they differ?
- What are sixteen important specialty areas in contemporary psychology?
- How do clinical psychologists and psychiatrists differ?

Read the section "Contemporary Psychology" and ***write*** *your answers to the following:*

1. The eight major perspectives in psychology are ____

____

____

2. The sixteen important specialty areas in contemporary psychology are ________________________

____

____

____

____

3. The difference between a clinical psychologist and a psychiatrist is ________________________

____

____

____

____

After you have carefully studied the preceding section, complete the following exercises.

Concept Check 2

Which specialty area is represented by each of the following?

1. Dr. Matthews studies the relationship between psychological processes and the body's physical systems and has a particular interest in the structure and activity of the intact brain. She would most likely be classified as a(n) ________________ psychologist.
2. Michele wants to study physical, social, and psychological changes that occur over the lifespan when she attends graduate school. Michele is planning to be a(n) ________________ psychologist.
3. Dr. Bowman studies the causes, treatment, and prevention of different types of behavioral and emotional disorders. Dr. Bowman is most likely a(n) ________________ psychologist.
4. Dr. Ying explores how individuals are affected by their social environments, how people think about and influence others, and the factors that influence conformity and obedience. Dr. Ying is a(n) ________________ psychologist.
5. Dr. Steinberg examines individual differences and the characteristics that make each person unique. He is most likely a(n) ________________ psychologist.
6. Ingrid is interested in investigating mental processes such as reasoning, thinking, memory, perception, and problem solving. Ingrid is probably planning a career as a(n) ________________ psychologist.
7. Dr. Whinney develops instructional methods and materials used to train people in both educational and work settings; she also studies how people of all ages learn. She is a(n) ________________ psychologist.
8. Dr. Barton is concerned with stress and coping, the relationship between psychological factors and physical health, and ways of promoting health-enhancing behaviors. Dr. Barton is probably a(n) ________________ psychologist.
9. Pitor, who just completed his Ph.D., applied for a job concerned with the relationship between people and work, including the study of job satisfaction, worker productivity, personnel selection and training, leadership, and group behavior within organizations. Pitor has applied for a job as a(n) ________________ psychologist.
10. Dr. Manhas has a medical degree plus years of specialized training in the treatment of mental disorders. He typically prescribes medication for his patients' psychological problems. Dr. Manhas is a ________________ .
11. Prosecutors used a psychologist who specializes in applying psychological principles and techniques to legal issues to determine the mental competency of the accused to stand trial. This specialist is most likely a ________________ psychologist.
12. To improve the swim team's performance the coach sought the advice of Dr. Cox, who uses psychological theory and knowledge to enhance athletic motivation, performance, and consistency. Dr. Cox is a ________________ psychologist.
13. While recovering from a stroke, Maurice was treated by a psychologist who applies psychological knowledge to help people with chronic and disabling health conditions adapt to their situation and attain optimal psychological, interpersonal, and physical functioning, a specialty area called ________________ psychology.
14. Dr. Telleman's interests are sensory and perceptual processes, principles of learning, emotion and motivation, and most of her time is spent conducting and supervising basic research projects. Her specialty area is ________________ psychology.

Graphic Organizer 1

The statements in the table below represent some of the major perspectives and specialty areas in contemporary psychology. Which perspective is reflected by each statement, and which specialty area is being described? Write your answers in the spaces provided.

Statement	Perspective	Specialty
1. I'm interested in how different parenting styles and techniques influence each child's individual potential for growth and self-determination.		
2. I study the relationship between people and work and, more specifically, how to increase productivity. I believe that by changing environmental factors, increasing the use of rewards and praise for correct behavior, and providing corrective feedback, workers' overt behavior can be changed.		
3. I study how people of all ages learn, and I develop instructional methods and materials to help the learning process. In particular, I stress the roles played by thinking, problem solving, memory, and mental imagery.		
4. Technological advances such as PET scans, MRIs, and functional MRIs have allowed me and my colleagues to study the relationship between psychological processes and the body's physical systems, in particular, the structure and activity of the brain. I am particularly interested in applying this knowledge to enhance athletic motivation and performance.		
5. I often travel to different countries to research people's attitudes and group relations. My research tends to show that many behavioral patterns—for instance, the amount of personal space people require to feel comfortable—vary from one country to another.		
6. I believe that unconscious conflicts, early childhood experiences, and repressed sexual and aggressive feelings make us who we are, and I use this point of view in my work on individual differences and in trying to determine which characteristics make each of us unique.		
7. I focus on the relationship between psychological factors and health, in particular on how people cope with stress in their lives. It is not what happens to us that is important; rather, how we perceive and think about potentially stressful events determines our well-being.		
8. When I went to graduate school, I conducted research in a relatively new area of psychology, which focuses on the conditions and processes that contribute to optimal functioning of people, groups, and institutions. My main task is to help people with disabling health conditions adapt to their situation and obtain optimal psychological, interpersonal, and physical functioning.		
9. Psychological processes that have helped individuals adapt to their environment have also helped them to survive, reproduce, and pass those abilities on to their offspring. I adopt this point of view in my investigations of interpersonal attraction, prejudice, and aggression.		

Graphic Organizer 2

Origins of Psychology, First Schools, and Key Figures

Flow diagram exercise: To help you develop the technique of creating your own graphic organizers, we encourage you to try making a flow diagram/timeline, using boxes, that contains the following information. Using a separate sheet of paper, generate your own graphic organizer, then compare it with the sample in the answer section. To help you in this early stage of your study, we've filled in portions of the first two boxes.

Philosophy (list key figures)	Physiology (list key figures)

1. Two areas that influenced the beginnings of psychology and the key figures in each.
2. The founder of psychology and the year the first psychology research laboratory was established.
3. First school in psychology and key figure.
4. First American school in psychology and key figures.
5. Two approaches (and key figures in each) that challenged the first two schools in psychology.
6. New school that emerged in the 1950s and key figures.

Review of Terms, Concepts, and Names 2

Use the terms in this list to complete the Matching Exercise, then to help you answer the True/False items correctly.

perspective
specialty area
biological perspective (biological psychology)
neuroscience
psychodynamic perspective
behavioral perspective
humanistic perspective
positive psychology perspective (positive psychology)
cognitive perspective (cognitive psychology)
cross-cultural perspective (cross-cultural psychology)
social loafing
evolutionary perspective (evolutionary psychology)
natural selection
culture
ethnocentrism
individualistic cultures
collectivistic cultures
clinical psychology (clinical psychologist)
counseling psychology
educational psychology
experimental psychology
developmental psychology
forensic psychology
health psychology
industrial/organizational psychology
personality psychology
rehabilitation psychology
social psychology
sports psychology
school psychology
military psychology
psychiatry and psychiatrist

Matching Exercise

Match the appropriate term/name with its definition or description.

1. ________________ Specialty area in psychology that involves on-site counseling for combat stress, helps returning soldiers and their families deal with the aftereffects of combat stress, deals with injuries, especially traumatic brain injuries, and helps select and train army personnel for particular roles or assignments.
2. ________________ Specialty area that studies the physical, social, and psychological changes that occur at different ages and stages of the lifespan, from conception to old age.
3. ________________ Specialty area in psychology that studies how people of all ages learn and is concerned with developing instructional methods and material used to train people.
4. ________________ Specialty area that investigates such basic psychological topics as sensory and perceptual processes, learning, emotion, and motivation.
5. ________________ Point of view or general framework that reflects a psychologist's emphasis in investigating psychological topics.
6. ________________ Specific area in psychology in which psychologists are trained and in which they work or practice.
7. ________________ Attitudes, values, beliefs, and behaviors shared by a group of people and communicated from one generation to another.
8. ________________ Perspective and specialty area that investigates mental processes, including reasoning, thinking, problem solving, language, perception, mental imagery, and memory.
9. ________________ Specialty area in psychology that examines individual differences and the characteristics that make each person unique, including how those characteristics originated and developed.

10. ________________ Perspective in psychology that studies how behavior is acquired or modified by environmental consequences and whose focus is on observable behavior and the fundamental laws of learning.

11. ________________ The tendency to use your own culture as the standard for judging other cultures.

12. ________________ Perspective and specialty area in psychology that studies the relationship between psychological processes and the body's physical systems, including the brain and the rest of the nervous system, the endocrine system, the immune system, and genetics.

13. ________________ Perspective and branch of psychology that studies the effects of culture on behavior and mental processes.

14. ________________ The study of the nervous system, especially the brain.

15. ________________ Principle that organisms that inherit characteristics that increase their chances of survival in their particular habitat are more likely to survive, reproduce, and pass on their characteristics to their offspring.

16. ________________ Specialty area in psychology that provides a variety of psychological services, including counseling and assessing students and consulting with parents and school staff.

True/False Test

Indicate whether each statement is true or false by placing T or F in the blank space next to each item.

1. ____ Psychiatrists work in a medical specialty area (psychiatry) that focuses on the diagnosis, treatment, causes, and prevention of mental and behavioral disorders, and can prescribe medications and other biomedical therapies.

2. ____ The evolutionary perspective (evolutionary psychology) uses the principles of evolution, including natural selection, to explain psychological processes and phenomena.

3. ____ Counseling psychology is concerned with the relationship between people and work, and it includes the study of job satisfaction, worker productivity, leadership, personnel selection and training, and group behavior within organizations.

4. ____ Forensic psychology applies psychological principles and techniques to legal issues, such as the assessment and treatment of offenders, mental competency to stand trial, child custody, jury selection, and eyewitness testimony.

5. ____ The specialty area that applies psychological knowledge to helping people with chronic and disabling health conditions adapt to their situation and attain optimal psychological, interpersonal, and physical functioning is called health psychology

6. ____ Psychologists who explore how people are affected by their social environments and what factors influence conformity, obedience, persuasion, interpersonal attraction, helping behavior, aggression, prejudice, social beliefs, and other related phenomena work in a specialty area called social psychology.

7. ____ Individualistic cultures emphasize the needs and goals of the group over the needs and goals of the individual.

8. ____ Rehabilitation psychology focuses on the role of psychological factors in the development, prevention, and treatment of illness and includes such areas as stress and coping, the relationship between psychological factors and physical health, and ways of promoting health-enhancing behaviors.

9. ____ Industrial/organizational psychology helps people of all ages adjust, adapt, and cope with personal and interpersonal problems in such diverse areas as relationships, work, education, marriage, child rearing, and aging.

10. ____ Psychologists who take the humanistic perspective emphasize the importance of unconscious influences, early life experiences, and interpersonal relationships in explaining the underlying dynamics of behavior or treating people with psychological problems.

11. ____ Collectivistic cultures emphasize the needs and goals of the individual over the needs and goals of the group.

12. ____ The psychodynamic perspective focuses on the motivation of people to grow psychologically, the influence of interpersonal relationships on a person's self-concept, and the importance of choice and self-direction in striving to reach one's potential.

13. ____ Sports psychology uses psychological theory and knowledge to enhance athletic motivation, performance, and consistency.

14. ____ The study of positive emotions and psychological states, positive individual traits, and the social institutions that foster positive qualities in individuals and communities is called positive psychology (the positive psychology perspective).

15. ___ Social loafing refers to a psychological finding that people in American and European cultures exert more effort on a task when working alone than when working as part of a group.

16. ___ Clinical psychologists work in a specialty area of psychology that studies the causes, diagnosis, treatment, and prevention of different types of behavioral and emotional disorders (clinical psychology), and have extensive training in evaluating and diagnosing psychological disorders, psychotherapy techniques, and psychological testing.

Check your answers and review any areas of weakness before going on to the next section.

The Scientific Method

Preview Questions

Consider the following questions as you study this section of the chapter.

- What are the four basic goals of psychology?
- What is the scientific method?
- What assumptions and attitudes guide psychologists?
- What is meant by empirical evidence, and what are the four basic steps of the scientific method?
- What role does statistics play in psychological research, what is meant by statistical significance, and what is a meta-analysis?
- What are theories, how do they differ from hypotheses, and what principle do they reflect?

Read the section "The Scientific Method" and ***write*** *your answers to the following:*

1. The four basic goals of psychology are to ______
2. The scientific method refers to ______
3. Psychologists are guided by the basic assumptions that ______
4. Psychologists share a set of attitudes, including ______
5. Empirical evidence refers to ______

   The four basic steps of the scientific method are ______
6. The role of statistics in psychological research is to ______

   A statistically significant result ______

   A meta-analysis is ______
7. A theory is ______

   A hypothesis is ______

   It is different from a theory in that ______
8. Theories can evolve and change because they reflect the ______

After you have carefully studied the preceding section, complete the following exercises.

Concept Check 3

Read the following and write the correct term in the space provided.

1. Dr. Marlow is interested in drinking-and-driving behavior and wants to know the frequency with which people will drive after receiving feedback from a Breathalyzer test. In one condition, she sets up her equipment in a bar and administers the test to patrons who are leaving and

planning to drive and then observes whether feedback on their level of intoxication influences their decision to drive. Dr. Marlow is using ________________ research.

2. In the previous example, Dr. Marlow makes this prediction: The majority of people who are told that they are over the legal limit will still drive; the higher the level on the Breathalyzer test, the more likely it is that they will drive. Dr. Marlow has formulated a ________________ .
3. After collecting data over many weeks, Dr. Marlow performs calculations and mathematical tests to see if her prediction was correct. Dr. Marlow is using ________________ to analyze her data.
4. Dr. Marlow next writes a report describing the background of this research and details her research design, data collection methods, results, analyses, and conclusions. She submits her report to a respected psychology journal for peer review and publication. She is following step __________ of producing scientific evidence by ________________ .
5. To examine the overall trends in this particular area of research, Dr. Marlow pools the results of a number of similar studies with her own data and does a single analysis of the collective data. She has used a statistical technique called ________________ .

Review of Terms and Concepts 3

Use the terms in this list to complete the Matching Exercise, then to help you answer the True/False items correctly.

scientific method	statistics
empirical evidence	statistically significant
hypothesis	practical significance
critical thinking	meta-analysis
variable	replicate
operational definition	theory (model)
descriptive methods	pseudoscience
experimental method	

Matching Exercise

Match the appropriate term/name with its definition or description.

1. ________________ Statistical technique that involves combining and analyzing the results of many research studies on a specific topic in order to identify overall trends.
2. ________________ To repeat or duplicate a scientific study in order to increase confidence in the validity of the original findings.
3. ________________ A set of assumptions, attitudes, and procedures that guide researchers in creating questions to investigate, in generating evidence, and in drawing conclusions.
4. ________________ Tentative statement about the relationship between two or more variables, often stated as a testable prediction or question.
5. ________________ Precise description of how the variables in a study will be manipulated or measured.
6. ________________ Method of investigation used to demonstrate cause-and-effect relationships by purposely manipulating a factor thought to produce change in a second factor.
7. ________________ Branch of mathematics used by researchers to organize, analyze, and interpret data.
8. ________________ Any factor that can vary, or change, in ways that can be observed, measured, and verified.

True/False Test

Indicate whether each statement is true or false by placing T or F in the blank space next to each item.

1. ____ A statistically significant finding is a mathematical indication that research results are likely to have occurred by chance.
2. ____ Empirical evidence is verifiable evidence based upon objective observation, measurement, and/or experimentation.
3. ____ A theory (or model) is a tentative explanation that tries to integrate and account for the relationships of various findings and observations.
4. ____ Descriptive methods are research strategies for observing and describing behavior and include naturalistic observation, surveys, case studies, and correlational studies.

5. ____ A pseudoscience is a fake or false science that makes claims based on little or no scientific evidence.
6. ____ Critical thinking is the active process of minimizing preconceptions and biases while evaluating evidence, determining what conclusions can reasonably be drawn from the evidence, and considering alternative explanations for research findings or other phenomena.
7. ____ Results of a study may be statistically significant but not have any *practical significance* or importance.

Check your answers and review any areas of weakness before going on to the next section.

Descriptive Research Methods

Preview Questions

Consider the following questions as you study this section of the chapter.

- What are descriptive research methods?
- How is naturalistic observation typically conducted?
- What are case studies, when are they normally used, and what is case-based research?
- What is a survey, and how do researchers ensure that their sample closely parallels the larger group on relevant characteristics?
- What is random selection, and why is it important for obtaining accurate results?
- What does a correlational study involve, and what are its limitations?
- What is the correlation coefficient, and how does a negative correlation differ from a positive correlation?

*Read the section "Descriptive Research Methods" and **write** your answers to the following:*

1. Descriptive research methods are ____________

2. Naturalistic observation involves the ____________

3. A case study is ____________

Case studies are typically used to ____________

In case-based research, information ____________

4. In a survey, the researcher ____________

5. Researchers ensure that their sample closely parallels the population of interest by ____________

6. Random selection refers to ____________

It is important because ____________

7. Correlational studies show ____________

They are limited because ____________

8. The correlation coefficient is ____________

The correlation coefficient has two parts:

____

____

____

9. A positive correlation is one in which ________

____

A negative correlation is one in which________

____

After you have carefully studied the preceding section, complete the following exercises.

Concept Check 4

Read the following and write the correct term in the space provided.

1. If a researcher found a correlation coefficient of –0.85 between amount of exercise and weight, this would indicate that the ______________ (more/less) people exercise, the ______________ (more/less) they weigh.
2. If an organization wants to find out about the spending habits of high-income people, they would be advised to conduct a ______________, using a representative ______________ that would be ______________ selected from this population.
3. Dr. Klatz is interested in whether there is a difference in the way men and women carry objects such as textbooks, bags, and other large items, so she sets up a hidden camera on the main quad of a large university and videotapes people at various times throughout the day. Dr. Klatz is using ______________________________.
4. A psychologist discovers that the more control people feel they have over what happens in their work environments, the more productive they are. The psychologist has discovered a ______________ correlation between perceived control and productivity.
5. A psychologist who is interested in finding out about the lives and experiences of people who claim to have been abducted by aliens and who wants to know how these people are viewed by their families, friends, and co-workers would be advised to use the ______________ method of research.
6. In his correlational research, Dr. Hamashima discovered that university graduates earn significantly more money than high school graduates. He also found that the more education people had, the less likely they were to be diagnosed with psychological problems. In this research, it appears that there is a ______________ correlation between education and income and a ______________ correlation between education and psychological health.

Graphic Organizer 3

Positive and Negative Correlations

The following box shows both positive and negative correlations between variables. In cells A through D the arrows indicate a relationship between the amount students study (variable X) and their grade point average (GPA) (variable Y). Fill in the appropriate term in each space provided.

Amount of Study (X)

GPA (Y)	High	Low
High	Cell A ↑ ↑	Cell B ↓ ↑
Low	Cell C ↑ ↓	Cell D ↓ ↓

1. Cell A indicates a ______________ correlation, and cell D indicates a ______________ correlation.
2. Cell C indicates a ______________ correlation, and cell B indicates a ______________ correlation.

3. Cell A: ________________ amounts of X are associated with ________________ levels of Y.

   Cell D: ________________ amounts of X are associated with ________________ levels of Y.

4. Cell C: ________________ amounts of X are associated with ________________ levels of Y.

   Cell B: ________________ amounts of X are associated with ________________ levels of Y.

Review of Terms and Concepts 4

Use the terms in this list to complete the Matching Exercise, then to help you answer the True/False items correctly.

descriptive research methods	representative sample
naturalistic observation	random selection
case study	correlational study
case-based research	correlation coefficient
survey	positive correlation
sample	negative correlation

Matching Exercise

Match the appropriate term with its definition or description.

1. ________________ A questionnaire or interview designed to investigate the opinions, behaviors, or characteristics of a particular group.
2. ________________ Scientific procedures that involve systematically observing behavior in order to describe the relationships among behaviors and events.
3. ________________ Selected segment of the population used to represent the group that is being studied.
4. ________________ Selected segment that very closely parallels the larger population being studied on relevant characteristics.
5. ________________ Research strategy that allows the precise calculation of how strongly related two factors are to each other.
6. ________________ Process in which participants are selected from the larger group such that every member has an equal chance of being included in the study.

True/False Test

Indicate whether each statement is true or false by placing T or F in the blank space next to each item.

1. ____ A case study is an intensive, in-depth investigation of a single individual, a family, or other social unit.
2. ____ A negative correlation is one in which two factors vary systematically in the same direction, increasing or decreasing together.
3. ____ Naturalistic observation is the systematic observation and recording of behaviors as they occur in their natural setting.
4. ____ A correlation coefficient is a numerical indication of the magnitude and direction of the relationship between two variables.
5. ____ A positive correlation is one in which the two variables move in opposite directions; as one factor increases, the other decreases.
6. ____ In case-based research, information from multiple case studies is systematically combined and analyzed.

Check your answers and review any areas of weakness before going on to the next section.

The Experimental Method and Ethics in Psychological Research

Preview Questions

Consider the following questions as you study these sections of the chapter.

- What is the experimental method, and what is its main purpose?
- What are independent and dependent variables, and what are extraneous variables?
- What is the experimental group, the placebo control group, the placebo, the placebo effect, and why do researchers use random assignment?
- What is the double-blind technique, why do researchers use this technique, and what is meant by demand characteristics, the practice effect, and the main effect?
- What is the control group (control condition), and what purpose does it serve?
- What is a natural experiment?
- What are the major imaging techniques used to study the brain and what are the limitations of this technology?

- What are five key provisions of the APA ethics code for research involving humans?
- What is comparative psychology?

Read the sections "The Experimental Method" and "Ethics in Psychological Research" and ***write*** *your answers to the following:*

1. The experimental method of investigation is used to ______________________________
2. The independent variable is the ______________________________

   The dependent variable is the ______________________________

   Extraneous variables are ______________________________
3. The experimental group (or experimental condition) is ______________________________

   The placebo control group is ______________________________
4. A placebo is ______________________________

   The placebo effect is ______________________________
5. Random assignment means that ______________________________

   It helps ensure that ______________________________
6. The double-blind technique is ______________________________

   It is used to ______________________________

   Demand characteristics are ______________________________

   Practice effects are ______________________________

   Main effects are ______________________________
7. The control group (or control condition) is ______________________________
8. Two limitations of experiments are ______________________________
9. A natural experiment is a study ______________________________
10. (Focus on Neuroscience) The major imaging techniques used to study the brain are ______________________________
11. (Focus on Neuroscience) Limitations of this technology are as follows: ______________________________
12. Five key provisions of the APA ethical guidelines regulating research with human participants are

    (a) ______________________________

    (b) ______________________________

    (c) ______________________________

    (d) ______________________________

    (e) ______________________________
13. (In Focus) Comparative psychology is ______________________________

After you have carefully studied the preceding section, complete the following exercises.

Concept Check 5

Read the following and write the correct term in the space provided.

Dr. Denton studies the effects of marijuana on memory. He designs an ethically approved experiment that consists of two groups: Group A are given a pill containing the active ingredient in cannabis, THC, and group B are given a harmless inert substance. Neither the researcher nor the participants know who is getting the drug and who is not. Participants are assigned to each group by chance, and all participants are told to learn a long list of word pairs and later take a memory test.

1. The independent variable in this study is ________________ and the placebo is ________________________ .
2. The dependent variable is the ________________________________ .
3. Group A is the ________________ group, and group B is the ________________________ group.
4. Dr. Denton has used a ______________ technique in designing the experiment; along with the control procedure used, this should help guard against ______________ and ____________ .
5. Participants ended up in group A or group B on the basis of ______________ .
6. Researchers were interested in determining whether changing a person's belief about the exercise benefits of a particular activity would result in health benefits. They recruited 84 female housekeeping staff from seven hotels and randomly assigned them to the informed group (told their work was good exercise) or the uninformed group (not told that their work was good exercise). At the end of the month-long study (during which all other conditions were held constant), health questionnaires were completed and measures of physical health were obtained.
   (a) The hypothesis in this study was ________________________________
   (b) The independent variable in this study was ________________________________
   The dependent variables were ________________________________
7. Psychologists investigating environmental factors and weight gain studied college freshmen who had been randomly assigned to college dorms. They compared weight changes in those who lived in dorms with on-site cafeterias and snack bars with those who lived in dorms without these facilities. This type of research is an example of a ________________ .

Review of Terms and Concepts 5

Use the terms in this list to complete the Matching Exercise, then to help you answer the True/False items correctly.

experimental method
independent variable (treatment variable)
dependent variable (outcome variable)
extraneous variable (confounding variable)
experimental controls
experimental group (or experimental condition)
placebo control group
placebo
placebo effect (expectancy effect)
random assignment
double-blind technique
single-blind study
demand characteristics
practice effect
main effect
control group (or control condition)
natural experiment
positron emission tomography (PET)
magnetic resonance imaging (MRI)
functional MRI (fMRI)
comparative psychology

Matching Exercise

Match the appropriate term with its definition or description.

1. ______________ Experimental technique in which the researchers, but not the participants, are aware of the critical information about the experiment.
2. ______________ Method of investigation used to demonstrate cause-and-effect relationships by purposely manipulating one factor thought to produce change in another factor.
3. ______________ In an experiment, the factor that is observed and measured for change and is thought to be influenced by the independent variable.
4. ______________ Branch of psychology that studies the behavior of different animal species.
5. ______________ Any change attributed to a person's beliefs and expectations rather than an actual drug, treatment, or procedure.
6. ______________ In an experiment, the group of participants who are exposed to all experimental conditions, except the independent variable, or treatment variable, and against which changes in the experimental group are compared.

7. ________________ In a research study, subtle cues or signals expressed by the researcher that communicate the kind of response or behavior that is expected from the participant.

8. ________________ A noninvasive imaging technique that produces highly detailed images of the body's structures and tissues using electromagnetic signals generated by the body in response to magnetic fields.

9. ________________ Specific strategies and procedures that help minimize the possibility that extraneous variables or some other uncontrolled factor will influence the outcome of the experiment.

10. ________________ An invasive imaging technique that provides color-coded images of brain activity by tracking the brain's use of a radioactively tagged compound, such as glucose, oxygen, or a drug.

11. ________________ A study investigating the effects of a naturally occurring event on the research participants.

True/False Test

Indicate whether each item is true or false by placing T or F in the blank space next to each item.

1. ____ Random assignment means that all participants have an equal chance of being assigned to any of the conditions or groups in the study.

2. ____ The placebo control group is the group of participants who receive a fake substance, treatment, or procedure that has no known direct effects.

3. ____ The experimental group (or experimental condition) is the group of participants who are exposed to all experimental conditions, including the independent variable or treatment variable.

4. ____ The independent variable (treatment variable) in an experiment is purposely manipulated in order to cause a change in another variable.

5. ____ A double-blind technique is one in which neither the participants nor the researcher interacting with the participants is aware of the group or condition to which participants have been assigned.

6. ____ A placebo is a fake substance, or procedure, that has no known direct effects.

7. ____ An extraneous, or confounding, variable is a factor or variable other than the ones being studied that, if not controlled, could affect the outcome of the experiment.

8. ____ Any change that can be directly attributed to the independent or treatment variable after controlling for other possible influences is called a main effect.

9. ____ Any change in performance that results from mere repetition of a task is called a practice effect.

10. ____ Functional magnetic resonance imaging (fMRI) is a noninvasive imaging technique that uses magnetic fields to map brain activity by measuring changes in the brain's blood flow and oxygen levels.

Check your answers and review any areas of weakness before going on to the next section.

Something to Think About

1. When family and friends find out you are taking a psychology course, someone typically makes some comment about "headshrinking" and "psychoanalyzing," or notes that "psychology is just plain common sense." To prepare yourself for these remarks, think about how you would explain what psychology really is and how you might "educate" your family and friends about the difference between psychiatry, clinical psychology, and psychoanalysis.

2. If you are like most introductory psychology students, you were probably motivated to take this course, at least in part, because of questions about human behavior and mental processes. For example, students often wonder if hypnosis can really help recover repressed memories and memories of past lives; if a lie detector really can detect lies; if "satanic messages" embedded in the lyrics of rock music can cause people to commit suicide; if ESP really exists; or whether subliminal tapes can really improve memory, clear up acne, or improve self-esteem. Now that you know more about the science of psychology, take one of your questions and think about how a psychologist would try to answer it.

Check your answers and review any areas of weakness before doing the following progress tests.

Progress Test 1

Review the complete chapter (including all boxed inserts), review all your study notes, and then test yourself on the following progress test. Check your answers. If you make a mistake, review your notes, check the relevant section in the study guide, and, if necessary, go back and read the appropriate part of your textbook.

1. Two disciplines influenced the founding of psychology. The discipline that concerns itself with questions such as mind–body dualism and the nature–nurture issue is ________________ ; the discipline that is a branch of biology and studies functions and structures of living organisms is ________________ .
   (a) physiology; philosophy
   (b) neuroscience; physiology
   (c) philosophy; neuroscience
   (d) philosophy; physiology

2. A Japanese psychologist investigating the relationship between worker satisfaction and productivity was surprised to find that North American workers were less productive when working as part of a group than when working alone. In some Asian countries, he had found the opposite to be true. This researcher probably has a ________________ perspective, and his specialty area is ________________ psychology.
   (a) cross-cultural; developmental
   (b) behavioral; health
   (c) behavioral; developmental
   (d) cross-cultural; industrial/organizational

3. Dr. Hammersly focuses on the role of unconscious factors in his patients' behaviors and spends time analyzing their dreams and delving into their early childhood experiences. Dr. Finkleman is more concerned with the way her patients think and reason, and her psychotherapy involves teaching her patients how to recognize irrational thinking and to find different ways of thinking about their situation. Dr. Hammersly's perspective is ________________ , and Dr. Finkleman's perspective is ________________ .
   (a) cognitive; behavioral
   (b) psychodynamic; cognitive
   (c) humanistic; biological
   (d) cognitive; psychodynamic

4. In a double-blind experiment testing the effects of memory-enhancing subliminal tapes, both the experimental and control groups were given a number of cognitive tests at the beginning (pretest) and end (posttest) of the three-month-long study. On the posttest, both groups showed improvement, but there was no difference in the level of improvement between the two groups. The researchers can conclude that
   (a) the improvement in both groups was probably because of demand characteristics.
   (b) the double-blind technique failed to eliminate extraneous variables.
   (c) the improvement in both groups was probably because of a practice effect.
   (d) memory-enhancing subliminal tapes work.

5. Dr. Lebel investigates how people differ on such characteristics as shyness, assertiveness, and self-esteem. It is most likely that she is a ________________ psychologist.
   (a) clinical
   (b) biological
   (c) developmental
   (d) personality

6. To ensure that differences among participants are evenly distributed across all conditions in the experiment and that there is no bias in how participants are assigned to their respective groups, a researcher studying the behavioral effects of playing violent video games should
   (a) operationally define each participant's role and assign participants on the basis of how closely they fit the definition.
   (b) make sure that the most aggressive people are assigned to the experimental condition.
   (c) make sure that the most aggressive people are assigned to the control group.
   (d) randomly assign the participants to each condition in the experiment.

7. A researcher is interested in how sleep deprivation affects performance and cognitive abilities. She proposes that there is a relationship between the amount of sleep deprivation and the ability to solve complex mental tasks; the more sleep-deprived people are, the more mistakes they are likely to make. She has
   (a) developed a theory.
   (b) formulated a hypothesis.
   (c) produced empirical evidence.
   (d) merely stated the obvious.

8. In a study investigating emotional arousal and memory, Dr. Alves discovers a statistically significant difference in recall ability between the high-arousal group and the low-arousal group. This finding indicates that
   (a) the participants were not randomly assigned to the two groups.
   (b) the difference between the two groups is likely to have occurred by chance.
   (c) extraneous variables were responsible for the difference in recall ability between the two groups.
   (d) the difference between the two groups is not likely to have occurred by chance.

9. Dr. Barbone and his colleagues decide to repeat the essence of an earlier study using different participants. They are
   (a) replicating the previous study.
   (b) wasting their time.
   (c) doing a meta-analysis.
   (d) violating one of the ethical codes of the American Psychological Association.

10. In an experiment designed to test the effects of alcohol on motor coordination, group 1 participants are given a precise amount of alcohol in a mixed drink and group 2 participants are given a drink that smells and tastes exactly like the alcoholic drink but contains no alcohol. Which of the following is true?
   (a) Group 1 is the placebo control group.
   (b) Group 2 is the experimental group.
   (c) Group 2 is the placebo control group.
   (d) Group 1 will have much more fun than group 2.

11. A researcher is interested in whether people talk when they are riding in elevators, so she and her research assistants spend many hours riding in elevators and unobtrusively noting when they hear a conversation. This researcher is using
   (a) naturalistic observation.
   (b) experimental research.
   (c) correlational research.
   (d) case study research.

12. In an attempt to understand how traumatic brain injuries affect behavior, Dr. Nicolai extensively and carefully observes and questions three accident victims who had suffered brain injuries. Which research method is Dr. Nicolai utilizing?
   (a) naturalistic observation
   (b) experimental method
   (c) correlational research
   (d) case study

13. In her research, Dr. Cranshaw focuses on the application of principles of natural selection to explain psychological processes and phenomena. Dr. Cranshaw is most likely a(n) ________ psychologist.
   (a) evolutionary
   (b) biological
   (c) behavioral
   (d) psychodynamic

14. Petra was injected with a small amount of radioactively tagged glucose. Then, while lying in a scanner, she tried to recall a list of words she had memorized earlier. The scanner tracked the glucose as her brain was using it. A computer then analyzed this data and produced color-coded images of her brain activity. Petra was participating in an experiment using
   (a) positron-emission tomography (PET).
   (b) magnetic resonance imaging (MRI).
   (c) transcranial magnetic stimulation (TMS).
   (d) functional magnetic resonance imaging (fMRI).

15. According to Science Versus Pseudoscience (What Is a Pseudoscience?), which of the following is true of pseudoscience?
   (a) It is a legitimate science that uses both established and unorthodox methods in the search for the truth.
   (b) It is a fake or false science that makes claims based on little or no scientific evidence.
   (c) It is not accepted by most of the scientific establishment because pseudoscientists have discovered truths that threaten all the fundamental laws and principles of science.
   (d) It has recently gained acceptance among the scientific commuity as new brain imaging techniques, such as MRI and fMRI, have provided evidence that backs up the claims made by pseudoscientists.

Progress Test 2

After you have checked your understanding of the material in Progress Test 1 and have done a complete chapter review with special focus on any areas of weakness, you are ready to assess your knowledge on Progress Test 2. Check your answers. If you make a mistake, review your notes and the relevant section of the study guide and, if necessary, review the appropriate part of your textbook.

1. In an experiment, children were randomly assigned to a group that watched a violent video or to a group that watched a nonviolent video; later, researchers measured the level of aggression in both groups under controlled laboratory conditions. In this example, the measure of the children's aggression was the
   (a) dependent variable.
   (b) independent variable.
   (c) extraneous variable.
   (d) naturalistic variable.

2. Dr. Ames researches changes in people's intellectual abilities as they grow older. Dr. Ames's specialty area is ________________ psychology.
   (a) social (c) developmental
   (b) educational (d) clinical

3. While researching a paper for her history of psychology course, Sangeeta noted that behaviorism and psychoanalysis dominated psychology for many decades early in the twentieth century. However, in the 1950s a new school of thought emerged that emphasized conscious experience and each person's unique potential for psychological growth, self-determination, creativity, and free will. This school of psychology is called
   (a) structuralism.
   (b) functionalism.
   (c) humanistic psychology.
   (d) cross-cultural psychology.

4. Dr. Sandman investigates the relationship between sleep deprivation and cognitive abilities. He decides to test research participants in his sleep research lab under varying conditions. First, he allows all his participants to get a number of uninterrupted nights' sleep and records how long each participant sleeps on average. Next, he decides that sleep deprivation would be either two, three, or four hours fewer than the average for each participant. Dr. Sandman
   (a) has operationally defined one of his variables.
   (b) is using cruel and unusual punishment.
   (c) is conducting correlational research.
   (d) has proposed a theory.

5. An educational psychologist is interested in whether having students evaluate instructors' performance is actually a good measure of teaching ability. A review of the literature showed some inconsistent findings across hundreds of different studies. To get a sense of the overall trends in this body of research, the investigator would be advised to use a technique called
   (a) the correlation coefficient.
   (b) meta-analysis.
   (c) case-based research.
   (d) replication.

6. Compared with clinical psychologists, psychiatrists are more likely to
   (a) prescribe drugs and other medical procedures for their clients.
   (b) assume that psychological disorders result from unconscious conflicts.
   (c) use a cognitively based therapy rather than a biologically based therapy.
   (d) favor a humanistic perspective rather than a psychoanalytic perspective.

7. To test the claim that listening to classical music improves cognitive functioning, researchers divided participants into three groups. Group A listened to classical music, group B listened to instrumental jazz, and group C spent the same amount of time in silence. All participants were given a standard cognitive reasoning test before and after being exposed to the treatment of interest. In this experiment, the independent variable was ________________ and the dependent variable was ________________ .
   (a) group C; groups A and B
   (b) the music and silent conditions; scores on the pretest and posttest
   (c) Groups A and B; group C
   (d) scores on the pretest and posttest; the music and silent conditions

8. In an experiment, participants were randomly assigned to one of three conditions. The purpose of random assignment is to
   (a) increase the probability that the same number of participants end up in each condition.
   (b) increase the likelihood that the participants are representative of people in general.
   (c) decrease the probability of expectancy effects.
   (d) reduce the possibility of bias and ensure that differences among participants are spread out across all experimental conditions.

9. Neither the researchers nor the participants in a study examining the effects of alcohol on inhibitions are aware of who actually received the active ingredient (the alcohol) and who were given a placebo. This study involves the use of
   (a) case-based research.
   (b) the single-blind procedure.
   (c) the double-blind technique.
   (d) correlational techniques.

10. Researchers using a form of descriptive research have found that the larger a person's line of credit, the more money he or she is likely to owe. The researchers have found a(n) ________________ between the size of a credit line and the amount of debt.
   (a) positive correlation
   (b) negative correlation
   (c) a cause-and-effect relationship
   (d) zero correlation

11. Mary is interviewed in depth, and her friends, family, and co-workers are contacted for further information. She also takes a number of psychological tests, and her behavior in various situations is observed. This is an example of
   (a) a survey.
   (b) correlational research.
   (c) a case study.
   (d) experimental research.

12. In an attempt to predict the winner in the next election, The Kneed to Know Kompany contacts a randomly selected representative sample of the voting population and questions them about their voting plans. This is an example of
   (a) correlational research.
   (b) a survey.
   (c) a case study.
   (d) experimental research.

13. When Drew goes to graduate school, he intends to pursue research in an area called positive psychology. Drew is most likely to
   (a) focus on the diagnosis, treatment, causes, and prevention of mental and behavior disorders.
   (b) study positive emotions and psychological states, positive individual traits, and the social institutions that foster positive qualities in individuals and communities.
   (c) apply the principles of evolution, including natural selection, to explain psychological processes and phenomena.
   (d) investigate the physical, social, and psychological changes that occur at different ages and stages of the lifespan.

14. According to Culture and Human Behavior, ethnocentrism is
   (a) the tendency to use one's own culture as the standard for judging other cultures.
   (b) introspective, self-centered analysis.
   (c) much more common in individualistic cultures than in collectivistic cultures.
   (d) much more common in collectivistic cultures than in individualistic cultures.

15. When evaluating media claims about psychology-related topics, Enhancing Well-Being with Psychology (Psychology in the Media: Becoming an Informed Consumer) makes the point that
   (a) anecdotal evidence is not scientific evidence.
   (b) there is no way to sort out true claims from false claims.
   (c) testimonials are the most reliable source of information.
   (d) correlational research is the most valid type of research because it can clearly establish cause-and-effect relationships between two variables.

Progress Test 3

After you have checked your understanding of the material in Progress Tests 1 and 2 and have done a complete chapter review with special focus on any areas of weakness, you are ready to assess your knowledge with Progress Test 3. Check your answers. If you make a mistake, review your notes and the relevant section of the study guide and, if necessary, review the appropriate part of your textbook.

1. An emphasis on the physical bases of behavior is to the ________________ perspective as an emphasis on how behavior is acquired or modified by environmental causes is to the ________________ perspective.
   (a) biological; evolutionary
   (b) behavioral; humanistic
   (c) biological; behavioral
   (d) behavioral; cognitive

2. The evolutionary perspective focuses on ______________, whereas the cognitive perspective emphasizes ______________ .
   (a) the physical bases of behavior; environmental influences on behavior
   (b) unconscious influences on behavior and personality; psychological growth and personal potential

(c) mental processes, information processing, problem solving, and thinking; the influence of culture on behavior
(d) the application of principles of natural selection to explain psychological processes and phenomena; information processing, problem solving, and thinking

3. Dr. Creedon believes in each person's unique potential for psychological growth, self-direction, and self-determination, and in the importance of free will in making choices about one's life. He also emphasizes the conscious experiences of his clients. His approach is most similar to one taken by
(a) John B. Watson and behaviorism.
(b) Sigmund Freud and psychoanalysis.
(c) Carl Rogers and humanistic psychology.
(d) Charles Darwin and evolutionary psychology.

4. In a memory experiment, half the participants were given the title of a passage before being asked to memorize it and the other half were simply told to memorize the passage but were not given the title. Later, all participants were given a memory test in which they were asked to recall as much of the passage as they could, and the overall results of both groups were compared. In this example, the independent variable was _______ and the dependent variable was _______ .
(a) the scores on the memory test; the title/no title manipulation
(b) the group given the title; the group not given the title
(c) the title/no title manipulation; the scores on the memory test
(d) the group not given the title; the group given the title

5. In conducting research on the effects of a new memory-enhancing drug, Dr. Simpleton used the double-blind technique. The purpose of doing so was to guard against the possibility that the researcher will inadvertently display
(a) expectancy effects.
(b) demand characteristics.
(c) placebo effects.
(d) ethnocentrism.

6. To learn students' opinions about the recent cutbacks at her university, Gira sent a questionnaire to every twentieth person on the list of currently enrolled students. Gira used the technique of
(a) replication.
(b) meta-analysis.
(c) random sampling.
(d) interviewing.

7. Research showing that students with the highest GPAs study approximately twice as many hours per week as those with the lowest GPAs would indicate that
(a) there is a positive correlation between study behavior and GPA.
(b) there is a negative correlation between study behavior and GPA.
(c) high GPA causes good study behavior.
(d) the correlation coefficient would probably exceed +1.50.

8. Ethical principles developed by the American Psychological Association require psychologists to
(a) always tell the participants the exact nature of the experiment and inform them of the hypothesis that will be tested.
(b) never, under any circumstances, use deception with potential participants.
(c) withhold all information about the nature, results, and conclusions of the study because of the confidentiality principle.
(d) obtain informed consent and voluntary participation of potential participants.

9. Dr. Joyce supports the view that the goal of psychology should be to discover the fundamental principles of learning and that psychologists should focus exclusively on overt behavior rather than on mental processes. Dr. Joyce favors the _________ perspective in psychology.
(a) behavioral
(b) cognitive
(c) psychodynamic
(d) humanistic

10. An experimenter found that variable A and variable B had a correlation coefficient of +.55, and variable C and variable D had a correlation coefficient of –.75. She can conclude that
(a) variables A and B have a stronger correlation than variables C and D.
(b) variable A causes variable B, but C and D are unrelated.
(c) variables A and B have a weaker correlation than variables C and D.
(d) variables A and B are strongly correlated, but C and D have no relationship.

11. Detailed descriptions of the ginkgo biloba and hotel experiments are presented in Chapter 1. In combination, the results of these two experiments demonstrated
    (a) that people's beliefs and expectations can have a significant influence on behavior and well-being.
    (b) conclusively that supplements, such as ginkgo biloba, improve memory, concentration, and mental focus in adults.
    (c) that demand characteristics, expectancy effects, and extraneous variables contributed to the main effect because the experimental designs did not adequately control for these factors.
    (d) that housekeeping work in hotels has beneficial health benefits for employees who take the daily recommended dose of ginkgo biloba.

12. Dr. Angellino stated, "Psychology should study the purpose of behavior and mental processes and how they function to allow organisms to adapt to their environment." It is most likely that Dr. Angellino belonged to the ________________ school of psychology.
    (a) functionalist
    (b) structuralist
    (c) behaviorist
    (d) psychoanalytic

13. When all the data were collected and analyzed, the researchers were confident that the observed change was not caused by placebo effects, practice effects, confounding variables, or other influences. Rather, the change could be directly attributed to the treatment variable, or independent variable, and this change is called the
    (a) practice effect.
    (b) main effect.
    (c) extraneous variable.
    (d) expectancy effect.

14. According to In Focus (Questions About the Use of Animals in Psychological Research), animal research is condoned by the American Psychological Association as long as the research
    (a) has an acceptable scientific purpose and will likely increase knowledge about behavior.
    (b) will likely increase understanding of the species under study.
    (c) produces results that benefit the health and welfare of humans or other animals.
    (d) has all of these characteristics.

15. According to Critical Thinking (What Is Critical Thinking?), critical thinking involves
    (a) minimizing the influence of preconceptions and biases while rationally evaluating evidence.
    (b) determining the conclusions that can be drawn from the evidence.
    (c) considering alternative explanations.
    (d) all of these characteristics.

Answers

Introduction: The Origins of Psychology

1. *Psychology is defined as* the scientific study of behavior and mental processes.
2. *The two disciplines that influenced the emergence of psychology were* philosophy and physiology.
3. *The person who established psychology as a distinct scientific discipline was* Wilhelm Wundt.
4. *The first two schools of psychology were* structuralism and functionalism, *and the people associated with their beginnings were* Edward B. Titchener and William James.
5. *Structuralism emphasized* studying the most basic components, or structures, of conscious experience using a procedure called introspection. *Functionalism stressed the importance of* how behavior functions to allow people and animals to adapt to their environments.
6. *Four students (and their accomplishments), who were influenced by William James were* G. Stanley Hall (awarded the first Ph.D. in psychology in the United States), Mary Whiton Calkins (first female president of the American Psychological Association), Margaret Floy Washburn (first female to be awarded a Ph.D. in psychology and second female president of the American Psychological Association), and Francis C. Sumner (first African American to receive a Ph.D. in psychology and who chaired the psychology department at Howard University).
7. *Psychoanalysis was founded by* Sigmund Freud. *This theory focused on* the role of unconscious conflicts in determining personality and behavior.
8. *Behaviorism focused on* the scientific study of overt behavior that could be objectively measured and verified *and rejected* the emphasis on

consciousness promoted by structuralism and functionalism, as well as Freudian notions of unconscious influences.

9. *The main proponents of behaviorism were* Ivan Pavlov, John B. Watson, and B. F. Skinner.

10. *Humanistic psychology emphasized* each person's unique potential for psychological growth, self-determination, and the importance of choice in human behavior. *Its two major advocates were* Carl Rogers and Abraham Maslow.

Concept Check 1

1. functionalist
2. psychoanalytic
3. behaviorism; humanistic psychology
4. interactive dualism
5. nature–nurture
6. structuralism

Matching Exercise 1

1. G. Stanley Hall
2. introspection
3. humanistic psychology
4. John B. Watson
5. functionalism
6. psychology
7. interactive dualism
8. Wilhelm Wundt
9. Edward B. Titchener
10. behaviorism
11. Carl Rogers
12. stimulus
13. learning
14. Francis C. Sumner

True/False Test 1

1. F
2. T
3. T
4. T
5. T
6. F
7. F
8. T
9. T
10. T
11. F
12. T
13. T

Contemporary Psychology

1. *The eight major perspectives in psychology are* biological, psychodynamic, behavioral, humanistic, positive psychology, cognitive, cross-cultural, and evolutionary.

2. *The sixteen important specialty areas in contemporary psychology are* biological, clinical, cognitive, counseling, educational, experimental, developmental, forensic, health, industrial/organizational, military, personality, rehabilitation, school, social, and sports psychology.

3. *The difference between a clinical psychologist and a psychiatrist is* that a clinical psychologist typically has a doctorate in clinical psychology, which includes extensive training in the different types of psychotherapy, and a psychiatrist has a medical degree plus additional specialized training in the treatment of mental disorders. A psychiatrist also can prescribe medications and other biomedical treatments.

Concept Check 2

1. biological
2. developmental
3. clinical
4. social
5. personality
6. cognitive
7. educational
8. health
9. industrial/organizational
10. psychiatrist
11. forensic
12. sports
13. rehabilitation
14. experimental

Graphic Organizer 1

Perspective	Specialty
1. humanistic	developmental
2. behavioral	industrial/organizational
3. cognitive	educational
4. biological	sports
5. cross-cultural	social
6. psychodynamic	personality
7. cognitive	health
8. positive psychology	rehabilitation
9. evolutionary	social

Graphic Organizer 2

Origins of Psychology, First Schools, and Key Figures

1. Philosophy: Aristotle, René Descartes — and — Physiology

2. Wilhelm Wundt; 1879

3. Structuralism: Edward B. Titchener

4. Functionalism: William James, G. Stanley Hall, Mary Whiton Calkins, Margaret Floy Washburn, Francis Sumner

5. Behaviorism: Ivan Pavlov, John B. Watson, B. F. Skinner — Psychoanalysis: Sigmund Freud

6. Humanistic Psychology: Carl Rogers, Abraham Maslow

Matching Exercise 2

1. military psychology
2. developmental psychology
3. educational psychology
4. experimental psychology
5. perspective
6. specialty area
7. culture
8. cognitive perspective (cognitive psychology)
9. personality psychology
10. behavioral perspective
11. ethnocentrism
12. biological perspective (biological psychology)
13. cross-cultural psychology
14. neuroscience
15. natural selection
16. school psychology

True/False Test 2

1. T	6. T	11. F	16. T
2. T	7. F	12. F	
3. F	8. F	13. T	
4. T	9. F	14. T	
5. F	10. F	15. T	

The Scientific Method

1. *The four basic goals of psychology are to* describe, explain, predict, and control or influence behavior and mental processes.
2. *The scientific method refers to* a set of assumptions, attitudes, and procedures that guide researchers in creating questions to investigate, in generating evidence, and in drawing conclusions.
3. *Psychologists are guided by the basic assumptions that* all events are lawful, which means that behavior and mental processes follow consistent patterns, and that events are explainable, which means that behavior and mental processes have a cause or causes that can be understood through careful, systematic study.
4. *Psychologists share a set of attitudes, including* open-mindedness, scientific skepticism, caution in making claims, and a willingness to critically evaluate the evidence for new findings.
5. *Empirical evidence refers to* evidence that is the result of objective observation, measurement, and experimentation. *The four basic steps of the scientific method are* formulate a testable hypothesis, design a study to collect relevant data, analyze the data to arrive at conclusions, and, finally, report the results.
6. *The role of statistics in psychological research is to* enable researchers to summarize, analyze, and draw conclusions about the data they have collected. *A statistically significant result is* one that is not very likely to have occurred by chance. *A meta-analysis is* a statistical technique that involves combining and analyzing the results of many research studies on a specific topic in order to identify overall trends.
7. *A theory is* a tentative explanation that tries to account for diverse findings on the same topic. *A hypothesis is* a specific question or prediction about the relationship between two or more variables that is to be tested. *It is different from a theory in that* a theory integrates and summarizes a large number of findings and observations and often generates predictions and new hypotheses that can be tested by further research.
8. *Theories can evolve and change because they reflect the* self-correcting nature of the scientific enterprise; when new research findings challenge established ways of thinking about a phenomenon, theories are expanded, modified, and even replaced.

Concept Check 3

1. experimental (in a natural setting)
2. hypothesis
3. statistics
4. 4; reporting her findings
5. meta-analysis

Matching Exercise 3

1. meta-analysis
2. replicate
3. scientific method
4. hypothesis
5. operational definition
6. experimental method
7. statistics
8. variable

True/False Test 3

1. F
2. T
3. T
4. T
5. T
6. T
7. T

Descriptive Research Methods

1. *Descriptive research methods are* scientific procedures that involve systematically observing behavior in order to describe the relationship among behaviors and events.
2. *Naturalistic observation involves the* systematic observation and recording of behaviors as they occur in their natural settings.
3. *A case study is* an intensive, in-depth investigation of a single individual, a family, or some other social unit. *Case studies are typically used to* develop a complete profile of a psychotherapy client and to investigate rare, unusual, or extreme conditions. *In case-based research, information* from multiple case studies is systematically combined and analyzed.
4. *In a survey, the researcher* develops a questionnaire or conducts an interview designed to investigate the opinions, behaviors, or characteristics of a particular group.
5. *Researchers ensure that their sample closely parallels the population of interest by* selecting a representative sample that matches the larger group on relevant characteristics, such as age, sex, race, marital status, and educational level.

6. *Random selection refers to* the process in which participants are selected randomly from a larger group such that every member has an equal chance of being included in the study. *It is important because* it ensures that the sample is representative, on relevant characteristics, of the larger population being studied.
7. *Correlational studies show* how strongly two factors, or variables, are related to each other and can sometimes be used for making meaningful predictions. *They are limited because* they cannot be used to demonstrate cause-and-effect relationships (experimental research is used to do that).
8. *The correlation coefficient is* a numerical indication of the magnitude and direction of the relationship between two variables; it always falls in the range from –1.00 to +1.00. *The correlation coefficient has two parts:* the number indicates the strength of the relationship (the bigger the number, the stronger the relationship) and the sign (+ or –) indicates the direction of the relationship between the two variables.
9. *A positive correlation is one in which* the two factors vary in the same direction, increasing together or decreasing together. *A negative correlation is one in which* the two variables move in opposite directions, one increasing as the other decreases.

Concept Check 4

1. more; less (or less; more)
2. survey; sample; randomly
3. naturalistic observation
4. positive
5. case study
6. positive; negative

Graphic Organizer 3

Positive and Negative Correlations

1. positive; positive
2. negative; negative
3. high; high; low; low
4. high; low; low; high

Matching Exercise 4

1. survey
2. descriptive research methods
3. sample
4. representative sample
5. correlational study
6. random selection

True/False Test 4

1. T
2. F
3. T
4. T
5. F
6. T

The Experimental Method and Ethics in Psychological Research

1. *The experimental method of investigation is used to* demonstrate cause-and-effect relationships by purposely manipulating one variable and observing the effect on a second variable.
2. *The independent variable is the* purposely manipulated factor thought to produce change in an experiment (also referred to as the treatment variable). *The dependent variable is the* factor that is observed and measured for change as a result of the manipulation of the independent variable in an experiment (also called the outcome variable). *Extraneous variables are* factors other than the ones being studied that, if not controlled, could affect the outcome of the experiment (also called confounding variables).
3. *The experimental group (or experimental condition) is* the group of participants who are exposed to all experimental conditions, including the independent (treatment) variable. *The placebo control group is* a control group in which participants are exposed to a fake independent variable, or placebo. The effects of the placebo are compared with the effects of the actual independent variable (treatment variable) on the experimental group. This group serves as a check for practice effects and placebo effects (expectancy effects).
4. *A placebo is* a fake substance, treatment, or procedure that has no known effects (commonly called a sugar pill). *The placebo effect is* any change attributed to a person's beliefs and expectations rather than the actual drug, treatment, or procedure (also called expectancy effect).
5. *Random assignment means that* all participants in the study have an equal chance of being assigned to any of the groups or conditions in an experiment. *It helps ensure that* potential differences among participants are spread out across all experimental conditions and that assignment is done in an unbiased manner.
6. *The double-blind technique is* an experimental control in which neither the participants nor the researchers interacting with the participants are aware of the group or condition to

which the participants have been assigned. *It is used to* guard against the possibility that the researcher will become an extraneous or confounding variable and display demand characteristics. *Demand characteristics are* subtle cues or signals expressed by the researcher that communicate the kind of response or behavior that is expected from the participant. *Practice effects are* any changes in performance that result from mere repetition of a task. *Main effects are* any changes that can be directly attributed to the independent variable after controlling for other possible influences.

7. *The control group (or control condition) is* the group of participants who are exposed to all experimental conditions, except the independent variable or treatment variable, and against which changes in the experimental group are compared.
8. *Two limitations of experiments are* (a) experiments are often conducted in highly controlled laboratory situations and consequently may not generalize well to real-world situations or to more general populations, and (b) the phenomena researchers want to study may be impossible or unethical to control experimentally (however, researchers may be able to take advantage of naturally occurring events or conditions and conduct a natural experiment)
9. *A natural experiment is a study* investigating the effects of a naturally occurring event on the research participants.
10. *(Focus on Neuroscience) The major imaging techniques used to study the brain are* positron emission tomography (PET scan), magnetic resonance imaging (MRI), and functional magnetic resonance imaging (fMRI).
11. *(Focus on Neuroscience) Limitations of this technology are as follows:* First, most brain-imaging studies involve small groups of participants, making it difficult to generalize the findings to a wider population. Second, most brain-imaging studies involve simple aspects of behavior and do not capture the extraordinary complexity of human behavior. Third, knowing what brain area is involved may reveal little about the psychological process under investigation. Finally, brain-imaging techniques are not necessarily more scientific than other techniques used by psychologists, and to be truly useful, brain images of a particular behavior must be accurately interpreted within the context of existing psychological knowledge about the behavior.
12. *Five key provisions of the APA ethical guidelines regulating research with human participants are*
    (a) Informed consent and voluntary participation is required.
    (b) Students must be given the choice of an alternative activity to fulfill the course requirement or earn extra credit.
    (c) Psychologists are restricted in their use of deception.
    (d) All records must be kept confidential.
    (e) Participants must be allowed the opportunity to obtain information about the study once it is completed and must be debriefed about the nature of their involvement in the study.
13. *(In Focus) Comparative psychology* is a branch of psychology that studies the behavior of different animal species, including the study of animal learning, memory, thinking, and language (animal cognition).

Concept Check 5

1. the actual drug given to group A (more precisely, THC, the active ingredient in marijuana); the harmless, inert or fake substance given to group B
2. participants' scores on the memory tests
3. experimental; placebo control
4. double-blind; placebo (expectancy) effects; demand characteristics
5. random assignment
6. (a) *The hypothesis in this study was* that changing a person's belief about the exercise benefits of a particular activity would result in health benefits.

   (b) *The independent variable in this study was* being informed, or not being informed, that housekeeping work was good exercise. *The dependent variables were* participants' responses to the questionnaire and the measure of physical health (weight, percentage of body fat, body mass index, and blood pressure).
7. natural experiment

Matching Exercise 5

1. single-blind study
2. experimental method
3. dependent variable
4. comparative psychology

5. placebo effect (expectancy effect)
6. control group (or control condition)
7. demand characteristics
8. MRI
9. experimental controls
10. PET scan
11. natural experiment

True/False Test 5

1. T	5. T	9. T
2. T	6. T	10. T
3. T	7. T	
4. T	8. T	

Something to Think About

1. (a) Psychology tackles questions that people have grappled with for thousands of years. Instead of using anecdotal evidence, intuition, philosophical discussion, and speculation, psychology uses the scientific method to answer questions that are amenable to empirical testing. It uses four steps in generating empirical evidence. First, questions are formulated into testable hypotheses; next, the study is designed and the data are collected; then statistical analyses are prepared and conclusions are drawn; and finally, the results are reported. Psychologists operationally define all variables and precisely specify the method of measurement or manipulation. Following this process, they can have more confidence in the accuracy of their results.

   (b) The difference between clinical psychologists and psychiatrists is training. Clinical psychologists have a doctorate in psychology and extensive training in the assessment, diagnosis, and treatment of people with psychological disorders. Psychiatrists, on the other hand, have an M.D. plus years of training in dealing with people with psychological disorders; because of their medical qualifications, they can prescribe drugs and order medical procedures such as electroconvulsive therapy (ECT) or transcranial magnetic stimulation (TMS).

   The term *psychoanalyze* is often used in popular jargon, and now that you are taking a psychology course people may say you are trying to "psychoanalyze" them. In the psychology literature, however, the term *psychoanalysis* has a more precise meaning and refers to Sigmund Freud's theory of personality and a method of psychotherapy that emphasizes the role of unconscious processes in determining behavior and personality. A psychoanalyst can be a clinical psychologist, psychiatrist, or other mental health professional who has extensive training in Freud's psychoanalytic method and psychological therapy.

2. Many of the questions posed by introductory psychology students can be tested empirically, and quite a few have, in fact, been answered. For example, how would you test the claim that subliminal (below awareness) messages can influence our behavior? It turns out that psychologists have done just that.

   The essence of their experimental design was the use of two subliminal tapes, one claiming to improve self-esteem and the other claiming to improve memory. They randomly assigned participants to one of four groups and gave them all pretests on measures of self-esteem and memory. Members of group 1 were given the memory tape to listen to for a set period and told it would help improve their memory; those in group 2 were given the same memory tape but were told it would improve their self-esteem. (By definition, on subliminal tapes you can't hear the messages, only the surface music.) Group 3 was given the self-esteem tape and told it would improve self-esteem, and group 4 was given the same self-esteem tape but were told that it would improve memory. All participants listened to their respective tapes for exactly the same length of time, at the same times of the day, etc. Later they were given another test of self-esteem and memory. The pretest and posttest scores for all conditions were compared.

   What do you think the results showed? If you believe the claims of those who promote the power of subliminal tapes, then groups 1 and 3 should have shown significant improvement in memory and self-esteem scores, respectively. And, one would assume, if the results were not due to some placebo effect, then groups 2 and 4 should have shown some change—memory improvement for group 2 and self-esteem improvement for group 4—because that is what they were actually exposed to.

   The results were clear and unequivocal: there was no improvement in any of the groups between their pretest and posttest scores. In contrast to the claims of their promoters, subliminal tapes were shown to be of no value in improving memory or self-esteem.

This is a good example of how useful the scientific method is in answering questions of a psychological nature. Can you apply what you know about scientific psychology to answer other questions you may have?

Progress Test 1

1. d
2. d
3. b
4. c
5. d
6. d
7. b
8. d
9. a
10. c
11. a
12. d
13. a
14. a
15. b

Progress Test 2

1. a
2. c
3. c
4. a
5. b
6. a
7. b
8. d
9. c
10. a
11. c
12. b
13. b
14. a
15. a

Progress Test 3

1. c
2. d
3. c
4. c
5. b
6. c
7. a
8. d
9. a
10. c
11. a
12. a
13. b
14. d
15. d

CHAPTER 2

Neuroscience and Behavior

PREVIEW

Reading the section below first will give you a general sense of the chapter's contents and an initial introduction to some of the major concepts and terms. This will prime you for what you are about to read and help you to develop a "cognitive map" that will guide your study of the material in this chapter. Likewise, reading the **preview questions** at the beginning of each major section will improve your ability to understand, learn, and retain the information.

CHAPTER 2 . . . AT A GLANCE

Chapter 2 first outlines the scope and diversity of biological psychology and notes that it is one of the scientific disciplines that makes important contributions to neuroscience. Biological psychologists (biopsychologists or psychobiologists) investigate the relationship between behavior and bodily processes and systems. The chapter begins with a description of the structure and functions of the neuron, as well as the functions of glial cells. Next, neural activation, synaptic transmission, and the role of neurotransmitters are outlined. The functions and effects of several neurotransmitters are discussed, as are the effects of certain drugs on neurotransmission.

The next section discusses the structures and functions of the divisions of the nervous system: the central nervous system, which consists of the brain and spinal cord; and the peripheral nervous system, which includes the somatic and autonomic nervous systems. The sympathetic and parasympathetic systems, which make up the autonomic nervous system, are described. This section ends by focusing on the endocrine system, its glands, and its chemical messengers, called hormones.

The section on the brain first discusses the neural pathways, functional and structural plasticity, as well as neurogenesis. The tour of the brain then takes you through the regions of the hindbrain, midbrain, and forebrain, including their structures and functions. The different roles of the four lobes of the brain's cerebral hemispheres (temporal, occipital, parietal, and frontal) are explained, and the functions of forebrain structures in the limbic system—the hippocampus, thalamus, hypothalamus, and amygdala—are described.

The chapter ends with a discussion of hemispheric specialization and the part played by split-brain patients in discovering the specialized functions of the brain's hemispheres. Enhancing Well-Being with Psychology suggests ways of maximizing your brain's potential.

Introduction: Neuroscience and Behavior

Preview Questions

Consider the following questions as you study this section of the chapter.

- What is biological psychology?
- What is neuroscience?
- What systems and structures are of interest to biopsychologists?

*Read the section "Introduction: Neuroscience and Behavior" and **write** your answers to the following:*

1. Biological psychology is ______
2. Neuroscience is ______
3. The systems and structures that lay an important foundation for psychological principles discussed in later chapters are ______

The Neuron: The Basic Unit of Communication

Preview Questions

Consider the following questions as you study this section of the chapter.

- What are the three main types of neurons, and how is information in the nervous system transmitted?
- What are the basic components of the neuron, and what are their functions?
- What are glial cells, and what are the four main types of glial cells?
- How is information communicated within and between neurons, and what are excitatory and inhibitory neurotransmitter messages?
- What are some common neurotransmitters, and what are their primary roles?
- How can drugs affect synaptic transmission?

*Read the section "The Neuron: The Basic Unit of Communication" and **write** your answers to the following:*

1. Information is transmitted in the nervous system by the three basic types of neurons: ______

   Their functions are ______

2. The basic components of the neuron and their functions are ______
3. Glial cells (glia) are ______

   Four types of glial cells (and their functions) are ______

4. Within the neuron, information is communicated (describe the complete process) ______
5. Communication between neurons may be electrical or chemical. When communication is electrical (in less than one percent of synapses in the brain) ______

   Chemically, communication involves ______

   Reuptake is the process by which ______

6. An excitatory neurotransmitter message ______

   An inhibitory neurotransmitter message ______

7. Some important neurotransmitters (and their primary roles) are ______________________________
____
____
____
____

8. Drugs can affect synaptic transmission by______
____
____

After you have carefully studied the preceding sections, complete the following exercises.

Concept Check 1

Read the following and write the correct term in the space provided:

1. Mrs. Cartwright's memory functions have deteriorated, and she has been diagnosed as suffering from Alzheimer's disease. The neurotransmitter implicated in this disease is ______________________________ .
2. The painkilling effect of morphine no longer worked after Hiu took the drug naloxone, which eliminated the effects of both ______________ and ______________ by blocking opiate receptors in his brain.
3. When Gerald was bitten by a black widow spider, he suffered severe, uncontrollable muscle spasms and had great difficulty breathing. The neurotransmitter involved is ______________________________ .
4. When Melanie was suffering from severe depression, her doctor prescribed Prozac, which he said would help alleviate the symptoms of her mood disorder by increasing the availability of a particular neurotransmitter called ______________________________ .
5. Patients afflicted with Parkinson's disease suffer from rigidity, muscle tremors, and poor balance and have trouble initiating movements. These symptoms are believed to result from diminished production of the neurotransmitter ______________________ .
6. George suffers from chronic anxiety. His doctor has prescribed the antianxiety drug Valium because it works by increasing ______________________________ , which inhibits action potentials and reduces brain activity.
7. Mr. Lee is undergoing the ancient Chinese medical technique called acupuncture for his back pain. Inserting needles in various parts of his body may reduce his perception of pain because of the involvement of ______________________________ .
8. Because of a problem with a specific neurotransmitter, Taniqua's body does not respond in a normal manner when she is faced with danger or threat. She also experiences problems with learning and memory retrieval, has trouble sleeping and is often depressed. The neurotransmitter involved is most likely ________________ .
9. Dr. Chou studies two types of glial cells. The ones that remove waste products from the nervous system, including dead and damaged neurons, are ________________ . The ones that provide connections between neurons and blood vessels and are involved in brain development and communication among neurons are ________________ .
10. Norman smokes cigarettes, which act as a stimulant because nicotine is chemically similar to acetycholine and binds to its receptor sites, stimulating skeletal muscles and causing his heart to beat faster. Nicotine would be classified as an ________________ (agonist/antagonist) drug.

Graphic Organizer 1

Identify the parts of the neuron in the figure below:

a. ________________ f. ________________

b. ________________ g. ________________

c. ________________ h. ________________

d. ________________ i. ________________

e. ________________

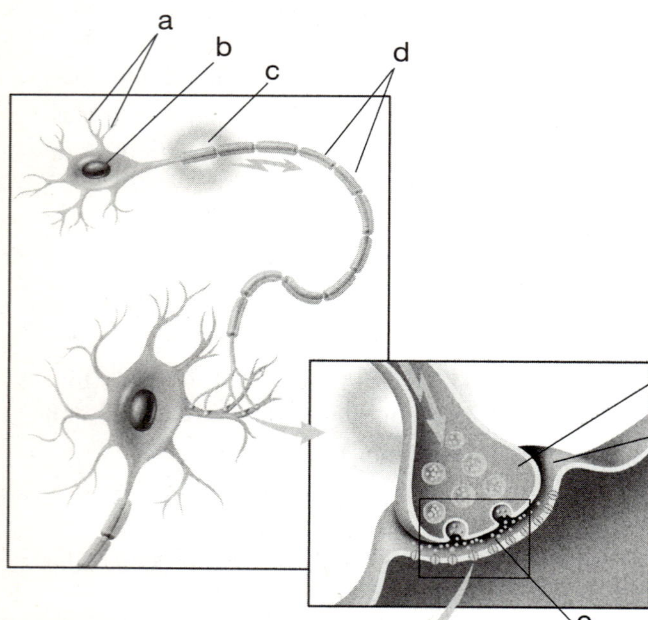

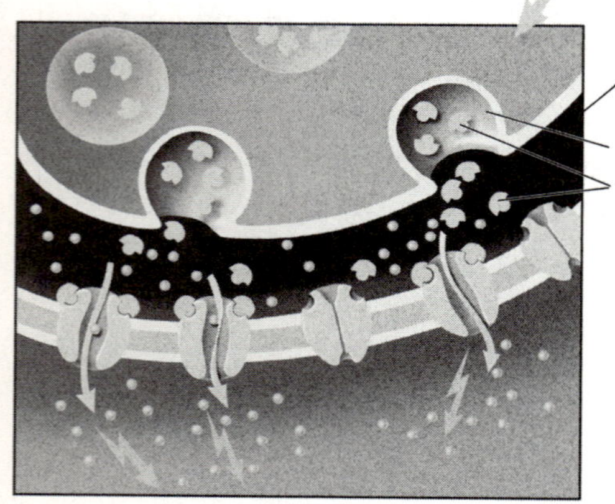

Review of Terms and Concepts 1

Use the terms in this list to complete the Matching Exercise, then to help you answer the True/False items correctly.

biological psychology (biopsychology or psychobiology)
neuroscience
neuron
sensory neuron
motor neuron
interneuron
cell body (soma)
nucleus
chromosomes
dendrites
axon
glial cells (glia)
microglia
astrocytes
oligodendrocytes and Schwann cells
myelin sheath
nodes of Ranvier (nodes)
multiple sclerosis
action potential
ions and ion channels
stimulus threshold
polarization
resting potential
depolarization
all-or-none law
refractory period
repolarization
synapse
presynaptic neuron/ postsynaptic neuron
synaptic gap
axon terminals
synaptic vesicles
neurotransmitter
synaptic transmission
reuptake
excitatory and inhibitory messages
acetylcholine
Alzheimer's disease
dopamine
Parkinson's disease
L-dopa
serotonin
norepinephrine
GABA (gamma-amniobutyric acid)
opiates
endorphins
acupuncture
selective serotonin reuptake inhibitors (SSRIs)
agonist
antagonist
curare
naloxone

Matching Exercise

Match the appropriate term from the list with its definition or description.

1. ________________ Highly specialized cell that communicates information in electrical and chemical form.
2. ________________ Neurotransmitter that usually communicates an inhibitory message.
3. ________________ Neurotransmitters that regulate pain perception.
4. ________________ Small gaps that separate segments of the myelin sheath that surrounds the axons of many neurons.
5. ________________ Neurotransmitter that is involved in sleep, sensory perception, moods, and emotional states.
6. ________________ The part of a neuron that contains the nucleus.
7. ________________ Disease that involves the degeneration of patches of the myelin sheath that surrounds many neurons and causes such symptoms as muscular weakness, loss of coordination, and disturbances in speech and vision.
8. ________________ Chemical messenger manufactured in the synaptic vesicles of a neuron.
9. ________________ Neural condition in which the axon's interior is more negatively charged than the exterior fluid surrounding it, which

occurs while the neuron is waiting for sufficient stimulation to activate it.

10. ________________ The point of communication between two neurons.

11. ________________ Tiny pouches, or sacs, in the axon terminals that contain chemicals called neurotransmitters.

12. ________________ Neurotransmitter involved in the regulation of bodily movements, thought processes, and pleasurable or rewarding sensations.

13. ________________ Minimum level of stimulation required to activate a particular neuron.

14. ________________ The scientific study of the nervous system, especially the brain.

15. ________________ Time period, lasting a thousandth of a second or less, that follows the action potential and during which the neuron is unable to fire.

16. ________________ Disease characterized by progressive loss of memory and deterioration of intellectual functioning, caused by severe depletion of several neurotransmitters, most notably, acetylcholine.

17. ________________ Specific group of painkilling drugs derived from the opium poppy that includes morphine, heroin, and codeine.

18. ________________ Ancient Chinese medical technique that involves inserting needles at various locations in the body.

19. ________________ Drug that eliminates the effects of both endorphins and opiates by blocking opiate receptor sites.

20. ________________ Disease characterized by rigidity, muscle tremors, poor balance, and difficulty in initiating movements, caused by the degeneration of neurons in one brain area that produces dopamine.

21. ________________ Twisted strands of DNA in the nucleus of the cell body.

22. ________________ Structure in the cell body that contains the cell's genetic material.

23. ________________ Drug or other chemical substance that binds to a receptor site and triggers a response in the cell.

24. ________________ Antidepressant medications, such as Prozac, Zoloft, and Paxil, that inhibit the reuptake of serotonin in certain neurons, increasing its availability in the brain.

25. ________________ Type of glial cell that removes waste products from the nervous system, including dead and damaged neurons.

26. ________________ Drug that converts to dopamine in the brain and alleviates the symptoms of Parkinson's disease.

True/False Test

Indicate whether each statement is true or false by placing T or F in the blank space next to each item.

1. ___ Norepinephrine is involved in activation of neurons throughout the brain, is critical in the body's response to danger, and plays a key role in the regulation of sleep and in learning and memory retrieval.

2. ___ Biological psychology (biopsychology or psychobiology) is the specialized branch of psychology that studies the relationship between behavior and bodily processes and systems.

3. ___ Reuptake is the process in which neurotransmitters are released by one neuron, cross the synaptic gap, and affect adjoining neurons.

4. ___ Glial cells (glia) assist neurons by providing structural support, nutrition, and removal of cell wastes.

5. ___ Interneurons communicate information from one neuron to the next.

6. ___ Synaptic transmission is the process by which neurotransmitter molecules detach from a postsynaptic neuron and are reabsorbed by a presynaptic neuron so that they can be recycled and used again.

7. ___ Axon terminals are branches at the end of the axon that contain tiny pouches, or sacs, called synaptic vesicles.

8. ___ Neurons that communicate information to the brain from specialized receptor cells in sense organs and internal organs are called motor neurons.

9. ___ Dendrites are multiple short fibers that extend from the neuron's cell body and receive information from other neurons or from sensory receptor cells.

10. ___ The myelin sheath is a white, fatty covering wrapped around the axons of some neurons that increases their speed of communication.

11. ___ The resting potential is a brief electrical impulse by which information is transmitted along the axon of a neuron.

12. ___ Acetylcholine is a neurotransmitter that causes muscle contractions and is involved in learning and memory.

13. ___ The synaptic gap is a tiny space between the axon terminal of one neuron and the dendrite of an adjoining neuron.
14. ___ The all-or-none law states that either a neuron is sufficiently stimulated and an action potential occurs or a neuron is not sufficiently stimulated and an action potential does not occur.
15. ___ Sensory neurons are a type of neuron that signal muscles to contract or relax.
16. ___ During an action potential a neuron is prepared to activate and communicate its message if it receives sufficient stimulation.
17. ___ The long, fluid-filled tube that carries a neuron's messages to other body areas is called the axon.
18. ___ The message-sending neuron is called the presynaptic neuron, and the message-receiving neuron is called the postsynaptic neuron.
19. ___ The drug curare mimics acetylcholine and blocks acetylcholine receptor sites, causing almost instantaneous paralysis.
20. ___ An excitatory message increases the likelihood that the postsynaptic neuron will activate, and an inhibitory message decreases the likelihood that the postsynaptic neuron will activate.
21. ___ The axon membrane opens and closes ion channels that allow electrically charged particles (ions) to flow into and out of the axon.
22. ___ When the neuron is sufficiently stimulated by other neurons or sensory receptors, the action potential begins, a process called *depolarization*.
23. ___ Oligodendrocytes and Schwann cells are the most abundant cell types in the human brain and provide communication between neurons and blood vessels, and are also involved in brain development and communication among neurons.
24. ___ Antagonists are drugs or other chemical substances that block a receptor site and inhibit or prevent a response in the receiving cell.
25. ___ Astrocytes are a type of glial cell that form the myelin sheath around the axons of some but not all neurons.
26. ___ During the refractory period *repolarization* reestablishes the negative-inside/positive-outside condition, creating the resting potential.

Check your answers and review any areas of weakness before going on to the next section.

The Nervous System and the Endocrine System: Communication Throughout the Body

Preview Questions

Consider the following questions as you study this section of the chapter.

- What are the two main divisions of the nervous system, and what does each include?
- What protects the central nervous system, and how are messages handled by the spinal cord?
- What are spinal reflexes?
- What are the key components of the peripheral nervous system, and what are their functions?
- What are the two branches of the autonomic nervous system, and what are their functions?
- What is the endocrine system, and how does it transmit information?
- How does the endocrine system interact with the nervous system?
- What are the specific functions of the hypothalamus, the pituitary gland, the adrenal glands, and the gonads?

*Read the section "The Nervous System and the Endocrine System: Communication Throughout the Body" and **write** your answers to the following:*

1. The two main divisions of the nervous system and their components are ______________________
____
____
2. The central nervous system is protected
____
____
The spinal cord handles ______________________
____
____
3. Spinal reflexes are ______________________
____
4. The key components of the peripheral nervous system and their functions are ______________
____
____
____
____
____

5. The two branches of the autonomic nervous system and their functions are ____________________
____
____
____
____

6. The endocrine system is made up of ____________
____
____

7. The endocrine system interacts with the nervous system in a number of ways: ____________
____
____
____
____
____
____
____

8. The hypothalamus serves as ____________
____
____

9. The pituitary gland's hormones affect ____________
____
____

The adrenal glands (adrenal cortex and adrenal medulla) are involved in ____________
____
____

The gonads are ____________
____
____

After you have carefully studied the preceding section, complete the following exercises.

Concept Check 2

Read the following and complete the sentence with the correct term.

1. Allison accidentally touched a hot stove top and immediately withdrew her hand before becoming consciously aware of the sensation or movement. She was able to do this because of her ____________________ .
2. Always a daredevil, Miguel dove off the cliff into the river below. Unfortunately, he landed on his head and is now paralyzed from the shoulders down. Fortunately, though, all his mental functions are intact, and he is attempting to complete his college degree. His present inability to move the lower part of his body is a result of permanent damage to his ____________________ .
3. At home alone late one night, Jason had just finished watching the most frightening video he had ever seen when there was a knock on the door. His heart rate suddenly increased, his breathing accelerated, and he began to sweat. These physiological changes were most likely triggered by his ____________________ .
4. When Jason answered the door, he discovered it was the pizza delivery; before long he calmed down and his blood pressure, heart rate, and breathing returned to their normal state. These physical reactions were most likely regulated by his ____________________ .
5. Jason's initial reaction to the knock on the door (his fight-or-flight response) resulted in his adrenal glands (in particular, the adrenal medulla) releasing the two hormones ____________ and ____________ .
6. Munro is a professional athlete and, like some of his colleagues, has suffered multiple concussions while engaged in various sports. As a result of these cumulative traumatic brain injuries (TBIs) he has now been diagnosed with a degenerative brain disease called ____________________ .
7. When Jannelle breast-feeds her baby, there is a complex interaction among the nervous system, the endocrine system, and behavior. The production of prolactin, which stimulates milk production, and oxytocin, which produces the let-down reflex, is a function of the ____________ gland, which is under the direction of a brain structure called the ____________ .

8. In a discussion about the brain and nervous system, Tom contends that there is no difference between nerves and neurons. His roommate Salvador, who is taking introductory psychology, explains the difference by pointing out that ________________ are made up of large bundles of ______________ axons.

9. Before entering ninth grade, Kristofer had to have most of his clothes replaced because he had grown almost five inches since the previous spring. This relatively sudden increase in height was probably the result of his ____________ gland producing ____________ .

10. Young Minnie and Max are twins. Minnie's sexual development will be regulated by the hormones ________________ and ________________ , which are produced by her ovaries, whereas Max's sexual development will be regulated by an androgen called ________________ , which is produced by his testes.

11. As Estelle was searching for some change in her purse she accidentally dropped her keys on the floor. She quickly reached down, retrieved her keys, and put them back in her purse. This voluntary reaction involved ____________ (motor/sensory) signals that were communicated to her muscles via the ____________ (somatic/autonomic) nervous system.

12. While Randolf is relaxing on the couch after lunch, his heart rate, blood pressure, breathing, and digestion all are functioning without any conscious effort on his part. This is because a subdivision of the ____________ nervous system called the ____________ regulates these involuntary functions.

Graphic Organizer 2

Mapping the Divisions and Functions of the Nervous System

In the following organizational chart of the nervous system, write the name of each division and choose the appropriate function of each from the list below:

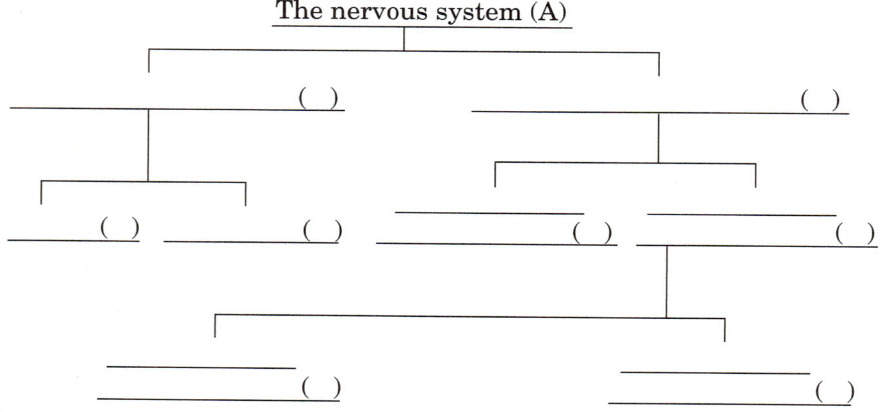

(e.g., A is the appropriate choice for the nervous system).

A. Complex, organized communication system of nerves and neurons.
B. Maintains normal bodily functions and conserves physical resources.
C. Produces rapid physical changes to perceived threats and emergencies.
D. Includes all nerves lying outside the central nervous system.
E. Communicates sensory and motor information.
F. Consists of the brain and the spinal cord.
G. Regulates involuntary functions such as heartbeat and respiration.
H. Main organ of the nervous system; made up of billions of neurons.
I. System that handles both incoming and outgoing messages to and from the brain.

Review of Terms and Concepts 2

Use the terms in this list to complete the Matching Exercise, then to help you answer the True/False items correctly.

nervous system	endocrine system
nerves	hormones
central nervous system (CNS)	hypothalamus
meninges	pituitary gland
cerebrospinal fluid	growth hormone
ventricles	prolactin
neural stem cells	oxytocin
spinal reflexes	adrenal glands
withdrawal reflex	adrenal cortex
peripheral nervous system	adrenal medulla
somatic nervous system	immune system
autonomic nervous system	epinephrine (adrenaline) and norepinephrine
sympathetic nervous system	gonads (ovaries and testes)
fight-or-flight response	estrogen, progesterone, and testosterone (an androgen)
parasympathetic nervous system	

Matching Exercise

Match the appropriate term with its definition or description.

1. ________________ Bundles of neuron axons that carry information in the peripheral nervous system.
2. ________________ System composed of glands located throughout the body that secrete hormones into the bloodstream.
3. ________________ Simple, automatic behaviors that are processed in the spinal cord without any brain involvement.
4. ________________ Pair of endocrine glands that are involved in the human stress response.
5. ________________ Hormones produced by the adrenal medulla that cause physical arousal in response to fear, anger, stress, and other strong emotions.
6. ________________ Brain structure that regulates the release of hormones by the pituitary gland.
7. ________________ Hormone secreted by the pituitary gland that stimulates normal skeletal growth during childhood.
8. ________________ Division of the nervous system that includes all the nerves lying outside the central nervous system.
9. ________________ In nursing mothers, the hormone produced by the pituitary gland that stimulates milk production.
10. ________________ Body's defense system against invading viruses and bacteria.
11. ________________ Hormone secreted by the pituitary gland that produces the let-down reflex, in which stored milk is "let down" into the nipple.
12. ________________ Endocrine glands that secrete hormones that regulate sexual characteristics and reproductive processes.
13. ________________ The three layers of membranous tissue surrounding and protecting the brain and spinal cord.
14. ________________ Specialized cells that line the inner surfaces of the ventricles and that generate neurons in the developing brain.
15. ________________ The brain and spinal cord are suspended in this fluid, which protects them from being jarred.

True/False Test

Indicate whether each statement is true or false by placing T or F in the blank space next to each item.

1. ____ The nervous system is the primary internal communication network of the body; it is divided into the central nervous system and the peripheral nervous system.
2. ____ The central nervous system is a major division of the nervous system and consists of the brain and the spinal cord.
3. ____ The pituitary gland is an endocrine gland attached to the base of the brain, which secretes hormones that affect the function of other glands as well as hormones that act directly on physical processes.
4. ____ The fight-or-flight response refers to physiological changes such as increased heart rate, accelerated breathing, dry mouth, and perspiration that occur in response to perceived threats or danger.
5. ____ The parasympathetic nervous system is a branch of the autonomic nervous system that produces rapid physical arousal in response to perceived emergencies or threats.
6. ____ Hormones are chemical messengers that are secreted into the bloodstream by endocrine glands.

7. ____ The somatic nervous system is a subdivision of the peripheral nervous system that regulates involuntary functions such as heartbeat, digestion, breathing, and blood pressure.
8. ____ The adrenal medulla is the inner portion of the adrenal glands that secretes epinephrine and norepinephrine.
9. ____ The branch of the autonomic nervous system that maintains normal bodily functions and conserves the body's physical resources is called the sympathetic nervous system.
10. ____ The adrenal cortex is the outer portion of the adrenal glands.
11. ____ The autonomic nervous system is a subdivision of the peripheral nervous system that communicates sensory information to the central nervous system and carries motor messages from the central nervous system to the muscles.
12. ____ Testosterone, estrogen, and progesterone are sex hormones that regulate sexual characteristics and reproductive processes.
13. ____ The withdrawal reflex occurs when a painful stimulus, such as something hot, electrified, or sharp, is touched.
14. ____ Ventricles are the four hollow cavities in the brain that are filled with cerebrospinal fluid and lined with neural stem cells.

Check your answers and review any areas of weakness before going on to the next section.

A Guided Tour of the Brain

Preview Questions

Consider the following questions as you study this section of the chapter.

- What are neural pathways, and why are they important?
- What are functional plasticity and structural plasticity?
- What is neurogenesis?
- What are the key structures of the hindbrain and midbrain, and what functions are associated with each structure?
- What does the forebrain include, and what functions have been identified with each of the four lobes of the cerebral cortex?
- What are the key limbic system structures, and what role do they play in behavior?

Read the section "A Guided Tour of the Brain" and ***write*** *your answers to the following:*

1. Neural pathways are ____________________

   ____

   They are important because ____________________

   ____

2. Neuroplasticity refers to ____________________

   ____

   Functional plasticity is ____________________

   ____

   Structural plasticity is ____________________

   ____

3. Neurogenesis refers to ____________________

   ____

   ____

4. The key structures of the hindbrain and their functions are ____________________

   ____

   ____

   ____

   ____

   ____

5. The midbrain is ____________________

   ____

   ____

6. The forebrain includes ____________________

   ____

   ____

7. The four lobes and their functions are ____________________

   ____

   ____

   ____

   ____

8. The main structures of the limbic system and their functions are ____________________

   ____

   ____

   ____

   ____

   ____

After you have carefully studied the preceding sections, complete the following exercises.

Concept Check 3

Read the following and write the name of the brain part or the correct term in the space provided.

1. Marcel had a stroke on the *right* side of his brain in an area that controls motor movement; as a result, he has trouble moving limbs on the *left* side of his body. This is because incoming sensory messages and outgoing motor messages cross over at the ________________ level of the brain.
2. If this area of your brain was electrically stimulated while you were fast asleep, you would wake up instantly. ____________________
3. After Larry was hit in the head by a baseball, his movements became jerky and uncoordinated, and he could no longer type or play his guitar. ________________
4. In the third round of a boxing match, Bruno caught a right hook that snapped his head back; when he hit the canvas, his breathing stopped. ______________
5. Ever since his automobile accident six months ago, Sam watches the same video day after day and each time responds to it as though he has never seen it before. All his other sensory functions appear to be intact, but it is clear that one brain area was damaged in the accident that prevents him from forming new memories. ____________________
6. Because of a tumor growing in her brain, Janna has lost her senses of taste, sight, hearing, and touch, but not her sense of smell. The area of the brain involved in regulating these behaviors is the ________________ .
7. Following an industrial accident, Harinder has lost his ability to plan, initiate, and execute voluntary movements, and he has problems with emotional control and in thinking clearly. It is most likely that the accident damaged his ____________________ .
8. Mr. Endo has been diagnosed with Parkinson's disease. Many of his movement-related symptoms are associated with the degeneration of dopamine-producing neurons in a midbrain structure called the ______________ .
9. When researchers electrically stimulated a forebrain structure in a cat, its back arched, its fur bristled, and it showed all the characteristic feline signs of rage and anger. The part of the cat's limbic system that was stimulated was the ______________ .
10. Morgana believes that you can tell a lot about a man's personality, character, and mental ability simply by examining the size and shape of his skull. Morgana's views are most like those of the popular nineteenth-century pseudoscience ______________ , which, strangely enough, triggered scientific interest in the notion that specific psychological and mental functions are located or localized in specific brain areas, an idea called ____________________ .
11. Following a stroke, Bruce was unable to talk coherently and was partially paralyzed on his right side. However, through rehabilitation therapy he "relearned" to talk and walk. It appears that undamaged areas in his brain have gradually assumed the ability to process and execute these once routine tasks, a process called ____________________ .
12. Dr. Lassiter and her colleagues conduct research on brain areas such as the hippocampus, the thalamus, the hypothalamus, and the amygdala. These are all components of the area of the forebrain called the ______________________________ .
13. During her ballet class, Emmalee executed a number of difficult moves, including a series of pirouettes on point. She is able to accomplish this difficult dance routine because somatosensory information about her muscles and joints, and the position of her arms and legs, are relayed to the ____________ lobe in her brain.
14. In her work on the Human Connectome Project, Dr. Weedon utilizes a new brain-scanning technique that allows neuroscientists to produce three-dimensional images of the neural pathways (tracts) that connect one part of the brain to another. This technique, called ____________________ , tracks the movement of water molecules in brain tissue along the axons.

Graphic Organizer 3

Chart Diagram Exercise: The Key Structures of the Limbic System

To help you develop the technique of creating your own graphic organizers, we encourage you to try to locate the structures listed below in the following outline of a brain. Then, on a separate piece of paper, write a description of each structure. Locate and describe the following:

(a) Hippocampus
(b) Hypothalamus
(c) Thalamus
(d) Amygdala

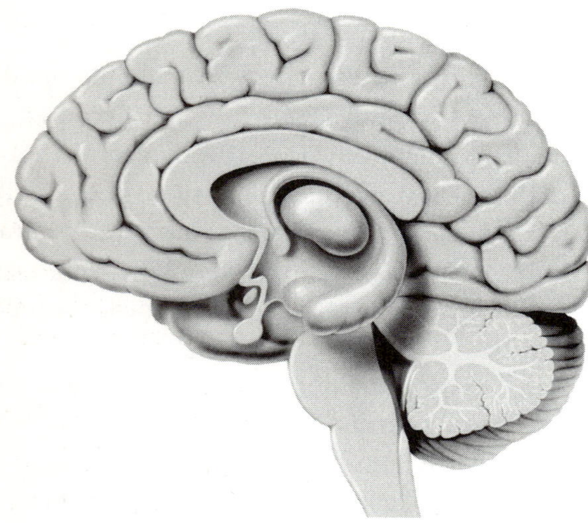

Review of Terms and Concepts 3

Use the terms in this list to complete the Matching Exercise, then to help you answer the True/False items correctly.

neural pathways
phrenology
cortical localization (localization of function)
neuroplasticity (or plasticity)
functional plasticity
structural plasticity
neurogenesis
olfactory bulb
brainstem
hindbrain
contralateral organization
medulla
pons
cerebellum
reticular formation (reticular activating system)
midbrain
substantia nigra
forebrain (cerebrum)
cerebral cortex
cerebral hemispheres
corpus callosum
gray matter
white matter
temporal lobe
primary auditory cortex
occipital lobe
primary visual cortex
parietal lobe
somatosensory cortex
frontal lobe
primary motor cortex
association areas
prefrontal association cortex
limbic system
hippocampus
thalamus
hypothalamus
suprachiasmatic nucleus (SCN)
amygdala

Matching Exercise

Match the appropriate term with its definition or description.

1. ______________ The nearly symmetrical left and right halves of the cerebral cortex.
2. ______________ The area on each cerebral hemisphere located above the temporal lobe that processes somatosensory information.
3. ______________ Midbrain area involved in motor control and containing a large concentration of dopamine-producing neurons.
4. ______________ The part of the temporal lobe that enables hearing.
5. ______________ Hindbrain structure that connects the medulla to the two sides of the cerebellum; helps coordinate and integrate movement on each side of the body.
6. ______________ Forebrain structure that processes motor information and sensory information from all the senses, except smell, and relays it to higher brain centers.
7. ______________ The part of the occipital lobe that receives information from the eyes.
8. ______________ The curved forebrain structure that is part of the limbic system and is involved in learning and forming new memories.
9. ______________ Region of the brain made up of the hindbrain and the midbrain.
10. ______________ Band of tissue in the frontal lobe on which the movements of different parts of the body are represented.
11. ______________ Large association area of the brain, situated in front of the primary motor cortex, that is involved in the planning of voluntary movements.
12. ______________ Hindbrain structure that controls vital life functions such as breathing, circulation, and heart rate.

13. ________________ Network of nerve fibers located at the center of the medulla and pons that helps regulate attention, arousal, and sleep.

14. ________________ Area of the hypothalamus that plays a key role in regulating daily sleep–wake cycles and other body rhythms.

15. ________________ The development of new neurons.

16. ________________ The brain's ability to shift functions from damaged to undamaged brain areas.

17. ________________ Pseudoscientific theory of the brain that claimed that personality characteristics, moral character, and intelligence could be determined by examining the bumps on a person's skull.

18. ________________ Networks formed by groups of neuron cell bodies in one area of the brain projecting their axons to other brain areas, forming communication circuits and links between them.

19. ________________ White myelinated axons that extend inward from the cerebral cortex.

20. ________________ Brain region responsible for odor perception.

True/False Test

Indicate whether each statement is true or false by placing T or F in the blank space next to each item.

1. ____ The frontal lobe is the largest lobe of the cerebral cortex; it processes voluntary muscle movement and is involved in thinking, planning, and emotional control.

2. ____ The somatosensory cortex is a band of tissue on the parietal lobe that receives information from touch receptors in different parts of the body.

3. ____ The midbrain is a region at the base of the brain that contains several structures that regulate basic life functions.

4. ____ The cerebellum is an almond-shaped structure at the base of the temporal lobe that is part of the limbic system and is involved in memory and a variety of emotional responses, including fear.

5. ____ The forebrain, the largest and most complex brain region, contains centers for complex behaviors and mental processes.

6. ____ The cerebral cortex is the wrinkled outer portion of the forebrain that contains the most sophisticated brain centers.

7. ____ The amygdala is the large, two-sided hindbrain structure at the back of the brain that is responsible for muscle coordination and maintaining posture and equilibrium.

8. ____ The occipital lobe is a region at the back of each cerebral cortex hemisphere that is the primary receiving area for visual information.

9. ____ The association areas, which make up the bulk of the cerebral cortex and are the regions in which sensory and motor information is combined, produce complex, sophisticated human behaviors.

10. ____ The temporal lobe is an area on each hemisphere that is the primary receiving area for auditory information.

11. ____ The hindbrain is the middle and smallest brain region that is involved in processing auditory and visual sensory information.

12. ____ Neuroplasticity (or plasticity) refers to the brain's ability to change structure and function.

13. ____ The limbic system is a group of forebrain structures that form a border around the brainstem and are involved in emotions, motivation, learning, and memory.

14. ____ The hypothalamus is a peanut-sized forebrain structure that is part of the limbic system and regulates behaviors related to survival, such as eating, drinking, and sexual activity.

15. ____ The thick band of nerve fibers that connects the two cerebral hemispheres and acts as a communication link between them is called the corpus callosum.

16. ____ Cortical localization (also known as localization of function) refers to the notion that different functions are located or localized in different areas of the brain.

17. ____ Contralateral organization refers to the crossing over of the right and left sensory and motor pathways in the hindbrain.

18. ____ Structural plasticity refers to the brain's ability to change its structure in response to learning, active practice, or environmental stimulation.

19. ____ The cerebral cortex is mainly composed of glial cells, neuron cell bodies, and axons and is sometimes described as being composed of *gray matter* because of its grayish appearance.

Check your answers and review any areas of weakness before going on to the next section.

Specialization in the Cerebral Hemispheres

Preview Questions

Consider the following questions as you study this section of the chapter.

- What did Broca and Wernicke contribute to our knowledge of the brain?
- What is lateralization of function?
- What is aphasia, Broca's aphasia, and Wernicke's aphasia?
- What is the split-brain operation, how did Roger Sperry test split-brain patients, and what did tests on split-brain patients reveal about differences in the abilities of the two hemispheres?

Read the section "Specialization in the Cerebral Hemispheres" and ***write*** *your answers to the following:*

1. Broca and Wernicke provided the first evidence that ______________________________
____

2. Lateralization of function is ______________________________
____
____
____

3. Aphasia refers to ______________________________
____

   Broca's aphasia results in ______________________________
____
____

   Wernicke's aphasia results in ______________________________
____
____

4. The split-brain operation involves ______________________________
____
____

5. In a specialized procedure, Roger Sperry directed split-brain patients to focus on a point in the middle of a screen and then ______________________________
____
____

   Split-brain patients can ______________________________
____
____
____

6. Tests on split-brain patients revealed that the left hemisphere is specialized for ______________________________
____
____

   and the right hemisphere is specialized for ______________________________
____
____

After you have carefully studied the preceding section, complete the following exercises.

Concept Check 4

Complete the following examples by placing the term right *or* left *in each blank:*

1. A blindfolded split-brain patient would be able to verbally identify an object placed in her ________________ hand but not in her ________________ hand.
2. When the picture of an apple was flashed to the ________________ of the midpoint on the screen during an experiment with a split-brain patient, the patient was *not* able to say what he saw. However, he could draw a picture of the object with his ________________ hand.
3. When a swear word was flashed to her ________________ hemisphere, a split-brain patient could not say what she saw but showed some nonverbal signs of embarrassment.
4. The fact that a split-brain patient had trouble assembling colored blocks to match a design with his left hand but not his right hand suggests that the ________________ hemisphere is superior to the ________________ hemisphere at perceptual tasks that involve deciphering visual cues, reading maps, copying designs, and so on.

Review of Terms, Concepts, and Names 4

Use the terms in this list to complete the Matching Exercise, then to help you answer the True/False items correctly.

cortical localization (localization of function)	aphasia
Pierre Paul Broca	Broca's aphasia (expressive aphasia)
Broca's area	Wernicke's aphasia (receptive aphasia)
Karl Wernicke	split-brain operation
Wernicke's area	Roger Sperry
lateralization of function	

Matching Exercise

Match the appropriate term/name with its definition or description.

1. ________________ U.S. psychologist and neuroscientist who received the Nobel Prize in 1981 for his pioneering research on brain specialization in split-brain patients.
2. ________________ The partial or complete inability to articulate ideas or understand spoken or written language due to brain damage or injury.
3. ________________ The language area on the left temporal lobe concerned with speech comprehension.
4. ________________ The notion that different functions are located, or localized, in different areas of the brain.
5. ________________ Language area on the lower left frontal lobe that plays a crucial role in speech production.
6. ________________ The notion that specific psychological or cognitive functions are processed primarily on one side of the brain.

True/False Test

Indicate whether each statement is true or false by placing T or F in the blank space next to each item.

1. ___ Karl Wernicke was a German psychiatrist and neurologist who discovered an area on the left temporal lobe that, when damaged, produces meaningless or nonsensical speech and difficulties in verbal or written comprehension.
2. ___ The split-brain operation is a surgical procedure that involves cutting the corpus callosum.
3. ___ People with Wernicke's aphasia find it difficult or impossible to produce speech, but their comprehension of verbal or written words is relatively unaffected.
4. ___ Pierre Paul Broca was a French surgeon and neuroanatomist who discovered an area on the lower left frontal lobe that, when damaged, produces speech disturbances but no loss of comprehension.
5. ___ People with Broca's aphasia can speak but may have problems finding the right words and typically have great difficulty understanding written or spoken communication.

Check your answers and review any areas of weakness before going on to the next section.

Something to Think About

1. A biological psychologist who specializes in the assessment and diagnosis of people with brain-related problems is faced with the following cases. On the basis of what you now know about biological psychology, the brain, and the functions of the nervous system, give some thought to what the specialist's assessment might be.
   (a) Fraser slipped on ice and hit the back of his head on the sidewalk, and now his vision is seriously affected. Which brain area is most likely affected?
   (b) Following an operation to remove a brain tumor, Yoko is able to read and understand written and spoken language but has difficulty speaking and expressing herself clearly. It is likely that she has damage in which part of the brain.
   (c) Ever since a part of her limbic system was destroyed, Vanessa has had trouble controlling her appetite and has had a constant urge to eat and drink. Which structure was most likely damaged?
   (d) Mr. Ashley has a disorder that is characterized by rigidity, muscle tremors, poor balance, and difficulty in initiating movements.
2. Family members and friends who know you are taking a psychology course may ask you some interesting and curious questions. One often-asked question is, "I know that regular exercise helps keep me in shape physically, but is there anything I can do to prevent mental deterioration?" What advice would you give in response to that question?

Check your answers and review any areas of weakness before doing the following progress tests.

Progress Test 1

Review the complete chapter (including all boxed inserts), review all your study notes, and then test yourself on the following progress test. Check your answers. If you make a mistake, review your notes, check the appropriate section in the study guide, and, if necessary, go back and read the relevant part of the chapter in your textbook.

1. A hunter in a South American jungle uses the poisonous drug curare on the tip of his arrow. When the arrow strikes an animal, the animal becomes almost instantly limp and quickly suffocates because its respiratory system has become paralyzed. The curare has ____________ the neurotransmitter acetylcholine.
   (a) blocked the release of
   (b) blocked the receptors for
   (c) increased the release of
   (d) increased the reuptake of

2. Miguel has been diagnosed with schizophrenia. His psychologist believes that Miguel's hallucinations and perceptual distortions may be caused, in part, by ________________ amounts of the neurotransmitter ________________ .
   (a) diminished; dopamine
   (b) excessive; dopamine
   (c) diminished; serotonin
   (d) excessive; serotonin

3. Jenny has just finished running a very tough marathon (26.22 miles) but seems to be very happy and elated. According to Focus on Neuroscience (Is "Runner's High" an Endorphin Rush?), one cause of her "runner's high" may be abnormally high levels of chemical substances in her brain called
   (a) acetylcholines.
   (b) serotonins.
   (c) endorphins.
   (d) dopamines.

4. Mrs. Danvers has multiple sclerosis. She experiences muscle weakness, loss of coordination and speech, and visual disturbances that result from the slowdown or interruption of neural transmission. The cause of these symptoms probably involves the degeneration of the
   (a) dendrites.
   (b) corpus callosum.
   (c) myelin sheath.
   (d) synaptic vesicles.

5. When Dr. Maxwell electrically stimulated a specific area of a patient's right cerebral hemisphere, the patient's left hand twitched. The part of the cortex that was stimulated was
   (a) Broca's area.
   (b) the primary motor cortex.
   (c) Wernicke's area.
   (d) the somatosensory cortex.

6. Neurotransmitters are to hormones as ________________ is (are) to ________________ .
   (a) nervous system; endocrine system
   (b) nerves; neurons
   (c) hypothalamus; pituitary gland
   (d) brain; spinal cord

7. When Mike was faced with a final exam worth 80 percent of his grade in his graduate statistics class, he was totally stressed out. The particular gland(s) in his endocrine system that is (are) likely to be stimulated is (are) the
   (a) thyroid.
   (b) pituitary gland.
   (c) adrenal glands.
   (d) nervous glands.

8. If researchers electrically stimulate the reticular formation in a sleeping cat, it is most likely that the cat will
   (a) aggressively attack the researchers.
   (b) stop breathing.
   (c) become paralyzed on both sides of the body.
   (d) instantly wake up, fully alert.

9. If researchers destroy the amygdala of a timid cat, it is likely that the cat will
   (a) become even more fearful.
   (b) lose its timidity and fearfulness.
   (c) become a vicious predator and start attacking large dogs.
   (d) stop breathing and die.

10. If a normal right-handed individual sustained severe damage to the right cerebral hemisphere, this would most likely reduce a number of abilities. Damage to the right hemisphere is NOT likely to affect his ability to
    (a) manipulate blocks to match a particular design.
    (b) recognize people's faces.
    (c) appreciate art and music and decipher visual cues related to emotional expression.
    (d) produce and understand written and spoken language.

11. The occipital lobe is to ____________ as the temporal lobe is to ____________ .
    (a) planning; seeing
    (b) seeing; planning
    (c) seeing; hearing
    (d) hearing; seeing

12. If someone taps you on the back, you sense the touch because the _________ cortex in the _________ lobe receives this tactile information.
    (a) primary motor; frontal
    (b) primary visual; occipital
    (c) primary somatosensory; parietal
    (d) primary auditory; temporal

13. Gye-Min was so engrossed in studying for his upcoming midterm exam that he did not notice how hungry and thirsty he was until his stomach started growling. The brain structure responsible for regulating behaviors related to survival, such as hunger and thirst, is called the _________ and is part of the _________ system.
    (a) hypothalamus; limbic
    (b) thalamus; endocrine
    (c) hippocampus; limbic
    (d) amygdala; limbic

14. According to Enhancing Well-Being with Psychology (Maximizing Your Brain's Potential), rats were exposed to either an enriched environment or an impoverished environment. Researchers found that enrichment
    (a) increases the number and length of dendrites, enlarges the size of neurons, and produces more synaptic connections.
    (b) results in a dramatic increase in the number of neurons in the brain.
    (c) has profound effects on the brains of young rats but no effect on those of mature rats.
    (d) dramatically affects the limbic system but has little or no effect on the cerebral cortex.

15. Phrenology was eventually dismissed as a pseudoscience. However, as Science Versus Pseudoscience (Phrenology: The Bumpy Road to Scientific Progress) points out, phrenology played a significant role in advancing the scientific study of the brain by triggering interest in
    (a) split-brain operations for epilepsy.
    (b) the role neurotransmitters play in regulating behavior.
    (c) cortical localization, or localization of function.
    (d) how drugs affect synaptic transmission.

Progress Test 2

After you have checked your understanding of the material in Progress Test 1 and have done a complete chapter review with special focus on any areas of weakness, you are ready to further assess your knowledge on Progress Test 2. Check your answers. If you make a mistake, review your notes, the appropriate parts of the study guide, and, if necessary, the relevant sections of your textbook.

1. Renata is suffering from a number of symptoms, including depression, sleep disturbances, and mood fluctuations; she also has problems in learning and memory retrieval. Her doctor prescribes Prozac and some other drugs because her problems are probably due to abnormal levels of the neurotransmitters
    (a) dopamine and acetylcholine.
    (b) serotonin and endorphins.
    (c) acetylcholine and norepinephrine.
    (d) serotonin and norepinephrine.

2. Signal reception is to ______________ as signal transmission is to ______________ .
    (a) myelin sheath; cell body
    (b) dendrite; axon
    (c) action potential; resting potential
    (d) axon; dendrite

3. As a result of a stroke, 75-year-old Mrs. Yee suffered brain damage. While she is no longer able to speak, she can understand what is being said to her. Mrs. Yee suffers from
    (a) damage to her occipital lobe.
    (b) Wernicke's aphasia.
    (c) damage to her left temporal lobe.
    (d) Broca's aphasia.

4. Your brain is involved in every perception, thought, and emotion, as are its neurons and their neurotransmitters. Neurotransmitters are chemical messengers that
    (a) carry information primarily in the endocrine system.
    (b) travel from the cell body along the axon and create an action potential.
    (c) assist neurons by providing physical support, nutrition, and waste removal.
    (d) travel across the synaptic gap and affect adjoining neurons.

5. If a patient suffers damage to the hippocampus, she is likely to have problems
   (a) learning and forming new memories.
   (b) remembering events and things that happened before her brain injury.
   (c) comprehending spoken and written language.
   (d) controlling emotions such as aggression, fear, anger, and disgust.

6. After Eduardo's serious skiing accident, doctors detected damage to his cerebellum. Eduardo is most likely to have trouble
   (a) swallowing, coughing, and breathing.
   (b) sleeping.
   (c) staying awake.
   (d) playing tennis, typing, and walking with a smooth gait.

7. In a typical test situation with a split-brain patient, a picture of an apple is briefly presented to the right of the center point (i.e., to her right visual field). If the patient is asked to name what she sees, she will
   (a) be unable to say what she saw.
   (b) be able to draw a picture of the apple with her left hand.
   (c) report that she saw nothing.
   (d) say she saw an apple.

8. A researcher anesthetizes the entire right hemisphere of a right-handed patient, then asks her to recite the alphabet aloud while reclining on the operating table with both arms extended upward. It is most probable that the patient's
   (a) left arm will fall limp but she will continue saying the alphabet.
   (b) right arm will fall limp but she will continue saying the alphabet.
   (c) left arm will fall limp and she will become speechless.
   (d) right arm will fall limp and she will become speechless.

9. A champion athlete loses his medal after officials discover that he has taken anabolic steroids, a synthetic version of the male sex hormone testosterone. Anabolic steroids, like other hormones, circulate through the ________ and act as chemical messengers in the ________ .
   (a) cerebrospinal fluid; central nervous system
   (b) bloodstream; endocrine system
   (c) cerebrospinal fluid; peripheral nervous system
   (d) bloodstream; limbic system

10. In response to an exam question, Leilani carefully draws a picture of a neuron and indicates the sequence of events that are typically involved when a neuron communicates. She is likely to note that information is carried from
    (a) the axon terminals to the cell body and then down the dendrites to the synapse.
    (b) from the cell body to the dendrites and then down the axon to the axon terminals and the synapse.
    (c) from the dendrites to the axon and then down the axon to the cell body and the synapse.
    (d) the dendrites to the cell body and then along the axon to the axon terminals and the synapse.

11. The parietal lobe is to ________________ as the frontal lobe is to ________________ .
    (a) anticipatory thinking; hearing
    (b) sensing touch; planning
    (c) seeing; hearing
    (d) tasting; smelling

12. The chapter Prologue tells the story of Asha, who suffered a stroke. This story illustrates that the brain has a remarkable ability to gradually shift functions from damaged to undamaged areas, a phenomenon called
    (a) lateralization of function.
    (b) structural plasticity.
    (c) synaptic transmission.
    (d) functional plasticity.

13. Lindsay had Botox injections in an attempt to eliminate her facial wrinkles. Botox contains minute amounts of botulin, which is an extremely lethal substance produced by bacteria; it works by blocking the release of a specific neurotransmitter from motor neurons, causing muscle paralysis. This neurotransmitter, found in all motor neurons, is called
    (a) dopamine.
    (b) serotonin.
    (c) GABA.
    (d) acetylcholine.

14. According to Critical Thinking (His and Her Brains), which of the following is (are) FALSE?
    (a) Differences between male and female brains are innate and hard-wired and are therefore fixed, permanent, and inevitable.
    (b) Men's brains tend to be much smaller than female brains.

(c) In general, female brains are more asymmetrical and functions are more lateralized than in the male brain.
(d) All of these statements are false.

15. According to Science Versus Pseudoscience (Brain Myths), which of the following is (are) a brain myth(s)?
(a) Skilled teachers can educate the right hemisphere of the brain (in isolation from the left) to become more creative and intuitive.
(b) The right hemisphere of the brain is solely responsible for creativity and intuition.
(c) We use only 10 percent of our brain.
(d) All of these are brain myths.

Progress Test 3

After you have checked your understanding of the material in Progress Tests 1 and 2 and have done a complete chapter review with special focus on any areas of weakness, you are ready to further assess your knowledge with Progress Test 3. Check your answers. If you make a mistake, review your notes, the appropriate parts of the study guide, and, if necessary, the relevant sections of your textbook.

1. When doctors removed a tumor from Andrew's occipital lobe, they also had to remove healthy brain tissue from the same area. When he recovers, Andrew is most likely to suffer some loss of
(a) language comprehension.
(b) muscular coordination.
(c) visual perception.
(d) taste perception.

2. Nancy suffers from severe epilepsy that so far has not responded to any treatment. As a final resort, her doctor operates on her brain and surgically cuts the
(a) amygdala.
(b) hippocampus.
(c) corpus callosum.
(d) adrenal cortex.

3. After a police car with flashing lights and blaring siren passes him and pulls over another driver for speeding, Jerry's heartbeat soon slows down, his blood pressure decreases, and he stops sweating so much. These calming physical reactions are most directly regulated by his
(a) sympathetic nervous system.
(b) parasympathetic nervous system.
(c) somatic nervous system.
(d) central nervous system.

4. While cooking dinner for a large family gathering, Mindy was so distracted by the conversations around her that she forgot to use an oven mitt when she grabbed a very hot roaster pan. She instantly withdrew her hand before becoming consciously aware of the sensation or her own hand movement. Mindy was able to do this because of her
(a) spinal reflexes.
(b) parasympathetic nervous system.
(c) high levels of endorphins.
(d) limbic system.

5. As a result of a stroke, Mr. Nelson can no longer understand what he reads or what is being said to him, and he often has trouble finding the right words when he tries to speak. Mr. Nelson suffers from
(a) Wernicke's aphasia.
(b) Broca's aphasia.
(c) Parkinson's disease.
(d) Alzheimer's disease.

6. During an experiment with a split-brain patient a picture of a hammer is flashed to the left of the midpoint (i.e., to her left visual field). If she is asked to indicate what she saw, she will
(a) verbally report what she saw.
(b) be able to draw a picture of the hammer with her right hand.
(c) be unable to verbally report what she saw.
(d) most likely draw a picture of a nail with her right hand.

7. When reading about the brain in his psychology textbook, Damon was surprised to learn that the brain is made up of specialized cells that outnumber neurons by about 10 to 1. These cells assist neurons by providing structural support, nutrition, and removal of cell wastes. Damon was reading about
(a) glial cells.
(b) sensory cells.
(c) motor cells.
(d) interneuron cells.

8. Sonny suffered brain damage when he was knocked down in a boxing match; he can no longer hear in one ear. It is most probable that one of his ________________ lobes was injured.
   (a) ear
   (b) occipital
   (c) temporal
   (d) frontal

9. In an effort to relax after a stress-filled week, Joanne had a couple of glasses of wine, and her co-worker Jim took a Valium. Both alcohol and Valium work by increasing the activity of the neurotransmitter ________________ , which inhibits action potentials and slows brain activity.
   (a) GABA
   (b) dopamine
   (c) norepinephrine
   (d) serotonin

10. If Dr. Doonan's research showed that the left hemisphere is dominant for speech and language in virtually all right-handed people and the majority of left-handers, this would argue strongly for the notion of
    (a) lateralization of function.
    (b) the all-or-none law.
    (c) structural plasticity.
    (d) functional plasticity.

11. Brian has been practicing his new hobby, juggling, every day for the last three months. If he is like most of the participants in the research described in Focus on Neuroscience (Juggling and Brain Plasticity) ________________
    (a) there will be an increase in gray matter in two brain regions that are involved in perceiving, remembering, and anticipating complex visual motions.
    (b) there will be structural changes in the left hemisphere of the cortex but not in the right hemisphere.
    (c) there will be a decrease in gray matter in two brain regions that are involved in perceiving, remembering, and anticipating complex visual motions.
    (d) there will be structural changes in the right hemisphere of the cortex, but not in the left hemisphere.

12. Sangeeta wakes up at 7:00 A.M. every day and is usually asleep by 11:00 P.M. every night. Her daily sleep–wake cycle is regulated by the area of her ________________ called the ________________ .
    (a) medulla; adrenal cortex
    (b) brainstem; pons
    (c) hypothalamus; suprachiasmatic nucleus (SCN)
    (d) hindbrain; corpus callosum

13. Researchers discovered that neural stem cells in the hippocampus developed into mature functioning neurons that appeared to become incorporated into the existing neural networks in the adult human brain. This development of new cells after birth is called
    (a) neurogenesis.
    (b) neurotransmission.
    (c) functional plasticity.
    (d) polarization.

14. Pierre is a professional ice hockey player and during his long career he has suffered many injuries to his head. As a consequence, Pierre may now suffer from chronic traumatic encepathalopathy (CTE). According to In Focus (Traumatic Brain Injury: From Concussions to Chronic Traumatic Encepathalopathy) which of the following statements is true?
    (a) Pierre's symptoms may include depression, anxiety, poor judgment, lack of impulse control, and problems with memory, concentration, and attention.
    (b) CTE is a progressive, degenerative brain disease that can only be diagnosed after death.
    (c) CTE may result form multiple concussions or traumatic brain injuries (TBIs).
    (d) All of the these statements are true.

15. For most right-handed people, the left hemisphere is dominant for language. According to Science Versus Pseudoscience (Brain Myths), for the majority of left-handed people (about 75 percent)
    (a) the right hemisphere is dominant for language.
    (b) language is processed equally in both hemispheres.
    (c) the left hemisphere is dominant for language.
    (d) language does not appear to be processed in either the left or the right hemisphere.

Answers

Introduction: Neuroscience and Behavior

1. *Biological psychology is* the specialized branch of psychology that studies the relationship between behavior and bodily processes and systems (also called biopsychology or psychobiology).
2. *Neuroscience is* the scientific study of the nervous system, especially the brain.
3. *The systems and structures that lay an important foundation for psychological principles discussed in later chapters are* the nervous system (the body's primary communication network), which is made up of neurons (the basic cells of the nervous system) and the endocrine system (a communication network closely linked to the nervous system). Also important is how certain brain areas are specialized to handle different functions such as language, vision, and touch.

The Neuron: The Basic Unit of Communication

1. *Information is transmitted in the nervous system by the three basic types of neurons:* sensory neurons, motor neurons, and interneurons. *Their functions are* to convey information from sense organs to the brain (sensory), communicate information between neurons (interneuron), and communicate information to the body's muscles and glands (motor).
2. *The basic components of the neuron and their functions are* the cell body (soma), which contains the nucleus and provides energy for the neuron to carry out its functions; the dendrites, which are short, branching fibers that extend out from the cell body and receive messages from other neurons or specialized cells; and the axon (often surrounded by the myelin sheath), which is a long, fluid-filled tube that carries information from the neuron to other cells in the body, including other neurons, glands, and muscles.
3. *Glial cells (glia) are* cells that assist neurons by providing structural support, nutrition, and removal of cell wastes; they also enhance the speed of communication between neurons by manufacturing myelin. Each type of glial cell performs a different function. *Four types of glial cells (and their functions)* are: microglia (remove waste products from the nervous system); astrocytes (provide connections between neurons and blood vessels and are involved in brain development and communication of information among neurons); oligodendrocytes and Schwann cells (form the myelin sheath).
4. *Within the neuron, information is communicated* in the form of brief electrical impulses, called action potentials, which are produced by the movement of electrically charged particles, called ions, across the membrane of the axon. The resting potential is the state in which a neuron is prepared to activate and communicate its message if it receives sufficient stimulation. For an action potential to occur and a neuron to be activated (depolarized), stimulation must be above the stimulus threshold. In addition, neurons either respond or they don't, the all-or-none law.
5. *Communication between neurons may be electrical or chemical. When communication is electrical (in less than one percent of synapses in the brain),* the synaptic gap is extremely narrow and special ion channels serve as a bridge between neurons, resulting in almost instantaneous communication. *Chemically, communication involves* neurotransmitters from the synaptic vesicles of one neuron diffusing across the synaptic gap, the space between two neurons, and affecting adjoining neurons. *Reuptake is the process by which* neurotransmitter molecules detach from a postsynaptic neuron and are reabsorbed by a presynaptic neuron so they can be recycled and used again.
6. *An excitatory neurotransmitter message* increases the likelihood that the postsynaptic neuron will activate and generate an action potential; *an inhibitory neurotransmitter message* decreases the likelihood that the postsynaptic neuron will activate.
7. *Some important neurotransmitters (and their primary roles) are* acetylcholine, which is involved in memory, learning, general intellectual functioning, and muscle contraction; dopamine, which is involved in movement, attention, learning, and pleasurable or rewarding sensations; serotonin, which is involved in sleep, moods, sensory perceptions, and emotional states, including depression; norepinephrine, which is involved in the activation of neurons, memory retrieval, learning, sleep, and physical arousal; GABA, which inhibits brain activity; and endorphins, which affect pain perceptions and positive emotions.
8. *Drugs can affect synaptic transmission by* increasing or decreasing the amount of neurotransmitter released by the neuron, by affecting the amount of time the neurotransmitter remains in the synaptic gap, by blocking the reuptake of the neurotransmitter by the send-

ing neuron, by mimicking specific neurotransmitters and producing the same effects (agonists), or by mimicking a neurotransmitter and blocking its effect by occupying its receptor sites and preventing it from acting (antagonists).

Concept Check 1

1. acetylcholine
2. endorphins; opiates
3. acetylcholine
4. serotonin
5. dopamine
6. GABA
7. endorphins
8. norepinephrine
9. microglia; astrocytes
10 agonist

Graphic Organizer 1

a. dendrites
b. cell body
c. axon
d. myelin sheath
e. synaptic gap
f. neurotransmitter
g. synaptic vesicles
h. postsynaptic neuron
i. presynaptic neuron

Matching Exercise 1

1. neuron
2. GABA (gamma-amniobutyric acid)
3. endorphins
4. nodes of Ranvier
5. serotonin
6. cell body
7. multiple sclerosis
8. neurotransmitter
9. polarization
10. synapse
11. synaptic vesicles
12. dopamine
13. stimulus threshold
14. neuroscience
15. refractory period
16. Alzheimer's disease
17. opiates
18. acupuncture
19. naloxone
20. Parkinson's disease
21. chromosomes
22. nucleus
23. agonist
24. selective serotonin reuptake inhibitors (SSRIs)
25. microglia
26. L-dopa

True/False Test 1

1. T	8. F	15. F	22. T
2. T	9. T	16. F	23. F
3. F	10. T	17. T	24. T
4. T	11. F	18. T	25. F
5. T	12. T	19. T	26. T
6. F	13. T	20. T	
7. T	14. T	21. T	

The Nervous System and the Endocrine System: Communication Throughout the Body

1. *The two main divisions of the nervous system and their components are* the central nervous system, which includes the brain and spinal cord, and the peripheral nervous system, which includes all the nerves lying outside the central nervous system.
2. *The central nervous system is protected* first by bone, then by three layers of membranous tissue called the meninges and is further protected by being suspended in cerebrospinal fluid. *The spinal cord handles* both incoming messages, via sensory receptors that send messages along sensory nerves to the spinal cord and brain, and outgoing messages, via messages from the brain along the spinal cord that are relayed out along motor neurons to activate muscles.
3. *Spinal reflexes are* simple, automatic behaviors that are processed in the spinal cord.
4. *The key components of the peripheral nervous system and their functions are* the somatic nervous system, which communicates sensory information to the central nervous system and carries motor messages from the central nervous system to the muscles, and the autonomic nervous system, which regulates involuntary functions, such as heartbeat, blood pressure, breathing, and digestion.

5. *The two branches of the autonomic nervous system and their functions are* the sympathetic nervous system, which produces rapid physical arousal in response to perceived threats or emergencies, and the parasympathetic nervous system, which maintains normal bodily functions and conserves the body's physical resources.
6. *The endocrine system is made up of* glands that transmit information via chemical messengers called hormones. Hormones regulate such things as metabolism, growth rate, digestion, blood pressure, and sexual development and reproduction. Hormones are also involved in emotional response and your response to stress.
7. *The endocrine system interacts with the nervous system in a number of ways:* Endocrine hormones can promote or inhibit the generation of nerve impulses; the release of hormones, in turn, can be stimulated or inhibited by certain parts of the nervous system; and finally, because some hormones and neurotransmitters are chemically identical, the same molecules can act as either a hormone or a neurotransmitter.
8. *The hypothalamus serves as* the main link between the endocrine system and the nervous system and directly regulates the release of hormones by the pituitary gland.
9. *The pituitary gland's hormones affect* the functions of other glands, as well as regulate the production of other hormones. *The adrenal glands (adrenal cortex and adrenal medulla) are involved in* the human stress response. *The gonads are* the sex organs: the ovaries in females, which secrete estrogen and progesterone, and the testes in males, which secrete androgens, the most important of which is testosterone (testosterone is also secreted by the adrenal glands in both males and females). In both males and females, the sex hormones influence sexual development, sexual behavior, and reproduction.

Concept Check 2

1. spinal reflex
2. spinal cord
3. sympathetic nervous system
4. parasympathetic nervous system
5. norepinephrine; epinephrine
6. chronic traumatic encephalopathy (CTE)
7. pituitary; hypothalamus
8. nerves; neuron
9. pituitary; growth hormone
10. estrogen; progesterone; testosterone
11. motor; somatic
12. peripheral; autonomic nervous system

Graphic Organizer 2

Mapping the Divisions and Functions of the Nervous System

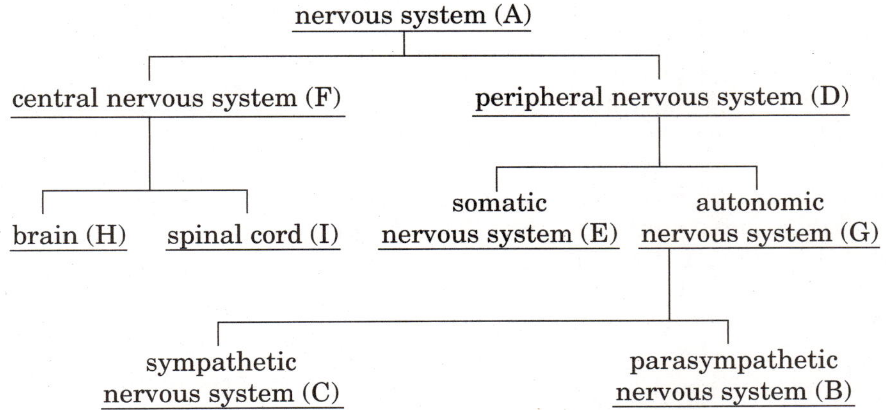

Matching Exercise 2

1. nerves
2. endocrine system
3. spinal reflexes
4. adrenal glands
5. epinephrine (adrenaline) and norepinephrine
6. hypothalamus
7. growth hormone
8. peripheral nervous system
9. prolactin

10. immune system
11. oxytocin
12. gonads
13. meninges
14. neural stem cells
15. cerebrospinal fluid

True/False Test 2

1. T	5. F	9. F	13. T
2. T	6. T	10. T	14. T
3. T	7. F	11. F	
4. T	8. T	12. T	

A Guided Tour of the Brain

1. *Neural pathways are* networks formed by groups of neuron cell bodies in one area of the brain that project their axons to other brain areas. *They are important because* they form communication networks and circuits that link different brain areas and are involved in many brain functions.
2. *Neuroplasticity refers to* the brain's ability to change structure and function. *Functional plasticity is* the brain's ability to shift functions from damaged to undamaged brain areas. *Structural plasticity is* the brain's ability to physically change its structure in response to learning, active practice, or environmental stimulation.
3. *Neurogenesis refers to* the development of new neurons in the brain.
4. *The key structures of the hindbrain and their functions are* the medulla, which controls breathing, heart rate, blood pressure, and other vital life functions; the pons, which connects the medulla to the two sides of the cerebellum and helps coordinate and integrate movements on each side of the body; and the cerebellum, which is responsible for muscle coordination and maintaining posture and equilibrium. The reticular formation, which is a network of nerve fibers in the center of the medulla and pons, plays a role in regulating attention, arousal, and sleep.
5. *The midbrain is* an important relay station that contains centers important to the processing of auditory and visual sensory information and an area called the substantia nigra that is involved in motor control and contains a large concentration of dopamine-producing neurons.
6. *The forebrain includes* the cerebral cortex (the wrinkled outer portion of the forebrain), which contains the most sophisticated brain centers, and the limbic system structures, which are involved in emotion, motivation, learning, and memory.
7. *The four lobes and their functions are* the temporal lobe, the primary receiving area for auditory information; the occipital lobe, the primary receiving area for visual information; the parietal lobe, which processes somatosensory information; and the frontal lobe, which processes voluntary muscle movements and is involved in thinking, planning, and emotional control. The association areas, on all four lobes, combine sensory and motor information and coordinate interaction among different brain areas.
8. *The main structures of the limbic system and their functions are* the hippocampus, which is involved in learning and forming new memories; the thalamus, which processes sensory information for all senses, except smell, and relays it to the cerebral cortex; the hypothalamus, which regulates behaviors related to survival, such as eating, drinking, and sexual behavior; and the amygdala, which is involved in emotions such as fear, anger, and disgust, and in memory. The amygdala also responds to appealing stimuli, such as to food when organisms are hungry.

Concept Check 3

1. hindbrain (more specifically, the pons is the point at which neural messages cross over)
2. reticular formation
3. cerebellum
4. medulla
5. hippocampus
6. thalamus
7. frontal lobes
8. substantia nigra
9. amygdala
10. phrenology; cortical localization (or localization of function)
11. functional plasticity
12. limbic system
13. parietal
14. diffusion spectrum imaging (DSI)

Graphic Organizer 3
Chart Diagram Exercise: The Key Structures of the Limbic System

(a) Hippocampus: a curved forebrain structure that is involved in learning and forming new memories
(b) Hypothalamus: a peanut-sized forebrain structure that regulates both divisions of the auto-

nomic nervous system, as well as behaviors related to survival, such as eating, drinking, and sexual activity

(c) Thalamus: a forebrain structure that processes motor information and sensory information for all the senses except smell and relays it to the cerebral cortex

(d) Amygdala: an almond-shaped forebrain structure that is involved in emotion and in forming memories

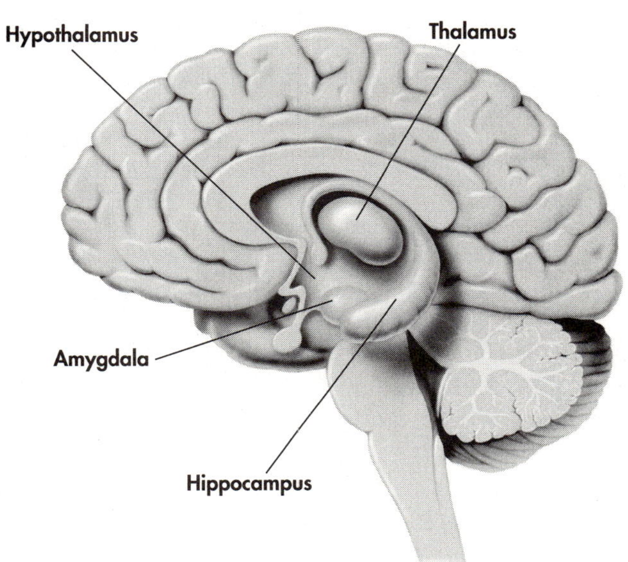

Matching Exercise 3

1. cerebral hemispheres
2. parietal lobe
3. substantia nigra
4. primary auditory cortex
5. pons
6. thalamus
7. primary visual cortex
8. hippocampus
9. brainstem
10. primary motor cortex
11. prefrontal association cortex
12. medulla
13. reticular formation (reticular activating system)
14. suprachiasmatic nucleus (SCN)
15. neurogenesis
16. functional plasticity
17. phrenology
18. neural pathways
19. white matter
20. olfactory bulb

True/False Test 3

1. T	7. F	13. T	19. T
2. T	8. T	14. T	
3. F	9. T	15. T	
4. F	10. T	16. T	
5. T	11. F	17. T	
6. T	12. T	18. T	

Specialization in the Cerebral Hemispheres

1. *Broca and Wernicke provided the first evidence that* the left and right hemispheres were specialized for different functions (cortical localization or localization of function), and in particular that language and speech functions are processed primarily in the left cerebral hemisphere.
2. *Lateralization of function is* the notion that specific psychological or cognitive functions are processed primarily on one side of the brain.
3. *Aphasia refers to* the partial or complete inability to articulate ideas or understand spoken or written language because of brain injury or damage. *Broca's aphasia results in* the inability to produce speech, but comprehension is relatively unaffected. *Wernicke's aphasia results in* problems in finding the correct word and difficulty in comprehension of written or spoken communication, but speech is relatively unaffected unless the damage is severe.
4. *The split-brain operation involves* surgically cutting the corpus callosum, the thick band of axons that connects the two hemispheres.
5. *In a specialized procedure, Roger Sperry directed split-brain patients to focus on a point in the middle of a screen and then* visual information was differentially projected either to the left or right hemisphere. *Split-brain patients can* verbally identify the object when it is projected to the left hemisphere but not the right; however, the left hand (which is controlled by the right hemisphere) can correctly pick out the object projected to the right hemisphere.
6. *Tests on split-brain patients revealed that the left hemisphere is specialized for* language abilities, speech, reading, and writing, and *the right hemisphere is specialized for* nonverbal emotional expression, visual-spatial tasks, deciphering complex visual cues, facial and emotional facial cue recognition, reading maps, copying designs, drawing, and musical appreciation or responsiveness (but not necessarily for musical ability, which involves the left hemisphere as well).

Concept Check 4

1. right; left
2. left; left
3. right
4. right; left

Matching Exercise 4

1. Roger Sperry
2. aphasia
3. Wernicke's area
4. cortical localization
5. Broca's area
6. lateralization of function

True/False Test 4

1. T
2. T
3. F
4. T
5. F

Something to Think About

1. (a) The occipital lobe is most likely affected because it includes the primary visual cortex where visual information is received, so damage to this area could affect vision.
   (b) Yoko probably has damage in the left frontal lobe, Broca's area. Damage here would not affect comprehension but would influence speech production.
   (c) Vanessa's hypothalamus was most likely damaged. The hypothalamus is part of the limbic system and regulates appetite, among its many functions.
   (d) Mr. Ashley suffers from Parkinson's disease, which is caused by the degeneration of neurons that produce dopamine in one brain area. Symptoms may be alleviated by the drug L-dopa, which converts to dopamine in the brain.
2. In answer to this question, the news is good. Because of the brain's structural plasticity, some brain structures can change in response to environmental stimulation. Research with rats and other animals has demonstrated that in addition to other changes, an enriched environment increases the number and length of dendrites, increases the number of glial cells, enlarges the size of neurons, increases the rate of neurogenesis, and increases the number of neural connections. Neuroscientists have identified an additional factor that improves brain function, even in aging mammals: exercise. Exercise appears to promote neurogenesis in the adult human brain, just as it does in other animals, and improved scores on several tests of mental abilities. Furthermore, research has shown that even moderate exercise can increase brain volume in previously sedentary, older adults. More important, there is an impressive amount of correlational research showing that the human brain also seems to benefit from enriched, stimulating environments. Getting a good education, as long as the process is challenging, is one way to "exercise" the brain. Another piece of advice is to remain mentally and physically active throughout the lifespan and to involve yourself in complex and stimulating activities rather than passively watching TV.

   It is important to point out that intellectual decline is not the inevitable result of aging. To increase the number of synaptic connections and dendritic growth, the best advice is to get involved in novel, challenging, and unfamiliar pursuits and read Enhancing Well-Being with Psychology (Maximizing Your Brain's Potential). Keep pumping those neurons and remember, "If you don't use it, you lose it!"

Progress Test 1

1. b
2. b
3. c
4. c
5. b
6. a
7. c
8. d
9. b
10. d
11. c
12. c
13. a
14. a
15. c

Progress Test 2

1. d
2. b
3. d
4. d
5. a
6. d
7. d
8. a
9. b
10. d
11. b
12. d
13. d
14. d
15. d

Progress Test 3

1. c
2. c
3. b
4. a
5. a
6. c
7. a
8. c
9. a
10. a
11. a
12. c
13. a
14. d
15. c

CHAPTER 3

Sensation and Perception

PREVIEW

Reading the section below first will give you a general sense of the chapter's contents and an initial introduction to some of the major concepts and terms. This will prime you for what you are about to read and help you to develop a "cognitive map" that will guide your study of the material in this chapter. Likewise, reading the **preview questions** at the beginning of each major section will improve your ability to understand, learn, and retain the information.

CHAPTER 3 . . . AT A GLANCE

Chapter 3 describes both sensation and perception. Sensation refers to the response of sensory receptors in the sense organs to stimulation and the transmission of that information to the brain. Perception is the process through which the brain integrates, organizes, and interprets sensory information.

The chapter begins with the basic principles of sensation—transduction and absolute and difference thresholds, Weber's law, and sensory adaptation. It then explains the senses of vision and hearing and the chemical and body senses, including smell (olfaction), taste (gustation), touch, and position (the kinesthetic and vestibular senses). In addition, pain sensation, the role of nociceptors and substance P, phantom limb pain, and the gate-control theory of pain are explored. Pain perception is the result of both physiological and psychological factors.

The discussion of perception first distinguishes between bottom-up (data-driven) processing and top-down (conceptually driven) processing. The Gestalt psychologists emphasized the perception of whole forms (gestalts). Figure–ground relationships and shape perception are then explained, followed by several principles of perceptual organization (laws of proximity, similarity, closure, good continuation, and Prägnanz). Depth perception, including monocular and binocular cues, is discussed next. The perception of motion is described; then perceptual constancies are explained. How we misperceive objects and events in our world is illustrated through various illusions. That perception is a psychological process is made clear through a discussion of how perceptual sets—expectations, learning experiences, and cultural factors—influence our interpretations.

Enhancing Well-Being with Psychology explains how we can use various perceptual strategies and techniques in the control of pain.

Introduction: What Are Sensation and Perception?

Preview Questions

Consider the following questions as you study this section of the chapter.

- What is the primary function of the nervous system?
- What are the definitions of *sensation* and *perception*?
- How do sensation and perception differ?

*Read the section "Introduction: What Are Sensation and Perception?" and **write** your answers to the following:*

1. The primary function of the nervous system is ______________________
2. Sensation refers to ______________________

   Perception occurs when ______________________
3. The difference between sensation and perception is ______________________

Basic Principles of Sensation

Preview Questions

Consider the following questions as you study this section of the chapter.

- What are sensory receptors; how do they help us hear, taste, smell, feel, and see? What is transduction?
- What are the two types of sensory thresholds?
- How does Weber's law relate to the just noticeable difference (jnd)?
- Why does sensory adaptation occur, and why is it important?

*Read the section "Basic Principles of Sensation" and **write** the answers to the following:*

1. We are able to hear, taste, smell, feel, and see by ______________________
2. Transduction is ______________________
3. The two types of sensory threshold (and what they refer to) are ______________________
4. Another name for the difference threshold is ______________________
5. Weber's law states ______________________
6. Sensory adaptation occurs because ______________________

   It is important because ______________________

After you have carefully studied the preceding sections, complete the following exercises.

Concept Check 1

Read the following and write the correct term in the space provided.

1. When Anton went to have his hearing tested, different tones were transmitted through the earphones he was wearing. Some tones were at such a low level of intensity he could not detect them. These sounds were below Anton's ______________ threshold.
2. When Jennifer was first presented with an auditory stimulus, she detected the sequence of sounds as only a series of different tones. After hearing the sequence of sounds a second time, she recognized them as a melody. This example illustrates the overlapping processes of ______________ and ______________ .
3. Jan was exposed to a 100-watt light. When its brightness was increased by 5 watts, she was not aware of the increase. However, when a 20-watt light was increased by 5 watts, she detected the increase immediately. Jan's ability to detect this difference is called the ______________ , or ______________ , and this may vary as a function of the size of the initial stimulus, a principle of sensation called ______________ .

4. The school bell rings at lunchtime. The process by which our ears convert the sound waves from the bell into a coded neural signal that can be processed by the nervous system is called ______________ .
5. Not realizing how cold it is after you have been on the ski slope for a while is an example of ______________ .
6. Dr. Jasenka's research demonstrated that simple information presented outside of conscious awareness influenced emotions, thoughts, and attitudes. These effects, however, were weak and short-lived. More complex messages had no effect. Dr. Jasenka's research is concerned with ______________ .

Review of Terms and Concepts 1

Use the terms in this list to complete the Matching Exercise, then to help you answer the True/False items correctly.

sensation	difference threshold (just noticeable difference or jnd)
perception	Weber's law
sensory receptors	subliminal perception
transduction	mere exposure effect
threshold	sensory adaptation
absolute threshold	

Matching Exercise

Match the appropriate term with its definition or description.

1. ______________ The point at which a stimulus is strong enough to be detected because it activates sensory receptors.
2. ______________ The process by which a form of physical energy is converted into a coded neural signal that can be processed by the nervous system.
3. ______________ The smallest possible strength of a stimulus that can be detected half the time.
4. ______________ Specialized cells unique to each sense organ that respond to a particular form of sensory stimulation.
5. ______________ The smallest possible difference between two stimuli that can be detected half the time.
6. ______________ The finding that repeated exposure to a stimulus increases a person's preference for that stimulus.

True/False Test

Indicate whether each statement is true or false by placing T or F in the blank space next to each item.

1. ___ Perception refers to the process of detecting a physical stimulus, such as sound, light, heat, or pressure.
2. ___ Sensory adaptation refers to the decline in sensitivity to a constant stimulus.
3. ___ Weber's law is a principle of sensation that holds that the size of the just noticeable difference will vary depending on its relation to the strength of the original stimulus.
4. ___ The process of integrating, organizing, and interpreting sensations is called sensation.
5. ___ The perception of stimuli that are below the threshold of conscious awareness is called subliminal perception.

Check your answers and review any areas of weakness before going on to the next section.

Vision: From Light to Sight

Preview Questions

Consider the following questions as you study this section of the chapter.

- How do we see, and what is the electromagnetic spectrum?
- What are the key structures of the eye, and what are their functions?
- What are the functions of the rods and cones, what is the optic disc, and how do the bipolar and ganglion cells process visual information for transmission to the brain?
- What properties of light determine our experience of color, how do the two theories of color vision explain the process, and what is the integrated explanation?

*Read the section "Vision: From Light to Sight" and **write** your answers to the following.*

1. The process of seeing begins with ______________
____
____

2. The electromagnetic spectrum is ______________________________

3. The key structures of the eye (and their functions) are ______________________________

4. The function of rods is to ______________________________

   The function of cones is to ______________________________

5. The optic disc is ______________________________

6. Bipolar cells process visual information by ______________________________

   The bundled axons of the ______________________________

7. Our experience of color involves ______________________________

8. According to the trichromatic theory, ______________________________

   This theory explains ______________________________

9. According to the opponent-process theory, ______________________________

   This theory explains ______________________________

10. An integrated explanation of color vision states that ______________________________

After you have carefully studied the preceding section, complete the following exercises.

Concept Check 2

Read the following and write the correct term in the space provided.

1. According to the trichromatic theory, if Mr. Colorado's red- and blue-sensitive cones are stimulated simultaneously, he should see ______________.
2. Constantino, who has normal vision, stares at a red circle for a couple of minutes, then shifts his eyes to a white surface. The afterimage of the circle will be ______________.
3. The fact that Constantino experiences an afterimage cannot be explained by the ______________ theory of color vision, but it can be explained by the ______________ theory.
4. Following an accident, the fovea in Harbinder's right eye was destroyed. Although he can still see with this eye, it is likely that he will have trouble seeing ______________ and ______________ when his left eye is closed.
5. Arica noted that her new T-shirt absorbed all the wavelengths of visible light and reflected none. The color of her T-shirt is ______________.
6. The story of Mike May was introduced in the Prologue. After surgery to restore vision to his right eye, Mike's retina and optic nerve were completely normal and he had excellent color perception and could easily identify simple shapes and lines that were oriented in different directions. According to Focus on Neuroscience (Vision, Experience, and the Brain), fMRI scans show that certain areas of Mike's brain never developed because they need experience and time to grow. As a result, even three years after surgery Mike is unable to ______________ ______________.

Graphic Organizer 1

Identify each part of the eye by writing the name on the appropriate line in the drawing below; then match its function by placing the corresponding number next to the name. (For example, "1. retina" is the first answer.)

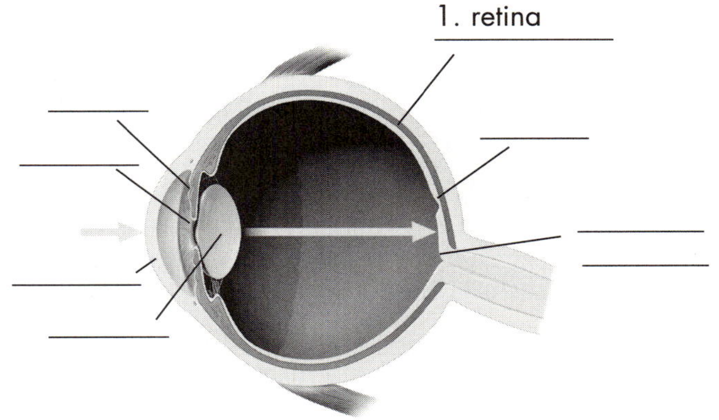

1. A light-sensitive membrane located at the back of the eye that contains sensory receptors for vision.
2. The black opening in the middle of the eye that changes size to let in different amounts of light.
3. A clear membrane covering the visible part of the eye that helps gather and direct incoming light.
4. The colored part of the eye that is the muscle that controls the size of the pupil.
5. A transparent structure located behind the pupil that actively focuses, or bends, light as it enters the eye.
6. A small area in the center of the retina that contains cones but not rods.
7. The area of the retina without rods or cones, where the optic nerve leaves the eye.

Review of Terms and Concepts 2

Use the terms in this list to complete the Matching Exercise, then to help you answer the True/False items correctly.

wavelength
cornea
sclera
pupil
iris
lens
accommodation
myopia (nearsightedness)
hyperopia (farsightedness)
presbyopia
astigmatism
retina
rods
cones
photoreceptors
fovea
optic disk
blind spot
ganglion cells
bipolar cells
visual acuity
optic nerve
optic chiasm
feature detectors
color
hue
saturation
brightness
trichromatic theory of color vision
color blindness
afterimage
opponent-process theory of color vision

Matching Exercise

Match the appropriate term with its definition or description:

1. ________________ The visual ability to see fine details.
2. ________________ Visual experience that occurs after the original source of stimulation is no longer present.
3. ________________ Distance from one wave peak to another.
4. ________________ Process by which the lens changes shape to focus incoming light so that it falls on the retina.
5. ________________ Perceived intensity of color that corresponds to the amplitude of the light wave.
6. ________________ Thick nerve that exits from the back of the eye and carries visual information to the visual cortex in the brain.
7. ________________ Theory that the sensation of color is due to cones in the retina that are especially sensitive to light that is red (long wavelengths), green (medium wavelengths), or blue (short wavelengths).
8. ________________ Short, thick, pointed sensory receptors of the eye that detect color and are responsible for color vision and visual acuity.
9. ________________ Property of wavelengths of light, known as color, in which different wavelengths correspond to our subjective experience of different colors.
10. ________________ Long, thin, blunt sensory receptors that are highly sensitive to light but not to color and are primarily responsible for peripheral vision and night vision.
11. ________________ Specialized neurons in the retina that collect sensory information from the rods and cones and then funnel it to other specialized neurons before it is transmitted to the brain.

12. ________________ Perceptual experience of different wavelengths of light, involving hue, saturation (purity), and brightness (intensity).

13. ________________ Area of the retina without rods or cones, where the optic nerve exits the back of the eye.

14. ________________ A form of farsightedness caused when the lens becomes brittle and inflexible during middle age.

15. ________________ A visual disorder in which an abnormally curved eyeball results in blurry vision for lines in a particular direction.

16. ________________ Specialized neurons in the visual cortex that detect, or respond to, particular aspects of more complex visual stimuli.

True/False Test

Indicate whether each statement is true or false by placing T or F in the blank space next to each item.

1. ____ The cornea is the transparent structure located behind the pupil that actively focuses, or bends, light as it enters the eye.
2. ____ The opponent-process theory states that color vision is the product of opposing pairs of color receptors, red–green, black–white, and blue–yellow; when one member of a color pair is stimulated, the other is inhibited.
3. ____ The lens is the clear membrane covering the visible part of the eye that helps gather and direct incoming light.
4. ____ Ganglion cells are the specialized neurons in the retina that connect to the bipolar cells and whose bundled axons form the optic nerve.
5. ____ The retina is a small area in the center of the back of the eye that is composed entirely of cones, where visual information is most sharply focused.
6. ____ The colored part of the eye, which is actually a ring of muscles that controls the size of the pupil, is called the iris.
7. ____ The pupil is the opening in the middle of the iris that changes size to let in different amounts of light.
8. ____ The fovea is a thin, light-sensitive membrane located at the back of the eye that contains two kinds of sensory receptors for light and vision.
9. ____ The optic chiasm is the point in the brain where the optic fibers from each eye meet and partly cross over to the opposite side of the brain.
10. ____ Saturation is the property of color that corresponds to the purity of the light wave.
11. ____ Color blindness is one of several forms of color deficiency or weakness in which an individual cannot distinguish between certain colors.
12. ____ The blind spot is the point where the optic nerve leaves the eye, producing a small gap in the field of vision.
13. ____ Nearsightedness occurs when close objects are seen clearly but distant objects appear blurry because the light from distant objects is focused behind the retina.
14. ____ The sclera, or white portion of the eye, is a tough, fibrous tissue that covers the eyeball, except for the cornea.
15. ____ Farsightedness occurs when distant objects are seen clearly but close objects appear blurry because the light from close objects is focused in front of the retina.
16. ____ Photoreceptors are sensory receptors that respond to light and undergo a chemical reaction that results in a neural signal.

Check your answers and review any areas of weakness before going on to the next section.

Hearing: From Vibration to Sound

Preview Questions

Consider the following questions as you study this section of the chapter.

- What is audition, and how do we hear?
- What properties of a sound wave correspond to our perception of sound?
- What are the key structures of the ear, and what are their functions?
- What does the process of hearing involve?
- How do place theory and frequency theory explain pitch perception?

*Read the section "Hearing: From Vibration to Sound" and **write** your answers to the following:*

1. Audition is ____
____
____

2. Our perception of sound is directly related to the physical properties of ____________________

3. The key structures of the ear are ____________________

4. The process of hearing begins when ____________________

It then involves ____________________

5. According to frequency theory ____________________

This theory explains ____________________

6. According to place theory ____________________

This theory explains ____________________

For intermediate frequencies or mid-range pitches ____________________

After you have carefully studied the preceding section, complete the following exercises.

Concept Check 3

Read the following and write the correct term in the space provided.

1. When Hamish whispered in Morag's ear, she could barely hear what he said. The loudness of his whisper was determined by the ____________________ of the sound waves, which are measured in units called ____________________ .

2. Rita, who has suffered damage to the bones in her middle ear, has been told by the experts that a hearing aid that artificially amplifies sounds will help restore her hearing. Rita probably has ____________________ deafness.

3. The three tiny bones in Rita's middle ear are called the ____________________ , the ____________________ , and the ____________________ .

4 Within seconds of answering the phone, Lacey recognized her old friend's voice even though they had not spoken for years. Her ability to do this is due, in part at least, to the fact that every human voice has its own distinctive ____________________ , a quality produced by the complexity of several sound-wave frequencies.

5. Dixon has attended so many rock concerts with extremely high decibel levels that he is now experiencing ringing in his ears. It is probable that this exposure to loud sounds has damaged the hair cells in his ____________________ ; he may eventually develop a form of deafness called ____________________ deafness.

6. During the first take in a recording session, Jelena adjusted the equipment in order to achieve a nice balance between the relative highness and lowness of the sounds produced by the musicians. Jelena is concerned with ____________________ , which is determined by the frequency of sound waves, measured in units called ____________________ .

7. Dr. Botchev's research is concerned with how sound waves produced by the rhythmic vibrations of air molecules are converted into neural messages in the inner ear, a process called ____________________ . He is most likely to be interested in the functions of the inner ear structure called the ____________________ and the ____________________ that lines its surface.

8. A researcher discovered that a sound wave of 100 hertz caused each hair along the basilar membrane to vibrate at 100 times per second and that neural impulses were sent to the brain at the same rate. This finding supports the ____________________ theory of pitch.

9. One question on the final exam required Seth to label three parts of the outer ear on a diagram. If he knows his material, he is likely to label these parts as the ________________ , the ________________ , and the ________________ .

Graphic Organizer 2

Identify each part of the ear by writing the name on the appropriate line and then match its function by placing the corresponding number next to the name. (For example, "1. pinna" is the first answer.)

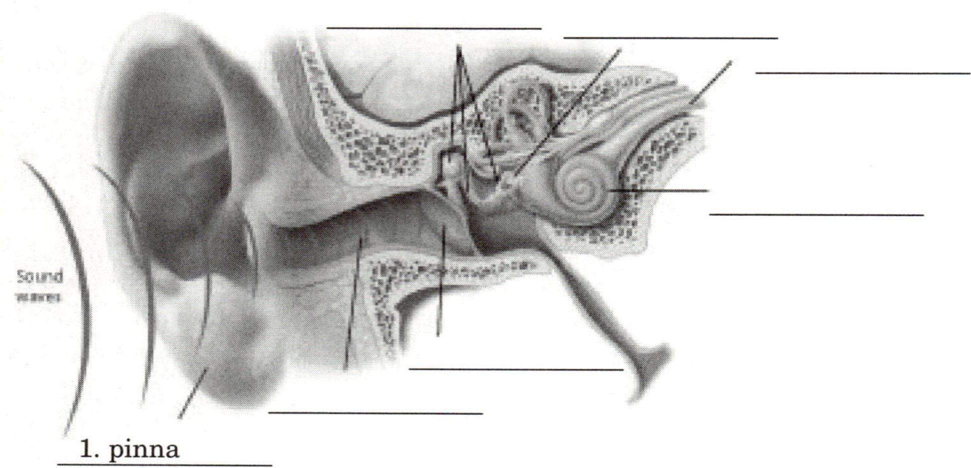

1. The oddly shaped flap of skin and cartilage that is attached to each side of the head.
2. A tightly stretched membrane at the end of the ear canal that vibrates when hit by sound waves.
3. A fluid-filled coiled structure that contains the sensory receptors for sound.
4. The tunnel through which sound waves travel to reach the eardrum.
5. The tightly stretched membrane that separates the middle ear from the inner ear.
6. The small structures of the middle ear whose joint action almost doubles the amplification of the sound.
7. The nerve that carries the neural information to the thalamus and the auditory cortex in the brain.

Review of Terms and Concepts 3

Use the terms in this list to complete the Matching Exercise, then to help you answer the True/False items correctly.

audition
sound waves
loudness
amplitude
decibel
pitch
frequency
hertz
timbre
outer ear
pinna
ear canal
eardrum
middle ear
hammer, anvil, and stirrup
oval window
conduction deafness
inner ear
cochlea
basilar membrane
hair cells
nerve deafness
frequency theory
place theory

Matching Exercise

Match the appropriate term with its definition or description.

1. ________________ The intensity (or amplitude) of a sound wave measured in decibels.
2. ________________ Technical term for the sense of hearing.
3. ________________ Rate of vibration, or number of waves per second.
4. ________________ Sensory receptors for sound embedded in the basilar membrane.
5. ________________ Physical stimuli that produce our sensory experience of sound.
6. ________________ The distinctive quality of a sound, determined by the complexity of the sound waves.
7. ________________ Part of the ear that collects sound waves and consists of the pinna, the ear canal, and the eardrum.

8. ________________ Relative highness or lowness of a sound, determined by the frequency of the sound wave.

9. ________________ Unit of measurement for loudness.

10. ________________ Intensity or amount of energy of a wave, reflected in the height of the wave; determines a sound's loudness.

11. ________________ The part of the ear that amplifies sound waves; consists of three small bones—the hammer, the anvil, and the stirrup.

12. ________________ The view that the basilar membrane vibrates at the same frequency as sound waves.

True/False Test

Indicate whether each statement is true or false by placing T or F in the blank space next to each item.

1. ____ Damage to the hair cells or auditory nerve can result in *conduction deafness.*

2. ____ The eardrum is a tightly stretched membrane that separates the middle ear from the inner ear.

3. ____ *Nerve deafness* results when the tiny bones of the middle ear are damaged or become brittle.

4. ____ The hammer, anvil, and stirrup are important structures in the middle ear that amplify sound.

5. ____ The cochlea is a coiled, fluid-filled structure that contains the sensory receptors for sound.

6. ____ Hertz refers to the number of wave peaks per second.

7. ____ The part of the outer ear that sound waves travel through to reach the eardrum is called the ear canal.

8. ____ The structure within the cochlea that contains the hair cells is called the basilar membrane.

9. ____ The oval window is a tightly stretched membrane at the end of the ear canal that vibrates when sound waves hit it.

10. ____ The pinna is the oddly shaped flap of skin and cartilage that is attached to each side of your head.

11. ____ The inner ear is the part of the ear where sound is transduced into neural impulses; it consists of the cochlea and semicircular canals.

12. ____ The view that different frequencies cause larger vibrations at different locations along the basilar membrane is called place theory.

Check your answers and review any areas of weakness before going on to the next section.

The Chemical and Body Senses: Smell, Taste, Touch, and Position

Preview Questions

Consider the following questions as you study this section of the chapter.

- How are *olfaction* and *gustation* defined, and what is meant by the chemical senses?
- How do airborne molecules result in the sensation of odor?
- What are the primary tastes, and how do we perceive different tastes?
- What are the skin and body senses, and what sensory receptors are involved in touch and temperature?
- How is the sensation of pain produced, and what causes pain?
- What nociceptors are involved in the fast and slow pain systems, and what is the gate-control theory of pain?
- What is phantom limb pain, and how can it be explained?
- What are the kinesthetic and vestibular senses, and where are their receptors located?

Read the section "The Chemical and Body Senses: Smell, Taste, Touch, and Position" and ***write*** *your answers to the following:*

1. Olfaction is the technical term for

   ____

   and gustation is the technical term for

   ____

2. They are called chemical senses because

   ____

   ____

3. Our sense of smell begins when ____________

   ____

The stimulation is then ______________________________
____
____

4. Our sense of taste begins when ______________________________
____

The stimulation is ______________________________
____
____

5. The five primary taste categories are ______________________________
____

6. The skin and body senses include ______________________________
____

7. The skin responds to ______________________________
____

8. One receptor for touch is ______________________________
which works by ______________________________
____
____

9. Pain is the unpleasant sensation of ______________________________
____

10. Two types of nociceptors are involved in pain.
(a) ____________________, which represent the fast pain system and transmit
____
____

(b) ____________________, which represent the slow pain system and transmit
____
____

11. According to the gate-control theory, ______________________________
____
____
____

12. The experience of pain can be influenced by psychological factors, such as ______________________________
____
____

13. Phantom limb pain refers to ______________________________
____

It is explained by ______________________________
____
____

14. Our kinesthetic sense involves ______________________________
____
____

15. Our vestibular sense provides us with ______________________________
____

16. The two sources of vestibular sensory information are ______________________________
____

After you have carefully studied the preceding sections, complete the following exercises.

Concept Check 4

Read the following and write the correct term in the space provided.

1. After eating his salad with vinegar dressing, Mario thinks that his very expensive vintage wine tastes strange. This change in perceived taste probably occurs because some vinegar remains on his ____________________.
2. Ever since he lost a finger in an industrial accident, Oswald experiences intense physical sensations in his nonexistent finger. Oswald is experiencing ____________________, which occurs because the neurons in the transmission pathways from the site of the amputation to the brain become ____________________.
3. As the result of an accident, Chih Fan experienced damage to his thalamus. The one sense that will be least affected by this brain damage is his sense of ____________________.
4. For dinner, Klara had a salad with lemon dressing, a teriyaki steak with mushrooms, a potato with sour cream, and ice cream for dessert. It is very likely that she has experienced the five basic taste sensations of
____________, ____________,
____________, ____________, and
____________.
5. On the day of her final statistics exam, Nadia has a sore ankle. According to the gate-control theory, it is likely that Nadia's anxiety about the exam will ____________________ her perception of the pain in her ankle.

6. While fishing in a small boat, Mortimer becomes nauseated from the motion of the waves. Mortimer's ________________ and ________________ are most likely responsible for making him feel ill.
7. Dr. Farnaz conducts research on pain pathways. He is likely to be interested in small sensory fibers called ______________________, or ______________________. In particular, he is interested in ______________________ fibers (fast pain system) and ______________________ fibers (slow pain system), which are triggered by bodily damage or injury.
8. If you are blindfolded and asked to touch your chin, nose, and forehead with your index finger, you probably will have no trouble doing so. This ability is due to your ______________________ sense.
9. Arleigh accidentally scrapes some skin off his knuckles while working on his car. The pain he feels following the injury is caused in part by the release of the neurotransmitter ______________________.

Review of Terms and Concepts 4

Use the terms in this list to complete the Matching Exercise, then to help you answer the True/False items correctly.

olfaction
gustation
anosmia
airborne chemical molecules
olfactory receptor cells
olfactory nerve
olfactory bulb
olfactory cortex
olfactory tract
pheromones
taste buds
umami
flavor
skin senses
body senses
Pacinian corpuscle
pain
nociceptors (free nerve endings)
A-delta fibers
C fibers
substance P
gate-control theory of pain
endorphins and enkephalins
phantom limb pain
sensitization
chronic pain
kinesthetic sense
proprioceptors
vestibular sense
semicircular canals and vestibular sacs

Matching Exercise

Match the appropriate term with its definition or description.

1. ________________ Technical term for our sense of taste.
2. ________________ Fluid-filled structures that are lined with hair-like receptor cells that shift in response to motion, changes in body position, or changes in gravity.
3. ________________ Touch receptor located beneath the skin; when stimulated by pressure, it converts the stimulation into neural messages that are relayed to the brain.
4. ________________ A condition characterized by a partial or complete loss of the sense of smell.
5. ________________ Specialized sensory receptors for pain that are found in the skin, muscles, or internal organs.
6. ________________ Cells located high in the nasal cavity that are stimulated by inhaled molecules in the air.
7. ________________ Enlarged ending of the olfactory cortex at the front of the brain, where the sensation of smell is registered.
8. ________________ Specialized sensory receptors for taste that are located on the tongue and inside the mouth and throat.
9. ________________ Tract formed by bundles of axons from the olfactory bulb that projects to different brain areas, including the temporal lobe and structures in the limbic system.
10. ________________ The sense of balance or equilibrium.
11. ________________ The body's natural painkillers that are produced in many parts of the brain and the body.
12. ________________ The sense of location and position of body parts in relation to one another.
13. ________________ A taste category that involves the distinctive taste of monosodium glutamate, aged cheeses, mushrooms, seaweed, and protein-rich foods such as meat.
14. ________________ A phenomenon in which a person continues to experience intense painful sensations in a limb that has been amputated.
15. ________________ Myelinated nociceptors involved in the fast pain system that transmit sharp, intense, but short-lived pain signals, immediately following injury.

True/False Test

Indicate whether each statement is true or false by placing T or F in the space next to each item.

1. ____ Pain is the unpleasant sensation of physical discomfort or suffering that can occur in varying degrees of intensity.
2. ____ Gate-control theory suggests that pain is the product of both physiological and psychological factors that cause spinal "gates" to open and relay patterns of intense stimulation to the brain, which perceives them as pain.
3. ____ Airborne chemical molecules are emitted by the substances we smell and are inhaled through the nose and through the opening in the palate at the back of the throat.
4. ____ The olfactory nerve connects directly to the olfactory bulb, where smells are perceived by the brain.
5. ____ Proprioceptors are neurotransmitters that are involved in the transmission of pain messages to the brain.
6. ____ Olfaction is the technical term for our sense of smell.
7. ____ Flavor involves several sensations, including the taste, aroma, temperature, texture, and appearance of food.
8. ____ The olfactory cortex is at the front of the brain and is directly linked to the outside world via neural pathways.
9. ____ The body senses provide essential information about our physical status and our physical interaction with objects in our environment.
10. ____ Substance P is found in the muscles and joints and provides information about body position and movement.
11. ____ The skin senses keep us informed as to our position and orientation in space.
12. ____ Pheromones are chemical signals released by animals that communicate information about social and sexual status and affect the behavior of other animals of the same species.
13. ____ C fibers are unmyelinated nociceptors that make up the slow pain system and create the longer-lasting, throbbing, burning kind of pain following injury.
14. ____ Sensitization is the opposite of sensory adaptation in that pain pathways in the brain become increasingly more responsive over time following severe injury or damage.
15. ____ Chronic pain involves the continuation of pain perception after the injury has healed; it may be caused by neurons in the pain pathways undergoing sensitization.

Check your answers and review any areas of weakness before going on to the next section.

Perception (Part 1)

Preview Questions

Consider the following questions as you study this section of the chapter.

- What is perception?
- How does bottom-up processing differ from top-down processing?
- What three questions does perception answer about the stimuli we sense?
- Who founded Gestalt psychology, and what is the main focus of this perspective?

*Read the section "Perception" (the introduction only) and **write** your answers to the following:*

1. Perception is the process of ____________________
   ____
   ____
2. Bottom-up processing refers to ____________________
   ____
   ____
3. Top-down processing refers to ____________________
   ____
   ____
4. The three basic questions of perception are
   ____
   ____
   ____
5. Gestalt psychology was founded by ____________________
   ____
   and is concerned with ____________________
   ____
   ____

Perception: The Perception of Shape (Part 2)

Preview Questions

Consider the following questions as you study this section of the chapter.

- What is the figure–ground relationship, and how significant is it to perception?
- What perceptual principles do we follow when we group visual elements?
- What is the law of Prägnanz, and what does it explain?

*Read the section "Perception: The Perception of Shape" (up to Depth Perception) and **write** your answers to the following:*

1. The figure–ground relationship describes ______________________

   ____

   It is important because it demonstrates that ______________________

   ____
2. The perceptual principles involved in grouping visual elements include ______________________

   ____

   ____
3. The law of Prägnanz states ______________________

   ____

   ____

   It is important because it encompasses ______________________

   and suggests that ______________________

   ____

Perception: Depth Perception (Part 3)

Preview Questions

Consider the following questions as you study this section of the chapter.

- How is depth perception defined, and why is it important?
- What are monocular cues, and how do they contribute to depth perception?
- What are binocular cues, and how do they differ from monocular cues?
- How is binocular disparity involved in our ability to see three-dimensional images in, for example, stereograms?

*Read the section "Perception: Depth Perception" (up to Motion Perception) and **write** your answers to the following:*

1. Depth perception refers to ______________________

   ____

   It is important because ______________________

   ____
2. Monocular cues are defined as ______________________

   ____

   and include ______________________

   ____
3. Binocular cues are defined as ______________________

   ____

   and include ______________________

   ____
4. A stereogram is ______________________

   ____

After you have carefully studied the preceding sections, complete the following exercises.

Concept Check 5

Read the following and write the correct term in the space provided.

1. When Tsung looked at the 16 numbers on his credit card—2314 5634 8679 1357—he perceived them as four groups of four numbers each. The tendency to perceive things that are close together as a single unit is called the ______________________ .
2. At a noisy party, Ben focuses on his girlfriend's conversation, while tuning out the other conversations. Using a Gestalt perceptual principle to analyze this example, the noisy environment is the ______________________ and his girlfriend's voice is the ______________________ .

3. While viewing a stereogram, Nina experiences the perceptual illusion of three-dimensional depth from the two-dimensional scene. The binocular cue responsible for this phenomenon is ______________________ .
4. Chan knows that the red bicycle in the parking lot is closer to him than the green bicycle because the red one casts a larger retinal image. This illustrates the distance cue known as ______________________ .
5. Emily paints a long garden pathway bordered with flowers. She shows the flowers as decreasing in size as they approach the horizon, where they seem to meet; Emily is using ________________ to convey depth on the canvas.
6. Although a number of individual lights had burned out on the flashing sign, Lizabet perceived the sign as complete and had no trouble reading the whole message. The tendency to fill in gaps in an incomplete image is called the ______________________ .
7. To make the task of completing the jigsaw puzzle more challenging, Zahra attempted to assemble it without the finished picture in front of her. Zahra is most likely to use ________________, or data-driven processing, to accomplish the task.

Review of Terms, Concepts, and Names 5

Use the terms in this list to complete the Matching Exercise, then to help you answer the True/False items correctly.

perception
bottom-up processing (data-driven processing)
top-down processing (conceptually driven processing)
ESP (extrasensory perception)
parapsychology
Gestalt psychology
Max Wertheimer
gestalt
figure–ground relationship
figure–ground reversal
law of similarity
law of closure
law of good continuation
law of proximity
law of Prägnanz (law of simplicity)
depth perception
monocular cues
pictorial cues
relative size
overlap (interposition)
aerial perspective
texture gradient
linear perspective
motion parallax
accommodation
binocular cues
convergence
binocular disparity
stereogram

Matching Exercise

Match the appropriate term with its definition or description.

1. ________________ School of psychology founded in Germany in the early 1900s that maintained that our sensations are actively processed according to consistent perceptual rules that result in meaningful whole perceptions.
2. ________________ Law that states that when several perceptual organizations are possible, the perceptual interpretation that will occur will be the one that produces the "best, simplest, and most stable shape."
3. ________________ Monocular cue that suggests that faraway objects often appear hazy or slightly blurred by the atmosphere.
4. ________________ Binocular cue that relies on the fact that our eyes are set a couple of inches apart, and thus slightly different images are cast on the retina of each eye.
5. ________________ Gestalt principle of perceptual organization that states that we automatically separate the elements of a perception into the feature that clearly stands out from its less distinct background.
6. ________________ Monocular cue in which an object partially blocked or obscured by another object is perceived as being farther away.
7. ________________ Distance or depth cues that require the use of both eyes.
8. ________________ Monocular cue that utilizes information about changes in the shape of the lens of the eye to help us gauge depth and distance.
9. ________________ Gestalt principle of organization that refers to the tendency to perceive objects that are close to one another as a unit or figure.
10. ________________ The use of monocular or binocular visual cues to perceive the distance or three-dimensional characteristics of objects.
11. ________________ The perception of an image in which the ground can be perceived as the figure and the figure as the ground; underscores that our perception of figure and ground is a psychological phenomenon.

12. ________________ German psychologist who founded Gestalt psychology in the early 1900s, studied the optical illusion of apparent movement, and described principles of perception.

13. ________________ The scientific investigation of claims of various paranormal phenomena.

14. ________________ Gestalt principle of organization that refers to the tendency to perceive objects of similar size, shape, or color as a unit or figure.

15. ________________ The German word that means unified whole, form, or shape.

True/False Test

Indicate whether each statement is true or false by placing T or F in the space next to each item.

1. ____ Perception refers to the process of integrating, organizing, and interpreting sensory information into meaningful representation.
2. ____The law of good continuation, a gestalt principle of organization, is the tendency to group elements that appear to follow in the same direction as a single unit or figure.
3. ____The monocular cue of linear perspective refers to the fact that if two or more objects are assumed to be similar in size, the object that appears larger is perceived as being closer.
4. ____ Monocular cues are distance or depth cues that can be processed by either eye alone.
5. ____ The depth cue that occurs when parallel lines seem to meet in the distance (and the closer together the lines appear to be, the greater the perception of depth) is called relative size.
6. ____ Convergence is a binocular cue that relies on the degree to which muscles rotate the eyes to focus on an object; the less convergence, the farther away the object appears to be.
7. ____ When we are in motion, we can use the speed of passing objects to estimate their distance; nearby objects will appear to move much faster relative to distant objects. This monocular cue is called motion parallax.
8. ____ Texture gradient is a monocular cue in which the details of a surface with distinct texture become gradually less clearly defined as the surface extends into the distance; it appears crisp and distinct when close, and fuzzy and indistinct when farther away.
9. ____ Top-down processing is information processing that emphasizes the importance of sensory receptors in detecting the basic features of a stimulus in the process of recognizing a whole pattern; it involves analysis from the parts to the whole.
10. ____ A stereogram is a picture that uses the principle of binocular disparity to create the perception of a three-dimensional image.
11. ____ Bottom-up processing is information processing that emphasizes the importance of the observer's knowledge, expectations, and other cognitive processes in arriving at meaningful perceptions and involves analysis from the whole to the parts.
12. ____ ESP (extrasensory perception) is based on the idea that sensory information can be detected by some means other than through the normal processes of sensation.
13. ____ The law of closure, a gestalt principle of organization, is the tendency to fill in gaps or contours in an incomplete image.
14. ____ Monocular cues used by artists to create the perception of distance or depth in paintings are called pictorial cues.

Check your answers and review any areas of weakness before going on to the next section.

Perception: The Perception of Motion (Part 4)

Preview Questions

Consider the following questions as you study this section of the chapter.

- Which sources of information contribute to our perception of motion?
- Who first studied induced motion, and what does this phenomenon involve?
- How does stroboscopic motion work, and how does it relate to the perception of motion?

*Read the section "Perception: The Perception of Motion" (up to Perceptual Constancies) and **write** your answers to the following:*

1. The perception of motion involves ________________
____
____

2. Induced motion refers to ______

   It was first studied by ______
3. Stroboscopic motion creates ______

   It is caused by ______

Perception: Perceptual Constancies (Part 5)

Preview Questions

Consider the following questions as you study this section of the chapter.

- What is perceptual constancy?
- What principles guide our perception of size constancy?
- What is shape constancy?

*Read the section "Perception: Perceptual Constancies" and **write** your answers to the following:*

1. Perceptual constancy refers to ______
2. Size constancy is ______

   An important aspect of size constancy is ______
3. Shape constancy is ______

Perceptual Illusions and The Effects of Experience on Perceptual Interpretations

Preview Questions

Consider the following questions as you study these sections of the chapter.

- What are perceptual illusions, and why are psychologists interested in them?
- How are the Müller-Lyer and moon illusions explained?
- What do illusions reveal about normal perceptual processes?
- What is a perceptual set, and what effect can it have?

*Read the sections "Perceptual Illusions" and "The Effects of Experience on Perceptual Interpretations" and **write** your answers to the following:*

1. A perceptual illusion involves ______
2. The Müller-Lyer illusion is ______
3. The moon illusion involves ______

   and may be the result of ______
4. Perceptual illusions reveal that ______
5. Perceptions can be influenced by ______
6. A perceptual set is ______

   A perceptual set can often determine ______

After you have carefully studied the preceding sections, complete the following exercises.

Concept Check 6

Read the following and write the correct term in the space provided.

1. Stereotypes are mental conceptions that we have about individuals belonging to specific racial or ethnic groups and can influence how we interpret their behaviors. Stereotypes are most similar to the perceptual phenomenon of ______, which is the tendency to perceive objects or situations from a particular frame of reference.
2. William noticed that the full moon seemed to be much larger on the horizon than when it was

overhead. His friend Jane, a psychology major, explained that the illusion results from distance cues that make the horizon moon seem ________________ (farther away/closer) than an overhead moon.

3. Your unopened introductory psychology textbook produces a trapezoidal retinal image, but you typically perceive it as a rectangular object. This is due to ________________ constancy.
4. When asked to judge the length of two equal lines, Desiree judged the one with outward-pointing arrows as being longer than the one with inward-pointing arrows. Desiree has experienced the ________________ illusion.
5. When Dave's dog runs down the lane to greet him after work, the image of the dog on his retinas gets bigger and bigger, yet Dave does not perceive Rex as the incredible growing dog. The *general term* for this tendency to perceive objects, particularly familiar objects, as constant and unchanging despite changes in sensory input is called ________________ .
6. Ricardo uses sequentially flashing Christmas lights in front of his house to make it look as though Santa and his sleigh are moving from the garden to the roof. Ricardo is using the perceptual illusion of ________________ .

Review of Terms, Concepts, and Names 6

Use the terms in this list to complete the Matching Exercise, then to help you answer the True/False items correctly.

induced motion	Müller-Lyer illusion
Karl Duncker	moon illusion
stroboscopic motion	Shepard Tables
perceptual constancy	perceptual set
size constancy	biofeedback
shape constancy	acupuncture
perceptual illusion	

Matching Exercise

Match the appropriate term with its definition or description.

1. ________________ The tendency to perceive objects or situations from a particular frame of reference.
2. ________________ The tendency to perceive objects, especially familiar ones, as constant and unchanging despite sensory input changes.
3. ________________ Famous visual illusion involving the misperception of the identical length of two lines, one with arrows pointed inward and one with arrows pointed outward.
4. ________________ The perception of an object as maintaining the same size despite changing images on the retina.
5. ________________ Gestalt psychologist who is best known for his studies on the perception of induced motion.
6. ________________ Ancient Chinese medical procedure involving the insertion and manipulation of fine needles into specific locations on the body to alleviate pain and treat illness (may also involve stimulation of the needles with mild electrical current).
7. ________________ Illusion in which one tabletop appears to be longer than another even though they are both identical in length.

True/False Test

Indicate whether each statement is true or false by placing T or F in the space next to each item.

1. ____ When we misperceive the true characteristics of an object or image, we experience a perceptual illusion.
2. ____ The moon illusion involves the misperception that the moon is larger when it is on the horizon than when it is directly overhead.
3. ____ The perception of a familiar object as maintaining the same shape regardless of the image produced on the retina is called shape constancy.
4. ____ Stroboscopic motion refers to an illusion of movement that results when two separate, carefully timed flashing lights are perceived as one light moving back and forth.
5. ____ Induced motion occurs because we have a strong tendency to assume that the background is stationary while the object or figure moves.
6. ____ Biofeedback is a technique that involves using auditory or visual feedback to learn to exert voluntary control over involuntary body functions, such as heart rate, blood pressure, blood flow, and muscle tension.

Check your answers and review any areas of weakness before going on to the next section.

Something to Think About

1. Many people have reported strange experiences that they interpret as extrasensory perception, or ESP. Suppose that a friend or family member told you about such an experience. This person might be convinced that something extraordinary has occurred. Based on what you have learned in this chapter, how would you go about explaining to your friend what has most likely taken place?
2. Imagine that you have decided to become an artist. You want to paint a picture that includes a variety of elements, such as buildings, fields, a river, a mountain, and some people and animals. Using what you know about sensation and perception, think of all the monocular cues that you could use to give your masterpiece a sense of depth. In addition, can you think of any perceptual components that might add interest to your canvas?

Check your answers and review any areas of weakness before doing the progress tests.

Progress Test 1

Review the complete chapter (including all boxed inserts), review all your study notes, and then test yourself on the following progress test. Check your answers. If you make a mistake, review your notes, check the appropriate section in the study guide, and, if necessary, go back and read the relevant part of the chapter in your textbook.

1. Dr. Kandola believes that we perceive whole objects as figures (gestalts) rather than isolated bits and pieces of sensory information. Dr. Kandola's research most likely focuses on
   (a) gate-control theory and the role of substance P in the perception of pain.
   (b) top-down processing and basic perceptual principles such as the laws of similarity, closure, good continuation, proximity, and simplicity.
   (c) theories of color vision and phenomena such as afterimages, color blindness, and the experience of hue, brightness, and saturation.
   (d) bottom-up processing and basic sensory phenomena such as transduction, difference threshold, sensory adaptation, and accommodation.
2. Dr. Frankenstein's younger brother built a monster but omitted a very important part of his anatomy. As a result, the monster cannot transform sounds into neural messages. The missing part is the
   (a) eardrum.
   (b) middle ear with its tiny bones.
   (c) vestibular sacs.
   (d) basilar membrane.
3. A red pen is displayed in Roger's peripheral vision while he stares straight ahead. He correctly identifies the object but is unable to name the color. The reason for this is that
   (a) there are many rods but very few cones in the periphery of the retina.
   (b) there are many cones but very few rods in the periphery of the retina.
   (c) there are no receptor cells for vision in the periphery of the retina.
   (d) the stimulus was below Roger's difference threshold.
4. After staring at a blue light for a few minutes, Yoko shifts her gaze to a white wall and experiences an afterimage in the color ________ . Yoko's experience provides support for the ________ theory of color vision.
   (a) red; opponent-process
   (b) yellow; opponent-process
   (c) red; trichromatic
   (d) yellow; trichromatic
5. Neville is color-blind and cannot see red or green, yet he can see blue with no problem. Which theory of color vision can most easily explain this?
   (a) trichromatic theory
   (b) gate-control theory
   (c) opponent-process theory
   (d) gestalt theory
6. Ever since her operation, Madame Castellucci can no longer experience the flavors of the gourmet foods and wines she serves in her restaurant. It is most likely that she has suffered damage to her
   (a) kinesthetic sense.
   (b) sense of smell.
   (c) sense of humor.
   (d) vestibular sense.
7. The dizziness and disorientation Shelly felt after rolling down the hill are a function of her
   (a) basilar membrane.
   (b) Pacinian corpuscles.
   (c) semicircular canals and vestibular sacs.
   (d) proprioceptors.

8. As Pancho gazed down the railway tracks it seemed to him that the two parallel rails actually met in the distance. Pancho is experiencing the monocular depth cue
   (a) linear perspective. (c) motion parallax.
   (b) aerial perspective. (d) texture gradient.

9. Many people have mistaken a floating log for Ogopogo, the alleged Okanagan Lake monster. The most likely reason for this misperception is
   (a) a perceptual set.
   (b) monocular vision.
   (c) rye whiskey.
   (d) extrasensory perception.

10. If Fred holds a letter he is reading very close to his nose and Charlie holds it at arm's length when he reads it, Fred will experience _______________ Charlie.
    (a) more convergence than
    (b) the identical level of convergence as
    (c) less convergence than
    (d) more motion parallax than

11. In an experiment, you are seated in a darkened room and shown a large lighted frame with a single dot of light inside it. The frame slowly moves to the left, and the dot remains stationary. It is very probable that you will perceive
    (a) induced motion.
    (b) the dot moving to the right.
    (c) the frame as remaining stationary.
    (d) all of these conditions.

12. As Demi moves away from the camera, her image in the viewfinder grows smaller and smaller, yet viewers do not perceive Demi as the incredible shrinking woman. This illustrates
    (a) convergence. (c) size constancy.
    (b) binocular disparity. (d) motion parallax.

13. Researchers at State University study nociceptors (free nerve endings) and, in particular, the role played by A-delta fibers and C fibers. They are most likely to be interested in
    (a) olfaction and gustation.
    (b) the sensation and perception of pain.
    (c) proprioception and kinesthesis.
    (d) extrasensory perception.

14. People in industrialized societies are more susceptible to the Müller-Lyer illusion than those in nonindustrialized societies. According to Culture and Human Behavior (The Carpentered-World Hypothesis), these differences in susceptibility to the Müller-Lyer illusion are
    (a) the result of biological factors rather than cultural influences.
    (b) due to the mere exposure effect.
    (c) the result of cultural factors rather than biological influences.
    (d) due to innate or inborn perceptual sets.

15. According to Science Versus Pseudoscience (Subliminal Perception), if advertisers were to expose moviegoers to the subliminally flashed words "Eat popcorn" and "Drink Coke" during a movie
    (a) sales of popcorn and Coke would increase dramatically.
    (b) the moviegoers would feel hungry and thirsty for days after seeing the movie.
    (c) the subliminal messages are not likely to have any discernible effect on the sale of popcorn and Coke.
    (d) the moviegoers will have recurring nightmares involving popcorn and Coke.

Progress Test 2

After you have checked your understanding of the material in Progress Test 1 and have done a complete chapter review with special focus on any areas of weakness, you are ready to further assess your knowledge on Progress Test 2. Check your answers. If you make a mistake, review your notes, the relevant sections of the study guide, and, if necessary, the appropriate parts of your textbook.

1. Detection of stimulus energy is to the interpretation of the information as _______________ is to _______________.
   (a) transduction; accommodation
   (b) hue; saturation
   (c) hearing; vision
   (d) sensation; perception

2. When Julius returns from getting a drink of water, he resumes weightlifting a 150-pound free weight and doesn't notice that someone has added a 5-pound ring to each end. For Julius the additional 10 pounds
   (a) is not a just noticeable difference (jnd).
   (b) is below his absolute threshold.
   (c) is not sensed because of sensory adaptation.
   (d) is easy to lift because water releases endorphins.

3. When Vincent arrived home, the first thing he noticed was the smell of freshly baked bread. The process by which the odor of baking bread was converted into neural signals that Vincent's brain could interpret is called
   (a) sensory adaptation.
   (b) transduction.
   (c) accommodation.
   (d) conduction.

4. Malgorzata is wearing headphones and is asked to indicate when she is first aware of hearing a sound. It is very likely that the researchers are investigating
   (a) her difference threshold.
   (b) sensory adaptation.
   (c) her absolute threshold.
   (d) subliminal perception.

5. When Tony was painting a landscape, he used many different colors. The technical term for each of the different wavelengths of light that produce the subjective sensation of different colors in Tony's painting is
   (a) saturation.
   (b) hue.
   (c) brightness.
   (d) timbre.

6. As Rodney was setting up the equipment for the concert, he adjusted the amplitude of the speaker system. This is most likely to affect the ________________ of the music.
   (a) pitch
   (b) frequency
   (c) timbre
   (d) loudness

7. Jasvir suffers from myopia; Carmen suffers from hyperopia. Both disorders involve abnormally shaped eyeballs that do not focus incoming light on the retina. In Jasvir's case, the light from a distant object is focused ________________________; for Carmen, the light is focused ________________________.
   (a) on the cornea; on the optic disk
   (b) behind her retina; in front of her retina
   (c) on the optic disk; on the cornea
   (d) in front of her retina; behind her retina

8. When Derrick looked up from the newspaper he was reading to see if the bus was coming, the lenses in his eyes changed shape in order to focus on his retina the distant image of the street. This process is called
   (a) accommodation.
   (b) transduction.
   (c) sensory adaptation.
   (d) saturation.

9. In terms of the transduction of physical energy into coded neural messages, the ______________ is to the eye as the ______________ is to the ear.
   (a) lens; oval window
   (b) fovea; auditory nerve
   (c) retina; cochlea
   (d) iris; eardrum

10. On the day of an important job interview, Madeline wakes up with a slight toothache. As the time for the stressful interview approaches, her anxiety increases and so does her perception of the pain from her tooth. When the interview is over, Madeline is elated because she feels it has gone well and, to her surprise, she feels hardly any pain from her tooth. Madeline's experience is best explained by the ________________ and the contribution of her psychological and emotional state.
    (a) opponent-process theory
    (b) gate-control theory
    (c) law of simplicity
    (d) law of good continuation

11. Astrid holds a pencil quite close to her nose and opens and closes her left and right eyes a couple of times in succession. She notices that the images are quite different. When she views the same pencil in a similar manner from across the room, she sees almost identical images. Astrid has demonstrated the ______________ cue of ______________.
    (a) binocular; binocular disparity
    (b) monocular; motion parallax
    (c) binocular; overlap
    (d) monocular; convergence

12. With his eyes closed, Shahin can accurately touch his nose, lips, and ears with his right index finger. Shahin's ability to do this is due to specialized sensory neurons called ________________ that are involved in his ________________ sense.
    (a) Pacinian corpuscles; vestibular
    (b) ganglion cells; visual
    (c) proprioceptors; kinesthetic
    (d) pheromones; olfactory

13. At a police roadblock, drivers are randomly checked for seatbelt violations and other driving offenses. The police officer sometimes shines a light into the driver's eye. This typically results in the contraction of the

________________, which controls the size of the ________________ and thus the amount of light entering the eye.

(a) pupil; lens
(b) iris; pupil
(c) cornea; fovea
(d) iris; optic disk

14. Culture and Human Behavior (Ways of Seeing) discusses research on differences in perception between collectivistic cultures and individualistic cultures and concludes that
    (a) people from collectivistic cultures perceive the world in completely different ways from those in individualistic cultures,
    (b) people from different cultures do not differ significantly in the way they perceive things, in what they pay attention to, or in how they think about things.
    (c) people from individualistic cultures have a more holistic perceptual style than those from collectivistic cultures.
    (d) all people use the same neural processes to make perceptual judgments, but there are cultural differences in what people pay attention to and in how they think about what they see.

15. Willard believes he can influence the mechanical systems within slot machines with the power of his mind alone. According to Critical Thinking (ESP), Willard is claiming to possess the power of
    (a) telepathy.
    (b) clairvoyance.
    (c) psychokinesis.
    (d) precognition.

Progress Test 3

After you have checked your understanding of the material in Progress Tests 1 and 2 and have done a complete chapter review with special focus on any areas of weakness, you are ready to further assess your knowledge with Progress Test 3. Check your answers. If you make a mistake, review your notes, the appropriate parts of the study guide, and, if necessary, the relevant sections of your textbook.

1. During a psychology lab demonstration, the instructor set up two flashing lights about three feet apart in a darkened room. About one-tenth of a second after the first light flashed, the second light flashed, and then the first light flashed again, and so on. Most of the students experienced the illusion of apparent motion, perceiving just one light traveling back and forth. The instructor is most likely to explain this phenomenon in terms of
    (a) the principles of stroboscopic motion.
    (b) the kinesthetic sense.
    (c) motion parallax.
    (d) binocular disparity.

2. You have just arrived at the beach and the texture of the sand toward the water appears smooth, even, and perfectly flat, yet the sand beneath your feet is rough and uneven, and you can see individual small stones, seashells, and other debris. You are experiencing the monocular distance cue of
    (a) motion parallax.
    (b) aerial perspective.
    (c) linear perspective.
    (d) texture gradient.

3. José notices that near the horizon the moon appears larger than when it is overhead in the sky. The effect is mainly the result of
    (a) distance cues that make the horizon moon seem farther away.
    (b) the retinal image of the horizon moon being larger than the retinal image of the overhead moon.
    (c) distance cues that make the horizon moon seem nearer.
    (d) having to tilt your head upward when looking at the overhead moon.

4. While carrying out a sensory demonstration in which a small object is positioned so that its retinal image would be cast on the exact spot where her optic nerve exits the eye, Deidre should expect the image of the object to
    (a) change to its opposite color.
    (b) look twice as large as it had before.
    (c) produce an afterimage if she shifts her gaze to a white surface.
    (d) disappear from sight.

5. Analysis that moves from the parts to the whole is to ________________ as analysis that moves from the whole to the parts is to ________________.
    (a) figure–ground relationship; figure–ground reversal
    (b) bottom-up processing; top-down processing
    (c) size constancy; shape constancy
    (d) the moon illusion; the Müller-Lyer illusion

6. While strolling through the garden, Jamal suddenly noticed the wonderful odor of roses. Jamal is using her ________________ sense, and the process by which the odor is converted into neural signals that her brain can understand is called ________________ .
   (a) gustatory; saturation
   (b) olfactory: transduction
   (c) gustatory; adaptation
   (d) olfactory; accommodation

7. Whenever Robyn looks at her boyfriend, her pupils dilate. The eye structure responsible for this response is called the
   (a) retina.
   (b) fovea.
   (c) iris.
   (d) optic disk.

8. When looking carefully at a picture of a country scene, we are able to detect fine visual details, especially those that are focused on the fovea. One reason for this visual acuity is that
   (a) the fovea contains rods, which have many individual neural connections to the cortex.
   (b) the fovea contains cones, which have many individual neural connections to the cortex.
   (c) the fovea is the spot where the optic nerve leaves the eye.
   (d) there are only bipolar cells in the fovea, and these are specialized for feature detection.

9. After Jackson has been in the hot tub for a few minutes, he no longer notices how hot the water is. This is because of
   (a) sensory adaptation.
   (b) the just noticeable difference.
   (c) Jackson's thick skin.
   (d) sensory saturation.

10. After playing in a heavy metal rock band for most of his young adult life, Edwin has suffered a significant hearing loss. Unfortunately for Edwin, his hearing problem cannot be helped by a hearing aid. It is most likely that he is suffering from
    (a) damage to the auditory cortex in his left temporal lobe.
    (b) nerve deafness.
    (c) damage to his proprioceptors.
    (d) conduction deafness.

11. Graham is nearsighted and Grace is farsighted. Corrective lenses work for both of them because their respective visual disorders are caused by
    (a) the lack of rods and cones in the visual disk.
    (b) clouding or occlusion of the cornea.
    (c) smaller than normal ganglion and bipolar cells in the retina.
    (d) a failure of the lens to properly focus incoming light on the retina.

12. Mehnroosh believes that the size of the just noticeable difference varies depending on its relation to the strength of the original stimulus. Her views are most consistent with
    (a) Weber's law.
    (b) the law of Prägnanz.
    (c) the opponent-process theory.
    (d) gate-control theory.

13. After a small area near the stirrup end of her basilar membrane was damaged, Harriet could no longer hear high-frequency sounds. This particular loss of hearing can best be explained by
    (a) trichromatic theory.
    (b) place theory.
    (c) gate-control theory.
    (d) frequency theory.

14. To control the arthritic pain in his knees, Frederick now wears magnetic insoles in his shoes and magnetic bracelets on his wrists. Frederick is convinced that his pain has been somewhat reduced since he started wearing these magnets. According to Enhancing Well-Being with Psychology (Maximizing Your Brain's Potential), Frederick's self-administered strategy of pain control is an example of
    (a) mainstream medical health therapy (MMHT).
    (b) biofeedback therapy (BFT).
    (c) complementary and alternative medicines (CAM).
    (d) distraction and counterirritation pain control strategy (DCPCS).

15. Maxwell is a male pig and, like most male pigs, he releases a chemical substance in the sweat glands to communicate territorial boundaries and sexual receptiveness. According to In Focus, these chemical signals, common in the animal kingdom, are called
    (a) chemosignals.
    (b) pheromones.
    (c) substance P.
    (d) umami.

Answers

Introduction: What Are Sensation and Perception?

1. *The primary function of the nervous system is* communication—the transmission of information from one part of the body to another.

2. *Sensation refers to* the detection and basic sensory experience of environmental stimuli. *Perception occurs when* we integrate, organize, and interpret sensory information in a way that is meaningful.
3. *The difference between sensation and perception is* that sensation involves responding to stimulation and transmitting it in usable form to the brain, whereas perception involves the organization and interpretation of sensation. However, there is no clear definitive boundary between the two.

Basic Principles of Sensation

1. *We are able to hear, taste, smell, feel, and see by* using specialized cells called sensory receptors that respond to stimulation by some form of energy (e.g., sound waves, chemicals, pressure, and light waves).
2. *Transduction is* the process by which a form of physical energy is converted into a coded neural signal that can be processed by the nervous system.
3. *The two types of sensory threshold (and what they refer to) are* the absolute threshold, which is the smallest possible strength of a stimulus that can be detected half the time, and the difference threshold, which is the smallest possible difference between two stimuli that can be detected half the time.
4. *Another name for the difference threshold is* the just noticeable difference (jnd).
5. *Weber's law states* that the size of the just noticeable difference (jnd) will vary depending on its relation to the strength of the original stimulus.
6. *Sensory adaptation occurs because* sensory receptor cells become less responsive to a constant stimulus; it is relative to the duration of exposure. *It is important because* it allows us to quickly notice new or changing stimuli and to avoid being overwhelmed with sensory information.

Concept Check 1

1. absolute
2. sensation; perception
3. difference threshold; just noticeable difference (jnd); Weber's law
4. transduction
5. sensory adaptation
6. subliminal perception

Matching Exercise 1

1. threshold
2. transduction
3. absolute threshold
4. sensory receptors
5. difference threshold (or jnd)
6. the mere exposure effect

True/False Test 1

1. F
2. T
3. T
4. F
5. T

Vision: From Light to Sight

1. *The process of seeing begins with* stimulation of visual receptor cells in the eye, which are sensitive to the physical energy of light.
2. *The electromagnetic spectrum is* made up of many different forms of electromagnetic energy, which vary in wavelength; humans are capable of visually detecting only a tiny portion of the spectrum (visible light).
3. *The key structures of the eye (and their functions) are* the cornea (helps gather and direct incoming light), the pupil (changes size to let in different amounts of light), the iris (the muscle that controls the size of the pupil), the lens (thins or thickens to focus or bend light as it enters the eye), and the retina (contains the rods and cones, the photoreceptors that respond to light).
4. *The function of rods is to* detect light (but not color). They are especially sensitive in dim light and at night. *The function of cones is to* detect color and fine details (most cones are concentrated in the fovea, the point of central focus in the retina).
5. *The optic disk is* the point at which the fibers that make up the optic nerve exit the back of the eye and project to the back of the brain. Because the disk has no photoreceptors, we have a tiny hole, or a blind spot, in our field of vision.
6. *Bipolar cells process visual information by* collecting information from the rods and cones and funneling it to the ganglion cells. *The bundled axons of the* ganglion cells form the optic nerve;

from the optic chiasm (the point of partial crossover of the optic nerves from each eye) information is sent to the thalamus and then on to the visual cortex.

7. *Our experience of color involves* three properties of light waves: hue (color), saturation (purity), and brightness (perceived intensity). Different wavelengths correspond to our subjective experience of different colors.
8. *According to the trichromatic theory,* there are three types of cones, each of which is especially sensitive to certain wavelengths: red light (long wavelengths), green light (medium wavelengths), or blue light (short wavelengths); other colors are a result of stimulation of a combination of cones. *This theory explains* the most common form of color blindness, red–green color blindness.
9. *According to the opponent-process theory,* there are four basic colors, which are divided into two pairs of color-sensitive neurons, red–green and blue–yellow (black and white also act as an opposing pair); when one member of a pair is stimulated, the other member is inhibited. *This theory explains* afterimages.
10. *An integrated explanation of color vision states that* both the trichromatic and the opponent-process theories are correct, but that each theory describes color vision at a different level or stage of visual processing.

Concept Check 2

1. purple
2. green
3. trichromatic; opponent-process
4. color; fine detail
5. black
6. recognize faces

Graphic Organizer 1

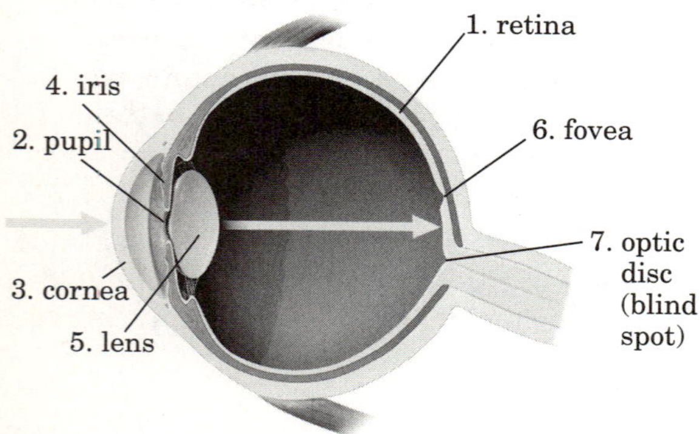

Matching Exercise 2

1. visual acuity
2. afterimage
3. wavelength
4. accommodation
5. brightness
6. optic nerve
7. trichromatic theory of color vision
8. cones
9. hue
10. rods
11. bipolar cells
12. color
13. optic disk
14. presbyopia
15. astigmatism
16. feature detectors

True/False Test 2

1. F	5. F	9. T	13. F
2. T	6. T	10. T	14. T
3. F	7. T	11. T	15. F
4. T	8. F	12. T	16. T

Hearing: From Vibration to Sound

1. *Audition is* the technical term for the sense of hearing.
2. *Our perception of sound is directly related to the physical properties of* sound waves; it involves loudness as determined by intensity (amplitude, measured in decibels), pitch (the relative highness or lowness of a sound, determined by frequency), and timbre (the distinctive quality of a sound).
3. *The key structures of the ear are* the outer ear (pinna, ear canal, and eardrum), the middle ear (the hammer, anvil, and stirrup), and the inner ear (cochlea, which contains the basilar membrane, and semicircular canals).
4. *The process of hearing begins when* sound waves are caught by the pinna and funneled down the ear canal to the eardrum, whose vibrations match the vibrations of the sound wave in intensity and frequency. *It then involves* the sound waves being amplified in the middle ear by the hammer, anvil, and stirrup. This amplified sound is transferred to the oval window, which relays the vibrations to the cochlea, where the sound waves are transduced (transformed into neural messages) by hair cells in the basilar membrane, which runs the

length of the cochlea in the inner ear. As the hair cells bend, they stimulate cells of the auditory nerve, which carries the neural information to the thalamus and the auditory cortex in the brain.

5. *According to frequency theory,* the basilar membrane vibrates at the same frequency as sound waves. *This theory explains* how low-frequency sound waves (up to about 1000 hertz) are transmitted to the brain but cannot explain transmission of higher-frequency sound waves.
6. *According to place theory,* different frequencies cause larger vibrations at different locations along the basilar membrane. *This theory explains* our discrimination of higher-pitched sounds, with the higher-pitched sounds being interpreted according to the place where the hair cells are most active. *For intermediate frequencies or mid-range pitches,* both place and frequency are involved.

Concept Check 3

1. amplitude; decibels
2. conduction
3. hammer; anvil; stirrup
4. timbre
5. basilar membrane; nerve
6. pitch; hertz
7. transduction; cochlea; basilar membrane
8. frequency
9. pinna; ear canal; eardrum

Graphic Organizer 2

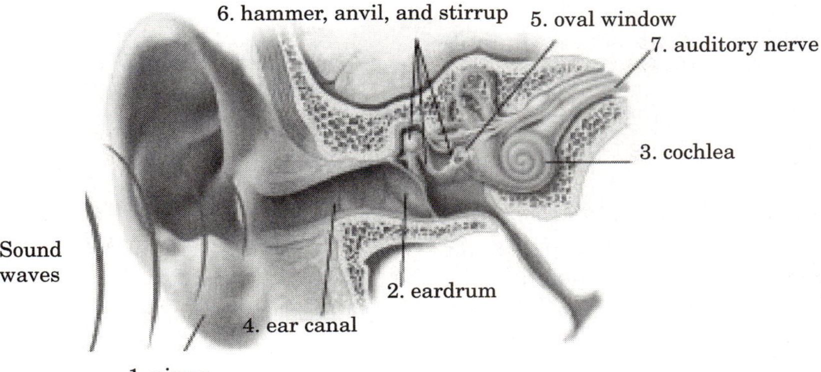

Matching Exercise 3

1. loudness
2. audition
3. frequency
4. hair cells
5. sound waves
6. timbre
7. outer ear
8. pitch
9. decibel
10. amplitude
11. middle ear
12. frequency theory

True/False Test 3

1. F	5. T	9. F
2. F	6. T	10. T
3. F	7. T	11. T
4. T	8. T	12. T

The Chemical and Body Senses: Smell, Taste, Touch, and Position

1. *Olfaction is the technical term for* the sense of smell, *and gustation is the technical term for* the sense of taste.
2. *They are called chemical senses because* the sensory receptors for taste and smell are specialized to respond to different types of chemical substances.
3. *Our sense of smell begins when* airborne molecules emitted by substances we inhale stimulate olfactory receptor cells high in the nasal cavity. *The stimulation is then* converted into neural messages that are passed along the olfactory nerves, which are directly connected to the olfactory bulb (the enlarged ending of the olfactory cortex). Axons from the olfactory bulb form the olfactory tract, along which messages pass to various brain areas, including the temporal lobe and structures in the limbic system.

4. *Our sense of taste begins when* specialized receptors in the taste buds located on the tongue, on the insides of our cheeks, on the roof of our mouth, and in our throat are stimulated. *The stimulation is* converted into neural messages that are sent along neural pathways to the thalamus, which, directs the information to several regions in the cortex.
5. *The five primary taste categories are* sweet, sour, salty, bitter, and umami.
6. *The skin and body senses include* touch and temperature, pain, movement, position, and balance.
7. *The skin responds to* stimulation such as pressure, warmth, and cold.
8. *One receptor for touch is* the Pacinian corpuscle, *which works by* converting pressure stimulation into a neural message that is relayed to the brain. If a pressure is constant, sensory adaptation takes place.
9. *Pain is the unpleasant sensation of* physical discomfort or suffering that can occur in varying degrees of intensity.
10. *Two types of nociceptors are involved in pain: (a)* myelinated A-delta fibers, *which represent the fast pain system and transmit* the sharp, intense, but short-lived pain of immediate injury (morphine and other opiates have virtually no effect on the system), and *(b)* unmyelinated C fibers, *which represent the slow pain system and transmit* the longer-lasting, throbbing, burning pain of injury (morphine and other opiates are effective with this system).
11. *According to the gate-control theory,* the sensation of pain is controlled by a series of gates in the spinal cord that open (pain is experienced or intensified) and close (pain is reduced); the gates open or close depending on how the brain interprets the pain experience, a process that is influenced by psychological, social, or situational factors; cultural beliefs about the meaning of pain and the appropriate response to pain also play a role (pain results from both physiological and psychological influences).
12. *The experience of pain can be influenced by psychological factors, such as* anxiety, fear, a sense of helplessness, and negative emotions (they intensify the experience of pain); positive emotions (good moods) and a sense of control reduce the sense of pain. Psychological factors can also influence the release of endorphins and enkephalins (the body's natural painkillers).
13. *Phantom limb pain refers to* the phenomenon in which a person continues to experience intense painful sensations in a limb that has been amputated. *It is explained by* sensitization, which is the opposite of sensory adaptation in that pain pathways from the site of the amputation to the brain become increasingly more responsive over time and produce the mental feeling of pain coming from the nonexistent limb.
14. *Our kinesthetic sense involves* stimulation of proprioceptors, which constantly communicate information to the brain about changes in body position and muscle tension and provide information about the location and position of body parts in relation to one another.
15. *Our vestibular sense provides us with* a sense of balance, or equilibrium, by responding to changes in gravity, motion, and body position.
16. *The two sources of vestibular sensory information are* the semicircular canals and the vestibular sacs, both of which are located in the ear.

Concept Check 4

1. taste buds
2. phantom limb pain; sensitized
3. smell (olfaction)
4. sweet; salty; sour; bitter; umami
5. intensify
6. semicircular canals; vestibular sacs
7. nociceptors; free nerve endings; A-delta; C
8. kinesthetic
9. substance P

Matching Exercise 4

1. gustation
2. semicircular canals and vestibular sacs
3. Pacinian corpuscle
4. anosmia
5. nociceptors (free nerve endings)
6. olfactory receptor cells
7. olfactory bulb
8. taste buds
9. olfactory tract
10. vestibular sense
11. endorphins and enkephalins
12. kinesthetic sense
13. umami
14. phantom limb pain
15. A-delta fibers

True/False Test 4

1. T
2. T
3. T
4. T
5. F
6. T
7. T
8. T
9. F
10. F
11. F
12. T
13. T
14. T
15. T

Perception (Part 1)

1. *Perception is the process of* integrating, organizing, and interpreting sensory information in a meaningful way.
2. *Bottom-up processing refers to* the flow of information from the sensory receptors to the brain; this type of analysis moves from the parts to the whole (data-driven processing).
3. *Top-down processing refers to* analysis that moves from the whole to the parts; it occurs when we use our knowledge, experience, expectations, and other cognitive processes to arrive at meaningful perceptions (conceptually driven processing).
4. *The three basic questions of perception are* What is it?, How far away is it?, and Where is it going? (Bottom-up and top-down processing are necessary for reaching perceptual conclusions.)
5. *Gestalt psychology was founded by* German psychologist Max Wertheimer *and is concerned with* the fact that we tend to perceive whole objects or figures (gestalts) rather than isolated bits and pieces of sensory information.

Perception: The Perception of Shape (Part 2)

1. *The figure–ground relationship describes* how we automatically separate the elements of perception into the feature that clearly stands out (the figure) and its less distinct background (the ground). *It is important because it demonstrates that* the separation of a scene into figure and ground is not a property of the actual elements in the scene but instead is a psychological accomplishment.
2. *The perceptual principles involved in grouping visual elements include* similarity, closure, good continuation, and proximity.
3. *The law of Prägnanz states* that when several perceptual organizations of an assortment of visual elements are possible, the perceptual interpretation that occurs will be the one that produces the "best, simplest, and most stable shape" (also called the law of simplicity). *It is important because it encompasses* all other gestalt principles, including the figure–ground relationship, *and suggests that* we actively and automatically construct a perception that reveals the "essence of something."

Perception: Depth Perception (Part 3)

1. *Depth perception refers to* the ability to perceive the distance of an object as well as its three-dimensional characteristics. *It is important because* being able to perceive the distance of an object has obvious survival value, especially regarding potential threats or danger.
2. *Monocular cues are defined as* distance or depth cues that can be processed by either eye alone *and include* relative size, overlap, aerial perspective, texture gradient, linear perspective, motion parallax, and accommodation.
3. *Binocular cues are defined as* distance or depth cues that require the use of both eyes *and include* convergence and binocular disparity.
4. *A stereogram is* a picture that uses the principles of binocular disparity to create the perception of a three-dimensional image.

Concept Check 5

1. law of proximity
2. ground; figure
3. binocular disparity
4. relative size
5. linear perspective
6. law of closure
7. bottom-up processing

Matching Exercise 5

1. Gestalt psychology
2. law of Prägnanz
3. aerial perspective
4. binocular disparity
5. figure–ground relationship
6. overlap (interposition)
7. binocular cues
8. accommodation
9. law of proximity
10. depth perception
11. figure–ground reversal
12. Max Wertheimer
13. parapsychology
14. law of similarity
15. gestalt

True/False Test 5

1. T
2. T
3. F
4. T
5. F
6. T
7. T
8. T
9. F
10. T
11. F
12. T
13. T
14. T

Perception: The Perception of Motion (Part 4)

1. *The perception of motion involves* the integration of information from several sources, including microfine eye-muscle movements, the changing retinal image, and the contrast of the moving object with its stationary background.
2. *Induced motion refers to* our strong tendency to assume that the background is stationary and that it is the object or figure that moves. *It was first studied by* Karl Duncker.
3. *Stroboscopic motion creates* an illusion of movement with two carefully timed flashing lights going on and off in succession. *It is caused by* the brain's visual system combining the rapid sequence of visual information (the two lights going on and off and being detected at two different points on the surface of the retina) and arriving at the conclusion of movement, even though no movement has occurred (the perception of smooth motion in movies is due to the same phenomenon).

Perception: Perceptual Constancies (Part 5)

1. *Perceptual constancy refers to* the tendency to perceive objects as constant and unchanging despite changes in sensory input.
2. *Size constancy is* the perception that an object remains the same size despite its changing retinal image. *An important aspect of size constancy is* that if the retinal image of an object does not change, but perception of its distance increases, the object is perceived as larger.
3. *Shape constancy is* the tendency to perceive familiar objects as having a fixed shape regardless of the image they cast on the retinas.

Perceptual Illusions and The Effects of Experience on Perceptual Interpretations

1. *A perceptual illusion involves* the misperception of an object's or image's true characteristics. These illusions are used to study perceptual principles.
2. *The Müller-Lyer illusion is* the misperception of the length of two identical lines, one with arrows pointing outward and one with arrows pointed inward.
3. *The moon illusion involves* the misperception that the moon is larger when it is on the horizon than when it is overhead *and may be the result of* the misapplication of the principles of overlap and size constancy—distance cues make the horizon moon seem farther away, and so we perceive it as larger, even though the retinal image of the moon remains constant.
4. *Perceptual illusions reveal that* what we see is not merely a reflection of the real world but instead is our subjective interpretation of it; we actively construct perceptual conclusions about the information detected through our senses (in a way, believing is seeing).
5. *Perceptions can be influenced by* a variety of learning experiences, including educational, cultural, and life experiences.
6. *A perceptual set is* the tendency to perceive objects or situations from a particular frame of reference. *A perceptual set can often determine* the interpretation of an ambiguous stimulus, such as seeing a person's face in a grilled cheese sandwich.

Concept Check 6

1. perceptual set
2. farther away
3. shape
4. Müller-Lyer
5. perceptual constancy
6. stroboscopic motion

Matching Exercise 6

1. perceptual set
2. perceptual constancy
3. Müller-Lyer illusion
4. size constancy
5. Karl Duncker
6. acupuncture
7. Shepard Tables

True/False Test 6

1. T	3. T	5. T
2. T	4. T	6. T

Something to Think About

1. First, you would note that these strange experiences happen to many people, that there is nothing particularly unique about them. The problem arises in the way people interpret these experiences. These experiences, of course, do not constitute proof of ESP, no matter how strongly someone believes they do. Two less extraordinary concepts can explain these occurrences: coincidence and the fallacy of positive instances. Coincidence, which refers to an event occurring simply by chance, can account for many of the experiences reported by people.

Combine coincidence with our tendency to remember coincidental events that seem to confirm our belief about unusual phenomena—the fallacy of positive instances—and the feeling that something unusual has happened can be very strong, even though there are no rational grounds for that belief. Finally, there is no strong scientific evidence for the existence of ESP, despite years of intensive study by psychologists interested in this topic. To date, no parapsychology experiment, including those using the ganzfeld procedure, that has claimed to show evidence of ESP has been successfully replicated. This, of course, does not prove conclusively that ESP does not exist; however, although one should keep an open mind, there is no evidence or any rational reason to believe in its existence.

2. Some of the most common monocular cues that are useful in conveying a sense of depth on the canvas are overlap, in which "nearer" objects are depicted as blocking or obscuring more "distant" objects; linear perspective, in which parallel lines are depicted as converging toward the top of the painting, for instance; and texture gradient, in which surfaces that are supposed to be close to the observer have distinct, clearly defined textures and those that are gradually less and less clearly defined depict distance. Relative size and aerial perspective are also useful devices to convey depth.

   To make your picture more interesting you might want to attempt to incorporate some misleading depth cues (such as in Escher drawings) or perceptual illusions.

Progress Test 1

1. b
2. d
3. a
4. b
5. a
6. b
7. c
8. a
9. a
10. a
11. d
12. c
13. b
14. c
15. c

Progress Test 2

1. d
2. a
3. b
4. c
5. b
6. d
7. d
8. a
9. c
10. b
11. a
12. c
13. b
14. d
15. c

Progress Test 3

1. a
2. d
3. a
4. d
5. b
6. b
7. c
8. b
9. a
10. b
11. d
12. a
13. b
14. c
15. b

Consciousness and Its Variations

PREVIEW

Reading the section below first will give you a general sense of the chapter's contents and an initial introduction to some of the major concepts and terms. This will prime you for what you are about to read and help you to develop a "cognitive map" that will guide your study of the material in this chapter. Likewise, reading the **preview questions** at the beginning of each major section will improve your ability to understand, learn, and retain the information.

CHAPTER 4 . . . AT A GLANCE

Chapter 4 examines the different forms of human consciousness, including the role of attention and how the limitations of attention affect human thought and behavior. Biological and environmental "clocks" that regulate our circadian rhythms, including our sleep–wake cycle, are addressed next. How the EEG is used to measure brain-wave activity is discussed, followed by an examination of the different stages of sleep and their associated brain-wave activity and behavioral patterns. The next section is an exploration of dreams and mental activity during sleep. Three major theories of the meaning of dreams and their relevance to psychological and physiological functioning are presented. This section ends with a discussion of the various sleep disorders (dyssomnias, such as insomnia, obstructive sleep apnea, and narcolepsy, and parasomnias, such as sleepwalking, sleep terrors, sleep-related eating disorder, sleepsex, and REM sleep behavior disorder).

Hypnosis and meditation are introduced next. Under hypnosis, profound sensory and perceptual changes may be experienced. This section focuses on phenomena such as posthypnotic suggestion, posthypnotic amnesia, and hypermnesia. Hilgard's notions of dissociation and the hidden observer are examined, and the controversy surrounding how to explain hypnosis is discussed. Finally, meditation is defined, and techniques for inducing a meditative state are presented along with research findings on the effects of meditation.

The final section is concerned with using drugs to alter consciousness. The psychoactive drugs are classified and listed along with their various effects on brain activity and physiological and psychological functioning. Drug dependence, drug tolerance, withdrawal symptoms, and drug abuse are discussed.

Enhancing Well-Being with Psychology offers some practical suggestions for minimizing sleep problems.

Introduction: Consciousness: Experiencing the "Private I"

Preview Questions

Consider the following questions as you study this section of the chapter.

- How is *consciousness* defined, and what did William James mean by *stream of consciousness*?
- What is attention, and what are the three characteristics of attention?
- What is multi-tasking, and how can it cause problems?

*Read the section "Introduction: Consciousness: The 'Private I'" and **write** your answers to the following:*

1. *Consciousness* is defined as the ______________________________

   ____

2. William James's idea of "stream of consciousness" refers to the fact that ______________________________

   ____

   ____

3. Attention is ______________________________

   ____

   The three characteristics of attention are

   ____

   ____

   ____

4. Multi-tasking refers to ______________________________

   ____

   Multi-tasking can cause problems when

   ____

   ____

   When a great deal of concentration is required

   ____

   ____

Biological and Environmental "Clocks" That Regulate Consciousness

Preview Questions

Consider the following questions as you study this section of the chapter.

- What are circadian rhythms?
- What roles do the suprachiasmatic nucleus (SCN), sunlight, and melatonin play in regulating circadian rhythms?
- How does the absence of all environmental time signals affect circadian rhythms?
- Why do people suffer jet lag symptoms, and what role does melatonin play in producing these symptoms?

*Read the section "Biological and Environmental 'Clocks' That Regulate Consciousness" and **write** the answers to the following:*

1. Circadian rhythms are ______________________________

   ____

2. The suprachiasmatic nucleus (SCN) is ______________________________

   ____

   ____

   Its role in sleep–wake cycles and other circadian rhythms is to ______________________________

   ____

   ____

3. Melatonin is a ______________________________

   ____

4. In the absence of all environmental time signals ______________________________

   ____

   As a result, ______________________________

   ____

   ____

   ____

5. People suffer from jet lag symptoms because

   ____

   ____

6. Melatonin plays a key role in jet lag symptoms by ______________________________

   ____

After you have carefully studied the preceding sections, complete the following exercises.

Concept Check 1

Read the following and write the correct term in the space provided.

1. After Sheena watched the sun set she began to feel sleepy and decided it was time for bed. It is likely that the decrease in available light was

detected by her _______________ ; this in turn triggered an increase in the production of a hormone called _______________ , which is manufactured by the _______________ .

2. Although Marvin was very tired after pulling an "all-nighter" to finish a paper, he began to feel much less drowsy as the morning proceeded. His reaction is probably due to decreased levels of the hormone _______________ .
3. David typically experiences a slump in mental alertness around midafternoon but feels very energetic in the early evening. These daily highs and lows are examples of _______________ .
4. During a history lecture, Alfie is listening and taking notes but at times he is also thinking about his girlfriend and the argument they had last night. He wonders what he will say to her when he phones her that afternoon, which gets him thinking about how often his parents fight and whether arguing is genetic, which reminds him about his biology exam next week. This description reflects Alfie's _______________ .
5. Dr. Parizeau arranges for volunteers to spend several weeks in special isolation units without exposure to sunlight, clocks, or other environmental time cues. During this time he monitors their sleep–wake cycles and other biological events. Dr. Parizeau is likely to discover that his participants' internal body clocks will drift to their natural, or intrinsic, rhythm of approximately _______________ hours.
6. Reena was listening to music on her radio (an auditory task) when she drove to school (a visual task). She is _______________ (likely/not likely) to experience inattentional blindness. Later, when walking across campus (a visual task), she was totally absorbed in conversation on her cell phone (an auditory task). In this instance, she is _______________ (likely/not likely) to experience inattentional blindness.

Review of Terms, Concepts, and Names 1

Use the terms in this list to complete the Matching Exercise, then to help you answer the True/False items correctly.

consciousness	circadian rhythm
William James	suprachiasmatic nucleus (SCN)
attention	melatonin
cocktail party effect	pineal gland
inattentional blindness	entrains
inattentional deafness	jet lag
change blindness	
multi-tasking	

Matching Exercise

Match the appropriate term/name with its definition or description:

1. _______________ Personal awareness of mental activities, internal sensations, and the external environment.
2. _______________ Behavior that involves a division of attention while doing two or more things at once or paying attention to two or more sources of stimuli at once.
3. _______________ Cluster of neurons in the brain's hypothalamus that governs the timing of circadian rhythms.
4. _______________ Symptoms such as physical and mental fatigue, depression or irritability, disrupted sleep, and fuzziness in concentration, thinking, and memory that result from circadian rhythms being out of sync with daylight and darkness cues.
5. _______________ Hormone manufactured by the pineal gland that produces sleepiness.
6. _______________ The capacity to selectively focus awareness on particular stimuli in your external environment or on your internal thoughts or sensations.
7. _______________ Selective attention to one stream of speech while ignoring others that compete for attention, unless there is something significant said, such as your name.

True/False Test

Indicate whether each statement is true or false by placing T or F in the blank space next to each item.

1. ____ Failure to notice some significant object or event that is in our clear field of vision because attention is being paid to other things is called inattentional deafness.

2. ___ William James was the American psychologist and philosopher who proposed that the subjective experience of consciousness is an ongoing stream of mental activity.
3. ___ The pineal gland is an endocrine gland located in the brain that regulates the production of the hormone melatonin.
4. ___ Exposure to environmental time signals, such as sunlight, regulates, or *entrains,* the SCN so that it keeps the circadian rhythms synchronized and operating on a 24-hour schedule.
5. ___ Circadian rhythm refers to a cycle or rhythm that is roughly 24 hours long and involves cyclical daily fluctuations in biological and psychological processes.
6. ___ Failure to notice a perceivable, significant, auditory stimulus because attention is being paid to other things is called inattentional blindness.
7. ___ Change blindness refers to not noticing when something changes because we fail to pay attention to the details.

Check your answers and review any areas of weakness before going on to the next section.

Sleep

Preview Questions

Consider the following questions as you study this section of the chapter.

- How did the invention of the electroencephalograph contribute to modern sleep research?
- What brain waves are associated with being alert and awake and with being drowsy and relaxed, and what are hypnagogic hallucinations?
- What are the characteristics of the NREM sleep stages and REM sleep?
- How do sleep patterns change over the lifespan?
- Why do we need sleep, and what is the evidence that we have a biological need for sleep?
- What do the phenomena of REM and NREM rebound indicate?

Read the section "Sleep" and ***write*** *your answers to the following:*

1. An electroencephalograph is ______________________

   ____

   The graphic record it produces is called an

   ____

2. By studying EEGs, sleep researchers established that ______________________

   ____

   They distinguish between two types of sleep:

   ____

3. Beta brain waves are associated with ________

   ____

   ____

   ____

   Alpha brain waves are associated with ________

   ____

   ____

   ____

4. Hypnagogic hallucinations are ______________

   ____

5. The four NREM sleep stages are characterized by different brain and body activity:

   Stage 1 NREM: ______________________

   ____

   Stage 2 NREM: ______________________

   ____

   Stages 3 and 4 NREM: ________________

   ____

6. REM sleep is characterized by______________

   ____

   ____

7. During the course of a typical night's sleep, stages 3 and 4 NREM usually______________

   ____

   As the night progresses,__________________

   ____

8. Over the course of the lifespan, the quantity and quality of our sleep ______________

   ____

   ____

   The newborn sleeps about________________

by about the third month of life ____________
____
and by age 5 ____________________
____
From childhood through late adulthood, total sleep time ____________________
____

9. The need to sleep serves ____________
____
____

The enormous variability in sleep patterns across different species is the result of ______
____
____

10. Sleep deprivation and sleep restriction studies demonstrate that ____________
____
____
____
____
____

11. The phenomena of REM and NREM rebound seem to indicate that ____________
____
____

Concept Check 2

Read the following and write the correct term in the space provided.

1. James went to bed a short while ago. Although his eyes are closed and he is very relaxed, he has not yet fallen asleep. If James's brain is relatively normal, it is probably generating __________ brain waves.
2. Shortly after falling asleep, James experiences a muscle spasm that jolts him awake. James has most likely experienced the most common hypnagogic hallucination of ____________ accompanied by a ____________ .
3. Every day during the past week, Richie got only about half his usual night's sleep. As a result, he is likely to be not only sleep deprived but also __________ deprived. When he is finally able to get a full night's sleep, he will probably experience ______________ .
4. Mrs. Eastman has just turned 65 and is worried because she is waking up more easily nowadays, sleeps less than 7 hours most nights, and feels less rested and less satisfied after sleeping. A sleep specialist is most likely to say that she ____________________ .
5. Azra has been asleep for about 10 minutes and is now in stage 2 sleep. Her brain-wave activity is likely to be predominantly ____________ waves and is defined by the appearance of ____________ and ____________ .
6. As part of a sleep deprivation study, Aiden was prevented from sleeping for 48 hours. If he is typical of participants in sleep deprivation research, he is likely to develop ____________ during wakefulness. He will also experience disruptions in ____________
____________ .
7. Vladimir was having a very frightening dream that heavily armed, masked burglars were breaking into his house and trying to kill him. He woke up suddenly and was even more alarmed because he was unable to move, a phenomenon called ____________ .
8. Researchers investigating whether the brain's emotional centers become more active in response to sleep deprivation found that sleep deprivation affects how we respond to positive stimuli as well as how we respond to negative stimuli. In sleep-deprived participants, the ____________________ activated 60 percent more strongly to images of aversive stimuli, and in response to pleasant images the
____
showed heightened activity.

Graphic Organizer 1

The diagram below shows the brain waves typical of each stage in a 90-minute (approximately) sleep cycle. Match the term or description with the correct brain-wave pattern.

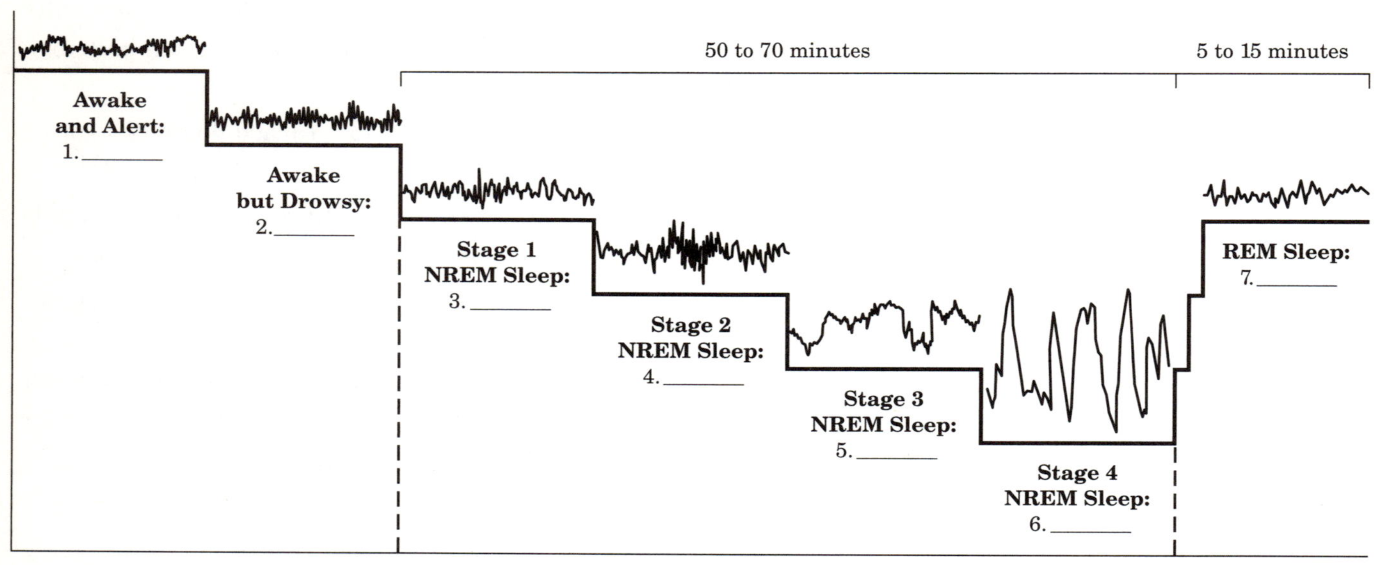

A. Brain waves associated with dreaming
B. Sleep spindles and K complexes
C. Beta brain waves
D. Mixture of theta and delta brain waves
E. Alpha brain waves
F. Delta brain waves
G. Mixture of alpha and theta brain waves

Review of Terms and Concepts 2

Use the terms in this list to complete the Matching Exercise, then to help you answer the True/False items correctly.

electroencephalograph
brain waves
EEG (electroencephalogram)
REM sleep (active sleep or paradoxical sleep)
NREM sleep (quiet sleep)
sleep paralysis
beta brain waves
alpha brain waves
hypnagogic hallucinations
myoclonic jerk (sleep start)
theta brain waves
sleep spindles
K complexes
delta brain waves
slow-wave sleep (SWS)
sleep deprivation studies
microsleeps
sleep restriction studies
REM rebound
NREM rebound

Matching Exercise

Match the appropriate term with its definition or description.

1. ______________ Brain-wave pattern associated with relaxed wakefulness and drowsiness.
2. ______________ Graphic record of brain activity produced by an electroencephalograph.
3. ______________ Short bursts of brain activity that characterize stage 2 NREM sleep.
4. ______________ Vivid sensory phenomena that can occur during the onset of sleep.
5. ______________ Term applied to the combination of stage 3 and stage 4 sleep.
6. ______________ Involuntary muscle spasm of the whole body that jolts the person completely awake and often accompanies the hypnagogic hallucination of falling.
7. ______________ Single but large high-voltage spikes of brain activity that characterize stage 2 NREM sleep.
8. ________ Phenomenon in which a person who is deprived of REM sleep greatly increases the amount of time spent in REM sleep at the first opportunity for sleep.
9. ______________ Instrument that uses electrodes placed on the scalp to measure and record the brain's electrical activity.
10. ______________ The rhythmical patterns of electrical brain activity.

True/False Test

Indicate whether each statement is true or false by placing T or F in the blank space next to each item.

1. ____ NREM rebound is a phenomenon in which a person who is deprived of stages 3 and 4 NREM sleep spends more time in these stages when permitted to sleep.
2. ____ Studies that reduce the amount of time people are allowed to sleep to as little as four hours per night are called sleep restriction studies.
3. ____ During REM sleep, rapid eye movements and dreaming usually occur, and voluntary muscle activity is suppressed; also called *active sleep* or *paradoxical sleep*.
4. ____ Beta brain waves are patterns of electrical activity that begin in stage 1 NREM sleep and predominate in stage 2 NREM sleep.
5. ____ Episodes of sleep lasting only a few seconds that occur during wakefulness are called microsleeps; they can occur after as little as one night's sleep deprivation.
6. ____ NREM sleep, or quiet sleep, is divided into four stages.
7. ____ Theta brain waves are small, fast brain waves that reflect an awake and reasonably alert state of consciousness.
8. ____ Delta brain waves are the long, slow waves associated with stage 3 and stage 4 NREM sleep.
9. ____ Sleep paralysis is a temporary condition in which a person is unable to move upon awakening in the morning or during the night.
10. ____ Sleep deprivation studies, in which people are not allowed to sleep, demonstrate a biological need for sleep.

Check your answers and review any areas of weakness before going on to the next section.

Dreams and Mental Activity During Sleep

Preview Questions

Consider the following questions as you study this section of the chapter.

- What is the difference between sleep thinking and dreaming?
- How many dream episodes do people typically have each night, and how long do they last?
- What patterns of brain activity are associated with REM sleep?
- How do the different stages of sleep contribute to the formation of episodic and procedural memories?
- What do people dream about, and what are nightmares?
- What is Freud's theory of the meaning of dreams, and what has research shown about this theory?
- How do the activation-synthesis and the neurocognitive models explain dreaming?

Read the section "Dreams and Mental Activity During Sleep" and ***write*** *your answers to the following:*

1. Sleep thinking (sleep mentation) refers to ______________________________

   whereas a dream is ______________________________
   ____
2. People usually have __________ dreaming episodes each night. The first REM period is ______________________________
   ____
   ____
   ____
3. Brain activity during REM sleep is __________
   ____
   ____
4. NREM slow-wave sleep contributes to __________
   ____
   ____

   whereas REM sleep and NREM stage 2 sleep seem to help ______________________________
   ____
5. Sleep strengthens and enhances new memories by ______________________________
   ____
   ____
   ____
6. Most dreams are ______________________________
   ____
   ____
   ____

7. The most common patterns and themes of dreams are as follows: ______________________
____

8. Nightmares are ______________________
____
____
____
The frequency of nightmares is closely related to ______________________
____
____

9. Freud's explanation for dreams suggests that ______________________
____
____

10. The manifest content refers to ______________________
____
The latent content is the ______________________
____
Freud believed that ______________________
____
were phallic symbols, and that ______________________
____
____
symbolized the vagina.
Psychological research has shown that ______________________
____
____

11. The activation–synthesis model of dreaming maintains that ______________________
____
____
This model does not contend ______________________
____

12. The neurocognitive model of dreams ______________________
____
____
This model suggests that ______________________
____

After you have carefully studied the preceding section, complete the following exercises.

Concept Check 3

Read the following and write the correct term in the space provided.

1. Meredith recalls having a dream about dancing in a ballet with a very big, strong, muscular male dancer when suddenly the music switches to loud rock music and the man disappears. According to Freud, Meredith's account represents the ______________________ of the dream.
2. Dr. Dormo believes that Meredith's dream could be the result of a burst of neural activity that spread upward from the brainstem and activated more sophisticated brain areas. This interpretation is most consistent with the ______________________ model of dreaming.
3. While Ricardo is asleep, his mind keeps returning to the material he has been studying all day in preparation for an exam the next morning. Ricardo is experiencing the most common form of mental activity during sleep, called ______________________ .
4. Sometimes when she is asleep, Madeline is aware that she is dreaming and can often deliberately guide the course of the dream, including backing it up and making it go in a different direction. These dreams are called ______________________ .
5. Maxwell claims that he has no recollection of any dream when he wakes up in the morning, and he is convinced that he never dreams. To demonstrate to Maxwell that he does dream you could awaken him after he has been asleep for about ______________________ minutes, when he is clearly in ______________________ sleep.
6. After a visit to the natural history museum, young Jamila had a scary dream about dinosaurs, which caused her to wake up in a very frightened state. Jamila has experienced an unpleasant anxiety dream called a ______________________ .

7. A PET scan of Danya's brain while she is in REM sleep is likely to reveal ________________ (increased/decreased) activity in the frontal lobes and primary visual cortex and ________________(increased/decreased) activity in areas of the limbic system and in association areas involved with generating visual images.
8. Dr. Dewar maintains that dreams are not a mishmash of random fragments of memories, images, and emotions, generated by lower brainstem circuits. Rather, dreams reflect our interests, personality, and individual worries and mirror our waking concerns in a way that is similar to normal thought processes. His views are consistent with the ________________________ model of dreaming.

Review of Terms, Concepts, and Names 3

Use the terms in this list to complete the Matching Exercise, then to help you answer the True/False items correctly.

sleep thinking (sleep mentation)	latent content
dream	phallic symbols
episodic memories	J. Allan Hobson and Robert W. McCarley
procedural memories	activation–synthesis model of dreaming
nightmare	neurocognitive model of dreaming
Sigmund Freud	
manifest content	

Matching Exercise

Match the appropriate term/name with its definition or description:

1. ________________ Neuroscientists who proposed the activation–synthesis model of dreaming.
2. ________________ Founder of psychoanalysis, who proposed that dream images are disguised and symbolic expressions of unconscious wishes and urges.
3. ________________ Vague, bland, thoughtlike ruminations about real-life events that usually occur during NREM slow-wave sleep.
4. ________________ A vivid and disturbing dream that typically involves fear, anxiety, or terror, and that often awakens the sleeper.
5. ________________ Dream images of sticks, swords, brooms, and other elongated objects that Freud believed represented the penis.
6. ________________ Memories of personally experienced events that tend to be formed during NREM slow-wave sleep.

True/False Test

Indicate whether each statement is true or false by placing T or F in the space next to each item

1. ___ REM sleep and NREM stage 2 sleep contribute to the consolidation of procedural memories, which are memories involved in learning a new skill or task until it can be preformed automatically.
2. ___ In Freud's psychoanalytic theory, the latent content of a dream refers to the elements that are consciously experienced and remembered by the dreamer.
3. ___ A dream is an unfolding sequence of perceptions, thoughts, and emotions during sleep that is experienced as a series of real-life events.
4. ___ The activation–synthesis model of dreaming states that dreaming is our subjective awareness of the brain's internally generated signals during sleep, which the activated brain synthesizes and imposes meaning on.
5. ___ In Freud's psychoanalytic theory, the manifest content of a dream refers to the unconscious wishes, thoughts, and urges that are concealed in the latent content of a dream.
6. ___ The neurocognitive model of dreams emphasizes the continuity of waking and dreaming cognition, and states that dreaming is like thinking under conditions of reduced sensory input and the absence of voluntary control.

Check your answers and review any areas of weakness before going on to the next section.

Sleep Disorders

Preview Questions

Consider the following questions as you study this section of the chapter.

- What are sleep disorders, and what is the difference between dyssomnias and parasomnias?

- How is insomnia defined, and what are transient insomnia and chronic insomnia?
- What are the characteristics of obstructive sleep apnea (OSA), narcolepsy, and cataplexy?
- What are sleep terrors, and how do they differ from nightmares?
- How are some of the other important parasomnias (sleepsex, sleepwalking, sleep-related eating disorder, and REM sleep behavior disorder) defined?

Read the section "Sleep Disorders" and ***write*** *your answers to the following:*

1. Sleep disorders involve ______________________________

2. Dyssomnias are ______________________________

   They include ______________________________

   Parasomnias are ______________________________

   They include ______________________________

3. Insomnia is characterized by ______________________________

   Transient insomnia lasts ______________________________

   Symptoms of chronic insomnia occur at least ______________________________

   The risk of insomnia is influenced by ______________________________

4. In obstructive sleep apnea (OSA) ______________________________

5. Narcolepsy is characterized by ______________________________

   Cataplexy is the ______________________________

   Autopsies of people who had narcolepsy have revealed ______________________________

6. In parasomnias, the brain is ______________________________

   Key characteristics of all the parasomnias are as follows: ______________________________

7. A parasomnia called sleep terrors, or night terrors, typically occurs ______________________________

   Sleep terrors involve ______________________________

   They differ from nightmares ______________________________

8. Sleepsex, or sexsomnia, is a parasomnia that involves ______________________________

9. Sleepwalking, or somnambulism, is characterized by ______________________________

10. Sleep-related eating disorder (SRED) involves ______________________________

11. REM sleep behavior disorder (RBD) involves ______________________________

After you have carefully studied the preceding section, complete the following exercises.

Concept Check 4

Read the following and write the correct term in the space provided.

1. Bjorn, who has been under a lot of stress ever since he started college a month ago, is having trouble sleeping. He repeatedly complains about the quality and duration of his sleep, and worrying about not sleeping well often keeps him awake at night. Bjorn is most likely to be diagnosed as suffering from ______________________ .
2. Researchers who study insomnia, obstructive sleep apnea, and narcolepsy are interested in disorders involving disruptions in the amount, quality, or timing of sleep, a broad category of sleep disorders called ______________________ .
3. Salim is enjoying a night out with several university friends at Yuk Yuks Comedy Club. While laughing heartily at a very funny act, he suddenly goes limp and falls asleep for a few minutes. It is likely that Salim is suffering from ______________________ and is experiencing ______________________ .
4. Ivana sometimes sleepwalks to the kitchen and compulsively eats mainly cake and cookies; typically, she has no memory of the nocturnal events when she awakens in the morning. Ivana is suffering from a parasomnia called ______________________ .
5. After being asleep for about 2 hours, 8-year-old Soo Mee suddenly sits up in bed screaming incoherently. Her mother has trouble waking her and calming her down. Soo Mee is experiencing ______________________ and is probably in stage ______________ or ______________ of NREM sleep.
6. Young Dominic suffers from sleep terrors and sometimes has episodes of sleepwalking. He is likely to be diagnosed with a general category of sleep disorders called ______________________ .
7. Percy has been diagnosed with a parasomnia called narcolepsy. It is probable that he has very low levels of a special class of neurotransmitters called ______________________ that are produced in the daytime by the hypothalamus to maintain a steady state of wakefulness.

Review of Terms and Concepts 4

Use the terms in this list to complete the Matching Exercise, then to help you answer the True/False items correctly.

sleep disorders
dyssomnias
parasomnias
insomnia
transient insomnia
chronic insomnia
obstructive sleep apnea (OSA)
continuous positive airway pressure (CPAP)
narcolepsy
sleep attacks (microsleeps)
cataplexy
hypocretins (orexins)
sleep terrors (night terrors)
sleepsex (sexsomnia)
sleepwalking (somnambulism)
sleep-related eating disorder (SRED)
REM sleep behavior disorder (RBD)

Matching Exercise

Match the appropriate term/name with its definition or description:

1. ______________________ Condition in which people repeatedly complain about the quality or duration of their sleep, have difficulty going to sleep or staying asleep, or wake up before it is time to get up.
2. ______________________ Sleep disorder in which the sleeper's airway becomes narrowed or blocked, causing shallow breathing or repeated pauses in breathing.
3. ______________________ Sleep disorder caused by a failure of the brain mechanisms that normally suppress voluntary actions during sleep, in which the sleeper verbally and physically responds to the dream story.
4. ______________________ A parasomnia that involves abnormal sexual behaviors and experiences during sleep.
5. ______________________ A sudden loss of voluntary muscle strength and control that is usually triggered by an intense emotion and often occurs during episodes of narcolepsy.

6. _______________ A sleep disorder characterized by excessive daytime sleepiness and brief, uncontrollable episodes of sleep.
7. _______________ Consistent abnormal sleep patterns that cause subjective distress and interfere with a person's daytime functioning.
8. _______________ Broad category of sleep disorders involving disruptions in the amount, quality, or timing of sleep that includes insomnia, obstructive sleep apnea, and narcolepsy.
9. _______________ Treatment for moderate to severe cases of obstructive sleep apnea (OSA).

True/False Test

Indicate whether each statement is true or false by placing T or F in the space next to each item

1. ____ Hypocretins (orexins) are a special class of neurotransmitters produced during daytime to maintain a steady state of wakefulness.
2. ____ People who suffer from narcolepsy experience overwhelming bouts of excessive sleepiness and brief, uncontrollable episodes of sleep called *microsleeps* or *sleep attacks*.
3. ____ Sleepwalking (somnambulism) is a sleep disturbance characterized by an episode of walking or performing other actions during stages 3 and 4 NREM sleep.
4. ____ Approximately 1 out of 10 adults experience *transient insomnia* with symptoms that occur at least three nights each week and persist for a month or longer.
5. ____ Sleep terrors (night terrors) typically occur during stages 3 and 4 NREM sleep and are characterized by increased physiological arousal, intense fear and panic, frightening hallucinations, and no recall of the episode the next morning.
6. ____ About 1 of 3 people occasionally experience *chronic insomnia,* which can last from one or two nights to a couple of weeks.
7. ____ Parasomnias are sleep disorders involving undesirable physical arousal, behaviors, or events during sleep or sleep transitions, and include sleep terrors, sleepsex, sleepwalking, sleep-related eating disorder, and REM sleep behavior disorder.
8. ____ Parasomnia in which the sleeper will sleepwalk and eat compulsively is called sleep-related eating disorder (SRED).

Check your answers and review any areas of weakness before going on to the next section.

Hypnosis

Preview Questions

Consider the following questions as you study this section of the chapter.

- What is hypnosis, and what are the characteristics of the hypnotic state?
- What are the main characteristics of people who are susceptible to hypnosis?
- What are some effects of hypnosis?
- How has hypnosis been explained?
- What are some of the limits and applications of hypnosis?

Read the section "Hypnosis" and ***write*** *your answers to the following:*

1. Hypnosis is a_______________________________
____
____
2. Hypnosis is characterized by_______________________________
____
____

   During hypnosis, the person _______________________________
____
____
3. The best candidates for hypnosis are _______________
____
____
____
4. The effects of hypnosis include _______________
____
____
____
____
5. Hilgard's neodissociation theory of hypnosis suggests that _______________________________
____
____
____
____
6. The limits of hypnosis are that _______________
____
____
____

Applications include ______________________________
____

Meditation

Preview Questions

Consider the following questions as you study this section of the chapter.

- What is meditation, and what is it intended to accomplish?
- What are the two general categories of meditation?
- What is the mindfulness meditation technique and what is transcendental meditation (TM)?
- What are the effects of meditation and what has research shown about these effects?

Read the section "Meditation" and ***write*** *your answers to the following:*

1. Meditation refers to ______________________________
____
Common to all forms of meditation is the goal of____
____
2. The two general categories of meditation are
____
They differ in that______________________________
____
____
Mindfulness is a meditation technique that____
____
____
____
____
____
____
Transcendental meditation is ____________________
____
____
____
____
____
____
3. The effects of meditation include ____________
____
____
____
Contemporary research on meditation has shown that meditation can ______________________
____
____
____
____

After you have carefully studied the preceding sections, complete the following exercises.

Concept Check 5

Read the following and write the correct term in the space provided.

1. Janna quickly becomes deeply absorbed while reading novels or watching movies. It is very likely that Janna is among the 15 percent of adults who are ________________ to hypnosis.
2. While under hypnosis, Karl describes a frightening experience of being lost at the fairgrounds when he was 6 years old. When his therapist makes the suggestion that Karl will soon forget this traumatic event, he is attempting to induce ______________________________.
3. During every final exam period, Declan becomes uptight and anxious. At the suggestion of a friend, he has tried using a meditation technique in which he focuses his awareness and attention by repeating a simple phrase over and over to himself. Declan is using a ________________ technique of meditation.
4. A researcher suggests to a hypnotized subject that the letter D does not exist. Afterward, the subject is asked to recite the alphabet; when she does, she skips the letter D. This example illustrates the use of
______________________________.

5. An eyewitness to a robbery (who couldn't remember much of the incident) was hypnotized. When the hypnotherapist suggested that there had been three white men and one black woman involved in the robbery, the subject agreed and described them in some detail. All the other five witnesses reported that only one white male robber was involved. The hypnotherapist has created a ________________________.
6. Lynda has an irrational fear and dislike of cats but has no conscious memory of when or how her phobia developed. In an attempt to enhance her memory, Lynda's therapist hypnotizes her. If the therapist's hypnotic suggestions actually work, this would demonstrate ______________.
7. Neuroscientists used PET scanners to investigate brain activity while hypnotized subjects performed three cognitive tasks as they viewed rectangular images: They were asked to see the images as they were, to mentally "drain" color from the images, and to mentally "add" color to the gray images. If the researchers' results are consistent with previous research, they are likely to conclude that hypnosis involves a distinct ______________ and is not simply ______________________, as the social-cognitive view of hypnosis proposes.
8. As part of a research study on meditation and neuroplasticity, participants learned to meditate during an 8-week stress-reduction course. MRI scans were taken two weeks before and two weeks after the course and were compared with those of participants who did not meditate. It is very likely that the scans of the new meditators will show ______________________ in several cortical areas, including the ______________________________.

Review of Terms, Concepts, and Names 5

Use the terms in this list to complete the Matching Exercise, then to help you answer the True/False items correctly.

hypnosis
posthypnotic suggestion
posthypnotic amnesia
hypermnesia
pseudomemories
Ernest R. Hilgard
dissociation
neodissociation theory of hypnosis
hidden observer
meditation
focused attention techniques
mantra
open monitoring techniques
mindfulness
transcendental meditation (TM)
primary somatosensory cortex
neuroplasticity

Matching Exercise

Match the appropriate term/name with its definition or description.

1. ______________ Theory proposed by Ernest Hilgard that explains hypnotic effects as being due to the splitting of consciousness into two simultaneous streams of mental activity, only one of which is available to the consciousness of the hypnotized subject.
2. ______________ Meditative technique that has been widely used in research in which practitioners sit quietly with eyes closed, mentally repeat the mantra they have been given, and practice a strategy for getting rid of distracting thoughts.
3. ______________ A cooperative social interaction in which the hypnotized person responds to the hypnotist's suggestions with changes in perception, memory, thoughts, and behavior.
4. ______________ The splitting of consciousness into two or more simultaneous streams of mental activity.
5. ______________ Suggestion made during hypnosis that the person carry out a specific instruction following the hypnotic session.
6. ______________ Hypnotic suggestion that supposedly enhances the person's memory for past events.
7. ______________ Hilgard's term for the dissociated stream of mental activity that continues during hypnosis.
8. ______________ Word or religious phrase that is mentally repeated during focused attention meditation.
9. ______________ The brain's capacity to change its structure as a function of experience.

True/False Test

Indicate whether each statement is true or false by placing T or F in the space next to each item.

1. ____ Ernest Hilgard is the American psychologist who studied hypnosis extensively and

advanced the neodissociation theory of hypnosis.

2. ____ The open monitoring meditative techniques involve a present-centered awareness of the passing moment (the here and now) without mental judgment; they do not involve concentrating on a mantra, visual image, or activity.
3. ____ The inability to recall specific information because of a posthypnotic suggestion is called posthypnotic amnesia.
4. ____ Pseudomemories are false memories (even though the person may be very confident that the memories are real) that result when suggestions are made during hypnosis that create distortions and inaccuracies in recall.
5. ____ Focused attention meditative techniques involve focusing awareness on a visual image or your breathing, or mentally repeating a sound or phrase called a mantra.
6. ____ Meditation is any one of a number of sustained concentration techniques that focus attention and heighten awareness.
7. ____ Mindfulness is a form of open monitoring meditation that has become increasingly popular in psychological research and clinical practice.
8. ____ The primary somatosensory cortex processes sensations of pain, touch, and pressure.

Check your answers and review any areas of weakness before going on to the next section.

Psychoactive Drugs

Preview Questions

Consider the following questions as you study this section of the chapter.

- What are psychoactive drugs, and what properties do they have in common?
- What is addiction, and what are some addiction-related conditions?
- What factors influence the effects of a drug, and what is drug abuse?
- How do depressants work, and what effects do alcohol, barbiturates, inhalants, and tranquilizers have?
- What are opiates, and what effects do they have?
- How do stimulants affect the brain and psychological functioning?
- How do the most common psychedelic drugs influence perception, mood, and thinking?
- What are designer "club" drugs, and what effects do they have?

Read the section "Psychoactive Drugs" and ***write*** *your answers to the following:*

1. Psychoactive drugs are ______________________

   ____

   They include ______________________

   ____
2. Addiction is a broad term that refers to

   ____

   ____

   Addiction-related conditions include ____________

   ____
3. The effects of a drug may be influenced

   ____

   ____

   ____
4. Drug abuse refers to______________________

   ____

   ____

   In the United States the most widely abused substance is ______________________

   ____
5. Depressants have several effects:

   ____

   ____

   ____

   Examples of depressants are ____________

   ____
6. Alcohol depresses ______________________

   ____

   Blood alcohol levels are affected by such factors as ______________________

   ____

   ____

   ____
7. Inhalants are ______________________

   ____

   They include ______________________

   ____

   ____

8. Barbiturates are depressant drugs that ______
______
______

   Common barbiturates are ______
______

9. Tranquilizers are depressants that ______
______
______

   and include ______
______

10. The opiates are a group of addictive drugs that
______
______

   Examples of opiates include ______
______

   Opiates produce their powerful effects by ______
______
______

11. Stimulant drugs ______
______
______

   Examples include ______
______

12. The psychedelic drugs create ______
______
______

   Examples of psychedelic drugs include ______
______

   LSD and psilocybin mimic ______
______
______

13. Marijuana's active ingredient, THC, produces
______
______

   THC has been shown to be useful in ______
______
______

14. Designer "club" drugs are ______
______
______

   Examples (and their effects) are ______
______
______
______
______

After you have carefully studied the preceding section, complete the following exercises.

Concept Check 6

Read the following and write the correct term in the space provided.

1. Sian regularly drinks five or six cups of strong coffee a day. If she is like most people, she would probably be surprised to find out that caffeine is a ______ drug and is ______ addictive.
2. Zachary has been using a mood-altering, euphoria-enhancing psychoactive drug. With continued use, he needs to take larger and larger doses in order to experience its original effects. Zachary is developing ______ .
3. At a party where he has had too much to drink, the normally shy Darryl keeps people entertained with his silly antics. Darryl probably behaves in this unusual way because alcohol lessens inhibitions by depressing the brain centers responsible for ______ and ______ .
4. While undergoing chemotherapy for cancer, Brendan is given marijuana to help prevent nausea and vomiting. Most likely, Brendan ______ (will/will not) develop drug tolerance and physical dependence.
5. Dora has been suffering from severe anxiety, so her doctor prescribes a depressant drug called Valium, which is a commonly prescribed ______ .
6. Shortly after "snorting" an illegal psychoactive drug, Samuel experiences intense euphoria, mental alertness, and self-confidence that lasts for several minutes. It is most likely that Samuel has inhaled the stimulant drug ______ .
7. After taking a designer drug at a party, Nadine experienced a combination of stimulant and mild psychedelic effects. It is most likely that Nadine has taken a club drug called ______ , or ______ .

8. After an accident, Trent was given medication to reduce his perception of pain. It is probable that he has been prescribed OxyContin, Percodan, or Demerol, drugs that belong to the category of psychoactive drugs called ________________ , or ________________ .

9. Kyle is a regular cocaine user. According to Focus on Neuroscience (The Addicted Brain: Diminishing Rewards), a PET scan of his brain would likely show little or no ________________ and a sharp reduction in the number of ________________ in his brain's reward system.

Graphic Organizer 2

Read the following examples, identify the drug involved, and indicate the type of drug it is.

Example	Drug Name	Drug Class
1. During a party Jordy becomes less and less inhibited as the night wears on, and by the time the party is nearly over, he is very uncoordinated and unbalanced and has trouble walking.		
2. After taking her prescription drug for a number of weeks, Janet no longer feels the intense anxiety she used to suffer.		
3. Mrs. Smothers, who suffers from glaucoma, and Mr. Hartley, who has asthma, have both been given an ordinarily illegal drug at the university hospital.		
4. Harold has used a powerful synthetic drug for a number of years to create sensory and perceptual distortions and to alter his mood, but now he is experiencing flashbacks, depression, and occasional psychotic reactions.		
5. Henrietta was a very heavy coffee drinker until she quit cold turkey. She is now experiencing headaches, irritability, drowsiness, and fatigue.		
6. Following surgery, Gregory was given a common prescription drug under medical supervision in order to alleviate his pain.		
7. Just before his exam, Juan smokes a couple of cigarettes and finds he is less tired, more mentally alert, and yet fairly relaxed.		

Review of Terms and Concepts 6

Use the terms in this list to complete the Matching Exercise, then to help you answer the True/False items correctly.

psychoactive drug
addiction
physical dependence
drug tolerance
withdrawal symptoms
drug rebound effect
drug abuse
depressants
additive
binge drinking
delirium tremens (DTs)
inhalants
barbiturates
tranquilizers
opiates (narcotics)
opium
morphine
codeine
stimulants
caffeine
adenosine
nicotine
amphetamines
cocaine
stimulant-induced psychosis (amphetamine-induced psychosis or cocaine-induced psychosis)
methamphetamine (meth)
psychedelic drugs
mescaline
psilocybin
LSD (lysergic acid diethylamide)
marijuana
THC (tetrahydrocannabinol)
hashish
anandamide
designer "club" drugs
MDMA (ecstasy)
dissociative anesthetics (PCP and ketamine)
stimulus control therapy

Matching Exercise

Match the appropriate term with its definition or description.

1. ________ The active ingredient of marijuana and other preparations derived from the hemp plant.

2. ________ Category of psychoactive drugs that inhibit brain activity.
3. ________ Stimulant drug found in tobacco products.
4. ________ Recurrent drug use that results in disruptions in academic, social, or occupational functioning or in legal or psychological problems.
5. ________ Drug that alters normal consciousness, perception, mood, and behavior.
6. ________ Schizophrenia-like symptoms that can occur as the result of prolonged amphetamine or cocaine use.
7. ________ Psychedelic drug derived from the peyote cactus.
8. ________ Condition in which increasing amounts of a physically addictive drug are needed to produce the original, desired effect.
9. ________ Potent form of marijuana made from the resin of the hemp plant.
10. ________ Unpleasant physical reactions, combined with intense drug cravings, that occur when a person abstains from a drug on which he or she is physically dependent.
11. ________ Stimulant drug derived from the coca tree.
12. ________ Class of stimulant drugs that arouse the central nervous system and suppress appetite.
13. ________ The collective term for withdrawal symptoms associated with high levels of alcohol dependence; may involve confusion, hallucinations, severe tremors, or seizures.
14. ________ A naturally occurring compound in the body that influences the release of several neurotransmitters in the central nervous system and whose receptors are blocked by caffeine.
15. ________ A natural opiate that can be derived from either opium or morphine.
16. ________ Synthetic "club" drug that combines stimulant and mild psychedelic effects.
17. ________ Naturally occurring brain chemical, structurally similar to THC, involved in pain sensations, mood, and memory.
18. ________ Chemical substances that produce an alteration in consciousness and include paint solvents, spray paint, gasoline, and aerosol sprays.
19. ________ Treatment for insomnia involving specific guidelines to create a strict association between the bedroom and rapid sleep onset.

True/False Test

Indicate whether each statement is true or false by placing T or F in the space next to each item.

1. ____ Marijuana is a psychoactive drug derived from the hemp plant.
2. ____ Opiates are a category of depressant drugs that reduce anxiety and produce sleepiness.
3. ____ The occurrence of withdrawal symptoms that are the opposite of a physically addictive drug's action is referred to as the drug rebound effect.
4. ____ Caffeine is the stimulant drug found in coffee, tea, cola drinks, chocolate, and many over-the-counter medications.
5. ____ Opium is a natural opiate derived from the opium poppy.
6. ____ Binge drinking is defined as five or more drinks in a row for men, or four or more drinks in a row for women.
7. ____ Psilocybin is a psychedelic drug derived from the Psilocybe mushroom, which is sometimes called "magic mushroom."
8. ____ LSD is a synthetic psychedelic drug.
9. ____ Morphine is the active ingredient of the natural opiate called opium.
10. ____ Tranquilizers such as Valium and Librium are depressants that are prescribed to relieve anxiety.
11. ____ Psychedelic drugs are a category of psychoactive drugs that increase brain activity, as reflected in aroused behavior and increased mental alertness.
12. ____ Physical dependence is a condition in which a person who has physically adapted to a drug must take the drug regularly in order to avoid withdrawal symptoms.
13. ____ Barbiturates are a category of psychoactive drugs that have strong pain-relieving properties and are chemically similar to morphine.
14. ____ Stimulants are a category of psychoactive drugs that create profound perceptual distortions, alter mood, and affect thinking.
15. ____ Designer "club" drugs are drugs that are synthesized in a laboratory rather than being derived from naturally occurring compounds.
16. ____ Dissociative anesthetics are a class of drugs that reduce sensitivity to pain and produce feelings of detachment, depersonalization, and dissociation.
17. ____ Methamphetamine is an illegal, highly addictive drug that provides an intense high

that is longer lasting than one from cocaine; it also causes brain damage and tissue loss.

18. ____ A condition in which a person feels psychologically and physically compelled to take a specific drug is called addiction.

19. ____ When depressants are combined, their sedative effects are *additive,* meaning that they are increased.

Check your answers and review any areas of weakness before going on to the next section.

Something to Think About

1. We've all heard the complaint, "There's so much to do, and so little time!" When people are busy and feel pressured, they are often also sleep-deprived, making them less efficient or productive than well-rested people. More important, they are more likely to make potentially dangerous mistakes. Those most at risk are shift workers (people who work night shifts or rotating shifts) or people who suffer jet lag symptoms for other reasons.

   Imagine you are a consultant and have been asked to prepare a report for an organization concerned with these problems among its employees. Based on what you have learned about the sleep–wake cycle, circadian rhythms, biological and environmental clocks, and so on, what would you recommend in your report?

2. Almost everybody is fascinated by dreams and what they mean. Some people believe that dreams can foretell the future or are important in other mysterious ways. Suppose a friend tells you that she has dreamed that she could not understand a single question on a very important math exam. She just stared at the exam until the professor announced the exam was over and removed the paper from in front of her. At this point, she awoke in a very anxious state. Now she is worried that when she takes the real exam next week, her dream will come true. What would you say to her about dreams and their meaning, theories of dreams, and such?

Check your answers and review any areas of weakness before doing the progress tests.

Progress Test 1

Review the complete chapter (including all boxed inserts), review all your study notes, and then test yourself on the following progress test. Check your answers. If you make a mistake, review your notes, check the appropriate section in the study guide, and, if necessary, go back and read the relevant part of the chapter in your textbook.

1. Nightmares are to ________ as sleep terrors are to ________ .
   (a) sleep spindles; beta waves
   (b) alpha waves; beta waves
   (c) REM sleep; slow-wave NREM sleep
   (d) slow-wave NREM sleep; REM sleep

2. Bernita witnessed a robbery, but her recall of the event was vague. Police investigators used hypnosis in an attempt to enhance her memory. The hypnotic effect that the investigators hope for is called ________ , which research shows is ________ to be successful.
   (a) hypermnesia; very likely
   (b) posthypnotic suggestion; not very likely
   (c) hypermnesia; not very likely
   (d) posthypnotic suggestion; very likely

3. After ingesting a small dose of a psychoactive drug, Graham experiences vivid visual hallucinations and other perceptual distortions; he feels as though he is floating above his body. Graham is most likely experiencing the effects of
   (a) cocaine.
   (b) barbiturates.
   (c) tranquilizers.
   (d) LSD.
   (e) cappuccino.

4. Curtis has been diagnosed with a sleep disorder after his wife complained about his sporadic abnormal sexual behaviors during the night. These episodes included behaviors such as masturbation, sex-talking, groping or fondling his wife's genitals, and sometimes very rough sexual intercourse. Curtis has no memory of these incidents. He has a parasomnia called
   (a) cataplexy.
   (b) sexsomnia (sleepsex).
   (c) transient insomnia.
   (d) somnambulism.

5. After flying from San Diego to New York, Jasmine experiences a restless, sleepless night; the next day, she is irritable and cannot concentrate on her work. Jasmine's problems are likely due to
   (a) disruption in her circadian rhythms.
   (b) high blood levels of melatonin.
   (c) jet lag.
   (d) all of these factors.

6. Justine believes that dreaming is simply our subjective awareness of the brain's internally generated signals during sleep, which start with automatic activation of brainstem circuits that then arouse more sophisticated brain areas. Justine's views are most consistent with which theory of dreams?
   (a) social-cognitive theory of dreams
   (b) neurocognitive model of dreaming
   (c) activation–synthesis model of dreaming
   (d) Freud's wish-fulfillment theory of dreams

7. To find out what goes on in people's brains during a typical night's sleep, researchers are most likely to
   (a) ask people to try to remember as much as possible when they awake in the morning.
   (b) closely watch the actions of subjects sleeping in the sleep research lab.
   (c) wake people up every 15 minutes and ask them what is going on in their minds.
   (d) use an electroencephalograph to measure their brain-wave activity throughout the night.

8. Just as you are about to fall asleep, you have the sudden feeling of falling and your body gives an involuntary spasm. You have experienced
   (a) a sleep spindle.
   (b) a myoclonic jerk.
   (c) sexsomnia.
   (d) cataplexy.

9. Harry has been asleep for about an hour or so, and his heart begins to beat faster, his breathing becomes irregular, his voluntary muscle activity is suppressed, and his closed eyes move rapidly back and forth. It is most probable that Harry is in ________ and is therefore experiencing ________ .
   (a) REM sleep; a myoclonic jerk
   (b) NREM; sleep spindles
   (c) REM; paradoxical sleep
   (d) NREM; quiet sleep

10. Eight-year-old Billy gets out of bed at 1 A.M. and starts to sleepwalk. He is most likely
    (a) in slow-wave stage 3 or 4 NREM sleep.
    (b) suffering from narcolepsy.
    (c) in REM sleep.
    (d) experiencing elevated brain levels of hypocretins.

11. After Zufina has been asleep for a period of time in the sleep lab, the EEG monitor indicates the presence of theta waves, sleep spindles, and K complexes. Zufina is in ________ sleep.
    (a) stage 3 NREM
    (b) REM
    (c) stage 2 NREM
    (d) stage 4 NREM

12. Mr. Jensen repeatedly complains about the quality and duration of his sleep. He claims that he can't fall asleep and stay asleep and usually wakes up before it is time to get up. Mr. Jensen apparently suffers from
    (a) obstructive sleep apnea (OSA).
    (b) narcolepsy.
    (c) cataplexy.
    (d) insomnia.

13. While participating in a research project, Teddy was confined to an isolation unit for a number of weeks and deprived of all external time signals. During this experiment, it is very probable that
    (a) Teddy's internal body clock will drift to its natural or intrinsic rhythm, which is about 24.2 hours long.
    (b) Teddy's SCN will keep his circadian cycles synchronized on a 24-hour schedule.
    (c) Teddy's internal body clock will drift to its natural or intrinsic rhythm, which is about 25.2 hours long.
    (d) Teddy will suffer major depression, irritability, memory loss, and both mental and physical fatigue because his SCN is no longer being entrained by sunlight.

14. According to Enhancing Well-Being with Psychology (Stimulus Control Therapy for Insomnia), which of the following is one of the recommendations for improving the quality of sleep and minimizing sleep problems?
    (a) continuous positive airway pressure (CPAP)
    (b) stimulus control therapy
    (c) transcendental meditation
    (d) take sleeping pills, herbal tea, or supplements that contain ginseng, ephedrine, or similar compounds

15. According to Critical Thinking (Is Hypnosis a Special State of Consciousness?), ________ theory suggests that hypnotic subjects are responding to social demands by acting the way they think good hypnotic subjects should act and by conforming to expectations and situational cues.
    (a) neodissociation
    (b) social-cognitive
    (c) imaginative suggestibility
    (d) activation–synthesis

Progress Test 2

After you have checked your understanding of the material in Progress Test 1 and have done a complete chapter review with special focus on any areas of weakness, you are now ready to assess your knowledge on Progress Test 2. Check your answers. If you make a mistake, review your notes, the relevant section of the study guide, and, if necessary, the appropriate part of your textbook.

1. Dr. Benjamin hypnotizes a client and suggests that she will no longer feel a craving for chocolates. Dr. Benjamin is making use of
   (a) posthypnotic suggestion.
   (b) hypermnesia.
   (c) posthypnotic amnesia.
   (d) meditation.

2. Amber sits in a relaxed position, closes her eyes, and begins to recite her mantra. Amber is practicing
   (a) hypnosis.
   (b) meditation.
   (c) stimulus control therapy.
   (d) dissociation.
   (e) laziness.

3. Researchers who have found evidence that subjects appear to have a "hidden observer" are likely to suggest that hypnosis involves
   (a) dissociation.
   (b) social factors.
   (c) stages 3 and 4 NREM sleep.
   (d) imaginative suggestibility.

4. John drinks five or six cups of coffee every day. If he doesn't, he feels irritable, drowsy, and fatigued. John is ________ a(n) ________ drug.
   (a) addicted to; psychedelic
   (b) physically dependent on; opiate
   (c) addicted to; depressant
   (d) physically dependent on; stimulant

5. Richard is heading to work shortly after sunrise and is enjoying the bright morning sunshine. The most likely effect of this exposure is that
   (a) he will experience a decrease in levels of melatonin, and the sunlight will help entrain his SCN so that it keeps his circadian rhythms on a 24-hour schedule.
   (b) he will become very drowsy and sleepy.
   (c) he will experience an increase in the production of melatonin.
   (d) his circadian rhythms will become desynchronized and he will experience symptoms of jet lag.

6. Nancy's husband took her to the doctor because she frequently sleepwalks to the kitchen and compulsively eats food from the cupboard and fridge but has no memory of doing so in the morning. The doctor is likely to diagnose her with a ________ called ________ .
   (a) parasomnia; night terror
   (b) dyssomnia; somnambulism
   (c) parasomnia; sleep-related eating disorder (SRED)
   (d) dyssomnia; sleep-related eating disorder (SRED)

7. Phelan has just had a very painful operation. His doctors are most likely to prescribe ________ for pain relief.
   (a) a tranquilizer
   (b) marijuana
   (c) morphine
   (d) alcohol

8. Mr. Godfrey has cancer and was given marijuana to counter the nausea and vomiting following chemotherapy. The active ingredient that makes this a useful drug in such cases is
   (a) psilocybin.
   (b) cannabis.
   (c) LSD.
   (d) THC.

9. Sleep researchers deprive participants of REM sleep for a number of nights but allow them an otherwise normal sleep; the participants are likely to experience ________ when next allowed to sleep.
   (a) narcolepsy
   (b) REM rebound
   (c) sleep terrors
   (d) NREM rebound

10. Harold dreams that he is on a train traveling through mountains in what he thinks is Switzerland. He can see the train very clearly going in and out of tunnels over and over again. Harold's therapist suggests that the dream is not about travel in a foreign country but about Harold's concern with his sexual performance. The therapist adheres to ________ theory of dreams and is attempting to reveal the ________ of Harold's dream.
    (a) the social-cognitive; manifest content
    (b) Freud's wish-fulfillment; manifest content
    (c) Freud's wish-fulfillment; latent content
    (d) the activation–synthesis; latent content

11. During a very intense game of pool, Gary is attempting a difficult shot that will win the game. However, he suddenly loses complete muscle control and falls fast asleep on the pool table. Gary probably suffers from ________ and is experiencing ________ .
    (a) obstructive sleep apnea (OSA); a sleep attack
    (b) narcolepsy; cataplexy
    (c) insomnia; somnambulism
    (d) REM sleep behavior disorder; sleep paralysis

12. Nicotine is to alcohol as a ________ drug is to a ________ .
    (a) stimulant; depressant
    (b) psychedelic; stimulant
    (c) depressant; stimulant
    (d) depressant; psychedelic

13. Dr. Tirian's research is concerned with the effects of psychedelic drugs on brain functioning. Which of the following is she most likely to test in her experiments?
    (a) LSD, psilocybin, and mescaline
    (b) amphetamines and cocaine
    (c) alcohol, nicotine, and caffeine
    (d) barbiturates and tranquilizers

14. According to In Focus (What You Really Wanted to Know About Sleep), which of the following is true?
    (a) Research suggests that high levels of a naturally occurring compound in the body called adenosine cause sleepiness.
    (b) It is not dangerous to wake a sleepwalker.
    (c) In a relatively common phenomenon called sleep paralysis, the paralysis of REM sleep carries over to the waking state for up to 10 minutes.
    (d) All of these statements are true.

15. According to In Focus (What You Really Want to Know About Dreams), which of the following is true?
    (a) People who have been blind all their lives don't dream.
    (b) Up until the widespread use of color TV, most people dreamed in black and white.
    (c) Virtually all mammals experience sleep cycles in which REM sleep alternates with slow-wave NREM sleep, and it is reasonable to conclude that they all dream.
    (d) Dreams can often be used to accurately predict the future.

Progress Test 3

After you have checked your understanding of the material in Progress Tests 1 and 2, and have done a complete chapter review with special focus on any areas of weakness, you are ready to further assess your knowledge with Progress Test 3. Check your answers. If you make a mistake, review your notes, the appropriate parts of the study guide, and, if necessary, the relevant sections of your textbook.

1. Mrs. Cadogan complains that her overweight 65-year-old husband snores and snorts throughout the night and appears to be gasping for breath. This happens most often when he is sleeping on his back. Mr. Cadogan suffers from
    (a) obstructive sleep apnea (OSA).
    (b) sleep terrors.
    (c) sleep-related eating disorder.
    (d) somnambulism.

2. Sleep researcher Seung-Schik Yoo and his colleagues deprived some participants of sleep for 35 hours while others were allowed to sleep normally. Then, all the participants viewed various images, some neutral and some unpleasant, while undergoing an fMRI brain scan. According to Focus On Neuroscience (The Sleep-Deprived Emotional Brain), the results showed that
    (a) the sleep-deprived brain is less emotional and less active compared with fully rested brains.
    (b) the participants who were sleep-deprived tended to demonstrate little or no emotional reaction to either the neutral or the unpleasant images.
    (c) the sleep-deprived participants were more responsive to the neutral images and less responsive to the unpleasant images.

(d) the sleep-deprived brain is much more prone to strong emotional reactions, especially in response to negative stimuli.

3. Brianna, who has a very warm, loving relationship with her husband, dreamed that she had an intense, emotional argument with him in which she shouted and screamed and called him horrible names. Her psychoanalyst suggested that Brianna must have some deeply repressed anger and frustration toward her father that is expressed symbolically in the dream about her husband. Brianna's account of the dream represents the ________ , and her therapist's account represents the ________ .
   (a) latent content; manifest content
   (b) activation phase; synthesis phase
   (c) manifest content; latent content
   (d) synthesis phase; activation phase

4. Stage 2 NREM sleep is to _____ as stage 4 NREM is to _____ .
   (a) beta waves; alpha waves
   (b) alpha waves; beta waves
   (c) sleep spindles and K complexes; delta waves
   (d) dreams; nightmares

5. Dr. Hayward uses hypnosis on a patient during a root canal procedure. When he asks her to raise her hand if some part of her can feel pain, she raises her hand. This illustrates
   (a) the hidden observer.
   (b) paradoxical sleep.
   (c) posthypnotic amnesia.
   (d) tolerance.

6. Nelson, who had been a heavy methamphetamine user, has not used the drug for the last two months. A PET scan of his brain now is likely to show
   (a) a relatively normal brain because any damage caused by the drug would be completely healed in two months.
   (b) a significant increase in the number of dopamine receptors, and improved neurological functioning, especially in the frontal lobes.
   (c) a significant reduction in the number of dopamine receptors, and extensive neurological damage, especially in the frontal lobes.
   (d) a significant decrease in the number of dopamine receptors in the brainstem and damage to brainstem areas that control breathing and heartbeat.

7. Due to prolonged and heavy use of cocaine, Andrew suffered schizophrenia-like symptoms, including auditory hallucinations of "voices" and bizarre paranoid ideas. Andrew's symptoms suggest that he has
   (a) stimulant-induced psychosis.
   (b) delirium tremens (DTs).
   (c) hypermnesia.
   (d) a parasomnia.

8. During a rave party, Drake was given a substance that reduced his sensitivity to pain and produced feelings of detachment, depersonalization, and dissociation. He is most likely to have used a class of club drug called ____________ , and, in particular, either ____________ or ____________ .
   (a) psychedelics; LSD; mescaline
   (b) the dissociative anesthetics; PCP (angel dust); ketamine (Special K)
   (c) depressants; methaqualone; quaalude
   (d) tranquilizers; Valium; Librium

9. After he abruptly stops taking a depressant drug, Ernie suffers from sleep problems, excitability, and restlessness. Ernie is suffering from
   (a) drug rebound effect.
   (b) parasomnia.
   (c) dyssomnia.
   (d) stimulant-induced psychosis.

10. Maya uses the zazen, or the "just sitting" technique of Zen Buddhism, in which she engages in quiet awareness of the "here and now" without any distracting thoughts. Maya is using a type of ________ meditation.
   (a) open monitoring
   (b) imaginative suggestibility
   (c) focused attention
   (d) stimulus control

11. According to his wife, 70-year-old Hugo sometimes jumps out of bed during the night and appears to be acting out his dreams. It is very likely that Hugo suffers from a sleep disorder called
   (a) narcolepsy.
   (b) REM sleep behavior disorder.
   (c) obstructive sleep apnea.
   (d) insomnia.

12. Gaetan is participating in a sleep research lab experiment. A PET scan reveals that, compared with when he is awake or in slow-wave sleep, his brain activity while in REM is likely to show decreased activity in ______________ , and increased activity in ______________ .
    (a) the limbic system; the frontal lobes and primary visual cortex
    (b) the left parietal lobe; both frontal lobes
    (c) the frontal lobes and primary visual cortex; the limbic system
    (d) brain areas associated with visual imagery; the temporal lobes

13. Farhana often becomes aware that she is dreaming while she is still asleep. Sometimes she can consciously guide the direction of the dream: even if she wakes up, she can go back to sleep and continue her interrupted dream. This example illustrates
    (a) lucid dreaming.
    (b) sleep mentation.
    (c) cataplexy.
    (d) parasomnia.

14. When Jasmine started college, she was extremely anxious about her courses and her ability to do well academically. Her doctor prescribed a tranquilizer to help her overcome her extreme nervousness. Which of the following drugs is NOT likely to have been prescribed?
    (a) Xanax
    (b) Valium
    (c) OxyContin
    (d) Librium

15. Jason suffers from a number of work- and school-related sleeping problems. According to Enhancing Well-Being with Psychology (Stimulus Control Therapy for Insomnia), Jason could improve the situation by
    (a) monitoring his intake of stimulants, especially those containing caffeine.
    (b) establishing a quiet bedtime routine and avoiding stimulating mental or physical activity for at least an hour before his bedtime.
    (c) creating the conditions for restful sleep; keeping the bedroom quiet, dark, and cool; and turning off his cell phone and computer so that they can't disrupt his sleep.
    (d) doing all of these things.

Answers

Introduction: Consciousness: Experiencing the "Private I"

1. Consciousness *is defined as the* personal awareness of mental activities, internal sensations, and the external environment.
2. *William James's idea of "stream of consciousness" refers to the fact that* although consciousness is always changing, it is perceived as unified and unbroken, in much the same way that a stream or river is seen as one thing, yet is constantly changing.
3. *Attention is* the capacity to selectively focus awareness on particular stimuli in your external environment or on your internal thoughts or sensations. *The three characteristics of attention are* attention has a limited capacity (we can't pay attention to all the stimuli in our external environment or to all the potential thoughts, memories, or fantasies available to us); attention is selective (it is like a spotlight that we focus on certain areas of our experience while ignoring others, a classic example being the *cocktail party effect*); attention can be blind (examples include inattentional blindness, inattentional deafness, and change blindness)
4. *Multi-tasking refers to* doing two or more things at once or paying attention to two or more sources of stimuli at once; it involves a division of attention. *Multi-tasking can cause problems when* the tasks are similar or require a great deal of concentration. *When a great deal of concentration is required,* absorption in a visual task can produce inattentional deafness, and absorption in an auditory task can produce inattentional blindness.

Biological and Environmental "Clocks" That Regulate Consciousness

1. *Circadian rhythms are* biological and psychological processes that systematically vary over a roughly 24-hour period.
2. *The suprachiasmatic nucleus (SCN) is* a tiny cluster of neurons in the brain's hypothalamus that governs the timing of circadian rhythms, including the sleep–wake cycle; thus, it is considered the master biological clock. *Its role in sleep–wake cycles and other circadian rhythms is to* detect, through its connections with the visual system, decreases in sunlight and, in turn, to trigger an increase in the production of melatonin, which makes you sleep. Exposure to sunlight suppresses melatonin levels.

3. *Melatonin is a* hormone manufactured by the pineal gland (an endocrine gland in the brain), which produces sleepiness.
4. *In the absence of all environmental time signals* people tend to drift to the natural, or intrinsic, rhythm of the SCN, which is approximately 24.2 hours long. *As a result,* the sleep–wake, body temperature, and melatonin circadian rhythms become desynchronized so that they are no longer coordinated with one another.
5. *People suffer from jet lag symptoms because* time cues are out of sync with their internal biological clocks. These symptoms can be produced by travel across multiple time zones, for example.
6. *Melatonin plays a key role in jet lag symptoms by* causing sleepiness, grogginess, and sluggishness, at a time when the external environmental cues suggest that you should be alert and awake (for example, your internal body clock says it is 3:00 A.M., so melatonin levels are high, but the external time is 10:00 A.M. and you need to be awake).

Concept Check 1

1. SCN (the body's clock); melatonin; pineal gland
2. melatonin
3. circadian rhythms
4. consciousness
5. 24.2
6. not likely; likely

Matching Exercise 1

1. consciousness
2. multi-tasking
3. suprachiasmatic nucleus (SCN)
4. jet lag
5. melatonin
6. attention
7. cocktail party effect

True/False Test 1

1. F	4. T	7. T
2. T	5. T	
3. T	6. F	

Sleep

1. *An electroencephalograph is* an instrument that uses electrodes placed on the scalp to measure and record the brain's electrical activity. *The graphic record it produces is called an* electroencephalogram (EEG).
2. *By studying EEGs, sleep researchers established that* brain-wave activity systematically changes throughout sleep. *They distinguish between two types of sleep:* REM (rapid-eye-movement) sleep, which is often called active sleep or paradoxical sleep, and NREM sleep (non-rapid-eye-movement sleep or quiet sleep).
3. *Beta brain waves are associated with* being alert and awake and are small, fast brain waves. *Alpha brain waves are associated with* drowsiness and relaxation and are slightly larger and slower than beta waves.
4. *Hypnagogic hallucinations are* vivid sensory phenomena that occur during the onset of sleep.
5. *The four NREM sleep stages are characterized by different brain and body activity:*

   Stage 1 NREM: a mixture of alpha and theta waves, lasts only a few minutes, and is a transitional stage from wakefulness to being asleep.

   Stage 2 NREM: the appearance of sleep spindles (bursts of brain activity that last a second or two), K complexes (single but large high-voltage spikes of brain activity), and mainly theta brain waves, although the slower delta waves begin to emerge.

   Stages 3 and 4 NREM: delta brain-wave activity (20 percent in stage 3, and 50 percent in stage 4); in combination, these stages are referred to as slow-wave sleep (SWS).
6. *REM sleep is characterized by* increased brain activity (smaller, faster brain waves), activation of visual and motor neurons, dreaming, suppression of voluntary muscle activity, and considerable physiological arousal.
7. *During the course of a typical night's sleep, stages 3 and 4 NREM usually* occur only during the first two 90-minute cycles. *As the night progresses,* REM sleep episodes become increasingly longer, and less time is spent in NREM.
8. *Over the course of the lifespan, the quantity and quality of our sleep* changes considerably; *the newborn sleeps about* 16 hours a day with up to 50 percent in REM and the rest in quiet sleep similar to NREM stages 1 and 2 sleep; *by about the third month of life* the deep, slow-wave sleep of NREM stages 3 and 4 appears, *and by age 5* the typical 90-minute sleep cycles of alternating REM and NREM sleep are established. *From childhood through late adulthood,*

total sleep time gradually decreases, and the amount of time devoted to slow-wave NREM sleep also gradually decreases. This is offset by an increase in NREM stages 1 and 2. The proportion of REM sleep increases during childhood and adolescence, remains stable throughout adulthood, and then decreases during late adulthood.

9. *The need to sleep serves* a variety of vital functions, including promoting physiological processes that restore and rejuvenate the body and mind, providing needed rest for muscles and body, maintaining immune system functioning, and regulating moods and emotions. *The enormous variability in sleep patterns across different species is the result of* evolutionary adaptation; different sleep patterns evolved as a way of conserving energy and preventing a particular species from interacting with the environment when doing so is most hazardous.
10. *Sleep deprivation and sleep restriction studies demonstrate that* we have a biological need to sleep; after a day or more without sleep we will experience impairments in mood, mental abilities (such as concentration and vigilance), reaction time, the ability to gauge risks, perceptual skills, and complex motor skills. Metabolic and hormonal disruptions also occur, and the immune system's effectiveness is diminished. All these changes become more pronounced as sleep restriction continues for night after night. When people are deprived of sleep (either REM or stages 3 and 4 NREM), they will experience rebound effects if allowed to sleep undisturbed.
11. *The phenomena of REM and NREM rebound seem to indicate that* the brain needs to experience the full range of sleep states, making up for missing components of sleep when given the chance.

Concept Check 2

1. alpha
2. falling; myoclonic jerk (sleep start)
3. REM; REM rebound
4. is experiencing sleep disturbances that are normal for her age
5. theta; sleep spindles; K complexes
6. microsleeps; mood, mental abilities, reaction time, perceptual skills, and complex motor skills
7. sleep paralysis
8. amygdala; brain's reward circuits

Graphic Organizer 1

1. C
2. E
3. G
4. B
5. D
6. F
7. A

Matching Exercise 2

1. alpha brain waves
2. electroencephalogram (EEG)
3. sleep spindles
4. hypnagogic hallucinations
5. slow-wave sleep
6. myoclonic jerk (sleep start)
7. K complexes
8. REM rebound
9. electroencephalograph
10. brain waves

True/False Test 2

1. T
2. T
3. T
4. F
5. T
6. T
7. F
8. T
9. T
10. T

Dreams and Mental Activity During Sleep

1. *Sleep thinking (sleep mentation) refers to* vague, bland, thoughtlike ruminations about real-life events that usually occur during NREM slow-wave sleep, *whereas a dream is* an unfolding sequence of perceptions, thoughts, and emotions during sleep (usually REM) that is experienced as a series of real-life events. Even if bizarre and illogical, dreams are accepted because disbelief is suspended when we dream.
2. *People usually have* four or five *dreaming episodes each night. The first REM period is* the shortest (about 10 minutes), and subsequent REM episodes average about 30 minutes and tend to get longer as the night continues, with early morning dreams the longest (40 minutes or longer) and most likely to be recalled.
3. *Brain activity during REM sleep is* different from that of waking and NREM sleep. Activity in the primary visual cortex and the frontal lobes is diminished, while activity in association areas of the visual cortex and the limbic centers associated with emotion, motivation, and memory increases.
4. *NREM slow-wave sleep contributes to* forming new episodic memories of personally experi-

enced events, *whereas REM and NREM stage 2 sleep seem to help* consolidate new procedural memories, which involve learning a new skill or task until it can be performed automatically.

5. *Sleep strengthens and enhances new memories by* reactivating daytime memories during the 90-minute cycles of sleep that occur throughout the night, and this repeated reactivation of newly encoded memories during sleep helps strengthen neuronal connections that contribute to forming long-term memories; it also helps integrate them into existing networks of memories.
6. *Most dreams are* fairly coherent, patterned, thoughtful, and by and large, a realistic simulation of waking life; they are overwhelmingly about everyday settings, people, activities, and events. They involve some unusual and perhaps nonsensical aspects, but only a relatively small amount of bizarreness.
7. *The most common patterns and themes of dreams are as follows:* Women report males and females in equal proportion but men are more likely to report other males as the story characters; negative feelings and events are more common than positive ones; instances of aggression, with the dreamer being the victim, are more common than instances of friendliness; physical aggression in dreams is more common for men than women but women report more emotions; sex or sexual behaviors seldom occur as elements of the dream story; and apprehension or fear is the most frequently reported dream emotion for both sexes, followed by happiness and confusion.
8. *Nightmares are* vivid and disturbing dreams that often awaken the sleeper and typically involve feelings of helplessness or powerlessness in the face of being aggressively attacked or pursued. Some nightmares involve intense feelings of sadness, anger, disgust, or embarrassment. *The frequency of nightmares is closely related to* age: nightmares occur most often during middle and late childhood, then decrease in frequency during adolescence and young adulthood (about 5 to 10 percent of adults experience nightmares on a weekly basis). Women have more nightmares than men, and daytime stress, anxiety, and emotional difficulties are often associated with nightmares. However, nightmares are not indicative of psychological or sleep disorders unless they occur frequently, cause difficulties returning to sleep, or cause daytime distress.
9. *Freud's explanation for dreams suggests that* because the sexual and aggressive instincts that motivate human behavior are so unacceptable to the conscious mind, they are pushed into the unconscious mind, or repressed. He believed that these repressed urges and wishes could surface in dream imagery.
10. *The manifest content refers to* the elements of a dream that are consciously experienced and remembered by the dreamer. *The latent content is the* disguised psychological meanings of the dream that are concealed in the manifest content. *Freud believed that* dream images of sticks, swords, brooms, and other elongated objects *were phallic symbols, and that* dream images of cupboards, boxes, and ovens *symbolized the vagina. Psychological research has shown that* Freud's belief that dreams represent the fulfillment of repressed wishes, and that dream images (the manifest content) are symbols that disguise the dream's true psychological meaning, has not been supported.
11. *The activation–synthesis model of dreaming maintains that* dreaming is our subjective awareness of the brain's internally generated signals during sleep; brain activity produces dream images (activation); these are combined by the brain into a dream story (synthesis) and meaning is imposed on them. *This model does not contend* that dreams are completely meaningless but that meaning may lie in the deeply personal way in which images are organized and in the way the dreamer makes sense of the progression of chaotic dream images.
12. *The neurocognitive model of dreams emphasizes* the continuity of waking and dreaming cognition, and states that dreaming is like thinking under conditions of reduced sensory input and the absence of voluntary control. *This model suggests that* dreams reflect our interests, personality, and individual worries, and mirror our waking concerns in a way that is similar to normal thought processes.

Concept Check 3

1. manifest content
2. activation–synthesis
3. sleep thinking (sleep mentation)
4. lucid dreams
5. 75; REM
6. nightmare
7. decreased; increased

8. neurocognitive

Matching Exercise 3

1. J. Allan Hobson and Robert W. McCarley
2. Sigmund Freud
3. sleep thinking (sleep mentation)
4. nightmare
5. phallic symbols
6. episodic memories

True/False Test 3

1. T
2. F
3. T
4. T
5. F
6. T

Sleep Disorders

1. *Sleep disorders involve* consistent abnormal sleep patterns that cause subjective distress and interfere with a person's daytime functioning (70 percent of people experience regular sleep disruptions).
2. *Dyssomnias are* sleep disorders involving disruptions in the amount, quality, or timing of sleep. *They include* insomnia, obstructive sleep apnea, and narcolepsy. *Parasomnias are* sleep disorders involving undesirable physical arousal, behaviors, or events during sleep or sleep transitions. *They include* sleep terrors, sleepsex, sleepwalking, sleep-related eating disorder, and REM sleep behavior disorder.
3. *Insomnia is characterized by* complaints about the quality or duration of sleep, difficulty going to sleep or staying asleep, or waking before it is time to get up. For insomnia to be diagnosed, these disruptions must also produce daytime sleepiness, fatigue, impaired social or occupational performance, or mood disturbances. *Transient insomnia lasts* from one or two nights to a couple of weeks. *Symptoms of chronic insomnia occur* at least three nights each week and persist for a month or longer. *The risk of insomnia is influenced by* age (increases with age), gender (women are twice as likely as men to suffer from insomnia), pregnancy, social factors, menopause, hyperarousal, use of stimulants, environmental factors (noise, temperature, and unfamiliar surroundings), anxiety over stressful life events (job or school difficulties, troubled relationships, illness or death of a loved one, financial problems), and worries about not being able to sleep, all of which may contribute to a self-perpetuating vicious cycle. Insomnia is the most common sleep complaint among adults (33 percent suffer transient insomnia, and 10 percent suffer chronic insomnia).
4. *In obstructive sleep apnea (OSA),* the sleeper's airway becomes narrowed or blocked, causing very shallow breathing or repeated pauses in breathing, disrupting the quality and quantity of a person's sleep. Sleep apnea can be treated with lifestyle changes, such as avoiding alcohol or losing weight, and severe to moderate cases are usually treated with continuous positive airway pressure, or CPAP.
5. *Narcolepsy is characterized by* overwhelming bouts of excessive daytime sleepiness and brief uncontrollable episodes of sleep, which are called microsleeps or sleep attacks. *Cataplexy is the* sudden loss of voluntary muscle strength and control, lasting from several seconds to several minutes; it is usually triggered by a sudden intense emotion, such as laughter, anger, fear, or surprise. *Autopsies of people who had narcolepsy have revealed* greatly reduced numbers of hypocretin-producing neurons in the brain (these neurotransmitters are produced exclusively by the hypothalamus during daytime to maintain a steady state of wakefulness).
6. *In parasomnias, the brain is* awake enough to carry out the actions, but not awake enough to be consciously aware of performing the actions. *Key characteristics of all the parasomnias are as follows:* lack of awareness while performing actions and total amnesia for the behaviors or events upon awakening; they arise during NREM stages 3 and 4 that occur in the first half of the night, are more common in children and decrease with age, may involve a genetic predisposition or susceptibility, and can be triggered by a wide range of stimuli (sleep deprivation, stress, erratic sleep schedules, medications, stimulants, pregnancy, and tranquilizers).
7. *A parasomnia called sleep terrors, or night terrors, typically occurs* during stage 3 or 4 NREM sleep and lasts for a minute or less and is more common in children than adults. *Sleep terrors involve* sharply increased physiological arousal, restlessness, sweating, a racing heart, and intense fear accompanied by a panic-stricken scream or cry for help with no recollection of the episode in the morning. *They differ from nightmares* in that nightmares are anxiety

dreams that involve a progressive unpleasant dream story and typically occur during REM sleep.

8. *Sleepsex, or sexsomnia, is a parasomnia that involves* abnormal sexual behaviors and experiences during NREM stages 3 and 4 slow-wave sleep; these include masturbation, sleep sex-talking, groping or fondling one's bed partner's genitals, or sexual intercourse.
9. *Sleepwalking, or somnambulism, is characterized by* an episode of walking or performing other actions, which may include elaborate and complicated behavior, and can range from benign to aggressive behavior; episodes typically occur during NREM stages 3 and 4 slow-wave sleep (15 percent of children have had one sleepwalking episode and 4 percent of adults are sleepwalkers).
10. *Sleep-related eating disorder (SRED) involves* episodes of frequent sleepwalking to the kitchen and compulsive eating during stages 3 and 4 NREM slow-wave sleep, with no memory of the episodes upon awakening in the morning (SRED affects 1 percent of Americans and females are twice as likely as males to sleep-eat).
11. *REM sleep behavior disorder (RBD) involves* a failure of the brain mechanisms that normally suppress voluntary actions during REM sleep; thus, the person verbally and physically responds to the unfolding dream story, which he remembers in vivid detail upon awakening (RBD typically occurs in males over 60 years of age; once it emerges, it gets progressively worse).

Concept Check 4

1. insomnia (or chronic insomnia)
2. dyssomnias
3. narcolepsy; cataplexy
4. sleep-related eating disorder (SRED)
5. sleep (night) terrors; 3; 4
6. parasomnias
7. hypocretins (orexins)

Matching Exercise 4

1. insomnia
2. obstructive sleep apnea (OSA)
3. REM sleep behavior disorder (RBD)
4. sleepsex (sexsomnia)
5. cataplexy
6. narcolepsy
7. sleep disorders
8. dyssomnias
9. continuous positive aiway pressure (CPAP)

True/False Test 4

1. T	4. F	7. T
2. T	5. T	8. T
3. T	6. F	

Hypnosis

1. *Hypnosis is a* cooperative social interaction in which the hypnotized person responds to the hypnotist's suggestions with changes in perception, memory, thoughts, and behavior.
2. *Hypnosis is characterized by* highly focused attention, increased responsiveness to suggestions, vivid images and fantasies, and a willingness to accept distortions of logic or reality. *During hypnosis, the person* temporarily suspends a sense of initiative and voluntarily accepts and follows the hypnotist's instructions.
3. *The best candidates for hypnosis are* individuals who approach the experience with positive, receptive attitudes and expect it to work and people who easily become absorbed in fantasy and imaginary experience—for example, they become absorbed in reading fiction, watching movies, or listening to music (about 15 percent of adults are highly susceptible to hypnosis, about 10 percent are difficult or impossible to hypnotize; children are more responsive to hypnosis than are adults).
4. *The effects of hypnosis include* sensory and perceptual changes (temporary blindness, deafness, or loss of sensation in some body part), hallucinations, and such behaviors as carrying out posthypnotic suggestions, posthypnotic amnesia, hypermnesia, and possibly creating false memories or pseudomemories.
5. *Hilgard's neodissociation theory of hypnosis suggests that* hypnotic effects are due to the splitting of consciousness into two simultaneous streams of memory activity, only one of which the participant is consciously aware of during hypnosis (the dissociated stream is called the hidden observer).
6. *The limits of hypnosis are that* you cannot be hypnotized against your will, you cannot become physically stronger than you are, you cannot exhibit talents that you don't already possess, and you cannot be made to perform

behaviors that are contrary to your morals and values. *Applications include* helping motivated people quit smoking (when combined with cognitive-behavioral therapy or other supportive treatments) and helping children and adolescents to stop thumb-sucking, nail-biting, and compulsive hair-pulling.

Meditation

1. *Meditation refers to* any one of a number of sustained concentration techniques that induce an altered state of focused attention and heightened awareness. *Common to all forms of meditation is the goal of* controlling or training attention.
2. *The two general categories of meditation are* focused attention techniques and open monitoring techniques. *They differ in that* the focused attention techniques involve focusing awareness on a visual image, your breathing, a word, or a phrase (such as a mantra), and open monitoring techniques involve a present-centered awareness of the passing moment (the here and now), without mental judgment (nonreflective awareness). *Mindfulness is a meditation technique that is* a form of open monitoring meditation; it has become increasingly popular in psychological research and clinical practice. Meditators report a state of heightened awareness and sensitivity to thoughts, internal sensations, and external stimuli. *Transcendental meditation is* a focused attention technique that involves mentally repeating a mantra given to the practitioner by a teacher, that was widely used in early research. TM practitioners experienced a state of lowered physical arousal.
3. *The effects of meditation include* relieving stress, improving cardiovascular fitness, a lowered state of physiological arousal, including a decrease in heart rate, lowered blood pressure, and changes in brain waves associated with relaxation. *Contemporary research on meditation has shown that meditation can* improve concentration, perceptual discrimination, and attention; it can increase working memory, improve emotional control and well-being, and reduce stress and minimize its physical effects.

Concept Check 5

1. highly susceptible
2. posthypnotic amnesia
3. focused attention
4. posthypnotic suggestion
5. pseudomemory
6. hypermnesia
7. brain state; role playing
8. gray-matter density; hippocampus, cerebellum, and other areas associated with memory, emotion, and awareness.

Matching Exercise 5

1. neodissociation theory of hypnosis
2. transcendental meditation (TM)
3. hypnosis
4. dissociation
5. posthypnotic suggestion
6. hypermnesia
7. hidden observer
8. mantra
9. neuroplasticity

True/False Test 5

1. T
2. T
3. T
4. T
5. T
6. T
7. T
8. T

Psychoactive Drugs

1. *Psychoactive drugs are* chemical substances that alter arousal, consciousness, perception, sensation, mood, and behavior. *They include* depressants, opiates, stimulants, and psychedelic drugs.
2. *Addiction is a broad term that refers to* a condition in which a person feels psychologically and physically compelled to take a specific drug. *Addiction-related conditions include* physical dependence, drug tolerance, withdrawal symptoms, and the drug rebound effect.
3. *The effects of a drug may be influenced* not only by biological factors (depending on race, age, gender, and weight) but also by psychological and environmental factors, including personality characteristics, mood, expectations, experience with the drug, and the setting in which the drug is taken.
4. *Drug abuse refers to* recurrent drug use that leads to disruptions in academic, social, or occupational functioning, or in legal or psychological problems. *In the United States the most widely abused substance is* alcohol.
5. *Depressants have several effects:* they inhibit central nervous system activity; produce drowsiness, sedation, or sleep; relieve anxiety; and

lower inhibitions. *Examples of depressants are* alcohol, barbiturates, inhalants, and tranquilizers.

6. *Alcohol depresses* the brain centers responsible for judgment and self-control and lessens inhibitions. *Blood alcohol levels are affected by such factors as* body weight, gender, food consumption, and the rate of alcohol consumption.
7. *Inhalants are* chemical substances that are inhaled to produce an alteration in consciousness. *They include* paint solvents, spray paint, gasoline, and aerosol sprays.
8. *Barbiturates are depressant drugs that* reduce anxiety and promote sleep by depressing activity in the brain centers that control arousal, wakefulness, and alertness. They also depress the brain's respiratory centers. *Common barbiturates are* the prescription sedatives Seconal and Nembutal and the illegal drug methaqualone (quaalude).
9. *Tranquilizers are depressants that* relieve anxiety. Although chemically different from barbiturates, they produce similar, but less powerful, effects, *and include* Xanax, Valium, Librium, and Ativan.
10. *The opiates are a group of addictive drugs that* relieve pain and produce feelings of euphoria. *Examples of opiates are* opium, morphine, codeine, heroin, methadone, oxycodone, and the prescription painkillers OxyContin, Vicodin, Percodan, Demerol, and Fentanyl. *Opiates produce their powerful effects by* mimicking the brain's own natural painkillers, endorphins.
11. *Stimulant drugs* increase brain activity, arouse behavior, and increase mental alertness. *Examples include* caffeine, nicotine, amphetamines, cocaine, and methamphetamine (caffeine is the most widely used psychoactive drug in the world).
12. *The psychedelic drugs create* profound perceptual distortions, alter mood, and affect thinking. *Examples of psychedelic drugs include* mescaline, psilocybin, LSD, and marijuana. *LSD and psilocybin mimic* the neurotransmitter serotonin (which is involved in regulating moods and sensations), stimulating serotonin receptor sites in the somatosensory cortex.
13. *Marijuana's active ingredient, THC, produces* a sense of well-being, mild euphoria, and a dreamy state of relaxation. *THC has been shown to be useful in* the treatment of pain, epilepsy, hypertension, nausea, glaucoma, arthritis, and asthma.
14. *Designer "club" drugs are* synthetic drugs used at dance clubs, parties, and "raves." *Examples (and their effects) are* MDMA (ecstasy), which acts as a stimulant and produces mild psychedelic effects and feelings of euphoria, friendliness, and increased well-being, and the dissociative anesthetics PCP (angel dust) and ketamine (Special K), which produce feelings of detachment from reality, depersonalization, and dissociation.

Concept Check 6

1. psychoactive; physically
2. drug tolerance
3. judgment; self-control
4. will not
5. tranquilizer
6. cocaine
7. MDMA; ecstasy
8. opiates; narcotics
9. dopamine response; dopamine receptors

Graphic Organizer 2

1. alcohol; depressant
2. tranquilizer; depressant
3. marijuana; psychedelic
4. LSD; psychedelic
5. caffeine; stimulant
6. morphine; opiate
7. nicotine; stimulant

Matching Exercise 6

1. THC
2. depressants
3. nicotine
4. drug abuse
5. psychoactive drug
6. stimulant-induced psychosis
7. mescaline
8. drug tolerance
9. hashish
10. withdrawal symptoms
11. cocaine
12. amphetamines
13. delirium tremens (DTs)
14. adenosine
15. codeine

16. MDMA (ecstasy)
17. anandamide
18. inhalants
19. stimulus control therapy

True/False Test 6

1. T	6. T	11. F	16. T
2. F	7. T	12. T	17. T
3. T	8. T	13. F	18. T
4. T	9. T	14. F	19. T
5. T	10. T	15. T	

Something to Think About

1. Generally speaking, humans are very adaptable; in fact, most people can easily adapt to shift work. If shifts are scheduled to take into account our natural tendencies and use knowledge about sleep–wake cycles, circadian rhythms, and the role of the SCN, they need not produce the usual jet lag symptoms.

   Begin your report with a discussion of how to rotate a person's shifts. Because we tend to drift to longer days (the 24.2-hour day rather than the 24-hour day), as we often do on weekends, it would seem best to rotate shifts forward: first shift, 8 A.M. to 4 P.M., second shift 4 P.M. to 12 midnight, and then midnight to 8 A.M. for the third shift.

   The length of the shift rotation is the next issue to address. Every shift change is going to take some time to get used to and will be accompanied by some jet-lag symptoms, so the less someone has to change the better. It would probably be best to have people do the same shift for at least a month before changing to the next shift.

   Shift workers should be given as much information as possible about circadian rhythms, sleep–wake cycles, and the role of the SCN in the production of melatonin. People finishing a night shift, for example, could be told the value of blackout curtains to avoid having their biological clock reset by bright light. Or, having bright lights, especially in the early part of the shift, can help people adjust to the night shift. For more specific suggestions, see the section Enhancing Well-Being with Psychology (Stimulus Control Therapy for Insomnia).

2. This dream sounds like a real nightmare. The first thing to tell your friend is that dreams cannot predict the future. She is not likely to fail the exam because of her dream. Her dream reflects the fact that she is concerned and worried about the course. The best way to do well on the exam, and to deal with exam anxiety, is to study the material completely. The text presents three theories of dreams. Freud's view is that the manifest content is relatively unimportant; he would suggest looking for disguised symbolic meaning that reflects the latent content. The activation–synthesis theory suggests that if someone is worried and anxious, these concerns are likely to show up in a dream if these well-worn neural pathways are activated. In other words, the brain produces dream images that are synthesized into a meaningful story, using memories about daily events, past experiences, concerns, and worries. In a similar vein the neurocognitive model of dreaming proposes that dreams reflect our interests, personality, and individual worries. But rather than suggesting that dreams are produced by random fragments of neural activity generated by the brainstem, this theory proposes that there is a continuity of waking and dreaming cognition in which dreaming is like thinking under conditions of reduced sensory input and lack of voluntary control.

   The person's interpretation of the dream may tell us more about the dreamer than anything else. If that is the case, it would be fairly safe to assume that this dreamer is experiencing some perceived difficulty with the course (or some aspect of it) and/or the course material itself.

Progress Test 1

1. c	6. c	11. c
2. c	7. d	12. d
3. d	8. b	13. a
4. b	9. c	14. b
5. d	10. a	15. b

Progress Test 2

1. a	6. c	11. b
2. b	7. c	12. a
3. a	8. d	13. a
4. d	9. b	14. d
5. a	10. c	15. c

Progress Test 3

1. a	6. c	11. b
2. d	7. a	12. c
3. c	8. b	13. a
4. c	9. a	14. c
5. a	10. a	15. d

CHAPTER 5

Learning

PREVIEW

Reading the section below first will give you a general sense of the chapter's contents and an initial introduction to some of the major concepts and terms. This will prime you for what you are about to read and help you to develop a "cognitive map" that will guide your study of the material in this chapter. Likewise, reading the **preview questions** at the beginning of each major section will improve your ability to understand, learn, and retain the information.

CHAPTER 5... AT A GLANCE

Chapter 5 answers the question "What is learning?" Conditioning focuses on how we form associations between environmental events and behavioral responses. Classical conditioning (discovered by Ivan Pavlov) involves repeatedly pairing a neutral stimulus with a stimulus that naturally elicits a response until the neutral stimulus elicits the same response. Behaviorism (founded by John B. Watson) is concerned with the scientific study of observable behaviors, especially as they pertain to learning. Classical conditioning is used to explain conditioned emotional reactions and conditioned drug effects, which seem to be involved in some placebo responses. Contemporary psychology has modified the basics of classical conditioning to account for cognitive functioning and evolutionary factors.

Operant conditioning (developed by B. F. Skinner) demonstrates how voluntary, active behaviors are acquired through reinforcement, punishment, and shaping. Once acquired, behaviors are maintained through different schedules of reinforcement. Behaviors that are partially reinforced are more resistant to extinction than are behaviors that are continuously reinforced. Behavior modification is the application of principles of operant conditioning to help people develop more adaptive behaviors. Operant conditioning principles have also been modified by contemporary views about the importance of cognitive and evolutionary factors.

Observational learning (studied by Albert Bandura) shows how new behaviors can be acquired through watching the actions of others. It involves the processes of attention, memory, motor skills, and motivation and has been applied in education, vocational and job training, psychotherapy, counseling, and entertainment–education programs to promote healthy behaviors and social change.

Enhancing Well-Being with Psychology suggests ways that learning principles can be used to improve your self-control.

Introduction: What Is Learning?

Preview Questions

Consider the following questions as you study this section of the chapter.

- How is learning defined?
- What is conditioning?
- What are three basic types of learning?

*Read the section "Introduction: What Is Learning?" and **write** your answers to the following:*

1. Learning refers to ______________________________

____

2. Conditioning is the ______________________________

____

3. Three basic types of learning are

____

____

Classical Conditioning: Associating Stimuli

Preview Questions

Consider the following questions as you study this section of the chapter.

- Who discovered classical conditioning, and how did he investigate it?
- What is the basic process of classical conditioning?
- What factors can affect the strength of a classically conditioned response?
- What five conditioning phenomena did Pavlov discover?

*Read the section "Classical Conditioning: Associating Stimuli" and **write** your answers to the following:*

1. The person who discovered classical conditioning was ______________________________
He investigated the phenomenon by ______________

____

____

____

2. Classical conditioning is the process of (describe the elements involved in the process)

____

____

____

____

3. Two factors that can affect the strength of a classically conditioned response are ______________

____

____

4. The five conditioning phenomena that Pavlov discovered were ______________________________

____

____

____

____

____

From Pavlov to Watson: The Founding of Behaviorism

Preview Questions

Consider the following questions as you study this section of the chapter.

- Who founded behaviorism, and what were its basic assumptions?
- What three innate emotions did Watson identify, and how can classical conditioning be used to create and explain conditioned emotional responses?
- What were the classical conditioning components in the Little Albert study?
- How does classical conditioning influence drug responses, and how are these effects involved in placebo responses?

*Read the section "From Pavlov to Watson: The Founding of Behaviorism" and **write** your answers to the following:*

1. Behaviorism was founded by ______________________________
and was defined as ______________________________

____

____

____

2. The fundamental assumptions of behaviorism as formulated by Watson are ______________

____

____

____

3. Watson identified three innate emotions, which are ______________________________
each of which could be ______________________________

____

With regard to these emotions, Watson showed that classical conditioning could be used to ______________________________

4. Classical conditioning can be used to create a conditioned emotional response (CR) to a previously neutral stimulus by ______________________________

5. The classical conditioning components in the Little Albert study were as follows:
   CS: ______________
   UCS: ______________
   UCR: ______________
   CR: ______________

6. Some people acquire classically conditioned responses to drugs such as caffeine, an active ingredient in coffee. In this example, the CS is ______________; the UCS is ______________; the UCR is ______________; and the CR is ______________.

7. A placebo response is ______________________________.

Contemporary Views of Classical Conditioning

Preview Questions

Consider the following questions as you study this section of the chapter.

- How does the cognitive explanation of learning differ from the behavioral explanation?
- What kinds of cognitive processes are involved in classical conditioning, and how have they been demonstrated experimentally?
- How does the evolutionary perspective account for the conditioning process?
- How do taste aversions challenge the basic principles of classical conditioning, and how can they be explained?
- What is biological preparedness?

Read the section "Contemporary Views of Classical Conditioning" and ***write*** *your answers to the following:*

1. According to the cognitive perspective, learning ______________________________

   The traditional behavioral perspective holds that ______________________________

2. In his research with rats, Robert Rescorla demonstrated that ______________________________

3. According to the evolutionary perspective, ______________________________

   This is because ______________________________

4. Taste aversion is a ______________________________

   Taste aversions violate three basic principles of classical conditioning: ______________________________

5. John Garcia demonstrated that taste aversions could be produced under controlled laboratory conditions by ______________________________

   He found that ______________________________

6. Biological preparedness refers to ______________________________

After you have carefully studied the preceding sections, complete the following exercises.

Concept Check 1

Read the following and write the correct term in the space provided.

1. Dr. Munchausen believes that the general principles of learning apply to virtually all species and all learning situations, whereas his colleague Dr. Milstein believes that an animal's natural behavioral patterns and unique characteristics can influence what it is capable of learning. Dr. Munchausen supports the traditional ____________________ perspective, and Dr. Milstein's views are consistent with a(n) ______________________ perspective.
2. Dr. Wells decided to classically condition some rats. He used a tone (CS) followed by a shock (UCS) for group 1; for group 2, he used a taste (CS) followed by a shock. It is very ______________ (likely/unlikely) that the rats in group 1 will be classically conditioned; it is very ______________ (likely/unlikely) that the rats in group 2 will be classically conditioned.
3. It appears that Dr. Wells in the above example is investigating how ______________________ affects learning through classical conditioning.
4. Dr. Manly believes that classical conditioning depends on the information the CS provides about the UCS and that for learning to occur, the CS must be a reliable signal that predicts the presentation of the UCS. Dr. Manly's views are most consistent with the ___________________________ perspective.
5. About five hours after extinguishing the classically conditioned response (CR) in an experimental animal, Dr. Taylor presented the conditioned stimulus (CS) and obtained a CR. Dr. Taylor has demonstrated ______________________________ .
6. Fido drools whenever he hears the sound of the electric can opener but does not drool when he hears the sound of the blender, which makes a similar noise. It appears that Fido has learned to ________________________ between the two sounds.
7. Ahmood, who has recently started drinking a lot of hot chocolate, notices that he now feels a positive emotional reaction at just the sight and smell of hot chocolate. In classical conditioning terms, Ahmood's response to these cues is called a ___________________________ .
8. Ahmood also observes that he has a similar emotional response to the smell of other beverages such as herbal tea and coffee. In this situation, he is experiencing a phenomenon called ___________________________ .
9. During basic training, Tremaine felt that the drill sergeant was very unfair in the way he demeaned and threatened him and some of the other new recruits. Tremaine was constantly angry and fearful during this period; today, although it's years later, just the mention of the sergeant's name is enough to elicit a strong negative emotional reaction. In this example of classical conditioning, the demeaning and threatening behavior was the ______________ , Tremaine's response of fear and anger was the ______________ , and the present negative emotional reaction to the sergeant's name is the ______________ .
10. In a research study, patients with high blood pressure regularly received a drug that reduced their hypertension. The drug was always given in the same location. When a similar-looking fake pill was given in the same place, the patients' blood pressure was reduced, much as it had been with the real drug. This example illustrates a ___________________________ .
11. Investigators attempting to replicate Watson's Little Albert study were unable to produce a conditioned response to wooden blocks, wooden ducks, or curtains. Recent research has also shown that both humans and monkeys acquire conditioned fear responses to pictures of snakes and spiders more rapidly than they do to neutral stimuli, such as flowers or mushrooms. These findings support the idea, proposed by psychologist ______________ , that we are ______________ to develop phobias for objects or situations that were of natural importance to the survival of the species.

Graphic Organizer 1

In his classic experiment, Pavlov repeatedly presented a neutral stimulus, such as a tone, just before putting food in the dog's mouth, which automatically elicited salivation. After several repetitions the tone alone triggered the salivation. Label the following graph using the correct terms (UCS, UCR, CS, CR):

Before Conditioning

Food in the mouth is the ____ and the salivation is the ____.	The neutral stimulus is the ___. It elicits no salivation before conditioning.

During Conditioning

The neutral stimulus is the ___.	+	Food in the mouth is the ____.	→	The salivation is the ____.

After Conditioning

The tone alone is the ___.	→	The salivation is now the ___.

Review of Terms, Concepts, and Names 1

Use the terms in this list to complete the Matching Exercise, then to help you answer the True/False items correctly.

learning
conditioning
Ivan Pavlov
reflex
stimulus
classical conditioning
elicit
unconditioned stimulus (UCS)
unconditioned response (UCR)
conditioned stimulus (CS)
conditioned response (CR)
neutral stimulus
stimulus generalization
stimulus discrimination
higher order conditioning (second-order conditioning)
extinction (in classical conditioning)
spontaneous recovery
John B. Watson
behaviorism
placebo response (placebo effect)
cognitive perspective
Robert A. Rescorla
theory of evolution by natural selection
taste aversion
John Garcia
biological preparedness

Matching Exercise

Match the appropriate term/name with its definition or description.

1. ________________ The gradual weakening and apparent disappearance of conditioned behavior; in classical conditioning, it occurs when the conditioned stimulus is repeatedly presented without the unconditioned stimulus.
2. ________________ The process of learning associations between environmental events and behavioral responses.
3. ________________ A process that produces a relatively enduring change in behavior or knowledge as a result of experience.
4. ________________ Classically conditioned dislike for and avoidance of a particular food that develops when an organism becomes ill after eating the food.
5. ________________ School of psychology and theoretical viewpoint that emphasizes the scientific study of observable behaviors, especially as they pertain to the process of learning.

6. ________________ American psychologist who founded behaviorism in the early 1900s.
7. ________________ Natural stimulus that reflexively elicits a response without the need for prior learning.
8. ________________ Russian physiologist who first described the basic learning process of associating stimuli that is now called classical conditioning.
9. ________________ Unlearned, reflexive response that is elicited by an unconditioned stimulus.
10. ________________ In learning theory, the idea that an organism is innately predisposed to form associations between certain stimuli and responses.
11. ________________ A largely involuntary, automatic response to an external stimulus.
12. ________________ An individual's psychological and physiological response to what is actually a fake treatment or drug.
13. ________________ Stimulus that, before conditioning, does not naturally elicit the response to be conditioned.

True/False Test

Indicate whether each statement is true or false by placing T or F in the blank space next to each item.

1. ____ Classical conditioning is the basic learning process that involves repeatedly pairing a neutral stimulus with a response-producing stimulus until the neutral stimulus elicits the same response.
2. ____ Elicit means to draw out or bring forth; a stimulus causes an existing behavior to occur.
3. ____ The psychologist who experimentally demonstrated the involvement of cognitive processes in classical conditioning is John Garcia.
4. ____ The occurrence of a learned response not only to the original stimulus but also to other, similar stimuli is called stimulus discrimination.
5. ____ The conditioned stimulus is a formerly neutral stimulus that acquires the capacity to elicit a reflexive response.
6. ____ The reappearance of a previously extinguished conditioned response after a period of time without exposure to the conditioned stimulus is called spontaneous recovery.
7. ____ Stimulus generalization occurs when a learned response is made to a specific stimulus but not to other, similar stimuli.
8. ____ Robert A. Rescorla is the American psychologist who experimentally demonstrated the learning of taste aversions in animals.
9. ____ The conditioned response is the learned, reflexive response to a conditioned stimulus.
10. ____ The cognitive perspective holds that mental processes as well as external events are important components in the learning of new behaviors.
11. ____ Anything perceptible to the senses is a stimulus.
12. ____ The procedure in which a conditioned stimulus from one learning trial functions as the unconditioned stimulus in a new conditioning trial and the second conditioned stimulus comes to elicit the conditioned response, even though it has never been directly paired with the unconditioned stimulus is called higher order conditioning.
13. ____ According to Darwin's theory of evolution by natural selection both physical characteristics and the natural behavior patterns of any species have been shaped by evolution to maximize adaptation to the environment.

Check your answers and review any areas of weakness before going on to the next section.

Operant Conditioning: Associating Behaviors and Consequences (Part 1)

Preview Questions

Consider the following questions as you study the first three parts of this section of the chapter (through Discriminative Stimuli).

- What was Thorndike's contribution to learning theory?
- What were B. F. Skinner's key assumptions, and what is the fundamental premise of operant conditioning?
- How are positive and negative reinforcement similar, and how are they different?
- What are primary and conditioned (secondary) reinforcers?
- What is punishment, and what factors influence its effectiveness?
- What negative effects are associated with the use of punishment?
- What are discriminative stimuli, and what important role do they play in operant conditioning?

Read the section "Operant Conditioning: Associating Behaviors and Consequences" (through Discriminative Stimuli) and ***write*** *your answers to the following:*

1. Edward L. Thorndike was the first person to ______

   He concluded that ______

2. B. F. Skinner believed that ______

3. Operant conditioning is ______

   It explains ______

4. The basic premise of operant conditioning is ______

5. Reinforcement refers to ______

6. Positive reinforcement involves ______

   Negative reinforcement involves ______

   Negative and positive reinforcement are similar in that ______

   They differ in that ______

7. A primary reinforcer is ______

   and a conditioned reinforcer (secondary reinforcer) is ______

8. Punishment is a ______

   It may involve ______

   It differs from negative reinforcement in that ______

9. The factors that influence the effectiveness of punishment are ______

   The drawbacks of punishment are that ______

10. Discriminative stimuli are ______

    According to Skinner, they are important because ______

After you have carefully studied the preceding section, complete the following exercises.

Concept Check 2

Read the following and write the correct term in the space provided.

1. Ashley holds the view that responses followed by a satisfying state of affairs are strengthened and are more likely to occur again in the same situation and that responses followed by an unpleasant or annoying state of affairs are less likely to recur. This view is most consistent with a fundamental principle of learning called the ________________________.
2. April burned her fingers when she picked up a hot saucepan with her bare hands. She now always dons her oven mitts before touching any hot pan or pot. The aversive stimulus of getting burned reduced her tendency to pick up pots with her bare hands and is therefore an example of ________________________; her increased tendency to use oven mitts because doing so reduces the possibility of getting burned is an example of ________________________.
3. Whenever young Simon wants something, such as a new toy or candy, he cries and screams until his parents give him what he wants. Simon's whining behavior is ______________ reinforced by his parents' giving him what he wants, and the parents' behavior is ______________ reinforced because it stops Simon's annoying crying and screaming.
4. While researching a term paper for his history of psychology class, Rupert discovered the name of the first psychologist to investigate how voluntary behaviors are influenced by their consequences. That psychologist was ______________.
5. The following are examples of negative reinforcement. Decide which illustrate *escape* and which illustrate *avoidance*.
   (a) You go to the dentist on a regular basis; as a result, you don't experience problems such as toothaches. This an example of ______________.
   (b) Your partner is complaining about your messy habits, so you put on your running gear and go for a five-mile jog. This is an example of ______________.
   (c) You study hard all semester because you don't want to end up with a low grade-point average. This is an example of ______________.
   (d) You turn the air conditioner on when the temperature in your room gets too hot and uncomfortable. This is an example of ______________.
6. For each of the following, decide whether the example illustrates negative reinforcement (NR), punishment by application (P/A), or punishment by removal (P/R).
   (a) _____ Marco always wears his seatbelt when he drives his car because he doesn't want to be thrown against the windshield if his car is hit from behind.
   (b) _____ Darryl has tried some new aftershave lotion. "It smells like diesel oil!" complains his girlfriend. Darryl never uses that aftershave lotion again.
   (c) _____ Maria does not misbehave at the dinner table because she knows that misbehavior will result in her forfeiting dessert.
   (d) _____ Greta's cigarette lighter ignites the hair spray she has just put on her hair and burns her bangs and eyebrows. Greta no longer smokes when she is doing her hair.
   (e) _____ Jim no longer picks up hitchhikers after the last one robbed him at gun point.
   (f) _____ Before pouring milk on her cereal, Carmelita smells the carton to make sure the milk has not gone sour.
   (g) _____ Astrid brushes her teeth after every meal because she wants to cut down on the number of visits she needs to make to the dentist.
7. A ringing telephone is a ________________________ for picking up the receiver.

Graphic Organizer 2

The following is a very useful way to organize the procedures used in operant conditioning. The arrow (↑ or ↓) indicates whether the behavior increases or decreases. Fill in the blanks in cells 1, 2, 3, and 4.

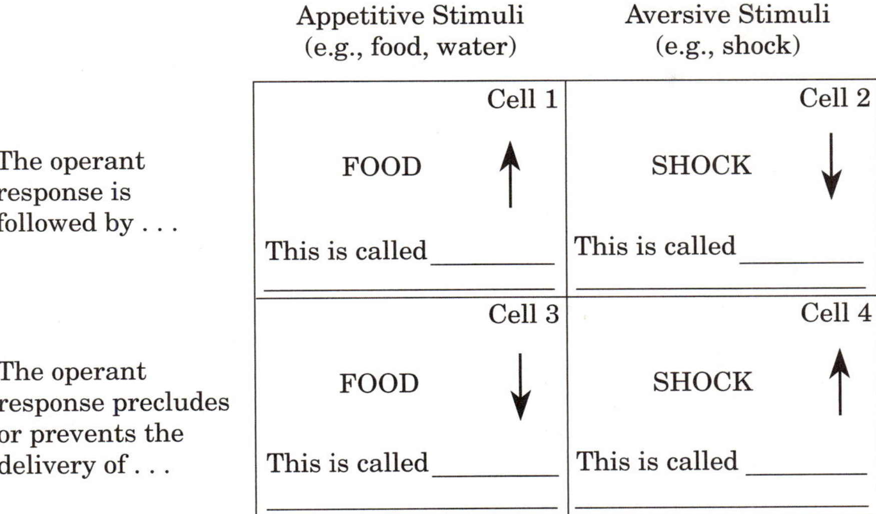

Review of Terms, Concepts, and Names 2

Use the terms in this list to complete the Matching Exercise, then to help you answer the True/False items correctly.

Edward L. Thorndike
law of effect
B. F. Skinner
operant
operant conditioning
reinforcement
reinforcing stimulus (reinforcer)
positive reinforcement
negative reinforcement
aversive stimuli
escape behavior
avoidance behavior
primary reinforcer
conditioned reinforcer (secondary reinforcer)
punishment
punishment by application (positive punishment)
punishment by removal (negative punishment)
discriminative stimulus

Matching Exercise

Match the appropriate term/name with its definition or description.

1. ________________ American psychologist who developed the operant conditioning model of learning.
2. ________________ Situation in which a response results in the removal of, avoidance of, or escape from a punishing stimulus, increasing the likelihood of the response being repeated in similar situations.
3. ________________ American psychologist who was the first to study animal behavior systematically and document how active behaviors are influenced by their consequences.
4. ________________ Presentation of a stimulus or event following a behavior that acts to decrease the likelihood of the behavior being repeated.
5. ________________ Stimulus or event that has acquired reinforcing value by being associated with a primary reinforcer.
6. ________________ Occurrence of a stimulus or event following a response that increases the likelihood of the response being repeated.
7. ________________ Skinner's term for an actively emitted behavior that operates on the environment to produce consequences.
8. ________________ A specific stimulus in the presence of which a particular response is more likely to be reinforced and in the absence of which a particular response is not reinforced.
9. ________________ In negative reinforcement, behavior that removes an aversive stimulus that is already present.

True/False Test

Indicate whether each statement is true or false by placing T or F in the blank space next to each item.

1. ____ A primary reinforcer is a stimulus or event that is naturally or inherently reinforcing for a given species, such as food, water, and other biological necessities.

2. ____ Punishment by application refers to a situation in which an operant is followed by the removal or subtraction of a reinforcing stimulus.
3. ____ Positive reinforcement refers to a situation in which a response is followed by the addition of a reinforcing stimulus, increasing the likelihood of the response being repeated in similar situations.
4. ____ Punishment by removal refers to a situation in which an operant is followed by the presentation or addition of an unpleasant or aversive event or stimulus.
5. ____ The law of effect states that responses followed by a satisfying effect become strengthened and are more likely to recur in a particular situation, whereas responses followed by a dissatisfying effect are weakened and less likely to recur in a particular situation.
6. ____ Operant conditioning is the basic learning process that involves changing the probability that a response will be repeated by manipulating the consequences of that response.
7. ____ Aversive stimuli involve physical or psychological discomfort that an organism seeks to escape or avoid.
8. ____ In negative reinforcement, behavior that precludes the delivery of an aversive stimulus is called avoidance behavior.
9. ____ A reinforcing stimulus (reinforcer) is the stimulus or event that is sought in a particular situation and is typically something desirable, satisfying, or pleasant.

Check your answers and review any areas of weakness before going on to the next section.

Operant Conditioning: Associating Behaviors and Consequences (Part 2)

Preview Questions

Consider the following questions as you study the last parts of this section of the chapter (through Applications of Operant Conditioning).

- What is shaping, and how does it work?
- How does partial reinforcement affect behavior?
- What is extinction in operant conditioning?
- What are the four basic schedules of reinforcement?
- What is behavior modification, and how has it been used to change human behavior?

Read the section "Operant Conditioning: Associating Behaviors and Consequences" (through Applications of Operant Conditioning) and ***write*** *your answers to the following:*

1. Shaping involves ____________________

   ____

   ____

   ____

   ____

   It works by ____________________

   ____

   ____

   ____

   ____

2. Partial reinforcement is more effective than continuous reinforcement because it ____________________

   ____

   ____

3. In operant conditioning, extinction refers to

   ____

   ____

4. The four basic schedules of reinforcement (and their patterns of responding) are ____________________

   ____

   ____

   ____

5. Behavior modification is ____________________

   ____

   ____

   ____

   ____

   It has been used in ____________________

   ____

   ____

   ____

   ____

After you have carefully studied the preceding section, complete the following exercises.

Concept Check 3

Read the following and write the correct term in the space provided.

1. Your instructor, Dr. Jones, gives surprise quizzes throughout the semester. Your studying will be reinforced on a ______________________ schedule.
2. Your instructor, Dr. Wong, schedules a quiz every two weeks throughout the semester. Your studying will be reinforced on a ______________________ schedule.
3. A rat gets a food pellet for every 20 responses. It is reinforced on a ______________________ schedule.
4. If parents use praise and encouragement to gradually teach a child how to dress herself, they are using a ______________ procedure.
5. Maria sells magazine subscriptions over the phone. She makes many calls but only gets paid for making a sale. She is reinforced on a ______________________ schedule.
6. Juanita and her colleagues assemble TV sets in a factory. They get paid a bonus for every 10 TVs they produce. They are being rewarded on a ______________ schedule.

Graphic Organizer 3

Fill in each cell with the name of the appropriate partial reinforcement schedule.

	Based on the number of responses made	Based on the elapsed time
Fixed	Cell 1 ______________	Cell 2 ______________
Variable	Cell 3 ______________	Cell 4 ______________

Review of Terms, Concepts, and Names 3

Use the terms in this list to complete the Matching Exercise, then to help you answer the True/False items correctly.

operant chamber (Skinner box)
shaping
continuous reinforcement
partial reinforcement
extinction (in operant conditioning)
partial reinforcement effect
schedule of reinforcement
fixed-ratio (FR) schedule
variable-ratio (VR) schedule
fixed-interval (FI) schedule
variable-interval (VI) schedule
behavior modification

Matching Exercise

Match the appropriate term/name with its definition or description:

1. ______________ The application of learning principles to help people develop more effective or adaptive behaviors.
2. ______________ Schedule of reinforcement in which every occurrence of a particular response is followed by a reinforcer.
3. ______________ The name of the experimental apparatus invented by B. F. Skinner to study the relationship between environmental events and active behaviors.
4. ______________ Reinforcement schedule in which a reinforcer is delivered after a fixed number of responses has occurred.
5. ______________ Operant conditioning procedure in which successively closer approximations of a goal behavior are selectively reinforced until the goal behavior is displayed.
6. ______________ Reinforcement schedule in which a reinforcer is delivered for the first response that occurs after a preset time interval has elapsed.

True/False Test

Indicate whether each statement is true or false by placing T or F in the blank space next to each item.

1. ____ Partial reinforcement refers to a situation in which the occurrence of a particular response is only sometimes followed by a reinforcer.
2. ____ A variable-ratio schedule is one in which a reinforcer is delivered for the first response that occurs after an average time interval has elapsed, but the time varies unpredictably from trial to trial.

3. ____ A variable-interval schedule is one in which a reinforcer is delivered after an average number of responses, but the number varies unpredictably from trial to trial.
4. ____ The partial reinforcement effect refers to the fact that behaviors conditioned using continuous reinforcement are more resistant to extinction than behaviors that are only sometimes followed by a reinforcer.
5. ____ The gradual weakening and disappearance of conditioned behavior in operant conditioning is called extinction; it occurs when an emitted behavior is no longer followed by a reinforcer.
6. ____ Schedule of reinforcement refers to the delivery of a reinforcer according to a preset pattern based on the number of responses or the time interval between responses.

Check your answers and review any areas of weakness before going on to the next section.

Contemporary Views of Operant Conditioning

Preview Questions

Consider the following questions as you study this section of the chapter.

- What factors do contemporary learning researchers suggest are involved in operant conditioning?
- How did Tolman's research demonstrate the involvement of cognitive processes in learning?
- What are cognitive maps, latent learning, and learned helplessness?
- How is operant conditioning influenced by an animal's natural behavior patterns?
- How does the phenomenon of instinctive drift challenge the traditional behavioral view of operant conditioning?

Read the section "Contemporary Views of Operant Conditioning" and ***write*** *your answers to the following:*

1. Contemporary learning researchers confirm the basic principles of operant conditioning but also acknowledge ______________________________
____

2. Unlike Skinner and Thorndike, Tolman believed that ______________________________
____

3. A cognitive map is ______________________________
____

Latent learning is ______________________________
____
____

4. Learned helplessness demonstrates the role of cognitive factors in learning in that __________
____
____
____

5. Operant conditioning may also be influenced by
____
____
____

6. The phenomenon of instinctive drift challenged the traditional behavioral view by______________
____
____
____

Observational Learning: Imitating the Actions of Others

Preview Questions

Consider the following questions as you study this section of the chapter.

- What is observational learning, and who is most strongly identified with work in this area?
- What four mental processes are involved in observational learning?
- What has research demonstrated about observational learning in nonhuman animals?
- How has observational learning been applied?

Read the section "Observational Learning: Imitating the Actions of Others" and ***write*** *your answers to the following:*

1. Observational learning is ______________________________
____

The person most strongly identified with work in this area is ______________________________

2. The four cognitive processes that interact to determine if imitation will occur are ____

3. Research with nonhuman animals has shown ____

4. Observational learning has been applied in a variety of settings, including ____

After you have carefully studied the preceding sections, complete the following exercises.

Concept Check 4

Read the following and write the correct term in the space provided.

1. Maria watches a popular cooking show on public TV on Saturday afternoons and often cooks one of the dishes she sees the chef prepare. Maria's culinary ability is the result of ______________ learning.
2. Dr. Bristow believes that reinforcement is not necessary for learning to occur but that the *expectation* of reinforcement can affect the performance of what has been learned. Dr. Bristow is emphasizing the importance of ____________ factors in learning.
3. A rat has been allowed to explore a maze for a number of trials without ever getting a reinforcer. When food is made available in the goal box, it is very ______________ (likely/unlikely) that the rat will find the food very quickly with few errors.
4. An animal trainer has a hard time operantly conditioning a pig to pick up a large wooden penny and put it in a big "piggy bank" because the pig seems to prefer to push the coin with its snout, even though it is not reinforced for this behavior. This phenomenon is called ______________________.
5. Mr. and Mrs. Delbrook both stopped smoking when they started a family because they wanted to model healthy behavior patterns for their children. They are apparently aware of the importance of ______________________ learning in children's development.
6. Dr. Rossi studies neural activity in brain areas that respond when actions are performed and when actions are simply perceived but not actually performed. According to Focus on Neuroscience, Dr. Rossi is most likely investigating ______________________.

Review of Terms, Concepts, and Names 4

Use the terms in this list to complete the Matching Exercise, then to help you answer the True/False items correctly.

Edward C. Tolman
cognitive map
latent learning
learned helplessness
Martin Seligman
instinctive drift
observational learning
Albert Bandura
mirror neurons

Matching Exercise

Match the appropriate term/name with its definition or description:

1. ______________ Learning that occurs through observing the actions of others.
2. ______________ Tolman's term for learning that occurs in the absence of reinforcement but is not behaviorally demonstrated until a reinforcer becomes available.
3. ______________ American psychologist whose experimental findings strongly suggested that cognitive factors play a role in animal learning.
4. ______________ Tolman's term for the mental representation of the layout of a familiar environment.
5. ______________ American psychologist who experimentally investigated observational learning, emphasizing the role of cognitive factors.

6. ________________ The tendency of an animal to revert to instinctive behaviors, which can interfere with the performance of an operantly conditioned response.
7. ________________ A phenomenon in which exposure to inescapable and uncontrollable aversive events produces passive behavior.
8. ________________ Neurons that fire both when an action is performed and when the action is simply perceived.
9. ________________ American psychologist who investigated the phenomenon of learned helplessness in dogs and later founded positive psychology.

Check your answers and review any areas of weakness before going on to the next section.

Something to Think About

1. Imagine that you are a behavioral therapist whose client has a real fear of going to the dentist. Despite the need for some important dental work, he can't bring himself to make an appointment. Using what you know about classical conditioning, explain how his irrational fear, or phobia, might have come about, and describe how to extinguish that fear.
2. Mrs. Denton can't understand why scolding her 10-year-old son for misbehaving only seems to make the problem worse. Using what you know about operant conditioning techniques, what advice would you give Mrs. Denton about how she might (a) reduce the disruptive behavior and (b) encourage more appropriate behavior?
3. Imagine that your family has decided to adopt a puppy. Using what you know about operant conditioning techniques, what advice would you give them about how they should train the dog to be obedient and do some neat pet tricks?

Check your answers and review any areas of weakness before doing the progress tests.

Progress Test 1

Review the complete chapter (including all boxed inserts), review all your study notes, and then test yourself on the following progress test. Check your answers. If you make a mistake, review your notes, check the appropriate section in the study guide, and, if necessary, go back and read the relevant part of the chapter in your textbook.

1. Dr. Ramos is a behavioral psychologist. He conducts basic research using animals in carefully controlled laboratory studies. The goal of his research is most probably to
   (a) train animals to do tricks.
   (b) collect and sell saliva from dogs and other animals.
   (c) identify the general principles of learning that apply across a wide range of species, including humans.
   (d) observe changes in animal behavior that result from biological maturation.

2. Dr. Frolov classically conditioned a dog to flex its hind leg at the sound of a bell by pairing the ringing of a bell with a mild electric shock to the leg. In this example, the ringing bell is the
   (a) unconditioned stimulus (UCS).
   (b) conditioned response (CR).
   (c) unconditioned response (UCR).
   (d) conditioned stimulus (CS).

3. Some forms of chemotherapy make patients sick. A patient who has eaten a pizza just before the therapy (and is then sick) later feels ill when she sees or smells pizza. In this example of taste aversion learning, the conditioned response is the
   (a) pizza.
   (b) chemotherapy.
   (c) illness induced by the therapy.
   (d) nausea felt at the sight or smell of pizza.

4. After establishing a classically conditioned response (CR) to a tone, the experimenter presents a new conditioned stimulus, a red light, followed repeatedly by the original conditioned stimulus, the tone. As a result the conditioned response (CR) is elicited by the red light alone, even though it had never been paired with the original UCS. The experimenter has demonstrated
   (a) spontaneous recovery.
   (b) higher order conditioning (second-order conditioning).
   (c) a placebo response (placebo effect).
   (d) punishment by application.

5. Dr. Redner believes that classical conditioning depends on the information the conditioned stimulus provides about the unconditioned stimulus. Also, for learning to occur, the conditioned stimulus must be a reliable signal that predicts the presentation of the unconditioned stimulus. Dr. Redner's views are most consistent with those of the learning theorist
   (a) Robert A. Rescorla.
   (b) Edward L. Thorndike.
   (c) Ivan Pavlov.
   (d) B. F. Skinner.

6. Ricardo always gets nervous and apprehensive when his professor uses the word *exam,* but he seldom feels the same anxiety when the word *quiz* is mentioned. Assuming that classical conditioning is involved in these two different reactions at the mention of tests, it appears that Ricardo is exhibiting
   (a) stimulus discrimination.
   (b) spontaneous recovery.
   (c) latent learning.
   (d) stimulus generalization.

7. About five hours after she had successfully extinguished a dog's classically conditioned response of salivating to the sound of a bell, Dr. Sheckenov discovered that the dog once again salivated in the presence of the bell. This example illustrates the phenomenon of
   (a) stimulus generalization.
   (b) spontaneous recovery.
   (c) latent learning.
   (d) instinctive drift.

8. Dr. Radersched conducts research on the phenomenon of biological preparedness. She is most likely to discover that
   (a) organisms are innately predisposed to form associations between some stimuli and responses and not to others.
   (b) the general principles of learning apply to virtually all animal species and all learning situations.
   (c) classical conditioning occurs because two stimuli are associated closely in time and that frequency and contiguity are the only variables that affect learning.
   (d) mental processes, but not innate predispositions, are the crucial variables involved in classical conditioning.

9. Sasha studied very hard last semester and earned good grades in all her courses. This semester, Sasha is once again studying hard. It appears that good grades are ______________ for Sasha's studying behavior.
   (a) conditioned stimuli
   (b) discriminative stimuli
   (c) positively reinforcing
   (d) negatively reinforcing

10. Rachel studies a lot to avoid getting bad grades because for her a bad grade is devastating. Rachel's studying behavior is maintained by
   (a) negative reinforcement.
   (b) primary reinforcement.
   (c) positive reinforcement.
   (d) punishment by removal.

11. Helmut is employed by his university as a telephone solicitor for a fundraising drive. He is paid a set amount of money for every 10 calls he makes whether or not he gets any donations. Helmut's telephoning is reinforced on a ______________ schedule of reinforcement.
   (a) fixed-interval (FI)
   (b) variable-interval (VI)
   (c) fixed-ratio (FR)
   (d) variable-ratio (VR)

12. Thelma turns her cell phone off at various times, such as when she is in class, studying in the library, watching her favorite TV show, or in a restaurant. Her parents don't know the best time to call her, so they try at random times. It appears that phoning Thelma is reinforced on a ______________ schedule.
   (a) fixed-interval (FI)
   (b) variable-interval (VI)
   (c) fixed-ratio (FR)
   (d) variable-ratio (VR)

13. After they had been watching Spider-Man cartoons all morning, 5-year-old Jim and 6-year-old John, using Mom's knitting yarn, climbed on top of the garage roof, tied the yarn around their waist, and got ready to leap. Their startled mother stopped them in time and realized the powerful influence of ______________ on behavior.
   (a) observational learning
   (b) classical conditioning
   (c) operant conditioning
   (d) stimulus generalization

14. In an operant conditioning experiment, a rat first learns to press a lever to get a food pellet. Then the researcher withholds all reinforcement, and the rat eventually stops pressing the lever. This example illustrates
    (a) the effect of negative reinforcement on behavior.
    (b) punishment by application.
    (c) extinction in operant conditioning.
    (d) instinctive drift in operant conditioning.

15. According to Critical Thinking (Is Human Freedom Just an Illusion?), B. F. Skinner maintained that
    (a) human freedom is an illusion.
    (b) all behavior arises from causes that are within the individual, and environmental factors have little or no influence.
    (c) cognitive factors are the crucial elements in all learning and that how we think about things determines our actions.
    (d) people should be held responsible for their actions because they have individual freedom (free will) and are self-determined.

Progress Test 2

After you have checked your understanding of the material in Progress Test 1 and have done a complete chapter review with special focus on any areas of weakness, you are now ready to assess your knowledge on Progress Test 2. Check your answers. If you make a mistake, review your notes, the relevant section of the study guide, and, if necessary, the appropriate part of your textbook.

1. Which of the following best illustrates classical conditioning?
    (a) Henry feels ill when he smells peanut butter because it once made him sick.
    (b) Annalee studies hard because she wants to get good grades.
    (c) Virginia goes shopping for new clothes fairly frequently because it makes her feel good.
    (d) Lyndle drives at the posted speed limit after getting a number of speeding tickets.

2. Erv developed a fear of attics after he was accidentally locked in his own attic by his wife. Erv's present fear of the attic is a(n)
    (a) example of instinctive drift.
    (b) conditioned emotional response.
    (c) form of observational learning.
    (d) operantly conditioned response.

3. Little Richard receives attention from his teacher in the form of a scolding every time he misbehaves. As a result, Richard misbehaves quite frequently. In this instance, it would appear that the teacher's scolding is a
    (a) form of punishment by application.
    (b) positively reinforcing stimulus.
    (c) form of punishment by removal.
    (d) negatively reinforcing stimulus.

4. A group of 4-year-old children watch a video showing an adult hitting, kicking, and punching a large Bobo doll. These children are later asked to imitate the model and are promised a reward for every behavior they can imitate. It is very probable that the children will
    (a) not imitate the adult model.
    (b) verbally describe what they saw but will refuse to imitate the adult model.
    (c) quite readily imitate the adult's aggressive behavior.
    (d) become very upset as a result of watching the aggressive behavior.

5. Lauren spent the first week of the semester exploring the campus. Later, she had no trouble locating the library, although she had never been there before. According to Tolman, Lauren
    (a) has developed biological preparedness.
    (b) has formed a cognitive map.
    (c) is suffering from instinctive drift.
    (d) has developed a sense of direction.

6. Gerry puts up her umbrella soon after it starts to rain in order to prevent her clothes from getting any wetter. This example illustrates ______________ behavior and ______________ reinforcement.
    (a) avoidance; positive
    (b) escape; negative
    (c) avoidance; negative
    (d) escape; positive

7. When Juanita gets paid, she uses her money to buy food to feed her family. For Juanita, money is a ______________ reinforcer and food is a ______________ reinforcer.
    (a) conditioned; primary
    (b) primary; negative
    (c) conditioned; secondary
    (d) primary; positive

8. At dinner one night, Amanda started using her spoon as a drumstick. Her mother told her that she would get no dessert if she persisted with her bad behavior. Amanda soon stopped the banging. This example most clearly illustrates
   (a) negative reinforcement.
   (b) punishment by removal.
   (c) positive reinforcement.
   (d) punishment by application.

9. When Cal first attended college, he either barely passed or failed almost all his courses despite his efforts to do well. After working at a low-paying job for a couple of years, Cal has returned to school. Overwhelmed with the demands of exams, term papers, library assignments, and the need to concentrate on his studies, Cal finds himself procrastinating and engaging in other self-defeating passive behaviors. This example illustrates the phenomenon of
   (a) observational learning.
   (b) spontaneous recovery.
   (c) learned helplessness.
   (d) biological preparedness.

10. Zeno uses operant conditioning principles to train animals to perform a variety of behaviors. However, he discovered that some behaviors were difficult, if not impossible, to condition because an animal's natural behavior patterns, even though never followed by a reinforcer, tended to interfere with the response he was trying to condition. This phenomenon is called
    (a) instinctive drift.
    (b) stimulus discrimination.
    (c) spontaneous recovery.
    (d) extinction.

11. Ashlynn loves playing the slot machines even though she wins money only once in a while. Ashlynn's gambling behavior is likely to be very resistant to extinction because of
    (a) the partial reinforcement effect.
    (b) spontaneous recovery.
    (c) the law of effect.
    (d) instinctive drift.

12. Dalbir believes that although reinforcement is not necessary for learning to occur, it does affect the performance of what has been learned. Dalbir's view is most consistent with the phenomenon of
    (a) instinctive drift.
    (b) biological preparedness.
    (c) shaping.
    (d) latent learning.

13. According to Critical Thinking (Does Exposure to Media Violence Cause Aggressive Behavior?), which of the following is (are) true?
    (a) A review of five decades of research concluded that exposure to violent media has little or no effect on aggression and violence.
    (b) Because the vast majority of studies on media violence and aggressive behavior are correlational, it is appropriate to conclude that watching violent media is a direct cause of aggression and violence.
    (c) Many psychologists are cautious in their conclusions about the effects of media violence, noting that violent behavior is a complex phenomenon and is unlikely to have a single cause.
    (d) According to the U.S. Surgeon General, substance abuse, poverty, and poor parenting are much more important risk factors for violence than exposure to violent media.

14. According to Enhancing Well-Being with Psychology, we often choose a short-term reinforcer over a more valuable long-term goal. Your text suggests that we do this because
    (a) the relative value of a reinforcer can shift over time.
    (b) as the availability of a reinforcer gets closer, the subjective value of the reinforcer increases.
    (c) when we make our decision, we'll choose whichever reinforcer has the greatest subjective value.
    (d) of all of these reasons.

15. According to Martin Seligman (In Focus: Evolution, Biological Preparedness, and Conditioned Fears), people are more likely to develop phobias of spiders, snakes, or heights—than to doorknobs, knives, washing machines, and ladders—because
    (a) of instinctive drift.
    (b) we are biologically prepared to do so.
    (c) doorknobs, knives, and ladders are inherently safer than spiders, snakes, and heights.
    (d) of latent learning.

Progress Test 3

After you have checked your understanding of the material in Progress Tests 1 and 2, and have done a complete chapter review with special focus on any areas of weakness, you are ready to further assess your knowledge with Progress Test 3. Check your answers. If you make a mistake, review your notes, the appropriate parts of the study guide, and, if necessary, the relevant sections of your textbook.

1. Arturo, a psychology major, was asked by his roommate to explain conditioning. He is most likely to point out that
   (a) conditioning is the process of learning associations between environmental events and behavioral responses.
   (b) there are two basic types of conditioning: operant conditioning and classical conditioning.
   (c) contemporary learning theorists also consider the process of observational learning.
   (d) all of these statements are true.

2. A monkey watches another monkey pick up and eat a peanut. Researchers discovered that the neuronal activity in this monkey's brain was the same as that of the monkey actually performing these actions. These researchers are investigating
   (a) cognitive maps and latent learning.
   (b) biological preparedness.
   (c) mirror neurons and the mirror neuron system.
   (d) higher order conditioning.

3. Justine got sick after eating a chicken burger. Now she not only has an intense dislike of chicken burgers but also feels nauseated at the sight of beef burgers, fish burgers, soybean burgers, or anything that even resembles a burger. It would appear that Justine has experienced the phenomenon Pavlov called
   (a) stimulus discrimination.
   (b) spontaneous recovery.
   (c) extinction.
   (d) stimulus generalization.

4. By presenting the CS over and over again without the UCS, Dr. Laslove discovered that the research participant's conditioned response (CR) gradually weakened and seemed to disappear. This decrease in responding is called
   (a) latent learning.
   (b) spontaneous recovery.
   (c) extinction.
   (d) stimulus discrimination.

5. Rolando got very sick after eating a big plate of oysters. Ever since that experience, Rolando feels ill whenever he sees or smells oysters. It appears that Rolando
   (a) has developed a taste aversion.
   (b) has experienced latent learning.
   (c) is suffering from instinctive drift.
   (d) is experiencing spontaneous recovery.

6. Dr. Alonzo takes a cognitive perspective in his research on learning. He is most likely to suggest that classical conditioning
   (a) involves learning the relationships between events and that the CS must be a reliable predictor of the UCS.
   (b) results from simply pairing the CS with the UCS for a number of trials.
   (c) is constrained by biological predispositions.
   (d) follows general principles of learning that apply to virtually all animal species and all learning situations.

7. Positive reinforcement is to ______________ as negative reinforcement is to ______________ .
   (a) decreased responding; increased responding
   (b) decreased responding; decreased responding
   (c) increased responding; decreased responding
   (d) increased responding; increased responding

8. When Billy used his knife to release a piece of toast that was jammed in the toaster he got a severe electric shock. Billy has never used his knife to get toast out of the toaster again. It appears that Billy's behavior has been changed by
   (a) punishment by application.
   (b) negative reinforcement.
   (c) punishment by removal.
   (d) extinction.

9. Whenever the doorbell rings, Rex runs to the door and barks and growls. For Rex the ringing doorbell is a(n) ______________ for his growling and barking behavior.
   (a) discriminative stimulus
   (b) unconditioned stimulus
   (c) reinforcing stimulus
   (d) primary reinforcer

10. Tammy wants to train her dog to "shake hands" with people, so she reinforces closer and closer approximations to the desired behavior. First she rewards the dog for sitting on command, then for slightly raising its front paw, then for fully raising the paw, then for moving the paw up and down until it is grasped, and so on. Tammy has used a process called
    (a) latent learning.
    (b) extinction.
    (c) partial reinforcement.
    (d) shaping.

11. Arnie always drives at the posted speed limit and obeys all the rules of the road because he can't afford to pay fines for driving offenses. Arnie's good driving habits are maintained by
    (a) positive reinforcement.
    (b) partial reinforcement.
    (c) secondary reinforcement.
    (d) negative reinforcement.

12. Harry works on an assembly line as part of a team of eight workers. They get paid a bonus for every 100 products they assemble. Harry and his co-workers are being rewarded on a ________________ schedule of reinforcement.
    (a) fixed-interval (FI)
    (b) variable-interval (VI)
    (c) fixed-ratio (FR)
    (d) variable-ratio (VR)

13. Wilma's psychology instructor schedules tests every two weeks throughout the semester, but her sociology instructor has surprise quizzes throughout the semester. The psychology instructor is using a ________________ schedule, and the sociology instructor is using a ________________ schedule.
    (a) fixed-interval (FI); variable-interval (VI)
    (b) variable-interval (VI); variable-ratio (VR)
    (c) fixed-ratio (FR); variable-ratio (VR)
    (d) variable-ratio (VR); fixed-interval (FI)

14. According to In Focus (Watson, Classical Conditioning, and Advertising), John B. Watson
    (a) believed that punishment was the best and most desirable way to change behavior.
    (b) vehemently opposed Skinner's idea that freedom is just an illusion.
    (c) was a pioneer in the application of classical conditioning principles to advertising.
    (d) discovered the phenomenon of latent learning.

15. According to In Focus (Changing the Behavior of Others), which of the following is true?
    (a) Punishment by removal is the most effective way to change undesirable behavior.
    (b) Punishment by application works better than any other behavioral strategy in changing undesirable behavior.
    (c) There are no effective strategies for reducing undesirable behaviors.
    (d) Several strategies other than punishment can be used to change undesirable behavior.

Answers

Introduction: What Is Learning?

1. *Learning refers to* a process that produces a relatively enduring change in behavior or knowledge as a result of past experience.
2. *Conditioning is the* process of learning associations between environmental events and behavioral responses.
3. *Three basic types of learning are* classical conditioning, operant conditioning, and observational learning.

Classical Conditioning: Associating Stimuli

1. *The person who discovered classical conditioning was* Ivan Pavlov. *He investigated the phenomenon by* studying how dogs learned to salivate to the presence of a stimulus (that would not normally elicit salivation) after it had been associated with food in the mouth, which reflexively elicits salivation.
2. *Classical conditioning is the process of (describe the elements involved in the process)* learning an association between two stimuli: the neutral stimulus (later to be the conditioned stimulus, or CS) that does not normally produce the response of interest and the unlearned natural stimulus (the unconditioned stimulus, or UCS), which automatically elicits the response (the unconditioned response, or UCR). Following this association, the CS will elicit a new learned response (the conditioned response, or CR).
3. *Two factors that can affect the strength of a classically conditioned response are* the frequency of the presentations of the two stimuli (the more frequently the CS and UCS are paired, the stronger the conditioning) and the timing of the stimulus presentations (the CS needs to be presented about a half-second before the UCS).
4. *The five conditioning phenomena that Pavlov discovered were* stimulus generalization, the ability to respond to new stimuli that were

similar to the CS; stimulus discrimination, the ability to distinguish between two stimuli, responding only to one stimulus but not to other, similar stimuli; higher order conditioning, in which a conditioned stimulus from one learning trial functions as the unconditioned stimulus in a new conditioning trial; extinction, the gradual weakening and apparent disappearance of the CR after repeated exposure to the CS alone (without the UCS); and spontaneous recovery, the reappearance of a previously extinguished conditioned response following a rest period when the CS is again presented.

From Pavlov to Watson: The Founding of Behaviorism

1. *Behaviorism was founded by* John B. Watson *and was defined as* the scientific study of observable behaviors, especially as they pertain to the process of learning.
2. *The fundamental assumptions of behaviorism as formulated by Watson are* that psychology is an objective experimental branch of natural science, the goals of which are the prediction and control of behavior; introspection and the study of consciousness are not part of scientific psychology; overt, observable, measurable behavior is the subject matter; and virtually all human behavior is a result of conditioning and learning.
3. *Watson identified three innate emotions, which are* fear, rage, and love, *each of which could be* reflexively triggered by a small number of specific stimuli. *With regard to these emotions, Watson showed that classical conditioning could be used to* deliberately establish a conditioned emotional response (i.e., a new learned response).
4. *Classical conditioning can be used to create a conditioned emotional response (CR) to a previously neutral stimulus by* pairing the neutral stimulus (now called the CS) with a stimulus (the UCS) that naturally and reflexively elicits the emotion in question (the UCR).
5. *The classical conditioning components in the Little Albert study were as follows: CS:* the sight of the white rat (initially neutral); *UCS:* the loud noise caused by clanging a steel bar; *UCR:* the fear experienced to the loud noise; *CR:* the fear experienced to the white rat after conditioning had taken place.
6. *Some people acquire classically conditioned responses to drugs such as caffeine, an active ingredient in coffee. In this example, the CS is* the sight, smell, and/or taste of coffee*; the UCS is* the caffeine; *the UCR is* increased arousal and alertness elicited by the caffeine; *and the CR is* the increased arousal and alertness in response to the CS (sight, smell, and/or taste of coffee) following a number of pairings of the CS and UCS.
7. *A placebo response is* an individual's psychological and physiological response to what is actually a fake treatment or drug; it is also called the placebo effect.

Contemporary Views of Classical Conditioning

1. *According to the cognitive perspective, learning* involves mental processes as well as external events. *The traditional behavioral perspective holds that* conditioning results from a simple association of the CS and the UCS.
2. *In his research with rats, Robert Rescorla demonstrated that* classical conditioning involves cognitive processes such as learning the relationship between events, assessing the reliability of signals, and actively processing information about the predictive value of stimuli in the environment.
3. *According to the evolutionary perspective,* biological predispositions, shaped by evolution, affect the conditioning process. *This is because* animals have developed unique forms of behavior to adapt to their natural environment, and so some responses and behavioral patterns are more readily conditioned than others.
4. *Taste aversion is a* classically conditioned dislike for and avoidance of a particular food that develops when an organism becomes ill after eating the food. *Taste aversions violate three basic principles of classical conditioning:* first, conditioning requires only a single pairing of the CS and UCS, not multiple pairings; second, the time span between the CS and UCS can be several hours, not necessarily a matter of seconds, as Pavlov claimed; and third, the particular CS used is important; some stimuli are more easy to associate than others, contrary to what Pavlov suggested.
5. *John Garcia demonstrated that taste aversions could be produced under controlled laboratory conditions by* pairing saccharin-flavored water (the CS) with a drug (the UCS), which produced illness (the UCR). *He found that* even though the interval between the presentation of the two stimuli was several hours, the rats developed a taste aversion (CR) to the CS and refused to drink the saccharin-flavored water.

6. *Biological preparedness refers to* the idea that organisms are innately predisposed to form associations between certain stimuli and responses.

Concept Check 1

1. behavioral; evolutionary
2. likely; unlikely
3. biological preparedness
4. cognitive
5. spontaneous recovery
6. discriminate
7. conditioned response (CR)
8. stimulus generalization
9. UCS; UCR; CR
10. placebo response (placebo effect)
11. Martin Seligman; biologically prepared

Graphic Organizer 1

Before Conditioning

Food in the mouth is the UCS and the salivation is the UCR.

The neutral stimulus is the CS. It elicits no salivation before conditioning.

During Conditioning

The neutral stimulus is the CS. + Food in the mouth is the UCS. → The salivation is the UCR.

After Conditioning

The tone alone is the CS. → The salivation is now the CR.

Matching Exercise 1

1. extinction
2. conditioning
3. learning
4. taste aversion
5. behaviorism
6. John B. Watson
7. unconditioned stimulus (UCS)
8. Ivan Pavlov
9. unconditioned response (UCR)
10. biological preparedness
11. reflex
12. placebo response (placebo effect)
13. neutral stimulus

True/False Test 1

1. T	5. T	9. T	13. T
2. T	6. T	10. T	
3. F	7. F	11. T	
4. F	8. F	12. T	

Operant Conditioning: Associating Behaviors and Consequences (Part 1)

1. *Edward L. Thorndike was the first person to* systematically study animal learning and how voluntary behaviors are influenced by their consequences. *He concluded that* (according to his law of effect) animals use the process of trial and error, rather than reasoning, to acquire new behaviors and that behaviors followed by satisfying outcomes were "strengthened" (more likely to occur again), and behaviors followed by unpleasant consequences were "weakened" (less likely to occur).
2. *B. F. Skinner believed that* psychology should restrict itself to studying only outwardly observable behavior and environmental events that could be objectively measured and verified; that internal factors such as thoughts, expectations, and perceptions should not be included in an objective, scientific explanation of behavior; and that the most important form of learning was demonstrated by new behaviors that were actively emitted by the organism (operants).

3. *Operant conditioning is* the basic learning process that involves changing the probability that a response will be repeated by manipulating the consequences of that response. *It explains* how we acquire everyday nonreflexive, voluntary behaviors.
4. *The basic premise of operant conditioning is* that behavior is shaped and maintained by its consequences.
5. *Reinforcement refers to* the occurrence of a stimulus or event following a response that increases the likelihood of that response being repeated.
6. *Positive reinforcement involves* following an operant with a reinforcing stimulus, thus increasing the likelihood that the response will be repeated in similar situations. *Negative reinforcement involves* the removal of an aversive, punishing, or unpleasant stimulus from a situation, thereby increasing the likelihood that the behavior that brought about the removal of the stimulus will be repeated in similar situations (can involve escape from, or avoidance of, the stimulus). *Negative and positive reinforcement are similar in that* they both increase the probability of the behavior occurring again. *They differ in that* positive reinforcement involves the addition of a reinforcing stimulus, and negative reinforcement involves the removal of, avoidance of, or escape from an aversive or punishing stimulus.
7. *A primary reinforcer is* one that is naturally reinforcing for a given species, *and a conditioned reinforcer (secondary reinforcer) is* one that has acquired reinforcing value by being associated with a primary reinforcer.
8. *Punishment is a* process in which a behavior is followed by an aversive consequence that decreases the future occurrence of that behavior. *It may involve* punishment by application (of an aversive stimulus) or punishment by removal (of a reinforcing stimulus). *It differs from negative reinforcement in that* it involves the presentation of an aversive stimulus or removal of a reinforcing stimulus following behavior, whereas negative reinforcement involves the removal of an aversive stimulus.
9. *The factors that influence the effectiveness of punishment are* the consistency and immediacy of the delivery of the punishment following the response. *The drawbacks of punishment are that* it doesn't teach the correct response, it may produce undesirable results, and its effects are likely to be temporary.
10. *Discriminative stimuli are* specific stimuli in the presence of which a particular response is more likely to be reinforced, and in the absence of which a particular response is not reinforced. *According to Skinner, they are important because* behavior is determined and controlled by the stimuli that are present in a given situation (discriminative stimuli) and not by personal choice or conscious decisions.

Concept Check 2

1. law of effect
2. punishment by application; negative reinforcement
3. positively; negatively
4. Edward L. Thorndike
5. (a) avoidance
   (b) escape
   (c) avoidance
   (d) escape
6. (a) NR (e) P/A
   (b) P/A (f) NR
   (c) P/R (g) NR
   (d) P/A
7. discriminative stimulus

Graphic Organizer 2

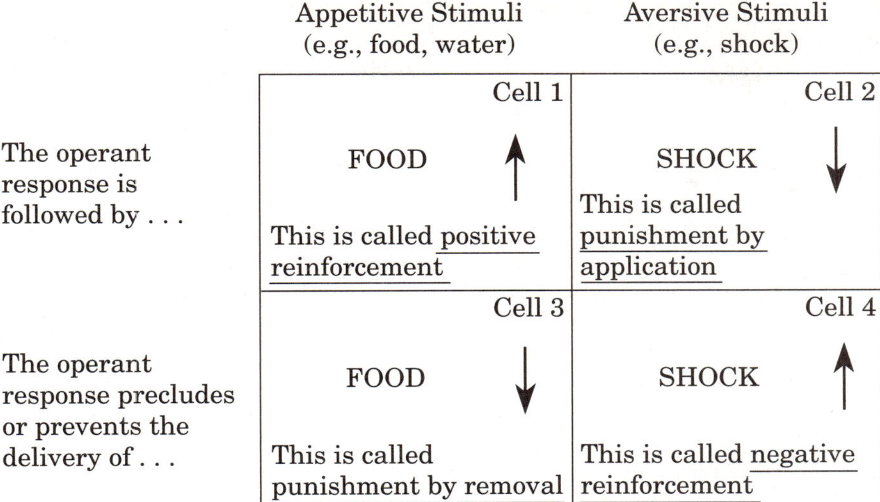

Matching Exercise 2

1. B. F. Skinner
2. negative reinforcement
3. Edward L. Thorndike
4. punishment
5. conditioned (secondary) reinforcer
6. reinforcement
7. operant
8. discriminative stimulus
9. escape behavior

True/False Test 2

1. T	4. F	7. T
2. F	5. T	8. T
3. T	6. T	9. T

Operant Conditioning: Associating Behaviors and Consequences (Part 2)

1. *Shaping involves* reinforcing successively closer approximations of a behavior until the correct behavior is displayed. *It works by* allowing the organism to gradually learn the correct response by making reinforcement dependent on getting closer and closer to the target behavior with each attempt.
2. *Partial reinforcement is more effective than continuous reinforcement because it* makes the target behavior more resistant to extinction than behavior that has been conditioned using continuous reinforcement (called the partial reinforcement effect).
3. *In operant conditioning, extinction refers to* the gradual weakening and disappearance of conditioned behavior; it occurs when an emitted behavior is no longer followed by a reinforcer.
4. *The four basic schedules of reinforcement (and their patterns of responding) are* fixed-ratio (FR), in which a fixed number of responses are required for reinforcement; variable-ratio (VR), in which an average number of responses, which varies from trial to trial, are needed for reinforcement; fixed-interval (FI), in which a reinforcer is delivered for the first response after a preset amount of time; and variable-interval (VI), in which a reinforcer is delivered for the first response after an average, and unpredictable, amount of time.
5. *Behavior modification is* the application of learning principles to help people develop more effective or adaptive behaviors. *It has been used in* such diverse situations as reducing public smoking by teenagers, improving student behavior in school cafeterias, reducing problem behaviors in school children, improving social skills and reducing self-destructive behaviors in people with autism and related disorders, increasing productivity in employees, and training animals to help the physically challenged.

Concept Check 3

1. variable-interval (VI)
2. fixed-interval (FI)
3. fixed-ratio (FR)
4. shaping
5. variable-ratio (VR)
6. fixed-ratio (FR)

Graphic Organizer 3

	Based on the number of responses made	Based on the elapsed time
Fixed	Cell 1 Fixed ratio	Cell 2 Fixed interval
Variable	Cell 3 Variable ratio	Cell 4 Variable interval

Matching Exercise 3

1. behavior modification
2. continuous reinforcement
3. operant chamber (Skinner box)
4. fixed-ratio (FR) schedule
5. shaping
6. fixed-interval (FI) schedule

True/False Test 3

1. T	3. F	5. T
2. F	4. F	6. T

Contemporary Views of Operant Conditioning

1. *Contemporary learning researchers confirm the basic principles of operant conditioning but also acknowledge* the importance of both cognitive factors and natural behavior patterns in operant conditioning.
2. *Unlike Skinner and Thorndike, Tolman believed that* cognitive processes played an important role in the learning of complex behavior, and he demonstrated their importance with his research on cognitive maps and latent learning.
3. *A cognitive map is* Tolman's term for the mental representation of the layout of a familiar environment. *Latent learning is* Tolman's term for learning that occurs in the absence of reinforcement but is not demonstrated in overt behavior until a reinforcer becomes available.
4. *Learned helplessness demonstrates the role of cognitive factors in learning in that* this behavior reflects a cognitive expectation that the organism cannot avoid the painful stimulus, no matter what it does to avoid or escape it. Exposure to inescapable and uncontrollable aversive events produces passive behavior.
5. *Operant conditioning may also be influenced by* biological predispositions to perform natural, or instinctive, behaviors that can interfere with the performance of an operantly conditioned response, a tendency called instinctive drift.
6. *The phenomenon of instinctive drift challenged the traditional behavioral view by* demonstrating that reinforcement is not the sole determinant of behavior and that instinctive behavior patterns can interfere with the operant conditioning of arbitrary responses.

Observational Learning: Imitating the Actions of Others

1. *Observational learning is* learning that occurs through observing the action of others. *The person most strongly identified with work in this area is* Albert Bandura.
2. *The four cognitive processes that interact to determine if imitation will occur are* attention (you must pay attention to the model), memory (you must remember the model's behavior), motor skills (you must be able to transform the mental representation into actions that you are capable of reproducing), and motivation (you must have some expectation of the outcome of your imitation of the behavior).
3. *Research with nonhuman animals has shown* that animals as diverse as orangutans, chimps, monkeys, dogs, golden hamsters, starlings, Caledonian crows, ring-tailed lemurs, rats, and guppies are all capable of forms of observational learning.
4. *Observational learning has been applied in a variety of settings, including* education, vocational and job training, psychotherapy, counseling, and medicine. It has also been used effectively in entertainment-education programs to promote healthy behaviors and social change.

Concept Check 4

1. observational
2. cognitive
3. likely
4. instinctive drift
5. observational
6. mirror neurons (or mirror neuron system)

Matching Exercise 4

1. observational learning
2. latent learning
3. Edward C. Tolman

4. cognitive map
5. Albert Bandura
6. instinctive drift
7. learned helplessness
8. mirror neurons
9. Martin Seligman

Something to Think About

1. The first assumption that someone who adheres to the behavioral perspective would make is that the phobia was the result of classical conditioning. In the past, the client had had a very unpleasant experience at a dentist's office. One could speculate that as a child he was taken to the dentist and experienced pain and fear when a hypodermic needle was inserted into his gum or a drill struck a nerve. If this were the case, the dentist (CS) has become associated with the needle or drill (UCS), which elicited pain and fear (UCR). The dentist (CS) now evokes a fear response (CR), which may have generalized to all dentists.

   One way to get rid of the irrational fear would be to use an extinction procedure in which the CS (the dentist) is presented over and over without the UCS until the fear subsides. This might mean that the client will have to find a very understanding dentist who will allow him to make many visits to the office without having any work done. The behavioral perspective predicts that this would eventually result in a reduction of the irrational fear and therefore allow the client to get some much-needed dental work done. It would also be important to point out that following a prolonged absence from the dentist, spontaneous recovery may occur.

2. It is possible that Mrs. Denton's "scolding" may in fact be reinforcing the undesirable behavior. Attention, in almost any form, from an adult can be a powerful positive reinforcer for a child. If this is the case, then withholding reinforcement (scolding) will tend to extinguish the target behavior, but only if it is consistent. Inconsistent or intermittent reinforcement will make the behavior very resistant to extinction.

   In addition, she should encourage desirable behavior. She should pay attention to any instance of good behavior, or any close approximation of the goal behavior, by praising her son or providing some other positive reinforcer. In other words, she should use a shaping procedure initially, then use partial reinforcement to ensure that the desirable behavior becomes resistant to extinction. It is also important that she model the appropriate behavior and avoid punishing the child, especially using punishment by application.

3. Operant conditioning techniques can be used to train animals. Decide on the target behavior(s) and start by using a shaping procedure and continuous positive reinforcement. Pick one of the behaviors you want to train—for example, having the dog sit at the command "sit"—and use a reinforcer such as "good dog!" while patting the dog on the head or rubbing its chest. The command "sit" should be followed with gentle pressure on the dog's rear end to make it sit; the dog should be reinforced immediately. After just a few trials, the dog will sit on command without the application of pressure to its back; the dog should always be immediately reinforced. It is important to let the dog know who is in command at all times without using punishment. After the dog is obeying the commands regularly, then switch to a partial reinforcement schedule, only occasionally reinforcing the dog for obeying. This will ensure greater resistance to extinction. Dogs can be trained to do many tricks in this manner, but remember to work with the animal's natural repertoire of behaviors (biological predispositions). Dogs can learn some behaviors more easily than others.

Progress Test 1

1. c	6. a	11. c
2. d	7. b	12. b
3. d	8. a	13. a
4. b	9. c	14. c
5. a	10. a	15. a

Progress Test 2

1. a	6. b	11. a
2. b	7. a	12. d
3. b	8. b	13. c
4. c	9. c	14. d
5. b	10. a	15. b

Progress Test 3

1. d
2. c
3. d
4. c
5. a
6. a
7. d
8. a
9. a
10. d
11. d
12. c
13. a
14. c
15. d

CHAPTER 6

Memory

PREVIEW

Reading the section below first will give you a general sense of the chapter's contents and an initial introduction to some of the major concepts and terms. This will prime you for what you are about to read and help you to develop a "cognitive map" that will guide your study of the material in this chapter. Likewise, reading the **preview questions** at the beginning of each major section will improve your ability to understand, learn, and retain the information.

CHAPTER 6 . . . AT A GLANCE

Chapter 6 examines memory and the mechanisms involved in remembering and forgetting. The first section begins by introducing the fundamental processes of encoding, storage, and retrieval, followed by a discussion of sensory memory, short-term memory, and long-term memory.

Short-term memory provides temporary storage for information transferred from sensory memory and from long-term memory; its effectiveness can be improved by maintenance rehearsal and chunking. The three components of Baddeley's model of working memory (the active manipulation of information) are explained.

Elaborative rehearsal and the three categories of information stored in long-term memory (procedural, episodic, and semantic) are explained. Explicit and implicit memories are explored, and the ways in which information is organized in long-term memory are discussed.

How retrieval works and the problems associated with retrieval failure are examined. The serial position effect, the encoding specificity principle, and flashbulb memories all contribute to our ability to remember, or not remember, and these topics are explored next.

Retrieval failure (forgetting) and the factors that contribute to forgetting (encoding failure, decay of memory traces, retroactive and proactive interference, suppression and repression) are covered in this section. Following this is a discussion of the constructive nature of memory and how the misinformation effect, source confusion, schemas, scripts, and imagination inflation all contribute to errors, distortions, and false memories.

Finally, the biological basis of memory is explained and the contributions of empirical research and case studies of people with amnesia are presented. The chapter ends with an examination of the role in memory played by several brain structures. Enhancing Well-Being with Psychology (Superpower Memory in Minutes per Day!), presents several effective strategies for improving memory.

Introduction: What Is Memory?

Preview Questions

Consider the following questions as you study this section of the chapter.

- How is *memory* defined?
- What are encoding, storage, and retrieval?
- What is the stage model of memory, and what are the characteristics of the three stages?
- How do the stages interact?

Read the section "What Is Memory?" and ***write*** *your answers to the following:*

1. Memory refers to the mental processes that enable us to acquire, retain, and retreive information.
2. Encoding is the process of transforming information into a form that can be entered and retained by the memory system.

   Storage is the process of retaining info in memory so that it can be used later.

   Retrieval is the process of recovering the stored info so that we are consciously aware of it.
3. The stage model of memory describes memory as being transferred from one memory stage to another. The 3 stages: sensory memory, short-term memory + long-term memory.
4. The three stages interact by ______

Sensory Memory: Fleeting Impressions of the World

Preview Questions

Consider the following questions as you study this section of the chapter.

- How long is information from the environment held in sensory memory?
- How did Sperling's experiment establish the duration of visual sensory memory?
- What is one of the important functions of sensory memory?

Read the section "Sensory Memory: Fleeting Impressions of the World" and ***write*** *your answers to the following:*

1. Information is held in sensory memory for a few seconds at the most.
2. Sperling's classic experiment demonstrated that our visual sensory memory holds a great deal of info very briefly, for about half a second.
3. An important function of sensory memory (iconic and echoic) is to very briefly store sensory impressions so that they overlap slightly with one another.

Short-Term, Working Memory: The Workshop of Consciousness

Preview Questions

Consider the following questions as you study this section of the chapter.

- What is the main function of short-term memory?
- What are the duration and capacity of short-term memory?
- How do we overcome the limitations of short-term memory?
- What is working memory, and what are the three components of Baddeley's model of working memory?

Read the section "Short-Term, Working Memory: The Workshop of Consciousness" and ***write*** *your answers to the following:*

1. Short-term memory is the stage of memory in which info is transferred from sensory memory + info from long-term memory becomes conscious.
2. The duration of short-term memory is about 20 seconds.
3. The capacity of short-term memory is limited.

   However, current research has found there are ways to increase the amount of info you want to remember.

It can be increased by "chunking": the grouping of numbers.

4. Working memory refers to the active conscious manipulation of temporarily stored information.

5. The three components of Baddeley's model of working memory are the phonological loop, visuospatial sketchpad, and the central executive.

Long-Term Memory

Preview Questions

Consider the following questions as you study this section of the chapter.

- How much information can be stored in long-term memory?
- What are three ways to increase the effectiveness of encoding?
- What are the characteristics of procedural, episodic, and semantic memory?
- What is the difference between explicit memory and implicit memory?
- How is information organized in long-term memory, and what is one of the best-known models of organization?

*Read the section "Long-Term Memory" and **write** your answers to the following:*

1. The amount of information that can be held in long-term memory is limitless
2. Three ways to increase the effectiveness of encoding are elaborative rehearsal, self-reference effect, and visual imagery.
3. Procedural memory refers to the long term memory of how to perform different skills, operations, and actions

   Episodic memory refers to specific events or episodes, including the time and place they occured.

   Semantic memory refers to general knowledge that includes facts, names, definitions, concepts, and ideas.

4. Explicit memory is memory with awareness

   Implicit memory is memory without awareness

5. Information is organized in long-term memory by clustering and assoicating.
6. The best-known model of how information is organized in memory is the semantic network model.

   which describes long-term memory as ______

After you have carefully studied the preceding sections, complete the following exercises.

Concept Check 1

Read the following and write the correct term in the space provided.

1. During a math exam, Trevor is desperately trying to think of the correct formula for the area of a triangle. Although he knew the formula when he was studying last week, it just won't come to mind, despite all his efforts. Trevor is experiencing trouble with one of the three fundamental processes of memory, called retrieval.
2. To help learn the number of days in each month, 8-year-old Gloria has been reciting a short rhyme over and over: "Thirty days hath September, April, June, and November; all the rest have thirty-one excepting February alone; and that has twenty-eight days clear; and twenty-nine in each leap year." She is using the fundamental process of encoding to transform the information into a form that can be entered and retained by the memory system.
3. In the above example, Gloria is using a type of rehearsal that is giving some meaning to an otherwise hard-to-remember string of numbers; this is called elaborative rehearsal.

4. After looking up a phone number, Alysha is able to remember it only long enough to press all the correct numbers on the keypad. The phone number is in her ______________ memory and is briefly stored there by the use of ______________ rehearsal.
5. Vito is an excellent chess player and can easily recall the exact positions of most of the chess pieces after a brief glance at the board. He explains his ability by pointing out that he does not try to memorize the locations of all the individual pieces but instead focuses on their relatively few attack patterns. Vito is using ______________ to improve the capacity of his short-term memory.
6. Fifty-five-year-old Mr. Adams puts on roller skates for the first time in over 40 years. Much to his surprise, he has no trouble remembering how to skate. In this instance, Mr. Adams is using one of the three categories of long-term memory, called ______________ memory.
7. When Stephan was consciously reviewing the information he had researched for a term paper, he was using a dimension of long-term memory called ______________ (or declarative memory). Later, when he was typing his paper without conscious awareness of the exact layout of the letters on the keyboard, he was using ______________ (or nondeclarative memory).
8. During an interview about his military accomplishments, General Rooyakkers described specific wartime episodes in which he was directly involved. He went on to reminisce about events in his early life that eventually led him to a career in the army. In the first instance, he was using ______________ memory to recall the time and place of wartime events; in the second case, he was using ______________ memory to recall his personal life history.

Review of Terms, Concepts, and Names 1

Use the terms in this list to complete the Matching Exercise, then to help you answer the True/False items correctly.

memory
encoding
storage
retrieval
stage model of memory
sensory memory
short-term memory
long-term memory
George Sperling
visual sensory memory (iconic memory)
auditory sensory memory (echoic memory)
maintenance rehearsal
chunking
working memory
phonological loop
visuospatial sketchpad
central executive
elaborative rehearsal
self-reference effect
visual imagery
procedural memory
episodic memory
autobiographical memory
semantic memory
explicit memory (declarative memory)
implicit memory (nondeclarative memory)
clustering
association
semantic network model

Matching Exercise

Match the appropriate term/name with its definition or description.

1. ______________ Rehearsal that involves focusing on the meaning of information to help encode and transfer it to long-term memory.
2. ______________ Model that describes units of information in long-term memory as being organized in a complex network of associations.
3. ______________ The process of recovering information stored in memory so that we are consciously aware of it.
4. ______________ Organizing items into related groups during recall from long-term memory.
5. ______________ The use of mental representations, or pictures, especially vivid ones, to enhance encoding.
6. ______________ Active stage of memory in which information is stored for about 20 seconds.
7. ______________ Category of long-term memory that includes memories of particular events.
8. ______________ The process of transforming information into a form that can be entered into and retained by the memory system.

9. ____________ Model that describes memory as consisting of three distinct stages: sensory memory, short-term memory, and long-term memory.
10. ____________ The mental processes that enable us to acquire, retain, and use information over time.
11. ____________ Category of long-term memory that includes memories of different skills, operations, and actions.
12. ____________ American psychologist who identified the duration of visual sensory memory in a series of classic experiments in 1960.
13. ____________ Memory that is closely related to episodic memory and involves memories of events in our lives and our personal life history.
14. ____________ The temporary storage and active, conscious manipulation of information needed for complex cognitive tasks, such as reasoning, learning, and problem solving.
15. ____________ Component of Baddeley's working memory that initiates retrieval and decision processes, integrates information, controls attention, and manages the activities of the other two components.

True/False Test

Indicate whether each statement is true or false by placing T or F in the blank space next to each item.

1. ____ Information or knowledge that can be consciously recollected is called implicit, or nondeclarative, memory.
2. ____ Auditory sensory memory is sometimes referred to as iconic memory because it is a brief memory of an image, or icon.
3. ____ Applying information to yourself to help you remember that information is called the self-reference effect.
4. ____ Semantic memory is the category of long-term memory that includes memories of general knowledge of facts, names, and concepts.
5. ____ When people are presented with the stimulus word *salt,* they frequently respond with the word *pepper,* this suggests that there is some logical *association* between bits of information in long-term memory.
6. ____ Storage is the process of retaining information in memory so that it can be used at a later time.
7. ____ Sensory memory is the stage of memory that registers information from the environment and holds it for a very brief period of time.
8. ____ Maintenance rehearsal involves the mental or verbal repetition of information in order to maintain it beyond the usual 20-second duration of short-term memory.
9. ____ Increasing the amount of information that can be held in short-term memory by grouping related items together as a single unit is called chunking.
10. ____ Visual sensory memory is sometimes referred to as echoic memory, because it is a brief memory that is like an echo.
11. ____ Information or knowledge that affects behavior or task performance but cannot be consciously recollected is called explicit, or declarative, memory.
12. ____ Long-term memory is the stage of memory that represents the storage of information over extended periods of time.
13. ____ The phonological loop is the component of Baddeley's working memory that is specialized for spatial or visual material.
14. ____ The visuospatial sketchpad is the component of Baddeley's working memory that is specialized for verbal material.

Check your answers and review any areas of weakness before going on to the next section.

Retrieval: Getting Information from Long-Term Memory

Preview Questions

Consider the following questions as you study this section of the chapter.

- How is *retrieval* defined, what is a retrieval cue, and what is retrieval cue failure?
- What do tip-of-the-tongue (TOT) experiences tell us about the nature of memory?
- How is retrieval tested, and what is the serial position effect?
- What is the encoding specificity principle, and how is it reflected in context effects and mood congruence?
- What role does distinctiveness play in retrieval, what are flashbulb memories, and how accurate are they?

*Read the section "Retrieval: Getting Information from Long-Term Memory" and **write** your answers to the following:*

1. Retrieval refers to ________________________________
____

   A retrieval cue is ________________________________
____

   Retrieval cue failure refers to ______________________
____

2. The tip-of-the-tongue (TOT) experience is
____
____

   It illustrates the fact that ________________________
____
____
____

3. Retrieval is tested by ____________________________
____
____
____

4. The serial position effect is ______________________
____
____

5. The encoding specificity principle states that
____
____

6. The context effect, an encoding specificity phenomenon, refers to ________________________
____
____

   Mood congruence, a different form of encoding specificity, refers to ________________________
____

7. Distinctiveness plays a role in retrieval because
____
____

8. A flashbulb memory is ____________________________
____

After you have carefully studied the preceding sections, complete the following exercises.

Concept Check 2

Read the following and write the correct term in the space provided.

1. When Cathy feels depressed, she remembers certain sad childhood events that she otherwise never thinks about. Cathy is experiencing the effects of Mood congruence
2. Hendrik vividly remembers exactly what he was doing when he felt the vibrations of the earthquake shake his house. This example illustrates a Flashbulb memory.
3. Although Jessie cannot remember the newer name of the small Central American country that was formerly called British Honduras, she has the distinct feeling that she knows the name. Jessie is experiencing a memory phenomenon called the Tip of the Tongue
4. When Jessie is told that the name of the country starts with the letter B she quickly remembers the name. The letter B acts as a Retrieval cue for the name *Belize*.
5. Professor Patheiger's exams consist of both multiple-choice questions and short essay questions. The multiple-choice questions involve retrieval that requires recognition, whereas the short essay questions measure the ability to recall information from long-term memory.
6. Research participants memorized long lists of words while in a room full of fresh flowers. Later, half the participants were tested in the same room, and half were tested in a room with no flowers. Those tested in the same room recalled significantly more words than those in the different room. This is one form of the encoding specificity principle, called the context effect.
7. When Beata was given a free recall test of a list of 20 words, she recalled words from the beginning and end of the list more easily than those in the middle of the list. The tendency to remember the first items is called the primary effect, and the tendency to remember the final items is called the recency effect.
8. The pattern of responses in the above example is called the serial position effect.

Graphic Organizer 1

Read the definitions and fill in the correct term next to the appropriate number in the puzzle below (items 1–6). When you have finished, the letters in the boxes will spell a significant memory term. Write out the definition of this term (item 7).

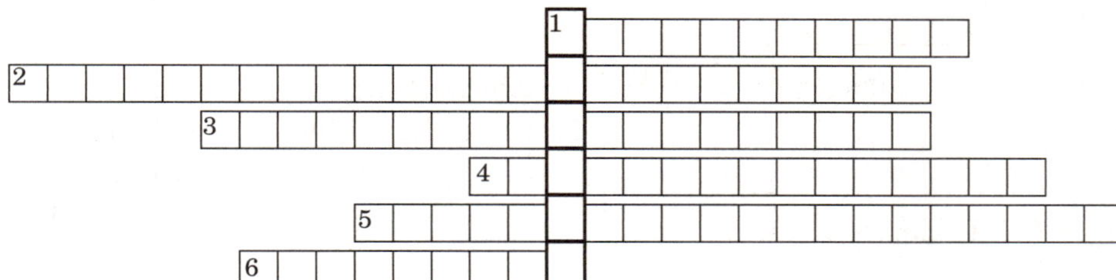

1. A test of long-term memory that involves identifying correct information out of several possible choices.
2. A memory phenomenon that involves the sensation of knowing that specific information is stored in long-term memory but being temporarily unable to retrieve it.
3. The inability to recall long-term memories because of inadequate or missing retrieval cues.
4. The recall of very specific images or details surrounding a vivid, rare, or significant personal event.
5. The tendency to remember items at the beginning and end of a list better than the items in the middle.
6. The process of accessing stored information.
7. Write the definition of the memory term:

____

____

Review of Terms and Concepts 2

Use the terms in this list to complete the Matching Exercise, then to help you answer the True/False items correctly.

retrieval
retrieval cue
retrieval cue failure
tip-of-the-tongue (TOT) experience
recall (free recall)
cued recall
recognition
serial position effect
primacy effect
recency effect
serial recall
encoding specificity principle
context effect
mood congruence
distinctiveness
flashbulb memory

Matching Exercise

Match the appropriate term with its definition or description.

1. ______________ Tendency to recover information more easily when the retrieval occurs in the same setting as the original learning of the information.
2. ______________ The process of accessing stored information.
3. ______________ Recall of very specific images or details surrounding a vivid, rare, or significant personal event.
4. ______________ The tendency to remember items at the beginning and end of a list better than items in the middle.
5. ______________ Test of long-term memory that involves remembering an item of information in response to a retrieval cue.
6. ______________ Clue, prompt, or hint that helps trigger recall of a given piece of information stored in long-term memory.
7. ______________ Encoding specificity phenomenon in which a given mood tends to evoke memories that are consistent with that mood.
8. ______________ Principle that when the conditions of information retrieval are similar to the conditions of information encoding, retrieval is more likely to be successful.

True/False Test

Indicate whether each statement is true or false by placing T or F in the blank space next to each item.

1. ______ The primacy effect refers to the tendency to recall the final items in a list during serial recall.

2. T A test of long-term memory that involves retrieving information without the aid of retrieval cues is called recall, or free recall.
3. T The tip-of-the-tongue (TOT) experience involves the sensation of knowing that specific information is stored in long-term memory, but being temporarily unable to retrieve it.
4. T Serial recall refers to remembering a list of items in their original order.
5. T When the encoded information represents a unique, different, or unusual memory, it is said to be characterized by a high degree of *distinctiveness.*
6. T The inability to recall long-term memories because of inadequate or missing retrieval cues is called retrieval cue failure.
7. F The recency effect refers to the tendency to recall the first items in a list during serial recall.
8. T Recognition refers to a test of long-term memory that involves identifying correct information from several possible choices.

Check your answers and review any areas of weakness before going on to the next section.

Forgetting: When Retrieval Fails

Preview Questions

Consider the following questions as you study this section of the chapter.

- How is *forgetting* defined?
- What did Ebbinghaus contribute to the study of forgetting?
- What are encoding failure, prospective memory, decay theory, and interference theory, and how do they contribute to forgetting?
- What is motivated forgetting (suppression and repression), and why is repression controversial?

*Read the section "Forgetting: When Retrieval Fails" and **write** your answers to the following:*

1. Forgetting is the ______________________________

____

2. The Ebbinghaus forgetting curve reveals two distinctive patterns about forgetting:

(a) ______________________________

____

(b) ______________________________

____

3. Encoding failure refers to ______________________________

____

It may contribute to ______________________________

____

4. Prospective memory is ______________________________

____

Prospective memory failure may be due to

____

____

5. According to decay theory ______________________________

____

____

6. Interference theory is the theory that ______________________________

____

____

The two basic types of interference affect memory in the following ways: ______________________________

____

____

7. Motivated forgetting refers to the idea that

____

____

There are two forms of motivated forgetting:

____

____

8. Repression is a controversial topic because

____

____

Imperfect Memories: Errors, Distortions, and False Memories

Preview Questions

Consider the following questions as you study this section of the chapter.

- Why do errors and distortions in memory occur during the process of retrieval?

- What are the misinformation effect and source confusion, and how can they distort memories?
- What is a false memory?
- What are schemas and scripts, and how can they contribute to memory distortions?
- What techniques can create false memories for events that never happened?
- How does imagination inflation contribute to the formation of false memories?

*Read the section "Imperfect Memories: Errors, Distortions, and False Memories" and **write** your answers to the following:*

1. Errors and distortions occur during the process of retrieval because ______________________________

2. The misinformation effect (one phenomenon that can reduce the accuracy of eyewitness testimony) refers to ______________________________

   It is a problem because ______________________________

3. Source confusion is ______________________________

4. A false memory is ______________________________

5. A schema is ______________________________

   Research has demonstrated that ______________________________

6. A script is ______________________________

7. The lost-in-the-mall technique is ______________________________

   It demonstrates that ______________________________

8. Imagination inflation is ______________________________

After you have carefully studied the preceding sections, complete the following exercises.

Concept Check 3

Read the following and write the correct term in the space provided.

1. When he first moved to his new apartment, Adam could not remember his new phone number; instead, he would give people his old phone number. Adam's inability to remember his new number is due to ______________ interference.
2. At a recent orientation meeting, Juan was introduced to five of the company's directors. Much to his embarrassment, after a short time he could not remember their names. Juan's memory lapse is probably due to ______________ .
3. Later that night, Juan thought about his embarrassment at the meeting and decided it was normal to forget names under such circumstances, so he was just not going to think about it any more. Juan is using a form of motivated forgetting called ______________ .
4. When Mr. Melvin questioned a witness, he deliberately kept referring to the murder weapon as a large pair of scissors instead of garden shears. When the witness was later asked to identify the garden shears as the murder weapon, he appeared slightly confused and said that he believed the weapon was a large pair of scissors. Mr. Melvin had successfully used the ______________ .
5. Giselle planned to return the library book before the due date but forgot to do so. Her inability to remember to do what she had planned is an example of prospective memory failure and was probably caused by ______________ .

6. Jackson has just finished a course in Spanish and is having problems remembering the Italian he learned last semester. Jackson's memory problem is a result of ________________ interference.
7. Cecil parked his car on the fifth floor of the parking garage; with flowers, chocolates, and magazines in hand he made his way to the hospital ward to visit his wife. When he was ready to go home, he could not remember where he had parked his car. This type of forgetting (resulting from divided attention) is called ________________ and is probably due to ________________ failure.
8. Mrs. Gerber's first phone was a rotary dial telephone. Now she uses a state-of-the-art cell phone with all the latest features. Most likely, Mrs. Gerber's ________________ for "telephone" has been changed to integrate recent technological innovations.
9. During one phase of an experiment a participant is encouraged to actively envision shaking hands with Mickey Mouse during a childhood visit to Disneyland. When asked about her visit to Disneyland later in the experiment, she was quite confident that she had met Mickey Mouse and shaken his hand (an event that never actually happened). This example illustrates an effect called ________________ .
10. Ferdie promised to text his girlfriend during the class break. Because he was distracted, he did not remember to do so. This example most clearly illustrates a failure in ________________ memory.

Graphic Organizer 2

Use the following to review forgetting due to interference in the test phase. Write in the type of interference that is responsible for forgetting in the test phase.

Memorizing Phase	Test Phase	Type of Interference
1. Learn A first; later learn B	Test A	
2. Learn A first; later learn B	Test B	

Review of Terms, Concepts, and Names 3

Use the terms in this list to complete the Matching Exercise, then to help you answer the True/False items correctly.

forgetting
Hermann Ebbinghaus
nonsense syllable
forgetting curve
encoding failure
absentmindedness
déjà vu experience
source memory (source monitoring)
prospective memory
decay theory
memory trace
interference theory
retroactive interference
proactive interference
motivated forgetting
suppression
repression
psychoanalysis
Elizabeth Loftus
misinformation effect
source confusion
false memory
schema
script
pseudoevent
lost-in-the-mall technique
imagination inflation

Matching Exercise

Match the appropriate term/name with its definition or description.

1. ________________ Motivated forgetting that occurs consciously; a deliberate attempt to not think about and remember specific information.
2. ________________ The inability to recall information that was previously available.

3. ________________ Theory that forgetting is due to normal metabolic processes that occur in the brain over time.
4. ________________ Motivated forgetting that occurs unconsciously; a memory that is blocked and unavailable to consciousness.
5. ________________ The theory that forgetting is caused by one memory competing with or replacing another.
6. ________________ German psychologist who originated the scientific study of forgetting and plotted the first forgetting curve, which describes the basic pattern of forgetting learned information over time.
7. ________________ Inability to recall specific information because of insufficient encoding of the information for storage in long-term memory.
8. ________________ Organized cluster of information about a particular topic.
9. ________________ Research strategy of using information from family members to help create or induce false memories of childhood experiences.
10. ________________ American psychologist who has conducted extensive research on the memory distortions that can occur in eyewitness testimony.
11. ________________ Memory distortion phenomenon in which a person's existing memories can be altered if the person is exposed to misleading information.
12. ________________ Memory failure that occurs when attention is divided and the relevant information is not encoded.
13. ________________ Remembering to do something in the future.
14. ________________ A memory illusion characterized by brief but intense feelings of familiarity in a situation that has never been experienced before.

True/False Test

Indicate whether each statement is true or false by placing T or F in the space next to each item.

1. ____ With retroactive interference, an old memory interferes with remembering a new memory; forward-acting memory interference.
2. ____ Motivated forgetting refers to the idea that we forget because a memory is unpleasant or disturbing.
3. ____ A distorted or inaccurate memory that feels completely real and is often accompanied by all the emotional impact of a real memory is called a false memory.
4. ____ Imagination inflation refers to a memory phenomenon in which vividly imagining an event markedly increases confidence that the event actually occurred.
5. ____ Hermann Ebbinghaus used *nonsense syllables* to study memory and forgetting of completely new material, and to avoid the potential bias of using words that had preexisting associations in memory.
6. ____ Proactive interference is forgetting in which a new memory interferes with remembering an old memory; backward-acting memory interference.
7. ____ Source confusion refers to a memory distortion that occurs when the true source of the memory is forgotten.
8. ____ The forgetting curve reveals two distinct patterns in the relationship between forgetting and the passage of time; much of what is learned is forgotten relatively quickly, and the amount of forgetting eventually levels off.
9. ____ A pseudoevent is an event that never really happened and is used in memory research to induce inaccurate or false childhood memories.
10. ____ A script is a schema for the typical sequence of actions and behaviors involved in an everyday event.
11. ____ Sigmund Freud's famous theory of personality and psychotherapy is called psychoanalysis.
12. ____ Source memory (source monitoring) refers to our ability to remember the original details or features of a memory, including when, where, and how a particular experience or piece of information was acquired.
13. ____ According to decay theory, when a new memory is formed, it creates a distinct structural or chemical change in the brain called a *memory trace.*

Check your answers and review any areas of weakness before going on to the next section.

The Search for the Biological Basis of Memory

Preview Questions

Consider the following questions as you study this section of the chapter.

- How did research by Karl Lashley and Richard Thompson contribute to our understanding of the physical basis of memory?
- How do neurons change when a memory is formed?
- What did Eric Kandel's research demonstrate, and what is long-term potentiation?
- What is amnesia, retrograde amnesia, memory consolidation, and anterograde amnesia?
- How have case studies of people with amnesia provided important insights into the brain structures involved in memory?
- What are dementia and Alzheimer's disease (AD)?

Read the section "The Search for the Biological Basis of Memory" and ***write*** *your answers to the following:*

1. Lashley and Thompson contributed to our understanding of the physical basis of memory by ______________________________
____
____
2. When a new memory is formed, neurons change in two ways: ______________________________
____
____
3. Eric Kandel showed that ______________________________
____
____
____

   Long-term potentiation refers to ______________________________
____
____
4. Amnesia refers to ______________________________
____

   Retrograde amnesia is ______________________________
____
____

   Memory consolidation refers to ______________________________
____

   Anterograde amnesia is ______________________________
____
____
5. Research with patients such as Henry Molaison (H.M.) has enabled investigators to ______________________________
____
____
____
____
6. The brain structures (and their functions) involved in normal memory are ______________________________
____
____
____
____
____
____
7. Dementia is the ______________________________
____
____

   Alzheimer's disease (AD) is a ______________________________
____
____

After you have carefully studied the preceding sections, complete the following exercises.

Concept Check 4

Read the following and write the correct term in the space provided.

1. Bruno, who was knocked out in his last boxing match, cannot remember anything about the fight or events that happened before the bout. Bruno is most likely suffering from a form of amnesia called ______________ amnesia.
2. Bruno's inability to remember details of events that happened before the knockout blow was most likely caused by the disruption of the process of ______________ .
3. Mrs. O'Meara, whose hippocampus was removed during a recent brain operation, is most likely to have trouble forming

_______________ (short-term/long-term) memories.

4. After many training trials, Pookie the dog will now sit on her hind legs and beg for food. Learning this new behavior has probably involved functional and structural neuronal changes in Pookie's brain that are collectively called _______________ .
5. Mr. Usselman has been diagnosed with a condition characterized by impairment of memory and intellectual functions. He is likely suffering from _______________ , a condition that is the most common cause of _______________ .
6. MRI images of Mr. Usselman's brain are likely to show an abundance of _______________ , which are dense deposits of proteins and other cell materials outside and around the neurons, and _______________ , which are twisted fibers that build up inside the neuron and interrupt the flow of nourishment to the neuron.
7. Reiner suffers from anterograde amnesia and has virtually no new memories (episodic or semantic) since a tumor destroyed his hippocampus. However, just like Henry Molaison, he is able to learn the procedures involved in solving certain puzzles, which suggests that he can form new _______________ memories. His lack of conscious awareness of his new ability indicates that these memories are _______________ memories.
8. When Annie viewed a picture of a dog, an fMRI scan of her brain is likely to show increased activity in areas of her _______________ . According to Focus On Neuroscience (Assembling Memories: Echoes and Reflections of Perception), when the memory of the picture is recalled, the _______________ (same/different) areas of the _______________ will be activated.

Review of Terms, Concepts, and Names 4

Use the terms in this list to complete the Matching Exercise, then to help you answer the True/False items correctly.

Karl Lashley
memory trace (engram)
cerebral cortex
Richard F. Thompson
cerebellum
Eric Kandel
long-term potentiation
amnesia
retrograde amnesia
memory consolidation
anterograde amnesia
hippocampus
Brenda Milner and Suzanne Corkin
amygdala
frontal lobes
prefrontal cortex
medial temporal lobes
dementia
Alzheimer's disease (AD)
beta-amyloid plaques and neurofibrillary tangles

Matching Exercise

Match the appropriate term/name with its definition or description.

1. _______________ Outermost covering of the brain that contains the most sophisticated brain areas.
2. _______________ American physiological psychologist who began the search for the memory trace, or engram, and attempted to find the specific brain location of particular memories.
3. _______________ The hypothetical brain changes associated with a particular stored memory.
4. _______________ Severe memory loss.
5. _______________ American psychologist and neuroscientist who conducted extensive research on the neurobiological foundations of learning and memory by studying the classically conditioned eye-blink response in rabbits.
6. _______________ The gradual, physical process of converting new long-term memories to stable, enduring long-term memory codes.
7. _______________ Long-lasting increase in synaptic strength between two neurons.
8. _______________ A lower-brain structure involved in classically conditioned simple reflexes, procedural memories, and motor skill memories.
9. _______________ A brain structure that plays an important role in working memory.

10. ________________ Memory researcher who won the Nobel Prize in 2000 for his work on the neural basis of learning and memory in the sea snail *Aplysia*.

True/False Test

Indicate whether each statement is true or false by placing T or F in the space next to each item.

1. ____ Anterograde amnesia is the loss of memory, especially for episodic information; backward-acting amnesia.
2. ____ Suzanne Corkin and Brenda Milner are psychologists who studied the famous amnesia patient H.M. (Henry Molaison) for 50 years before he died in 2008.
3. ____ Beta-amyloid plaques are dense deposits of protein and other cell materials outside and around neurons, and neurofibrillary tangles are twisted fibers that build up inside the neuron and interrupt the flow of nourishment to the neuron.
4. ____ The frontal lobes are involved in retrieving and organizing information that is associated with autobiographical and episodic memories.
5. ____ Retrograde amnesia is the loss of memory caused by the inability to store new memories; forward-acting amnesia.
6. ____ The critical role of the hippocampus is to encode new memories of events and information and transfer them from short-term memory to long-term memory.
7. ____ The amygdala is involved in encoding and storing the emotional qualities associated with particular memories.
8. ____ Dementia is a condition characterized by impairment of memory and intellectual functions.
9. ____ The medial temporal lobes are involved in encoding complex memories by forming links among pieces of information stored in multiple brain regions.
10. ____ Alzheimer's disease (AD) is a progressive disease that destroys the brain's neurons gradually, impairing memory, thinking, language, and other cognitive functions and is the most common cause of dementia.

Check your answers and review any areas of weakness before going on to the next section.

Something to Think About

1. You may have met that rare person who seems to have a perfect memory—seldom forgetting anything. Most of us, however, have to struggle to learn and retain at least some of the vast amount of material we are constantly exposed to in the "information age." If someone were to ask you what you have learned about memory and forgetting that could be of help, what would you say?
2. Suppose a friend of yours is falsely identified as being the culprit in a grocery store hold-up and comes to you for help. Based on what you know about eyewitness testimony and related phenomena, what advice would you give him?

Check your answers and review any areas of weakness before doing the progress tests.

Progress Test 1

Review the complete chapter (including all boxed inserts), review all your study notes, and then test yourself on the following progress test. Check your answers. If you make a mistake, review your notes, check the appropriate section in the study guide, and, if necessary, go back and read the relevant part of the chapter in your textbook.

1. In preparation for his biology exam, Lionel repeats the list of terms and their definitions over and over. Lionel's rehearsal strategy involves the fundamental memory process of
   (a) encoding.
   (b) storage.
   (c) retrieval.
   (d) wasting his time.
2. Michael, whose aggressive, arrogant behavior and indifferent attitude have resulted in the break-up of many relationships, is contemplating getting married for the third time. Michael is confident that this time it will work and that his previous relationship problems were never his fault. Michael is either actively ________________ or unconsciously ________________ memory of his own behavior.
   (a) consolidating; schematizing
   (b) schematizing; consolidating
   (c) suppressing; repressing
   (d) repressing; suppressing

3. Five-year-old Betty can recite the alphabet perfectly every time she is asked to do so. Betty's ability to do this involves the fundamental memory process of
   (a) repression.
   (b) retrieval.
   (c) retrograde amnesia.
   (d) encoding.

4. Sarina repeated the 10-digit telephone number over and over in her mind as she walked from the living room to the kitchen to make her call. Paige created an acronym for the names of the different brain waves associated with various states of wakefulness and sleep, BATD—Beta, Alpha, Theta, Delta. Sarina is using ________________ rehearsal, and Paige is using ________________ rehearsal.
   (a) distributed; massed
   (b) maintenance; elaborative
   (c) massed; distributed
   (d) elaborative; maintenance

5. Dirk can remember in vivid detail where he was and what he was doing when he heard about the terrorist attacks in New York City and Washington, D.C. Dirk's flashbulb memory is stored in his
   (a) iconic memory.
   (b) short-term memory.
   (c) long-term memory.
   (d) echoic memory.

6. Whenever Killian is introduced to someone, he usually remembers the name by repeating it over and over to himself. Killian is using a memory strategy called
   (a) rehearsal.
   (b) retroactive interference.
   (c) clustering.
   (d) chunking.

7. One conclusion that can be drawn from Ebbinghaus's work on forgetting is that
   (a) we can remember only about seven nonsense syllables at one time.
   (b) when we memorize new information, most forgetting occurs relatively soon after we learn it.
   (c) the duration of visual sensory memory is less than half a second.
   (d) the capacity of long-term memory is large but temporary.

8. Mrs. Carson phoned her husband and quickly listed the 12 items she wanted him to pick up at the store. After his wife hung up, Mr. Carson attempted to write down the items. It is likely that he will
   (a) forget the items in the middle.
   (b) remember only the middle and the last items.
   (c) remember only the first and middle items.
   (d) forget the first and last items and remember the items in the middle.

9. At her high school reunion, Chychi met a girl who used to sit next to her in tenth grade, but she could not recall the girl's name. In an attempt to jog her memory, Chychi began reciting the alphabet. When she came to the letter M, she immediately remembered that her schoolfriend's name was Maureen. In this example, the letter of the alphabet
   (a) eliminated source confusion.
   (b) served as a retrieval cue.
   (c) provoked a flashbulb memory.
   (d) reversed encoding failure.

10. Charlie finds it easier to remember a list of words that includes *automobile, cigarettes, encyclopedia, lampshade, geranium,* and *seashell* than a list of the same length that includes *philosophy, processes, justice, abstraction, fundamental,* and *inherent.* This is because with the first list it is easier to use
    (a) echoic processing.
    (b) maintenance rehearsal.
    (c) procedural memory.
    (d) visual imagery.

11. Karen can remember very clearly when and where she met Jim and how she felt when he first spoke to her. This information, which is stored in Karen's long-term memory, is called
    (a) procedural memory.
    (b) episodic memory.
    (c) semantic memory.
    (d) retroactive memory.

12. After his hippocampus was destroyed by a tumor, Mr. Locke is likely to experience problems ____________ and is likely to be classified as suffering from ____________ .
    (a) forming procedural memories; retrograde amnesia
    (b) recognizing common objects; Alzheimer's disease
    (c) correctly repeating items over and over; Alzheimer's disease
    (d) transferring short-term memories into long-term memory; anterograde amnesia

13. When Mitra entered the famous cathedral for the first time she had a brief but intense feeling that she had walked through the doorway before but could not recall when or where. According to In Focus (Déjà Vu Experiences), which of the following is true?
    (a) Déjà vu is the result of precognition, clairvoyance, telepathy, or a past life experience.
    (b) Déjà vu can be explained by basic memory concepts such as disruptions in source memory, encoding failure, or inattentional blindness.
    (c) The remembered feeling of familiarity is caused by an overabundance of beta-amyloid plaques and neurofibrillary tangles in the brain.
    (d) Frequent episodes of déjà vu are associated with early-onset dementia and, in particular, Alzheimer's disease (AD).

14. According to Enhancing Well-Being with Psychology (Superpower Memory in Minutes per Day!), one way to make memories last is to learn material over several sessions rather than cramming learning into one long session. This method of study is called
    (a) distributed practice.
    (b) massed practice.
    (c) maintenance rehearsal.
    (d) serial position learning.

15. According to Critical Thinking (The Memory Wars), which of the following regarding childhood sexual abuse is true?
    (a) Physical and sexual abuse in childhood is a serious social problem and can contribute to psychological problems in adulthood.
    (b) Some psychologists contend it is possible that memories of abuse can become repressed in childhood and surface later in life.
    (c) Repressed memories recovered in therapy need to be regarded with caution; a person's confidence in those memories is no guarantee that they are accurate.
    (d) All of these statements are true.

Progress Test 2

After you have checked your understanding of the material in Progress Test 1 and have done a complete chapter review with special focus on any areas of weakness, you are ready to assess your knowledge on Progress Test 2. Check your answers. If you make a mistake, review your notes, the relevant section of the study guide, and, if necessary, the appropriate part of your textbook.

1. When Gary was preparing for an exam, he tried to make the material more meaningful by using strategies such as visual imagery, creating short stories involving the terms, self-referencing, and so on. Gary is using __________ to help him remember the information.
    (a) elaborative rehearsal
    (b) maintenance rehearsal
    (c) clustering
    (d) the encoding specificity principle

2. Shortly after he finished reading an exciting novel, Sean fell down the stairs and suffered a concussion; now, he has no recall of ever having read the novel. Sean's memory problem is probably the result of __________ , and he is most likely to be classified as suffering from __________ .
    (a) retrieval cue failure; anterograde amnesia
    (b) source confusion; dementia
    (c) disruption of memory consolidation; retrograde amnesia
    (d) source amnesia; dementia

3. Dr. Chung's research is concerned with three components of memory: the phonological loop, the visuospatial sketchpad, and the central executive. He is most likely investigating aspects of
    (a) memory consolidation and long-term potentiation.
    (b) the encoding specificity principle.
    (c) Baddeley's model of working memory.
    (d) motivated forgetting such as suppression and repression.

4. Richard F. Thompson classically conditioned rabbits to eye-blink to a tone. He found that after learning, the brain activity in the rabbit's cerebellum changed. This result suggests that some long-term memories
    (a) are stored in a localized region of the brain.
    (b) are distributed and stored across multiple brain locations.
    (c) have no biological or physical basis in the brain.
    (d) are very vulnerable if they are not given enough time to consolidate.

5. Dr. Dement believes that forgetting is due to memory traces being eroded by normal metabolic processes in the brain. Dr. Dement supports the
   (a) interference theory.
   (b) motivated forgetting theory.
   (c) semantic network theory.
   (d) decay theory.

6. When Manfred, who used to be a compulsive gambler, is asked how much money he won or lost, he recalls losing much less money than was actually the case. Manfred's memory failure best illustrates
   (a) motivated forgetting.
   (b) retrieval cue failure.
   (c) retroactive interference.
   (d) proactive interference.

7. Natasha has memorized the new personal identity code she was given by security; now, she can't remember her old personal identity code. Natasha is experiencing the effects of
   (a) mood congruence.
   (b) source confusion.
   (c) proactive interference.
   (d) retroactive interference.

8. Jeffery, who was an eyewitness to a robbery, initially thought the robber was a female. During questioning, a police detective suggested to him many times that the robber was probably a man with long hair. Later, when he was giving testimony on the witness stand, Jeffery was quite sure that it was a man who robbed the store. This example illustrates
   (a) the serial position effect.
   (b) mood congruence.
   (c) a flashbulb memory.
   (d) the misinformation effect.

9. Faizal was given a list of words to remember. On a later test of his long-term memory, he recalled the words according to how he had grouped them into categories, such as vegetables, furniture, and colors. When Korina is given a list of letters to study and recall—CPADNIDCTMVDASABM—she groups them into familiar units—CD PC ATM DVD NASA and IBM. Faizal is using a strategy for improving long-term memory called ____________ , and Korina is using ____________ to increase the amount of information she can hold in short-term memory.
   (a) clustering; chunking
   (b) echoic memory; iconic memory
   (c) chunking; clustering
   (d) long-term potentiation; memory consolidation

10. The smell of cherry blossoms awakened in Mrs. Yamomoto vivid memories of her childhood in Osaka. The aroma of the blossoms apparently acted as an effective
    (a) schema.
    (b) echoic cue.
    (c) flashbulb cue.
    (d) retrieval cue.

11. During a discussion about old movies, Grace could not bring to mind the name of the actor who played Sidney Greenstreet's sidekick in *The Maltese Falcon*, despite the fact that she felt she knew the name and had, in fact, talked about his role in the movie on other occasions. Grace is experiencing
    (a) the serial position effect.
    (b) encoding failure.
    (c) the tip-of-the-tongue (TOT) phenomenon.
    (d) anterograde amnesia.

12. Harold, who was in the kitchen, asked Jane, who was reading a book in the living room, whether she wanted a diet or a regular soft drink. Jane replied, "What did you say?" Before Harold could respond, Jane said, "Make it a regular Coke, please." This example illustrates
    (a) iconic memory.
    (b) repression.
    (c) echoic memory.
    (d) a flashbulb memory.

13. According to Culture and Human Behavior (Cultural Differences in Early Memories), which of the following is true?
    (a) Autobiographical memories may be shaped by cultural and social contexts.
    (b) European American and Taiwanese and Chinese college students' earliest memories were very similar in content, and both groups had their earliest memories at the same average age.
    (c) Autobiographical memories are relatively independent of culture and context and reflect universal and innate biological developments in the brain.
    (d) The memories of Asian students tended to be longer, more elaborate, and more self-focused than those of the American students.

14. When his hippocampus was removed, Henry Molaison (H.M.) lost the ability to quickly encode new semantic and episodic memories. According to In Focus (H.M. and Famous People), research with H.M. (and the famous people test) demonstrated that
    (a) most of Henry's memory problems were related to retrograde amnesia.
    (b) most of Henry's new memories were the result of source confusion and imagination inflation.
    (c) his brain had an abundance of two abnormal structures, beta-amyloid plaques and neurofibrillary tangles.
    (d) some limited declarative semantic learning can occur without the hippocampus.

15. Regarding the critical issue of recovered memories versus false memories, Critical Thinking (The Memory Wars) notes that
    (a) every act of remembering involves reconstructing a memory.
    (b) the details of memory can be distorted with disturbing ease.
    (c) false or fabricated memories can seem just as detailed, vivid, and real as accurate ones.
    (d) all of these statements are true.

Progress Test 3

After you have checked your understanding of the material in Progress Tests 1 and 2 and have done a complete chapter review with special focus on any areas of weakness, you are ready to further assess your knowledge with Progress Test 3. Check your answers. If you make a mistake, review your notes, the appropriate parts of the study guide, and, if necessary, the relevant sections of your textbook.

1. Memory with awareness is to ______________ as memory without awareness is to ______________ .
    (a) explicit memory; implicit memory
    (b) retroactive interference; proactive interference
    (c) implicit memory; explicit memory
    (d) proactive interference; retroactive interference

2. Dr. Rhodes believes that when the conditions of information retrieval are similar to the conditions of information encoding, retrieval is more likely to be successful. This view is most consistent with
    (a) the stage model of memory.
    (b) the semantic network model.
    (c) the encoding specificity principle.
    (d) interference theory.

3. Elizabeth Loftus's story, presented in the Prologue, demonstrates how it is possible to form an extremely vivid, but inaccurate, memory. A common cause of such false memories is
    (a) retrograde amnesia.
    (b) source confusion.
    (c) anterograde amnesia.
    (d) retrieval cue failure.

4. The ______________ is to encoding emotional aspects of memory as the ______________ is to the encoding and transfer of new information from short-term to long-term memory.
    (a) amygdala; hippocampus
    (b) prefrontal cortex; amygdala
    (c) hippocampus; amygdala
    (d) cerebellum; hippocampus

5. Research participants were first presented with a visual stimulus (a picture of a cat and the word *cat*). Another group heard an auditory stimulus (the sound of a dog barking and the word *dog*). Next, both groups were given a retrieval cue (cat or dog) and asked to recall the original stimulus (visual or auditory). If the results of this experiment are similar to those in the Focus on Neuroscience, fMRI scans during the recall phase are likely to show that remembering the sound activates the ______________ and remembering the picture activates the ______________ .
    (a) visual cortex; auditory cortex
    (b) prefrontal cortex; cerebellum
    (c) auditory cortex; visual cortex
    (d) hippocampus; amygdala

6. Neddy cannot accurately remember the order of the keys on the computer keyboard he has used quite frequently for 10 years. Neddy's problem in recall is most likely a function of
    (a) retrieval cue failure.
    (b) proactive interference.
    (c) encoding failure.
    (d) retroactive interference.

7. Most participants in an experiment responded with *sky* and *grass* to the stimulus words *blue* and *green*. Results such as these support
    (a) the semantic network model.
    (b) decay theory.
    (c) the tip-of-the-tongue (TOT) experience.
    (d) interference theory.

8. Emelia can quite easily list all 50 U.S. states and Canada's 10 provinces and 3 territories. This type of information in long-term memory is called ______________ information.
   (a) procedural (c) semantic
   (b) episodic (d) implicit

9. During a memory experiment, Amy was given lists of words to remember. Which component of her working memory is most likely to be used for this verbal task?
   (a) the phonological loop
   (b) visual sensory memory
   (c) the visuospatial sketchpad
   (d) auditory sensory memory

10. Lisa took a strong mood-altering prescription drug while studying for her exam; the following week, she took the same pills before the exam because she wanted to be in the same positive emotional state on both occasions. Lisa appears to believe in the effects of
   (a) maintenance rehearsal.
   (b) elaborative rehearsal.
   (c) mood congruence.
   (d) source confusion.

11. When Kirk was given a long list of items to memorize, he found it easier to remember them when he regrouped all the items according to whether they were plants, animals, minerals, and so on. Kirk is using a memory aid called
   (a) the serial position effect.
   (b) the self-referencing technique.
   (c) the context effect.
   (d) chunking.

12. When she first transferred from a junior college to a university, Kelly had trouble remembering her new student number; she would always recall her old college student number instead. Kelly's memory problem is an example of
   (a) retrograde amnesia.
   (b) proactive interference.
   (c) anterograde amnesia.
   (d) retroactive interference.

13. Mrs. Kahn experienced no trouble skiing despite the fact that she had not been on the slopes for almost 15 years. Mrs. Kahn's current skiing ability is probably due to a category of long-term memory called ______________ memory.
   (a) procedural (c) semantic
   (b) episodic (d) repressed

14. Professor Isernia uses short essay questions on all her exams. In contrast, Professor Stregger relies on multiple-choice questions to test his students. Professor Isernia's exams involve a test of long-term memory called ______________ , whereas Professor Stregger's exam questions involve ______________ .
   (a) cued recall; chunking
   (b) recall (free recall); recognition
   (c) cued recall; clustering
   (d) recognition; recall (free recall)

15. According to Enhancing Well-Being with Psychology (Superpower Memory in Minutes per Day!), which of the following strategies is NOT good for boosting memory?
   (a) Focus your attention and avoid distractions.
   (b) Use massed practice and take ginkgo biloba.
   (c) Organize the information and elaborate on it.
   (d) Use visual imagery, mnemonic devices, contextual cues, and sleep after studying

Answers

Introduction: What Is Memory?

1. *Memory refers to* the mental processes that enable us to acquire, retain, and use information over time.
2. *Encoding is the process of* transforming information into a form that can be entered into and retained by the memory system. *Storage is the process of* retaining information in memory so that it can be used at a later time. *Retrieval is the process of* recovering information stored in memory so that we are consciously aware of it.
3. *The stage model of memory describes memory as* consisting of three distinct stages: sensory memory (the stage that registers information from the environment for a brief period of time), short-term memory (the active, working stage in which information is stored for up to about 20 seconds), and long-term memory (the stage that represents the potentially permanent storage of information).
4. *The three stages interact by* transferring information from one stage to another, with transfer between short-term and long-term memory going two ways.

Sensory Memory: Fleeting Impressions of the World

1. *Information is held in sensory memory for* about one-quarter to one-half second for visual

sensory memory and up to three or four seconds for auditory sensory memory.

2. *Sperling's classic experiment demonstrated* that our visual sensory memory holds a great deal of information very briefly; this information is available just long enough for us to pay attention to specific elements that are significant to us at that moment.
3. *An important function of sensory memory (iconic and echoic) is* to store sensory impressions very briefly so that they overlap slightly with one another. Consequently, we perceive the world around us as continuous, rather than as a series of disconnected images or disjointed sounds.

Short-Term, Working Memory: The Workshop of Consciousness

1. *Short-term memory is the stage of memory in which* information transferred from sensory memory and retrieved from long-term memory is temporarily stored and enters conscious awareness.
2. *The duration of short-term memory is* approximately 20 seconds, unless the information is rehearsed (maintenance rehearsal).
3. *The capacity of short-term memory is,* according to George Miller, limited to about seven items, or bits of information, plus or minus two. *However, current research has found that* four plus or minus one is more likely. *It can be increased by* maintenance rehearsal and by chunking (grouping related items together into a single unit or chunk).
4. *Working memory refers to* the temporary storage and active, conscious manipulation of information needed for complex cognitive tasks, such as reasoning, learning, and problem solving.
5. *The three components of Baddeley's model of working memory are* the phonological loop (specialized for verbal material), the visuospatial sketchpad (specialized for spatial or visual material), and the central executive (controls attention, integrates information, initiates retrieval and decision processes, and manages the activities of the other two components).

Long-Term Memory

1. *The amount of information that can be held in long-term memory is* essentially unlimited.
2. *Three ways to increase the effectiveness of encoding are* to engage in elaborative rehearsal (focus on the meaning of information), use self-referencing (apply information to yourself), and use visual imagery.
3. *Procedural memory refers to* the long-term memory of how to perform different skills, operations, and actions. *Episodic memory refers to* the long-term memory of specific events or episodes, including the time and place that they occurred (autobiographical memory is closely related and refers to memory of events in your life). *Semantic memory refers to* memory of general knowledge that includes facts, names, definitions, concepts, and ideas.
4. *Explicit memory is* information or knowledge that can be consciously recollected (also called declarative memory). *Implicit memory is* information or knowledge that affects behavior or task performance but cannot be consciously recollected (also called nondeclarative memory).
5. *Information is organized in long-term memory by* clustering and by association.
6. *The best-known model of how information is organized in memory is* the semantic network model, *which describes long-term memory as* units of information organized in a complex network of associations.

Concept Check 1

1. retrieval
2. encoding
3. elaborative
4. short-term; maintenance
5. chunking
6. procedural
7. explicit memory; implicit memory
8. episodic; autobiographical

Matching Exercise 1

1. elaborative rehearsal
2. semantic network model
3. retrieval
4. clustering
5. visual imagery
6. short-term memory
7. episodic memory
8. encoding
9. stage model of memory

10. memory
11. procedural memory
12. George Sperling
13. autobiographical memory
14. working memory
15. central executive

True/False Test 1

1. F	6. T	11. F
2. F	7. T	12. T
3. T	8. T	13. F
4. T	9. T	14. F
5. T	10. F	

Retrieval: Getting Information from Long-Term Memory

1. *Retrieval refers to* the process of recovering information stored in memory so that we are consciously aware of it. *A retrieval cue is* a clue, prompt, or hint that helps trigger recall of a given piece of information stored in long-term memory. *Retrieval cue failure refers to* the inability to recall long-term memories because of inadequate or missing retrieval cues.
2. *The tip-of-the-tongue (TOT) experience is* a memory phenomenon that involves the sensation of knowing that specific information is stored in long-term memory, but being temporarily unable to retrieve it. *It illustrates the fact that* retrieving information is not an all-or-nothing process; in many instances, information is stored in memory but is not accessible without the right retrieval cues. It also shows that information stored in memory is organized and connected in relatively logical ways.
3. *Retrieval is tested by* recall (retrieving information without the aid of retrieval cues), cued recall (remembering an item of information in response to a retrieval cue), and recognition (identifying correct information out of several possible choices).
4. *The serial position effect is* the tendency to remember items at the beginning of a list (primacy effect) and at the end of a list (recency effect) better than items in the middle of the list.
5. *The encoding specificity principle states that* when the conditions of information retrieval are similar to the conditions of information encoding, retrieval is more likely to be successful.
6. *The context effect, an encoding specificity phenomenon, refers to* the tendency to recover information more easily when retrieval occurs in the same setting as the original learning of the information. *Mood congruence, a different form of encoding specificity, refers to* the idea that a given mood tends to evoke memories that are consistent with that mood.
7. *Distinctiveness plays a role in retrieval because* highly unusual, surprising, or even bizarre experiences are easier to retrieve from memory than are routine events.
8. *A flashbulb memory is* the recall of very specific images or details surrounding a vivid, rare, or significant event. Although confidence about the recollection is usually high, accuracy is not (confidence in a memory is no guarantee of accuracy).

Concept Check 2

1. mood congruence
2. flashbulb
3. tip-of-the-tongue phenomenon
4. retrieval cue
5. recognition; recall
6. encoding specificity; context effect
7. primacy effect; recency effect
8. serial position effect

Graphic Organizer 1

1 RECOGNITION
2 TIPOFTHETONGUEEXPERIENCE
3 RETRIEVALCUEFAILURE
4 FLASHBULBMEMORY
5 SERIALPOSITIONEFFECT
6 RETRIEVAL

7. Recall is a test of long-term memory that involves retrieving information without the aid of retrieval cues (also called free recall).

Matching Exercise 2

1. context effect
2. retrieval
3. flashbulb memory
4. serial position effect
5. cued recall
6. retrieval cue
7. mood congruence
8. encoding specificity principle

True/False Test 2

1. F	5. T
2. T	6. T
3. T	7. F
4. T	8. T

Forgetting: When Retrieval Fails

1. *Forgetting is the* inability to recall information that was previously available.
2. *The Ebbinghaus forgetting curve reveals two distinct patterns about forgetting: (a)* much of what we forget is lost relatively soon after we originally learned it; *(b)* the amount of forgetting eventually levels off, with information that is not quickly forgotten remaining quite stable in memory over long periods.
3. *Encoding failure refers to* the inability to recall specific information because of insufficient encoding of the information for storage in long-term memory. *It may contribute to* absent-mindedness, which occurs when attention is divided at the time of encoding and the relevant information is therefore not transferred into long-term memory.
4. *Prospective memory is* remembering to do something in the future. *Prospective memory failure may be due to* retrieval cue failure rather than encoding failure.
5. *According to decay theory,* forgetting is due to normal metabolic processes that occur in the brain over time.
6. *Interference theory is the theory that* forgetting is caused by one memory competing with or replacing another memory. *The two basic types of interference affect memory in the following ways:* in retroactive interference, a new memory interferes with remembering an old memory (backward-acting memory interference); in proactive interference, an old memory interferes with remembering a new memory (forward-acting memory interference).
7. *Motivated forgetting refers to the idea that* we forget because we are motivated to forget, usually because a memory is unpleasant or disturbing. *There are two forms of motivated forgetting:* suppression (a deliberate, conscious effort to forget) and repression (unconscious motivation to forget).
8. *Repression is a controversial topic because* (a) it is based on the Freudian (psychoanalytic) belief that psychologically threatening emotions, conflicts, and urges (especially those from childhood) can become repressed, yet can still unconsciously influence a person's thoughts, behavior, and personality, often in maladaptive or unhealthy ways; and (b) The construct of repression has not been scientifically validated and, while many clinical psychologists and others believe in the notion, the evidence from research on false and distorted memories suggests that claims of recovered repressed memories in psychotherapy should be regarded with caution.

Imperfect Memories: Errors, Distortions, and False Memories

1. *Errors and distortions occur during the process of retrieval because* retrieval involves the active construction and reconstruction of memories and may be affected by the information stored before and after the memory occurred.
2. *The misinformation effect (one phenomenon that can reduce the accuracy of eyewitness testimony) refers to* a memory-distortion phenomenon in which a person's existing memories can be altered if the person is exposed to misleading information. *It is a problem because* post-event exposure to misinformation can distort the recollection of the original event.
3. *Source confusion is* memory distortion that occurs when the true source of the memory is forgotten.
4. *A false memory is* a distorted or fabricated recollection of an event that did not actually occur.
5. *A schema is* an organized cluster of knowledge and information about a particular topic. *Research has demonstrated that* our schemas can influence what we remember; that they can prompt us to fill in missing details with schema-consistent information; and that memories can easily become distorted.
6. *A script is* one kind of schema that involves the typical sequence of actions and behaviors at a common event.

7. *The lost-in-the-mall technique is* a research strategy using information from family members to help create or induce false memories of childhood experiences (pseudoevents). *It demonstrates that* people are capable of developing beliefs and memories for events that definitely did not happen to them.
8. *Imagination inflation is* a memory phenomenon in which vividly imagining an event markedly increases confidence that the event (pseudoevent) actually happened.

Concept Check 3

1. proactive
2. encoding failure
3. suppression
4. misinformation effect
5. retrieval cue failure
6. retroactive
7. absentmindedness; encoding
8. schema
9. imagination inflation
10. prospective

Graphic Organizer 2

1. retroactive interference
2. proactive interference

Matching Exercise 3

1. suppression
2. forgetting
3. decay theory
4. repression
5. interference theory
6. Hermann Ebbinghaus
7. encoding failure
8. schema
9. lost-in-the-mall technique
10. Elizabeth Loftus
11. misinformation effect
12. absentmindedness
13. prospective memory
14. déjà vu experience

True/False Test 3

1. F	5. T	9. T	13. T
2. T	6. F	10. T	
3. T	7. T	11. T	
4. T	8. T	12. T	

The Search for the Biological Basis of Memory

1. *Lashley and Thompson contributed to our understanding of the physical basis of memory by* demonstrating that memories have the potential to be both localized and distributed: Very simple memories are localized in a specific area, and more complex memories are distributed throughout the brain.
2. *When a new memory is formed, neurons change in two ways:* functionally, they increase the amount of neurotransmitters they produce, and structurally, they show an increase in the number of interconnecting branches between neurons as well as in the number of synapses on each branch.
3. *Eric Kandel showed that* functional and structural changes in neurons are associated with acquiring a classically conditioned response (in the sea snail *Aplysia*). *Long-term potentiation refers to* a long-lasting increase in synaptic strength between two neurons.
4. *Amnesia refers to* severe memory loss. *Retrograde amnesia is* loss of memory, especially for episodic information about recent events (backward-acting amnesia). *Memory consolidationg refers to* the gradual, physical process of converting new long-term memories to stable, enduring memory codes; if disrupted before the process is complete, the vulnerable memory may be lost. *Anterograde amnesia is* loss of memory caused by the inability to store new memories (forward-acting amnesia).
5. *Research with patients such as Henry Molaison (H.M.) has enabled investigators to* relate the type and extent of amnesia to the specific brain areas that have been damaged and has also contributed to our understanding of the distinction between implicit and explicit memory.
6. *The brain structures (and their functions) involved in normal memory are* the cerebellum (motor skill memories, classically conditioned simple reflexes, and procedural memories), the amygdala (encodes and stores the emotional aspects of memories), prefrontal cortex (plays an important role in working memory), the frontal lobes (retrieve and organize information associated with autobiographical and episodic memories), the medial temporal lobes (encode complex memories by forming links among multiple brain regions), and the hippocampus (encodes and transfers new explicit memories to long-term memory).
7. *Dementia is the* progressive deterioration and impairment of memory, reasoning, language,

and other cognitive functions occurring as the result of a disease or a condition. *Alzheimer's disease (AD) is a* progressive disease that destroys the brain's neurons, gradually impairing memory, thinking, language, and other cognitive functions, resulting in the complete inability to care for oneself. It is the most common cause of dementia.

Concept Check 4

1. retrograde
2. memory consolidation
3. long-term
4. long-term potentiation
5. Alzheimer's disease (AD); dementia
6. beta-amyloid plaques; neurofibrillary tangles
7. procedural; implicit
8. visual cortex; same; visual cortex

Matching Exercise 4

1. cerebral cortex
2. Karl Lashley
3. memory trace (engram)
4. amnesia
5. Richard F. Thompson
6. memory consolidation
7. long-term potentiation
8. cerebellum
9. prefrontal cortex
10. Eric Kandel

True/False Test 4

1. F	5. F	9. T
2. T	6. T	10. T
3. T	7. T	
4. T	8. T	

Something to Think About

1. We are all vulnerable to forgetting, and sometimes the consequences can be serious. What can we do to improve memory? Fortunately, a number of strategies can help us to remember important information. You might begin your answer with a discussion of the fundamental processes of encoding, storage, and retrieval, then explain the function, capacity, and duration of each of the three stages of memory. Of course, no discussion of the topic of memory would be complete without mentioning Ebbinghaus's work on forgetting, as well as the contributions of the various factors that contribute to forgetting to our understanding of memory. Finally, mention the important strategies that could help improve memory, as described in Enhancing Well-Being with Psychology (Superpower Memory in Minutes per Day!).
2. It is a real nightmare to contemplate the prospect of being falsely accused of a crime and having an eyewitness point at you and say very confidently, "Yes, that is the person. There's no doubt about it, he (or she) did it!" What can be done in such a situation? If you don't have an alibi, the jury is very likely to believe a confident eyewitness who, under oath, points a finger at the accused. First, you might consider hiring an expert witness, such as Elizabeth Loftus, to testify to the problems inherent in eyewitness testimony. Such testimony, based on scientific evidence, is difficult to refute.

    If your friend cannot afford the testimony of an expert witness, then we suggest he or she try to educate his defense lawyer about the relevant research findings in this important area of psychology. These include source confusion, the personal schema of the eyewitness, the power of the misinformation effect, suggestion, and imagination inflation, evidence related to false memories, and relevant aspects of the encoding specificity principle.

Progress Test 1

1. a	6. a	11. b
2. c	7. b	12. d
3. b	8. a	13. b
4. b	9. b	14. a
5. c	10. d	15. d

Progress Test 2

1. a	6. a	11. c
2. c	7. d	12. c
3. c	8. d	13. a
4. a	9. a	14. d
5. d	10. d	15. d

Progress Test 3

1. a	6. c	11. d
2. c	7. a	12. b
3. b	8. c	13. a
4. a	9. a	14. b
5. c	10. c	15. b

CHAPTER 7

Thinking, Language, and Intelligence

PREVIEW

Reading the section below first will give you a general sense of the chapter's contents and an initial introduction to some of the major concepts and terms. This will prime you for what you are about to read and help you to develop a "cognitive map" that will guide your study of the material in this chapter. Likewise, reading the **preview questions** at the beginning of each major section will improve your ability to understand, learn, and retain the information.

CHAPTER 7... AT A GLANCE

Chapter 7 combines thinking, language, and intelligence, three closely related cognitive functions. The section on thinking begins with discussions of the use of mental imagery and concept formation. This leads to a description of problem-solving strategies, followed by an explanation of two common obstacles to effective problem solving: functional fixedness and mental sets. The section concludes with a discussion of different decision-making models.

The next section, on our remarkable cognitive capacity for language, first explains the characteristics of language, then discusses bilingualism and its effect on cognitive abilities. Animal communication and cognition (comparative cognition), as well as the question of whether animals are capable of language are included in this section.

Our ability to think and use language are aspects of what we call intelligence. Because the measurement of intelligence has been a controversial issue, this section provides some background into the development of intelligence testing and the contributions of various psychologists. The difference between aptitude tests and achievement tests is explained, and standardization, reliability, and validity are described as requirements of good test design.

The debate over the nature of intelligence centers on whether intelligence is a single, general ability or a cluster of different abilities, and on whether intelligence should be narrowly or broadly defined. Four theories regarding this issue are presented. The heredity–environment debate regarding the origins of intelligence is examined in detail. Enhancing Well-Being With Psychology: A Workshop on Creativity, presents a number of suggestions for enhancing our ability to think creatively.

Introduction: Thinking, Language, and Intelligence

Preview Questions

Consider the following questions as you study this section of the chapter.

- What is cognition?
- How is *thinking* defined, and what does it typically involve?
- What are mental images, and how do we manipulate them?
- What has neuroscience demonstrated about mental images?
- What are concepts, and how are they formed?
- What are prototypes and exemplars, and what role do they play in concept formation?

*Read the section "Introduction: Thinking, Language, and Intelligence" and **write** your answers to the following:*

1. Cognition is mental activities involved in acquiring, retaining, and using knowledge.
2. Thinking is defined as manipulation of mental representations to draw ______
   It typically involves ______
3. A mental image is ______
4. We manipulate mental images ______
   Mental images are potentially subject to error and distortion because ______
5. Neuroscientists have shown that when people view faces ______
   When they view places ______
   The same two brain areas were activated ______
6. Concepts are mental categories of objects or ideas based on shared properties.
   The two ways of forming concepts are formal concept and natural concept.
7. A prototype is ______
   The more closely an item matches a prototype, ______
8. Exemplars are ______
   When we encounter a new object, ______

Solving Problems and Making Decisions

Preview Questions

Consider the following questions as you study this section of the chapter.

- How is *problem solving* defined?
- What are four problem-solving strategies, and what are the advantages and/or disadvantages of each?
- What are functional fixedness and mental sets, and how do they interfere with problem solving?

*Read the section "Solving Problems and Making Decisions" and **write** your answers to the following:*

1. *Problem solving* is defined as ______
2. The trial-and-error strategy involves trying different ways of doing things until something works.
3. An algorithm involves ______
4. A heuristic is a "rule-of-thumb"
5. Insight is the sudden realization of how a problem can be solved.

Intuition means coming to a conclusion without conscious awareness of the thought processes involved.

6. Functional fixedness is a type of mental set.

   It may prevent seeing an object as having a function other than its usual one.

7. A mental set is ______

   It may prevent ______

Decision-Making Strategies

Preview Questions

Consider the following questions as you study this section of the chapter.

- What are the single-feature, additive, and elimination-by-aspects models of decision making?
- Under what conditions is each strategy most appropriate?
- What strategies do good decision makers use?
- When are the availability and representativeness heuristics used, and what potential problems are associated with each?

Read the section "Decision-Making Strategies" and ***write*** *your answers to the following:*

1. The single-feature model involves making a decision by focusing on only one feature.

   It is appropriate when ______

2. Using the additive model, you first systematically evaluate the important features of each alternative.

   It is appropriate for ______

3. Using the elimination-by-aspects model, you rate choices based on features

   It is appropriate when ______

4. Good decision makers adapt their strategy ______

5. The availability heuristic is a strategy by ______

   One problem with this strategy is that ______

6. The representativeness heuristic is a strategy where you judge probability of an event based on how it matches a prototype.

   This strategy can produce faulty estimates if ______

After you have carefully studied the preceding sections, complete the following exercises.

Concept Check 1

Read the following and write the correct term in the space provided.

1. After a chimpanzee tries unsuccessfully to get bananas that are out of reach, she sits for a long time staring at them. Suddenly, she looks around the cage, picks up a stick, and uses it to pull the bananas within her reach, something she has never done before. Her solution to the banana problem is probably the result of ______ .

2. You learn that one of the Russell children is taking ballet classes. You immediately conclude that it is their one daughter rather than any of their three sons. You reached a possibly erroneous conclusion by using the ______ .

3. Dr. Mendleson studies how people manipulate mental representations to draw inferences and conclusions. Dr. Mendleson is most likely a ______ psychologist interested in people's ______ ability.

4. You are asked to decide which city is farther north, Edinburgh, Scotland, or Stockholm, Sweden, so you try to picture a map of Europe in your mind. You are using a ______ .

5. Marisa has learned the rules and features that define a square, a rectangle, and a right-angle triangle. Marisa has learned a ______________ concept.
6. Henry, an avid fisherman, had trouble recognizing that a seahorse is a fish because it does not closely resemble his ________________ concept of fish.
7. To convert liters into U.S. gallons, Natalie multiplies the number of liters by 0.264178. She is using a(n) ________________ to arrive at the correct answer.
8. Hilda is asked to complete the sequence "J, F, M, A, _, _, _, _, _, _, _, _." After trying a few different possibilities, she comes up with the correct answer—M, J, J, A, S, O, N, D (the first letter of the months of the year). It appears that Hilda is using a(n) __________________________________ strategy to solve the problem.
9. Anatole is trying to decide which of two equally affordable and attractive cars to purchase, so he makes a list of the advantages and disadvantages of each using an arbitrary rating scale. Anatole is using the ________________ model to help him make a decision.
10. When he first tried an avocado, Keeton compared his memory of other types of fruits in order to decide whether an avocado is a fruit. In this case, Keeton is using an ________________ to help him categorize the food item.
11. Researchers used fMRI scans of people's brains while the people were viewing actual photos of faces and places or just imagining faces and places. If their results are similar to those reported in the text (Focus On Neuroscience: Seeing Faces and Places in the Mind's Eye) they are likely to find that imagining a face or a scene activated ________________ (different/ the same) brain areas compared with when they were perceiving the actual photos.

Review of Terms and Concepts 1

Use the terms in this list to complete the Matching Exercise, then to help you answer the True/False items correctly.

cognition
thinking
mental image
concept
formal concept
natural concept
prototype
exemplars
problem solving
trial and error
algorithm
heuristic
analysis of subgoals
working backward
insight
intuition
guiding stage and integrative stage
fixation
functional fixedness
mental set
single-feature model
additive model
elimination by aspects model
availability heuristic
representativeness heuristic

Matching Exercise

Match the appropriate term with its definition or description.

1. ________________ Decision-making model in which all the alternatives are evaluated one characteristic at a time, starting with the most important feature and scratching each alternative off the list of possible choices if it fails to meet the criteria.
2. ________________ The manipulation of mental representations of information in order to draw inferences or conclusions.
3. ________________ Most typical instance of a particular concept.
4. ________________ Sudden realization of how a problem can be solved.
5. ________________ Decision-making strategy in which the choice among many alternatives is simplified by basing the decision on one feature.
6. ________________ Strategy in which the likelihood of an event is estimated by comparing how similar it is to the typical prototype of the event.
7. ________________ Problem-solving strategy that involves following a specific rule, procedure, or method that inevitably produces the correct solution.
8. ________________ Problem-solving strategy that involves attempting different solutions and eliminating those that do not work.

9. ________________ Mental category that is formed by learning the rules or features that define it.
10. ________________ The mental activities involved in acquiring, retaining, and using knowledge.
11. ________________ Mental category of objects or ideas based on properties that they share.
12. ________________ Problem-solving strategy that involves following a general rule of thumb to reduce the number of possible solutions.
13. ________________ Individual instances of a concept or category, held in memory.

True/False Test

Indicate whether each statement is true or false by placing T or F in the blank space next to each item.

1. ____ Working backward is a common heuristic used to break a problem down into a series of smaller problems; as each subproblem is solved, you get closer to solving the larger problem.
2. ____ A mental representation of objects or events that are not physically present is called a mental image.
3. ____ Problem solving is thinking and behavior directed toward attaining a goal that is not readily available.
4. ____ The tendency to persist in solving problems with solutions that have worked in the past is called functional fixedness.
5. ____ The additive model of decision making involves generating a list of the most important factors, then using an arbitrary rating scale to rate each alternative on each factor, and finally adding the ratings together for comparison purposes.
6. ____ The availability heuristic is a strategy in which the likelihood of an event is estimated on the basis of how easily other instances of the event are available in memory.
7. ____ A natural concept is a mental category that is formed as a result of everyday experience.
8. ____ A useful heuristic in which you start at the end point and determine the steps necessary to reach your goal uses the analysis of subgoals.
9. ____ A mental set is the tendency to view objects as functioning only in their usual or customary manner.
10. ____ Intuition refers to the process of coming to a conclusion or making a judgment without conscious awareness.
11. ____ The two-stage model of intuition involves a guiding stage (a pattern in the information is perceived unconsciously) and an integrative stage (a representation of the pattern becomes conscious).
12. ____ Fixation refers to the use of old, inappropriate heuristics, ideas, or problem-solving strategies that block the generation of new, more effective approaches.

Check your answers and review any areas of weakness before going on to the next section.

Language and Thought

Preview Questions

Consider the following questions as you study this section of the chapter.

- How is *language* defined?
- What are the five most important characteristics of language?
- What is bilingualism, and what has research shown about its influence on cognitive abilities?
- What has research shown about nonhuman animal communication and cognition?
- What is animal cognition, or comparative cognition?

*Read the section "Language and Thought" and **write** your answers to the following:*

1. *Language* is defined as a system for combining arbitrary symbols to produce an infinite number of meaningful statements.
2. The five most important characteristics of language are as follows:

   (a) ____

   (b) ____

   (c) ____

   (d) ____

   (e) ____

3. Bilingualism is defined as ______

Research on bilingualism has shown that ______

4. Animals communicate with one another, and ______

Bonobos, dolphins, and parrots have ______

5. Animal cognition, or comparative cognition, is ______

Recent studies have shown ______

Measuring Intelligence

Preview Questions

Consider the following questions as you study this section of the chapter.

- How is *intelligence* defined?
- What roles did Binet, Terman, and Wechsler play in the development of intelligence tests?

Read the section "Measuring Intelligence" and **write** *your answers to the following:*

1. *Intelligence* is defined as the global capacity to think rationally, act purposefully, and deal effectively with the environment.
2. Alfred Binet, along with psychiatrist Théodore Simon, devised the first intelligence test, Binet-Simon test developed in France, 1905.
3. Lewis Terman translated and adapted ______
4. David Wechsler developed a new intelligence test, the Wechsler tests, used more widely now.

Principles of Test Construction: What Makes a Good Test?

Preview Questions

Consider the following questions as you study this section of the chapter.

- How do achievement tests differ from aptitude tests?
- What does it mean to standardize a test?
- What is the role of norms in standardization, and what is the normal curve?
- How are *reliability* and *validity* defined, and how are they determined?

Read the section "Principles of Test Construction: What Makes a Good Test?" and **write** *your answers to the following:*

1. Achievement tests are designed to ______

   Aptitude tests are designed to ______
2. Standardization refers to administered to large groups of people under uniform conditions to establish norms.

   Norms are the ______
3. The normal curve, or normal distribution, is ______
4. Reliability is defined as ability to produce consistent results when administered on repeated occasions under similar conditions.

   It is determined by ______
5. Validity is defined as ability to measure what the test is intended to measure.

   One way to determine validity is by ______

After you have carefully studied the preceding sections, complete the following exercises.

Concept Check 2

Read the following and write the correct term in the space provided.

1. A Norwegian visitor to England asks the hotel clerk, "Can you please my key to my room give me?" This visitor has apparently not yet mastered the ________________ of the English language.
2. To fulfill one of the three requirements of good test design, Dr. Houseman administered his new test, under uniform conditions, to a large number of people who were representative of the population of interest. Dr. Houseman has gone through a procedure called ________________, and the scores of this representative group will be used to establish the ________________ against which an individual score will be compared and interpreted.
3. Ten-year-old Jean performed at the same level as most 12-year-olds on Binet's test. Her ________________ age is different from her ________________ age.
4. According to his score on the Stanford–Binet test, Marcel's mental age is identical to his chronological age. Marcel's IQ score would be ________________.
5. When 25-year-old Dagmar applied for a position with the Department of Defense, she was given a test. She scored slightly above the norm on overall verbal ability but well above the norm in overall performance for her age group. The test Dagmar was given was a(n) ________________, called the ________________.
6. The test and retest scores on the new Zander jealousy scale were highly similar but lacked predictive value; furthermore, it was not clear exactly what human attribute it was measuring. The Zander test was high in ________________ but low in ________________.
7. Marta is thoroughly enjoying reading the latest book in a series that recounts the adventures of children who attend a special school for wizards and witches. The author of these books has an extraordinary talent for telling interesting and exciting tales about nonexistent places and people. This ability to communicate meaningfully about imaginary events and characters demonstrates two important characteristics of language; one is called ________________, and the second is that language is ________________, or ________________.
8. Twelve-year-old Golnaz was given a standardized intelligence test, specially designed for children. She is most likely to have taken the ________________.

Review of Terms, Concepts, and Names 2

Use the terms in this list to complete the Matching Exercise, then to help you answer the True/False items correctly.

language
symbols
syntax
generative
displacement
bilingualism
balanced proficiency
Alzheimer's disease (dementia)
cognitive reserve
linguistic relativity hypothesis (Whorfian hypothesis)
animal cognition (comparative cognition)
intelligence
Alfred Binet
mental age
Lewis Terman
Stanford–Binet Intelligence Scale
intelligence quotient (IQ)
Army Alpha and Army Beta tests
David Wechsler
Wechsler Adult Intelligence Scale (WAIS)
verbal score
performance score
Wechsler Intelligence Scale for Children (WISC) and the Wechsler Preschool and Primary Scale of Intelligence (WPPSI)
achievement test
aptitude test
standardization
norms
normal curve (normal distribution)
reliability
validity

Matching Exercise

Match the appropriate term/name with its definition or description.

1. ________________ Every language's unique rules for combining words.
2. ________________ The French psychologist who, along with French psychiatrist Théodore Simon, developed the first widely used intelligence test.
3. ________________ The ability to communicate meaningfully about ideas, objects, and activities that are not physically present.

4. ________________ Measure of intelligence in which an individual's mental level is expressed in terms of the average abilities of a given age group.
5. ________________ Name of Lewis Terman's translation and revision of the Binet-Simon intelligence test.
6. ________________ The ability of a test to measure what it is intended to measure.
7. ________________ Characteristic of language that allows one to create an infinite number of new and different phrases and sentences.
8. ________________ The study of animal learning, memory, thinking, and language.
9. ________________ Bell-shaped distribution of individual differences in a normal population in which most scores cluster around the average score.
10. ________________ The global capacity to think rationally, act purposefully, and deal effectively with the environment.
11. ________________ System for combining arbitrary symbols to produce an infinite number of meaningful statements.
12. ________________ Two tests developed by David Wechsler for testing children's intelligence.
13. ________________ Term used for sounds, written words, or, as in American Sign Language, formalized gestures.
14. ________________ Fluency in two or more languages.
15. ________________ Condition whose symptoms include deterioration in memory and other cognitive functions.

True/False Test

Indicate whether each item is true or false by placing T or F in the space next to each item.

1. ____ Lewis Terman was the American psychologist who translated and adapted the Binet-Simon intelligence test for use in the United States.
2. ____ David Wechsler was the American psychologist who developed the Wechsler Adult Intelligence Scale (WAIS), the most widely used intelligence scale.
3. ____ An aptitude test is designed to measure a person's level of knowledge, skill, or accomplishments in a particular area, such as mathematics or a foreign language.
4. ____ The intelligence quotient (IQ) is a measure of general intelligence derived by comparing an individual's score with that of others in the same age group.
5. ____ The *verbal score* on the WAIS reflects scores on subtests such as identifying missing parts in incomplete pictures, arranging pictures to tell a story, or arranging blocks to match a given pattern.
6. ____ Reliability refers to the ability of a test to produce consistent results when administered on repeated occasions under similar conditions.
7. ____ Standardization is the process of administering a test to a large, representative sample of people under uniform conditions for the purpose of establishing norms.
8. ____ An achievement test is designed to measure a person's capacity to benefit from education or training.
9. ____ The *performance score* on the WAIS represents scores on subtests of vocabulary, comprehension, knowledge of general information, and other similar tasks.
10. ____ The Wechsler Adult Intelligence Scale (WAIS) is an adult intelligence test with scores on 11 subtests that are grouped to provide an overall verbal score and a performance score.
11. ____ The scores of the large number of representative subjects for whom the test is designed establish the *norms* or the standards against which an individual score is compared and interpreted.
12. ____ The notion that differences among languages causes differences in the thoughts of their speakers is called the linguistic relativity hypothesis.
13. ____ Speakers who are equally fluent in two languages have *balanced proficiency.*
14. ____ The Army Alpha test was administered in writing and the Army Beta tests was administered orally to recruits and draftees who could not read.
15. ____ Speaking two or more languages appears to build up a cognitive reserve that can help protect against cognitive decline in late adulthood.

Check your answers and review any areas of weakness before going on to the next section.

The Nature of Intelligence

Preview Questions

Consider the following questions as you study this section of the chapter.

- What are the two key issues involved in the debate over the nature of intelligence?
- What is the *g* factor (general intelligence), and who first proposed a theory regarding its existence?
- What was Louis L. Thurstone's contribution to the debate about the nature of intelligence?
- Who proposed the idea of "multiple intelligences," and what are his eight distinct intelligences?
- What are autism, Asperger's syndrome, and mental retardation, and what distinguishes autism from Asperger's syndrome?
- What is the triarchic theory of intelligence, and who proposed it?

*Read the section "The Nature of Intelligence" and **write** your answers to the following:*

1. The two key issues involved in the debate over the nature of intelligence are as follows:
   (a) ____________________
   ____
   (b) ____________________
   ____
2. The *g* factor (or general intelligence) is the notion ____________________
   ____
   It was proposed by ____________________
3. Louis L. Thurstone proposed the notion that
   ____
   ____
4. The idea of "multiple intelligences" was proposed by ____________________
   The eight intelligences he proposed are ____________________
   ____
   ____
   ____
5. The triarchic theory of intelligence proposes that ____________________
   ____
   ____
   It was developed by ____________________
6. Autism is ____________________
   ____
   ____
   Asperger's syndrome is ____________________
   ____
   ____
   ____
   Mental retardation is ____________________
   ____
   ____
   Unlike children with autism, children with Asperger's syndrome show ____________________
   ____
   ____
   ____

The Roles of Genetics and Environment in Determining Intelligence

Preview Questions

Consider the following questions as you study this section of the chapter.

- What is the heredity–environment issue?
- How are twin studies used to measure genetic and environmental influences?
- What is heritability, and why can't heritability estimates be used to explain differences between groups?
- What social, psychological, and cultural factors affect performance on intelligence tests?
- Are IQ tests culturally biased?

*Read the section "The Roles of Genetics and Environment in Determining Intelligence" and **write** your answers to the following:*

1. The basic heredity–environment issue is concerned with ____________________
   ____
   ____
   ____
2. Twin studies have been used because ____________________
   ____
   ____
   ____
   ____

3. *Heritability* is defined as ____

   Heritability estimates cannot be used to explain differences between groups because ____

4. Factors that affect performance on intelligence tests are
   (a) ____
   (b) ____
   (c) ____

5. It is virtually impossible to create a culture-free IQ test because ____

After you have carefully studied the preceding sections, complete the following exercises.

Concept Check 3

Read the following and write the correct term in the space provided.

1. Although Dr. Bowman recognizes that particular individuals might excel in specific areas, she believes that a factor, called general intelligence, or the *g* factor, is responsible for overall performance on mental ability tests. Her belief about the nature of intelligence is most consistent with the approach taken by psychologist ________________ .
2. Jamal is a highly valued maintenance worker because of his almost uncanny ability to fix nearly any piece of equipment that breaks down. Jamal is demonstrating what Robert Sternberg would call ________________ intelligence.
3. Selma is a very successful, highly motivated, goal-directed, and creative graphic designer. These aspects of her intelligence are ________________ (not likely/very likely) to be assessed and measured on a conventional intelligence test.
4. Dicky and Ricky are identical twins and have almost identical IQ scores despite the fact that they were separated at birth and raised in different environments. Fraternal twins Joel and Joanna were raised together but their IQ scores are much less similar than Dicky and Ricky's scores. This example provides the most support for the ________________ side in the heredity–environment debate.
5. Compared with the scores of two randomly selected unrelated people of the same age, the IQ scores of fraternal twins Joel and Joanna are much more similar. This finding provides the most support for the ________________ side in the heredity–environment debate.
6. Dr. Yokomoto, like the majority of experts on intelligence testing, is most likely to attribute the finding that Japanese and Chinese children outperform American children on mathematics achievement tests to ________________ factors.
7. When Dr. Parsei, an expert on intelligence testing, was asked if a completely culture-free intelligence test could be designed, he replied that it ________________ (was possible/was not possible) because group ability tests reflect the values, knowledge, and communication strategies of their culture of origin.
8. Professor Kensington suggests that there are seven "primary mental abilities," which are relatively independent elements of intelligence. These abilities include verbal comprehension, numerical ability, reasoning, and perceptual speed. Dr. Kensington's views of intelligence are most consistent with those of ________________ .
9. Constantino is a very successful salesperson. His success is due, in part at least, to his ability to understand and respond appropriately to other people's emotions, motives, and intentions. Constantino demonstrates ________________ intelligence, one of the eight intelligences proposed by ________________ .

10. Yan is an expert chess player with an exceptional ability to mentally visualize the relationship of the various chess pieces following different moves. Howard Gardner labeled this type of intelligence ______________________ .
11. Before taking a challenging math test Chung Yee was reminded of the cultural stereotype that Asian Americans have superior math skills. She scored significantly higher than her equally gifted friend Jee Young, who was reminded before the same test of the stereotype that females are poor at math. The unexpected difference in their performance on the same test may be the result of what psychologist Claude Steele called the ______________________ .
12. Researchers calculated that approximately 50 percent of the differences in IQ scores within a given population was due to genetic factors. They have calculated the ______________________ of the variation within that group that is due to heredity.
13. According to the Prologue, Tom is intellectually gifted but has a number of problems, including cognitive rigidity, inflexible thinking, a tendency toward functional fixedness, and some impairments in social aspects of his life. Tom has been diagnosed with a condition called ______________________ .

Graphic Organizer 1

Read the following statements and decide which psychologist is most associated with each.

Statement	Psychologist
1. I define intelligence as the global capacity to think rationally, act purposefully, and deal effectively with the environment; a good IQ test should have both verbal and performance scores representing subtests that measure a variety of abilities.	
2. My theory of intelligence emphasizes both universal aspects of intelligent behavior and the importance of adapting to the individual's particular social and cultural environment; there are essentially three forms of intelligence: analytical, creative, and practical intelligence.	
3. I'm not sure I have a fully developed theory of intelligence, but I do believe that we can help children do better in school if we devise tests that can identify those who need help and then provide that help. There is a great deal of variation in intelligence in any age group of children.	
4. I am convinced that a factor called general intelligence, or the *g* factor, is responsible for overall performance on mental ability tests. Furthermore, I would go so far as to say that intelligence can be accurately expressed as a single number that reflects an individual's intellectual abilities.	
5. I disagree with those who say that intelligence is a single, general mental capacity. On the basis of my observations of what is valued in different cultures, I've concluded that there are eight intelligences, each independent of the other, and these must be viewed in the context of a particular culture.	
6. I tend to agree with statement 4 above. In addition, I believe that intelligence can best be expressed by a number I call the intelligence quotient, or IQ, which is derived by dividing the mental age by the chronological age and multiplying the result by 100.	

Graphic Organizer *(contnued)*

Statement	Psychologist
7. I do not agree with the notion that intelligence is a single general mental capacity. Instead, I believe that there are a number of different "primary mental abilities" such as verbal comprehension, numerical ability, reasoning, and perceptual speed, and that each one is a relatively independent element of intelligence. In my view, the so-called *g* factor is simply an overall average score of these independent abilities and is therefore less important than an individual's specific pattern of mental abilities.	

Review of Terms, Concepts, and Names 3

Use the terms in this list to complete the Matching Exercise, then to help you answer the True/False items correctly.

Charles Spearman	successful intelligence
general intelligence, or the *g* factor	analytic intelligence
Louis L. Thurstone	creative intelligence
Howard Gardner	practical intelligence
autism	identical twins
Asperger's syndrome	fraternal twins
mental retardation	heritability
Robert Sternberg	Claude Steele
triarchic theory of intelligence	Flynn effect
	stereotype threat
	creativity

Matching Exercise

Match the appropriate term/name with its definition or description.

1. ________________ Contemporary American psychologist whose triarchic theory of intelligence identifies three forms of intelligence (analytical, creative, and practical).
2. ________________ The percentage of variation within a given population that is due to heredity.
3. ________________ Factor of intelligence that is thought by some to be responsible for a person's overall performance on tests of mental ability.
4. ________________ Group of cognitive processes used to generate useful, original, and novel ideas or solutions to problems.
5. ________________ American psychologist who advanced the theory that intelligence is composed of several primary mental abilities and cannot be accurately described by an overall general, or *g*, factor measure.
6. ________________ Sternberg's type of intelligence that involves the ability to adapt to the environment and often reflects what is commonly described as street smarts.
7. ________________ British psychologist who advanced the theory that a general intelligence factor, called the *g* factor, is responsible for overall intellectual functioning.
8. ________________ According to Sternberg, a form of intelligence that involves the ability to deal with novel situations by drawing on existing skills and knowledge.
9. ________________ Psychological predicament in which fear that you will be evaluated in terms of a negative stereotype about a group to which you belong creates anxiety and self-doubt, lowering performance in a particular domain that is important to you.
10. ________________ Behavioral syndrome associated with differences in brain functioning and sensory responses, and which is characterized by impaired social interaction, impaired verbal and nonverbal communication skills, repetitive or odd motor skills, and highly restricted interests and routines.

True/False Test

Indicate whether each item is true or false by placing T or F in the space next to each item.

1. ____ Howard Gardner is a contemporary American psychologist who expanded on Thurstone's basic notion of intelligence as different mental abilities, proposing that there are eight independent intelligences that are biologically distinct and controlled by different parts of the brain.
2. ____ Identical twins develop from two different fertilized eggs and are 50 percent genetically similar to each other.

3. ____ Mental retardation is a disorder characterized by intellectual function that is significantly below average, usually defined as a measured IQ of 70 or below and which is caused by brain injury, disease, or a genetic disorder.
4. ____ Analytic intelligence refers to the mental processes used in learning how to solve problems, that is, in picking a problem-solving strategy and applying it to solve problems.
5. ____ Fraternal twins share exactly the same genes because they developed from a single fertilized egg that split into two.
6. ____ Sternberg's theory that there are three forms of intelligence—analytic, creative, and practical—is called the triarchic theory of intelligence.
7. ____ Successful intelligence involves three distinct types of mental ability—analytic, creative, and practical.
8. ____ Claude Steele is a contemporary American social psychologist whose research has focused on the effects of stereotypes and who is credited with coining the term *stereotype threat*.
9. ____ Asperger's syndrome is a behavioral syndrome characterized by varying degrees of difficulty in social and conversational skills but normal-to-above-average intelligence and language development; often accompanied by obsessive preoccupation with particular topics or routines.
10. ____ The Flynn effect refers to the finding that average IQ scores have improved in several cultures and countries during the past few generations, a phenomenon that points to the importance of environmental factors in determining IQ scores.

Check your answers and review any areas of weakness before going on to the next section.

Something to Think About

1. Many people mistakenly believe that creativity is restricted to a few gifted, genius-level, artistic people. What would you tell someone who wants to be creative but does not believe he or she possesses an artistic temperament?
2. People vary in their IQ test scores, but about 68 percent of scores on tests such as the WAIS-IV are between 85 and 115, the range for normal intelligence. A friend comes to you and says, "Wouldn't it be great if we all had above-average IQ scores? Just think how wonderful life would be and how happy and successful we'd be!" How might you enlighten your friend about IQ tests and IQ scores?

Check your answers and review any areas of weakness before doing the progress tests.

Progress Test 1

Review the complete chapter (including all boxed inserts), review all your study notes, and then test yourself on the following progress test. Check your answers. If you make a mistake, review your notes, check the appropriate section in the study guide, and, if necessary, go back and read the relevant part of the chapter in your textbook.

1. In applying for a job at O'Hare Airport, Lynda is given a test to see if she is suited to be an air traffic controller. This is an example of ________________ testing.
   (a) intelligence
   (b) achievement
   (c) aptitude
   (d) motivational
2. When Aaron is asked to define *weapon,* he responds that it is anything you could use to beat someone with. Aaron is using the word *weapon* as a
   (a) natural concept.
   (b) algorithm.
   (c) formal concept.
   (d) heuristic.
3. Like Aaron, Michelle is asked to define *weapon.* She replies that a weapon is one of a variety of instruments, or objects, that can be used to defend, attack, hurt, maim, or kill. Furthermore, the term *weapon* can even refer to words in a phrase, as in "the pen is mightier than the sword." Michelle is using the word *weapon* as a
   (a) natural concept.
   (b) prototype.
   (c) formal concept.
   (d) heuristic.
4. When 3-year-old Claudia is asked which letter of the alphabet comes before *g*, she recites the alphabet from the beginning until she arrives at the solution. Claudia is using ________________ to solve the problem.
   (a) trial and error
   (b) insight
   (c) an algorithm
   (d) a heuristic

5. Louis forgot to bring his pillow when he went camping for the weekend, so he spent a very uncomfortable night. It didn't occur to Louis that he could use his down-filled jacket as a pillow. This example best illustrates
   (a) functional fixedness.
   (b) mental set.
   (c) the availability heuristic.
   (d) use of an algorithm.

6. When Vasilis is faced with the decision of which of two equally attractive apartments to rent, he makes a list of what is most important and gives each factor a numerical rating. It appears that Vasilis is using the ________________ model of decision making.
   (a) elimination-by-aspects
   (b) additive
   (c) single-feature
   (d) heuristic

7. Jerome recently saw a TV special in which most of the psychologists interviewed were middle-aged, bearded males. When he took his first psychology class, he was surprised to find that his professor was a young female rather than an older, bearded male. Jerome's surprise is probably due to his use of the
   (a) availability heuristic.
   (b) elimination-by-aspects model.
   (c) single-feature model.
   (d) additive model.

8. When Heidi tells Hans that she is going to enter a foot race to raise funds to end the arms race, he has no trouble understanding that she is going to run in a race to generate support for an anti-weapons cause. Hans's correct interpretation best illustrates the importance of
   (a) syntax. (c) generativity.
   (b) displacement. (d) prototypes.

9. In the course of doing some research for a term paper, Anet read about the psychologist who is best known for developing the first intelligence test. She also discovered that this psychologist believed his test could help identify children who needed special help. Anet was reading about
   (a) Charles Spearman. (c) Alfred Binet.
   (b) Lewis Terman. (d) Louis L. Thurstone.

10. Six-year-old Bruce's performance on an intelligence test is at a level characteristic of an average 4-year-old. Bruce's mental age is
    (a) 8. (c) 6.
    (b) 4. (d) 5.

11. Scott is a very bright 10-year-old with a mental age of 13. If tested on the Stanford–Binet Intelligence Scale, his IQ score would most likely be
    (a) 100. (c) 150.
    (b) 77. (d) 130.

12. Twenty-year-old Val has just taken a test that includes vocabulary, comprehension, general knowledge, object assembly, and other subtests. Val has completed the
    (a) WAIS. (c) WISC.
    (b) WPPSI. (d) Stanford–Binet.

13. In Dr. Wilson's survey of intelligence test scores around the world, 14 nations were found to have shown significant gains in average IQ scores in just one generation. Based on these results and evidence from similar studies, Dr. Wilson is most likely to conclude that
    (a) average scores increased significantly because IQ tests were revised and made "culture-free" or "culture-fair."
    (b) IQ scores cannot be improved by environmental factors because intelligence is genetically determined.
    (c) the changes in IQ test scores can be accounted for by mutations in the gene that influences intellectual potential, and this can happen in one generation.
    (d) the changes in IQ test scores can be accounted for only by environmental factors because the amount of time involved was too short for genetic influences.

14. As discussed in the Prologue, Tom has been diagnosed with Asperger's syndrome. According to Critical Thinking (Neurodiversity: Beyond IQ), Tom is likely to
    (a) have a low score on the Raven's Progressive Matrices test (50 or below) and a high score on the WAIS (100 or above).
    (b) have an IQ score of 70 or below accompanied by intellectual functioning that is significantly below average, but still have a high level of social competence.
    (c) show abnormal and retarded language development, to have narrow interests and inflexible behavior, and by definition, have an IQ of 70 or below

(d) show normal, even advanced language development, to have narrow interests and inflexible behavior, and by definition, have an IQ in the normal-to-above-average level.

15. Critical Thinking (The Persistence of Unwarranted Beliefs) discusses how unwarranted beliefs in pseudosciences or other areas can persist, and how contradictory evidence can actually strengthen a person's established beliefs. A number of obstacles to logical thinking about unwarranted beliefs are discussed. Which of the following is NOT one of those obstacles?
(a) the belief-bias effect
(b) the confirmation bias
(c) the underestimation effect
(d) the fallacy of positive instances

Progress Test 2

After you have checked your understanding of the material in Progress Test 1 and have done a complete chapter review with special focus on any areas of weakness, you are now ready to assess your knowledge on Progress Test 2. Check your answers. If you make a mistake, review your notes, the relevant section of the study guide, and, if necessary, the appropriate part of your textbook.

1. As part of his overall vocational assessment, Steven took a test that measured his level of knowledge, skills, and accomplishments in particular areas such as mathematics and writing ability. Steven took a(n) ______________ test.
(a) aptitude (c) intelligence
(b) achievement (d) motivational

2. When Katrina is asked to identify the letters of the alphabet that do not have curved lines, she tries to mentally picture each letter as she completes the task. Katrina is using
(a) mental imagery. (c) a formal concept.
(b) a natural concept. (d) a prototype.

3. Shawn is asked to memorize a map of an island that has a hut, a lake, a tree, a beach, and a grassy area, all clearly marked at distinct locations. Later, he is asked to imagine a specific location, such as the hut; when a second location, the tree, is named, he has to press a button when he reaches the tree on the visual image in his mind. What are the results of this experiment most likely to reveal about the relationship between the distance between the two points and the time it will take Shawn to scan the mental image of the map?
(a) The greater the distance, the more time it will take Shawn to scan the mental image.
(b) The greater the distance, the less time it will take Shawn to scan the mental image.
(c) The shorter the distance, the more time it will take Shawn to scan the mental image.
(d) All of these statements are false; there is no relationship between distance and time taken to mentally scan points on a map.

4. When Earl is asked what object or objects come to mind in response to the word *vegetable,* he answers "potatoes and carrots." For Earl, potatoes and carrots are
(a) formal concepts. (c) algorithms.
(b) prototypes. (d) heuristics.

5. Dr. Naidu's research is concerned with the study of animal learning, memory, thinking, and language. Dr. Naidu is most likely interested in
(a) understanding the stereotype threat.
(b) investigating the triarchic theory of intelligence.
(c) heritability and heritability estimates.
(d) comparative cognition.

6. When Elana got her new DVD recorder, she spent a lot of time trying different approaches to programming the machine rather than consulting the manual. Elana is using the ____________ approach to problem solving.
(a) algorithm (c) heuristic
(b) trial-and-error (d) insight

7. After spending weeks studying a variety of sources and materials, Terry still couldn't decide on a topic for her seminar presentation. However, when she was out for her daily jog, she suddenly had a flash of inspiration about her topic. Terry solved her problem
(a) through insight.
(b) by using an algorithm.
(c) through functional fixedness.
(d) by using the representativeness heuristic.

8. Whenever his TV picture became fuzzy, Lloyd would bang the top of the TV set, which usually cleared the picture. Recently, when he was viewing a film on his new DVD player, tracking problems created a fuzzy picture; Lloyd banged the top of the TV over and over but to no avail. Lloyd appears to be experiencing a problem-solving obstacle called
   (a) functional fixedness.
   (b) subgoal analysis.
   (c) a mental set.
   (d) confirmation bias.
   (e) prototypical male stupidity.

9. Maria is perfectly fluent in English and Spanish. Research has shown that such balanced proficiency in two languages
   (a) may result in delayed language development in both languages, learning problems, and lower intelligence.
   (b) helps build up a cognitive reserve that can protect against cognitive decline in late adulthood.
   (c) decreases control over attention and lowers the ability to switch attention to new stimuli when needed.
   (d) can accelerate the onset of Alzheimer's disease by four or five years.

10. Dr. Peerless has designed a test to measure the level of scientific knowledge in high school graduates. To establish a norm against which individual scores may be interpreted and compared, she is presently administering the test to a large representative sample of high school graduates. Dr. Peerless is in the process of
   (a) establishing the test's reliability.
   (b) establishing the test's validity.
   (c) standardizing the test.
   (d) determining the test's aptitude.

11. Dr. Peerless needs to check whether her test on the level of scientific knowledge measures what it was designed to measure. She does this by comparing scores on her test with students' grades in high school science courses. In this instance, Dr. Peerless is in the process of
   (a) establishing the test's reliability.
   (b) establishing the test's validity.
   (c) standardizing the test.
   (d) determining the test's aptitude.

12. Arnie is very adept at dealing with novel situations by drawing on previous experience and can often find unusual ways to relate old information to solve new problems. Robert Sternberg would call this ________ intelligence.
   (a) analytic (c) creative
   (b) practical (d) motivational

13. As part of a bizarre experiment in a science fiction story, Dr. Igor places 100 genetically identical infants in different homes. Because the infants are all identical, the heritability of intelligence (that is, the percentage of variation within the group that is due to genetic factors) should be ____________ percent.
   (a) 0 (c) 65
   (b) 50 (d) 100

14. According to In Focus (Does a High IQ Score Predict Success in Life?), which of the following is true?
   (a) IQ scores reliably predict academic success.
   (b) Academic success is no guarantee of success beyond school.
   (c) Many different personality factors are involved in achieving success, such as motivation, emotional maturity, commitment to goals, creativity, and a willingness to work hard.
   (d) All of these statements are true.

15. According to Enhancing Well-Being with Psychology (A Workshop on Creativity), which of the following is NOT a way to increase your creative potential?
   (a) Focus almost exclusively on extrinsic motivation.
   (b) Try different approaches.
   (c) Acquire relevant knowledge.
   (d) Engage in problem finding.

Progress Test 3

After you have checked your understanding of the material in Progress Tests 1 and 2, and have done a complete chapter review with special focus on any areas of weakness, you are ready to further assess your knowledge with Progress Test 3. Check your answers. If you make a mistake, review your notes, the appropriate parts of the study guide, and, if necessary, the relevant sections of your textbook.

1. Adrian took the WAIS test. One aspect of his general cognitive ability that is NOT likely to have been measured is his
   (a) linguistic ability.
   (b) problem-solving ability.

(c) general knowledge.
(d) creativity.

2. Dr. Larch is a renowned researcher and theorist in the area of intelligence testing. Like most experts in his field, Dr. Larch is most likely to agree that
   (a) genetic factors, rather than environmental influences, are the primary cause of any IQ differences found between racial groups.
   (b) within a given racial group, the differences among people are due at least as much to environmental influences as they are to genetic influences.
   (c) the IQ of any individual, regardless of his or her race, is determined almost exclusively by genetic factors and is relatively uninfluenced by environmental influences.
   (d) the IQ of any given individual, regardless of his or her race, is determined almost exclusively by environmental factors and is relatively uninfluenced by genetics.

3. With little or no hesitation, Matthew was able to state that cats and dogs are both examples of the concept of mammal; he was slower to respond when asked whether dolphins and whales were also examples of mammals. This example suggests that
   (a) formal concepts have fuzzy boundaries and that cats and dogs are prototypes of the category.
   (b) natural concepts have fuzzy boundaries and that cats and dogs are prototypes of the category.
   (c) formal concepts have fuzzy boundaries and that dolphins and whales are prototypes of the category.
   (d) natural concepts have fuzzy boundaries and that dolphins and whales are prototypes of the category.

4. Tom created the novel sentence, "The faceless bureaucrat was finally faced with making a face-saving decision but could not face up to the fact that he was in a fatal face-off with his favorite facetious faculty." Tom's ability to do this illustrates the ________________ nature of language.
   (a) syntactic (c) generative
   (b) inflexible (d) practical

5. Dr. Adatia, a cross-cultural psychologist, discovered that children of immigrant Buraku families living in the United States had IQ scores no different from other Japanese Americans, but that the Burakumin in Japan had IQ scores 10 to 15 points lower than those of other Japanese. Dr. Adatia is most likely to conclude that
   (a) IQ scores are genetically determined.
   (b) social discrimination can affect IQ scores.
   (c) better nutrition is the main factor that influences IQ scores.
   (d) the U.S. educational system is better than that of Japan.

6. Dr. Bishop assesses the correlation between scores obtained on two halves of her new abstract reasoning test in order to measure the ________________ of her test.
   (a) reliability (c) norms
   (b) validity (d) aptitude

7. Miguel is extremely adept at learning how to solve problems; that is, he is very good at picking problem-solving strategies and applying them to problems. Robert Sternberg would call this ability a form of
   (a) analytic intelligence.
   (b) creative intelligence.
   (c) practical intelligence.
   (d) general intelligence, or the *g* factor.

8. Dr. Welch believes that there are multiple independent intelligences that cannot be reflected in a single measure of mental ability and that each intelligence must be viewed within a cultural context. Dr. Welch's position is most consistent with the views of
   (a) Charles Spearman.
   (b) L. L. Thurstone.
   (c) Howard Gardner.
   (d) Robert Sternberg.

9. When Allison goes to graduate school, she plans to investigate aspects of the heredity–environment debate as it relates to intelligence. She is most likely to
   (a) use animals, such as rats and pigeons, in her research.
   (b) get involved in twin studies.
   (c) study the language abilities of primates.
   (d) explore creativity and intuition.

10. Maja is writing a paper for her course in comparative cognition. After reviewing all the relevant research on animal language, Maja is likely to conclude that
    (a) only humans possess language capabilities.
    (b) animals can communicate with one another but are not capable of mastering any aspect of language.
    (c) some species have demonstrated an elementary understanding of syntax and certain other aspects of language.
    (d) many animal species can "think," use language, and possess self-awareness.

11. Martin has had some difficulties in school and has fallen behind in academic achievement. His chronological age is 10 and his IQ score on the Stanford–Binet is 70. Martin's mental age is
    (a) 7.
    (b) 10.
    (c) 13.
    (d) 5.

12. Cynthia always buys the brand of paper towels that is on sale, even if it is not the highest quality towel. Cynthia makes her decision about which paper towel to purchase based on the ______________ model of decision making.
    (a) single-feature
    (b) additive
    (c) elimination-by-aspects
    (d) heuristic

13. Jan is orderly, neat, quiet, and shy. She enjoys reading in her spare time and is an avid chess player. Given this description, most people would guess that she is a librarian rather than a real estate agent. This tendency to classify Jan as a librarian illustrates the influence of
    (a) the availability heuristic.
    (b) belief bias.
    (c) the representativeness heuristic.
    (d) the elimination-by-aspects strategy.

14. According to Culture and Human Behavior (The Effect of Language on Perception), the linguistic relativity hypothesis (Whorfian hypothesis)
    (a) proposes that the differences among languages cause differences in the thoughts of their speakers.
    (b) has been supported by the results of dozens of cross-cultural studies.
    (c) suggests that the ability to count and use numerical concepts is an innate capacity of all human beings.
    (d) proposes that color perception does not depend on the language used and that people from cultures that vary in the number of color words used will perceive differences between colors in much the same manner.

15. According to Culture and Human Behavior (Performing with a Threat in the Air: How Stereotypes Undermine Performance), which of the following is (are) true?
    (a) Older people always score lower on memory tests than younger people because forgetfulness and an inability to remember new material is the inevitable consequence of growing old.
    (b) Performance on relatively fair and objective tests may be susceptible to social and cultural influences such as the stereotype threat.
    (c) What other people expect and believe about a person's performance on a test will have no influence on his or her score as long as the test has been standardized.
    (d) Females always score lower than males on advanced math tests because they do not possess the same level of logical-mathematical intelligence as males.

Answers

Introduction: Thinking, Language, and Intelligence

1. *Cognition is* a general term that refers to the mental activities involved in acquiring, retaining, and using knowledge.
2. *Thinking is defined as* the manipulation of mental representations of information in order to draw inferences and conclusions. *It typically involves* active mental processes and is often directed toward some goal, purpose, or conclusion.
3. *A mental image is* a mental representation of objects or events that are not physically present.
4. *We manipulate mental images* in much the same way as we manipulate the actual objects they represent. *Mental images are potentially subject to error and distortion because* they are not perfect duplicates of our actual sensory experience; instead, they are memories of visual images and are actively constructed.
5. *Neuroscientists have shown that when people view faces* specific brain areas such as the fusiform facial area (FFA) become active; *when they view places,* a different brain area called the parahippocampal place area (PPA) becomes active. *The same two brain areas were activated* when people formed a mental image of faces and places.

6. *Concepts are* mental categories of objects, events, ideas, or situations based on properties they share. *The two ways of forming concepts are* learning the rules or features that define the particular concept (formal concept) and as a result of everyday experiences (natural concept).
7. *A prototype is* the most typical instance of a particular concept. *The more closely an item matches a prototype,* the more quickly we can identify it as being an example of the concept.
8. *Exemplars are* individual instances of a concept or category, held in memory. *When we encounter a new object,* we compare it with the exemplars that we have stored in memory to determine whether it belongs to that category.

Solving Problems and Making Decisions

1. *Problem solving is defined as* thinking and behavior directed toward attaining a goal that is not readily available.
2. *The trial-and-error strategy involves* attempting different solutions and eliminating those that do not work. It is useful when there is a limited range of possible solutions.
3. *An algorithm involves* following a specific rule, procedure, or method that inevitably produces the correct solution (such as a mathematical formula). Using an algorithm may not always be practical because of the amount of time it can take to solve some problems.
4. *A heuristic is a* general rule-of-thumb strategy that reduces the number of possible solutions. While it tends to simplify problem solving, it is not guaranteed to solve a given problem.
5. *Insight is the* sudden realization of how a problem can be solved. *Intuition means* coming to a conclusion without conscious awareness of the thought processes involved. Insights, intuitions, or hunches are likely to be accurate only in contexts in which you already have a broad base of knowledge and experience.
6. *Functional fixedness is* the tendency to view objects as functioning only in their usual or customary way. *It may prevent* us from seeing the full range of ways in which an object can be used.
7. *A mental set is* the tendency to persist in solving problems with solutions that have worked in the past. *It may prevent* us from coming up with new, and possibly more effective, solutions.

Decision-Making Strategies

1. *The single-feature model involves* making a decision based on a single feature. *It is appropriate when* the decision is a minor one.
2. *Using the additive model, you first* generate a list of factors that are most important to you, next you rate each alternative using an arbitrary rating scale, and finally, you add up the ratings for each alternative. *It is appropriate for* complex decisions and useful in identifying the most acceptable choice from a range of possible decisions.
3. *Using the elimination-by-aspects model, you* evaluate all the alternatives one characteristic at a time (starting with what you consider to be the most important feature) and systematically eliminate all alternatives that don't meet that criterion until only the one choice that satisfies your criteria remains. *It is appropriate when* the decision is complex and there is a need to narrow down a range of choices with multiple features.
4. *Good decision makers adapt their strategy* to the demands of the specific situation. When there are just a few choices, they tend to use the additive model, but when the decision involves the comparison of many choices that have multiple features they often use more than one strategy (one key to successful problem solving is flexibility).
5. *The availability heuristic is a strategy* in which the likelihood of an event is estimated on the basis of how readily available other instances of the event are in memory. *One problem with this strategy is that* if our memory of the event's frequency is inaccurate, then our estimate of the probability of the event occurring will also be inaccurate.
6. *The representative heuristic is a strategy* in which the likelihood of an event is estimated by comparing how similar its essential features are to our prototype of the event. *This strategy can produce faulty estimates if* we fail to consider possible variations from the prototype or if we fail to consider the approximate number of prototypes that actually exist.

Concept Check 1

1. insight
2. representativeness heuristic
3. cognitive; thinking
4. mental image
5. formal

6. natural
7. algorithm
8. trial-and-error
9. additive
10. exemplar
11. the same

Matching Exercise 1

1. elimination-by-aspects model
2. thinking
3. prototype
4. insight
5. single-feature model
6. representativeness heuristic
7. algorithm
8. trial and error
9. formal concept
10. cognition
11. concept
12. heuristic
13. exemplars

True/False Test 1

1. F	5. T	9. F
2. T	6. T	10. T
3. T	7. T	11. T
4. F	8. F	12. T

Language and Thought

1. *Language is defined as* a system for combining arbitrary symbols to produce an infinite number of meaningful statements.
2. *The five most important characteristics of language are as follows: (a)* The purpose of language is to communicate; to do so, language requires the use of symbols; their connection to meaning is arbitrary. *(b)* The meaning of these arbitrary symbols is shared by others who speak the same language. *(c)* Language is a highly structured system that follows rules for combining words (syntax). *(d)* Language is creative, allowing for the generation of an infinite number of new and different phrases and sentences (generative). *(e)* Language involves displacement, the ability to communicate meaningfully about ideas, objects, and activities that are not physically present.
3. *Bilingualism is defined as* having fluency in two or more languages. *Research on bilingualism has shown that* when speakers are equally fluent in two languages (balanced proficiency) they are better able to control attention and inhibit distracting information than are monolinguals (they have increased mental agility); they are better at switching attention to new stimuli when they need to; they are better at taking the perspective of others. In addition, bilingualism helps build a cognitive reserve that can protect against cognitive decline in late adulthood.
4. *Animals communicate with one another, and* some can be taught to communicate with humans. *Bonobos, dolphins, and parrots have demonstrated* an elementary grasp of the rules of syntax.
5. *Animal cognition, or comparative cognition,* is the study of animal learning, memory, thinking, and language. *Recent studies have shown* many instances of cognitive abilities in various bird species and elephants.

Measuring Intelligence

1. *Intelligence is defined as* the global capacity to think rationally, act purposefully, and deal effectively with the environment.
2. *Alfred Binet, along with psychiatrist Théodore Simon, devised* a series of tests to measure different elementary mental abilities, such as memory, attention, and the ability to understand similarities and differences; his research led Binet to the idea of a mental age.
3. *Lewis Terman translated and adapted* Binet's intelligence test (the Stanford–Binet Intelligence Scale) and developed the concept of the intelligence quotient, or IQ.
4. *David Wechsler developed a new intelligence test,* the Wechsler Adult Intelligence Scale (WAIS), which was designed specifically for adults, and its 11 subtest scores (measuring a variety of abilities) can be grouped to provide an overall verbal score and performance score. He also devised the WISC and WPPSI.

Principles of Test Construction: What Makes a Good Test?

1. *Achievement tests are designed to* measure a person's level of knowledge, skill, or accomplishment in a particular area. *Aptitude tests are designed to* assess a person's capacity to benefit from education or training.
2. *Standardization refers to* the administration of a test to a large, representative sample of

people under uniform conditions for the purpose of establishing norms. *Norms are the* standards against which an individual score is compared and interpreted.

3. *The normal curve, or normal distribution, is* a bell-shaped distribution of individual differences in a normal population in which most scores cluster around the average score.
4. *Reliability is defined as* the ability of a test to produce consistent results when administered on repeated occasions under similar conditions. *It is determined by* administering two similar, but not identical, versions of the test at different times, or by comparing the scores on one half of the test to the scores on the other half of the test.
5. *Validity is defined as* the ability of a test to measure what it is intended to measure. *One way to determine validity is by* demonstrating the predictive value of a test.

Concept Check 2

1. syntax
2. standardization; norms
3. mental; chronological
4. 100
5. IQ test; WAIS
6. reliability; validity
7. displacement; creative; generative
8. Wechsler Intelligence Scale for Children (WISC)

Matching Exercise 2

1. syntax
2. Alfred Binet
3. displacement
4. mental age
5. Stanford–Binet Intelligence Scale
6. validity
7. generative
8. animal cognition (comparative cognition)
9. normal curve (normal distribution)
10. intelligence
11. language
12. Wechsler Intelligence Scale for Children (WISC) and Wechsler Preschool and Primary Scale of Intelligence (WPPSI)
13. symbols
14. bilingulism
15. Alzheimer's disease

True/False Test 2

1. T	5. F	9. F	13. T
2. T	6. T	10. T	14. T
3. F	7. T	11. T	15. T
4. T	8. F	12. T	

The Nature of Intelligence

1. *The two key issues involved in the debate over the nature of intelligence are as follows: (a)* Is intelligence a single, general ability or is it better described as a cluster of different mental abilities? *(b)* Should the definition of intelligence be restricted to the mental abilities measured by IQ and other intelligence tests, or should it be defined more broadly? (There is much disagreement among psychologists about the nature of intelligence and how it should be defined and measured.)
2. *The* g *factor (or general intelligence) is the notion* of a general intelligence factor that is responsible for a person's overall performance on tests of mental ability. *It was proposed by* Charles Spearman.
3. *Louis L. Thurstone proposed the notion that* intelligence is a cluster of seven different primary mental abilities, each a relatively independent element of intelligence.
4. *The idea of multiple intelligences was proposed by* Howard Gardner. *The eight intelligences he proposed are* linguistic, logical-mathematical, musical, spatial, bodily-kinesthetic, interpersonal, intrapersonal, and naturalist.
5. *The triarchic theory of intelligence proposes that* there are three distinct forms of intelligence: analytic, creative, and practical. *It was developed by* Robert Sternberg.
6. *Autism is a* behavioral syndrome associated with differences in brain functioning and sensory responses. It is characterized by impaired social interaction, impaired verbal and nonverbal communication skills, repetitive or odd motor skills, and highly restricted interests and routines. *Asperger's syndrome is* a behavioral syndrome characterized by varying degrees of difficulty in social and conversational skills but normal-to-above-average intelligence and language development and is often accompanied by obsessive preoccupation with particular topics and routines. *Mental retardation is* a

disorder characterized by intellectual function that is significantly below average, usually defined as a measured IQ of 70 or below. It is caused by brain injury, disease, or a genetic disorder. *Unlike children with autism, children with Asperger's syndrome show* normal, even advanced, language development; they may exhibit unusually narrow interests and inflexible behavior, but to a much lesser degree than people with autism; and, by definition, they have an IQ in the normal-to-above-average range.

The Roles of Genetics and Environment in Determining Intelligence

1. *The basic heredity–environment issue is concerned with* whether we inherit our intelligence from our parents (genes, or nature) or whether our intellectual potential is primarily determined by our environment and upbringing (nurture). (Because of research by molecular biologists, the issue has become one of how environment influences gene expression.)
2. *Twin studies have been used because* identical twins share exactly the same genes, and any differences between them must be due to environmental factors rather than hereditary differences.
3. *Heritability is defined as* the percentage of variation within a given population that is due to heredity. *Heritability estimates cannot be used to explain differences between groups because* unless the environmental conditions of the two groups are identical, it is impossible to estimate the overall genetic differences between the groups; even if intelligence were primarily determined by heredity, which is not the case, IQ differences between groups could still be due entirely to the environment (socioeconomic conditions, cultural values, and so on).
4. *Factors that affect performance on intelligence tests are (a)* social discrimination; the average IQ is lower for members of discriminated-against minority groups. Children belonging to these minority groups have lower IQ scores than children of the dominant group in their societies; belonging to a stigmatized group can negatively affect performance on tests of many different abilities, and cross-cultural research on minority groups around the world find consistent effects of discrimination on test scores in many different societies. *(b)* psychologically, test scores can be negatively affected by the stereotype threat (a psychological predicament in which fear that you will be evaluated in terms of a negative stereotype about a group to which you belong creates anxiety and self-doubt, lowering performance in a particular domain that is important to you). This applies to many different groups: females made aware of the gender stereotype of math ability get lower scores than would be expected, African Americans score lower than whites when the test is presented as measuring "intellectual ability" rather than "problem-solving skills," white males reminded of their racial identity do worse on a math test when they believe they are competing with Asian males, children from lower socioeconomic backgrounds perform more poorly than those from higher socioeconomic backgrounds, older individuals reminded of the stereotype "elderly are forgetful" scored lower on a memory test than did a matched group not given that reminder (on the other hand, awareness of positive expectations—the stereotype lift—can improve performance on tests). *(c)* cultural factors such as motivation, attitude, familiarity with test-taking, and previous experience with test-taking can affect performance and scores on tests. Cultural differences can be involved in test-taking behavior when people from different cultural backgrounds use strategies in problem solving or organizing information that are different from those required on standard intelligence tests, and intelligence tests tend to favor the people from the culture in which they were developed.
5. *It is virtually impossible to create a culture-free IQ test because* ability tests reflect the values, knowledge, and communication strategies of their culture of origin. Cultural differences in test-taking behavior may also affect results. Finally, the stereotype threat can cause students to perform as they think they are expected to perform.

Concept Check 3

1. Charles Spearman
2. practical
3. not likely
4. heredity
5. environment
6. environmental
7. was not possible
8. Louis L. Thurstone
9. interpersonal; Howard Gardner
10. spatial intelligence

11. stereotype threat
12. heritability (or heritability estimate)
13. Asperger's syndrome

Graphic Organizer 1

1. David Wechsler
2. Robert Sternberg
3. Alfred Binet
4. Charles Spearman
5. Howard Gardner
6. Lewis Terman
7. Louis L. Thurstone

Matching Exercise 3

1. Robert Sternberg
2. heritability
3. *g* factor (general intelligence)
4. creativity
5. Louis L. Thurstone
6. practical intelligence
7. Charles Spearman
8. creative intelligence
9. stereotype threat
10. autism

True/False Test 3

1. T	4. T	7. T	10. T
2. F	5. F	8. T	
3. T	6. T	9. T	

Something to Think About

1. Many people would like to be more creative. Fortunately, much can be done to increase our creative potential. The first thing to tell someone is that creativity is hard to define precisely but that most cognitive psychologists agree that creativity is a group of cognitive processes used to generate useful, original, novel ideas and solutions. Creativity is not confined to artistic expression; as indicated in the definition, creativity involves usefulness as well as originality. Based on information in Enhancing Well-Being with Psychology: A Workshop on Creativity, you could then conduct your own mini-workshop on creativity. You can summarize the workshop by using the letters of the word **CREATE** as an acronym: **C**hoose the goal of creativity; **R**einforce creative behavior; **E**ngage in problem finding; **A**cquire relevant knowledge; **T**ry different approaches; **E**xert effort and expect setbacks.
2. First, you could tell your friend that we can't all be above average. The distribution of intelligence scores tends to follow a normal, or bell-shaped, curve, in which most scores cluster around the average score. Next, you could talk a little about the problems involved in defining intelligence. Not even the experts agree. Some think that performance on mental ability tests reflects a general intelligence, or *g* factor; others think there are three forms of intelligence; and some postulate as many as eight types of intelligence. Despite these disagreements, psychologists do agree that intelligence involves such elements as abstract thinking, problem solving, and the capacity to acquire knowledge. They also tend to agree that aspects of intelligent behavior such as creativity, motivation, goal-directed behavior, and adaptation to one's environment are not measured by conventional intelligence tests. Thus, IQ scores reflect the limitations of existing intelligence tests. Finally, although IQ scores may predict academic success, doing well in school is no guarantee of success and happiness in life in general. Many different personality factors are involved in achieving success, such as motivation, emotional maturity, commitment to goals, creativity, and, perhaps most important of all, a willingness to work hard. None of these attributes are measured by traditional IQ tests.

Progress Test 1

1. c	6. b	11. d
2. a	7. a	12. a
3. c	8. a	13. d
4. c	9. c	14. d
5. a	10. b	15. c

Progress Test 2

1. b	6. b	11. b
2. a	7. a	12. c
3. a	8. c	13. a
4. b	9. b	14. d
5. d	10. c	15. a

Progress Test 3

1. d
2. b
3. b
4. c
5. b
6. a
7. a
8. c
9. b
10. c
11. a
12. a
13. c
14. a
15. b

CHAPTER 8

Motivation and Emotion

PREVIEW

Reading the section below first will give you a general sense of the chapter's contents and an initial introduction to some of the major concepts and terms. This will prime you for what you are about to read and help you to develop a "cognitive map" that will guide your study of the material in this chapter. Likewise, reading the **preview questions** at the beginning of each major section will improve your ability to understand, learn, and retain the information.

CHAPTER 8 . . . AT A GLANCE

Chapter 8 is concerned with motivation and emotion. Motivation refers to the forces that act on or within an organism to initiate and direct behavior. Instinct theories, drive theories, incentive theories, arousal theory, and humanistic theories are introduced.

The motivation to eat is influenced by psychological, biological, social, and cultural factors. Set-point theory and the rate at which the body uses energy (basal metabolic rate, or BMR) are discussed in relation to the regulation of body weight. Settling-point models of weight regulation help explain why baseline body weight can change over time. Factors involved in becoming overweight or obese are presented.

Human sexuality is discussed next. The four stages of the human sexual response cycle are presented, and sexual motivation in both humans and other animals is explored. Research findings on genetic factors and brain structures associated with sexual orientation are critically examined.

The section on psychological needs as motivators covers Maslow's hierarchy of needs and Deci and Ryan's self-determination theory (SDT). Competence motivation and achievement motivation are compared, and the Thematic Apperception Test (TAT) is introduced.

Emotions, which involve a subjective experience, a physiological response, and a behavioral or expressive response, are associated with distinct response patterns by the sympathetic nervous system and in the brain. The functions and value of emotions are explained from an evolutionary perspective. Facial expressions for some basic emotions seem to be universal and innate, but expression is also influenced by cultural display rules. The James–Lange, two-factor, and cognitive appraisal theories of emotion are examined. Researchers tend to agree that some emotions do not require a conscious cognitive appraisal.

Enhancing Well-Being with Psychology discusses Albert Bandura's concept of self-efficacy and describes methods for turning our goals into reality.

Introduction: Motivation and Emotion

Preview Questions

Consider the following questions as you study this section of the chapter.

- How is *motivation* defined?
- What three characteristics are associated with motivation?
- How is emotion related to motivation?

Read the section "Introduction: Motivation and Emotion" and ***write*** *your answers to the following:*

1. Motivation refers to ____________________
2. The three characteristics associated with motivation are ____________________
3. Emotions are closely tied to motivational processes (and vice versa) because ____________________

Motivational Concepts and Theories

Preview Questions

- What five categories of theories have historically been included in the study of motivation?
- How does each theory explain motivation, and what are some of the limitations of these theories?
- What lasting ideas did each theory contribute to the study of motivation?

Read the section "Motivational Concepts and Theories" and ***write*** *your answers to the following:*

1. According to the earliest theories of motivation, instinct theories, people are motivated to ____________________

   The limitation of these theories is ____________________

2. According to drive theories, behavior is motivated by ____________________

   Their limitations are ____________________

3. Incentive theories proposed that behavior is motivated by ____________________

   Their limitation is ____________________

   In combination, drive and incentive theories account for ____________________

   The combination is limited because ____________________

4. Arousal theory is based on the notion that people are motivated to ____________________

   What constitutes an optimal level of arousal ____________________

   Sensation seekers tend to ____________________

5. Humanistic theories emphasize the importance of ____________________

   (Limitations of this model are covered later in the chapter.)

6. The key ideas and concepts from each theory that come into play in understanding many human behaviors include ____________________

After you have carefully studied the preceding section, complete the following exercises.

Concept Check 1

Read the following and write the correct term in the space provided.

1. Amber is a graduate student studying the biological, emotional, cognitive, and social forces that activate and direct behavior. Her area of research is ________________ .
2. When Trevor is hungry, he eats. The consumption of food serves to maintain ________________________ .
3. Gurjinder loves bungee jumping, skydiving, and hang gliding. Because of her need for novel and exciting sensory stimulation, she is likely to be dubbed a ________________________ .
4. Mrs. Lewis gives a gold star to any child in her class who gets 100 percent on the weekly spelling test. This example illustrates ________________ theory.
5. Bruno the bear hibernates every winter. This behavior is an example of a(n) ________________ .
6. When Bernice finished her first 10-mile race in less than 100 minutes, she felt totally exhilarated and overjoyed by having achieved her goal. Her intense feelings suggest that ________________ are closely tied to motivation.

Review of Terms and Concepts 1

Use the terms in this list to complete the Matching Exercise, then to help you answer the True / False items correctly.

motivation
activation
persistence
intensity
emotion
instinct theories
fixed action patterns
evolutionary perspective
drive theories
homeostasis
drive
drive state
incentive theories
arousal theory
sensation seeking
humanistic theories of motivation

Matching Exercise

Match the appropriate term / name with its definition or description.

1. ________________ Theories that emphasize the importance of psychological and cognitive components in human motivation, especially the notion that people are motivated to realize their personal potential.
2. ________________ The biological, emotional, cognitive, or social forces that activate and direct behavior.
3. ________________ Basic characteristic commonly associated with motivation that is seen in a person's continued efforts or determination to achieve a particular goal, often in the face of obstacles.
4. ________________ Automatic and innate instinctual behavior patterns, such as migration or mating rituals, displayed by animals.
5. ________________ Need or internal motivational state that activates behavior to reduce the need and restore homeostasis.
6. ________________ Theories that view certain human behaviors as innate and due to evolutionary programming.
7. ________________ Degree to which an individual is motivated to experience high levels of sensory and physical arousal associated with varied and novel activities.
8. ________________ Point of view that considers how our heritage influences human behaviors such as eating habits or the expression of emotions.

True/False Test

Indicate whether each statement is true or false by placing T or F in the blank space next to each item.

1. ____ Incentive theories propose that behavior is motivated by the pull of external goals, such as rewards.
2. ____ Arousal theory is the view that people are motivated to maintain a level of arousal that is optimal—neither too high nor too low.
3. ____ Activation, one of the basic characteristics commonly associated with motivation, is seen in the greater vigor of responding that usually accompanies motivated behavior.
4. ____ Drive theories propose that behavior is motivated by the desire to reduce internal tension caused by unmet biological needs.
5. ____ Homeostasis refers to the notion that the body monitors and maintains internal states, such as body temperature and energy supplies, at relatively constant levels; in general, the tendency to reach or maintain equilibrium.

6. ____ Intensity, one of the basic characteristics commonly associated with motivation, is seen in the initiation or production of behavior.

7. ____ Emotion is a complex psychological state that involves a subjective experience, a physiological response, and a behavioral or expressive response.

8. ____ An unmet biological need, such as hunger, creates a *drive state* that motivates or energizes behavior.

Check your answers and review any areas of weakness before going on to the next section.

Biological Motivation: Hunger and Eating

Preview Questions

Consider the following questions as you study this section of the chapter.

- What factors interact and influence the motivation to eat?
- What is energy homeostasis, and what role do glucose, insulin, the basal metabolic rate, and adipose tissue play in energy homeostasis?
- What is the difference between positive and negative energy balance?
- What are the physiological short-term signals associated with eating, and what role does ghrelin play in hunger?
- What psychological factors trigger eating, and what roles do cholecystokinin (CCK) and sensory-specific satiety play in satiation?
- What are the long-term chemical signals that regulate body weight, and what influences do leptin, insulin, and neuropeptide Y (NPY) have in the long-term regulation of stable body weight?
- What are set-point theory and settling-point models of weight reduction, and how do they differ?

Read the section "Biological Motivation: Hunger and Eating" and ***write*** *your answers to the following:*

1. Eating behavior reflects the complex interaction of ______________________________
____

2. Energy homeostasis refers to ______________________________
____
____

3. Energy homeostasis (energy balance) involves
(a) glucose (blood sugar), which is a ______________________________
____
____
(b) insulin, which is a ______________________________
____
____
(c) basal metabolic rate (BMR), which is
____
____
(d) adipose tissue, which is ______________________________
____

4. Positive energy balance occurs when
____
____
Negative energy balance occurs when
____
____

5. Short-term signals that regulate eating behavior include physiological changes:
About 30 minutes before eating there is
____
____
Once a meal has begun ______________________________
____
____

6. An important internal signal involved in eating is provided by the hormone ghrelin, which is
____
____
Blood levels of ghrelin ______________________________
____
____

7. Psychological factors that trigger eating behavior include
(a) classical conditioning, in which ______________________________
____
____
(b) operant conditioning, in which ______________________________
____
____

8. Satiation refers to ______

Satiation involves signals from ______

and ______

9. Sensory-specific satiety refers to ______

10. Long-term chemical signals that regulate body weight are

(a) leptin, a hormone secreted by the ______

(b) insulin, a hormone secreted by the ______

(c) neuropeptide Y (NPY), a neurotransmitter manufactured ______

The two factors correlated with how much of each hormone is secreted are ______

and ______

11. According to set-point theory ______

According to settling-point models of weight regulation ______

After you have carefully studied the preceding section, complete the following exercises.

Excess Weight and Obesity

Preview Questions

Consider the following questions as you study this section of the chapter.

- What is the body mass index (BMI), and what is the difference between being overweight and being obese?
- What factors contribute to people becoming overweight?
- What factors contribute to people becoming obese?
- How do genetics and environment interact in people susceptible to becoming obese, and what factors are involved in obesity?

Read the section "Excess Weight and Obesity" and ***write*** *your answers to the following:*

1. The body mass index (BMI) is a ______

2. People are considered overweight if ______

Obesity is a condition characterized by ______

3. A number of factors are involved in creating a positive energy balance (when caloric intake consistently exceeds energy expenditure) and in becoming overweight:

(a) Going without sleep disrupts ______

(b) the positive incentive value of certain foods, defined as ______

(c) the "Supersize It" syndrome, a phenomenon in which ______

(d) the cafeteria diet effect, which is ______

(e) the sedentary lifestyle of many people (40 percent of Americans) who never________________

(f) individual differences and lifespan changes are involved because ________________

4. Several factors contribute to obesity:

(a) The interaction of genetics and environment, because ________________

(b) leptin resistance, which refers to ________________

(c) weight cycling (yo-yo dieting), which is ________________

(d) and finally, as noted in Focus on Neuroscience, obese people's brains tend to have fewer________________

which may lead to ________________

After you have carefully studied the preceding section, complete the following exercises.

Concept Check 2

Read the following and write the correct term in the space provided.

1. Shortly before lunch, Farah begins to feel hungry. It is likely that blood levels of the hormone ________________, which is primarily manufactured by cells lining the stomach, have ________________ (increased/decreased).
2. By the end of her family's holiday dinner, Federica declared that she was so full she couldn't eat another bite. Federica is experiencing ____________, a feeling that is promoted, in part at least, by the chemical ________________.
3. Although she was feeling full after her turkey dinner, Federica was still able to eat a plate of her favorite dessert. It appears that her feeling of being full after eating the main course was a ________________ satiety.
4. Although he leads a somewhat sedentary lifestyle, 35-year-old Joshua has been about the same weight, give or take a pound or two, since his late teens. Joshua's relatively consistent weight is called his ________________; instances of stable weight over time, such as Joshua's, provide support for ________________ theory.
5. The regulatory process of matching food intake with energy expenditure that allows Joshua to maintain his typical body weight over time is called ________________.
6. If Dr. Hamagoochi studies the long-term signals that regulate body weight, he is most likely to investigate the effects of three chemical messengers: ________________.
7. Bruno the bear eats large quantities of food during the summer months in order to help him survive hibernation in the winter. His reserve of stored energy or calories is called ____________, or ________________.
8. Benjamin, a lively 60-year-old, noted that as he aged his weight tended to increase somewhat, then stabilize, increase again, and stabilize once again, and so on. Now he is 30 pounds heavier than when he was a young adult. This phenomenon can best be accounted for by the ________________.
9. Mikka multiplied her weight in pounds by 703 and divided the product by her height in inches squared. She has just calculated her ________________. If the resulting number is 30 or greater, she is considered ________________.
10. During his afternoon statistics lecture, Dimitri's mind wandered as he contemplated

the pleasure of having souvlaki, salad, olives, feta cheese, and pita bread for dinner. These foods obviously have a high ________________ for Dimitri.

11. Alice has experienced weight cycling (yo-yo dieting) throughout most of the time she has been attempting to lose weight. Her inability to maintain weight loss may be due in part to ____ ____.

12. Whenever Saul and his friends eat at the International Self-Serve Smorgasbord Deli, which has a wide variety of wonderful foods, they tend to consume substantially more food than they would at the school cafeteria. This phenomenon is called the ____.

13. Charles's calculated BMI is 27.7. Assuming that his BMI is due to fat rather than muscle or bone, he would be considered ________________ (normal/overweight/obese).

Review of Terms and Concepts 2

Use the terms in this list to complete the Matching Exercise, then to help you answer the True/False items correctly.

glucose (blood sugar)
glycogen
insulin
basal metabolic rate (BMR)
adipose tissue
baseline body weight
energy homeostasis (energy balance)
positive energy balance
negative energy balance
ghrelin
positive incentive value
satiation
stretch receptors
cholecystokinin (CCK)
sensory-specific satiety
leptin
neuropeptide Y (NPY)
set-point theory and set-point weight
settling-point models of weight regulation and settling-point weight
body mass index (BMI)
overweight
obese (or obesity)
cafeteria diet effect
leptin resistance
weight cycling (yo-yo dieting)

Matching Exercise

Match the appropriate term with its definition or description.

1. ________________ An organism's typical body weight.
2. ________________ When the body is at rest, the rate at which it uses energy for vital functions, such as heartbeat and respiration.
3. ________________ Compound formed and stored in the liver and the muscles that can easily be reconverted into glucose for energy.
4. ________________ A numerical scale indicating adult height in relation to weight that is calculated by multiplying weight in pounds by 703 and dividing the product by height in inches squared.
5. ________________ Body fat that is the main source of stored or reserve energy.
6. ________________ Hormone produced by the pancreas that regulates blood levels of glucose and signals the hypothalamus, regulating hunger and eating behavior.
7. ________________ In the stomach, specialized sensory receptors that communicate sensory information to the brainstem.
8. ________________ In eating behavior, the long-term matching of caloric intake and caloric energy expenditure.
9. ________________ Reduced desire to continue consuming a particular food.
10. ________________ A condition in which higher-than-normal blood levels of the hormone leptin do not produce the expected physiological response.
11. ________________ Repeated cycles of dieting, weight loss, and weight regain.
12. ________________ Hormone manufactured primarily by cells lining the stomach that stimulates appetite and the secretion of growth hormone by the pituitary gland.
13. ________________ Neurotransmitter found in several brain areas, including the hypothalamus, that stimulates eating behavior and reduces metabolism, promoting a positive energy balance and weight gain.

True/False Test

Indicate whether each statement is true or false by placing T or F in the blank space next to each item.

1. ____ Set-point theory suggests that body weight (the set-point weight) settles, or stabilizes, around the point at which there is a balance between the factors influencing energy intake and energy expenditure.
2. ____ Glucose is the simple sugar that provides energy and is primarily produced by conversion of carbohydrates and fats.
3. ____ In eating behavior, a negative energy balance occurs when caloric intake exceeds calories expended for energy; produced by overeating or overconsumption.
4. ____ In eating behavior, satiation is the feeling of fullness and diminished desire to eat that accompanies eating a meal, and in general, refers to fully or excessively satisfying an appetite or desire.
5. ____ Leptin is a hormone produced by fat cells that signals the hypothalamus, regulating hunger and eating behavior.
6. ____ Cholecystokinin (CCK) is a hormone that is secreted primarily by the small intestines that promotes satiation; also acts as a neurotransmitter in the brain.
7. ____ Settling-point models of weight regulation propose that humans and other animals have a natural or optimal body weight (the settling-point weight) that the body defends from becoming higher or lower by regulating feelings of hunger and metabolism.
8. ____ In eating behavior, positive incentive value is the anticipated pleasure of consuming a particular food and, in general, the expectation of pleasure or satisfaction in performing a particular task.
9. ____ In eating behavior, a positive energy balance occurs when calories expended for energy exceed caloric intake; produced by fasting, dieting, or starvation.
10. ____ Obesity is a condition characterized by excessive body fat and a body mass index (BMI) equal to or greater than 30.
11. ____ People are considered overweight if their BMI is between 25 and 29.9, and is due to fat and not muscle or bone.
12. ____ The tendency to eat more when a wide variety of palatable foods is available is called the cafeteria diet effect.

Check your answers and review any areas of weakness before going on to the next section.

Human Sexuality

Preview Questions

Consider the following questions as you study this section of the chapter.

- What are the four stages of the human sexual response?
- How does sexual motivation differ for lower and higher animals?
- What factors are involved in human sexual behavior?
- What have neuroscientists shown about activity in the brains of people in love?

Read the section "Human Sexuality" and ***write*** *your answers to the following:*

1. The four stages of the human sexual response (and the characteristics of each) are ____________
____
____
____
____
____
____
2. In nonhuman animals, sexual behavior is
____
____

   In higher animals, sexual behavior is ____________
____
____
3. In humans, sexual behavior is not____________
____
____

   For females ____________________
____

   When human males experience lowered levels of testosterone ____________________
____
____

In both men and women, sexual motivation is ______________________________

____

4. Neuroscientists have shown that romantic love activates ______________________________

____

____

Sexual Orientation

Preview Questions

Consider the following questions as you study this section of the chapter.

- What does sexual orientation refer to?
- Why is sexual orientation sometimes difficult to identify?
- What factors have been associated with sexual orientation?
- What has research shown about same-sex couples and their children?

*Read the section "Sexual Orientation" and **write** your answers to the following:*

1. Sexual orientation refers to ______________________________

____

2. Sexual orientation is difficult to identify because ______________________________

____

____

____

____

3. Factors associated with sexual orientation are as follows: ______________________________

____

____

____

____

4. Research on same-sex couples and their children has shown that

(a) ______________________________

____

(b) ______________________________

____

(c) ______________________________

____

After you have carefully studied the preceding section, complete the following exercises.

Concept Check 3

Read the following and write the correct term in the space provided.

1. Mary and her husband James have just shared a fulfilling sexual experience. Unlike Mary, James is not likely to be able to experience another orgasm for a period of time; this is called the ______________ period.
2. Mrs. Jacobson had her ovaries removed because of cancer and is now in perfect health. As a result of the operation, the level of the female sex hormone estrogen will ______________ ; the level of her interest in sexual activity will ______________ (increase/decrease/stay the same).
3. Dr. Jamison surgically removed the testes of an experimental laboratory rat. It is very probable that the rat will experience a(n) ______________ in sexual activity and interest.
4. Hamish, a 25-year-old medical student, is heterosexual; his brother Stuart, a 21-year-old philosophy major, is homosexual. The two brothers differ in their ______________ .
5. Barney and Bailey are identical twins. Barney is gay. Therefore, there is a ______________ (low probability/high probability) that Bailey will also be homosexual.
6. Young Simon has a rather passive, weak-willed father and a strong-willed, assertive mother. Research on early life experiences and sexual orientation indicates that such atypical family relationships ______________ (are/are not) one of the main causes of homosexuality.
7. Kaleigh and Graeme are madly and passionately in love. A brain scan using functional magnetic resonance imaging (fMRI) is likely to show activation in four brain areas associated

with the emotion of happiness. According to Focus on Neuroscience (Romantic Love and the Brain), these four brain areas are also activated in response to ________________ , such as ________________ .

8. Dr. Krebs is an evolutionary psychologist who is interested in cultural patterns of male and female mate preferences and mating behavior. If her results are consistent with previous cross-cultural research, she is likely to find that ________________ are the most important factors in selecting a mate in all cultures studied.
9. To avoid the potential problem of memory bias in the recall of childhood events, researchers followed the development of two groups of boys for approximately 15 years, then compared them on a number of different traits and characteristics. The researchers are trying to avoid the problems associated with ________________ studies by conducting a ________________ study.

Review of Terms, Concepts, and Names 3

Use the terms in this list to complete the Matching Test, then to help you answer the True / False items correctly.

William Masters and Virginia Johnson
excitement phase
plateau phase
orgasm
resolution phase
refractory period
estrus
estrogen
testosterone
sexual orientation
heterosexual
homosexual
bisexual
lesbian
gay
retrospective study
prospective study

Matching Exercise

Match the appropriate term / name with its definition or description.

1. ________________ American scientists who conducted pioneering research in the field of human sexuality and sex therapy.
2. ________________ The second stage in the human sexual response cycle in which physical arousal builds as pulse and breathing rates continue to rise; the penis becomes fully erect, the testes enlarge, the clitoris withdraws but remains sensitive, the vaginal entrance tightens, and vaginal lubrication continues.
3. ________________ A person who is sexually attracted to individuals of the other sex.
4. ________________ For a male, a period of time following orgasm during which he is incapable of having another erection or orgasm.
5. ________________ A person who is attracted to individuals of the same sex.
6. ________________ The first stage in the human sexual response cycle that marks the beginning of sexual arousal and can occur in response to sexual fantasies or other sexually arousing stimuli, physical contact with another person, or masturbation.
7. ________________ Term typically used by male homosexuals to describe their sexual orientation.
8. ________________ Type of study in which a group of people are systematically observed over time in order to discover what factors are associated with a particular trait, characteristic, or behavior.
9. ________________ The direction of a person's emotional and erotic attraction toward members of the opposite sex, the same sex, or both sexes.

True/False Test

Indicate whether each statement is true or false by placing T or F in the blank space next to each item.

1. ____ Estrus refers to the cyclical period during which a nonhuman female animal is fertile and receptive to male sexual advances.
2. ____ The fourth stage of the sexual response cycle, during which both sexes tend to experience a warm physical glow and sense of well-being and arousal returns to normal, is called the resolution phase.
3. ____ A bisexual is sexually attracted to individuals of both sexes.
4. ____ Testosterone, the female sex hormone produced by the ovaries, influences a woman's monthly reproductive cycle.
5. ____ Orgasm is the third and shortest phase of the sexual response cycle, during which blood pressure and heart rate reach their peak and muscles in the vaginal walls and uterus contract rhythmically, as do the muscles in and around the penis as the male ejaculates.
6. ____ Estrogen, the male sex hormone produced by the testes, is responsible for male sexual development.

7. ____ Female homosexuals are usually called lesbians.
8. ____ A retrospective study involves asking people to recall or remember childhood events and behaviors.

Check your answers and review any areas of weakness before going on to the next section.

Psychological Needs as Motivators

Preview Questions

Consider the following questions as you study this section of the chapter.

- What are the key questions associated with theories that emphasize the motivation to satisfy fundamental psychological needs?
- How does Maslow's hierarchy of needs explain human motivation?
- What are some important criticisms of Maslow's theory?
- Which psychologists are associated with self-determination theory, and what are its basic premises?
- What roles do intrinsic and extrinsic motivation play in human behavior?

Read the section "Psychological Needs as Motivators" (up to Competence and Achievement Motivation) and ***write*** *your answers to the following:*

1. The key questions associated with motivational theories that emphasize fundamental psychological needs are
(a) ____________________
(b) ____________________
____
(c) ____________________
____

2. Maslow's hierarchy of needs divides motivation into ____________________
____
____
Maslow believed that people ____________________
____
____
____

3. Criticisms of Maslow's model of motivation are
(a) The concept of self-actualization is ____________________
____
____
(b) Maslow's initial studies on self-actualization
____
____
(c) Despite the claim that self-actualization is an innate motivational goal of all people,
____
____
(d) Maslow's notion that we must satisfy needs at one level before moving to the next level
____
____

4. Self-determination theory is associated with psychologists ____________________
____________________, who contend that in order to realize optimal psychological functioning we must meet three innate and universal psychological needs:
(a) autonomy, which is ____________________
____
____
(b) competence, which is ____________________
____
____
(c) relatedness, which is ____________________
____
____

5. Intrinsic motivation refers to ____________________
____
Extrinsic motivation refers to ____________________
____

Competence and Achievement Motivation

Preview Questions

Consider the following questions as you study this section of the chapter.

- How does competence motivation differ from achievement motivation, and how is achievement motivation measured?

- What characteristics are associated with a high level of achievement motivation, and how does culture affect achievement motivation?

*Read the section "Competence and Achievement Motivation" and **write** your answers to the following:*

1. Competence motivation is displayed when ____
____

2. Achievement motivation refers to ____________
____

   It is measured by the ____________________
____

3. People who score high in achievement motivation tend to ____________________________
____
____
____
____

4. In individualistic cultures, the need to achieve emphasizes ____________________________
____
____

   In collectivistic cultures ________________
____
____

After you have carefully studied the preceding sections, complete the following exercises.

Concept Check 4

Read the following and write the correct term in the space provided.

1. Young Alec practices at the golf range for at least two or three hours most days because he plans to become a professional golfer. His goal and behavior suggest that Alec has a high level of ________________ motivation.
2. Yen Shih and her fellow students believe that it is unacceptable to express pride for personal achievements, but it is acceptable to feel pride in achievements that benefit others. Yen Shih most likely lives in a ____________________ culture.
3. Young Mindy loves painting and spends many enjoyable hours carefully drawing and coloring flowers, butterflies, and birds. Her focused behavior is most likely a result of ________________ motivation
4. Allison wants to prove to herself that she is capable of mastering basic mathematical concepts, so she enrolls in an algebra course and an introductory statistics course. Allison is demonstrating ________________ motivation.
5. Dr. Rosenbaum believes that people are actively growth-oriented and that to realize optimal psychological functioning and growth, three innate and universal psychological needs must be satisfied. Dr. Rosenbaum's views are most consistent with ________________ theory.
6. Sarah studies and rehearses her spelling list because those children who get 100 percent on the weekly test receive a gold star and have their name and prize posted on the bulletin board. Sarah's studying behavior appears to be a function of ________________ motivation.
7. In her counseling practice, Dr. Harrar is often interested in her clients' achievement motivation; to measure their need for achievement (nAch) she is likely to use the ______________________.

Graphic Organizer 1

Identify the theory associated with each of the following statements (note that this covers all the sections on motivation):

Statement	Theory
1. I support the view that behavior is motivated by the desire to reduce internal tension caused by unmet biological needs that push us to behave in certain ways.	
2. I believe in the importance of psychological and cognitive factors in motivation, and especially the notion that people are motivated to realize their personal potential.	
3. I take my lead from Charles Darwin and support the perspective that we are motivated to engage in certain behaviors because of evolutionary programming.	
4. We are of the opinion that people are actively growth-oriented and that optimal human functioning can occur only if the psychological needs of autonomy, competence, and relatedness are satisfied.	
5. We do what we do because of the pull of external goals, such as obtaining rewards, money, or recognition. I believe that learning and cognitive theorists have it right when they say reinforcement, and the expectation of reinforcement, are key factors in motivation.	
6. In my view, we are motivated to maintain an optimal level of arousal that is neither too high nor too low. When arousal is too low, we experience boredom and try to increase arousal by seeking out stimulating experiences; when it is too high, we seek to reduce arousal in less stimulating environments.	

Review of Terms, Concepts, and Names 4

Use the terms in this list to complete the Matching Exercise, then to help you answer the True/False items correctly.

Abraham Maslow
hierarchy of needs
self-actualization
Edward L. Deci and Richard M. Ryan
self-determination theory (SDT)
autonomy
competence
relatedness
intrinsic motivation
extrinsic motivation
internalize and integrate
competence motivation
achievement motivation
Thematic Apperception Test (TAT)
power motivation

Matching Exercise

Match the appropriate term with its definition or description:

1. ________________ The theory that optimal functioning can occur only if the psychological needs for autonomy, competence, and relatedness are satisfied.
2. ________________ Maslow's division of motivation into levels that progress from basic physical needs to psychological needs to self-actualization needs.
3. ________________ To incorporate societal evaluations, rules, and regulations as values or rules that one personally endorses.
4. ________________ A projective test developed by Christiana Morgan and Henry Murray that involves creating stories about vague scenes that can be interpreted in a variety of ways.
5. ________________ Behavior motivated by the desire to attain power or control or influence the behavior of other people or groups.
6. ________________ American humanistic psychologist who developed a hierarchical model of human motivation in which basic needs must first be satisfied before people can strive for self-actualization.
7. ________________ In self-determination theory (SDT), the need to effectively learn and master appropriately challenging tasks.

8. ________________ In self-determination theory (SDT), the need to determine, control, and organize one's own behavior and goals so that they are in harmony with one's own interests and values.

True/False Test

Indicate whether each statement is true or false by placing T or F in the blank space next to each item.

1. ____ Edward L. Deci and Richard M. Ryan developed self-determination theory, which contends that optimal psychological functioning and growth can occur only if the psychological needs of autonomy, competence, and relatedness are satisfied.
2. ____ Extrinsic motivation refers to the desire to engage in tasks that the person finds inherently satisfying and enjoyable, novel, or optimally challenging.
3. ____ Self-actualization was defined by Maslow as "a person's full use and exploitation of talents, capacities, and potentialities."
4. ____ In self-determination theory (SDT), the need to feel attached to others and experience a sense of belongingness, security, and intimacy is called relatedness.
5. ____ The desire to direct one's behavior toward demonstrating competence and exercising control in a situation is called achievement motivation.
6. ____ Intrinsic motivation refers to external factors or influences on behavior, such as rewards, consequences, or social expectations.
7. ____ The desire to direct one's behavior toward excelling, succeeding, or outperforming others at some task is called competence motivation.

Check your answers and review any areas of weakness before going on to the next section.

Emotion

Preview Questions

Consider the following questions as you study this section of the chapter.

- How is *emotion* defined, and what are the three components of emotion?
- How do emotions and moods differ, what functions do emotions serve, and what is emotional intelligence?
- How do evolutionary psychologists view emotions?
- What are the basic emotions, and how are they classified?
- How does culture influence emotional experience?
- What has research shown about gender differences in emotion?

Read the section "Emotion" and ***write*** *your answers to the following:*

1. Emotion is defined as ____

____

____

2. Emotions tend to be ____

____

____

Moods involve ____

____

3. Emotions have many functions, including triggering ____

____

____

____

4. Emotional intelligence is the capacity to

____

____

____

5. According to evolutionary psychologists, emotions are the ____

____

____

____

6. The most common basic emotions that all humans, in every culture, experience are

____

____

7. Cross-cultural research has shown ____________

____

____

8. Cross-cultural researchers have noted that Japanese subjects also categorized emotions along a dimension of ______

   which reflects ______

9. Research has shown that men and women ______

   Compared with men, women tend to be ______

The Neuroscience of Emotion

Preview Questions

Consider the following questions as you study this section of the chapter.

- How is the sympathetic nervous system involved in intense emotional responses?
- What brain structures are involved in emotional experience, and what neural pathways make up the brain's fear circuit?
- How does the evolutionary perspective explain the dual brain pathways for transmitting fear-related information?

Read the section "The Neuroscience of Emotion" and ***write*** *your answers to the following:*

1. The physiological component of emotions such as fear and anger involves the ______

2. The amygdala, which is part of the limbic system, is an ______

   It is involved in ______

3. From an evolutionary perspective, evidence of a direct thalamus→amygdala pathway makes adaptive sense because the amygdala can be activated by ______

   When the amygdala is activated, it sends information along ______

   The second (indirect) pathway, thalamus→cortex→amygdala, allows more complex stimuli to be ______

The Expression of Emotion: Making Faces

Preview Questions

Consider the following questions as you study this section of the chapter.

- What evidence supports the notion that facial expressions for basic emotions are universal?
- What are display rules, and how does culture affect the behavioral expression of emotion?
- How can emotional expression be explained in terms of evolutionary theory?

Read the section "The Expression of Emotions: Making Faces" and ***write*** *your answers to the following:*

1. Research on facial expressions suggests that ______

2. Display rules are social and cultural rules that ______

3. Display rules can vary greatly from culture to culture (and even for different groups within a given culture, such as men and women); consequently, ______

4. The overall conclusion is that the expression of emotions ______________________________

____

____

____

Theories of Emotion: Explaining Emotion

Preview Questions

Consider the following questions as you study this section of the chapter.

- What are the basic principles and key criticisms of the James–Lange theory of emotion?
- What challenges did Walter Cannon present to the James–Lange theory?
- What is the facial feedback hypothesis, and how does this hypothesis and other contemporary research support aspects of the James–Lange theory?
- What are the two-factor and cognitive appraisal theories of emotion, and how do the two theories differ?

Read the section "Theories of Emotion: Explaining Emotion" and write your answers to the following:

1. The James–Lange theory of emotions states that ______________________________

____

____

2. Walter Cannon criticized the James–Lange theory on a number of grounds:

(a) Bodily reactions are ______________________________

____

____

(b) Our emotional reaction to a stimulus is

____

____

(c) When physiological changes are artificially induced, ______________________________

____

(d) People cut off from feeling body changes

____

____

3. Support for some aspects of the James–Lange theory comes from

(a) Damasio's work, which demonstrated that

____

____

(b) the facial feedback hypothesis, which states that ______________________________

____

____

4. Schachter and Singer's two-factor theory of emotion suggests that ______________________________

____

____

5. Cognitive appraisal theory proposes that

____

____

____

6. Although both the two-factor theory and the cognitive appraisal theory emphasize the importance of cognitive appraisal, the two-factor theory states ______________________________

____

____

____

while the cognitive appraisal theory stresses that ______________________________

____

____

After you have carefully studied the preceding sections, complete the following exercises.

Concept Check 5

Read the following and write the correct term in the space provided.

1. Since the end of the semester, Ellen had been feeling very content and relaxed. When she received her transcript in the mail and discovered that she had received an A+ in statistics, she was overwhelmed with excitement and relief. Ellen's two different states (content-

ment and excitement) illustrate the difference between a(n) ________________ and a(n) ________________ .

2. Walking to the parking lot late at night, Camellia suddenly hears footsteps behind her. Her heartbeat and blood pressure increase, her muscles tense, her mouth goes dry, and she begins to perspire. These physiological reactions were activated by her ________________ nervous system and are called the ________________________ response.
3. Mr. Kobayashi is very careful to hide his true feelings and control his facial expressions when in the presence of his company's chief executive officers. This example illustrates the ________________ of his culture.
4. Although Kasper is known for his superior reasoning skills, he appears to lack the ability to manage his own emotions and does not seem to understand or respond appropriately to the emotions of others. It is probable that Kasper is low in ________________ .
5. When Pavel got his layoff notice after five years with the company, he simultaneously experienced a number of emotions—anger, sadness, anxiety, and even relief and a degree of excitement about what the future would hold for him. Pavel has experienced ________________ emotions.
6. Opening what he thought was simply a can of peanuts, generously given to him by his older sister, young Kyle was totally startled and alarmed by the "jack-in-the-box" snake that flew out of the can. His instantaneous startle response was most likely the result of stimulation of the ________________ neural pathway in his brain.
7. In an experiment testing the two-factor theory of emotion, Milbourne was injected with a hormone called ________________ that activated his sympathetic nervous system, causing accelerated heartbeat, rapid breathing, trembling, and so on.
8. Dr. Rhienhard believes that the cognitive interpretation of an event or situation and the personal meaning of that appraisal for the individual determine the emotion experienced. Dr. Rhienhard's view is most consistent with the ________________ theory of emotion.
9. As the result of an accident that damaged her spinal cord, Gerri is paralyzed from the waist down. The fact that her experience of fear, anger, grief, sentimentality, and joyfulness has not been affected by her injury is ________________ (consistent/not consistent) with the proposal made by William James.
10. Whenever she feels a bit gloomy, Danica sings the song "Pretend You're Happy When You're Blue." If she follows the advice of the song, she actually experiences an elevation in her mood. This example is consistent with the ________________ .
11. When Harbinder first rode on the High Peak ski lift, he looked down at the steep slopes beneath him and became aware of his high level of physiological arousal. Suddenly, he felt fearful. Harbinder's experience is best explained by the ________________ theory of emotion.
12. Cecelia decided to tackle the challenging task of becoming a proficient piano player. Although she knew that progress would likely be gradual and that there would be some setbacks along the way, she nevertheless felt that engaging in what Bandura called a ________________ would help strengthen her sense of self-efficacy.

Graphic Organizer 2

Identify the emotion (contentment, alarm, annoyance, boredom, astonishment) associated with each of the following descriptions and indicate where it should go on the matrix below.

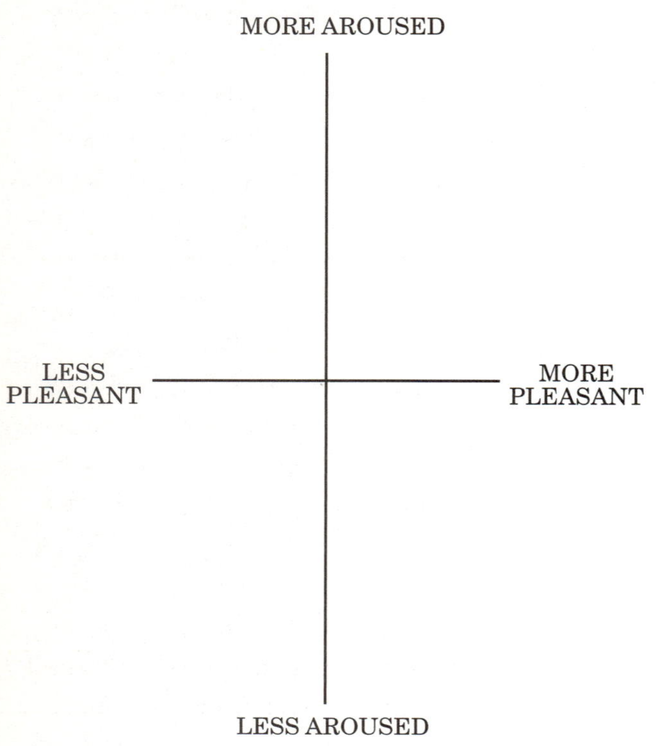

1. Natasha receives an A+ in her third-year history course and can hardly believe it. ________________
2. In the middle of the night, Harry, who lives alone, is startled out of a deep sleep by strange noises coming from the basement. ________________
3. During his three o'clock calculus class, Nathan finds the topic totally uninteresting and starts losing his concentration. ________________
4. On Saturday, Dawn sleeps in and spends most of the morning propped up on comfortable pillows reading a romantic novel. ________________
5. Five minutes after the meter has expired Dhillon arrives at his car only to find he has been given a $20 ticket. ________________

Review of Terms, Concepts, and Names 5

Use the terms in this list to complete the Matching Exercise, then to help you answer the True/False items correctly.

emotion	anthropomorphism
mood	William James
emotional intelligence	James–Lange theory of emotion
Charles Darwin	Walter Cannon
basic emotions	epinephrine (adrenaline)
mixed emotions	somatosensory cortex
interpersonal engagement	facial feedback hypothesis
fight-or-flight response	two-factor theory of emotion
amygdala	cognitive appraisal theory of emotion
limbic system	self-efficacy
thalamus	
Paul Ekman	
emblems	
display rules	

Matching Exercise

Match the appropriate term/name with its definition or description:

1. ________________ English naturalist who was one of the earliest scientists to systematically study emotions and who published *The Expression of the Emotions in Man and Animals* in 1872.
2. ________________ The most fundamental set of categories of emotion, which are biologically innate, evolutionarily determined, and culturally universal.
3. ________________ The capacity to understand and manage your own emotional experiences and to perceive, comprehend, and respond appropriately to the emotional responses of others.
4. ________________ The almond-shaped cluster of neurons in the brain's temporal lobe, involved in memory and emotional responses, especially fear.
5. ________________ Psychologist and emotion researcher who is best known for his work in classifying basic emotions, analyzing facial expressions, and demonstrating that basic emotions and facial expressions are culturally universal.
6. ________________ View that expressing a specific emotion, especially facially, causes the subjective experience of that emotion.

7. ________________ Specific gestures or other nonverbal behaviors that have a particular meaning in a given culture but may vary across cultures.
8. ________________ Schachter and Singer's theory that emotion is the interaction of physiological arousal and the cognitive label we apply to explain the arousal.
9. ________________ The attribution of human traits, motives, emotions, or behaviors to nonhuman animals or inanimate objects.
10. ________________ Hormone secreted by the adrenal glands that is released into the bloodstream in response to physical or emotional stress or excitement.
11. ________________ A complex psychological state that involves a subjective experience, a physiological response, and a behavioral or expressive response.
12. ________________ Group of brain structures involved in emotion, memory, and basic motivational drives, such as hunger, thirst, and sex.

True/False Test

Indicate whether each item is true or false by placing T or F in the space next to each item.

1. ____ The fight-or-flight response is a rapidly occurring series of automatic physical reactions, including accelerated breathing and heart rate, a surge in blood pressure, increased perspiration, dilation of the pupils, and dryness of the mouth.
2. ____ Display rules are social and cultural regulations governing the expression of emotions, especially facial expressions.
3. ____ In more complex situations we may experience mixed emotions, in which very different emotions are experienced simultaneously or in rapid succession.
4. ____ In comparison to an emotion, a mood involves a milder emotional state that is more general and pervasive and may last for a few hours or even days.
5. ____ Interpersonal engagement is a dimension of emotion reflecting the degree to which emotions involve a relationship with another person or people.
6. ____ Walter Cannon was an American psychologist who challenged the James–Lange theory.
7. ____ The James–Lange theory suggests that emotions arise from the perception of body changes.
8. ____ The cognitive appraisal theory of emotion proposes that emotions result from the cognitive appraisal of the situation or stimulus and the personal meaning of events and experiences.
9. ____ Self-efficacy refers to the degree to which a person is convinced of his or her ability to effectively meet the demands of a particular situation.
10. ____ William James was an American psychologist who developed an influential theory of emotion called the James–Lange theory of emotion.
11. ____ All incoming sensory information, with the exception of olfactory sensations, is processed in the *thalamus* before being relayed to sensory centers in the cerebral cortex.
12. ____ The somatosensory cortex processes sensory information from the skin, muscles, and internal organs.

Check your answers and review any areas of weakness before going on to the next section..

Something to Think About

1. Many Americans are obsessed with achieving, or at least getting closer to, the socially desirable goal of thinness. Approximately one-third of all American women and one-quarter of all American males are trying to lose weight, and the weight-loss industry is a multibillion-dollar-a-year enterprise. Based on what you have read in the text, what advice would you give to a friend who is trying to lose weight?
2. Imagine that you have been asked to write a report outlining ways that would help people actually accomplish their goals. Using psychological research presented in the text, consider the various strategies that you might include in your paper on motivation and behavior.

Check your answers and review any areas of weakness before doing the progress tests.

Progress Test 1

Review the complete chapter (including Concept Reviews and the boxed inserts), review all your study notes, and then test yourself on the following progress test. Check your answers. If you make a mistake, review your notes, review the relevant section of the study guide, and, if necessary, go back and read the appropriate part of your textbook.

1. It is an innate characteristic of the European cuckoo to lay her eggs in other birds' nests. This behavior is called ________ and is an example of ________ .
   (a) a fixed action pattern; an instinct
   (b) energy homeostasis; a drive
   (c) a drive; incentive motivation
   (d) anthropomorphism; competence motivation

2. Harland got up in the middle of the night to go to the bathroom. In the dark, he accidentally tripped over his sleeping dog. Both the dog and Harland were instantaneously startled and frightened; the dog barked and Harland screamed. In this instance, it is very probable that the neural pathway involved in their immediate emotional reactions was the
   (a) thalamus→cortex→amygdala pathway.
   (b) hypothalamus→pituitary→cortex pathway.
   (c) thalamus→amygdala pathway.
   (d) amygdala→cortex→thalamus pathway.

3. About 10 or 15 minutes into his weightlifting routine Scott usually begins to perspire heavily. His body's tendency to maintain a steady temperature through the cooling action of sweating is a function of
   (a) instinct.
   (b) incentive motivation.
   (c) energy homeostasis.
   (d) self-actualization.

4. Dr. Range's views are consistent with self-determination theory (SDT). He believes that for people to realize optimal psychological functioning and growth throughout the lifespan, a number of innate and universal needs must be met, namely,
   (a) autonomy, competence, and relatedness.
   (b) competence, interpersonal engagement, and self-efficacy.
   (c) self-actualization, mastery, and self-efficacy.
   (d) relatedness, satiation, and homeostasis.

5. Morrie is a very successful business consultant. His success, in part at least, is due to his capacity to manage and understand his own emotional experiences, and his ability to correctly perceive, comprehend, and respond appropriately to the emotional reactions of his clients. Morrie has a high level of
   (a) emotional intelligence.
   (b) self-determination.
   (c) interpersonal engagement.
   (d) power motivation.

6. Tim buys a lottery ticket every Friday with the expectation that he is going to win some money. His behavior illustrates
   (a) competence motivation.
   (b) incentive motivation.
   (c) drive theory.
   (d) self-actualization.

7. Nicole feels that she has all the material possessions she needs in life and is now determined to devote all her energy to her art. According to Maslow's hierarchy of needs, Nicole is probably striving
   (a) to fulfill her fundamental biological need to paint.
   (b) to fulfill her basic safety needs.
   (c) toward the realization of her personal potential.
   (d) toward the realization of her social needs.

8. Fast-Fat-Fuds offers a double helping of fries with its Sooper Dooper Whooper Burger for only an extra 15 cents; not surprisingly, many people buy the larger meal. This phenomenon is referred to as
   (a) the "Supersize It" syndrome.
   (b) the cafeteria diet effect.
   (c) positive incentive value.
   (d) the energy homeostasis effect.

9. Whenever he sees Amanda, Richard's heart beats faster and he gets a trembling feeling inside. Richard's personal interpretation of his physiological reaction to the sight of Amanda led him to experience the emotion of romantic love. Which theory of emotion is represented in this example?
   (a) self-determination theory (SDT)
   (b) drive theory
   (c) facial feedback theory
   (d) cognitive appraisal theory

10. Dr. LaSage conducted twin studies on sexual orientation. If his findings are consistent with previous research on this topic, he is likely to conclude that
    (a) having an inadequate male role model or having an overly dominant mother is the primary cause of homosexuality.
    (b) sexual orientation is almost completely influenced by environmental factors.
    (c) sexual orientation is at least partly influenced by genetics.
    (d) homosexuality is the result of unpleasant early heterosexual experiences.

11. Zomobia is easily bored and constantly seeks new and stimulating situations; she loves the outdoors and includes among her many interests skydiving, downhill skiing, white water kayaking, and hang gliding. Based on this information about her, it is most probable that Zomobia would be classified as
    (a) a sensation seeker.
    (b) fully self-actualized.
    (c) emotionally intelligent.
    (d) having high extrinsic motivation.

12. As part of his overall vocational assessment, Bertram took the Thematic Apperception Test (TAT). His score on this test is most likely to reveal his level of
    (a) competence motivation.
    (b) need for achievement (nAch).
    (c) self-actualization.
    (d) emotional intelligence.

13. When Rex was a young pup, his owners took him to the vet to have him neutered. If Rex is like most animals, the removal of his testes will very likely result in a(n) ________________ in the levels of the hormone testosterone, and a(n) ________________ in sexual interest and sexual activity.
    (a) increase; decrease
    (b) decrease; decrease
    (c) decrease; increase
    (d) increase; increase

14. One of the most persistent and pervasive gender stereotypes is that women are more emotional than men. Critical Thinking (Are Women Really More Emotional Than Men?) concludes that
    (a) males and females differ significantly in their *experience* of emotion.
    (b) the expression of emotions is strongly influenced by genes and inherited tendencies and relatively unaffected by culturally determined display rules.
    (c) the female role encourages the expression of powerful emotions (anger, hostility, contempt) and the male role encourages the expression of powerless emotions (sadness, shame, guilt).
    (d) women are more emotionally *expressive* than men, but men and women experience emotions in a similar manner.

15. Tracylynne usually starts the semester with the intention of studying hard, achieving high grades, eating a properly balanced diet, and getting lots of exercise. Unfortunately, these good intentions are rarely translated into actual behavior. According to Enhancing Well-Being with Psychology (Turning Your Goals into Reality), which of the following strategies might help Tracylynne?
    (a) Transform general intentions into specific, concrete, measurable goals.
    (b) Create implementation intentions, such as specifying exactly where, when, and how the behaviors will be carried out.
    (c) Strengthen self-efficacy through mastery experiences and by observing and imitating the behavior of those already competent at these tasks.
    (d) All of these strategies would be useful.

Progress Test 2

After you have checked your understanding of the material in Progress Test 1 and reviewed the chapter with special focus on any areas of weakness, you are ready to assess your knowledge on Progress Test 2. Check your answers. If you make a mistake, review your notes, the relevant section of the study guide, and, if necessary, the appropriate part of your textbook.

1. Sachiyo had lunch more than an hour later than usual. Before lunch, she probably had high blood levels of the "hunger hormone"
   (a) ghrelin.
   (b) cholecystokinin (CCK).
   (c) neuropeptide Y (NPY).
   (d) leptin.

2. Farina was curious about the physiological changes that correlate with eating behavior. A review of the relevant literature would likely reveal that
   (a) eating is triggered by a drastic drop in blood glucose levels and a drastic increase in blood levels of insulin.
   (b) about 30 minutes before eating there is a *slight* decrease in blood glucose levels and a *slight* increase in blood levels of insulin.
   (c) eating is triggered by a drastic increase in blood glucose levels and a drastic decrease in blood levels of insulin.
   (d) about 30 minutes before eating there is a *slight* increase in blood glucose levels and a *slight* decrease in blood levels of insulin.

3. If he's feeling sad or unhappy, Milton "puts on a happy face." When he does this, his mood often improves. This result is best predicted by the
   (a) cognitive appraisal theory.
   (b) two-factor theory.
   (c) self-determination theory.
   (d) facial feedback hypothesis.

4. After his fifth slice of pizza, Massimo felt quite full. His feeling of satiation was most likely triggered by
   (a) stretch receptors in his stomach and cholecystokinin (CCK).
   (b) leptin, ghrelin, and insulin.
   (c) homeostasis, adipose, and insulin.
   (d) glycogen, leptin, ghrelin, and insulin.

5. Professor DeVoir's area of research is concerned with the long-term signals that regulate body weight. The chemical messengers of most interest to the professor are likely to be
   (a) leptin, insulin, and neuropeptide Y (NPY).
   (b) glucose, insulin, glycogen, and adipose.
   (c) CCK, BMR, and BMI.
   (d) BMR, NPY, and CCK.

6. Dr. Ushiro scanned the brains of his subjects using positron emission tomography (PET) while they recalled emotionally charged memories that made them feel sad, happy, angry, disgusted, and so on. If his research is consistent with neuroscience data reported in the text, he is likely to find that
   (a) there is a single "emotional center" in the brain that controls all emotions.
   (b) negative emotions such as fear and anger have distinct circuits in the brain, but positive emotions such as happiness and joy are governed by a single emotion center.
   (c) each emotion involves distinct neural circuits in the brain.
   (d) negative emotions such as fear and anger are governed by a single emotion center, but positive emotions such as happiness and joy have distinct circuits in the brain.

7. Dr. Zascow conducts research on the facial feedback hypothesis. Her results are consistent with previous research showing that expressing a specific emotion, especially facially, causes people to subjectively experience that emotion. Collectively, this evidence provides support for the ______________ theory of emotion.
   (a) arousal
   (b) cognitive appraisal
   (c) two-factor
   (d) James–Lange

8. While writing a term paper for her motivation course, Cara notes that the majority of people do not experience or achieve self-actualization, despite the claim that it is a goal common to all people. She decides that this is an important limitation of
   (a) instinct theories.
   (b) drive theories.
   (c) incentive theories.
   (d) Maslow's hierarchy of needs.

9. Set-point theory provides the best explanation for which of the following?
   (a) Gladys finds that when she is alone and feeling bored her arousal level is uncomfortably low; in order to regain her normal or optimal level of arousal she seeks a more stimulating environment.
   (b) At age 60, Edwina noted that her weight had fluctuated over the years and had progressively increased to the point where she is now about 25 pounds heavier than she was 35 years ago.
   (c) After eating a very filling and satisfying main meal, Ken manages to eat and enjoy a delicious slice of banana cream pie.
   (d) Although she leads a somewhat sedentary lifestyle, 40-year-old Andrea has been about the same weight, give or take a pound or two, since her late teens.

10. In an investigation of culture and emotional experience, researchers discovered that Japanese people categorize emotions not only along pleasantness and activation dimensions but also along a third dimension. This dimension, called _______ , reflects the idea that some emotions result from relationships and interactions with other people.
    (a) interpersonal engagement
    (b) the self-efficacy dimension
    (c) anthropomorphism
    (d) emotional intelligence

11. Nithya has been carrying extra pounds for many years. If she is like most of the obese experimental participants examined by neuroscientists who were studying obesity and the brain (Focus on Neuroscience), a PET scan is likely to reveal ________________ in her brain, compared with normal-weight control participants.
    (a) higher levels of cholecystokinin (CCK)
    (b) more dopamine receptors
    (c) lower levels of neuropeptide Y (NPY)
    (d) fewer dopamine receptors

12. Laureen is a lesbian. It is very probable that
    (a) she experienced some early childhood sexual abuse by a member of the opposite sex.
    (b) her father was overly domineering and her mother was ineffectual and provided her with a poor feminine role model.
    (c) her first sexual experience occurred in childhood with a member of the same sex.
    (d) her sexual orientation was determined before adolescence and before any sexual activity occurred.

13. Dr. Heilbron studies a neurotransmitter, manufactured throughout the brain, that increases during periods of negative energy balance and triggers eating behavior, reduces body metabolism, and promotes fat storage. If there is a positive energy balance, the activity of this neurotransmitter decreases. Dr. Heilbron's research is concerned with
    (a) ghrelin.
    (b) leptin.
    (c) cholecystokinin (CCK).
    (d) neuropeptide Y (NPY).

14. According to Critical Thinking (Has Evolution Programmed Us to Overeat?), the tendency for people in industrialized countries to overeat and become overweight or obese is the result of
    (a) the high positive incentive value of many of our foods.
    (b) an evolutionary propensity to eat a wide variety of foods, which promoted survival by ensuring that essential nutrients, vitamins, and minerals were obtained.
    (c) a tendency to overeat when food is available, which was adaptive in our ancestral past.
    (d) all of these things.

15. Doyne typically approaches any difficult task as a challenge to be mastered; he exerts a strong motivational effort, persists in the face of obstacles, and looks for creative ways to solve the problem. According to Enhancing Well-Being with Psychology (Turning Your Goals into Reality), Doyne has a high level of
    (a) self-efficacy.
    (b) self-actualization.
    (c) power motivation.
    (d) interpersonal engagement.

Progress Test 3

After you have checked your understanding of the material in Progress Tests 1 and 2, and have done a complete chapter review with special focus on any areas of weakness, you are ready to further assess your knowledge with Progress Test 3. Check your answers. If you make a mistake, review your notes, the appropriate parts of the study guide, and, if necessary, the relevant sections of your textbook.

1. When Sean went for his annual medical checkup, his doctor calculated his body mass index (BMI) and told him that he was overweight but not obese. Sean's BMI is most likely
    (a) between 25 and 29.9.
    (b) less than 20.
    (c) between 30 and 39.9.
    (d) less than 15.

2. Five-year-old Nemanja was excited and very curious about the various animals he saw when he was taken to the zoo for the first time. His exploratory behavior and curiosity were quickly inhibited, however, when he was suddenly startled and frightened by a loud roar from the lion's enclosure. According to the _______ theory of emotion, Nemanja's negative emotions were the result of cognitive appraisal of the meaning of the event or stimulus, whereas the _______ theory would say that they were the result of the perception of the physiological response to the event or stimulus.
   (a) arousal; two-factor
   (b) James–Lange; arousal
   (c) cognitive appraisal; James–Lange
   (d) two-factor; cognitive appraisal

3. The desire to drink when thirsty is to _______ as the desire to avoid boredom is to _______ .
   (a) sensory-specific satiety; sensation seeking
   (b) set-point theory; settling-point theory
   (c) drive theory; arousal theory
   (d) two-factor theory; cognitive appraisal theory

4. As Leopold aged he had to pay more attention to how much he ate in order to maintain his typical weight. One factor that may be involved in this tendency to gain weight as we age is that
   (a) the positive incentive value of food increases substantially over time.
   (b) leptin resistance increases with age.
   (c) as age increases, the basal metabolic rate (BMR) decreases.
   (d) as age increases, the basal metabolic rate (BMR) increases.

5. Dr. Fleming studies how food is converted into energy in the body. It is very likely that she is interested in
   (a) glucose.
   (b) insulin.
   (c) basal metabolic rate (BMR).
   (d) all of these factors.

6. Lazy Lou's food intake tends to exceed the amount of calories he expends on energy. On the other hand, Frenetic Frank's caloric intake is often less than the calories he expends on energy. It is likely that Lou has _______ and Frank has _______ .
   (a) a low set-point weight; a high set-point weight
   (b) a positive energy balance; a negative energy balance
   (c) a low settling-point weight; a high settling-point weight
   (d) a negative energy balance; a positive energy balance

7. Despite minor seasonal fluctuations, Phil's weight has been fairly consistent all his adult life. One reason for this stability over time is that the number of calories he consumes tends to match the number of calories he expends, a process called
   (a) positive incentive value.
   (b) satiation.
   (c) fixed action pattern.
   (d) energy homeostasis.

8. Kramer argues that from an evolutionary perspective, our need for autonomy, competence, and relatedness had an adaptive advantage. The need for relatedness, for example, promoted resource sharing, mutual protection, and the division of labor; it thus increased the likelihood that both the individual and the group would survive. Kramer's views of motivation are most like those of
   (a) Maslow's self-actualization theory.
   (b) Ryan and Deci's self-determination theory.
   (c) Bandura's self-efficacy theory.
   (d) Schachter and Singer's two-factor theory.

9. Graham, an assistant manager, has a strong need to attain a higher status so that he can control and influence the behavior of other employees; he has his heart set on becoming general manager. It is probable that Graham has a high level of
   (a) self-actualization.
   (b) emotional intelligence.
   (c) anthropomorphism.
   (d) power motivation.

10. When Keiho first arrived in North America from Japan, she was surprised to find that people vigorously nodded their heads in answer to a question to indicate the affirmative "Yes" instead of "Maybe" or "No way." Nodding the head is a specific gesture called _______ that can have a different meaning in different cultures.
   (a) an emblem
   (b) anthropomorphism
   (c) a fixed action pattern
   (d) self-efficacy

11. Ulricke lost 20 pounds on her latest diet, and her weight fell below her set-point weight. She is likely to experience a(n) _______ in her basal metabolic rate and energy level; when she goes off the diet she is likely to _______ .
    (a) increase; maintain her weight loss
    (b) decrease; regain the lost pounds
    (c) increase; regain the lost pounds
    (d) decrease; maintain her weight loss

12. Sharon is writing a term paper on human sexuality. Her library research is likely to indicate that the normal order of the four stages in the human sexual response cycle is
    (a) excitement, plateau, orgasm, and resolution.
    (b) plateau, resolution, excitement, and orgasm.
    (c) excitement, plateau, resolution, and orgasm
    (d) excitement, resolution, orgasm, and plateau.

13. Miguella was born blind and deaf. Despite her inability to observe or hear others, she still expresses joy, anger, and pleasure using the same expressions as sighted children. This example provides support for
    (a) the idea that basic emotions are innate.
    (b) the notion that emotional expressions are culturally determined.
    (c) the idea that both genetics and the environment are involved in the expression of basic emotions.
    (d) all of these ideas.

14. Self-determination theory is to ________ as self-actualization is to ________
    (a) William James and Carl Lange; Walter Cannon
    (b) Edward Deci and Richard Ryan; Abraham Maslow
    (c) Walter Cannon; William James and Carl Lange
    (d) Abraham Maslow; Edward Deci and Richard Ryan

15. According to Culture and Human Behavior (Evolution and Mate Preferences), the evolutionary explanation of sex differences
    (a) has been criticized on the grounds that it is overly deterministic and does not sufficiently acknowledge the role of culture, gender-role socialization, and other social factors.
    (b) provides clear evidence that sexual inequality is natural, correct, and justified.
    (c) proposes that kindness, intelligence, emotional stability, health, and a pleasing personality are much less important than a prospective mate's financial resources or good looks.
    (d) theorizes that men are more likely to look for a mate who has high status and wealth and will be a "good provider," and women are more attracted to males who are young and fertile and would make good "trophy husbands."

Answers

Introduction: Motivation and Emotion

1. *Motivation refers to* the biological, emotional, cognitive, or social forces that activate and direct behavior.
2. *The three characteristics associated with motivation are* activation (the initiation of behavior), persistence (continued efforts to achieve a goal), and intensity (the vigor of responding).
3. *Emotions are closely tied to motivational processes (and vice versa) because* we may be motivated to achieve certain emotions, and emotions may motivate us to take action. Also, many forms of motivation have an emotional component, which is involved in the initiation and persistence of behavior.

Motivational Concepts and Theories

1. *According to the earliest theories of motivation, instinct theories, people are motivated to* engage in certain behaviors because of evolutionary programming. *The limitation of these theories is* that they merely describe and label behaviors rather than actually explain them.
2. *According to drive theories, behavior is motivated by* the desire to reduce internal tension caused by unmet biological needs, such as hunger or thirst. *Their limitations are* that people engage in behaviors that are not a reflection of internal drives (we sometimes eat when we are not hungry or don't eat when we are hungry) and that many behaviors involve psychological influences, such as buying a lottery ticket, that are not related to filling unmet biological needs.
3. *Incentive theories proposed that behavior is motivated by* the "pull" of external goals, such as rewards. In addition, cognitive factors, such as the expectation that a behavior will lead to a particular reward, may be involved. *Their limitation is* that many behaviors are not primarily motivated by any kind of external incentive

(we sometimes engage in behaviors for their own sake without any obvious reinforcement). *In combination, drive and incentive theories account for* a broad range of "pushes" and "pulls" motivating many behaviors. *The combination is limited because* in some situations our behavior seems to be directed toward increasing tension and physiological arousal and is not motivated by either internal drives or external incentives.

4. *Arousal theory is based on the notion that people are motivated to* maintain an optimal level of arousal. When arousal is too low, we are motivated to seek stimulation; when it is too high, we seek to reduce arousal in a less stimulating environment. *What constitutes an optimal level of arousal* varies from person to person, time to time, and from one situation to another. *Sensation seekers tend to* seek out varied, novel, and unique sensory experiences because they find high levels of arousal pleasurable.
5. *Humanistic theories emphasize the importance of* psychological and cognitive components in human motivation, especially the notion that people are motivated to realize their personal potential.
6. *The key ideas and concepts from these theories that come into play in understanding many human behaviors include* drive, homeostasis, incentive, and arousal.

Concept Check 1

1. motivation
2. homeostasis
3. sensation seeker
4. incentive
5. instinct
6. emotions

Matching Exercise 1

1. humanistic theories of motivation
2. motivation
3. persistence
4. fixed action patterns
5. drive
6. instinct theories
7. sensation seeking
8. evolutionary perspective

True/False Test 1

1. T	3. F	5. T	7. T
2. T	4. T	6. F	

Biological Motivation: Hunger and Eating

1. *Eating behavior reflects the complex interaction of* psychological, biological, and social factors.
2. *Energy homeostasis refers to* the long-term matching of food intake to energy expenditure.
3. *Energy homeostasis (energy balance) involves (a) glucose (blood sugar), which is a* simple sugar that provides energy and is primarily produced by the conversion of carbohydrates and fats; *(b) insulin, which is a* hormone produced by the pancreas that regulates blood levels of glucose and signals the hypothalamus, regulating hunger and eating behavior; *(c) basal metabolic rate (BMR), which is* the rate at which your body at rest uses energy for vital body functions, such as generating body heat, heartbeat, respiration, and brain activity; *(d) adipose tissue, which is* body fat that is the main source of stored, or reserve, calories (energy).
4. *Positive energy balance occurs when* caloric intake exceeds the amount of calories expended for energy and the excess glucose is stored as fat (reserve energy). *Negative energy balance occurs when* caloric intake falls short of the calories expended as energy; if continued, body fat stores will shrink.
5. *Short-term signals that regulate eating behavior include physiological changes: About 30 minutes before eating, there is* a slight increase in blood levels of insulin, a slight decrease in blood levels of glucose, body temperature increases, and metabolism decreases. *Once a meal has begun,* blood glucose levels return to baseline, body temperature decreases, and metabolism increases.
6. *An important internal signal involved in eating is the hormone ghrelin, which is* manufactured primarily by cells lining the stomach and stimulates appetite and the secretion of growth hormone by the pituitary gland. *Blood levels of ghrelin* rise sharply before meals and fall abruptly after meals.
7. *Psychological factors that trigger eating behavior involve (a) classical conditioning, in which* the conditioned stimulus (the time you normally eat, the setting, the sight of food cues, etc.) elicits the conditioned response (internal physiological changes, such as changes in blood

levels of insulin, glucose, and ghrelin, increased body temperature, and decreased metabolism). *(b) operant conditioning, in which* voluntary eating behaviors are followed by a reinforcing stimulus (the taste of food) and are thus positively reinforced (preferred foods acquire positive incentive value).

8. *Satiation refers to* the feeling of fullness and diminished desire to eat that accompanies eating a meal. *Satiation involves signals from* stretch receptors in the stomach that communicate sensory information to the brainstem *and* cholecystokinin (CCK), a hormone/neurotransmitter that promotes satiety effects.
9. *Sensory-specific satiety refers to* the reduced desire to continue consuming a particular food, especially the food that is being eaten; this may be due to a decline in the food's positive incentive value.
10. *Long-term chemical signals that regulate body weight are (a) leptin, a hormone secreted by the* body's adipose tissue (fat) into the bloodstream and detected by receptors in various locations in the hypothalamus and also by neurons in the stomach and gut that have leptin receptors; *(b) insulin, a hormone secreted by the* pancreas; high brain levels of insulin are associated with reduced food intake and body weight; *(c) neuropeptide Y (NPY), a neurotransmitter manufactured* throughout the brain, including the hypothalamus; increased levels trigger eating behavior, reduce body metabolism, and promote fat storage. *The two factors correlated with how much of each hormone is secreted are* the amount of body fat and the degree of negative or positive energy balance.
11. *According to set-point theory,* the body has a natural or optimal body weight, called the set-point weight, that the body defends from becoming higher or lower by regulating feelings of hunger and body metabolism. *According to settling-point models of weight regulation,* the body weight tends to settle, or stabilize, around the point at which an equilibrium, or balance, is achieved between energy expenditure and calorie consumption; settling-point weight may go up or down depending on whether the factors affecting food consumption and energy expenditure change.

Excess Weight and Obesity

1. *The body mass index (BMI) is a* numerical scale indicating adult height in relation to weight; it is calculated as 703 × weight (in pounds) divided by height in inches squared (BMI, however, is not the most accurate measure of weight status if a high score is due to bone or muscle rather than to fat).
2. *People are considered overweight if* they have a BMI between 25 and 29.9 that is due to fat and not to muscle or bone. *Obesity is a condition characterized by* an abnormally high proportion of body fat and a body mass index equal to or greater than 30.
3. *A number of factors are involved in creating a positive energy balance (when caloric intake consistently exceeds energy expenditure) and in becoming overweight:*
(a) Going without adequate sleep disrupts the hunger-related hormones leptin (appetite-suppressing) and ghrelin (appetite-increasing), resulting in increased feelings of hunger, especially for foods with high carbohydrate content.
(b) the positive incentive value of certain foods, defined as the anticipated pleasure of consuming particular highly palatable foods.
(c) the "Supersize It" syndrome, a phenomenon in which restaurants, fast-food outlets, etc. offer substantially increased portions of food for very little extra money, an offer many find hard to resist. *(d) the cafeteria diet effect, which is* the tendency to eat more when a wide variety of palatable foods is available. *(e) the sedentary lifestyle of many people (40 percent of Americans) who never* exercise, play sports, or engage in physically active hobbies. *(f) individual differences and lifespan changes are involved because* people vary greatly in their basal metabolic rate (which accounts for about two-thirds of energy expenditure), females have a slightly lower BMR than males, metabolism decreases slightly over the lifespan (2 to 3 percent per decade), and weight gain will occur over time if food intake is not reduced.
4. *Several factors contribute to obesity: (a) the interaction of genetics and environment, because* when a genetic predisposition to become obese is combined with a high-risk environment characterized by ample easily obtainable high-fat, high-calorie, palatable food, obesity is more likely to occur. *(b) leptin resistance, which refers to* a condition in which higher-than-normal blood levels of the hormone leptin do not produce the expected physiological response of reduced eating behavior and weight loss.
(c) weight cycling (yo-yo dieting), which is the repeated cycles of dieting, weight loss, and weight regain experienced by many overweight and obese dieters. *(d) and finally, as noted in*

Focus on Neuroscience, obese people's brains tend to have fewer dopamine receptors than normal-weight individuals, *which may lead to* compulsive eating to stimulate brain reward centers.

Concept Check 2

1. ghrelin; increased
2. satiation; cholecystokinin (CCK)
3. sensory-specific
4. baseline body weight; set-point
5. energy homeostasis or energy balance
6. leptin, insulin, and neuropeptide Y (NPY)
7. adipose tissue; body fat
8. settling-point models of weight regulation
9. body mass index (BMI); obese
10. positive incentive value
11. her body defending against weight loss by decreasing her basal metabolic rate and energy level
12. cafeteria diet effect
13. overweight

Matching Exercise 2

1. baseline body weight
2. basal metabolic rate (BMR)
3. glycogen
4. body mass index (BMI)
5. adipose tissue
6. insulin
7. stretch receptors
8. energy homeostasis (energy balance)
9. sensory-specific satiety
10. leptin resistance
11. weight cycling (yo-yo dieting)
12. ghrelin
13. neuropeptide Y (NPY)

True/False Test 2

1. F	5. T	9. F
2. T	6. T	10. T
3. F	7. F	11. T
4. T	8. T	12. T

Human Sexuality

1. *The four stages of the human sexual response (and the characteristics of each) are* excitement (which can occur in response to sexual fantasies or other sexually arousing stimuli, physical contact with another person, or masturbation), plateau (physical arousal builds as pulse and breathing rates continue to increase), orgasm (blood pressure and heart rate reach their peak), and resolution (arousal slowly subsides and returns to normal; at this point, males experience a refractory period during which they are incapable of having another erection or orgasm).
2. *In nonhuman animals, sexual behavior is* biologically determined and triggered by hormonal changes in the female (during estrus, females are fertile and receptive to male sexual advances). *In higher animals, sexual behavior is* more strongly influenced by learning and environmental factors and is less limited to the goal of reproduction; in some species, sexual interactions serve important social functions.
3. *In humans, sexual behavior is not* limited to a female's fertile period, and motives are not limited to reproduction. *For females,* fluctuations in sexual interest and motivation may be related to hormonal cycles, but these changes are highly influenced by social and psychological factors. *When human males experience lowered levels of testosterone,* a drop in sexual interest tends to occur, although the effects vary among individuals (testosterone is also involved in female sexual motivation). *In both men and women, sexual motivation is* biologically influenced by the levels of the hormone testosterone in the body.
4. *Neuroscientists have shown that romantic love activates* brain areas (anterior cingulate cortex, caudate nucleus, putamen, and insula) that are involved in positive emotions, such as happiness, but in a way that represents a unique pattern, and that respond to euphoria-producing drugs, such as opiates and cocaine.

Sexual Orientation

1. *Sexual orientation refers to* whether a person is sexually aroused by members of the same sex, the opposite sex, or both sexes; a heterosexual is sexually attracted to individuals of the other sex, a homosexual is attracted to individuals of the same sex, and a bisexual is attracted to individuals of both sexes.

2. *Sexual orientation is difficult to identify because* there is not always a perfect correspondence between a particular person's sexual identity, sexual desires, and sexual behaviors. In addition, determining accurate numbers depends on how researchers structure survey questions, how they define their criteria, where the survey is conducted, and how survey participants are selected.
3. *Factors associated with sexual orientation are as follows:* First, twin studies suggest that genetics may play a role in determining sexual orientation, but genetic predisposition alone is not a sufficient explanation. Second, genetic influences are complex and involve multiple genes (not a single "gay" gene). Beyond heredity, other biological influences, such as prenatal exposure to sex hormones or other aspects of the prenatal environment may play a role. Third, the more older biologically related brothers a man has, the more likely he is to be homosexual. Research suggests that carrying successive male children might trigger an immune response in the mother that, in turn, might influence brain development in the male fetus. Fourth, some small and inconclusive studies have found differences in brain function and structure among gay, lesbian, and heterosexual males and females, but it is not known if these differences are the cause or the effect of different patterns of sexual behavior. Fifth, homosexuality is not the result of disturbed or abnormal family relationships. Finally, research has shown that sexual orientation is determined before adolescence and long before the beginning of sexual activity, and that psychological, biological, social, and cultural factors are involved in determining sexual orientation. Researchers are unable to say precisely what those factors are and how they interact.
4. *Research on same-sex couples and their children has shown that (a)* gays and lesbians can be found in every occupation and at every socioeconomic level in our society, and like heterosexual couples many are involved in long-term, committed, and caring relationships. *(b)* children who are raised by gay or lesbian parents are as well adjusted as children who are raised by heterosexual parents. *(c)* children who are raised by gay or lesbian parents are no more likely to be gay or lesbian in adulthood than children who are raised by heterosexual parents.

Concept Check 3

1. refractory
2. decrease; stay the same
3. decrease
4. sexual orientation
5. high probability
6. are not
7. euphoria-producing drugs; opiates and cocaine
8. mutual attraction and love
9. retrospective; prospective

Matching Exercise 3

1. William Masters and Virginia Johnson
2. plateau phase
3. heterosexual
4. refractory period
5. homosexual
6. excitement phase
7. gay
8. prospective study
9. sexual orientation

True/False Test 3

1. T	4. F	7. T
2. T	5. T	8. T
3. T	6. F	

Psychological Needs as Motivators

1. *The key questions associated with motivational theories that emphasize fundamental psychological needs are*
   (a) Are there universal psychological needs?
   (b) Are we internally or externally motivated to satisfy psychological needs?
   (c) What psychological needs must be satisfied for optimal human functioning?
2. *Maslow's hierarchy of needs divides motivation into* levels that progress from basic physiological needs to psychological needs to self-actualization needs. *Maslow believed that people* are motivated to satisfy the needs at each level of the hierarchy before moving up to the next level and that they are ultimately motivated by the desire to achieve self-actualization (the "full use and exploitation of talents, capacities, and potentialities").
3. *Criticisms of Maslow's model of motivation are (a) The concept of self-actualization is* very

vague and difficult to define in a way that would allow it to be tested scientifically. *(b) Maslow's initial studies on self-actualization* had limited samples, and many were based on biographical and autobiographical accounts of famous historical figures selected by Maslow. *(c) Despite the claim that self-actualization is an innate motivational goal of all people,* most people do not experience or achieve self-actualization. *(d) Maslow's notion that we must satisfy needs at one level before moving to the next level* has not been supported (has not stood the test of time).

4. *Self-determination theory is associated with psychologists* Edward L. Deci and Richard M. Ryan, *who contend that in order to realize optimal psychological functioning we must meet three innate and universal psychological needs: (a) autonomy, which is* the need to determine, control, and organize one's own behavior and goals so that they are in harmony with one's own interests and values. *(b) competence, which is* the need to effectively learn and master appropriately challenging tasks. *(c) relatedness, which is* the need to feel attached to others and experience a sense of belongingness, security, and intimacy.
5. *Intrinsic motivation refers to* the desire to engage in tasks that the person finds inherently satisfying and enjoyable, novel, or optimally challenging (the desire to do something for its own sake). *Extrinsic motivation refers to* external factors or influences on behavior, such as rewards, social evaluations, rules, and responsibilities.

Competence and Achievement Motivation

1. *Competence motivation is displayed when* a person strives to use his or her cognitive, social, and behavioral skills to be capable and exercise control in a situation (provides much of the "push" for tackling new challenges).
2. *Achievement motivation refers to* the desire to direct one's behavior toward excelling, succeeding, or outperforming others at some task. *It is measured by* the Thematic Apperception Test (TAT).
3. *People who score high in achievement motivation tend to* expend their greatest efforts when faced with moderately challenging tasks, work long hours, display original thinking, seek expert advice, value feedback about their performance, and have the capacity to delay gratification. They also tend to be independent and to attribute their successes to their own abilities and efforts and explain their failures as being due to external factors or bad luck.
4. *In individualistic cultures, the need to achieve emphasizes* personal, individual success rather than the success of the group. *In collectivistic cultures* there is a social orientation with a focus on the well-being of others and a desire to fulfill the expectations of family members and to fit into the larger group.

Concept Check 4

1. achievement
2. collectivistic
3. intrinsic
4. competence
5. self-determination
6. extrinsic
7. Thematic Apperception Test (TAT)

Graphic Organizer 1

1. drive theory
2. humanistic theory
3. instinct theory
4. self-determination theory (SDT)
5. incentive theory
6. arousal theory

Matching Exercise 4

1. self-determination theory (SDT)
2. hierarchy of needs
3. internalize and integrate
4. Thematic Apperception Test (TAT)
5. power motivation
6. Abraham Maslow
7. competence
8. autonomy

True/False Test 4

1. T
2. F
3. T
4. T
5. F
6. F
7. F

Emotion

1. *Emotion is defined as* a complex psychological state involving three distinct components: a subjective experience, a physiological response, and a behavioral or expressive response.

2. *Emotions tend to be* intense and rather short-lived, and they have a specific cause, are directed toward a particular object, and motivate a person to take some form of action. *Moods involve* a milder emotional state that is more general and pervasive, such as gloominess or contentment, and they may last for a few hours or days.
3. *Emotions have many functions, including triggering* motivated behavior, and they contribute to rational decision making, purposeful behavior, and setting appropriate goals. People who have lost the capacity to feel emotion tend to make disastrous decisions.
4. *Emotional intelligence is the capacity to* understand and manage your own emotional experiences, and to perceive, comprehend, and respond appropriately to the emotional responses of others.
5. *According to evolutionary psychologists, emotions are the* product of evolution, they help us solve important adaptive problems posed by the environment, they move us toward potential resources and away from potential dangers, ultimately they help survival and reproductive success, and their expression informs other organisms about our internal state.
6. *The most common basic emotions that all humans, in every culture, experience are* happiness, sadness, anger, fear, surprise, and disgust.
7. *Cross-cultural research has shown* general agreement among cultures regarding the "pleasant/unpleasant" and "activated/not activated" emotional dimensions.
8. *Cross-cultural researchers have noted that Japanese subjects also categorized emotions along a dimension of* interpersonal engagement, *which reflects* the degree to which emotions involve a relationship with another person or other people.
9. *Research has shown that men and women* do not really differ in the frequency or intensity of emotional experience (but both men and women *believe* that women are "more emotional" than men). *Compared with men, women tend to be* more emotionally expressive, more emotionally aware, more at ease expressing emotions and thinking about emotions, and better at recalling emotional experiences.

The Neuroscience of Emotion

1. *The physiological component of emotions such as fear and anger involves the* activation of the sympathetic branch of the autonomic nervous system, which gears people for action, affecting heart rate, blood pressure, respiration, perspiration, and other bodily activities (the fight-or-flight response).
2. *The amygdala, which is part of the limbic system, is an* almond-shaped cluster of neurons in the brain's temporal lobe. *It is involved in* memory and emotional responses, especially fear, and has connections with other brain structures, including the cortex, the thalamus, and the hypothalamus.
3. *From an evolutionary perspective, evidence of a direct thalamus→amygdala pathway makes adaptive sense because the amygdala can be activated by* a threatening stimulus, even before we become consciously aware of the stimulus, an adaptive response. *When the amygdala is activated, it sends information along* two pathways, one to the hypothalamus, then to the medulla, which, in combination, trigger arousal of the sympathetic nervous system. Another pathway projects from the amygdala to a different hypothalamus area that, in concert with the pituitary gland, triggers the release of stress hormones. *The second (indirect) pathway, thalamus→ cortex→amygdala, allows more complex stimuli to be* evaluated in the cortex before triggering the amygdala's alarm system.

The Expression of Emotions: Making Faces

1. *Research on facial expressions suggests that* expressions of the basic emotions are innate and probably hard-wired in the brain, and appear to be universal across different cultures.
2. *Display rules are social and cultural rules that* regulate the expression of emotions, particularly facial expressions.
3. *Display rules can vary greatly from culture to culture (and even for different groups within a given culture, such as men and women); consequently,* the expression of different emotions may vary depending on the culture and its display rules.
4. *The overall conclusion is that the expression of emotions* is biologically determined, the result of evolutionary processes, serves the adaptive function of communicating internal states to friends and enemies, helps us recognize and respond quickly to the emotional state of others, and ultimately helps in survival.

Theories of Emotion: Explaining Emotion

1. *The James–Lange theory of emotions states that* emotions arise from the perception and

interpretation of body changes; in other words, the experience of emotion results from the perception of the internal physical responses to a stimulus—you feel afraid because your heart pounded.

2. *Walter Cannon criticized the James–Lange theory on a number of grounds: (a) Body reactions are* similar for many emotions, yet our subjective experience of various emotions is very different. *(b) Our emotional reaction to a stimulus is* often faster than our physiological reaction; the subjective experience of emotion is often virtually instantaneous. *(c) When physiological changes are artificially induced,* people do not necessarily report feeling a related emotion. *(d) People cut off from feeling body changes* do experience true emotions (the perception of physical arousal does not seem to be essential to the experience of emotion).
3. *Support for some aspects of the James–Lange theory comes from (a) Damasio's work, which demonstrated that* each of the basic emotions produced a distinct pattern of brain activity and that the subjective sense of feeling an emotion follows from physiological feedback from the skin, muscles, internal organs, and the sympathetic nervous system, and *(b) the facial feedback hypothesis, which states that* expressing a specific emotion, especially facially, causes the subjective experience of that emotion.
4. *Schachter and Singer's two-factor theory of emotion suggests that* emotion is a result of the interaction of physiological arousal and the cognitive label that we apply to explain the arousal.
5. *Cognitive appraisal theory proposes that* the most important aspect of an emotional experience is our cognitive interpretation, or appraisal, of the personal meaning of events and experiences.
6. *Although both the two-factor theory and the cognitive appraisal theory emphasize the importance of cognitive appraisal, the two-factor theory states that* emotion results from physiological arousal plus a cognitive label, *while the cognitive appraisal theory stresses that* cognitive appraisal is the essential trigger for an emotional response, and all other components of emotion, including physiological arousal, follow from the initial cognitive appraisal.

Concept Check 5

1. mood; emotion
2. sympathetic; fight-or-flight
3. display rules
4. emotional intelligence
5. mixed
6. thalamus→amygdala
7. epinephrine
8. cognitive appraisal
9. not consistent
10. facial feedback hypothesis
11. James–Lange
12. mastery experience

Graphic Organizer 2

1. astonishment
2. alarm
3. boredom
4. contentment
5. annoyance

Matching Exercise 5

1. Charles Darwin
2. basic emotions
3. emotional intelligence
4. amygdala
5. Paul Ekman
6. facial feedback hypothesis
7. emblems
8. two-factor theory of emotion
9. anthropomorphism
10. epinephrine (adrenaline)
11. emotion
12. limbic system

True/False Test 5

1. T	5. T	9. T
2. T	6. T	10. T
3. T	7. T	11. T
4. T	8. T	12. T

Something to Think About

1. Losing weight and keeping it off is a big problem for many people. You might begin your discussion by noting that our motivation to eat is influenced by psychological, biological, and social factors. For example, biologically, hunger and satiation are regulated by stretch receptors in the stomach, and chemicals such as CCK,

insulin, ghrelin, and leptin. Of course, genetic factors also play a role, but there is usually an interaction between genetic susceptibility and environmental factors. Psychological factors include classically conditioned stimuli, the positive incentive value of certain foods acquired through operant conditioning and reinforcement, and memory of previous meals eaten. Socially, people are affected by the cultural norms and attitudes about what constitutes the ideal weight.

First, knowing a little about how food is converted to energy in the body is useful in understanding the regulation of hunger and eating behavior. Food provides glucose, the main source of the body's energy, which is regulated by insulin. Excess glucose is stored in adipose tissue (fat) and the basal metabolic rate reflects the rate at which your body at rest uses energy for vital body functions. Energy homeostasis and chemicals such as leptin, insulin, and neuropeptide Y (NPY) help people maintain their baseline body weight, which tends to remain stable over time unless conditions of positive or negative energy balance occur. When the former happens, we gain weight. Body mass index (BMI) is one way to calculate weight status, and someone with a BMI of 30 or more is classified as obese.

So what are the major factors involved in becoming overweight and what might we do to minimize or prevent weight gain?

First is the positive incentive value of many easily available and very palatable foods, which can easily lead to overeating. You have to become aware of this factor and try to avoid these foods.

Second, when faced with the opportunity of a double portion of a tasty food for only a few cents more (the "Supersize It" syndrome) most people can't resist. These situations are optimized to pack on those extra calories, so do your best to stay away from them.

Third is the cafeteria diet effect. This happens when a wide variety of highly palatable foods are offered, such as at a cafeteria or an all-you-can-eat buffet. Your "eyes are bigger than your stomach," as the expression goes, and sure enough people tend to pile up their plates with food, a sure-fire formula for packing on the pounds.

Fourth are individual differences in basal metabolic rate (BMR). Two people, matched on all the essential variables, can maintain the same approximate weight even though one of the pair consumes twice as much as the other. Yes, it's true, and no, life is not fair. In addition, your BMR decreases with age, so as you get older you have to watch carefully what you eat or you'll gain weight (the old "middle-age spread" idea). People also differ in the amount of energy they use for normal daily activities.

Finally, weight gain for many people is a result of a sedentary lifestyle. Forty percent of Americans report that they never exercise, play sports, or engage in physical activities such as walking the dog or gardening. Make exercise a regular part of your routine and give the time spent doing some physical activity the highest priority. When you get busy and anxiety levels are high, the very last thing you should give up is your regular exercise program.

Having said all that, it is important to note that this is a complex problem with no magic bullet or easy solution. For example, obesity certainly involves genetic susceptibility, but environmental factors also play a role. Obese people also develop leptin resistance, a condition in which higher-than-normal blood levels of the hormone leptin do not produce the expected physiological response of reduced hunger and eating. Frequent dieting may lead to weight cycling, a phenomenon in which the weight lost during dieting is regained in a matter of weeks or months and is then maintained until the next attempt at dieting begins. Research has also shown that obese people tend to have fewer dopamine receptors in their brains than normal-weight people, which may lead some individuals to engage in compulsive eating to stimulate brain reward centers. And, as Critical Thinking: Has Evolution Programmed Us to Overeat points out, we may be programmed by evolution for the propensity to overeat and store energy as fat. Obviously, obesity is not a simple problem with a simple solution.

So, the best advice for losing weight is to become aware of all the factors (especially those just mentioned) that can contribute to weight gain, modify your eating patterns accordingly, and follow a regular exercise program. It's an uphill battle, and despite the gloomy statistics, many people have successfully kept weight off by following this advice.

2. You might first want to define the two important and related topics of motivation and emotion. Motivation refers to the forces that act on or within an organism to initiate and direct behavior and involves three characteristics: activation, persistence, and intensity. It is closely related to emotion because we are often motivated to achieve certain emotional states, and

emotions, in turn, may motivate us to achieve certain goals.

As the text makes clear, these are complicated topics involving a variety of theories and a large volume of research findings. Fortunately, there is some relevant psychological research that directly addresses the issue of how to change our goals (usually easy to formulate) into actual accomplishments (much harder to achieve).

Psychologist Albert Bandura has investigated this topic and proposed the notion of self-efficacy—the degree to which a person believes his or her ability can meet the demands of a specific situation and produce the desired results. Those who have an optimistic sense of self-efficacy tend to approach a tough task as a challenge to be overcome rather than an aversive event that needs to be avoided. Those who view themselves as capable, competent, and effective in dealing with obstacles and challenges are more likely to pursue higher personal goals than those who have self-doubts about their abilities. The big question for most of us, then, is how do we build our sense of self-efficacy, especially when confronted with tough challenges and when our confidence level is not as high as it might be. Enhancing Well-Being with Psychology provides a number of strategies and suggestions that can help motivate people to pursue and achieve their goals, and these should be a central part of your report.

Bandura noted that one of the most effective ways to build self-efficacy is through mastery experiences. Experiencing success at moderately challenging tasks can lead to the desire to tackle somewhat more difficult goals. In addition, realizing that setbacks can and do occur can teach us that success usually requires persistent effort. Social modeling (observational learning) is a useful strategy because it allows us to observe and imitate the behavior of those who are already competent at the task of interest. Gaining knowledge about what works and what doesn't work is a very important part of building a sense of self-efficacy. The two steps for turning goals into actions, forming a goal intention, and creating implementations, should be discussed next in your report. Finally, you should provide information about the power of mental rehearsal in improving performance. Mentally rehearsing the process (the skills that will be effectively used and the steps that will be taken in achieving the desired outcome) is better than simply imagining a positive outcome.

Progress Test 1

1. a
2. c
3. c
4. a
5. a
6. b
7. c
8. a
9. d
10. c
11. a
12. b
13. b
14. d
15. d

Progress Test 2

1. a
2. b
3. d
4. a
5. a
6. c
7. d
8. d
9. d
10. a
11. d
12. d
13. d
14. d
15. a

Progress Test 3

1. a
2. c
3. c
4. c
5. d
6. b
7. d
8. b
9. d
10. a
11. b
12. a
13. a
14. b
15. a

CHAPTER 9

Lifespan Development

PREVIEW

Reading the section below first will give you a general sense of the chapter's contents and an initial introduction to some of the major concepts and terms. This will prime you for what you are about to read and help you to develop a "cognitive map" that will guide your study of the material in this chapter. Likewise, reading the **preview questions** at the beginning of each major section will improve your ability to understand, learn, and retain the information.

CHAPTER 9 . . . AT A GLANCE

Chapter 9 examines the scope of developmental psychology and major themes such as the stages of lifespan development, the nature of change, and the interaction between heredity and environment. The first two sections describe genetic contributions to development, the new science of epigenetics, and the stages of prenatal development.

The capacities and capabilities of the newborn and development during infancy and childhood are explored. Special attention is paid to the nature of temperament, the concept of attachment, and the stages of language development. *Gender, gender role, gender identity,* and *sex* are defined, and gender differences that develop during childhood are presented. Social learning theory and gender schema theories explain current thinking about how gender roles develop. The section concludes with a detailed analysis of Piaget's theory of cognitive development and an examination of Vygotsky's sociocultural theory and the information-processing model.

Adolescence, the transition from childhood to adulthood, involves important changes in physical, sexual, and social development. Adolescent–parent relationships undergo some changes during this period, and peer relationships and influence become increasingly relevant. Erikson's theory of psychosocial development and Kohlberg's theory of moral development are examined next.

The final sections describe early (emerging), middle, and late adult development, including physical, social, and cognitive changes typical of each stage. Love and work are the key themes that dominate adult development. Late adulthood does not necessarily involve a steep decline in physical and cognitive functioning. In discussing dying and death, the text outlines Kübler-Ross's five-stage model of dying, noting that dying is an individual process, like any other during the lifespan.

Enhancing Well-Being with Psychology presents some basic principles of parenting that have been shown to foster the development of psychologically well-adjusted and competent children.

Introduction: Your Life Story

Preview Questions

Consider the following questions as you study this section of the chapter.

- What do developmental psychologists study?
- What are the major themes in developmental psychology?
- What are the eight major stages of the life span?

Read the section "Introduction: Your Life Story" and ***write*** *your answers to the following:*

1. Developmental psychology is the ____________________
2. The major themes in developmental psychology are ____________________
3. The eight major stages of the lifespan are ____________________

Genetic Contributions to Your Life Story

Preview Questions

Consider the following questions as you study this section of the chapter.

- What is a zygote?
- What are chromosomes, DNA, and genes?
- How do genes guide the development of living organisms?
- What are genotypes, alleles, and phenotypes, and what role does environment play in the relationship between genotype and phenotype?
- Why is the "genetic blueprint" analogy inaccurate?
- What are genetic predispositions, and what triggers gene expression?
- What does the field of epigenetics study?
- What factors are important in the relationship between genotype and phenotype?

Read the section "Genetic Contributions to Your Life Story" and ***write*** *your answers to the following:*

1. A zygote is ____________________
2. Chromosomes are ____________________
3. Deoxyribonucleic acid (DNA) is ____________________
4. Genes are ____________________

   Genes direct the manufacture of ____________________
5. Genotype refers to the ____________________

   The human genome is ____________________
6. Alleles are ____________________

   The best-known pattern of allele variation is the ____________________ gene pair. These alleles operate as follows: ____________________
7. Phenotype refers to the ____________________
8. The "genetic blueprint" analogy is not accurate because ____________________
9. Scientists use the term *genetic predispositions* to refer to ____________________
10. Gene expression can be triggered by ____________________
11. Epigenetics researchers study ____________________

They investigate how ______________________

____

____

____

12. Epigenetic research is providing insight into ______________________

____

____

13. The five critical factors in the relationship between genotype and phenotype are

____

____

____

____

____

Prenatal Development

Preview Questions

Consider the following questions as you study this section of the chapter.

- What happens to the single-celled zygote during prenatal development?
- What are the three phases of the prenatal stage?
- What are teratogens?
- What is the neural tube, what is the function of stem cells, and what brain structures does the neural tube form?
- What is the fetal period, and what happens to neurons after birth?

Read the section "Prenatal Development" and ***write*** *your answers to the following:*

1. During prenatal development, the single-celled zygote ______________________

____

____

2. The three phases of the prenatal stage are

____

____

____

____

3. Teratogens are ______________________

____

____

Other factors that can affect the unborn child are ______________________

____

____

4. The neural tube is ______________________

____

Stem cells are ______________________

____

5. The top of the neural tube develops to eventually form ______________________

____

6. The fetal period is ______________________

____

After birth, the neurons ______________________

____

____

After you have carefully studied the preceding sections, complete the following exercises.

Concept Check 1

Read the following and write the correct term in the space provided.

1. Dr. Dalliwhal's research focuses on the relationship between various teratogens and birth defects. Dr. Dalliwhal is most likely a ______________________ psychologist.
2. Researchers at State University are working to understand the processes that guide and determine gene expression. In particular, they want to know how gene activity is regulated within a cell and what signals switch genes to "on" or "off." These researchers work in a new field called ______________________.
3. Dr. Markowitz argues against the "genetic blueprint" analogy and the idea of a fixed, inevitable master plan. He is most likely to suggest that people with a specific genetic configuration develop in a particular way because they may be more or less sensitive to certain environmental factors, a tendency called a ______________________.

4. It is now six weeks since Jennifer conceived. The human organism she is carrying is called a(n) ________________ ; at the third month, it will be called a(n) ________________ .
5. When Myra became pregnant, she decided that she would not drink any alcohol because she did not want to risk causing abnormal development or birth defects in her unborn child. Myra is aware that alcohol is a ________________ .
6. Dr. Zhang conceptualizes the lifespan in terms of eight basic stages of development. She is most likely to label the stage from birth to 2 years of age as ________________ , the stage from 2 to 6 years as ________________ , and the stage from 6 to 12 years as ________________ .
7. When answering an exam question about what makes each individual unique, Philipa is most likely to note that every cell in the body has 23 pairs of ________________ . Each of these long, thread-like structures is composed of twisted strands of ________________ , which are arranged in thousands of segments called ________________ .
8. Sapna read that the development of freckles appears to be controlled by a single gene, which can be dominant or recessive. To have the potential for freckles you need to inherit a dominant version of the freckles gene from either or both your parents. Sapna is reading about one of the best-known patterns of allele variation, called the ________________ .
9. Dr. Ramsey conducts research on ________________ , which are undifferentiated cells that divide and give rise to cells that can develop into any one of the body's different cell types.

Graphic Organizer 1

Identify the parts of the cell in the diagram below.

1.	cell nucleus	3.	gene
2.	chromosome	4.	DNA

Then match each numbered part with one of the following descriptions.

A. ____ Unit of DNA on a chromosome that encodes instructions for making a particular molecule.

B. ____ Double-stranded molecule that encodes genetic instructions.

C. ____ Long, thread-like structure composed of twisted parallel strands of DNA.

D. ____ Part of the cell that contains the 23 pairs of chromosomes.

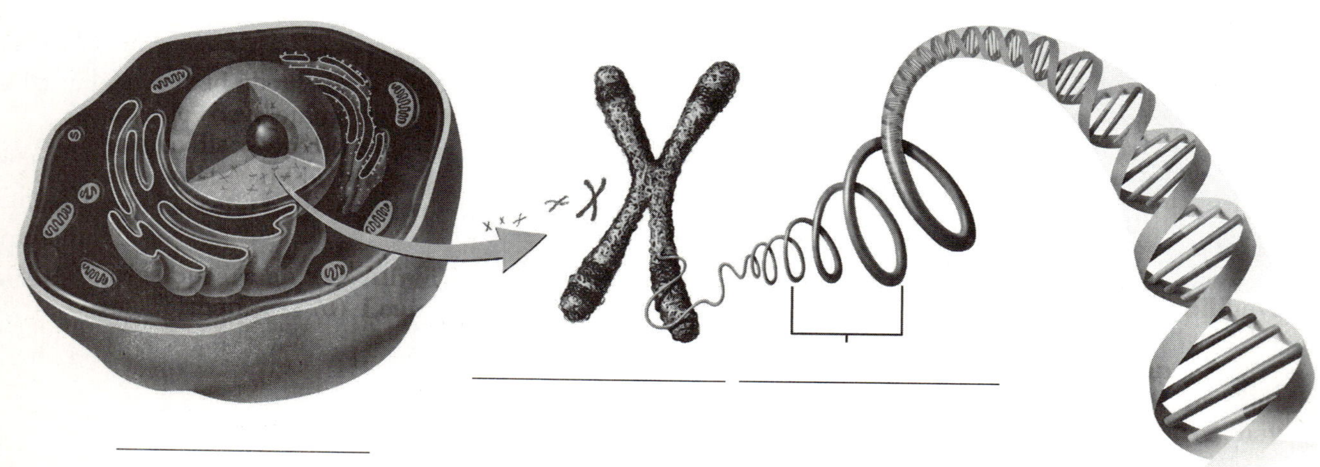

Review of Terms and Concepts 1

Use the terms in this list to complete the Matching Exercise, then to help you answer the True/False items correctly.

developmental psychology
critical period
nature–nurture issue
zygote
chromosome
deoxyribonucleic acid (DNA)
gene
genotype
human genome
allele
phenotype
genetic predispositions
epigenetics
mutation
prenatal stage
germinal period (zygotic period)
embryo
embryonic period
amniotic sac
umbilical cord
placenta
teratogens
fetal alcohol syndrome
neural tube
stem cells
ventricles
fetal period
quickening

Matching Exercise

Match the appropriate term with its definition or description.

1. ________________ The stage of development before birth; divided into the germinal, embryonic, and fetal periods.
2. ________________ The basic unit of heredity that directs the manufacture of proteins, which are used in virtually all of your body's functions; the individual unit of DNA instructions on a chromosome.
3. ________________ The branch of psychology that studies how people change over the lifespan.
4. ________________ Particular genetic configurations that are more or less sensitive to specific environmental factors and influence how development unfolds.
5. ________________ Harmful agents or substances that can cause malformations or defects in an embryo or a fetus.
6. ________________ Long, thread-like structure composed of twisted parallel strands of DNA; found in the cell nucleus.
7. ________________ Spontaneous change in genes from one generation to another.
8. ________________ The first two weeks of prenatal development.
9. ________________ Cluster of cells that develops from the single-celled zygote by the end of the two-week germinal period.
10. ________________ The scientific description of the complete set of DNA in the human organism.
11. ________________ One of the different forms of a particular gene.
12. ________________ Disk-shaped vascular organ that acts as a filter to prevent the mother's blood from directly mingling with that of the developing embryo.
13. ________________ Study of the cellular mechanisms that control gene expression and its impacts on health and behavior.
14. ________________ Undifferentiated cells that can divide and give rise to cells that can develop into any one of the body's different cell types.

True/False Test

Indicate whether each statement is true or false by placing T or F in the blank space next to each item.

1. ____ Fetal alcohol syndrome is characterized by physical and mental problems; symptoms include abnormal facial features, poor coordination, learning disabilities, behavior problems, and mental retardation.
2. ____ A critical period during development is a time during which the child is maximally sensitive to environmental influences.
3. ____ Deoxyribonucleic acid (DNA) is the double-stranded molecule that encodes genetic instructions and is the chemical basis of heredity.
4. ____ The fetal period is the second period of prenatal development, extending from the third week through the eighth week.
5. ____ The single cell formed at conception from the union of the egg cell and sperm cell is called a zygote.
6. ____ The umbilical cord delivers nourishment, oxygen, and water to the embryo and carries away carbon dioxide and other wastes.
7. ____ The embryonic period is the third and longest period of prenatal development, extending from the ninth week until birth.
8. ____ An important theme in developmental psychology is the interaction between heredity and environment; traditionally called the nature–nurture issue.

9. ____ Genotype refers to observable traits or characteristics of an organism as determined by the interaction of genetic and environmental factors.

10. ____ Phenotype refers to the genetic makeup of an individual organism.

11. ____ The embryo is protectively housed in the fluid-filled amniotic sac.

12. ____ During the fourth month of pregnancy, the mother can feel the fetus moving, an experience called quickening.

13. ____ Cavities, filled with cerebrospinal fluid and found at the core of the fully developed brain, are called ventricles.

14. ____ The neural tube is a sheet of primitive neural cells that curls to form a hollow tube that is lined with stem cells.

Check your answers and review any areas of weakness before going on to the next section.

Development During Infancy and Childhood: Physical Development

Preview Questions

Consider the following questions as you study this section of the chapter.

- What reflexes and sensory capabilities are physically helpless infants equipped with that enhance their chances for survival?
- How do the sensory capabilities of the newborn promote the development of relationships with caregivers?
- How does the brain develop after birth?
- What are the major milestones in infant motor development, and at what average age do they take place?

Read the section "Physical Development" and ***write*** *your answers to the following:*

1. Newborn infants enter the world equipped with ____________________

   Their senses of vision, hearing, smell, and touch are ____________________

2. The infant's sensory capabilities promote the development of relationships with caregivers, as evidenced by the fact that they ____________________

3. After birth, a number of physical changes in the brain and body take place: ____________________

4. Some of the major milestones in infant motor development (and the average age range of each) are ____________________

   The basic sequence of motor-skill development is ____________________

Development During Infancy and Childhood: Social and Personality Development

Preview Questions

Consider the following questions as you study this section of the chapter.

- What is temperament, and what temperamental patterns have been identified?
- What is attachment, and what is the basic premise of attachment theory?
- How is attachment measured?

Read the section "Social and Personality Development" and ***write*** *your answers to the following:*

1. Temperament refers to ____________________

The three broad temperamental patterns are ______

Two other temperamental patterns that have been identified are ______

2. Attachment is the ______

The basic premise of attachment theory is ______

3. Attachment is measured using a procedure called the ______
In this procedure, ______

Development During Infancy and Childhood: Language Development

Preview Questions

Consider the following questions as you study this section of the chapter.

- How does a biological predisposition to learn language function in language development?
- How is language development encouraged by caregivers?
- What are the stages of language development?

Read the section "Language Development" and ***write*** *your answers to the following:*

1. According to Noam Chomsky ______
2. Language development is encouraged by ______
3. The stages of language development are ______

Development During Infancy and Childhood: Gender-Role Development

Preview Questions

Consider the following questions as you study this section of the chapter.

- How do the terms *gender, gender role, gender identity,* and *sex* differ in meaning?
- What gender differences develop during childhood?
- How do social learning theory and gender schema theory explain gender-role development?

Read the section "Development During Infancy and Childhood: Gender-Role Development" and ***write*** *your answers to the following:*

1. Gender refers to ______

   Gender roles consist of ______

   Gender identity refers to ______

   Sex is defined as ______

2. Gender differences that develop during childhood include the following:
   (a) ______
   (b) ______
   (c) ______
   (d) ______

3. According to social learning theory, gender roles are ______

4. Gender schema theory contends that ______

After you have carefully studied the preceding sections, complete the following exercises.

Concept Check 2

Read the following and write the correct term in the space provided.

1. Dr. Snow is interested in the abilities of newborns. While testing visual perception, she is likely to find that newborns will look longer at the image of a(n) ________________ than at other visual patterns.
2. To determine whether a child is securely or insecurely attached, researchers are likely to use the ________________________ procedure.
3. Kathy just gave birth to a normal, healthy, eight-and-a-half-pound baby. In terms of brain development, the baby's brain weighs ________________ (25 percent/50 percent/75 percent/100 percent) of its adult weight.
4. When Kathy touched her newborn's right cheek, the infant turned to the right and opened her mouth, a response called the ________________; touching her lips elicited the ________________; and when Kathy put a finger on each of the infant's palms, she grasped them tightly, a response called the ________________.
5. As Kathy's infant develops, she readily adapts to new experiences, displays positive moods and emotions, and has regular sleeping and eating patterns. She is likely to be classified as a temperamentally ________________ infant.
6. In contrast, Kathy's first child Kamron tended to be tense, frightened, and somewhat shy when exposed to new experiences, strangers, and novel objects. According to Jerome Kagan, who classified temperament in terms of reactivity, Kamron is likely to be categorized as a(n) ________________ infant.
7. Kathy and her husband are consistently warm, responsive, and sensitive to their infant's needs, and the infant has developed the expectation that her needs will be met. It is very probable that the infant will form a(n) ________________ attachment to her parents.
8. When Kathy tells 12-month-old Kaila to "Bring Mommy the dolly," Kaila immediately does so, even though she cannot say the words *bring, Mommy,* or *dolly.* This suggests that Kaila's ________________ vocabulary is larger than her ________________ vocabulary.
9. Jerome is 10 months old and has mastered all the motor skills of the typical infant his age. During the next three to four months, he is very likely to be able to master two more motor skills, ________________ and ________________.
10. Malcolm's parents really liked the "Baby Video" that claimed to enhance infant's vocabulary and believed that their infant greatly benefited from watching the video. According to Science Versus Pseudoscience (Can a DVD Program Your Baby to Be a Genius) Malcolm's parents may have misattributed normal developmental progress to the baby's exposure to the video, a phenomenon called ________________.
11. After watching an action-packed movie on TV, young Ho Wai started practicing kung fu kicks and karate chops. According to ____________________ theory, Ho Wai's present behavior is the result of observing and imitating the movie characters, a process called ____________________.
12. Sheila contends that children actively develop cognitive categories for masculinity and femininity, and that these mental representations influence how children perceive, interpret, and remember relevant aspects of what is appropriate for boys and girls. Sheila's views are most consistent with ____________________ theory.
13. Liam describes his girlfriend's behavior as gentle, caring, empathic, and very feminine. Liam is referring to his girlfriend's ________________________.

Review of Terms, Concepts, and Names 2

Use the terms in this list to complete the Matching Exercise, then to help you answer the True/False items correctly.

rooting reflex
sucking reflex
grasping reflex
cephalocaudal pattern
proximodistal trend
temperament
easy temperament
difficult temperament
slow-to-warm-up temperament
high-reactive infant
low-reactive infant
attachment
Mary D. Salter Ainsworth
secure base
secure attachment
insecure attachment
Strange Situation
multiple attachments
motherese (parentese or infant-directed speech)
cooing and babbling stage
comprehension vocabulary
production vocabulary
one-word stage
two-word stage
gender
gender roles
gender identity
sex
social learning theory of gender-role development
modeling
gender schema theory
schemas

Matching Exercise

Match the appropriate term/name with its definition or description.

1. ________________ Kagan's term for infants who react to new experiences, strangers, and novel objects by being fearful, tense, shy, and inhibited.
2. ________________ Procedure for measuring attachment devised by Mary D. Salter Ainsworth, typically used with infants who are between 1 and 2 years old.
3. ________________ Automatic response elicited by touching a newborn's lips.
4. ________________ Temperamental category for babies who have a low activity level, who withdraw from new situations and people, and who adapt to new experiences very gradually.
5. ________________ Universal style of speech used with babies and characterized by very distinct pronunciation, a simplified vocabulary, short sentences, a high pitch, and exaggerated intonation and expression.
6. ________________ Biologically programmed stage in language development that occurs between about 3 and 9 months of age.
7. ________________ Emotional bond that forms between infants and their caregiver(s), especially parents.
8. ________________ Words that are understood by an infant or child.
9. ________________ Form of attachment that may develop when parents are neglectful, inconsistent, or insensitive to their infant's moods or behaviors and reflects an ambivalent or detached emotional relationship between the infant and his or her parents.
10. ________________ Universal stage in language development, starting around 2 years of age, in which infants combine two words to construct simple "sentences" that reflect the first understanding of grammar.
11. ________________ Bonds that are formed between the infant and other consistent caregivers in his or her life, such as relatives or workers at day-care centers.
12. ________________ The tendency of infants to develop motor control from the center of their bodies outwards.
13. ________________ The cultural, social, and psychological meanings that are associated with masculinity or femininity.
14. ________________ Theory that gender roles are acquired through the basic processes of learning, including reinforcement, punishment, and modeling.
15. ________________ The behaviors, attitudes, and personality traits that are designated as either "masculine" or "feminine" in a given culture.
16. ________________ Theory that gender-role development is influenced by the formation of schemas, or mental representations, of masculinity and femininity.

True/False Test

Indicate whether each statement is true or false by placing T or F in the blank space next to each item.

1. ____ Mary D. Salter Ainsworth is the psychologist who devised the Strange Situation procedure to measure attachment; contributed to attachment theory.
2. ____ Production vocabulary refers to the words that an infant or child can speak.
3. ____ An infant's response to having his or her palms touched is called the rooting reflex.

4. ____ Babies with a difficult temperament tend to be intensely emotional, irritable, and fussy; cry a lot; and have irregular sleeping and eating patterns.

5. ____ During the one-word stage, babies use a single word and vocal intonation to stand for an entire sentence.

6. ____ Secure attachment is likely to develop when parents are consistently warm, responsive, and sensitive to their infant's needs.

7. ____ According to attachment theory, parents or caregivers function as a secure base for the infant, providing a sense of comfort, security, and a safe haven from which the infant can explore and learn about the environment.

8. ____ Babies with an easy temperament readily adapt to new experiences, generally display positive moods and emotions, and have regular sleeping and eating patterns.

9. ____ Touching the newborn's cheek elicits the grasping reflex; the infant turns toward the source of the touch and opens the mouth.

10. ____ Temperament is the inborn predisposition to consistently behave and react in a certain way.

11. ____ A low-reactive infant tends to be calm, uninhibited, sociable, not shy, and shows interest rather than fear when exposed to new people, experiences, and objects.

12. ____ The term *cephalocaudal pattern* refers to the fact that physical and motor skill development tends to follow a "top to bottom" sequence with the top of the body developing faster than the bottom.

13. ____ Children learn about gender differences by observing and imitating the sex-typed behaviors of significant adults and other children, a process called *modeling*.

14. ____ In gender schema theory, the mental categories or representations of masculinity and femininity are called *schemas*.

15. ____ Sex refers to the biological category of male or female.

16. ____ Gender identity refers to a person's psychological sense of being male or female.

Check your answers and review any areas of weakness before going on to the next section.

Development During Infancy and Childhood: Cognitive Development

Preview Questions

Consider the following questions as you study this section of the chapter.

- What are Piaget's four stages of cognitive development, and what are the characteristics of each stage?
- What are three criticisms of Piaget's theory?
- What factors did Vygotsky emphasize in his theory of cognitive development?
- What is the zone of proximal development?
- What is the information-processing model of cognitive development?

Read the section "Cognitive Development" and ***write*** *your answers to the following:*

1. The four stages (and their characteristics) in Piaget's theory are

   (a) ____

   ____

   ____

   (b) ____

   ____

   ____

   (c) ____

   ____

   ____

   (d) ____

   ____

   ____

2. Piaget's theory has been criticized because

   ____

   ____

   ____

   ____

   ____

3. Vygotsky believed that ______________________

   ____

   ____

   The zone of proximal development refers to

   ____

   ____

4. The information-processing model of cognitive development views cognitive development as ______________________________ ______________________________ ______________________________

After you have carefully studied the preceding sections, complete the following exercises.

Concept Check 3

Read the following and write the correct term in the space provided.

1. Four-year-old Tiborg is not completely egocentric, and 5-year-old Natasha exhibits some understanding of conservation. Observations such as these suggest that Piaget may have ______________ (overestimated/underestimated) the cognitive abilities of infants and children.
2. Eight-year-old Nadia has the ability to think logically about visible and tangible objects and situations. She is in the ______________________ stage of cognitive development.
3. Young Adrienne attempts to retrieve her toy bear after her father hides it under a blanket. This suggests that Adrienne has developed a sense of ________________ .
4. When Mrs. Goodley cut Janet's hot dog into eight pieces and Simon's into six pieces, Simon started to cry and complained that he wasn't getting as much hot dog as Janet. Piaget would say that Simon doesn't understand the principle of ____________ .
5. Three-year-old Rita calls all unfamiliar four-legged animals "doggies." She appears to be ____________ these new experiences into her existing concept of a dog.
6. Piaget would call Rita's mental representation or concept of dog a ____________ .
7. During a tutorial devoted to the pros and cons of genetic engineering, Vasilis raised some important issues about the ownership of fertilized eggs and whether destroying them constitutes taking a life. Piaget would say that Vasilis is in the ____________ operational stage of cognitive development.
8. While Coral was still in high school, she imagined that most of her college professors would be older bearded males. During her first year, she was surprised to find that many were relatively young females. Because of these new experiences, she has changed her way of thinking about college professors, a process Piaget called ________________ .
9. Dr. Ramenian believes that infants have limited physical coordination and are therefore incapable of clearly demonstrating their mental abilities in tasks involving manual responses. The results of Dr. Ramenian's research using visual tasks suggest that Piaget confused ______________ limitations with ______________ limitations.
10. Dr. Ramenian also believes that cognitive development is a process of continuous change over the lifespan, not a series of distinct stages, as Piaget proposed. His views are consistent with the ____________ model of cognitive development.

Review of Terms, Concepts, and Names 3

Use the terms in this list to complete the Matching Exercise, then to help you answer the True/False items correctly.

Jean Piaget
qualitatively different thinking
assimilation
accommodation
sensorimotor stage
object permanence
schemas
preoperational stage
operations
symbolic thought
egocentrism
irreversibility
centration
conservation
concrete operational stage
formal operational stage
Renée Baillargeon
Lev Vygotsky
zone of proximal development
information-processing model of cognitive development

Matching Exercise

Match the appropriate term/name with its definition or description.

1. ____________ The ability to use words, images, and symbols to represent the world.

2. _______________ Psychologist whose studies of cognitive development during infancy using visual rather than manual tasks challenged beliefs about the age at which object permanence first appears.
3. _______________ The understanding that an object continues to exist even when it can no longer be seen.
4. _______________ Piaget's fourth stage of cognitive development, which lasts from adolescence through adulthood and is characterized by the ability to think logically about abstract principles and hypothetical situations.
5. _______________ Swiss child psychologist whose influential theory proposed that children progress through distinct stages of cognitive development.
6. _______________ The model that views cognitive development as a process of continuous change over the lifespan and that studies the development of fundamental mental processes such as attention, memory, and problem solving.
7. _______________ Piaget's term for the mental representations of the world that children acquire as their memories improve and as they gain an understanding of object permanence.
8. _______________ Piaget's first stage of cognitive development, from birth to about age 2; the period during which the infant explores the environment and acquires knowledge through sensing and manipulating objects.
9. _______________ In Piaget's theory, the inability to take another person's perspective or point of view.
10. _______________ Russian psychologist who stressed the importance of social and cultural influences on cognitive development.

True/False Test

Indicate whether each statement is true or false by placing T or F in the blank space next to each item.

1. ____ In Piaget's theory, the word *operations* refers to logical, mental activities.
2. ____ Changing one's mental representation of the world, and the way one thinks about things on the basis of new information and experiences, is a process Piaget called accommodation.
3. ____ In Piaget's theory, the concrete operational stage is the second stage of cognitive development, which lasts from about age 2 to age 7 and is characterized by increasing use of symbols and prelogical thought processes.
4. ____ In Piaget's theory, irreversibility is the inability to reverse a sequence of events or logical operations mentally.
5. ____ In Piaget's theory, centration refers to the understanding that two equal quantities remain equal even though the form or appearance is rearranged, as long as nothing is added or subtracted.
6. ____ According to Piaget, as children advance to a new stage, their thinking is *qualitatively different* from that used in the previous stage; each new stage represents a fundamental shift in *how* children think and understand the world.
7. ____ In Piaget's theory, the tendency to focus on only one aspect of a situation and ignore other important aspects of the situation is called conservation.
8. ____ Assimilation is the process of incorporating and interpreting new information in terms of existing mental representations of the world.
9. ____ In Piaget's theory, the preoperational stage is the third stage of cognitive development, which lasts from about age 7 to adolescence and is characterized by the ability to think logically about concrete objects and situations.
10. ____ Zone of proximal development refers to the gap between what children can accomplish on their own and what they can accomplish with the help of others who are more competent.

Check your answers and review any areas of weakness before going on to the next section.

Adolescence

Preview Questions

Consider the following questions as you study this section of the chapter.

- How is *adolescence* defined?
- What is puberty, and what are primary and secondary sex characteristics?
- What is the adolescent growth spurt, and, in females, what is menarche?
- What factors affect the timing of puberty?

- What characterizes adolescent relationships with parents and peers?
- What factors are involved in romantic and sexual relationships during adolescence?
- How do adolescents begin the process of identity formation?
- What is Erikson's psychosocial theory of lifespan development?
- What are the key psychosocial conflicts facing adolescents, and what is involved in forming an integrated identity?
- What is moral reasoning?
- What does each level and stage of Kohlberg's theory of moral development involve, and what are some of the criticisms and limitations of the theory?

*Read the section "Adolescence" and **write** your answers to the following:*

1. Adolescence is ______

2. Puberty is the ______

3. Puberty involves the development of primary sex characteristics, which are ______

   and secondary sex characteristics, which are ______

4. The adolescent growth spurt is ______

5. Menarche refers to ______

6. Factors that affect the timing of puberty include ______

   When adolescents are "off time" in maturation, they ______

   Off-time" development is stressful for ______

   Early-maturing girls have ______

   and while early maturation has advantages for boys, these boys are ______

7. The relationship between parents and their adolescent children is ______

8. Romantic and sexual relationships during adolescence are influenced by ______

9. Identity refers to ______

10. Adolescents begin the process of identity formation by ______

11. According to Erikson's psychosocial theory of lifespan development ______

    The key psychosocial conflict facing adolescents is ______

    The path to an integrated identity usually begins with ______

    This is followed by ______

    Gradually ______

12. Moral reasoning is ______

13. Kohlberg's levels (and stages) of moral development are ______________________________
____
____
____
____

14. Criticisms and limitations of Kohlberg's theory are that
(a) ______________________________
____
(b) ______________________________
____
(c) ______________________________
____
(d) ______________________________
____
(e) ______________________________
____

After you have carefully studied the preceding section, complete the following exercises.

Concept Check 4

Read the following and write the correct term in the space provided.

1. Thomas, who is now a young adult, had a typical adolescent period of conflict over identity issues but now feels comfortable with the choices and commitments he has made. According to Erikson, Thomas has achieved an ________________, and the next psychosocial task he is facing is likely to be ________________.
2. Seventeen-year-old Brendan questions his parents' values but is not sure that his peer group's standards are totally correct either. His confusion about what is really important in life suggests that Brendan is struggling with the problem of ________________.
3. Prior to adolescence, Brendan very likely struggled with other conflicts. According to Erikson, his first psychosocial conflict during infancy was about ______________; his second, during toddlerhood (18 months to 3 years), involved ______________; his third, which is likely to have happened during early childhood (3 to 6 years), was concerned with ______________; and his fourth psychosocial conflict in middle to late childhood (6 to 12 years) dealt with ______________.
4. Mr. and Mrs. Atkins have three adolescent children. If they are like most parents, their relationships with their children are likely to be generally ________________ (negative/positive).
5. When she was almost 13, Manjit experienced her first menstrual period. She has reached ________________.
6. Adam is 15 and has gained both height and weight, some body hair, and a deeper voice during the past year. These changes are referred to as ________________ sex characteristics.
7. During the final months of Darrel's prenatal development, there was fierce competition among the neurons in his brain to make connections, and those that did not make connections were eliminated. According to Focus on Neuroscience (The Adolescent Brain), this process is called ______________.
8. Mr. and Mrs. Kartwright both have jobs they enjoy, are involved in community activities, and have two young children. Erikson would say that they have successfully dealt with the psychosocial conflict called ______________, which is typical of the ______________ stage of life.
9. Delbert resists stealing cookies from the cookie jar because he is afraid his mother will punish him if he does. According to Kohlberg's theory, Delbert is demonstrating stage ______________ of the ______________ level of moral reasoning.
10. In her studies of women's moral reasoning, Dr. Haydari found that women tend to stress the importance of maintaining interpersonal relationships and responding to the needs of others rather than focusing primarily on individual rights. Her findings are consistent with those of psychologist ______________, who developed a model of women's moral development that is based on the ethic of ______________.

11. When her daughter chided her about driving slowly, Mrs. Estafani replied that she would not drive faster than the posted speed limit because responsible, law-abiding citizens should always obey traffic laws. According to Kohlberg's theory of moral development, Mrs. Estafani is probably at stage _______ of the _______ level of moral development.

Graphic Organizer 2

For each of the following, identify the appropriate stage of Piaget's theory and the stage and level of Kohlberg's theory.

Statement	Theory	Stage/Level
1. Jeremy refuses to pay taxes and risks going to jail because he does not believe in supporting a government that spends so many tax dollars on weapons of mass destruction. Jeremy enjoys discussing his position and is very articulate in developing logical arguments for ideals such as nonviolence, equality, and human dignity.		
2. Mary is convinced that her older sister Natalie has more soda than she does after her mother pours Natalie's can of soda into a long, thin glass and hers into a short, fat one. Despite being tempted to take a big drink out of Natalie's glass when she is in the washroom, Mary refrains because she thinks she might be punished.		
3. While playing a game of cards with his friends, Mark insists that everyone should have a chance to be dealer because that is the fair thing to do. Mark is also able to explain the rules to everyone by dealing a couple of practice hands; later, he has difficulty trying to explain the game to his Dad without using the cards.		
4. During a discussion with her therapist, Mrs. Bradshaw is asked to describe her husband. Among other things, she notes that he is very law abiding, always drives with extreme care, and frequently boasts that he has never received a ticket. He never completed high school because he couldn't handle all that abstract, hypothetical stuff and is fairly content working as a custodian in an office building.		

Review of Terms, Concepts, and Names 4

Use the terms in this list to complete the Matching Exercise, then to help you answer the True/False items correctly.

adolescence
puberty
primary sex characteristics
secondary sex characteristics
adolescent growth spurt
menarche
identity
Erik Erikson
role confusion
moratorium period
integrated identity
moral reasoning
Lawrence Kohlberg
levels and stages of moral reasoning
preconventional level
conventional level
postconventional level
ethic of individual rights and justice
ethic of care and responsibility

Matching Exercise

Match the appropriate term/name with its definition or description.

1. ________________ A person's sense of self, including his or her memories, experiences, and the values and beliefs that guide his or her behavior.
2. ________________ In Erikson's theory, the period following role confusion, during which the adolescent experiments with different roles, values, and beliefs.
3. ________________ Transitional stage between late childhood and the beginning of adulthood, during which sexual maturity is reached.
4. ________________ The stage of adolescence in which an individual reaches sexual maturity and becomes physiologically capable of sexual reproduction.
5. ________________ A female's first menstrual period, which occurs during puberty.
6. ________________ Period of accelerated growth during puberty, involving rapid increases in height and weight.
7. ________________ American psychologist who proposed an influential theory of moral development.
8. ________________ Carol Gilligan's categorization of women's moral development and reasoning, based on her research that showed women tended to stress the importance of maintaining interpersonal relationships and responding to the needs of others, rather than focusing primarily on individual rights.
9. ________________ The aspect of cognitive development related to the way an individual reasons about moral decisions.
10. ________________ Kohlberg's level of moral reasoning that begins in late childhood and continues through adolescence and adulthood; characterized by moral reasoning that emphasizes social roles, rules, and obligations.

True/False Test

Indicate whether each item is true or false by placing T or F in the space next to each item.

1. ____ Secondary sex characteristics are the sexual organs that are directly involved in reproduction, such as the uterus, ovaries, penis, and testicles.
2. ____ In Erikson's theory, the adolescent's path to successfully achieving an identity begins with *role confusion,* which is characterized by little sense of commitment to the various issues he or she has to grapple with and the social demands made on him or her.
3. ____ Following the moratorium period, during which the adolescent experiments with different roles, values, and beliefs, he or she may then choose among alternatives and make commitments, gradually arriving at an *integrated identity.*
4. ____ Erik Erikson was the psychoanalyst who proposed an influential theory of psychosocial development throughout the lifespan.
5. ____ Primary sex characteristics are sexual characteristics that develop during puberty and are not directly involved in reproduction but differentiate between the sexes, such as male facial hair and female breasts.
6. ____ In Kohlberg's theory, stage 6 of the postconventional level is characterized by moral reasoning that reflects self-chosen ethical principles that are universally applied and take precedence if there is a conflict.
7. ____ The ethic of individual rights and justice is Carol Gilligan's term for the ethic that she believes is the basis for Kohlberg's theory and that she suggests is a more common perspective for males.
8. ____ In Kohlberg's theory, there are three distinct levels of moral reasoning, and each level has two stages that represent different degrees of sophistication in thinking about moral dilemmas.

9. ____ In Kohlberg's theory, stage 1 of the preconventional level is characterized by moral reasoning based on self-interest; it is guided by external consequences, such as avoiding punishment and maximizing personal gain, rather than by internalized values and rules.

Check your answers and review any areas of weakness before going on to the next section.

Adult Development

Preview Questions

Consider the following questions as you study this section of the chapter.

- What are the two fundamental themes that dominate adulthood, and what are the primary psychosocial tasks of early and middle adulthood?
- What is emerging adulthood, and what are some important aspects of this period of lifespan development?
- What physical changes take place in adulthood?
- How does the transition to parenthood affect marital satisfaction?
- What is the nature of intimate relationships and family structures during adulthood?
- What characterizes career paths in adulthood?

Read the section "Adult Development" and ***write*** *your answers to the following:*

1. According to Erikson, the two fundamental themes that dominate adulthood are ____________________

   and the primary psychosocial task of early adulthood is ____________________

   and for middle adulthood ____________________

2. In industrialized countries, emerging adulthood is ____________________

3. Some important aspects of this period of lifespan development are as follows:

   (a) ____________________

   (b) ____________________

   (c) ____________________

   (d) ____________________

   (e) ____________________

4. The physical changes that take place during adulthood include ____________________

5. The nature of intimate relationships and family structures varies widely in the United States. For example, ____________________

6. In relation to having children, marital satisfaction ____________________

7. In terms of careers in adulthood, ____________________

Late Adulthood and Aging

Preview Questions

- What cognitive and physical changes take place in late adulthood?
- What factors can influence social development during this period?
- What is the psychosocial conflict in late adulthood?

Read the section "Late Adulthood and Aging" and ***write*** *your answers to the following:*

1. Regarding mental and physical abilities in late adulthood ______________________________ ______________________________ ______________________________ ______________________________

2. According to the activity theory of aging, ______________________________ ______________________________ ______________________________

3. According to Erikson, the psychosocial conflict of late adulthood is ______________________________ ______________________________

The Final Chapter: Dying and Death

Preview Question

- How did Kübler-Ross describe the stages of dying, and how valid is her theory?

Read the section "The Final Chapter: Dying and Death" and ***write*** *your answers to the following:*

1. According to Kübler-Ross's theory of dying and death, the five stages are ______________________________ ______________________________ ______________________________ ______________________________ ______________________________ ______________________________

2. Problems with Kübler-Ross's theory are that ______________________________ ______________________________

After you have carefully studied the preceding sections, complete the following exercises.

Concept Check 5

Read the following and write the correct term in the space provided.

1. Forty-eight-year-old Dr. Gretinger has three grown children, a thriving dental practice, and is very involved in local community activities. Dr. Gretinger is in the ______________ stage of life and, according to Erikson, has achieved the psychosocial task of ______________ .

2. Compared with their grandparents, Mr. and Mrs. Belmont's children are likely to marry for the first time at ______________ (an earlier/a later) age.

3. David, a 65-year-old retired civil servant, feels that his life has been unproductive and ultimately meaningless. David is in the ______________ stage of life and, according to Erikson, is experiencing ______________ .

4. Andrew, a 45-year-old accountant, has just learned he has a terminal illness. According to Kübler-Ross, as soon as Andrew gets over his initial denial, he will experience ______________ .

5. Geoffrey and Allison have been married for four years and Allison is now pregnant. If they are typical of couples having their first child, they can expect that satisfaction with their marital relationship will ______________ (increase/decline) after the baby is born.

6. The last of the Sandwells' four children has just left home to pursue a career with NASA. If the Sandwells are like most parents whose children have left home, they are likely to experience a steady ______________ (decline/increase) in marital satisfaction.

7. Mort and Harry, who are in their seventies, belong to a club called the "Active Ancients Association." Both men feel that their lives have been meaningful and satisfying, and they are not disappointed in their accomplishments. Erikson would say that Mort and Harry have achieved ______________ .

8. Harry and Mort pursue hobbies, such as fishing, golf, and chess, travel occasionally, take an interest in their grandchildren and great-grandchildren, and do occasional volunteer work. Mort and Harry appear to epitomize the ______________ theory of aging.

9. Jane and Barbara are both in their late sixties and have physically active lives. They walk four or five miles three times a week, take Zumba exercise classes, and are generally actively involved in their community center programs. According to Focus On Neuroscience (Boosting the Aging Brain) one area of the brain that is likely to benefit from this level of aerobic activity is the ________________ .

Graphic Organizer 3

Identify the theorist related to each of the following statements. (Note: This covers theorists discussed throughout the chapter.)

Statement	Theorist
1. I believe that social and cultural influences are the most important factors in cognitive development.	
2. I study attachment, and I have devised a procedure for measuring attachment called the Strange Situation.	
3. In my view, people have an innate understanding of the basic principles of language, which I call a "universal grammar."	
4. I believe that development continues throughout the lifespan and that individuals pass through eight distinct stages during which they are faced with resolving important psychosocial conflicts.	
5. My primary interest is in how children develop intellectually and cognitively, and my theory proposes that children progress through four distinct stages in succession, each stage characterized by a qualitatively different way of thinking from the previous stage.	
6. I believe that there are distinct stages of moral development that unfold in an age-related step-by-step fashion and that are closely associated with age-related cognitive abilities.	
7. Piaget underestimated the cognitive abilities of infants and young children. My studies using visual rather than manual tasks challenged beliefs about the age at which object permanence first appears.	

Review of Terms and Concepts 5

Use the terms in this list to complete the Matching Exercise, then to help you answer the True/False items correctly.

emerging adulthood
early adulthood
middle adulthood
late adulthood
menopause
hot flashes
andropause
generativity
activity theory of aging
ego integrity
despair
life review
Kübler-Ross's stages of dying (denial, anger, bargaining, depression, acceptance)
authoritarian parenting style
permissive parenting style
authoritative parenting style
induction

Matching Exercise

Match the appropriate term/name with its definition or description.

1. ________________ Discipline technique that combines parental control with explaining why a behavior is prohibited.

2. ________________ The natural cessation of menstruation and the end of reproductive capacity in women.
3. ________________ Baumrind's term for a parenting style in which parents are extremely tolerant and not demanding.
4. ________________ Stage of adulthood, roughly from the forties to the mid-sixties, when physical strength and endurance gradually decline.
5. ________________ Psychosocial theory that life satisfaction in late adulthood is highest when people maintain the level of activity they displayed earlier in life.
6. ________________ Erikson's eighth psychosocial task that involves the feeling that one's life has been meaningful.
7. ________________ Process through which the themes of ego integrity or despair emerge as older adults think about or retell their life story to others.
8. ________________ The gradual decline in testosterone levels in middle-aged men.
9. ________________ In industrialized countries, the stage of lifespan from approximately the late teens to the mid- to late-twenties, which is characterized by exploration, instability, and flexibility in social roles, vocational choices, and relationships.

True/False Test

Indicate whether each item is true or false by placing T or F in the space next to each item.

1. ___ In Erikson's theory, the primary psychosocial task of middle adulthood in which the person contributes to future generations through children, career, and other meaningful activity is called generativity.
2. ___ Early adulthood refers to the stage of development during the twenties and thirties when physical strength typically peaks.
3. ___ Authoritarian parenting style is Diana Baumrind's term for describing parents who set clear standards for their children's behavior but are also responsive to the children's needs and wishes.
4. ___ Late adulthood refers to the stage of development beginning in the mid-sixties, when physical stamina and reaction time tend to decline further and faster.
5. ___ According to Baumrind, authoritative parents are demanding and expect obedience from their children; they are unresponsive toward their children's needs or wishes.
6. ___ According to Kübler-Ross, people who are facing death go through five stages—denial, anger, bargaining, depression, and acceptance.
7. ___ During Erikson's eighth stage of psychosocial development, older adults who are filled with regrets or bitterness about past mistakes, missed opportunities, or bad decisions experience despair.
8. ___ For some women, menopause involves some unpleasant symptoms, such as *hot flashes,* which are rapid and extreme increases in body temperature.

Check your answers and review any areas of weakness before going on to the next section.

Something to Think About

1. A popular and controversial topic in any discussion of raising children is the effect of day care on a child's development. Such discussions can become quite heated, with people holding strong views on both sides of the debate. On the basis of what you have read in this chapter, what light could you shed on this controversial topic?
2. You may be planning to have a family one day, if you haven't already started one. For most people this is quite a responsibility and a lot of work. Unlike many other areas in life, no formal training is available or required for the job of parent. You, however, are fortunate because you are taking an introductory psychology course and have learned a few things about child development. What advice would you give to people who are planning to have a family?

Check your answers and review any areas of weakness before doing the progress tests.

Progress Test 1

Review the complete chapter (including all boxed inserts), review all your study notes, and then test yourself on the following progress test. Check your answers. If you make a mistake, review your notes, check the appropriate section in the study guide, and, if necessary, go back and read the relevant part of the chapter in your textbook.

1. When Thomas was conceived, he was a single fertilized egg called a(n)
   (a) zygote. (c) fetus.
   (b) embryo. (d) infant.

2. Young Misty has dark curly hair and freckles; her friend Paige has straight blonde hair and no freckles. In both children, the underlying genetic makeup and genetic instructions for these traits are their ____________ , and the observable traits that they actually display are their ____________.
   (a) dominant characteristics; recessive characteristics
   (b) phenotypes; genotypes
   (c) recessive characteristics; dominant characteristics
   (d) genotypes; phenotypes

3. In her research, Dr. Joacim found that a pregnant mother's use of a certain chemical substance caused harm to the fetus. The chemical substance could be classified as
   (a) DNA. (c) a phenotype.
   (b) a chromosome. (d) a teratogen.

4. When Samira was an infant, she was usually calm, uninhibited, sociable, and typically showed interest rather than fear when exposed to new people, novel experiences, and unfamiliar objects. In terms of Kagan's classification of temperamental patterns, Samira is likely to be categorized as
   (a) a low-reactive infant.
   (b) a slow-to-warm-up infant.
   (c) a high-reactive infant.
   (d) an insecurely attached infant.

5. When Mrs. Euland touched her newborn's lips, he produced an automatic response called the ____________ reflex.
   (a) rooting (c) grasping
   (b) sucking (d) greedy

6. It has become apparent to Mr. and Mrs. Euland that their baby has a low activity level, tends to withdraw from new situations and people, and adapts to new experiences very gradually. The baby would be classified as a(n) ____________ baby.
   (a) easy (c) slow-to-warm-up
   (b) difficult (d) securely attached

7. When 2-year-old Kerry was tested in the Strange Situation, she did not explore the environment even when her mother was present. She appeared very anxious, and she became extremely distressed when her mother left the room. Kerry is a(n)
   (a) insecurely attached infant.
   (b) securely attached infant.
   (c) slow-to-warm-up infant.
   (d) concrete operational infant.

8. Donald believes in law and order, obeys all rules and regulations, and has respect for authorities just because they are authorities. Donald is likely at Kohlberg's ____________ level of moral reasoning.
   (a) preconventional
   (b) postconventional
   (c) conventional
   (d) care and responsibility

9. When Neil's mother hides his favorite toy under a blanket, Neil acts as though it no longer exists and makes no attempt to retrieve it. Neil is in Piaget's ________________ stage, and his behavior suggests that he ________________.
   (a) sensorimotor; has developed object permanence
   (b) sensorimotor; has not yet developed object permanence
   (c) concrete operational; is capable of reversible thinking
   (d) formal operational; understands the principle of conservation

10. Lincoln is a normal 8-month-old infant. According to Chomsky's theory of language development, Lincoln
   (a) has a biological predisposition to learn any language and can distinguish among speech sounds of all the world's languages.
   (b) has a much larger production vocabulary than comprehension vocabulary.
   (c) can only distinguish among the speech sounds of the language spoken by his parents.
   (d) is capable of speaking quite clearly but only in motherese (infant-directed speech).

11. Danielle has switched college majors four times and does not know what she wants to do after she gets her degree. Erikson would suggest that Danielle has not achieved
    (a) an integrated identity.
    (b) a sense of generativity.
    (c) the zone of proximal development.
    (d) the formal operational stage of development.

12. Sarah believes that gender roles develop as young children observe others modeling particular gender-appropriate behaviors and that children are rewarded when they behave accordingly and punished when they don't. Sarah's view is most consistent with ________________ theory of gender-role development.
    (a) gender schema
    (b) Erikson's psychosocial
    (c) social learning
    (d) Piaget's cognitive

13. Gordon, a 50-year-old lawyer, has just learned from his physician that he has only one year to live. According to Kübler-Ross, his first reaction to hearing the news is likely to be
    (a) "No, it's not possible, there's obviously been some mix-up, some terrible mistake."
    (b) "Life is not worth living any more."
    (c) "Why me? This is very unfair and makes me mad."
    (d) "Well, that's the way it goes, I guess."

14. According to Enhancing Well-Being with Psychology, a parenting style in which parents set clear standards for their children's behavior but are also responsive to the children's needs and wishes is called
    (a) authoritarian.
    (b) permissive-indulgent.
    (c) permissive-indifferent.
    (d) authoritative.

15. According to Culture and Human Behavior (Where Does the Baby Sleep?), infants typically sleep in their own bed and in a separate room from their parents in
    (a) all cultures.
    (b) all Western cultures.
    (c) the United States.
    (d) all Latin cultures.

Progress Test 2

After you have checked your understanding of the material in Progress Test 1 and have done a complete chapter review with special focus on any areas of weakness, you are ready to assess your knowledge on Progress Test 2. Check your answers. If you make a mistake, review your notes, the relevant section of the study guide, and, if necessary, the appropriate part of your textbook.

1. Dr. Strayer is conducting longitudinal research on factors that correlate with getting older. She is likely to find that
    (a) intelligence declines sharply with age.
    (b) there is severe memory impairment as people reach late adulthood.
    (c) most people maintain their intellectual abilities as they age.
    (d) no matter how much older people practice their mental skills, they still do very poorly on intellectual tasks.

2. Oliver, who is almost 30, has finished his graduate studies at State University and is now considering a number of career options. He is not married or in a long-term committed relationship and enjoys the flexibility that his single life allows. Which of the following statements is most likely to be true of Oliver?
    (a) He would be classified as being in the emerging adult stage of lifespan development.
    (b) He is in Piaget's concrete operational stage of development.
    (c) He has not resolved the primary psychosocial conflict of autonomy versus doubt.
    (d) He would be classified as being in the middle adulthood stage of lifespan development.

3. When he was 13, Kyle experienced several physical changes: his testicles started to enlarge, his height and weight increased, and his voice deepened. Kyle experienced
    (a) menarche.
    (b) a germinal period.
    (c) puberty.
    (d) irreversibility.

4. Dominique is participating in a class debate on the issue of whether war is ever justified. She argues that war is never justified because it involves killing people, which is against the law, and obeying the law is something everyone

must do. Dominique is in the __________ stage of __________ .

(a) postconventional; Kohlberg's model of moral development
(b) conventional; Kohlberg's model of moral development
(c) moratorium; Erikson's model of psychosocial development
(d) concrete operational; Piaget's model of cognitive development

5. Mrs. Grant is 49 years old and has recently ceased to menstruate. Mrs. Grant has experienced
   (a) moratorium.
   (b) menopause.
   (c) menarche.
   (d) centration.

6. According to Erikson's psychosocial theory of development, late adulthood is to __________ as adolescence is to __________ .
   (a) ego integrity; generativity
   (b) generativity; intimacy
   (c) intimacy; ego integrity
   (d) ego integrity; integrated identity

7. In a term paper on child development, Simon made the case that children actively develop categories for masculinity and femininity and suggested that these mental representations influence how children perceive, interpret, and remember relevant aspects of what is appropriate for girls and boys. Simon's position is most consistent with __________ of gender-role development.
   (a) gender schema theory
   (b) Erikson's psychosocial theory
   (c) Kohlberg's moral theory
   (d) social learning theory

8. Sixteen-year-old Jade is reading books about different religions and philosophies and is trying out different approaches to how one should live one's life. Jade is in Erikson's
   (a) moratorium period.
   (b) generativity stage.
   (c) ego integrity period.
   (d) formal operational stage.

9. According to Focus on Neuroscience (The Adolescent Brain), MRI studies of normal children and adolescents
   (a) demonstrated clearly that there was a causal connection between high levels of sex hormones and emotional problems in adolescents.
   (b) indicated that only about 10 percent of the neurons in adolescent brains were ever active or were ever used.
   (c) showed overproduction of a second wave of gray matter just prior to puberty, followed by a second round of neuronal pruning during the teenage years.
   (d) indicated that as the brain matures the amount of gray matter increases significantly and the amount of white matter steadily diminishes.

10. Marcel is researching a paper for his child development course and discovers the work of Lev Vygotsky. In summarizing Vygotsky's contribution to developmental psychology, Marcel is likely to note that the theorist emphasized
    (a) genetic factors.
    (b) clearly defined biological stages of cognitive development.
    (c) clearly defined biological stages of physical development.
    (d) social and cultural factors in cognitive development.

11. Kelly is 5 years old and has a good imagination. Recently, for example, she used a discarded box as a make-believe castle and made up a very interesting dialogue between the "king" and "queen" of her castle. This illustrates
    (a) centration.
    (b) conservation.
    (c) symbolic thought.
    (d) object permanence.

12. In the Strange Situation procedure, little Anthony used his mother as a safe base from which to explore the environment, showed distress when she left the room, and greeted her warmly when she returned. Anthony would be classified as a(n)
    (a) difficult baby.
    (b) securely attached baby.
    (c) insecurely attached baby.
    (d) slow-to-warm-up baby.

13. The development of freckles appears to be controlled by a single gene, which can be either dominant or recessive. Colleen has freckles, just like her mother, so it is likely that she inherited a dominant version of the freckle gene from her mother. The simple dominant–recessive pattern is a fairly common example of gene variation. The different versions of genes are called
    (a) alleles.
    (b) phenotypes.
    (c) sex chromosomes.
    (d) karyotypes.

14. According to Critical Thinking (The Effects of Child Care on Attachment and Development), putting young children in a high-quality day-care facility
    (a) is detrimental to their physical health.
    (b) severely disrupts the attachment process.
    (c) has no detrimental effect on the children.
    (d) is detrimental to their psychological health.

15. According to Enhancing Well-Being with Psychology, psychologist Diana Baumrind has described a number of basic parenting styles. In her research, she found that children of _______ parents were likely to be moody, unhappy, fearful, withdrawn, unspontaneous, and irritable.
    (a) permissive-indulgent
    (b) permissive-indifferent
    (c) authoritative
    (d) authoritarian

Progress Test 3

After you have checked your understanding of the material in Progress Tests 1 and 2, and have done a complete chapter review with special focus on any areas of weakness, you are ready to further assess your knowledge with Progress Test 3. Check your answers. If you make a mistake, review your notes, the appropriate parts of the study guide, and, if necessary, the relevant sections of your textbook.

1. In looking back at his life, 70-year-old Redner experiences regret, dissatisfaction, and disappointment about his accomplishments. According to Erikson, Redner, who is in late adulthood, is experiencing _______________ and has failed to achieve a sense of _______________ .
    (a) inferiority; generativity
    (b) despair; ego integrity
    (c) stagnation; ego identity
    (d) isolation; intimacy

2. Nine-year-old Adam has acquired the mental operations to comprehend such things as conservation and reversibility and can solve tangible problems in a logical manner. Adam is in Piaget's _______________ stage of development.
    (a) sensorimotor
    (b) preoperational
    (c) concrete operational
    (d) formal operational

3. Piaget is to _______________ development as Erikson is to _______________ development.
    (a) cognitive; language
    (b) psychosocial; cognitive
    (c) language; cognitive
    (d) cognitive; psychosocial

4. Despite the fact that he uses only one-word utterances when he attempts to talk, 1-year-old Vincent immediately does what he is told when his mother says, "Bring Mommy the teddy bear, Vincent." This suggests that
    (a) Vincent's comprehension vocabulary is much larger than his production vocabulary.
    (b) Vincent is in the embryonic stage of language development.
    (c) Vincent has reached the concrete operational stage of development.
    (d) Vincent's production vocabulary is much larger than his comprehension vocabulary.

5. When asked if he had a brother, 3-year-old Kiran said, "Yes, and his name is Mike." When Kiran was asked if Mike had a brother, he replied, "No." This example illustrates Kiran's preoperational way of thinking and demonstrates
    (a) conservation.
    (b) egocentrism.
    (c) a problem in production vocabulary.
    (d) that he has not yet entered the zone of proximal development.

6. Nine months after conception, baby Tracy is born. The stages of her prenatal development, from first to last, were
    (a) embryonic, fetal, germinal.
    (b) fetal, embryonic, germinal.
    (c) germinal, embryonic, fetal.
    (d) germinal, fetal, embryonic.

7. Mrs. Hoff uses very distinct pronunciation, a simplified vocabulary, short sentences, a high pitch, and exaggerated intonation and expression whenever she interacts with her baby. This is an example of
   (a) motherese, parentese, or infant-directed speech.
   (b) comprehension vocabulary.
   (c) an insecurely attached mother.
   (d) cooing and babbling.

8. Dr. Kalbiar believes that there is a gap between what children can accomplish on their own and what they can accomplish with the help of others who are more competent. Vygotsky's theory suggested that such guidance can help "stretch" the child's cognitive abilities to new levels, an idea he called
   (a) induction.
   (b) event-specific expectations.
   (c) centration.
   (d) the zone of proximal development.

9. During Mr. Guerno's seventieth birthday party, his grandchildren had a chance to ask him about some of his many adventures and travels. While listening to his colorful stories, they realized that their grandfather had lived a very meaningful life and was very satisfied with his many accomplishments. Mr. Guerno is in the ________________ stage of life and has achieved what Erikson called ________________.
   (a) middle adulthood; generativity
   (b) late adulthood; ego integrity
   (c) middle adulthood; initiative
   (d) late adulthood; ego identity

10. According to Focus on Neuroscience (The Adolescent Brain), neuroscientists studying brain changes during childhood are likely to find that between age 6 and early adolescence
   (a) there is a steady increase in the actual number of neurons in the brain.
   (b) unused dendrites, synaptic connections, and neurons are selectively pruned and discarded, and those neurons that are most used strengthen their interconnections with other neurons.
   (c) the neurons that are least used tend to proliferate and those that are most used tend to wear out and decrease in number.
   (d) there is an explosive proliferation of synaptic connections in all neurons regardless of whether they are used.

11. Young Allison doesn't understand that adding together one and three is the same as adding together three and one. Allison is demonstrating ________________ and is in Piaget's ________________ stage of development.
   (a) conservation; concrete operational
   (b) egocentrism; preoperational
   (c) centration; sensorimotor
   (d) irreversibility; preoperational

12. Fourteen-year-old Jason has the ability to reason abstractly and think logically even about hypothetical situations. Jason is in Piaget's ______________ stage of cognitive development.
   (a) sensorimotor
   (b) preoperational
   (c) concrete operational
   (d) formal operational

13. According to Kohlberg's theory of moral development, preconventional morality is to postconventional morality as ______________ is to ______________.
   (a) social approval; ethical principle
   (b) self-interest; ethical principle
   (c) self-interest; social approval
   (d) social approval; self-interest

14. Dr. Bradshaw and his colleagues have conducted research on a relatively new trend on college campuses called "hooking up." If their findings are similar to those reported in the text (In Focus: Hooking Up On Campus) they are likely to find that
   (a) both men and women report that hooking up had overall been a more negative than positive experience.
   (b) alcohol does not appear to be a factor implicated in hooking-up behavior.
   (c) about 80 percent of students report hooking up at least once while in college.
   (d) compared with women, men tend to report more negative emotional reactions after hooking up.

15. Tracy is now 18 months old; during her development her parents read to her every day. On the other hand, 18-month-old Tommy's parents frequently showed their child a DVD that claimed to enhance language skill development. According to Science Versus Pseudoscience (Can a DVD Program Your Baby to Be a Genius?) it is very likely that
    (a) Tommy and Tracy will have learned an equal number of words.
    (b) Tommy will have learned more words than Tracy.
    (c) Both children will have retarded language development compared with children whose parents simply talked to their children.
    (d) Tracy will have learned more words than Tommy.

Answers

Introduction: Your Life Story

1. *Developmental psychology is the* study of how people change physically, mentally, and socially over the lifespan.
2. *The major themes in developmental psychology are* the common patterns of growth and change and how people differ in their development and life stories; the abrupt age-related stages people go through over the lifespan and those aspects of development that reflect gradually unfolding changes; and the nature of the interaction between heredity (nature) and environment (nurture) throughout development.
3. *The eight major stages of the lifespan are* prenatal (conception to birth); infancy and toddlerhood (birth to 2 years); early childhood (2 to 6 years); middle childhood (6 to 12 years); adolescence (12 to 18 years); young adulthood (18 to 40 years); middle adulthood (40 to 65 years); late adulthood (65 years to death).

Genetic Contributions to Your Life Story

1. *A zygote is* a single cell formed at conception from the union of the egg cell and the sperm cell that contains the unique set of genetic instructions inherited from our biological parents.
2. *Chromosomes are* long, thread-like structures composed of twisted parallel strands of DNA; they are found in the cell nucleus.
3. *Deoxyribonucleic acid (DNA) is* the double-stranded molecule that is the chemical basis of heredity and carries genetic instructions in the cell.
4. *Genes are* the basic units of heredity and consist of units of DNA strung like beads along the chromosomes; each gene is a unit of DNA code for making a particular protein molecule. *Genes direct the manufacture of* proteins, which are used in virtually all body functions, such as building cells, producing hormones, and regulating brain activity.
5. *Genotype refers to the* underlying genetic makeup of a particular organism, including the genetic instructions for traits that are not actually displayed. *The human genome is* the scientific description of the complete set of DNA in the human organism.
6. *Alleles are* different versions of a particular gene; the combination of these makes our unique genotype (some genes have only a few different versions, others have 50 or more). *The best-known pattern of allele variation is the* dominant–recessive *gene pair. These alleles operate as follows:* The dominant gene contains genetic instructions that may be expressed when paired with another dominant gene or with a recessive gene, and the recessive gene contains genetic instructions that will not be expressed unless paired with another recessive gene.
7. *Phenotype refers to the* observable traits or characteristics of an organism as determined by the interaction of genetics and environmental factors.
8. *The "genetic blueprint" analogy is not accurate because* (a) genes don't directly control physical development, traits, or behavior (they direct the synthesis and production of particular proteins, which ultimately influence development and behavior); (b) environmental factors influence the phenotype that is actually displayed (freckles will not develop, even if you have the dominant "freckle" gene, without exposure to sunlight); and (c) different genotypes react differently to environmental factors, and people with a particular genetic configuration (their genotype) will be more or less sensitive to particular environmental factors (redheads sunburn more easily because their genotype is especially sensitive to the effects of ultraviolet light).
9. *Scientists use the term genetic predispositions to refer to* the tendency of certain genotypes to be sensitive to specific environmental factors, to a lesser or greater degree, influencing their development in a particular way.
10. *Gene expression can be triggered by* the activity of other genes, internal chemical changes, or by

environmental factors and is thus flexible (rather than being a fixed master plan or blueprint).

11. *Epigenetics researchers study* the mechanisms that control gene expression and their effects on behavior and health. *They investigate how* gene activity is regulated within a cell, such as identifying the signals that switch genes to "on" or "off."

12. *Epigenetic research is providing insight into* how the environment affects gene expression and the final phenotype that develops.

13. *The five critical factors in the relationship between genotype and phenotype are* (a) interactions among genes; (b) interactions between genotype and environmental influences; (c) genetic mutations (genes can spontaneously change from one generation to the next); (d) genetic damage (DNA can be damaged by environmental factors); and (e) errors can occur in the genetic code, which can disrupt production of correct proteins and lead to birth defects or genetic disorders.

Prenatal Development

1. *During prenatal development, the single-celled zygote* undergoes rapid cell division before it is implanted on the wall of the mother's uterus. Eventually, it develops into a full-term fetus.

2. *The three phases of the prenatal stage are* the germinal period, which is also called the zygotic period (the first two weeks), the embryonic period (from the third through the eighth week), and the fetal period (from the ninth week until birth).

3. *Teratogens are* harmful agents or substances that can cross the placenta and cause malformations or defects in an embryo or fetus. The greatest vulnerability to teratogens is during the embryonic stage. Some teratogens can damage the developing fetus at any stage. *Other factors that can affect the unborn child are* the mother's psychological state, including depression, chronic stress, and anxiety, as well as poor nutrition, lack of sleep, and other unhealthy behaviors.

4. *The neural tube is* a sheet of primitive neural cells that curls to form a hollow tube that is lined with stem cells. *Stem cells are* cells that can divide indefinitely, renew themselves, and give rise to a variety of other types of cells.

5. *The top of the neural tube develops to eventually form* the three main regions of the brain: the hindbrain, midbrain, and forebrain.

6. *The fetal period is* the final and longest stage of prenatal development; during this seven-month period, body systems grow and reach maturity in preparation for life outside the mother's body. *After birth, the neurons* grow in size and continue to develop new dendrites and interconnections with other neurons, myelin forms on axons in key areas of the brain, and the axons also grow longer and their branching ends become more dense.

Concept Check 1

1. developmental
2. epigenetics
3. genetic predisposition
4. embryo; fetus
5. teratogen
6. infancy; early childhood; middle childhood
7. chromosomes; deoxyribonucleic acid (DNA); genes
8. dominant–recessive pattern
9. stem cells

Graphic Organizer 1

1. cell nucleus: D
2. chromosome: C
3. gene: A
4. DNA: B

See next page for graphic depiction of cell.

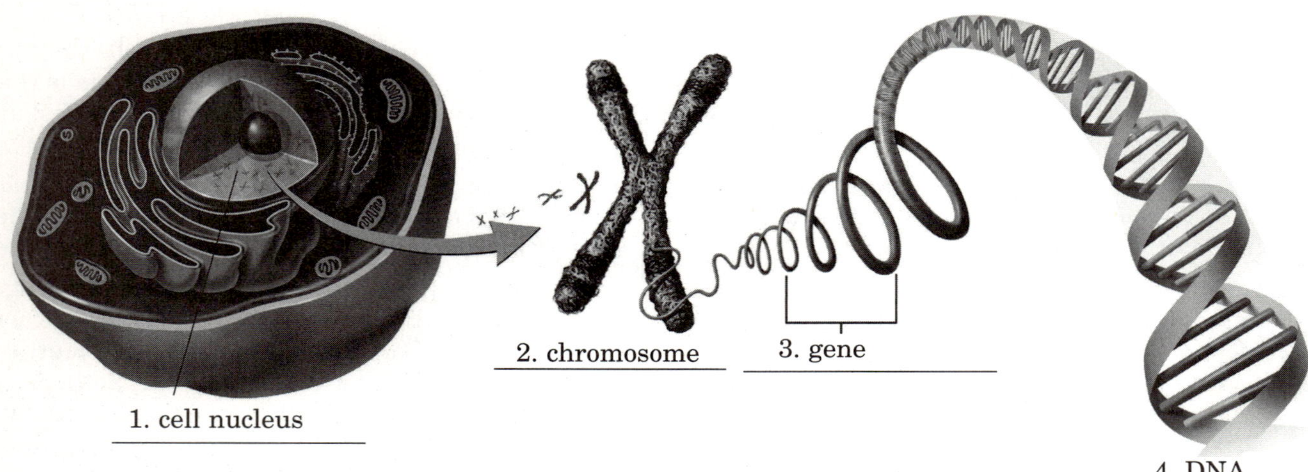

Matching Exercise 1

1. prenatal stage
2. gene
3. developmental psychology
4. genetic predisposition
5. teratogens
6. chromosome
7. mutation
8. germinal period (zygotic period)
9. embryo
10. human genome
11. allele
12. placenta
13. epigenetics
14. stem cells

True/False Test 1

1. T	5. T	9. F	13. T
2. T	6. T	10. F	14. T
3. T	7. F	11. T	
4. F	8. T	12. T	

Development During Infancy and Childhood: Physical Development

1. *Newborn infants enter the world equipped with* the rooting reflex, the sucking reflex, and the grasping reflex. *Their senses of vision, hearing, smell, and touch are* keenly attuned to people, and this ability helps them differentiate between their mothers and other people.
2. *The infant's sensory capabilities promote the development of relationships with caregivers, as evidenced by the fact that they* stare at human faces longer than at other images, make eye contact with adults who position themselves close to the newborn (about 6 to 12 inches), and display a preference for their mother's voice and face.
3. *After birth, a number of physical changes in the brain and body take place:* At birth, the brain is about 25 percent of its adult weight, whereas birth weight is only about 5 percent of the body's eventual adult weight. During infancy, the brain will grow to about 75 percent of its adult weight, whereas body weight will reach approximately 20 percent of adult weight. Physical and motor skill development follows a cephalocaudal pattern (a top to bottom sequence) and development of motor control goes from the center of the body outwards, a pattern called the proximodistal trend.
4. *Some of the major milestones in infant motor development (and the average age range of each) are* rolling over (2 to 5.5 months), grasping a rattle (2.5 to 4.5 months), sitting without support (5 to 8 months), standing while holding on (5 to 10 months), standing alone well (10 to 14 months), walking well (11 to 14.5 months), building tower of two cubes (12 to 20 months), walking up steps (14 to 22 months). *The basic sequence of motor skill development is* universal, but the average age of mastery of each skill

varies a great deal, with each infant having his or her own inborn timetable of physical maturation and developmental readiness.

Development During Infancy and Childhood: Social and Personality Development

1. *Temperament refers to* the inborn predispositions to consistently behave and react in a certain way. *The three broad temperamental patterns are* easy, difficult, and slow-to-warm-up. *Two other temperamental patterns that have been identified are* high and low reactivity. High-reactive infants react intensely to new experiences, strangers, and novel objects and tend to be tense, fearful, and inhibited (shy); low-reactive infants tend to be calmer, uninhibited, bolder, and more sociable and show interest rather than fear when exposed to new people, experiences, and objects.
2. *Attachment is the* emotional bond that forms between the infant and his or her caregivers, especially the parents. *The basic premise of attachment theory is* that an infant's ability to thrive physically and psychologically depends in part on the quality of attachment. When parents are consistently warm, responsive, and sensitive to their infant's needs, the infant develops a secure attachment; if parents are neglectful, inconsistent, or insensitive to the infant's moods or behaviors, he or she may suffer insecure attachment.
3. *Attachment is measured using a procedure called the* Strange Situation. *In this procedure,* the infant and mother are brought into an unfamiliar room with a variety of toys, and a few minutes later a stranger enters. The mother stays with the infant for a few moments, then departs and returns a short time later, she again spends a little time with the infant, and then departs and returns again. Observers record the infant's behavior through a one-way window.

Development During Infancy and Childhood: Language Development

1. *According to Noam Chomsky,* all children are born with a biological predisposition to learn language; in effect, they possess a "universal grammar," which allows them to easily extract grammatical rules from what they hear.
2. *Language development is encouraged by* the use of infant-directed speech (motherese or parentese) that adults instinctively use with babies.
3. *The stages of language development are* the cooing and babbling stage, the one-word stage (in which comprehension vocabulary is usually much larger than production vocabulary), the two-word stage, and finally, fully developed language comprehension and production.

Development During Infancy and Childhood: Gender-Role Development

1. *Gender refers* to the cultural, social, and psychological meanings that are associated with masculinity and femininity. *Gender roles consist* of the behaviors, attitudes, and personality traits that are designated as either masculine or feminine in a given culture. *Gender identity refers to* a person's psychological sense of being male or female. *Sex is defined as* biologically determined physical characteristics such as differences in reproductive anatomy and function.
2. *Gender differences that develop during childhood in our culture include the following: (a)* From about the age of 18 to 24 months sex differences in behavior begin to emerge and become more pronounced throughout childhood *(b)* Toddler girls play more with soft toys and dolls and ask for adult help, whereas toddler boys play more with blocks and trucks or wagons, and play more actively than do girls. *(c)* Between the ages of 2 and 3, preschoolers start acquiring gender-role stereotypes for toys, clothes, household objects, games, and work; and *(d)* they also develop a strong preference for playing with members of their own sex, tendencies that continue throughout childhood.
3. *According to social learning theory,* gender roles are developed through the basic processes of learning, including reinforcement, punishment, and modeling.
4. *Gender schema theory contends that* children actively develop mental categories, or schemas, for masculinity and femininity, and these mental representations influence gender-role development.

Concept Check 2

1. human face
2. Strange Situation
3. 25 percent
4. rooting reflex; sucking reflex; grasping reflex
5. easy
6. high-reactive
7. secure

8. comprehension; production
9. standing alone well; walking well
10. an illusory correlation
11. social learning; modeling
12. gender schema
13. gender role

Matching Exercise 2

1. high-reactive infant
2. Strange Situation
3. sucking reflex
4. slow-to-warm-up temperament
5. motherese (parentese or infant-directed speech)
6. cooing and babbling stage
7. attachment
8. comprehension vocabulary
9. insecure attachment
10. two-word stage
11. multiple attachments
12. proximodistal trend
13. gender
14. social learning theory of gender-role development
15. gender roles
16. gender schema theory

True/False Test 2

1. T	5. T	9. F	13. T
2. T	6. T	10. T	14. T
3. F	7. T	11. T	15. T
4. T	8. T	12. T	16. T

Development During Infancy and Childhood: Cognitive Development

1. *The four stages (and their characteristics) in Piaget's theory are (a)* The sensorimotor stage, from birth to about age 2, during which the infant explores the environment and acquires knowledge through experiencing and manipulating objects. Object permanence develops by the end of this stage. *(b)* The preoperational stage, from about age 2 to age 7, during which the use of symbols and prelogical thought processes increase. Characteristics of this stage include the increasing use of symbolic thought; the tendency for egocentrism, irreversibility, and centration; and the inability to understand conservation. *(c)* The concrete operational stage, from about age 7 to adolescence, during which the child develops the ability to think logically about concrete objects and situations. Characteristics of this stage are the tendency to be less egocentric in their thinking, the ability to reverse mental problems, and the ability to understand the principle of conservation. *(d)* The formal operational stage, from adolescence through adulthood, during which the person acquires the ability to think logically about abstract principles and hypothetical situations. This stage is characterized by more systematic and logical problem-solving abilities.
2. *Piaget's theory has been criticized because* he underestimated the cognitive abilities of infants and young children, confusing motor skill limitations with cognitive limitations; he underestimated the impact of social and cultural factors on cognitive development; and he overestimated the degree to which people achieve formal operational thought processes.
3. *Vygotsky believed that* cognitive development is strongly influenced by social and cultural factors, such as the support and guidance that children receive from parents, other adults, and older children. *The zone of proximal development refers to* the gap between what children can accomplish on their own and what they can accomplish with the help of others who are more competent.
4. *The information-processing model of cognitive development views cognitive development as* a process of continuous change over the lifespan. Researchers in this area focus on the development of fundamental mental processes, such as attention, memory, and problem solving.

Concept Check 3

1. underestimated
2. concrete operational
3. object permanence
4. conservation
5. assimilating
6. schema
7. formal
8. accommodation
9. motor skill; cognitive
10. information-processing

Matching Exercise 3

1. symbolic thought
2. Renée Baillargeon
3. object permanence
4. formal operational stage
5. Jean Piaget
6. information-processing model of cognitive development
7. schemas
8. sensorimotor stage
9. egocentrism
10. Lev Vygotsky

True/False Test 3

1. T	6. T
2. T	7. F
3. F	8. T
4. T	9. F
5. F	10. T

Adolescence

1. *Adolescence is* the transitional stage between late childhood and the beginning of adulthood, during which sexual maturity is reached.
2. *Puberty is the* physical process of attaining sexual maturation and reproductive capacity that begins during the early adolescent years.
3. *Puberty involves the development of primary sex characteristics, which are* the sexual organs that are directly involved in reproduction, such as the uterus, ovaries, penis, and testicles, *and secondary sex characteristics, which are* not directly involved in reproduction but differentiate between the sexes, such as male facial hair and female breasts.
4. *The adolescent growth spurt is* the period of accelerated growth during puberty, involving rapid increases in height and weight (occurs about two years earlier in females than in males).
5. *Menarche refers to* a female's first menstrual period (typically occurs around 12 or 13, but may be as early as 9 or 10 or as late as 16 or 17).
6. *Factors that affect the timing of puberty include* genetics, nutrition, health, body size, degree of physical activity, family stress, and absence of the biological father. *When adolescents are "off time" in maturation, they* experience maturation noticeably earlier or later than the majority of their peers. *"Off-time" development is stressful for* both boys and girls, who may experience teasing, social isolation, and exclusion from social activities. Girls who develop early and boys who develop late are most likely to have problems. *Early-maturing girls have* higher rates of sexual risk-taking, substance use, and delinquent behavior. *While early maturation has advantages for boys, these boys are* more prone to symptoms of depression, problems at school, and engaging in drug or alcohol abuse.
7. *The relationship between parents and their adolescent children is* generally positive, and parents remain influential, but relationships with friends and peers become increasingly important.
8. *Romantic and sexual relationships during adolescence are influenced by* social and cultural factors; that is, these factors have an influence on when, why, and how adolescents engage in romantic and sexual behavior.
9. *Identity refers to* a person's sense of self, including his or her memories, experiences, and the values and beliefs that guide his or her behavior.
10. *Adolescents begin the process of identity formation by* evaluating themselves on several different dimensions, such as social acceptance by peers, academic and athletic abilities, work abilities, personal appearance, and romantic appeal.
11. *According to Erikson's psychosocial theory of lifespan development,* each of the eight stages of life is associated with a particular psychosocial conflict that can be resolved in either a positive or negative direction. *The key psychosocial conflict facing adolescents is* identity versus role confusion. *The path to an integrated identity usually begins with* role confusion, which is characterized by little commitment to issues such as selecting a potential career; formulating religious, moral, and political beliefs; adopting social roles involved in interpersonal relationships, sexuality, and long-term commitment. *This is followed by a* moratorium period, during which the adolescent experiments with different roles, values, and beliefs. *Gradually,* by choosing among alternatives and making commitments, the adolescent forms an integrated identity (note that identity continues to evolve over the lifespan, not just during the adolescent years).

12. *Moral reasoning is* the aspect of cognitive development that has to do with how an individual reasons about moral and ethical decisions.
13. *Kohlberg's levels (and stages) of moral development are* the preconventional level (stage 1: punishment and obedience and stage 2: mutual benefit), the conventional level (stage 3: interpersonal expectations and stage 4: law and order), and the postconventional level (stage 5: legal principles and stage 6: universal moral principles).
14. *Criticisms and limitations of Kohlberg's theory are that (a)* moral reasoning doesn't always predict moral behavior (people are flexible in their real-world moral behavior), and moral decisions in the real world are frequently affected by nonrational processes (often without awareness), such as emotions, customs, traditions, and social contexts; *(b)* the theory may not be as universal as claimed; *(c)* it reflects a male perspective and may not accurately depict the development of moral reasoning in women; *(d)* it is based on the ethic of individual rights and justice and does not consider the ethic of care and responsibility; *(e)* as a 2000 meta-analysis found, the evidence indicates that both men and women used a mix of the care/responsibility ethic and the rights/justice ethic, and so the theory does not adequately reflect the way humans actually experience moral decision making; and *(f)* aspects of moral reasoning in other cultures do not appear to be reflected in the theory.

Concept Check 4

1. integrated identity; intimacy versus isolation
2. identity
3. trust versus mistrust; autonomy versus doubt; initiative versus guilt; industry versus inferiority
4. positive
5. puberty
6. secondary
7. pruning
8. generativity versus stagnation; middle adulthood
9. 1; preconventional
10. Carol Gilligan; care and responsibility
11. 4; conventional

Graphic Organizer 2

1. Piaget: formal operational stage; Kohlberg: postconventional level, stage 6
2. Piaget: preoperational stage; Kohlberg: preconventional level, stage 1
3. Piaget: concrete operational stage; Kohlberg: preconventional level, stage 2
4. Piaget: concrete operational stage; Kohlberg: conventional level, stage 4

Matching Exercise 4

1. identity
2. moratorium period
3. adolescence
4. puberty
5. menarche
6. adolescent growth spurt
7. Lawrence Kohlberg
8. ethic of care and responsibility
9. moral reasoning
10. conventional level

True/False Test 4

1. F	4. T	7. T
2. T	5. F	8. T
3. T	6. T	9. T

Adult Development

1. *According to Erikson, the two fundamental themes that dominate adulthood are* love and work *and the primary psychosocial task of early adulthood is* to form a committed, mutually enhancing, intimate relationship with another person *and for middle adulthood* it is generativity- to contribute to future generations through children, career, or other meaningful activities.
2. *In industrialized countries, emerging adulthood is* the stage of lifespan development from approximately the late teens to the mid- to late-twenties, which is characterized by exploration, instability, and flexibility in social roles, vocational choices, and relationships.
3. *Some important aspects of this period of lifespan development are as follows: (a)* Although some emerging adults find the instability of this period unsettling, several studies have found that well-being and self-esteem rise steadily during this time. *(b)* While some emerging adults establish long-term, stable relationships,

in general, relationships during this period are characterized by exploration (hooking up during college and postcollege years is common—see In Focus: Hooking Up On Campus). *(c)* Compared with previous generations, today's emerging adults wait longer to get married (median age is 28 years for men and 26 for women). *(d)* Emerging adults actively explore different career options (they have an average of seven different jobs during their twenties). *(e)* Emerging adulthood is not universal, it only exists in industrialized or postindustrialized countries where adult roles and responsibilities are postponed until the 20s; members of minority groups, immigrants, and young people who enter the workforce directly from high school are all less likely to experience emerging adulthood as a developmental period.

4. *The physical changes that take place during adulthood include* genetically influenced changes such as menopause (the cessation of menstruation) and thinning, graying hair; and environmentally influenced changes such as the formation of wrinkles, a decrease in the efficiency of various body organs, and a decline in physical strength and endurance.
5. *The nature of intimate relationships and family structures varies widely in the United States. For example,* adult social development does not always follow a predictable pattern such as the "traditional" path of finding a mate, getting married, starting and raising a family; the number of unmarried couples living together increased dramatically at the end of the twentieth century; more than 30 percent of children are being raised by a single parent; more than half of all first marriages end in divorce, and remarrying and starting a second family later in life is not uncommon; among married couples some are opting for a child-free life together; and there are many gay and lesbian couples committed to a long-term monogamous relationship.
6. *In relation to having children,* marital satisfaction tends to decline after the first child is born and to increase after children leave home.
7. *In terms of careers in adulthood,* dual-career families have become more common. Although the combination of work and family roles can be demanding, multiple roles can provide both men and women with increased feelings of self-esteem, happiness, and competence; the quality of their experiences on the job, in marriage, and as a parent are vital factors for both males and females. The career tracks of men and women often differ, especially if they have children; married women with children are much more likely to interrupt their careers, leave jobs, or switch to part-time work because of child-rearing responsibilities.

Late Adulthood and Aging

1. *Regarding mental and physical abilities in late adulthood,* they do not necessarily show a steep decline. A small but steadily increasing percentage of older adults show a slight decline on tests of general intellectual abilities beginning around age 60, and these declines can be minimized or eliminated with a physically active and mentally stimulating lifestyle.
2. *According to the activity theory of aging,* life satisfaction in late adulthood is highest when you maintain your previous level of activity, either by continuing old activities or by finding new ones.
3. *According to Erikson, the psychosocial conflict of late adulthood is* ego integrity (feeling that one's life has been meaningful) versus despair (a deep sense of disappointment in life).

The Final Chapter: Dying and Death

1. *According to Kübler-Ross's theory of death and dying, the five stages are* denial (people deny that death is imminent); anger (people feel and express indignation and rage); bargaining (people try to work out a deal with doctors, relatives, or God); depression (people become despondent about their fate); and acceptance (people realize what lies ahead and resign themselves to their fate).
2. *Problems with Kübler-Ross's theory are that* dying individuals do not necessarily progress through the predictable sequence of stages that she described. Dying is as individual a process as living; people cope with the prospect of dying much as they have coped with other stresses in their lives.

Concept Check 5

1. middle adulthood; generativity
2. a later
3. late adulthood; despair
4. anger
5. decline
6. increase
7. ego integrity
8. activity
9. hippocampus

Graphic Organizer 3

1. Lev Vygotsky
2. Mary D. Salter Ainsworth
3. Noam Chomsky
4. Erik Erikson
5. Jean Piaget
6. Lawrence Kohlberg
7. Renée Baillargeon

Matching Exercise 5

1. induction
2. menopause
3. permissive parenting style
4. middle adulthood
5. activity theory of aging
6. ego integrity
7. life review
8. andropause
9. emerging adulthood

True/False Test 5

1. T	4. T	7. T
2. T	5. F	8. T
3. F	6. T	

Something to Think About

1. Most psychologists today agree that the *quality* of the child-care arrangements is the key factor in promoting secure attachment in early childhood and preventing problems in later childhood. In fact, many studies have found that children who experience high-quality day care tend to be more sociable, better adjusted, and more academically competent than children who experience low-quality day care. They also have fewer behavioral problems than children who experience low-quality day care. Child care is just one aspect of a child's developmental environment; research has shown that sensitive parenting and quality of caregiving in the child's home have an even greater influence on social, emotional, and cognitive development than the quality of child care.

   High-quality day care is characterized by a number of key factors: caregivers should be warm and responsive, developmentally appropriate activities and a variety of learning materials and toys should be available, caregivers should have some training and education in child development and learning, low staff turnover is essential, the ratio of caregivers to children should be low, and groups should be small enough to provide the individual attention young children need.

2. A short discussion of the various stages of cognitive and psychosocial development would be appropriate. Raising psychologically healthy children is possible if parents adopt some of the strategies suggested by the experts. Psychologist Diana Baumrind has described three basic parenting styles: authoritarian, permissive, and authoritative. Research has shown that the authoritative style produces the best results. Can parents learn to be authoritative in their parenting style? Enhancing Well-Being with Psychology has a number of practical suggestions: let your children know that you love them, listen to your children, use induction to teach as you discipline, work with your children's temperamental qualities, understand your children's age-related cognitive abilities and limitations, and don't expect perfection and learn to go with the flow.

   Although all children inherit genetic predispositions from both parents, research has shown that environmental factors, such as social and cultural influences, educational experiences, and parenting style have very powerful effects on a child's development.

Progress Test 1

1. a	6. c	11. a
2. d	7. a	12. c
3. d	8. c	13. a
4. a	9. b	14. d
5. b	10. a	15. c

Progress Test 2

1. c	6. d	11. c
2. a	7. a	12. b
3. c	8. a	13. a
4. b	9. c	14. c
5. b	10. d	15. d

Progress Test 3

1. b	6. c	11. d
2. c	7. a	12. d
3. d	8. d	13. b
4. a	9. b	14. c
5. b	10. b	15. d

CHAPTER 10

Personality

PREVIEW

Reading the section below first will give you a general sense of the chapter's contents and an initial introduction to some of the major concepts and terms. This will prime you for what you are about to read and help you to develop a "cognitive map" that will guide your study of the material in this chapter. Likewise, reading the **preview questions** at the beginning of each major section will improve your ability to understand, learn, and retain the information.

CHAPTER 10 . . . AT A GLANCE

Chapter 10 focuses on the four major perspectives on personality and how each has been evaluated. Sigmund Freud's psychoanalysis stresses the unconscious, the importance of sex and aggression, and the influences of early childhood experiences. The major defense mechanisms, as well as the psychosexual stages of development and the various conflicts associated with each, are examined. The contributions of Freud's early followers, the neo-Freudians, are explored.

Humanistic theory and its optimistic view of human nature are examined, including Carl Rogers's ideas about the self-concept, unconditional positive regard, actualizing tendency, and the fully functioning person.

The social cognitive perspective stresses the role of conscious thought processes, goals, self-regulation, and reciprocal determinism. The influence of self-efficacy on behavior, performance, motivation, and persistence is explored. The notion that the interaction of multiple factors determines personality and behavior is examined.

The trait perspective focuses on measuring and describing individual differences. Raymond Cattell initially suggested 16 basic personality factors, then Hans Eysenck proposed three dimensions. The five-factor model is the current view of the number of source traits. The text concludes that traits are generally stable over time and across situations. Behavioral genetics research uses twin and adoption studies to measure the effects of genes and heredity on behavior. Their findings indicate that the influence of environmental factors on personality traits is at least equal to the influence of genetic factors.

The final section examines projective tests and self-report inventories, noting some of their strengths and weaknesses. Enhancing Well-Being with Psychology discusses the concept of "possible selves" and explains how we can apply research findings to our own lives.

Introduction: What Is Personality?

Preview Questions

Consider the following questions as you study this section of the chapter.

- How is *personality* defined, and what is a personality theory?
- What are the four major theoretical perspectives on personality?

Read the section "Introduction: What Is Personality?" and ***write*** *your answers to the following:*

1. Personality is defined as an individual's unique
2. A personality theory is
3. The four basic perspectives on personality (and the main emphasis of each) are

The Psychoanalytic Perspective on Personality

Preview Questions

Consider the following questions as you study this section of the chapter.

- Who was the founder of psychoanalysis, and what did he consider to be the main factors that influenced personality development?
- What were some of the key influences on Freud's thinking?

Read the section "The Psychoanalytic Perspective on Personality" and ***write*** *your answers to the following:*

1. Psychoanalysis—Freud's theory of personality—stresses
2. Some of the key factors in the development of Freud's ideas were

The Psychoanalytic Perspective: Freud's Dynamic Theory of Personality

Preview Questions

Consider the following questions as you study this section of the chapter.

- How are unconscious mental processes revealed?
- What are the three basic structures of personality, and what are their functions?
- What are the main defense mechanisms, and what role do they play?

Read the section "The Psychoanalytic Perspective: Freud's Dynamic Theory of Personality" and ***write*** *your answers to the following:*

1. The content of the unconscious can surface in disguised form in
2. The three basic structures of personality (and their functions) are
3. The three main ego defense mechanisms (and the roles they play) are

   Other ego defense mechanisms include

The Psychoanalytic Perspective: Personality Development

Preview Questions

Consider the following questions as you study this section of the chapter.

- What are the five psychosexual stages of personality development, and what is the focus of each?
- What is the consequence of failure to resolve the developmental conflict of a particular psychological stage?
- What role does the Oedipus complex play in personality development?

Read the section "The Psychoanalytic Perspective: Personality Development" and ***write*** *your answers to the following:*

1. The psychosexual stages are age-related developmental periods in which ______________________________
____
____

2. The five psychosexual stages (and the focus of each) are ______________________________
____
____
____
____

3. If the developmental conflict of a particular stage is not resolved ______________________________
____
____

4. The Oedipus complex refers to ______________________________
____
____

5. Identification (which is one way of resolving the Oedipus complex) is an ego defense mechanism that ______________________________
____

After you have carefully studied the preceding sections, complete the following exercises.

Concept Check 1

Read the following and write the correct term in the space provided.

1. Birkley was feeling irritable and bad-tempered all day. When she arrived home from work, she accused her husband of being moody and grumpy. According to Freud, Birkley may be using an ego defense mechanism called ______________ .
2. Colleen, who is suffering from some puzzling physical and psychological symptoms that don't appear to have any physiological cause, has decided to seek help from a Freudian psychoanalyst. The therapist is most likely to use ______________ in an attempt to explore Colleen's unconscious.
3. During a heated argument, David inadvertently called his wife, Joanne, by his mother's name. From the psychoanalytic perspective, this "Freudian slip" reveals something about David's ______________ (conscious/preconscious/unconscious) motivation.
4. Amelia had a very strange dream in which she was with a very handsome man on a train traveling through the Swiss Alps. The train kept going in and out of tunnels and going faster and faster as it made its way through the mountains. According to Freudian theory, the ______________ (manifest/latent) content of the dream should give some clue to Amelia's unconscious conflicts.
5. When 2-year-old Tyler was told that he would get no dessert unless he finished eating all his vegetables, he turned the plate upside down and said he hated his Mom and Dad. Freud would have said that Tyler was responding to the demands of the ______________ .

6. Kato found a wallet containing $200 in cash. For just a moment he was tempted to keep the money, but the thought of doing so made him feel guilty and anxious, and he immediately took the wallet to the lost-and-found office. According to Freud, Kato's good deed was motivated by his _______________ .
7. Leslie sometimes thinks that the real reason her husband became a psychotherapist was to provide himself with a socially acceptable way to indulge his excessive curiosity about other people's private lives. Leslie is suggesting that her husband's unconscious sexual urges are being rechanneled into productive work, a special form of displacement called _______________ .
8. Nine-year-old Danny looks up to his father and wants to be an engineer just like him. Freud would suggest that Danny is exhibiting signs of the process of _______________ .
9. When Gregory did not get the promotion he applied for, he told his family and colleagues that, in retrospect, he was much happier staying in his present position and glad he didn't have to deal with all the hassles associated with the higher-paying position. It appears that Gregory is using an ego defense mechanism called _______________ .

Graphic Organizer 1

Read the following and match each one with the appropriate stage of psychosexual development:

Description	Stage
1. Sixteen-year-old Graham has started going steady with Julie and is experiencing all the sensations of being in love.	
2. Five-year-old Annette has become very competitive with her mother for her father's affections and quite defiantly states that she is "Going to marry Daddy when I grow up!"	
3. Vivian is 8 years old and does not like boys very much. In fact, she plays with her girlfriends almost exclusively.	
4. No matter what Marie gives her baby to play with, the baby immediately puts it in her mouth.	
5. Darcy is not quite 2 but seems to take great pleasure in refusing to obey his parents and asserting his control and independence. His favorite word is "No!"	

Review of Terms, Concepts, and Names 1

Use the terms in this list to complete the Matching Exercise, then to help you answer the True/False items correctly.

personality
personality theory
Sigmund Freud
psychoanalysis
catharsis
free association
conscious
preconscious
unconscious
manifest content
latent content
id
Eros (life instinct)
libido
Thanatos (death instinct)
pleasure principle
ego
reality principle
superego
ego defense mechanisms
repression
displacement
sublimation
psychosexual stages
oral stage
anal stage
phallic stage
fixation
Oedipus complex
castration anxiety
identification
penis envy
latency stage
genital stage

Matching Exercise

Match the appropriate term/name with its definition or description.

1. ________________ In Freud's theory, the psychological and emotional energy associated with expressions of sexuality; the sex drive.
2. ________________ An individual's unique and relatively consistent patterns of thinking, feeling, and behaving.
3. ________________ In Freud's theory, the partly conscious, self-evaluative, moralistic component of personality that is formed through the internalization of parental and societal rules.
4. ________________ In Freud's theory, a child's unconscious sexual desire for the opposite-sex parent, usually accompanied by hostile feelings toward the same-sex parent.
5. ________________ Latin for "I"; in Freud's theory, the partly conscious, rational component of personality that regulates thoughts and behavior and is most in touch with the demands of the external world.
6. ________________ Level of awareness that contains information not currently in conscious awareness but easily accessible.
7. ________________ Psychosexual stage of development during which the child derives pleasurable and gratifying sensations through feeding and exploring objects with his or her mouth.
8. ________________ In psychoanalytic theory, the ego defense mechanism that involves unconsciously shifting the target of an emotional urge to a substitute target that is less threatening or dangerous.
9. ________________ Founder of psychoanalysis, whose legacy continues to influence psychology, philosophy, literature, art, and psychotherapy.
10. ________________ Psychosexual stage of development during which the infant derives pleasurable sensations through acquiring control over elimination via toilet training.
11. ________________ Theory that attempts to describe and explain similarities and differences in people's patterns of thinking, feeling, and behaving.
12. ________________ Latin for "the it"; in Freud's theory, the completely unconscious, irrational component of personality that seeks immediate satisfaction of instinctual urges and drives; ruled by the pleasure principle.
13. ________________ Psychosexual stage of development during which sexual urges become repressed and dormant as the child develops same-sex friendships with peers and focuses on school, sports, and other activities.
14. ________________ Sigmund Freud's theory of personality, which emphasizes unconscious determinants of behavior, sexual and aggressive instinctual drives, and the enduring effects of early childhood experiences on later personality development.
15. ________________ In psychoanalytic theory, largely unconscious distortions of thought or perception that act to reduce anxiety.
16. ________________ In Freud's theory, age-related developmental periods in which the child's sexual urges are focused on different areas of the body and are expressed through the activities associated with those areas.
17. ________________ In Freud's psychoanalytic theory, the elements of a dream that are consciously experienced and remembered by the dreamer.

True/False Test

Indicate whether each statement is true or false by placing T or F in the blank space next to each item.

1. ____During the phallic psychosexual stage of development, the adolescent reaches physical sexual maturity and the genitals become the primary focus of pleasurable sensations, which the person seeks to satisfy in heterosexual relationships.
2. ____As the Oedipus complex unfolds, the little boy feels affection for his mother and hostility and jealousy toward his father but realizes that his father is more physically powerful than he is; the boy experiences *castration anxiety,* or the fear that his father will punish him by castrating him.
3. ____Fixation occurs if the child is frustrated or overindulged in his or her attempts to resolve the conflict associated with a psychosexual stage; the individual will continue to seek pleasure through behaviors that are similar to those associated with that stage.
4. ____In Freud's theory, the death instinct, reflected in aggressive, destructive, and self-destructive actions, is called Eros.
5. ____In psychoanalytic theory, repression refers to the unconscious exclusion of anxiety-provoking thoughts, feelings, and memories from conscious awareness; the most fundamental ego defense mechanism.
6. ____The term *unconscious* is used in Freud's theory to describe thoughts, feelings, wishes, and drives that are operating below the level of conscious awareness.
7. ____Catharsis is a phenomenon that occurs when puzzling physical and psychological problems disappear after a person expresses pent-up emotions associated with traumatic events that may have been related to his or her problems.
8. ____As part of the resolution of her Oedipus complex, the little girl discovers that little boys have a penis and that she does not; she experiences a sense of loss, or deprivation, that Freud referred to as *penis envy.*
9. ____During the genital stage of psychosexual development, the genitals are the primary focus and the child derives pleasurable sensations through sexual curiosity, masturbation, and sexual attraction toward the opposite-sex parent.
10. ____In psychoanalytic theory, sublimation is an ego defense mechanism that involves reducing anxiety by imitating the behavior and characteristics of another person.
11. ____The reality principle refers to the awareness of environmental demands and the capacity to accommodate them by postponing gratification until the appropriate time or circumstances exist.
12. ____In Freud's theory, Thanatos refers to the self-preservation, or life, instinct, reflected in the expression of basic psychological urges that perpetuate the existence of the individual as well as the species.
13. ____Free association is a psychoanalytic technique in which the patient spontaneously reports all thoughts, feelings, and mental images as they come to mind.
14. ____All thoughts, feelings, and sensations that a person is aware of at any given moment represent the conscious level of awareness.
15. ____The pleasure principle refers to the motive to obtain pleasure and avoid tension or discomfort; the most fundamental human motive and the guiding principle of the id.
16. ____In psychoanalytic theory, identification is the ego defense mechanism that involves redirecting sexual urges toward productive, socially acceptable, nonsexual activities.
17. ____In Freud's psychoanalytic theory, the latent content of a dream refers to the unconscious wishes, thoughts, and urges that are concealed as symbols in a dream.

Check your answers and review any areas of weakness before going on to the next section.

The Psychoanalytic Perspective: The Neo-Freudians

Preview Questions

Consider the following questions as you study this section of the chapter.

- What are the similarities and differences in the approaches taken by Freud and the neo-Freudians?

- What are the key ideas of Jung, Horney, and Adler?

*Read the section "The Psychoanalytic Perspective: The Neo-Freudians" and **write** your answers to the following:*

1. The neo-Freudians followed Freud in stressing ______________________________

   However, they developed independent personality theories, because they disagreed with Freud on three key points:

   (a) ______________________________

   (b) ______________________________

   (c) ______________________________

2. Carl Jung emphasized ______________________________

3. Karen Horney stressed ______________________________

4. Alfred Adler believed ______________________________

The Psychoanalytic Perspective: Evaluating Freud and the Psychoanalytic Perspective on Personality

Preview Questions

Consider the following questions as you study this section of the chapter.

- What are three criticisms of Freud's theory and, more generally, the psychoanalytic perspective?
- Which Freudian ideas have been substantiated by empirical research?

*Read the section "Evaluating Freud and the Psychoanalytic Perspective on Personality" and **write** your answers to the following:*

1. Although Sigmund Freud's ideas have had a profound and lasting effect on psychology and on society, the main criticisms of Freud's theory and psychoanalysis are

   (a) ______________________________

   (b) ______________________________

   (c) ______________________________

2. Several of Freud's ideas have been substantiated by empirical evidence, including ______________________________

After you have carefully studied the preceding sections, complete the following exercises.

Concept Check 2

Read the following and write the correct term in the space provided.

1. Wilfred suffered physical hardship and abuse as a child; as an adult, he lacks confidence, can't hold a job for long, and feels that nothing is really worth striving for. Adler would have said that Wilfred suffers from feelings of

   ______________ .

2. In a class discussion, Louanne disputed Freud's assumption that women are inferior to men and that they suffer from penis envy; instead, she suggested that men suffer from womb envy and feel inadequate because they are incapable of bearing children. Louanne's views are most consistent with those of personality theorist

   ______________ .

3. During a lecture on personality, Dr. Shornagel suggested that the deepest aspect of the individual psyche is a part inherited from previous generations, which contains universally shared experiences and ideas called archetypes. Dr. Shornagel is describing the ______________________________, which is central to ____________ theory of personality.
4. Terry has an excessive need to exert power over people; his competitiveness and need to feel superior to others stem from his childhood feelings of being isolated and helpless in a potentially hostile world. Horney would have suggested that Terry is attempting to deal with __________________________ by moving ________________ (toward/against/away from) others.
5. Frank is very sociable and outgoing and has a keen interest in sports and outdoor activities. Jung would probably describe Frank as an ________________ personality type.
6. When Merrilee recently watched the video *Lord of the Rings,* she became aware of some of the universal themes and preoccupations depicted in the movie. In particular, she noted the hero's quest for psychological growth, self-knowledge, selfhood, and wisdom. According to Jung, these inherited images of human instincts, themes, and preoccupations are called ________________ and are the main components of the ____________.
7. According to his psychotherapist, Adrian can achieve psychological harmony only if he recognizes and accepts the feminine aspect of his personality. The therapist is referring to the ________________, an important archetype in ________________ theory of personality.
8. Shelby is always trying to improve himself, to master challenges, to grow and develop intellectually and psychologically, and to move forward toward self-realization. Adler would say that Shelby is exhibiting the most fundamental human motive of __________________________.

Review of Terms, Concepts, and Names 2

Use the terms in this list to complete the Matching Exercise, then to help you answer the True/False items correctly.

neo-Freudians	basic anxiety
Carl Jung	womb envy
collective unconscious	Alfred Adler
archetypes	striving for superiority
anima	feelings of inferiority
animus	inferiority complex
introvert	superiority complex
extravert	
Karen Horney	

Matching Exercise

Match the appropriate term/name with its definition or description.

1. ________________ German-born American psychoanalyst who emphasized the role of social relationships and culture in personality; sharply disagreed with Freud's characterization of female psychological development, especially his notion that women suffer from penis envy.
2. ________________ In Jung's theory, the inherited mental images of universal human instincts, themes, and preoccupations that are the main components of the collective unconscious.
3. ________________ In Adler's theory, the desire to improve oneself, master challenges, and move toward self-perfection and self-realization, considered to be the most fundamental human motive.
4. ________________ Fundamental emotion that Horney described as a child's feeling of being isolated and helpless in a potentially hostile world.
5. ________________ Adler's term for the personality characteristic developed by people who are unable to compensate for specific weaknesses; it includes a general sense of inadequacy, weakness, and helplessness.
6. ________________ In Jung's theory, the basic personality type that focuses attention and energy toward the outside world.
7. ________________ In Jung's theory, the hypothesized part of the unconscious mind that is inherited from previous generations and that contains universally shared ancestral experiences and ideas.
8. ________________ According to Jung, an important archetype that represents the feminine side of every person.

True/False Test

Indicate whether each statement is true or false by placing T or F in the blank space next to each item.

1. ____ The term *neo-Freudians* was given to the early followers of Freud who developed their own theories yet still recognized the importance of many of Freud's basic notions, such as the influence of unconscious processes and early childhood experiences.
2. ____ Alfred Adler was an Austrian physician who broke with Freud and developed his own psychoanalytic theory of personality, which emphasized social factors and motivation toward self-improvement and self-realization, and overcoming feelings of inferiority.
3. ____ According to Adler's theory, people can overcompensate for their feelings of inferiority and develop a *superiority complex,* which is characterized by exaggeration of one's accomplishments and importance in an effort to cover up weaknesses and limitations.
4. ____ Horney used the term *womb envy* to describe the envy that men feel about women's capacity to bear children.
5. ____ In Jung's theory, the introvert is a basic personality type that focuses attention inward.
6. ____ Carl Jung was the Swiss psychiatrist who broke with Freud to develop his own psychoanalytic theory of personality, which stressed striving toward psychological harmony and included the key ideas of the collective unconscious and archetypes.
7. ____ According to Adler's theory, striving for superiority arises from universal *feelings of inferiority* that are experienced during infancy and childhood, when the child is helpless and dependent on others.
8. ____ In Jung's theory of personality, the animus is the archetype that represents the masculine side of every person.

Check your answers and review any areas of weakness before going on to the next section.

The Humanistic Perspective on Personality

Preview Questions

Consider the following questions as you study this section of the chapter.

- Who were the major contributors to humanistic psychology?
- What is the focus of the humanistic perspective?
- What role do the self-concept, actualizing tendency, and conditional and unconditional positive regard play in Rogers's personality theory?
- What characterizes the fully functioning person?
- What are key strengths and weaknesses of the humanistic perspective?

Read the section "The Humanistic Perspective on Personality" and ***write*** *your answers to the following:*

1. The major contributors to humanistic psychology were ______________ and ______________.
2. The humanistic perspective emphasizes ______________
3. The actualizing tendency is ______________
4. The self-concept is ______________
5. Conditional positive regard is ______________

   Unconditional positive regard is ______________
6. The fully functioning person experiences ______________
7. The humanistic perspective has been criticized on two particular points: ______________

   The humanistic perspective has contributed to ______________

The Social Cognitive Perspective on Personality

Preview Questions

Consider the following questions as you study this section of the chapter.

- What is the focus of the social cognitive perspective, and what specifically does Bandura emphasize in his social cognitive theory?
- What is the principle of reciprocal determinism, and what is the role of self-efficacy beliefs in personality, according to this perspective?
- What are some key strengths and weaknesses of the social cognitive perspective?

Read the section "The Social Cognitive Perspective on Personality" and ***write*** *your answers to the following:*

1. The social cognitive perspective stresses ____

2. Bandura's social cognitive theory emphasizes ____

3. Reciprocal determinism suggests that human functioning and personality ____

4. Self-efficacy is ____

5. A key strength of the social cognitive perspective is ____

6. Some weaknesses of the social cognitive perspective are that ____

The Trait Perspective on Personality

Preview Questions

Consider the following questions as you study this section of the chapter.

- What is the focus of trait theories?
- How are *traits* defined, and what is the difference between surface traits and source traits?
- What models of personality did Cattell and Eysenck propose, and what is the five-factor model of personality?
- What is the focus of behavioral genetics?
- To what degree are personality traits inherited?
- What are the key strengths and weaknesses of the trait perspective?

Read the section "The Trait Perspective on Personality" and ***write*** *your answers to the following:*

1. Trait theories focus on ____

2. Traits are ____

   Surface traits are ____

   Source traits are ____

3. Raymond Cattell believed that ____

4. Hans Eysenck proposed that ____

5. According to the five-factor model ____

6. The field of behavioral genetics studies ____

7. Factors that seem to have a significant genetic component are ____

The influence of environmental factors on personality traits ______________________________
____
____

8. The trait perspective is useful in ______________________________
____

9. Some criticisms of trait theories are ______________________________
____
____
____
____

After you have carefully studied the preceding sections, complete the following exercises.

Concept Check 3

Read the following and write the correct term in the space provided.

1. Dunja is confident in her ability to service her own car but is less sure of her ability to bake cakes and cookies. According to Bandura, Dunja's different beliefs about her own abilities are her ______________ beliefs.
2. Eileen is consistently cheerful, optimistic, talkative, and impulsive. These traits, which are inferred from her observable behavior, are referred to as ______________ traits.
3. Navi is viewed by her family and friends as a flexible, creative, spontaneous, open, caring person who likes and is liked by most people. Carl Rogers would probably describe her as a(n) ______________ person.
4. Arthur believes that human behavior and personality are caused by the interactions of behavioral, cognitive, and environmental factors, and that each factor both influences and is influenced by the other factors. Arthur's explanation of human functioning and personality is most consistent with the ______________ theory on personality, and the process he describes is called ______________ .
5. Dr. Bhatt is concerned with describing, classifying, and measuring the many ways in which individuals may differ from one another. Her approach is most characteristic of the ______________ perspective on personality.
6. Whenever her son misbehaves, Rochelle makes sure he clearly understands that his behavior is not acceptable while taking care to reassure him that he is loved and valued. Rochelle is using Rogers's concept of ______________ .
7. Dr. Lavalle studies the effects of heredity on behavior. In his research, he studies identical and fraternal twins who were separated at birth, identical and fraternal twins raised together, and the similarities and differences between adopted children and their adoptive and biological parents. Dr. Lavalle works in the field of ______________ .
8. According to research described in Focus On Neuroscience (The Neuroscience of Personality: Brain Structure and the Big Five), increased brain tissue volume in various areas of the brain correlates with the personality traits of ______________ , ______________ , and ______________ , but not with ______________ or ______________ .
9. Dr. Porter collected data on a large sample of people who were rated on each of 150 personality characteristics. He then used a statistical technique called factor analysis to identify the traits that were most closely related; eventually, he reduced his list to 12 key personality factors. Dr. Porter's approach is most similar to that of trait theorist ______________ , who developed one of the most widely used personality tests, called the ______________ .

Graphic Organizer 2

Read the following statements and match the personality theorist and theory/perspective associated with each. This chart covers all four perspectives.

Statement	Theory/ Theorist	Perspective
1. I believe that people can be classified into four basic types: introverted–neurotic, introverted–stable, extraverted–neurotic, and extraverted–stable.		
2. It is my belief that people have an innate drive to maintain and enhance themselves. This actualizing tendency is the most basic human motive, and all other motives, whether biological or social, are secondary.		
3. I reduced Allport's 4,000 terms to 171, and then, by using factor analysis, I eventually came up with 16 personality factors that represent the essential source of human personality.		
4. My theory of personality stresses the influence of unconscious mental processes, the importance of sexual and aggressive instincts, and the enduring effects of early childhood experiences on personality.		
5. For me, the most fundamental human motive is striving for superiority, which arises from universal feelings of inferiority. Depending on how people deal with these feelings, they may develop either an inferiority complex or a superiority complex.		
6. My research suggests that human functioning is caused by the interaction of behavioral, cognitive, and environmental factors, a process I call reciprocal determinism.		
7. For me, the impact of social relationships and the nature of the parent–child interaction are the main determinants of personality. Different patterns of behavior develop as people try to deal with their basic anxiety. Males have an additional problem to deal with: womb envy.		
8. I am most well known for my theory of motivation and the notion of a hierarchy of needs. I also identified the qualities most associated with self-actualized people.		
9. It is apparent to me, from my observations of different cultures and my own patients, that the deepest part of the individual psyche is the collective unconscious, which contains universal archetypes. Personality can be described on two basic dimensions: introversion and extraversion.		

Review of Terms, Concepts, and Names 3

Use the terms in this list to complete the Matching Exercise, then to help you answer the True/False items correctly.

humanistic psychology
Abraham Maslow
Carl Rogers
actualizing tendency
self-concept
positive regard
conditional positive regard
incongruence
unconditional positive regard
fully functioning person
congruence
Albert Bandura
observational learning
social cognitive theory
reciprocal determinism
self-system
self-efficacy
mastery experience
trait
trait theory
surface traits
source traits
Raymond Cattell
Hans Eysenck
introversion
extraversion
neuroticism
stability
psychoticism
five-factor model of personality
behavioral genetics

Matching Exercise

Match the appropriate term/name with its definition or description.

1. ______________ A relatively stable, enduring predisposition to consistently behave in a certain way.
2. ______________ People's beliefs about their ability to meet the demands of a specific situation; feelings of self-confidence or self-doubt.
3. ______________ Contemporary psychologist who is best known for his research on observational learning and his social cognitive theory of personality.
4. ______________ In Rogers's theory, the innate drive to maintain and enhance the human organism.
5. ______________ Trait theory of personality that identifies five basic source traits (extraversion, neuroticism, agreeableness, conscientiousness, and openness to experience) as the fundamental building blocks of personality.
6. ______________ Psychologist who was one of the main contributors to the humanistic perspective and who developed the hierarchy of needs and the idea of self-actualization.
7. ______________ In Eysenck's theory, a third dimension of personality; a person high on this trait is antisocial, cold, hostile, and unconcerned about others, whereas a person low on this trait is warm and caring toward others.
8. ______________ In Rogers's theory, the term for the sense of being loved and valued by other people, especially one's parents.
9. ______________ Bandura's theory of personality, which emphasizes the importance of observational learning, conscious cognitive processes, social experiences, self-efficacy beliefs, and reciprocal determinism.
10. ______________ Theory of personality that focuses on identifying, describing, and measuring individual differences in behavioral predispositions.
11. ______________ In Eysenck's theory, the dimension of personality that describes people who direct their energies outward toward the environment and other people; a person high on this dimension would be outgoing and sociable, enjoying new experiences and stimulating environments.
12. ______________ American psychologist who was one of the main contributors to the humanistic perspective; developed a theory of personality and form of psychotherapy that emphasized the actualizing tendency, the importance of the self-concept, and unconditional positive regard.
13. ______________ Theoretical viewpoint on personality that generally emphasizes the inherent goodness of people, human potential, self-actualization, the self-concept, and healthy personality development.
14. ______________ Albert Bandura's model that explains human functioning and personality as caused by the interaction of behavioral, cognitive, and environmental factors.
15. ______________ In Eysenck's theory, a personality dimension in which the person directs his or her energies inward, toward inner, self-focused experiences; a person high on this dimension is quiet, solitary, and reserved, avoiding new experiences.
16. ______________ In Bandura's theory, the term for the successful performance of a task that results in enhanced self-efficacy.

True/False Test

Indicate whether each statement is true or false by placing T or F in the blank space next to each item.

1. ____ Behavioral genetics is an interdisciplinary field that studies the effects of genes and heredity on behavior.
2. ____ In Rogers's theory, people are in a state of congruence when their feelings and experiences are denied and distorted because they contradict or conflict with their self-concept.
3. ____ Raymond Cattell developed a trait theory that identifies 16 essential source traits or personality factors; also developed the widely used self-report personality test, the Sixteen Personality Factor Questionnaire (16PF).
4. ____ Personality characteristics or attributes that can easily be inferred from observable behavior are called source traits.
5. ____ In Rogers's theory, the sense that you will be valued and loved only if you behave in a way that is acceptable to others is called conditional positive regard.
6. ____ Self-concept is the set of perceptions and beliefs that you hold about yourself.
7. ____ In Eysenck's theory, neuroticism refers to a person's predisposition to become emotionally upset.
8. ____ In Rogers's theory, the fully functioning person has a flexible, constantly evolving self-concept and is realistic, open to new experiences, and capable of changing in response to new experiences.
9. ____ Unconditional positive regard, in Rogers's theory, is the sense that you will be valued and loved even if you don't conform to the standards and expectations of others.
10. ____ Surface traits are the most fundamental dimensions of personality; these broad basic traits are hypothesized to be universal and relatively few in number.
11. ____ In Rogers's theory, people are in a state of incongruence when their sense of self (their self-concept) is consistent with their emotions and experiences.
12. ____ Hans Eysenck was a British psychologist who developed a trait theory of personality that identifies the three basic dimensions of personality as neuroticism–emotional stability, introversion–extraversion, and psychoticism.
13. ____ In Eysenck's theory, stability reflects a person's predisposition to be emotionally even.
14. ____ Cognitive skills, abilities, and attitudes that emerge through developmental experiences involving the interaction of behavioral, cognitive, and environmental factors represent the person's self-system.
15. ____ In Bandura's theory, observational learning refers to learning that occurs through watching and then imitating the behavior of other people, noting the consequences and the rules and standards that apply to behavior in specific situations.

Check your answers and review any areas of weakness before going on to the next section.

Assessing Personality: Psychological Tests

Preview Questions

Consider the following questions as you study this section of the chapter.

- What are psychological tests, and what two criteria must be met to make them useful?
- What are projective tests and self-report inventories, and how are they used to measure personality?
- What are some key strengths and limitations of projective tests and self-report inventories?

*Read the section "Assessing Personality: Psychological Tests" and **write** your answers to the following:*

1. A psychological test is ______________________________

____

____

Any psychological test is useful if (a)______________

____

and (b) ______________________________

____

2. A projective test is ______________________________

____

Examples are ______________________________

____

____

3. A self-report inventory is______________________________

____

Examples include______________________________

____

____

4. Projective tests provide qualitative data but their limitations are that ____

5. The strengths of self-report inventories such as the MMPI, CPI, and 16PF are that ____

The Myers–Briggs Type Indicator (MBTI) differs from other self-report inventories in that it ____

6. Problems with self-report inventories (MMPI, CPI, and 16PF) are that ____

The MBTI has several problems: ____

After you have carefully studied the preceding section, complete the following exercises.

Concept Check 4

Read the following and write the correct term in the space provided.

1. Michelle was given a psychological test in which she was asked to look at a series of cards with ambiguous scenes and make up stories for each one. She was told to give as much detail as possible about what the characters are feeling and how the story ends. Michelle was given a ______________ called the ______________________.

2. When Roger was assessed for his suitability to be a police officer, he was given a 500-item test that was used to evaluate his mental health. The test he was given was most likely the ______________.

3. Mr. and Mrs. Sheldrake want to get some idea of how their son is going to do in high school. The test that is best at predicting their son's high school grades is the ______________.

4. In his psychoanalytic practice, Dr. Coles tries to understand his client's unconscious conflicts, motives, psychological defenses, and personality traits. It is very probable that Dr. Coles uses either the ______________ or the ______________, which are both ______________ tests.

5. Dr. Cera sees a lot of married couples in his counseling practice. In an effort to help them resolve their conflicts, he frequently administers a test to each partner, which generates a profile of their personality characteristics. Dr. Cera most likely uses the ______________________.

6. Sheldon's personality test results indicated that he has a distinct personality type, ESTF (extraverted, sensing, thinking, feeling). It is very likely that Sheldon has taken the ______________________ personality test.

Review of Terms and Concepts 4

Use the terms in this list to complete the Matching Exercise, then to help you answer the True/False items correctly.

psychological test
projective test
projection
Rorschach Inkblot Test
Thematic Apperception Test (TAT)
graphology
validity
reliability
self-report inventory (objective personality test)
Minnesota Multiphasic Personality Inventory (MMPI)
California Psychological Inventory (CPI)
Sixteen Personality Factor Questionnaire (16PF)
Myers-Briggs Type Indicator (MBTI)
possible selves

Matching Exercise

Match the appropriate term with its definition or description.

1. ______________ Type of psychological test in which a person's responses to standardized questions are compared with established norms.

2. ______________ Projective test that uses inkblots, developed by Swiss psychiatrist Hermann Rorschach in 1921.

3. ________________ Self-report inventory that assesses personality characteristics in normal populations.
4. ________________ Test that assesses a person's abilities, aptitudes, interests, or personality on the basis of a systematically obtained sample of behavior.
5. ________________ Self-report inventory developed by Raymond Cattell that generates a personality profile with ratings on 16 trait dimensions.
6. ________________ The consistency of test results on repeated occasions under similar conditions.
7. ________________ Pseudoscience that claims to assess personality, social, and occupational attributes based on a person's distinctive handwriting, doodles, and drawing styles.

True/False Test

Indicate whether each statement is true or false by placing T or F in the blank space next to each item.

1. ____ A projective test is a type of personality test in which a person interprets an ambiguous image; it is used to assess unconscious motives, conflicts, psychological defenses, and personality traits.
2. ____ Possible selves refers to an aspect of the self-concept that includes images of the selves that you hope, fear, or expect to become in the future.
3. ____ The Minnesota Multiphasic Personality Inventory (MMPI) is a projective personality test that involves creating stories about each of a series of ambiguous scenes.
4. ____ The Thematic Apperception Test (TAT) is a self-report inventory that assesses personality characteristics and psychological disorders; used to assess both normal and disturbed populations.
5. ____ Projection is a major ego defense mechanism that involves attributing one's own unacceptable urges or qualities to others.
6. ____ Validity is the ability of a test to measure what it is intended to measure.
7. ____ The Myers–Briggs Type Indicator is a self-report test designed to assess personality *types* rather than personality *traits*.

Check your answers and review any areas of weakness before going on to the next section.

Something to Think About

1. The use of psychological tests has been and will continue to be an interesting topic of discussion for most people. Almost everyone has heard of the famous inkblot test, but not everyone knows its purpose or its limitations. Considering what you have learned about psychological tests in this chapter, what would you tell someone about the inkblot test and psychological tests in general?
2. This chapter focuses on contemporary theories of personality, as well as personality assessment and measurement. Long before psychology became interested in the topic of personality, people developed various ways of thinking about personality and how to assess and measure it. For example, astrology can be traced back over 4,000 years. Astrology's basic premise is that the positions of the planets and stars at the time and place of your birth determine your personality and destiny. As discussed in the text, Science Versus Pseudoscience, another popular belief, graphology, maintains that your handwriting, the way you shape letters, and so on, reveal your personality and true inner nature. How do you think scientific psychologists might go about testing the claims of graphologists, and how might you enlighten people about scientific research on graphology?

Check your answers and review any areas of weakness before completing the progress tests.

Progress Test 1

Review the complete chapter (including all boxed inserts), review all your study notes, and then test yourself on the following progress test. Check your answers. If you make a mistake, review your notes, check the appropriate section in the study guide, and, if necessary, go back and read the relevant part of the chapter in your textbook.

1. Marvin is angry and upset after an argument with his boss. At home that evening he is harshly and unreasonably critical of his son for not completing all his homework assignments.

According to Freud, Marvin is using an ego defense mechanism called
(a) identification.
(b) repression.
(c) rationalization.
(d) displacement.

2. Seven-year old Salvatore prefers to play with his male friends and does not like playing with girls very much. Salvatore is probably in the __________ stage of psychosexual development.
(a) anal
(b) phallic
(c) latency
(d) genital

3. Although Tim has many fond memories of his college days, he only vaguely remembers the girl he was engaged to but who left him suddenly for another man. Tim's unconscious forgetting is an ego defense mechanism called
(a) identification.
(b) sublimation.
(c) displacement.
(d) repression.

4. Every time 2-year-old Kate is given a bath, she plays with her genital area. If her parents chastise or punish her, she is likely to experience frustration and so be unable to resolve the developmental conflict of that stage. The result is
(a) fixation.
(b) undoing.
(c) displacement.
(d) denial.

5. Zachary considers himself to be an outgoing, fun-loving type of person, and he goes to a lot of parties. Sondra, on the other hand, thinks of herself as fairly quiet and shy, and she enjoys being by herself, reading a book, and listening to classical music. In Jung's theory, Zachary's and Sondra's different behaviors reflect
(a) the two basic personality types, the extravert and the introvert.
(b) the two important archetypes, the hero and the nurturing mother.
(c) a superiority complex and an inferiority complex.
(d) penis envy and womb envy.

6. Mary is an outgoing, extraverted person, and John is introverted and shy. According to social cognitive theory, the different personalities of Mary and John reflect the interaction of behavioral, cognitive, and environmental factors, a process Bandura called
(a) identification.
(b) striving for superiority.
(c) the actualizing tendency.
(d) reciprocal determinism.

7. As part of a research project, Jasbinder was given the same psychological test three times at 2-month intervals by three different therapists. Her results on the tests were all very different. It is most probable that she was given the
(a) MMPI.
(b) 16PF.
(c) CPI.
(d) TAT.

8. The actualizing tendency and the self-concept are to __________ as reciprocal determinism and self-efficacy are to __________ .
(a) Abraham Maslow; Hans Eysenck
(b) Alfred Adler; Albert Bandura
(c) Raymond Cattell; Carl Jung
(d) Carl Rogers; Albert Bandura

9. When asked to describe her husband, Mrs. Roech said that he is prone to exaggerating his accomplishments and importance, seems unaware of the reality of his limitations, and tends to overcompensate for his feelings of inferiority and weakness. Adler would probably have said that Mr. Roech has
(a) an inferiority complex.
(b) an extraverted personality.
(c) a superiority complex.
(d) an anal fixation.

10. Katrina thinks of herself as fairly laid back, easygoing, and relatively calm. She believes that she is above average academically and intellectually and sees herself as very conscientious at work and caring and loving with her family. Carl Rogers's term for Katrina's perceptions and beliefs about herself would be
(a) self-efficacy.
(b) self-concept.
(c) self-system.
(d) possible selves.

11. Miguel is giving a lecture on the five-factor model of personality. Which of the following personality dimensions is NOT likely to be included in his talk?
(a) anal retentiveness
(b) extraversion and conscientiousness
(c) neuroticism
(d) agreeableness and openness to experience

12. Dr. Markowitz studies the effects of heredity on behavior. One of his areas of research focuses on similarities and differences in identical twins who were separated at birth or early infancy and raised by different families. Dr. Markowitz is most probably a
    (a) psychoanalyst.
    (b) humanistic psychologist.
    (c) social cognitive psychologist.
    (d) behavioral geneticist.

13. In Freudian theory, retreating to a behavior pattern characteristic of an earlier stage of development is to __________ as thinking or behaving in a way that is the extreme opposite of unacceptable urges or impulses is to __________ .
    (a) rationalization; projection
    (b) regression; reaction formation
    (c) sublimation; displacement
    (d) repression; undoing

14. According to Enhancing Well-Being with Psychology (Possible Selves: Imagine the Possibilities), the term *possible selves* refers to
    (a) the unconscious part of the mind that motivates our behavior.
    (b) the major symptom of a fixated personality.
    (c) the aspect of the self-concept that includes images of the selves that you hope, fear, or expect to become in the future.
    (d) delusional thought processes.

15. According to Critical Thinking (Freud Versus Rogers on Human Nature), which of the following is true?
    (a) Freud's view of human nature was deeply pessimistic.
    (b) Rogers's view of human nature was deeply pessimistic.
    (c) Freud believed that humans are positive, forward-moving, constructive, realistic, and trustworthy.
    (d) Rogers believed that the essence of human nature is destructive but that societal, religious, and cultural restraints make people behave in good and moral ways.

Progress Test 2

After you have checked your understanding of the material in Progress Test 1 and have done a complete chapter review with special focus on any areas of weakness, you are ready to assess your knowledge on Progress Test 2. Check your answers. If you make a mistake, review your notes, the relevant section of the study guide, and, if necessary, the appropriate part of your textbook.

1. Nathan chews the end of his pen, bites his nails, overeats, smokes cigarettes, and talks incessantly. According to Freud, Nathan has probably fixated at the ________________ stage of psychosexual development due to some unresolved conflict.
    (a) oral
    (b) anal
    (c) phallic
    (d) genital

2. Dr. Jivraj, like many contemporary trait theorists, believes that the 16-trait model is too complex, and that the three-dimensional trait theory is too limited. Instead, he favors a model in which five basic dimensions represent the structural organization of personality traits. These five factors are
    (a) extraversion, neuroticism, agreeableness, conscientiousness, and openness to experience.
    (b) submissiveness, apprehensiveness, dominance, sociability, and venturesomeness.
    (c) inferiority, superiority, introversion, extraversion, and actualizing tendencies.
    (d) self-efficacy, self-concept, reciprocal determining tendencies, defensiveness, and openness to experience.

3. Sheila was often rejected by her parents; as a result, she mistrusts other people and treats them with hostility, which leads to their rejection of her. This cycle of rejection, mistrust, hostility, and further rejection illustrates what Bandura called
    (a) self-efficacy.
    (b) identification.
    (c) displacement.
    (d) reciprocal determinism.

4. During a class discussion of various perspectives on personality, Sasha points to all the evidence that human beings are destructive and aggressive. He points to the millions who died in two world wars and the ongoing killings and massacres that continue in many parts of the world today. Sasha's observation about basic human nature supports the ________________ perspective and is a criticism of the ________________ perspective.
    (a) humanistic; psychoanalytic
    (b) trait; social cognitive
    (c) social cognitive; trait
    (d) psychoanalytic; humanistic

5. Dr. Sheenan is a clinical psychologist who wants to assess the extent to which a client is suffering from depression, delusions, and other mental health problems. Dr. Sheenan is most likely to use the
   (a) 16PF.
   (b) CPI.
   (c) MMPI.
   (d) MBTI.

6. When Cindy was given the Rorschach Inkblot Test, she reported seeing a number of inanimate objects and some animal figures and tended to concentrate on very small details in each inkblot. Her therapist observed her behavior, gestures, and reactions as she responded to each card. It is most probable that her therapist is
   (a) interested in her unconscious conflicts, motives, and psychological defenses.
   (b) assessing her suitability for a particular occupation, such as police officer or pilot.
   (c) trying to generate a personality profile based on a number of personality traits.
   (d) trying to predict how she will perform academically when she goes to college.

7. Lukasz was given a forced-choice personality test in which he was required to respond to each item by choosing one of three alternatives. The results generated a personality profile with ratings on a number of trait dimensions that helped Lukasz decide which career path he should pursue. Lukasz was most likely given the
   (a) Thematic Apperception Test (TAT).
   (b) Minnesota Multiphasic Personality Inventory (MMPI).
   (c) California Psychological Inventory (CPI).
   (d) Sixteen Personality Factor Questionnaire (16PF).

8. Five-year-old Dunstan has recently become very possessive of his mother and appears to be jealous of his father. He is sometimes openly hostile, telling his father, "Don't kiss my Mommy!" According to Freud, Dunstan is in the ________________ stage of psychosexual development and showing manifestations of ________________.
   (a) oral; fixation
   (b) anal; fixation
   (c) phallic; the Oedipus complex
   (d) latency; the Oedipus complex

9. Wendy believes that the most fundamental human motive is striving for superiority. She thinks that this drive arises from global feelings of inferiority and that human personality and behavior reflect our attempts to compensate for or overcome our perceived weaknesses. Which personality theorist is most likely to agree with Wendy's views?
   (a) Freud
   (b) Jung
   (c) Horney
   (d) Adler

10. David is very quiet, pessimistic, anxious, and moody and becomes emotionally upset very easily. In terms of Eysenck's four basic personality types, he would be classified as
    (a) introverted–neurotic.
    (b) introverted–stable.
    (c) extraverted–neurotic.
    (d) extraverted–stable.

11. In a term paper on Carl Jung's theory of personality, Justin quoted Jung as saying that the ________________ contains "the whole spiritual heritage of mankind's evolution, born anew in the brain structure of every individual."
    (a) personal preconscious
    (b) collective conscious
    (c) personal unconscious
    (d) collective unconscious

12. Ursula's therapist instructs her to relax, close her eyes, and state aloud whatever thoughts come to mind no matter how trivial, silly, or absurd they seem. The therapist is using a technique called
    (a) free association.
    (b) displacement.
    (c) unconditional positive regard.
    (d) repression.

13. Leanne studies very hard, but she always feels that she hasn't studied enough. If she takes a break to socialize with her friends, she starts feeling guilty and anxious. Freud would say that Leanne has a
    (a) strong superego.
    (b) strong id.
    (c) weak superego.
    (d) weak id.

14. According to Science Versus Pseudoscience (Graphology), graphologists' claims that handwriting reveals temperament, personality traits, intelligence, and reasoning ability
    (a) have been tested and supported by numerous scientific studies.
    (b) have not been supported by scientific research.
    (c) should be believed because thousands of companies have used graphologists to assist in hiring new employees.
    (d) have been compared with astrologers' claims, and graphology has been shown clearly to have greater validity and reliability.

15. According to In Focus (Explaining Those Amazing Identical-Twin Similarities), which of the following is true?
    (a) Any two randomly chosen people of the same age, sex, and culture will likely have virtually no similarities.
    (b) Some similarities between separated identical twins may be genetically influenced.
    (c) Personality is almost completely determined by genes.
    (d) Personality is almost completely determined by environmental factors.

Progress Test 3

After you have checked your understanding of the material in Progress Tests 1 and 2, and have done a complete chapter review with special focus on any areas of weakness, you are ready to further assess your knowledge with Progress Test 3. Check your answers. If you make a mistake, review your notes, the appropriate parts of the study guide, and, if necessary, the relevant sections of your textbook.

1. During a class reunion, Adeil reminisced with some of his high school friends about their last year at school. He had no problem recalling many of the fun times they had together. In terms of Freud's theory of personality, Adeil's ability to recall these events would suggest that they are stored at the ________________ level of awareness.
    (a) unconscious
    (b) conscious
    (c) latency
    (d) preconscious

2. Researchers conducting twin and adoption studies are likely to conclude that
    (a) in general, the influence of environmental factors on personality traits is at least equal to the influence of genetic factors.
    (b) certain personality traits, such as extraversion and neuroticism, are significantly influenced by genetics.
    (c) identical twins are more alike early in life, but as they grow up, leave home, and have different experiences in different environments, their personalities become more different.
    (d) all of these statements are true.

3. Juan is an experienced car mechanic who believes he can fix just about any problem in any make of car or truck. According to Bandura, Juan's confidence in his ability to handle mechanical problems is his
    (a) self-concept.
    (b) superiority complex.
    (c) self-efficacy.
    (d) actualizing tendency.

4. When Romwaldo was given the results of his psychological test, he was told that he scored high on the extraverted–stable dimension and that he has a tendency to be sociable, outgoing, talkative, and responsive. This description of Romwaldo's source and surface traits is most consistent with
    (a) Hans Eysenck's view of personality.
    (b) Hermann Rorschach's theory of personality.
    (c) Alfred Adler's model of personality.
    (d) Carl Rogers's humanistic approach to personality.

5. The pleasure principle is to ________________ as the reality principle is to ________________ .
    (a) the oral stage; the anal stage
    (b) Thanatos; Eros
    (c) the id; the ego
    (d) the ego; the superego

6. When Kaysone was researching a term paper for her history of psychology course, she was intrigued by the ideas of neo-Freudian Alfred Adler. She noted that for Adler the most fundamental human motive was ________________ , which arises from universal ________________ .
    (a) driven by basic anxiety; feelings of womb and penis envy
    (b) the need to achieve psychological growth, self-realization, and psychic harmony; archetypes in the collective unconscious
    (c) sexual and aggressive in nature; feelings of guilt and anxiety repressed in the unconscious
    (d) striving for superiority; feelings of inferiority

7. Dr. Selnick believes in the importance of unconscious psychological conflicts, sexual and aggressive drives, and the formative influence of early childhood experiences. Dr. Selnick's views are most consistent with the ________________ perspective.
   (a) psychoanalytic
   (b) humanistic
   (c) social cognitive
   (d) trait

8. Raffi is shown a series of cards with ambiguous scenes and is told to make up a story about each one, describing the characters' feelings and their motives. Raffi has been given the
   (a) Thematic Apperception Test (TAT).
   (b) Rorschach Inkblot Test.
   (c) California Psychological Inventory (CPI).
   (d) Myers–Briggs Type Indicator (MBTI).

9. Sheldon has frequently been rebellious, inconsiderate, and self-centered. His parents are consistent in disciplining him for his inappropriate behaviors while communicating to him that they value and love him. The person most likely to agree with their parenting approach and use of unconditional positive regard is
   (a) Sigmund Freud.
   (b) Carl Rogers.
   (c) Joseph Breuer.
   (d) Carl Jung.

10. Dr. Welch is a clinical psychologist who uses the MMPI and the 16PF. If asked to identify the key strength of these tests, he is most likely to note that
   (a) they provide a wealth of qualitative information about the individual.
   (b) scoring relies on the examiner's subjective judgment and clinical experience and expertise.
   (c) they accurately measure the individual's unconscious motives and conflicts.
   (d) they are standardized and objectively scored.

11. Researchers interested in brain structure differences and personality traits first gave participants a personality test that measures the Big Five personality traits. Next, the participants were given MRI scans. If the results are similar to those reported in Focus On Neuroscience (The Neuroscience of Personality: Brain Structure and the Big Five) they are likely to find that __________ had no significant correlation with brain structure differences.
   (a) extraversion
   (b) agreeableness
   (c) openness to experience
   (d) conscientiousness

12. Tracy was given a widely used personality test called the Myers–Briggs Type Indicator (MBTI). This test differs from other self-report inventories, such as the MMPI, CPI, and 16PF, in that
   (a) it has high reliability and validity, and test results are consistent on different test-taking occasions.
   (b) the results can be applied to accurately determine the best vocational choice and predict future occupational success.
   (c) it is designed to assess unconscious motives, conflicts, psychological defenses, and personality traits.
   (d) it is designed to measure personality types rather than personality traits, and suffers from validity and reliability problems.

13. When Dr. Mainprize was going through a very painful divorce, he tended to mark students' papers more harshly than usual and he also constructed much tougher exams. A psychoanalyst would most likely view the professor's treatment of his students as an example of
   (a) reciprocal determinism.
   (b) repression.
   (c) Thanatos (death instinct).
   (d) displacement.

14. Dr. Abrahams believes that people experience psychological problems when their self-concept conflicts with their actual experience and they continually have to defend against genuine feelings and experiences. Consistent with humanistic theory, Dr. Abrahams is likely to say that such people are ____________ , which is caused by ____________ .
   (a) extraverts with neuroticism; a lack of self-efficacy
   (b) in a state of congruence; unconditional positive regard
   (c) overcompensating; feelings of inferiority
   (d) in a state of incongruity; conditional positive regard

15. After reading Freud's theory, Edwin was convinced that there are two conflicting instinctual drives. One consists of biological urges that perpetuate the existence of the individual and the species, and the other is destructive energy reflected in aggressive, reckless, and life-threatening, self-destructive behavior. Freud called these two constructs ______ and ______ .
   (a) introversion; extraversion
   (b) neuroticism; psychoticism
   (c) the pleasure principle; the reality principle
   (d) Eros; Thanatos

Answers

Introduction: What Is Personality?

1. *Personality is defined as* an individual's unique and relatively consistent patterns of thinking, feeling, and behaving.
2. *A personality theory is* an attempt to describe and explain similarities and differences in people's patterns of thinking, feeling, and behavior—in other words, how people are similar, how they are different, and why every individual is unique.
3. *The four basic perspectives on personality (and the main emphasis of each) are* the psychoanalytic perspective, which emphasizes the importance of unconscious processes and the influence of early childhood experience; the humanistic perspective, which represents an optimistic look at human nature, emphasizing the self and the fulfillment of a person's unique potential; the social cognitive perspective, which emphasizes learning and conscious cognitive processes, including the importance of beliefs about the self, goal setting, and self-regulation; and the trait perspective, which emphasizes the description and measurement of specific personality differences among individuals.

The Psychoanalytic Perspective on Personality

1. *Psychoanalysis—Freud's theory of personality—stresses* the influence of unconscious mental processes, the importance of sexual and aggressive instincts, and the enduring effects of early childhood experiences on later personality development.
2. *Some of the key factors in the development of Freud's ideas were* his collaboration with Joseph Breuer on the cause of hysteria and the concept of catharsis; the development of free association to study the unconscious; the importance of dreams and their interpretation; and the impact of war on culture and society.

The Psychoanalytic Perspective: Freud's Dynamic Theory of Personality

1. *The content of the unconscious can surface in disguised form in* free association, dreams, slips of the tongue, mistakes, instances of forgetting, and what, on the surface, appear to be accidental or unintentional actions.
2. *The three basic structures of personality (and their functions) are* the id (the completely unconscious, irrational component of personality that seeks immediate satisfaction of instinctual urges and is ruled by the pleasure principle); the ego (the partly conscious rational component of personality that regulates thoughts and behavior, that is most in touch with the real world, and that is governed by the reality principle); and the superego (the partly conscious, self-evaluative, moralistic component of personality that is formed through the internalization of parental and societal rules).
3. *The three main ego defense mechanisms (and the roles they play) are* repression (the unconscious exclusion of anxiety-provoking thoughts, feelings, and memories from conscious awareness, which is involved in all other ego defense mechanisms), displacement (unconscious shifting of the target of an emotional urge to a substitute target that is less threatening or dangerous), and sublimation (a form of displacement in which sexual urges are rechanneled into productive, sociably acceptable, nonsexual activities). *Other ego defense mechanisms include* rationalization, projection, reaction formation, denial, undoing, and regression.

The Psychoanalytic Perspective: Personality Development

1. *The psychosexual stages are age-related developmental periods in which* the child's sexual impulses are focused on different bodily zones and are expressed through the activities associated with these areas.
2. *The five psychosexual stages (and the focus of each) are* the oral stage (the mouth is the primary focus of pleasurable and gratifying sensations, which are achieved via feeding and exploring objects with the mouth); the anal stage (the anus is the primary focus of pleasurable sensations, which are derived from developing control over elimination via toilet training); the phallic stage (the genitals are the primary focus of pleasurable sensations derived through sexual curiosity, masturbation, and sexual attraction to the opposite-sex parent); the latency stage (sexual impulses become repressed and dormant as the child develops same-sex friendships with peers and focuses on school, sports, and other activities); and the genital stage (at physical sexual maturity, the genitals become the focus of pleasurable sensations, which are satisfied in heterosexual relationships).
3. *If the developmental conflict of a particular stage is not resolved,* the result may be fixation,

and the person will continue to seek pleasure through behaviors that are similar to those associated with that psychosexual stage.

4. *The Oedipus complex refers to* a child's unconscious sexual desire for the opposite-sex parent, usually accompanied by hostile feelings toward the same-sex parent.
5. *Identification (which is one way of resolving the Oedipus complex) is an ego defense mechanism that* involves reducing anxiety by imitating the behavior and characteristics of another person.

Concept Check 1

1. projection
2. free association
3. unconscious
4. latent
5. id
6. superego
7. sublimation
8. identification
9. rationalization

Graphic Organizer 1

1. genital
2. phallic
3. latency
4. oral
5. anal

Matching Exercise 1

1. libido
2. personality
3. superego
4. Oedipus complex
5. ego
6. preconscious
7. oral stage
8. displacement
9. Sigmund Freud
10. anal stage
11. personality theory
12. id
13. latency stage
14. psychoanalysis
15. ego defense mechanisms
16. psychosexual stages
17. manifest content

True/False Test 1

1. F	6. T	11. T	16. F
2. T	7. T	12. F	17. T
3. T	8. T	13. T	
4. F	9. F	14. T	
5. T	10. F	15. T	

The Psychoanalytic Perspective: The Neo-Freudians

1. *The neo-Freudians followed Freud in stressing* the importance of the unconscious and early childhood experiences. *However, they developed independent personality theories, because they disagreed with Freud on three key points: (a)* They took issue with Freud's belief that behavior was primarily motivated by sexual desires. *(b)* They disagreed with Freud's contention that personality is fundamentally determined by early childhood experiences; instead, they believed that personality can also be influenced by experiences throughout the lifespan. *(c)* They departed from Freud's generally pessimistic view of human nature and society.
2. *Carl Jung emphasized* psychological growth, self-realization, and psychic wholeness and harmony. He proposed the existence of the collective unconscious, which contains archetypes of universal human instincts, themes, and preoccupations. He was the first to describe two basic personality types: introverts and extraverts.
3. *Karen Horney stressed* the role of social relationships in protecting against basic anxiety; she objected to Freud's views of female development, particularly his idea of penis envy (she proposed that males often have womb envy).
4. *Alfred Adler believed* that the most fundamental human motive was to strive for superiority, which arose from universal feelings of inferiority. He proposed the notions of the inferiority complex and the superiority complex.

The Psychoanalytic Perspective: Evaluating Freud and the Psychoanalytic Perspective on Personality

1. *Although Sigmund Freud's ideas have had a profound and lasting effect on psychology and on society, the main criticisms of Freud's theory and psychoanalysis are (a)* Freud's theory relies wholly on data derived from a relatively small

sample of patients and from self-analysis. He did not take notes during his private therapy sessions, and so we have only Freud's interpretations of the cases; this problem has to do with the ability to objectively evaluate the evidence. *(b)* Many psychoanalytic concepts, because they are so vague and ambiguous, are very difficult to measure or confirm scientifically. In addition, because even seemingly contradictory information can be used to support Freud's theory, psychoanalytic concepts are often impossible to disprove. Psychoanalysis is also better at explaining past behavior than at predicting future behavior. *(c)* Many people feel that Freud's theories reflect a sexist view of women; Freud's theory uses male psychology as a prototype, and women are essentially viewed as a deviation from the norm of masculinity.

2. *Several of Freud's ideas have been substantiated by empirical evidence, including* the idea that much of mental life is unconscious; that early childhood experiences have a critical influence on interpersonal relationships and psychological adjustment; and that people differ significantly in the degree to which they are able to regulate their impulses, emotions, and thoughts toward adaptive and socially acceptable ends.

Concept Check 2

1. inferiority
2. Karen Horney
3. collective unconscious; Jung's
4. basic anxiety; against
5. extravert
6. archetypes; collective unconscious
7. anima; Jung's
8. striving for superiority

Matching Exercise 2

1. Karen Horney
2. archetypes
3. striving for superiority
4. basic anxiety
5. inferiority complex
6. extravert
7. collective unconscious
8. anima

True/False Test 2

1. T
2. T
3. T
4. T
5. T
6. T
7. T
8. T

The Humanistic Perspective on Personality

1. *The major contributors to humanistic psychology were* Abraham Maslow *and* Carl Rogers.
2. *The humanistic perspective emphasizes* free will, self-awareness, and psychological growth.
3. *The actualizing tendency is* the innate drive to maintain and enhance the human organism.
4. *The self-concept is* the set of perceptions and beliefs that you have about yourself, including your nature, your personal qualities, and your typical behavior.
5. *Conditional positive regard is* the sense that you will be loved and valued only if you behave in a way that is acceptable to others; this can cause a person to deny or distort genuine feelings and experience, leading to a state of incongruence with regard to the self-concept. *Unconditional positive regard is* the sense that you will be valued and loved even if you don't conform to the standards and expectations of others; this leads to a state of congruence, where your sense of self is consistent with your emotions and experiences.
6. *The fully functioning person experiences* congruence, the actualizing tendency, and psychological growth.
7. *The humanistic perspective has been criticized on two particular points*: first, humanistic theories are hard to validate or test scientifically; second, according to many psychologists, the humanistic perspective's view of human nature is too optimistic. *The humanistic perspective has contributed to* psychotherapy, counseling, education, and parenting; has prompted the scientific study of the healthy personality and creativity; and has stressed the importance of subjective experience and the self-concept.

The Social Cognitive Perspective on Personality

1. *The social cognitive perspective stresses* the role of conscious thought processes, self-regulation, and the importance of situational influences.
2. *Bandura's social cognitive theory emphasizes* the importance of observational learning, conscious cognitive processes, social experiences, self-efficacy beliefs, self-regulation, and reciprocal determinism.

3. *Reciprocal determinism suggests that human functioning and personality* are caused by the interaction of behavioral, cognitive, and environmental factors.
4. *Self-efficacy is* a person's belief about his or her ability to meet the demands of a specific situation (feelings of self-confidence or self-doubt); self-efficacy influences behavior, performance, motivation, and persistence.
5. *A key strength of the social cognitive perspective is* that it is grounded in empirical, laboratory research; it is built on research in learning, cognitive psychology, and social psychology, rather than on clinical impressions. Unlike the vague psychoanalytic and humanistic concepts, the concepts of social cognitive theory are scientifically testable; they can be operationally defined and measured.
6. *Some weaknesses of the social cognitive perspective are that* real-life, everyday situations are not adequately captured in the typical laboratory research situation because they are more complex, with multiple factors converging to affect behavior and personality. Other psychologists argue that the social cognitive perspective ignores unconscious influences, conflicts, or emotions.

The Trait Perspective on Personality

1. *Trait theories focus on* identifying, measuring, and describing individual differences in behavioral predispositions.
2. *Traits are* relatively stable, enduring predispositions to consistently behave in certain ways. *Surface traits are* personality characteristics or attributes that can easily be inferred from observing behavior. *Source traits are* the most fundamental dimensions of personality and are thought to be universal and relatively few in number.
3. *Raymond Cattell believed that* there are 16 basic personality factors (he developed the 16PF personality test).
4. *Hans Eysenck proposed that* there are three personality dimensions, introversion–extraversion, neuroticism–emotional stability, and psychoticism.
5. *According to the five-factor model,* there are five basic personality dimensions: extraversion, neuroticism, agreeableness, conscientiousness, and openness to experience.
6. *The field of behavioral genetics studies* the effects of genes and heredity on behavior.
7. *Factors that seem to have a significant genetic component are* extraversion and neuroticism, but openness to experience, conscientiousness, and agreeableness are also influenced by genetics, although to a lesser extent. *The influence of environmental factors on personality traits* is at least equal to the influence of genetic factors.
8. *The trait perspective is useful in* describing and comparing people.
9. *Some criticisms of trait theories are* that they don't really explain human personality or how or why individual differences develop. Also, they generally fail to address other important personality factors, such as the basic motives that drive human personality, the role of unconscious mental processes, how beliefs about the self influence personality, or how psychological change and growth occur.

Concept Check 3

1. self-efficacy
2. surface
3. fully functioning
4. social cognitive; reciprocal determinism
5. trait
6. unconditional positive regard
7. behavioral genetics
8. extraversion; agreeableness; conscientiousness; neuroticism; openness to experience.
9. Raymond Cattell; Sixteen Personality Factor Questionnaire (16PF)

Graphic Organizer 2

1. Hans Eysenck; trait
2. Carl Rogers; humanistic
3. Raymond Cattell; trait
4. Sigmund Freud; psychoanalytic
5. Alfred Adler; psychoanalytic (neo-Freudian)
6. Albert Bandura; social cognitive
7. Karen Horney; psychoanalytic (neo-Freudian)
8. Abraham Maslow; humanistic
9. Carl Jung; psychoanalytic (neo-Freudian)

Matching Exercise 3

1. trait
2. self-efficacy
3. Albert Bandura
4. actualizing tendency

5. five-factor model of personality
6. Abraham Maslow
7. psychoticism
8. positive regard
9. social cognitive theory
10. trait theory
11. extraversion
12. Carl Rogers
13. humanistic psychology
14. reciprocal determinism
15. introversion
16. mastery experience

True/False Test 3

1. T	6. T	11. F
2. F	7. T	12. T
3. T	8. T	13. T
4. F	9. T	14. T
5. T	10. F	15. T

Assessing Personality: Psychological Tests

1. *A psychological test is* a test that assesses a person's abilities, aptitudes, interests, or personality on the basis of a systematically obtained sample of behavior. *Any psychological test is useful if (a)* it accurately and consistently reflects a person's characteristics on some dimension, *and (b)* it predicts a person's future psychological functioning or behavior.
2. *A projective test* is a type of personality test that involves the client's interpreting an ambiguous image; it is used to assess unconscious motives, conflicts, psychological defenses, and personality traits. *Examples are* the Rorschach Inkblot Test and the Thematic Apperception Test (TAT).
3. *A self-report inventory is* a type of psychological test in which a person's responses to standardized questions are compared with established norms. *Examples include* the Minnesota Multiphasic Personality Inventory (MMPI), the California Psychological Inventory (CPI), the Sixteen Personality Factor Questionnaire (16PF), and the Myers–Briggs Type Indicator (MBTI).
4. *Projective tests provide qualitative data but their limitations are that* responses may be affected by the examiner or the situation, scoring is very subjective, results may be inconsistent, and they do not predict behavior well.
5. *The strengths of self-report inventories such as the MMPI, CPI, and 16PF are that* they are objectively scored, and the scores are compared with norms established by previous research; they differentiate among people on particular personality characteristics; and they have high reliability, validity, and predictive value. *The Myers–Briggs Type Indicator (MBTI) differs from other self-report inventories in that it* is designed to assess personality types rather than measure personality traits (types are distinct categories that don't overlap, whereas traits can be displayed to varying degrees).
6. *Problems with self-report inventories (MMPI, CPI, and 16PF) are that* people do not always respond honestly or accurately, people can successfully fake responses and answer in socially desirable ways, and some people may respond in a set way to all questions. *The MBTI has several problems:* (a) it lacks reliability (people can receive different MBTI results on different test-taking occasions); (b) it has no validity (research does not support the claim that MBTI personality types have a relationship with occupational success); and (c) there is no evidence that there are 16 distinctly different personality types (caution is also advised in interpreting MBTI results and applying them to vocational choices or predicting occupational success).

Concept Check 4

1. projective test; Thematic Apperception Test (TAT)
2. MMPI
3. CPI
4. Rorschach Inkblot Test; TAT; projective
5. 16PF
6. MBTI

Matching Exercise 4

1. self-report inventory
2. Rorschach Inkblot Test
3. California Psychological Inventory (CPI)
4. psychological test
5. Sixteen Personality Factor Questionnaire (16PF)
6. reliability
7. graphology

True/False Test 4

1. T	3. F	5. T	7. T
2. T	4. F	6. T	

Something to Think About

1. In any discussion of psychological testing it is always a good idea to point out the important characteristics of a good test, namely, reliability and validity. In terms of personality testing, you should first describe the two categories of tests, projective tests and self-report inventories.

   The famous Rorschach Inkblot Test is, of course, a projective test. In other words, it is assumed that people will project their unconscious feelings, motives, drives, thoughts, and so on in their responses to the series of inkblots. Similarly, the Thematic Apperception Test (TAT) gives people an opportunity to project unconscious information into the stories they make up about ambiguous scenes. Both tests developed out of the psychoanalytic approaches to personality, and scoring involves the subjective interpretations of the examiner. A brief discussion of Freud's theory as it relates to personality would probably be in order. A review of the most damaging criticisms of psychoanalysis may shed light on the topic, and the issue of the validity and reliability of projective tests should not be overlooked. Despite the criticisms, projective tests are widely used and can provide a wealth of qualitative data about an individual.

   Self-report inventories are used by clinical psychologists to evaluate both normal and abnormal populations in a variety of settings and for a variety of purposes. Three of the most commonly used objective self-report tests are the MMPI, the CPI, and the 16PF. These are called objective personality tests because they are standardized and objectively scored and measured against established norms. Self-report inventories are far more reliable and valid than are projective tests. These tests do have some drawbacks, including a person's ability to fake responses and answer in a socially desirable manner, some people's tendency to answer in a set way to all questions, and the fact that people are not always the best judges of their own behavior.

   Another widely used personality test is the Myers–Briggs Type Indicator (MBTI). It differs from other self-report inventories in that it is designed to assess personality *types* rather than personality *traits* (types are distinct categories that don't overlap, whereas traits can be displayed to varying degrees). The MBTI has several problems: (a) it lacks reliability (people can receive different MBTI results on different test-taking occasions); (b) it has no validity (research does not support the claim that MBTI personality types have a relationship with occupational success); and (c) there is no evidence that there are 16 distinctly different personality types (caution is also advised in interpreting MBTI results and applying them to vocational choices or predicting occupational success).

   Personality tests are generally useful strategies that can provide insights about the psychological makeup of a person. However, no personality test, by itself, is likely to provide a definitive description of a given individual. In addition, because people can and often do change over time, any personality test provides a profile of the person only at the time of the test.

2. You should begin by noting that nonscientific belief systems about personality, and what forms and shapes it, have existed long before psychology became interested in the topic. However, ancient origins and popular belief does not make them true or accurate. Nor does the fact that so many people today—from all walks of life—believe in astrology, palmistry, or graphology provide evidence that they work as claimed. In fact, most scientists consider these belief systems to be pseudosciences.

   For example, proponents of handwriting analysis (graphologists) claim that people's handwriting reveals their personality traits, temperamental qualities, intelligence levels, and cognitive capacities, and can even be used to accurately measure job applicants' honesty, reliability, leadership ability, and cooperativeness. Graphology is very popular and has been used by many businesses, both large and small, and even by some government agencies, to help in employee selection, hiring, promotion, and other personnel matters. Clearly, many people believe graphology to be a valid measure of personality traits.

   And, as is the case with many strongly held beliefs, it is often difficult to get true believers to listen to any information that might contradict what they feel is a valid point of view. It is always important to be aware of this and to respect their right to believe whatever they wish. However, if you have an opportunity for an open-minded discussion with them, you might be able to show how the claims of graphologists have been rigorously tested under scientific conditions.

For instance, a study by Edwards and Armitage (1992) investigated graphologists' ability to distinguish among people in three different groups, successful versus unsuccessful secretaries, successful business entrepreneurs versus librarians and bank clerks, and actors and actresses versus monks and nuns.

In designing the study, researchers included suggestions made by leading graphologists, who agreed that the methodology was appropriate and a fair test of graphology. In addition, and this is important, the graphologists hypothesized that they would have a high degree of success in discriminating among the people in each group (one graphologist even predicted that the graphologists would have a 100 percent level of accuracy).

All participants in the study (170 in total from the various groups) indicated their age, sex, and hand preference; they all also submitted 20 lines of spontaneous handwriting on a neutral topic. Four leading graphologists independently assessed the handwriting samples and then assigned each handwritten sample to one category or another of each group in the study.

Two control conditions were also included for comparison purposes (four ordinary people with no graphology or psychology training analyzed the samples and a typewritten copy of the handwritten samples was assessed by four psychologists). How did the graphologists do in comparison to the two control groups? Remember the prediction they made before the study?

Overall, they fared very poorly. The completely inexperienced judges achieved a success rate of 59 percent compared with the slightly better rate of 65 percent achieved by the graphologists. The psychologists had a success rate of 54 percent overall. If graphology were indeed as accurate and reliable as the claims made for it, they would surely have performed at a much higher rate than they did. Of course, one study does not rule out the possibility that graphology is a good measure of personality. So, as good scientific psychologists are supposed to do, researchers have carried out hundreds of other similar studies to test the claims of the graphologists. Every one of these studies reached the same conclusion as the Edwards and Armitage study. After a comprehensive review of the evidence, researchers noted that graphologists have completely failed to demonstrate the validity or reliability of predicting work performance, personality traits, aptitudes, temperamental qualities, human talents and leanings, and so on. In a word, the evidence is clear, graphology is a pseudoscience. The handwriting is on the wall!!!

Progress Test 1

1. d	6. d	11. a
2. c	7. d	12. d
3. d	8. d	13. b
4. a	9. c	14. c
5. a	10. b	15. a

Progress Test 2

1. a	6. a	11. d
2. a	7. d	12. a
3. d	8. c	13. a
4. d	9. d	14. b
5. c	10. a	15. b

Progress Test 3

1. d	6. d	11. c
2. d	7. a	12. d
3. c	8. a	13. d
4. a	9. b	14. d
5. c	10. d	15. d

CHAPTER 11

Social Psychology

PREVIEW

Reading the section below first will give you a general sense of the chapter's contents and an initial introduction to some of the major concepts and terms. This will prime you for what you are about to read and help you to develop a "cognitive map" that will guide your study of the material in this chapter. Likewise, reading the **preview questions** at the beginning of each major section will improve your ability to understand, learn, and retain the information.

CHAPTER 11 . . . AT A GLANCE

Social psychology is the study of how a person's thoughts, feelings, and behavior are influenced by the presence of other people and by the social and physical environment. It is broadly divided into two major research areas: social cognition and social influence. The chapter first explores person perception, then discusses the process of attribution and the fundamental attribution error, blaming the victim, hindsight bias, the just-world hypothesis, and the self-serving bias. Cross-cultural differences in attributional processes are also explored.

Once we form impressions of people, we tend to interpret their behavior in terms of our attitudes about them. The conditions under which attitudes determine behavior are identified. The role of cognitive dissonance in behavior and cognition is explored. In discussing prejudice, the text describes such cognitive influences as stereotypes, in-groups and out-groups, and implicit attitudes. The emotional roots of prejudice and techniques for reducing prejudice are also considered.

Conformity occurs when people change their behavior, attitudes, or beliefs in response to real or imagined group pressure. The original experimental design and the results of Stanley Milgram's research on obedience are presented in detail. Conditions that influence people to obey and to resist obeying authority figures are identified.

Latané and Darley's research on helping behavior and the bystander effect is discussed, and their model of bystander intervention is presented. In this context, individual behavior can be strongly influenced by the presence of others.

Enhancing Well-Being with Psychology provides some practical suggestions that will help you to avoid being taken in by techniques used by professional persuaders.

Introduction: What Is Social Psychology?

Preview Questions

Consider the following questions as you study this section of the chapter.

- What is social psychology?
- What is the sense of self, and why is it important?
- What is meant by social cognition and social influence?

*Read the section "Introduction: What Is Social Psychology?" and **write** your answers to the following:*

1. Social psychology is ______________________________

   ____

   The sense of self refers to ______________________________

   ____

   It is important because ______________________________

   ____

2. Social cognition refers to ______________________________

   ____

3. Social influence focuses on ______________________________

   ____

Person Perception: Forming Impressions of Other People

Preview Questions

Consider the following questions as you study this section of the chapter.

- What is person perception?
- What four principles does the mental process of forming judgments of others follow and what do they demonstrate?
- What is social categorization, and what do the terms *explicit cognition* and *implicit cognition* refer to?
- How do social categories, implicit personality theories, physical appearance cues, and physical attractiveness influence person perception?

*Read the section "Person Perception: Forming Impressions of Other People" and **write** your answers to the following:*

1. Person perception refers to ______________________________

   ____

   ____

2. The four basic principles of person perception are

   (a) ______________________________

   (b) ______________________________

   (c) ______________________________

   (d) ______________________________

3. In combination, these four basic principles underscore that person perception is ______________________________

   ____

   ____

   ____

4. Social categorization is ______________________________

   ____

   ____

   Explicit cognition refers to ______________________________

   ____

   ____

   Implicit cognition refers to ______________________________

   ____

   ____

5. An implicit personality theory is ______________________________

   ____

   Like social categories, implicit personality theories are useful ______________________________

   ____

6. Physical appearance cues play ______________________________

   ____

   ____

   Research has shown that physical attractiveness is correlated with ______________________________

   ____

   ____

   Neuroscientists have shown that when people make direct eye contact with a physically attractive person ______________________________

   ____

   ____

   ____

7. General conclusions about the process of person perception are that

   (a) ______________________________

   (b) ______________________________

   (c) ______________________________

   (d) ______________________________

Attribution: Explaining Behavior

Preview Questions

Consider the following questions as you study this section of the chapter.

- How is *attribution* defined?
- What are the fundamental attribution error, blaming the victim, hindsight bias, and the just-world hypothesis?
- What is the self-serving bias?

*Read the section "Attribution: Explaining Behavior" and **write** your answers to the following:*

1. Attribution is ______________________________
____
____

2. The fundamental attribution error is the tendency to ______________________________
____
____

   When it comes to explaining our own behavior, we tend to use ______________________________
____

3. Blaming the victim is the tendency to __________
____
____

4. Hindsight bias is ______________________________
____

   In the case of blaming the victim ______________
____

5. The just-world hypothesis is ______________
____
____

6. The self-serving bias is the tendency to __________
____
____

After you have carefully studied the preceding sections, complete the following exercises.

Concept Check 1

Read the following and write the correct term in the space provided.

1. When Adam earned an A in his philosophy class, he concluded that he had quite a talent for writing coherently and thinking logically. When he earned a C in his sociology class, he expressed dissatisfaction with the course content, the teaching ability of the professor, and the quality and clarity of the exams. This best illustrates the ______________________________ .

2. Rachel has just learned that her neighbor's teenaged son Brad was involved in an automobile accident at a nearby intersection. She said to her husband, "Well, Brad's recklessness has finally got him into trouble!" Rachel's comment suggests that she has made the

   ______________________________ .

3. While Susan was having lunch at her local deli, her wallet and cell phone were taken from her handbag, which was hanging on the back of her chair. When she reported the incident to the police, the duty officer said, "I can't believe you didn't see that coming. You should have kept your bag on your lap." It appears that the police officer was engaged in a common explanatory pattern called ______________________________ , and his suggestion that she should have anticipated being robbed is a cognitive bias called

   ______________________________ .

4. When Cheryl first met Charles, who is an archivist at the university library, she concluded that he was probably very quiet, introverted, and introspective. She was later surprised to learn that he was the lead singer in a heavy metal band. Cheryl's surprise is probably the result of using a(n) ______________________________
______________________________ , that is, the tendency to judge people on the basis of the traits and behaviors associated with certain types of people.

5. After learning about some interesting social psychology phenomena in his introductory class, Patrick decided he would like to test one of the concepts by facing the back instead of the front while riding the elevator. Much to his surprise, he found that he could not carry out his plan. After a second or two, he was overcome with embarrassment and ended up facing the front like everyone else. Patrick's behavior was governed by the ______________________ of the situation.
6. Grover does not support any charities because he believes that people who are poor, hungry, or homeless did something to deserve their situation. Grover's explanatory style is called ______________________; it probably reflects his strong need to believe the world is fair, an assumption called the ______________________.
7. Byron is tall, dark, and handsome. Like most physically attractive people, he is likely to be *perceived* as being ______________________ ______________________ than less attractive people.
8. When people make direct eye contact with Byron, an area of their brain called the ventral striatum is likely to ______________________; if he disengages from eye contact and averts his gaze, it is likely ______________________.
9. Using fMRI, researchers showed that when we make direct eye contact with a physically attractive person, a specific area on each side of the brain is activated. Other researchers have expanded on these findings and identified three brain areas (the ______________________, the ______________________, and the ______________________) that are selectively responsive to the reward value of attractive faces.
10. When Theresa got on the bus, she glanced at the young person in the front seat and noticed he had a backpack on the seat next to him, iPod earplugs in his ears, and a cell phone holding the page of a book open; she decided that he must be a college student. Theresa has used ______________________ (implicit/explicit) cognition in categorizing the person on the bus.

Graphic Organizer 1

The following statements represent attributional processes. Decide which is the fundamental attribution error, blaming the victim, hindsight bias, the self-serving bias, or the self-effacing (modesty) bias.

Statement	Attribution
1. I solved the local newspaper puzzle because I'm smart; I couldn't solve the *New York Times* puzzle because it was tricky and unfair and asked questions about facts unknown to most people.	
2. I think I got that A+ in my math class because the exams were easy and there was not much competition. I have to study much harder for my English exam, because I got a low grade on the last English exam.	

Statement	Attribution
3. I don't care what he said about his car breaking down; he was 15 minutes late for the first class, so he must be one of those inconsiderate professors who is more concerned with his research than with his students.	
4. When I invested and lost all my money with that fraudulent investment manager, I should have known that the big returns were just too good to be true and that I'd eventually get ripped off.	
5. I know it is tragic that she died so young, but if only she had adopted a more positive attitude toward her illness she could have beaten it.	

Review of Terms and Concepts 1

Use the terms in this list to complete the Matching Exercise, then to help you answer the True/False items correctly.

social psychology
sense of self
evolutionary psychology
social cognition
social influence
person perception
interpersonal context
social norms
social categorization
explicit cognition
implicit cognition
implicit personality theory
schemas
attribution
fundamental attribution error
blaming the victim
hindsight bias
just-world hypothesis
self-serving bias
self-effacing bias (modesty bias)

Matching Exercise

Match the appropriate term with its definition or description.

1. ________________ The "rules," or expectations, for appropriate behavior in a particular social situation.
2. ________________ Mental process of inferring the causes of people's behavior, including one's own. Also used to refer to the explanation made for a particular behavior.
3. ________________ Tendency to attribute successful outcomes of one's own behavior to internal causes and unsuccessful outcomes to external, situational causes.
4. ________________ Branch of psychology that studies how a person's thoughts, feelings, and behavior are influenced by the presence of other people and by the social and physical environment.
5. ________________ Network of assumptions or beliefs about the relationships among various types of people, traits, and behaviors.
6. ________________ Perspective in psychology that is based on the premise that certain psychological processes and behavior patterns changed over hundreds of thousands of years because they were adaptive.
7. ________________ Tendency to find fault with an innocent casualty of misfortune for having somehow caused the problem or for not having taken steps to avoid or prevent it.
8. ________________ The assumption that the world is fair and that therefore people get what they deserve and deserve what they get.
9. ________________ The tendency, after an event has occurred, to overestimate one's ability to have foreseen or predicted the outcome.
10. ________________ The mental processes we use to form judgments and draw conclusions about the characteristics and motives of others.

True/False Test

Indicate whether each statement is true or false by placing T or F in the blank space next to each item.

1. ____ The effect that situational factors and other people have on an individual's behavior is called social cognition.
2. ____ The fundamental attribution error refers to the tendency to attribute the behavior of others to internal, personal characteristics while ignoring or underestimating the effects of external, situational factors; an attributional bias that is common in individualistic cultures.

3. ____ Implicit cognition refers to deliberate, conscious mental processes involved in perceptions, judgments, decisions, and reasoning.
4. ____ Social categorization refers to the mental process of classifying people into groups (or social categories) on the basis of their shared characteristics.
5. ____ Social influence refers to the mental processes people use to make sense of their social environment.
6. ____ The self-effacing bias (modesty bias) involves blaming failure on internal, personal factors while attributing success to external, situational factors; more common in collectivistic cultures than in individualistic cultures.
7. ____ Interpersonal context involves the characteristics of the person being perceived, your own self-perception, your goals in the situation, and the specific situation in which the process occurs.
8. ____ Through previous social experiences, we form cognitive *schemas,* or mental frameworks, about the traits and behaviors associated with different types of people.
9. ____ *Sense of self* refers to an individual's unique sense of identity that has been influenced by social, cultural, and psychological experiences; who you are in relation to other people.
10. ____ Explicit cognition refers to automatic, nonconscious mental processes that influence perceptions, judgments, decisions, and reasoning.

Check your answers and review any areas of weakness before going on to the next section.

The Social Psychology of Attitudes

Preview Questions

Consider the following questions as you study this section of the chapter.

- How is the term *attitude* defined, and what are its three components?
- Under what conditions are attitudes most likely to determine behavior?
- What is cognitive dissonance, and how does it affect behavior?

Read the section "The Social Psychology of Attitudes" and ***write*** *your answers to the following:*

1. An attitude is defined as ________________

____

2. The three components of an attitude are
   (a) ________________________
   (b) ________________________
   (c) ________________________
3. You are most likely to behave in accordance with your attitudes in any of five conditions:
   (a) ________________________
   (b) ________________________
   (c) ________________________
   (d) ________________________
   (e) ________________________
4. Cognitive dissonance is ________________

____

____

It commonly occurs in situations in which

____

____

____

____

5. Cognitive dissonance can also change ________

____

____

6. Cognitive dissonance also operates when you have to choose ________________

____

____

____

____

____

Understanding Prejudice

Preview Questions

Consider the following questions as you study this section of the chapter.

- How is *prejudice* defined?
- What are stereotypes, stereotype threats, in-groups, out-groups, the out-group homogeneity effect, the in-group bias, ethnocentrism, and discrimination?

- What are implicit attitudes, and how are they measured?
- How can prejudice be overcome, and how have the results of Sherif's study been applied?

*Read the section "Understanding Prejudice" and **write** your answers to the following:*

1. Prejudice is defined as ____________________
____
2. A stereotype is ____________________
____
____
Stereotype threat refers to the fact that
____
____
3. An in-group is ____________________
____
An out-group is ____________________
____
4. The out-group homogeneity effect refers to
____
The in-group bias is ____________________
____
5. Ethnocentrism is the belief ____________________
____
____
6. The emotional component of prejudice includes negative feelings, such as ____________________
____
Behaviorally, prejudice can result in __________
____
7. Implicit attitudes are ____________________
____
They are measured by ____________________
____
8. In his classic study on overcoming prejudice, psychologist Muzafer Sherif demonstrated that
____
____
____
In the educational system ____________________
____
____
____

After you have carefully studied the preceding sections, complete the following exercises.

Concept Check 2

Read the following and write the correct term in the space provided.

1. In Zeegland, where Majib grew up, women manage all the household finances, make all the major decisions regarding the family, and earn most of the family income. The men, on the other hand, tend to spend their time "hanging out" and trying to impress each other with the way they dress. Majib's belief that all women are naturally more assertive and domineering than men reflects her ________________ about gender.
2. In a discussion about gun-control laws, Jerrilee said, "In my opinion, easy access to guns is the major contributing factor to the high homicide rate in the United States." This statement reflects the ________________ component of Jerrilee's attitude about gun control.
3. At lunch one day, a group of fine arts majors happened to sit next to a group of engineering students. During a discussion after lunch, one of the fine arts students remarked, "Boy, those engineering students are all alike. They are so loud, pushy, and aggressive, and, unlike us, they haven't got a scrap of creativity among them!" This statement reflects the ____________________________ effect.
4. During a sociology class, the instructor mentioned that the Heckawe tribe considers chopped-up earthworms, sheep's eyeballs, water buffalo testicles, and live caterpillars to be delicacies. Later, while having a hamburger and fries for lunch, a student remarked that the Heckawe diet was disgusting and repulsive. Another suggested that the tribe would someday become civilized and maybe even start eating good food "just like us." These remarks illustrate a form of in-group bias called ____________________ .

5. When Sylvester decided to buy the very expensive Z5000 Spartan computer, he was happy with all the features of this model but was also very concerned about the cost. However, after talking with many enthusiastic Z5000 Spartan owners, he is now convinced that he made the right decision. It is very likely that Sylvester experienced ____________________ when he purchased his PC, and his subsequent behavior was an attempt to ______________ this unpleasant state of psychological tension.
6. Miss Graham's elementary class is made up of students from a variety of backgrounds and cultures. To increase cooperation and decrease negative stereotypes and intergroup hostility, Miss Graham has students cooperate in small ethnically diverse groups in which each individual has responsibility for one aspect of the overall project. This is called the ______________________ .
7. Dr. Gandham believes that stereotypes are closely related to the tendency to view others in terms of two very basic social categories, "us" and "them," referred to as the ____ and the ____________________ .
8. In a class discussion, Klarissa points out that negative attitudes toward people who belong to a specific group are ultimately based on the exaggerated notion that members of other social groups are very different from members of our own social group. Klarissa is discussing the topic of ____________________ .
9. In response to Klarissa's comment, Selena suggests that certain groups *are* different from others. She notes that Italians are emotional and passionate, the English are cold and aloof, the Japanese are inscrutable, and the Scots are hairy and argumentative. These comments indicate that Selena is engaging in the process of ____________________ these particular groups.
10. While researching a paper on interpersonal attraction Jasmine discovered that the most significant factor in attraction is ____________________ . She also found that familiarity; being happy, intoxicated, or physically aroused by exercise; or similarity in physical characteristics, personality traits, attitudes, and health ____________________ (are also/are not) associated with judgments of attractiveness.
11. Harry considers himself to be open-minded, nonjudgmental, nonsexist, and nonracist. The computer-based test he took indicated that he had overt and covert social preferences and stereotypes. This test is called ________________________ and was designed to measure ____________________ .

Graphic Organizer 2

The following statements reflect attitudes about certain topics. Decide which component—cognitive, affective, or behavioral—is represented by each statement.

Statement	Component
1. I believe that the automobile is the single most destructive element on this planet.	
2. I consistently recycle paper, plastic, soda cans, glass, and other waste.	

Statement	Component
3. I vote for anti-gun-control advocates and give them my full support.	
4. I get really angry when I see people carelessly throwing their litter on the ground.	
5. I don't want to contribute to the pollution of our city, so I ride my bicycle or take public transportation.	
6. I am very happy when I see women doing well in what used to be male-dominated occupations.	
7. In my opinion, a woman's place is in the home, raising the kids and doing housework.	
8. I get really upset when motorists are rude and inconsiderate.	
9. I believe that the automobile is the greatest invention ever and that we need to elect politicians who will promise to build more roads and freeways.	

Review of Terms, Concepts, and Names 2

Use the terms in this list to complete the Matching Exercise, then to help you answer the True/False items correctly.

attitude
cognitive component
affective component
behavioral component
Philip Zimbardo
cognitive dissonance
prejudice
stereotype
stereotype threat
in-group
out-group
out-group homogeneity effect
heterogeneous
in-group bias
ethnocentrism
discrimination
implicit attitudes
Implicit Association Test (IAT)
Muzafer Sherif
jigsaw classroom technique

Matching Exercise

Match the appropriate term/name with its definition or description.

1. ________________ Social psychologist who is best known for his "Robbers Cave" experiments to study prejudice, conflict resolution, and group processes.
2. ________________ The belief that one's own culture or ethnic group is superior to all others and the related tendency to use one's own culture or ethnic group as a standard by which to judge other cultures or ethnic groups.
3. ________________ Learned tendency to evaluate some object, person, or issue in a particular way; such evaluations may be positive, negative, or ambivalent.
4. ________________ A social group to which one belongs.
5. ________________ Unpleasant state of psychological tension or arousal that occurs when two thoughts or perceptions are inconsistent; typically results from awareness that attitudes and behavior are in conflict.
6. ________________ A social group to which one does not belong.
7. ________________ Component of an attitude that involves thoughts, ideas, and conclusions about a given topic or object.
8. ________________ Cluster of characteristics that are associated with all members of a specific social group, often including qualities that are unrelated to the objective criteria that define the category.
9. ________________ Social psychologist who is known for his research on cognitive dissonance and social influence, and especially for the Stanford Prison Experiment, which demonstrated how situational factors can have an impact on human behavior.

10. ________________ Preferences and biases toward particular groups that are automatic, spontaneous, unintentional, and often unconscious.

True/False Test

Indicate whether each statement is true or false by placing T or F in the blank space next to each item.

1. ____ Prejudice is a negative attitude toward people who belong to a specific social group.
2. ____ When prejudice is displayed behaviorally, it is called discrimination.
3. ____ The out-group homogeneity effect refers to the tendency to judge the behavior of in-group members favorably and out-group members unfavorably.
4. ____ The jigsaw classroom technique is a teaching technique that stresses cooperative, rather than competitive, learning situations.
5. ____ The in-group bias refers to the tendency to see members of out-groups as very similar to one another.
6. ____ The affective component of an attitude is reflected in the feelings that people have about a given event, object, or topic.
7. ____ Members of an in-group typically see themselves as being quite varied, or *heterogeneous*.
8. ____ The behavioral component of an attitude is reflected in people's actions.
9. ____ Stereotype threat refers to the fact that awareness that your social group is associated with a particular stereotype can negatively affect your performance on tests or tasks that measure abilities thought to be associated with that stereotype.
10. ____ The Implicit Association Test (IAT) is a computer-based test that measures the degree to which people associate particular groups of people with specific characteristics or attributes.

Check your answers and review any areas of weakness before going on to the next section.

Conformity: Following the Crowd

Preview Questions

Consider the following questions as you study this section of the chapter.

- What is social influence, and how is *conformity* defined?
- Which psychologist first studied conformity, and what did he find?
- Why do people conform, and what factors influence the degree to which people conform and do not conform?
- How does culture affect conformity?

*Read the section "Conformity: Following the Crowd" and **write** your answers to the following:*

1. Social influence is ________________________________
____
____
2. Conformity is the tendency to ____________________
____
____
3. In studying the degree to which people would conform to the group even when the group opinion was clearly wrong, social psychologist, ________________________, found that
____
____
4. We conform to the larger group for two basic reasons:
(a) ____
____
(b) ____
____
5. You are more likely to conform to groups norms when
(a) ____
(b) ____
(c) ____
(d) ____
(e) ____
(f) ____
6. Conformity decreases under certain conditions:
(a) ____
____
____

(b) ______________________________

(c) ______________________________

7. In a cross-cultural meta-analysis, British psychologists found that ______________________________

Obedience: Just Following Orders

Preview Questions

Consider the following questions as you study this section of the chapter.

- How is *obedience* defined?
- What was the basic procedure in Milgram's original obedience experiment, and what were the results?
- What aspects of the experimental situation increased the likelihood of obedience?
- What factors did Milgram later discover that decreased the level of obedience?
- What are some of the important implications of the scientific study of conformity and obedience?

Read the section "Obedience: Just Following Orders" and ***write*** *your answers to the following:*

1. Obedience is defined as ______________________________

2. The basic design of Milgram's obedience experiment was as follows: ______________________________

3. In contrast to predictions, the results of Milgram's original experiment showed that ______________________________

4. Aspects of the experimental situation that had a strong impact on the subjects' willingness to continue obeying the experimenter's orders were as follows: ______________________________

5. Some of the situational factors that made people less willing to obey were as follows: ______________________________

6. The scientific study of conformity and obedience has some important implications:

   (a) ______________________________

   (b) ______________________________

   (c) ______________________________

   (d) ______________________________

Helping Behavior: Coming to the Aid of Strangers

Preview Questions

Consider the following questions as you study this section of the chapter.

- What is altruism, and how does it differ from prosocial behavior?
- What factors increase or decrease the likelihood that people will help a stranger?
- What is the bystander effect, and what causes it?
- What factors decrease the likelihood that people will help a stranger?

*Read the section "Helping Behavior: Coming to the Aid of Strangers" and **write** your answers to the following:*

1. Altruism is ________________________________

____

____

whereas prosocial behavior is ________________

____

____

2. According to Latané and Darley's general model, six factors increase the likelihood of bystander intervention. We tend to be more helpful when

(a) ________________________________

____

(b) ________________________________

____

(c) ________________________________

____

(d) ________________________________

____

(e) ________________________________

____

(f) ________________________________

____

3. The bystander effect refers to ________________

____

____

4. There are two reasons for the bystander effect:

(a) ________________________________

____

____

(b) ________________________________

____

____

5. Other factors that decrease the likelihood of helping behavior are

(a) ________________________________

____

(b) ________________________________

____

(c) ________________________________

____

After you have carefully studied the preceding sections, complete the following exercises.

Concept Check 3

1. Trent hates to wear ties but wears one to his sister's wedding to avoid the disapproval of his family. Trent's behavior illustrates the importance of ________________ social influence.
2. Harold is a subject in a replication of Milgram's obedience experiment. If he is like most subjects in the experiment, he __________ (will/will not) administer high levels of shock to the learner.
3. If Harold was allowed to act as his own authority and freely choose the shock level, it is very ________________ (likely/unlikely) that he will use a shock over 150 volts, the first point at which the learner is likely to protest.
4. At the end of a music concert featuring his *favorite* group, Jason joined everyone else in giving the group a standing ovation. Jason's behavior ________________ (is/is not) an example of conformity.
5. Carmichael was elated when he won $1,000 in the lottery. Later that day, he gladly volunteered to spend a few hours helping collect food for the local food bank. This illustrates the "________________________" effect.
6. While about 20 people were filling out a questionnaire in a classroom, an odorless vapor started seeping into the room from one of the heating vents. The room slowly began to fill with the vapor, yet none of the people stopped what they were doing, and no one went to report the incident. This bystander effect occurred because the presence of other people creates a ________________________.
7. Leonarda volunteers for the crisis line at her university because she believes that not only is the work experience valuable but it will also look good on her application to graduate school. Leonarda's volunteer work would be considered an example of ________________________.
8. When Jaffar, the student representative, attended the first meeting of the College Education Committee, a vote was taken on an

agenda item that he knew little about. Jaffar voted for the motion because he assumed that the rest of the committee members, who voted in favor of the motion, must have accurate information about the proposal. Jaffar's conformity in this case was the result of

________________________________ .

9. Bryan is short of cash and needs about another $20 for an evening out with his girlfriend. He asks his friend Jared if he can borrow $150; before Jared can say no, Bryan appears to back off and makes a much smaller request—to borrow $20. Jared says, "OK, I can't lend you $150, but I guess I can cough up $20." Bryan has cleverly utilized a strategy called the

____

technique, which is based on the rule of

________________________________ .

10. Kaila read about Zimbardo's controversial Stanford Prison Experiment and was surprised at how quickly the participants adopted their randomly assigned roles as either guards or prisoners. She realized that when people are not certain about what to do, they tend to rely on cues provided by others and conform their behavior to those in their immediate social group, showing that implied ________________ can be just as powerful as explicit orders.

Graphic Organizer 3

Describe the main research findings of the following social psychologists. (For example, Zimbardo's grasshopper study showed how behavior can change attitude through the process of cognitive dissonance.)

Researcher	Main Research Findings
1. Asch	
2. Sherif	
3. Milgram	
4. Latané and Darley	

Review of Terms, Concepts, and Names 3

Use the terms in this list to complete the Matching Exercise, then to help you answer the True/False items correctly.

conformity
Solomon Asch
normative social influence
informational social influence
Stanley Milgram
obedience
Bibb Latané and John M. Darley
altruism
prosocial behavior
"feel good, do good" effect
bystander effect
diffusion of responsibility
persuasion

Matching Exercise

Match the appropriate term/name with its definition or description.

1. ________________ Social psychologist who is best known for his controversial investigation of destructive obedience to an authority figure.
2. ________________ Adjusting your opinions, judgments, or behavior so that it matches the opinions, judgments, or behavior of other people, or the norms of a social group or situation.
3. ________________ Social psychologists who are best known for their pioneering studies of bystander intervention in emergency situations.
4. ________________ Performance of a behavior in response to a direct command.
5. ________________ Social psychologist who is best known for his pioneering studies of conformity.
6. ________________ Helping another person with no expectation of personal reward or benefit.
7. ________________ Any behavior that helps another, whether the underlying motive is self-serving or selfless.

True/False Test

Indicate whether each item is true or false by placing T or F in the space next to each item.

1. ____ Persuasion is the deliberate attempt to influence the attitudes or behavior of another person in a situation in which that person has some freedom of choice.
2. ____ The bystander effect refers to a phenomenon in which the greater the number of people present, the less likely each individual is to help someone in distress.
3. ____ A phenomenon in which the presence of other people makes it less likely that any individual will help someone in distress because the obligation to intervene is shared among all the onlookers is called diffusion of responsibility.
4. ____ Source of behavior that is motivated by the desire to gain social acceptance and approval is called informational social influence.
5. ____ The "feel good, do good" effect refers to the fact that when people feel good, successful, happy, or fortunate, they are more likely to help others.
6. ____ Source of behavior that is motivated by the desire to be correct is called normative social influence.

Check your answers and review any areas of weakness before going on to the next section.

Something to Think About

1. People often ask, "Why are so many people reluctant to help others who are in distress and need help?" The most usual responses are that people suffer from apathy and that big cities alienate and depersonalize people. What would you say if someone asked you that question?
2. We are subjected to a wide variety of situations and stimuli that are designed to influence our attitudes or behavior. The most obvious of these are media advertisements, but we regularly encounter many other more subtle sources of attempted influence. These attempts to influence us all use techniques of persuasion. Imagine that you are hired by a company, and management wants you to write a brief summary of the factors that are most powerful in changing people's attitudes or behaviors. What would you put in your report?

Check your answers and review any areas of weakness before completing the progress tests.

Progress Test 1

Review the complete chapter (including all boxed inserts), review all your study notes, and then test yourself on the following progress test. Check your answers. If you make a mistake, review your notes, check the appropriate section in the study guide, and, if necessary, go back and read the relevant part of the chapter in your textbook.

1. Dr. Lopez is a social psychologist who studies the mental processes people use to make sense of their social environment, including person perception, attribution, attitudes, and prejudice. His specific area of research is called
   (a) social cognition.
   (b) perception.
   (c) social influence.
   (d) personality.

2. About a dozen students were sitting in a small research laboratory room filling out a questionnaire when they heard a crash followed by groaning from the room next door. While many of them appeared to notice, nobody went to inform the researcher, who said he would be in his office just down the hall. This example illustrates
   (a) hindsight bias.
   (b) diffusion of responsibility.
   (c) obedience.
   (d) informational social influence.

3. Michael, who is an accountant, often wonders why people are surprised when they find out that he is also a skydiving instructor on the weekends. The most obvious explanation is that people form cognitive schemas for different types of people and occupations. The use of these types of assumptions is called
   (a) the fundamental attribution error.
   (b) ethnocentrism.
   (c) implicit personality theory.
   (d) the self-serving bias.

4. In her field research, Dr. Safarian observes that people generally avoid sitting next to strangers on buses or trains when there are other seats vacant. This behavior may be the result of mental processes associated with automatic, nonconscious, social evaluations, a phenomenon called
   (a) prosocial behavior.
   (b) explicit cognition.
   (c) ethnocentrism.
   (d) implicit cognition.

5. Sally did very poorly on her last math test. If her fifth-grade teacher concludes that Sally did poorly because she is not motivated to do well in school, the teacher may be
   (a) committing the fundamental attribution error.
   (b) suffering from cognitive dissonance.
   (c) engaged in prosocial behavior.
   (d) using the rule of reciprocity.

6. When Allison landed a big contract for her firm, she accepted the credit for her hard work and smart "wheeling and dealing." When she failed to get the contract in another situation, she blamed the sneaky and dishonest tactics of the competition. This illustrates
   (a) informational social influence.
   (b) the self-serving bias.
   (c) the self-effacing bias.
   (d) hindsight bias.

7. During a discussion on fast food and fast-food outlets, Reginald stated, "Fast food is great. I just love southern fried chicken, fries, coleslaw, and milkshakes." This statement represents the ________________ component of Reginald's positive attitude toward fast-food restaurants.
   (a) cognitive
   (b) affective
   (c) behavioral
   (d) ambivalent

8. When Jill tried on the very fashionable but expensive coat, she thought it looked great on her. However, she initially felt guilty about buying the coat because she couldn't really afford it. Later that night she rationalized her decision by saying that the coat was one of a kind, and, considering how lovely it looked on her, it was surely quite a bargain. This example illustrates
   (a) diffusion of responsibility.
   (b) conformity.
   (c) prejudice.
   (d) cognitive dissonance.

9. One of Manfred's college classmates was from Turkey, and he loved turkey sandwiches, turkey pizza, turkey burgers, and turkey sausages. Manfred now believes that all people from Turkey eat mostly foods made from turkey meat, and so he has little doubt why the country is called Turkey. Manfred's beliefs about the culture of Turkey reflect
   (a) ethnic stereotyping.
   (b) ethnocentrism.
   (c) the stereotype threat.
   (d) in-group bias.

10. Jackson joined the Alpine cross-country ski club because he couldn't afford the cost of downhill skiing. Many members of his club think that downhill skiing is destroying the natural environment, and they often make derogatory remarks about downhillers. Since joining the club, Jackson has changed his attitude about downhill skiing; he now promotes the benefits of cross-country skiing and joins his new buddies in categorizing all downhill skiers as self-centered, uncaring destroyers of the environment. This example illustrates
    (a) the out-group homogeneity effect.
    (b) in-group bias.
    (c) stereotyping.
    (d) all of these effects.

11. Greg, who is a new faculty member, is on a college committee concerned with student evaluation. Greg disagrees with the proposal to institute a collegewide percentage system for grading. The other five members have already stated that they are in favor of the proposal. Greg decides that it would be in his best interests to go along with his colleagues and not risk antagonizing them, so he votes in favor of the proposed policy. This example best illustrates
    (a) obedience.
    (b) informational social influence.
    (c) in-group bias.
    (d) normative social influence.

12. All the members of the MacGregor household are enthusiastic supporters of the new community recycling program. They consistently sort their garbage by placing paper, plastic, glass, and aluminum in their respective bins. The actions of the MacGregors best illustrate the __________ component of attitudes.
    (a) emotional
    (b) behavioral
    (c) biological
    (d) cognitive

13. Just moments after dozens of people get off a crowded bus, a badly dressed man stumbles and falls on the sidewalk near the bus stop. Research on bystander intervention would suggest that
    (a) he will get immediate help from many people.
    (b) the presence of others will decrease the diffusion of responsibility.
    (c) if one person stops to help him, other people are likely to help as well.
    (d) no one in the crowd will perceive that he may need help.

14. According to Critical Thinking (Abuse at Abu Ghraib), which of the following factors contributed to the events that occurred at Abu Ghraib prison?
    (a) prejudice and negative stereotypes
    (b) dehumanization
    (c) in-group versus out-group thinking
    (d) all of these factors

15. According to Enhancing Well-Being with Psychology (The Persuasion Game), which of the following is correct?
    (a) Persuasion refers to the deliberate attempt to influence the attitudes or behaviors of another person in a situation in which the person has some freedom of choice.
    (b) Persuasion techniques are not effective in manipulating people in any way.
    (c) Professional persuaders can easily manipulate and change the attitudes and behaviors of the vast majority of people.
    (d) Because of the flexible nature of social norms, the vast majority of people can resist conforming to any societal standards.

Progress Test 2

After you have checked your understanding of the material in Progress Test 1 and have done a complete chapter review with special focus on any areas of weakness, you are ready to assess your knowledge on Progress Test 2. Check your answers. If you make a mistake, review your notes, the relevant section of the study guide, and, if necessary, the appropriate part of your textbook.

1. Jake lost his job two months ago when his company downsized its operations. Despite his efforts, he has not yet found another job. One of his neighbors stated that Jake is just like most unemployed people—irresponsible, unmotivated, and basically lazy. The neighbor has
    (a) violated the rule of commitment.
    (b) used the self-serving bias in her categorization of Jake.
    (c) been influenced by the stereotype threat in her categorization of Jake.
    (d) committed the fundamental attribution error.

2. When their town was threatened by a flood, two families who had been enemies for years ended up working together to try to save the town from the overflowing river. Generalizing from Sherif's findings, you might conclude that this act of cooperative behavior may lead to

(a) increased antagonism once the danger has passed.
(b) an increase in cognitive dissonance.
(c) reduced conflict and increased harmony between the two families.
(d) diffusion of responsibility.

3. Liliana thinks that people her parents' age are old-fashioned, critical, intolerant, and unconcerned about important social issues. Liliana is assuming that people in a particular age category have certain characteristics, even though these qualities may be unrelated to the objective criteria that define this particular age group. This example illustrates
(a) the just-world hypothesis.
(b) stereotyping.
(c) ethnocentrism.
(d) the self-effacing (modesty) bias.

4. When Rachel found out that she had straight As in all her courses, she was elated. Later that day, when she was asked if she could donate some money to the restore-the-church fund, she readily made a donation, even though she is not religious and does not go to church. This illustrates
(a) cognitive dissonance.
(b) the "feel good, do good" effect.
(c) conformity.
(d) informational social influence.

5. When young Tia saw the movie *Snow White,* she thought that Snow White was very pretty and sweet and that her evil stepmother was ugly and cruel. Tia's beliefs about the characters in the movie represent _________ called _____________ .
(a) a form of social categorization; the self-serving bias
(b) a type of fundamental attribution error; blaming the victim
(c) an implicit personality theory; the "what is beautiful is good" myth
(d) a form of person perception; the "feel good, do good" myth.

6. When Inge was first elected to the student finance committee, she was asked to make a decision on an important but unfamiliar financial matter. All the other members of the committee stated that they were going to vote against the proposal. Inge voted with the group because she assumed that they must have the correct information. This example illustrates
(a) the bystander effect.
(b) normative social influence.
(c) informational social influence.
(d) diffusion of responsibility.

7. Martha is participating in a replication of Milgram's original obedience experiment that involves female subjects only. Compared with a similar study involving only male subjects,
(a) at least 60 percent of the females will refuse to continue with the experiment at the 300-volt level.
(b) a much higher percentage of the females will obey the experimenter and progress to the 450-volt level.
(c) only about 10 percent of the female subjects will obey the experimenter and progress to the 450-volt level.
(d) the results of the all-female replication will be the same as the all-male condition.

8. Explicit cognition is to ________________ as implicit cognition is to ________________ .
(a) automatic, nonconscious mental processes that influence perceptions, judgments, decisions, and reasoning; deliberate, conscious mental processes involved in perceptions, judgments, decisions, and reasoning
(b) the mental processes people use to make sense of their social environments; the effects of situational factors and other people on an individual's behavior
(c) deliberate, conscious mental processes involved in perceptions, judgments, decisions, and reasoning; automatic, nonconscious mental processes that influence perceptions, judgments, decisions, and reasoning
(d) the effects of situational factors and other people on an individual's behavior; the mental processes people use to make sense of their social environments

9. In preparing a term paper on conformity and obedience, Quincy has reviewed all the relevant literature. He is most likely to conclude that
(a) virtually nobody is capable of resisting group or authority pressure.
(b) all people are innately predisposed to be cruel and aggressive.
(c) conformity and obedience are not necessarily bad in and of themselves and are important for an orderly society.
(d) all of these statements are true.

10. Jorge thought that either horse, Con Brio or White Lightning, had an equal chance of winning the next race and was debating which one to bet on. After he placed his money on Con Brio, however, he felt very confident that he had backed the winner. This example illustrates the effect of
    (a) cognitive dissonance.
    (b) the self-serving bias.
    (c) conformity.
    (d) social influence.

11. Jenny's score on her biology midterm exam was 90 percent, Jean's was 60 percent, and Jackie's was 75 percent. On the basis of these scores, Jackie thinks to herself that Jenny must be really intelligent and that Jean must be a little slow. Which of the following is true?
    (a) Jackie has made an attribution.
    (b) Jackie's assessment of her classmates' intelligence is accurate.
    (c) Jackie's evaluation reflects the in-group bias.
    (d) Jackie's assessment of her classmates' intelligence reflects her prejudice.

12. In a replication of a classic experiment, Joey joined a group of six other people whose task it was to state which of three comparison lines (A, B, or C) matched the standard line in length. This is a replication of ________________ experiment(s) investigating ________________ .
    (a) Solomon Asch's; conformity
    (b) Muzafer Sherif's; factors that produce intergroup conflict and harmony
    (c) Phillip Zimbardo's; cognitive dissonance
    (d) Stanley Milgram's; obedience

13. Rose Marie contends that kindness and thoughtfulness are the most important factors in judging a person's attractiveness and that physical factors are relatively unimportant. According to In Focus (Interpersonal Attraction and Liking) research has shown that
    (a) a preference for thinner women is more common in societies where resources are scarce; in societies where food and resources are abundant, men prefer heavier women.
    (b) warmth, trustworthiness, and social status are more important than physical appearance in influencing judgments of attractiveness.
    (c) every culture has its own standards of what constitutes attractiveness, and there are no factors that are consistently associated with attractiveness across cultures.
    (d) physical appearance, especially facial features, is probably the most significant factor in attraction.

14. Yoko was late for work because the traffic was particularly heavy. When she arrived at the office, she apologized to her boss, insisting that it was her fault for being late; if she were less lazy, it wouldn't have happened. According to Culture and Human Behavior (Explaining Failure and Murder), blaming an accidental occurrence on an internal, personal disposition rather than on situational factors is called the
    (a) self-serving bias.
    (b) self-effacing bias (modesty bias).
    (c) hindsight bias.
    (d) fundamental attribution error.

15. A number of persuasion techniques are used by professional marketers. According to Enhancing Well-Being with Psychology (The Persuasion Game), which of the following is NOT one of those techniques?
    (a) the door-in-the-face technique
    (b) the that's-not-all technique
    (c) the foot-in-the-mouth technique
    (d) the foot-in-the-door technique

Progress Test 3

After you have checked your understanding of the material in Progress Tests 1 and 2, and have done a complete chapter review with special focus on any areas of weakness, you are ready to further assess your knowledge with Progress Test 3. Check your answers. If you make a mistake, review your notes, the appropriate parts of the study guide, and, if necessary, the relevant sections of your textbook.

1. Dr. Saroya is a social psychologist whose research interests focus on how our behavior is affected by situational factors and other people, and in particular why we conform to group norms and why we help or don't help strangers. The basic area of social psychology that Dr. Saroya studies is called
    (a) social cognition.
    (b) social perception.
    (c) social influence.
    (d) social categorization.

2. When Ruby stepped into the subway car, she quickly looked around and decided it would be safer to sit next to the middle-aged, well-dressed woman than the man with bright orange hair and earrings. Ruby has engaged in the process of
   (a) blaming the victim.
   (b) person perception.
   (c) ethnocentrism.
   (d) cognitive dissonance.

3. When Mr. Denbridge was asked to donate to a fund to help people infected with hepatitis B and the HIV virus, he responded that he would not help these people because they caused their own misfortunes. It appears that Mr. Denbridge is
   (a) blaming the victim.
   (b) demonstrating the out-group homogeneity effect.
   (c) responding to normative social influence.
   (d) reducing his cognitive dissonance.

4. During a tour of a Latin American country, Susanne was surprised to find that almost everyone took a three-hour break in the middle of the day. She concluded that, compared with the United States, this country was not doing well economically because everyone was lazy, lacked motivation, and spent too much time sleeping. Susanne's conclusion reflects a form of in-group bias called
   (a) ethnocentrism.
   (b) the self-effacing bias.
   (c) the self-serving bias.
   (d) altruism.

5. In her fifth-grade class, Miss Tausig uses a technique for improving cooperation that involves students working together in small, ethnically diverse groups on a mutual project. Miss Tausig is using the
   (a) out-group homogeneity procedure.
   (b) jigsaw classroom technique.
   (c) normative social influence technique.
   (d) rule-of-reciprocity technique

6. Rita volunteers three or four evenings a week at a local shelter for the homeless because she believes in helping those less fortunate than herself. Richard also volunteers at the shelter because he believes the work experience will increase his chances of getting accepted in the master's degree program in social work. In this situation, Rita's motivation is guided by ________________ and Richard's motivation reflects ________________ .
   (a) prosocial behavior; altruism
   (b) normative social influence; informational social influence
   (c) altruism; prosocial behavior
   (d) informational social influence; normative social influence

7. Kyle is in sixth grade and, like most children in his school, believes that his school is better than all the other schools in town. This best illustrates
   (a) in-group bias.
   (b) ethnic stereotyping.
   (c) cognitive dissonance.
   (d) the fundamental attribution error.

8. In an experiment, half the female participants were told that males typically did better than females on the math test they were about to take; the other half were told that test results did not show gender differences. The first group scored lower on the test than did the second group. These results are explained by a phenomenon called
   (a) ethnocentrism.
   (b) the stereotype threat.
   (c) hindsight bias.
   (d) the just-world hypothesis.

9. Pietro notices that when there are empty seats on the bus, nobody ever sits beside a stranger; however, when the bus is crowded, people sit beside strangers all the time. He noticed that the same thing happens in movie theaters, the cafeteria, and even the classroom. Pietro's observation suggests that people's behavior in these situations is governed by
   (a) prejudice.
   (b) social categorization.
   (c) stereotypes.
   (d) social norms.

10. Fraser loves wearing sandals or thongs and hates wearing shoes. However, when he went out to dinner with his girlfriend's family, he wore shoes because he did not want them to think he was a sloppy dresser. Fraser's behavior best illustrates the importance of
    (a) informational social influence.
    (b) normative social influence.
    (c) diffusion of responsibility.
    (d) obedience.

11. Lyle is studying alone late Friday night in the almost deserted library. His concentration is interrupted when he notices another student nearby slumped over his desk, making sounds that suggest he might be in pain. In this situation, it is very likely that Lyle will engage in ________________ , because he is not constrained by ________________ .
   (a) prosocial behavior; the bystander effect
   (b) social categorization; social norms
   (c) blaming the victim; diffusion of responsibility
   (d) altruism; self-serving bias

12. When Mary Jane steps into the elevator, she quickly looks at the other passengers and decides that the gray-haired man with the beard must be a professor at the college. Mary Jane has engaged in the process of
   (a) prejudicial thinking.
   (b) discrimination.
   (c) social categorization.
   (d) ethnocentrism.

13. During cross-examination, a witness repeatedly offers his opinion in answer to the lawyer's questions, so the judge orders him to confine his answers to a simple *yes* or *no*. Following the judge's rebuke, the witness stops offering his opinions. This example best illustrates
   (a) obedience.
   (b) conformity.
   (c) persuasion.
   (d) prejudice.

14. According to Critical Thinking (Abuse at Abu Ghraib), the events of Abu Ghraib prison have the most parallels and similarities to two famous social psychology studies: ________________ and ________________ .
   (a) Latané and Darley's bystander studies; Asch's conformity research
   (b) Sherif's Robbers Cave prejudice experiments; Cialdini's persuasion studies
   (c) Lerner's just-world hypothesis research; Zimbardo's cognitive dissonance research
   (d) Milgram's obedience studies; Zimbardo's Stanford Prison Experiment

15. In the run-up to a fiercely contested local election, Birkley believes she can win if she can only get enough people to display her large poster on their front lawns. First, her supporters ask homeowners if they would be willing to put a very small poster in their window. Later, when they asked these same people if they could put a large poster on their front lawn, most agreed to the request. According to Enhancing Well-Being with Psychology (The Persuasion Game), Birkley is using a technique called the ________________________ , which capitalizes on a powerful social norm, the ________________________ .
   (a) door-in-the-face technique; rule of reciprocity
   (b) foot-in-the-door-technique; rule of commitment
   (c) low-ball technique; rule of reciprocity
   (d) foot-in-the-mouth technique; rule of commitment

Answers

Introduction: What Is Social Psychology?

1. *Social psychology is* the branch of psychology that studies how a person's thoughts, feelings, and behavior are influenced by the presence of other people and by the social and physical environment. *The sense of self refers to* an individual's unique sense of identity that has been influenced by social cultural, and psychological experiences and involves who you are in relation to other people. *It is important because* the sense of self is shaped by interactions with others, by our psychological experiences, and by our social environments, including our culture, and it plays a key role in how we perceive and react to others.
2. *Social cognition refers to* the mental processes people use to make sense out of their social environment.
3. *Social influence focuses on* the effects of situational factors and other people on an individual's social behavior.

Person Perception: Forming Impressions of Other People

1. *Person perception refers to* the mental processes we use to form judgments and draw conclusions about the characteristics and motives of others; it is an active, interactive, and subjective process that always occurs in some interpersonal context.
2. *The four basic principles of person perception are (a)* Your reactions to others are determined by your perceptions of them, not by who or what they really are. *(b)* Your self-perception influences how you perceive others and how you act on your perceptions. *(c)* Your goals in a particular situation determine the amount and kind of information you collect about others.

(d) In every situation, how you expect people to act in that situation partly determines how you evaluate them (you make reference to the social norms for the appropriate behavior in a particular social situation).

3. *In combination, these four basic principles underscore that person perception is* not a one-way process in which we objectively survey other people, then logically evaluate their characteristics. Instead, the context, our self-perceptions, and the perception we have of others all interact.
4. *Social categorization is* the mental process of classifying people into groups (or social categories) on the basis of their shared characteristics. *Explicit cognition refers to* deliberate, conscious mental processes involved in perceptions, judgments, decisions, and reasoning. *Implicit cognition refers to* automatic, nonconscious mental processes that influence perceptions, judgments, decisions, and reasoning.
5. *An implicit personality theory is* a network of assumptions or beliefs about the relationships among various types of people, traits, and behaviors. *Like social categories, implicit personality theories are useful* as mental shortcuts in perceiving other people; however, they are not always accurate in that we come to sweeping conclusions about the people we meet based on very limited information.
6. *Physical appearance cues play* an important role in person perception and social categorization; they are particularly influential in the implicit personality theory that most people have for physically attractive people (e.g., that "what is beautiful is good" and that physical attractiveness is perceived to be associated with a wide range of desirable characteristics). *Research has shown that physical attractiveness is correlated with* being more popular, being happier, having higher self-esteem, being more intelligent, earning higher salaries, and being more satisfied with life. *Neuroscientists have shown that when people make direct eye contact with a physically attractive person,* a brain area that predicts rewards (the ventral striatum) is activated; when the attractive person's gaze is averted away from the viewer, activity in this brain area decreases. In addition, the orbital frontal cortex, the nucleus accumbens, and the amygdala are selectively responsive to the reward value of attractive faces.
7. *General conclusions about the process of person perception are that (a)* both deliberate and automatic thought processes influence our impressions of others; *(b)* we use mental shortcuts, such as social categories and implicit personality theories, and whether we react positively or negatively depends on previous social and cultural experience; *(c)* social categories are natural, adaptive, and efficient cognitive processes and may have conferred survival value in our evolutionary past; *(d)* however, relegating someone to a social category on the basis of superficial information ignores that person's unique qualities and our conclusions can be wrong.

Attribution: Explaining Behavior

1. *Attribution is* the mental process of inferring the causes of people's behavior, including one's own (also refers to the explanation made for a particular behavior).
2. *The fundamental attribution error is the tendency to* spontaneously attribute the behavior of others to internal, personal characteristics, while ignoring or underestimating the effects of external, situational factors. *When it comes to explaining our own behavior, we tend to use* external, situational attributions, in part, because we have more information about the potential causes of our own behavior than we do about the causes of other people's behavior.
3. *Blaming the victim is the tendency to* blame an innocent victim of misfortune for having somehow caused the problem or for not having taken steps to avoid or prevent it.
4. *Hindsight bias is* the tendency, after an event has occurred, to overestimate one's ability to have foreseen or predicted the outcome. *In the case of blaming the victim,* hindsight bias makes it seem as though the victim should have been able to predict and prevent what happened.
5. *The just-world hypothesis is* the assumption that the world is fair and that therefore people get what they deserve and deserve what they get.
6. *The self-serving bias is the tendency to* attribute successful outcomes of our own behavior to internal causes and unsuccessful outcomes to external, situational causes.

Concept Check 1

1. self-serving bias
2. fundamental attribution error
3. blaming the victim; hindsight bias
4. implicit personality theory

5. social norms
6. blaming the victim; just-world hypothesis
7. more intelligent, stronger, happier, and more sensitive, honest, sociable, assertive, and emotionally stable
8. become activated; that activity in this area of the brain will decrease
9. orbital frontal cortex; amygdala; nucleus accumbens
10. explicit

Graphic Organizer 1

1. self-serving bias
2. self-effacing (modesty) bias
3. fundamental attribution error
4. hindsight bias
5. blaming the victim

Matching Exercise 1

1. social norms
2. attribution
3. self-serving bias
4. social psychology
5. implicit personality theory
6. evolutionary psychology
7. blaming the victim
8. just-world hypothesis
9. hindsight bias
10. person perception

True/False Test 1

1. F	3. F	5. F	7. T	9. T
2. T	4. T	6. T	8. T	10. F

The Social Psychology of Attitudes

1. *An attitude is defined as* a learned tendency to evaluate some object, person, or issue in a particular way; such evaluations may be positive, negative, or ambivalent.
2. *The three components of an attitude are (a)* cognitive (your thoughts and conclusions about the attitude object); *(b)* affective (your feelings or emotions about the object of your attitude); and *(c)* behavioral (your attitude is reflected in your actions).
3. *You are most likely to behave in accordance with your attitudes in any of five conditions: (a)* you anticipate a favorable outcome or response from others; *(b)* your attitudes are extreme or are frequently expressed; *(c)* your attitudes have been formed through direct experience; *(d)* you are very knowledgeable about the subject; and *(e)* you have a vested interest in the subject.
4. *Cognitive dissonance is* an unpleasant state of psychological tension or arousal (dissonance) that occurs when two thoughts or perceptions (cognitions) are inconsistent. *It commonly occurs in situations in which* you become uncomfortably aware that your behavior and your attitudes are in conflict. If you can easily rationalize your behavior to make it consistent with your attitude, then any dissonance can be quickly and easily resolved. When your behavior cannot be easily justified, you will tend to change your attitude to make it consistent with your behavior.
5. *Cognitive dissonance can also change* the strength of an attitude so that it is consistent with some behavior you've already performed.
6. *Cognitive dissonance also operates when you have to choose* between two basically equal alternatives; each choice has desirable and undesirable features, creating dissonance. Once a choice is made, however, attitudes are brought more closely in line with the commitment made, which reduces the dissonance. The negative features of the rejected option are emphasized ("sour grapes" rationalization), and the positive features of the chosen option are seen more favorably ("sweet lemons" rationalization).

Understanding Prejudice

1. *Prejudice is defined as* a negative attitude toward people who belong to a specific social group.
2. *A stereotype is* a cluster of characteristics that are associated with all members of a specific social group, often including qualities that are unrelated to the objective criteria that define a given category. *Stereotype threat refers to the fact that* awareness that your social group is associated with a particular stereotype can negatively affect your performance on tests or tasks that measure abilities thought to be associated with that stereotype.
3. *An in-group is* a social group to which one belongs. *An out-group is* a social group to which one does not belong.

4. *The out-group homogeneity effect refers to* the tendency to see members of out-groups as very similar to one another. *The in-group bias is* the tendency to judge the behavior of in-group members favorably and out-group members unfavorably.
5. *Ethnocentrism is the belief* that one's own culture or ethnic group is superior to all others and the related tendency to use one's own culture or ethnic group as a standard by which to judge other cultures and groups.
6. *The emotional component of prejudice includes negative feelings such as* hatred, contempt, fear, and loathing. *Behaviorally, prejudice can result in* some form of discrimination.
7. *Implicit attitudes are* preferences and biases toward particular groups that are automatic, spontaneous, unintentional, and often unconscious. *They are measured by* the Implicit Association Test (IAT), a computer-based test that measures the degree to which people associate particular groups of people with specific characteristics or attributes, including age, sexual orientation, weight, disability, and racial or ethnic groups (the degree to which implicit attitudes affect actual behavior is still an open question, but some studies suggest they do).
8. *In his classic study on overcoming prejudice, psychologist Muzafer Sherif demonstrated that* prejudice can be overcome when rival groups cooperate to achieve a common goal. *In the educational system,* cooperative learning, as used in the jigsaw classroom technique, is one way of reducing prejudice in the classroom.

Concept Check 2

1. stereotype
2. cognitive
3. out-group homogeneity
4. ethnocentrism
5. cognitive dissonance; reduce
6. jigsaw classroom technique
7. in-group; out-group
8. prejudice
9. stereotyping
10. physical appearance (especially facial features); are also
11. Implicit Association Test (IAT); implicit attitudes

Graphic Organizer 2

1. cognitive
2. behavioral
3. behavioral
4. affective (emotional)
5. behavioral
6. affective (emotional)
7. cognitive
8. affective (emotional)
9. cognitive

Matching Exercise 2

1. Muzafer Sherif
2. ethnocentrism
3. attitude
4. in-group
5. cognitive dissonance
6. out-group
7. cognitive component
8. stereotype
9. Philip Zimbardo
10. implicit attitudes

True/False Test 2

1. T	3. F	5. F	7. T	9. T
2. T	4. T	6. T	8. T	10. T

Conformity: Following the Crowd

1. *Social influence is* the psychological study of the effects of situational factors and other people on an individual's behavior.
2. *Conformity is the tendency to* adjust your opinions, judgments, or behavior so that it matches the opinions, judgments, or behavior of other people, or the norms of a social group or situation.
3. *In studying the degree to which people would conform to the group even when the group opinion was clearly wrong, social psychologist,* Solomon Asch, *found that* the vast majority conformed with the group judgment on at least one of the critical trials in the line judgment task.
4. *We conform to the larger group for two basic reasons: (a)* normative social influence (we want to be liked and accepted by the group); *(b)* informational social influence (we want to be right;

when we're uncertain or doubt our own judgment, we may look to the group as a source of accurate information).

5. *You are more likely to conform to groups norms when (a)* you are facing a unanimous group of at least four or five people; *(b)* you must give your response in front of the group; *(c)* you have not already expressed commitment to a different idea or opinion; *(d)* you find the task ambiguous or difficult; *(e)* you doubt your abilities or knowledge in the situation; *(f)* you are strongly attracted to a group and want to be a member of it.
6. *Conformity decreases under certain conditions: (a)* when just one other person goes against the majority; *(b)* when there is dissent even if the dissenting person's opinion is wrong; *(c)* when there is dissent even if the dissenter's competence is questionable.
7. *In a cross-cultural meta-analysis, British psychologists found that* conformity is generally higher in collectivistic cultures than in individualistic cultures.

Obedience: Just Following Orders

1. *Obedience is defined as* the performance of a behavior in response to a direct command.
2. *The basic design of Milgram's obedience experiment was as follows:* the subject (the "teacher") thought he was delivering ever-increasing levels of electric shock to another person (the "learner") when the learner answered incorrectly on a simple memory task. If the teacher protested that he wished to stop, he was instructed by the experimenter to continue with the experiment.
3. *In contrast to predictions, the results of Milgram's original experiment showed that* most of the subjects (two-thirds) obeyed the experimenter and progressed to the maximum shock level.
4. *Aspects of the experimental situation that had a strong impact on the subjects' willingness to continue obeying the experimenter's orders were as follows:* The subjects had a previously well-established mental framework to obey; the context or situation influenced them (they believed the experiment would advance scientific knowledge and may have felt that defying the experimenter's orders would make them appear arrogant, rude, disrespectful, or uncooperative); the gradual, repetitive escalation of the task; the experimenter's behavior and reassurances (the experimenter took responsibility for the learner's well-being); and the physical and psychological separation from the learner.
5. *Some of the situational factors that made people less willing to obey were as follows:* The buffers that separated the teacher from the learner were lessened or removed, such as when both of them were put in the same room; subjects (teachers) were allowed to act as their own authority and freely choose the shock level (95 percent of them did not go beyond 150 volts); and the teacher observed two other teachers rebel and refuse to continue (the obedience rate dropped to 10 percent).
6. *The scientific study of conformity and obedience has some important implications: (a)* Situational factors influence our behavior; as a result, our judgments and perceptions can be distorted, and we may act in ways that violate our conscience. *(b)* Each of us has the capacity to resist group or authority pressure (see text Table 11.5). *(c)* No specific personality trait consistently produces conformity or obedience in experimental situations (situational factors can overcome personality traits like independence). *(d)* Conformity and obedience are not completely bad in and of themselves and may be necessary for an orderly society (the critical issue is whether the norms we conform to reflect values that respect the rights, well-being, and dignity of others).

Helping Behavior: Coming to the Aid of Strangers

1. *Altruism is* the act of helping another person with no expectation of personal reward or benefit, *whereas prosocial behavior is* any behavior that helps another person, whether the underlying motive is self-serving or selfless.
2. *According to Latané and Darley's general model, six factors increase the likelihood of bystander intervention: We tend to be more helpful when (a)* we're feeling good, successful, happy, or fortunate (the "feel good, do good" effect); *(b)* we're feeling guilty, such as after telling a lie or inadvertently causing an accident; *(c)* we see others who are willing to help; *(d)* we perceive people as deserving, such as people who are in need through no fault of their own; *(e)* we know how to help; and *(f)* we have any sort of personal relationship (even the most minimal social interaction, such as making eye contact or engaging in small talk).

3. *The bystander effect refers to* a phenomenon in which the greater the number of people present, the less likely each individual is to help someone in distress.
4. *There are two reasons for the bystander effect: (a)* The presence of other people creates a diffusion of responsibility, which means that the responsibility to intervene is shared (or diffused) among the other onlookers (because no one person feels all the pressure to respond, each bystander becomes less likely to help). *(b)* Each of us is motivated to some extent by the desire to behave in a socially acceptable way (normative social influence) and to appear correct (informational social influence), and consequently we often rely on the reactions of others to help us define the situation and guide our responses.
5. *Other factors that decrease the likelihood of helping behavior are (a)* being in a big city or a very small town (people are less likely to help a stranger in very big cities or in very small towns); *(b)* when situations are vague or ambiguous and people are not certain that help is needed, such as in domestic disputes or a lovers' quarrel; and, *(c)* as a general rule, when the cost of helping outweighs the benefit.

Concept Check 3

1. normative
2. will
3. unlikely
4. is not
5. feel good, do good
6. diffusion of responsibility
7. prosocial behavior
8. informational social influence
9. door-in-the-face; reciprocity
10. social norms

Graphic Organizer 3

1. Naive subjects yielded to group pressure in the line-judging task, even though the group opinion was wrong.
2. The Robbers Cave study helped clarify the conditions that produce intergroup conflict and harmony and led to the use of the jigsaw classroom technique to promote cooperative behavior.
3. Dramatic illustration of the pressure to obey an authority figure's request to shock another person in a mock learning experiment.
4. Showed the conditions under which people are more likely to help a stranger in distress, as well as the factors that decrease helping behavior.

Matching Exercise 3

1. Stanley Milgram
2. conformity
3. Bibb Latané and John M. Darley
4. obedience
5. Solomon Asch
6. altruism
7. prosocial behavior

True/False Test 3

1. T
2. T
3. T
4. F
5. T
6. F

Something to Think About

1. Why is it that people do not help others who are in obvious distress? What prevents bystanders from intervening? In some instances, such as in the Kitty Genovese case, people could easily help simply by making a phone call, but often they don't. Latané and Darley have conducted extensive research that addresses the question of why people don't intervene.

   Latané and Darley's final model identifies six specific factors that increase the likelihood that bystanders will help: (1) the "feel good, do good" effect, (2) feeling guilty, (3) seeing others who are willing to help, (4) perceiving others as deserving help, (5) knowing how to help, and (6) a personal relationship with the person who needs help.

   A number of factors decrease the likelihood of bystanders helping: (1) the presence of others, called the *bystander effect,* and the resulting diffusion of responsibility; (2) being in a big city or a very small town; (3) a vague or ambiguous situation; and (4) when the personal costs for helping outweigh the benefits. In a discussion of this issue, it is important to be able to explain and give examples of each factor.
2. The summary in Enhancing Well-Being with Psychology (The Persuasion Game) provides

the information you need to answer this question. First, define *persuasion,* then paraphrase the main strategies that professional persuaders use to manipulate people's attitudes and behaviors. These include the role of reciprocity, the door-in-the-face technique, the that's-not-all technique, the rule of commitment, the foot-in-the-door technique, and the low-ball technique. You might also want to integrate material from the chapter, such as the role of cognitive dissonance in changing cognitions and behavior, and various aspects of conformity and obedience research. Finally, you should discuss the ways in which people can defend themselves against professional persuasion techniques—for example, sleeping on it, playing the devil's advocate, and paying attention to gut feelings.

Progress Test 1

1. a
2. b
3. c
4. d
5. a
6. b
7. b
8. d
9. a
10. d
11. d
12. b
13. c
14. d
15. a

Progress Test 2

1. d
2. c
3. b
4. b
5. c
6. c
7. d
8. c
9. c
10. a
11. a
12. a
13. d
14. b
15. c

Progress Test 3

1. c
2. b
3. a
4. a
5. b
6. c
7. a
8. b
9. d
10. b
11. a
12. c
13. a
14. d
15. b

CHAPTER 12

Stress, Health, and Coping

PREVIEW

Reading the section below first will give you a general sense of the chapter's contents and an initial introduction to some of the major concepts and terms. This will prime you for what you are about to read and help you to develop a "cognitive map" that will guide your study of the material in this chapter. Likewise, reading the **preview questions** at the beginning of each major section will improve your ability to understand, learn, and retain the information.

Chapter 12 . . . AT A GLANCE

Chapter 12 deals with the effects of stress on health and the ways that people cope with stress. Health psychologists, who study stress and other psychological factors that influence health, illness, and medical treatment, are guided by the biopsychosocial model. The life events approach to stress, first developed in the 1960s, is critically examined. More recently, researchers investigating stress have focused on the importance of daily hassles, trauma, resilience, work and burnout, social factors, and acculturation.

The physical effects of stress are discussed. Walter Cannon's fight-or-flight response and Hans Selye's three-stage general adaptation syndrome are described. Chronic stress and the role that telomeres play in premature aging and disease are discussed. Psychoneuroimmunology, the scientific study of the connections among psychological processes, the nervous system, and the immune system, is introduced, along with research findings on the effects of stress on the immune system.

Psychological factors can also influence our response to stress. People's sense of personal control and their explanatory style—optimistic or pessimistic—are important in determining how a person responds to stress. The text notes that chronic negative emotions are related to the development of some chronic diseases and that the hostility component of the Type A behavior pattern can predict the development of heart disease. Positive emotions are associated with physical and psychological well being. The role of social support in how people deal with stressful situations is explored.

The final section covers coping strategies. Depending on the situation, people use problem-focused or emotion-focused coping. Individualistic and collectivistic coping strategies are compared and contrasted. Enhancing Well-Being with Psychology offers some important advice for minimizing the effects of stress.

Introduction: Stress and Health Psychology

Preview Questions

Consider the following questions as you study this section of the chapter.

- How is *stress* defined, what is the cognitive appraisal model of stress, and who developed it?
- What is the main focus of health psychology?
- What is the biopsychosocial model?

Read the section "Introduction: Stress and Health Psychology" and ***write*** *your answers to the following:*

1. Stress is defined as ____________________
2. The cognitive appraisal model of stress, developed by ____________________, emphasizes ____________________
3. Health psychologists focus on ____________________
4. The biopsychosocial model is ____________________

Stress and Health Psychology: Sources of Stress

Preview Questions

Consider the following questions as you study this section of the chapter.

- What are stressors, and what are some of the most important sources of stress?
- What is the life events approach, what problems are associated with this approach, and why is it still useful?
- What are traumatic events, post-traumatic stress disorder, and resilience?
- What are daily hassles, and how do they contribute to stress?
- How can work affect stress levels, what is burnout, and what factors produce it?
- How can social and cultural factors become sources of stress?

Read the section "Stress and Health Psychology: Sources of Stress" and ***write*** *your answers to the following:*

1. Stressors are ____________________
2. Early stress researchers Thomas Holmes and Richard Rahe believed that ____________________
3. Several problems with the life events approach have been pointed out:

   (a) ____________________

   (b) ____________________

   (c) ____________________

   However, the Social Readjustment Rating Scale (SRRS) is still a useful tool for quickly measuring exposure to stress, and so ____________________
4. Traumatic events are ____________________

   Post-traumatic stress disorder (PTSD) is ____________________
5. Both high and low levels of accumulative adversity are associated with ____________________
   Moderate levels of cumulative adversity are associated with ____________________

   Resilience refers to ____________________
6. Daily hassles are ____________________

   The number of daily hassles people experience is ____________________

7. Work can affect stress levels because of ______
______
Burnout is ______
______
It is characterized by ______
______
Factors that produce burnout include ______
______
______

8. Social factors that are a source of stress include
______
______

9. In terms of culture, stress can result when
______
______

After you have carefully studied the preceding sections, complete the following exercises.

Concept Check 1

Read the following and write the correct term in the space provided.

1. Dr. Woodworth studies stress and how biological, behavioral, and social factors influence health, illness, treatment, and health-related behaviors. Dr. Woodworth is a ______ psychologist.
2. If Dr. Woodworth is like most psychologists in his specialty area, he adheres to the theory that health and illness are determined by the complex interaction of biological, psychological, and social factors. In other words, he is guided by the ______ model.
3. In the past year, Frank has been divorced, has moved twice, and has started a new relationship. He has also received a promotion and a big raise at work but now has many more responsibilities. His score on the Social Readjustment Rating Scale is likely to be ______ (high/low); according to the scale's developers, Thomas Holmes and Richard Rahe, Frank has a(n) ______ (increased/decreased) likelihood of developing serious physical or psychological problems.
4. According to Richard Lazarus, Frank's major life events may create a ripple effect and generate a host of ______ (such as having to pack and repack all his belongings twice) that may accumulate to cause even greater stress.
5. Researchers conducted a survey to learn about the relationship between racism and chronic stress. They found that three-quarters of African-American adolescents reported being treated as incompetent or dangerous, or both, because of their race. Such subtle instances of racism are called ______ .
6. When Kailen got a speeding ticket, he complained bitterly about the unfairness of it all. When Kylie got a ticket, he perceived it as a lesson learned and decided that if he didn't want to waste his scarce resources, he should stop speeding. The two reactions to the same stressor were due, in part at least, to Kailen and Kylie's different ______ of the experience.
7. When Serena married Hiroyuki and went to live in Japan, she continued to value her North American customs and way of life, but she was also very determined to become part of her new culture. She now speaks fluent Japanese and moves comfortably between her new society and her original culture and feels almost equally at home in both countries. In terms of acculturation, Serena would be classified as ______, and her level of acculturative stress would be ______ (high/low).

8. Dr. Keelahan emphasizes the importance of cognitive appraisal in the stress response and believes that ordinary irritations in daily life—not just major life events—are significant sources of stress. His approach is most similar to that of ______________________ .
9. Pat has many daily hassles, mainly associated with family and friends, and experiences high levels of psychological stress, which tend to spill over into spousal interactions. On the other hand, Dana's main source of stress is work-related, and coping with this stress typically involves withdrawing from social interactions. It is very probable that Pat is ______________________ (male/female) and Dana is ______________________ (male/female).
10. Jake complains that his job leaves him emotionally and physically drained, that he often feels unappreciated and unfairly treated, and that he gets no sense of accomplishment from his work. Jake is most likely suffering from ______________________ .
11. Tania recently experienced some difficult and unforeseen events. However, she managed quite well and soon rebounded from the negative events. Her ability to cope so well with this adversity is called ______________________ .

Review of Terms, Concepts, and Names 1

Use the terms in this list to complete the Matching Exercise, then to help you answer the True/False items correctly.

stress
cognitive appraisal model of stress
Richard Lazarus
health psychology
biopsychosocial model
stressors
Social Readjustment Rating Scale (SRRS)
life change units
traumatic events
post-traumatic stress disorder (PTSD)
cumulative adversity
resilience
daily hassles
burnout
work overload, lack of control, and low sense of community
chronic stress
microaggressions
acculturative stress

Matching Exercise

Match the appropriate term/name with its definition or description.

1. ________________ Psychologist who emphasized the importance of cognitive appraisal in the stress response and demonstrated the significance of daily hassles in producing stress.
2. ________________ Everyday minor events that annoy and upset people.
3. ________________ The branch of psychology that studies how biological, behavioral, and social factors influence health, illness, medical treatment, and health-related behaviors.
4. ________________ Model that suggests that physical health and illness are determined by the complex interaction of biological, psychological, and social factors.
5. ________________ On the Social Readjustment Rating Scale, the numerical rating assigned to each life event that estimates its relative impact on a person.
6. ________________ Type of stress that is persistent and ongoing.
7. ________________ Unhealthy condition caused by chronic, or prolonged, work stress that is characterized by exhaustion, cynicism, and a sense of failure and inadequacy.
8. ________________ The ability to cope with stress and adversity, to adapt to negative or unforeseen circumstances, and to rebound after negative experiences.
9. ________________ Anxiety disorder that involves intrusive thoughts of the traumatic event, emotional numbness, and physical symptoms of anxiety, such as nervousness, sleep disturbances, and irritability.

True/False Test

Indicate whether each statement is true or false by placing T or F in the blank space next to each item.

1. ____ Stress refers to events or situations that are perceived as harmful, threatening, or challenging.
2. ____ The Social Readjustment Rating Scale was developed by Thomas Holmes and Richard Rahe in an attempt to measure the amount of stress people experienced as a function of life events that are likely to require some level of adaptation.
3. ____ Subtle instances of racism, such as being perceived as incompetent or dangerous, or

both, because of one's race, are called microaggressions.

4. ____ Stressors refer to negative emotional states that occur in response to events that are perceived as taxing or exceeding a person's resources or ability to cope.

5. ____ The stress that results from the pressure of adapting to a new culture is called acculturative stress.

6. ____ The cognitive appraisal model of stress emphasizes the role of an individual's evaluation (appraisal) of events and situations and of the resources that he or she has to deal with the event or situation.

7. ____ Workplace conditions that commonly produce burnout are work overload, lack of control, and low sense of community at work.

8. ____ Cumulative adversity refers to the total amount of negative events experienced over a lifetime.

9. ____ Traumatic events are events or situations that are negative, severe, and far beyond our expectations for everyday life or life events.

Check your answers and review any areas of weakness before going on to the next section.

Physical Effects of Stress: The Mind–Body Connection

Preview Questions

Consider the following questions as you study this section of the chapter.

- How can stress contribute to health problems both directly and indirectly?
- What is the fight-or-flight response, and what role do catecholamines play?
- What did Hans Selye's research reveal about prolonged stress, and what endocrine pathways are involved?
- What is the general adaptation syndrome?
- What are telomeres and telomerase, and what role do they play in stress-related aging?

*Read the section "Physical Effects of Stress: The Mind–Body Connection" (up to "Stress and the Immune System") and **write** your answers to the following:*

1. Stress can indirectly affect a person's health by ______________________________
____

2. High levels of stress can also interfere with ______________________________
____

3. Stress can directly affect physical health by ______________________________
____

4. The fight-or-flight response refers to ______________________________
____
____

5. Catecholamines are ______________________________
____
____

6. Hans Selye found that prolonged stress activates a ______________________________
____
____

7. The general adaptation syndrome is ______________________________
____
____

8. Telomeres are ______________________________
____
____

9. Telomeres may play a role in stress-related aging in a number of ways:
(a) with each cell division the string of telomeres ______________________________
____
____
(b) shorter telomeres have been linked with ______________________________
(c) chronic stress may lead to ______________________________
____

and (d) elevated levels of the stress hormones cortisol and the catecholamines have been linked to ______________________________

____

____

10. Telomerase is ______________________________

____

Acute, short-term stress produces ____________

____

________________ and chronic stress has a

____

____

Physical Effects of Stress: Stress and the Immune System

Preview Questions

Consider the following questions as you study this section of the chapter.

- What is the immune system, what is its function, and what are lymphocytes?
- What is psychoneuroimmunology, and how does it explain the interaction of the immune system with the nervous system?
- What kinds of stressors affect immune system functioning?
- What have neuroscientists demonstrated about the role of placebos in the perception of pain?

Read the section "Physical Effects of Stress: Stress and the Immune System" and ***write*** *your answers to the following:*

1. The immune system consists of ____________

____

____

The function of this system is ____________

____

____

2. Lymphocytes are ______________________________

____

3. Psychoneuroimmunology is ____________________

____

____

4. The three main findings of psychoneuroimmunological research are

(a) ______________________________

____

(b) ______________________________

____

(c) ______________________________

____

5. Extremely stressful events reduce ____________

____

____

____

6. Subsequent research has shown that immune system functioning was also affected by

____

____

____

7. Neuroscientists investigating the placebo effect using positron emission tomography (PET) have shown that ______________________________

____

____

____

After you have carefully studied the preceding sections, complete the following exercises.

Concept Check 2

Read the following and write the correct term in the space provided.

1. When Hans was hiking on a trail in the wilderness, he unexpectedly encountered a large brown bear and her two cubs. Hans froze in his tracks, and his heartbeat, blood pressure, and pulse increased dramatically. Fortunately, the bear and the cubs took off into the bush. The rapidly occurring chain of internal physical reactions that Hans experienced was described by Walter Cannon as the ____________________ response.

2. The physiological changes that Hans experienced when he was startled resulted from his sympathetic nervous system stimulating the ________________ to secrete hormones called ________________ .
3. After overcoming the initial shock of finding her new car badly damaged by a hit-and-run driver, Wilma phones the police and becomes actively involved in seeking witnesses to the incident. At this point, it is most likely that Wilma is in the ________________ stage of the general adaptation syndrome.
4. Dr. Laslo believes that there is an interaction among psychological processes, the nervous and endocrine systems, and the immune system and that each system influences and is influenced by the other systems. It is very likely that Dr. Laslo works in the new interdisciplinary field called ________________ .
5. When Georgia was under a lot of stress, she became ill from a viral infection. In response to this infection, the most important elements in her immune system, called ________________ , will try to defend against the foreign invader.
6. Dr. Batisic gave a painkilling drug to half the group of participants who were exposed to a painful stimulus and a placebo to the other half. A PET scan of their brains is likely to reveal that ________________ (a different/the same) area of the brain was activated in each group.
7. In a replication of Selye's work on the effects of prolonged stress, researchers confirmed the existence of a second endocrine pathway that involves the hypothalamus, the pituitary gland, and the adrenal cortex. Like Selye, they found that in response to a stressor the hypothalamus signals the pituitary gland to secrete a hormone called ________________ , which in turn stimulates the adrenal cortex to release stress-related hormones called ________________ , the most important of which is ________________ .
8. Eng-Seng had a tooth extracted just before going on summer vacation. Yihong had his tooth removed just before taking stressful final exams. Research by investigating the effect of psychological stress and immune system functioning suggests that Eng-Seng's gum will heal ________________ (faster/slower) than Yihong's.
9. Researchers investigating immune system functioning and factors that are linked to susceptibility to respiratory infections, the common cold, and influenza are likely to discover that ________________ is (are) related to becoming ill.
10. Marsha has been caring for her chronically ill child for many years and perceives the ongoing responsibility as extremely stressful. It is likely that Marsha's telomeres are ________________ (shorter/longer) than the telomeres of mothers who experience normal levels of stress.
11. Dr. Astor investigates telomerase activity as a function of short-term stress and chronic stress. If her findings are similar to those reported in the text, she is likely to find that acute, short term-stress produces ________________ on telomerase activity, and that chronic long-term stress has ________________ on telomerase activity.

Review of Terms, Concepts, and Names 2

Use the terms in this list to complete the Matching Exercise, then to help you answer the True/False items correctly.

fight-or-flight response	alarm stage
Walter Cannon	resistance stage
catecholamines	exhaustion stage
Hans Selye	telomeres
adrenocorticotropic hormone (ACTH)	telomerase
corticosteroids	immune system
cortisol	lymphocytes
general adaptation syndrome	psychoneuroimmunology

Matching Exercise

Match the appropriate term/name with its definition or description.

1. ________________ American physiologist who made many lasting contributions to psychology, including an influential theory of emotion, and who found that the fight-or-flight response involved both the sympathetic nervous system and the endocrine system.
2. ________________ Specialized white blood cells that are responsible for immune defenses.
3. ________________ Hormones, including adrenaline and noradrenaline, secreted by the adrenal medulla that cause rapid physiological arousal.
4. ________________ Canadian endocrinologist who was a pioneer in stress research; described a three-stage response to prolonged stress that he called the general adaptation syndrome.
5. ________________ Hormones released by the adrenal cortex that play a key role in the body's response to long-term stressors.
6. ________________ The first stage of the general adaptation syndrome, during which intense arousal occurs as the body mobilizes internal physical resources to meet the demands of the stress-producing event.
7. ________________ Body system that produces specialized white blood cells that protect the body from viruses, bacteria, and tumor cells.
8. ________________ The most important of the stress-related hormones called corticosteroids.

True/False Test

Indicate whether each statement is true or false by placing T or F in the blank space next to each item.

1. ____ Telomerase is an enzyme that has the capacity to add DNA to shortened telomeres, rebuilding and extending the length of telomeres.
2. ____ The rapidly occurring chain of internal physical reactions that prepare people to either fight or take flight from an immediate threat is called the general adaptation syndrome.
3. ____ In the resistance stage of the general adaptation syndrome, the body actively tries to resist or adjust to the continuing stressful situation.
4. ____ Telomeres are repeated, duplicate DNA sequences that are found at the very tips of chromosomes and that protect the chromosomes' genetic data during cell division.
5. ____ The fight-or-flight response is Hans Selye's term for the three-stage progression of physical changes that occur when an organism is exposed to intense and prolonged stress.
6. ____ Psychoneuroimmunology is an interdisciplinary field that studies the interconnections among psychological processes, nervous and endocrine system functions, and the immune system.
7. ____ In the exhaustion stage of the general adaptation syndrome, the symptoms of the alarm stage reappear, only this time irreversibly; as the body's energy reserves become depleted, adaptation begins to break down, leading to exhaustion, physical disorders, and, potentially, death.
8. ____ In response to stress, a hormone called adrenocorticotropic hormone (ACTH) is released by the pituitary gland after it receives a signal from the hypothalamus.

Check your answers and review any areas of weakness before going on to the next section.

Individual Factors That Influence the Response to Stress: Psychological Factors

Preview Questions

Consider the following questions as you study this section of the chapter.

- What psychological factors can affect our response to stress?
- How do feelings of control, explanatory style, and negative and positive emotions influence stress and health?
- What are Type A aqnd Type B behaviors, and what role does hostility play in the relationship between Type A behavior and health?

Read the section "Individual Factors That Influence the Response to Stress" (up to "Social Factors") and ***write*** *your answers to the following:*

1. Psychological factors that influence responses to stressful events include ______________________________

   Feeling a lack of control over events produces ______________________________

2. According to psychologist Martin Seligman, how people characteristically explain ______________________________

3. Explanatory style is related to health consequences in that ______________________________

4. Two effects of chronic negative emotions on health are that ______________________________

   Positive emotions are associated with ______________________________

5. The Type A behavior pattern refers to ______________________________

   The critical component (and strongest predictor of cardiac disease) in the Type A behavior pattern is ______________________________

   The Type B behavior pattern is ______________________________

6. High levels of hostility are associated with ______________________________

Individual Factors That Influence the Response to Stress: Social Factors

Preview Questions

Consider the following questions as you study this section of the chapter.

- What is meant by social support, and how does it benefit health?
- How can relationships with others sometimes increase stress?
- What gender differences have been found in social support and its effects?

Read the section "Individual Factors That Influence the Reaction to Stress: Social Factors" and ***write*** *your answers to the following:*

1. Social support refers to ______________________________

2. Social support may benefit our health and improve our ability to cope with stressors by
   (a) ______________________________
   (b) ______________________________
   (c) ______________________________

3. Conversely, relationships with others can also be a significant source of stress for four reasons:
   (a) ______________________________
   (b) ______________________________

(c) ______________________________

(d) ______________________________

4. Some of the main gender differences in social support are
(a) ______________________________
(b) ______________________________
(c) ______________________________
(d) ______________________________

Coping: How People Deal with Stress

Preview Questions

Consider the following questions as you study this section of the chapter.

- How is *coping* defined, and what is involved in adaptive and maladaptive coping?
- What are the two basic forms of coping, and when is each typically used?
- What are some of the most common coping strategies, and how does culture affect coping style?

Read the section "Coping: How People Deal with Stress" and ***write*** *your answers to the following:*

1. Coping refers to ______________________________

   Adaptive coping is ______________________________

   Maladaptive coping can involve ______________________________

2. The two basic types of coping (and their uses) are ______________________________

3. Problem-focused coping strategies include
(a) ______________________________
(b) ______________________________

4. Emotion-focused coping strategies include
(a) ______________________________
(b) ______________________________
(c) ______________________________
(d) ______________________________
(e) ______________________________
(f) ______________________________

5. In terms of coping strategy, members of individualistic cultures tend to ______________________________

   Members of collectivistic cultures tend to ______________________________

After you have carefully studied the preceding sections, complete the following exercises.

Concept Check 3

Read the following and write the correct term in the space provided.

1. When Marie turned down Massimo's offer to go out for dinner on Friday night, he was disappointed. Upon reflection, however, he decided that Marie was really not his type anyway, and he'd be better off going out with someone else. Massimo's rationalization of the situation reflects a ______________ explanatory style.

2. When asked by her therapist to describe her husband, Cheryl said that he was very competitive and ambitious, he was always very busy, and any demands made on his time angered and irritated him. Cheryl's description suggests that her husband may exhibit a(n) ________________ behavior pattern.
3. In the case of Cheryl's husband, the critical component and the strongest predictor that he will suffer cardiac disease in his particular behavior pattern is ________________ .
4. Irene constantly complains about her health, her job, and in general everything about her life. She tends to dislike most of the people she meets and always seems to be in a grouchy mood. It appears that Irene suffers from ______________________ emotions.
5. Masayuki is an engineer in a large industrial plant in Tokyo. When things get stressful, Masayuki tries to control the outward expression of his emotions and endeavors to accept the situation with maturity, serenity, and flexibility. Masayuki is using a(n) ________________ coping strategy, which is more characteristic of collectivistic cultures than of individualistic cultures.
6. Shortly after he lost his job and his relationship with his girlfriend ended, Jim went to visit his family. Unfortunately, being with his family made him feel worse. He felt better only when he was with the family dog. It is possible that Jim perceived his family as being ______________ (judgmental/nonjudgmental) and the dog as being ______________ and unconditionally supportive.
7. Although Lambert was very disappointed when he didn't even come close to winning his first mountain bike race, he concluded that all his training and the knowledge he gained from the experience were beneficial. Lambert is using a very constructive emotion-focused strategy called ____________________ .
8. Researchers have found some gender differences in the stress response. The evolutionary perspective suggests that women have developed a "________________________" behavioral response to stress, because this response is more likely to promote the survival of both the individual and the individual's offspring. The researchers have speculated that the effects of the hormone ______________ , which is higher in females than in males, may be a factor.
9. Most evenings after work—especially if she has had a stressful day—Laureena deals with her high level of tension by swimming and exercising in the pool. Laureena is using a(n) ______________________-focused coping strategy called ______________________ .
10. The Bickersons have been married for five difficult years. When asked about his marriage, Mr. Bickerson admits that he and his wife have some "disagreements," but he thinks the fights are "no big deal." He also jokes about the relationship, saying about women: "You can't live with them, but you can't live without them." On the other hand, Mrs. Bickerson thinks their marriage is not going well and openly discusses her problems with friends and family. Mr. Bickerson appears to be using a coping strategy called ______________________ , and his wife deals with her marital problems by ____________________________ .
11. When Mrs. Holt was recently widowed, she sought comfort in prayer, attending church services and activities, and believing that her personal experience of loss and grief were spiritually meaningful. Mrs. Holt is using a(n) ______________________ coping strategy called ______________________ coping.

Graphic Organizer 1

Read the following statements and decide which researcher(s) is (are) most likely to have expressed these views. These statements cover material throughout the chapter.

Statement	Researcher(s)
1. I believe that when we are faced with danger or any threatening or stress-producing situation, we have an immediate physical reaction that involves the sympathetic nervous system and the endocrine system and the release of catecholamines. I call these internal physical changes the fight-or-flight response.	
2. We were two of the earliest researchers to study stress. In an attempt to measure the amount of stress people experienced, we developed the Social Readjustment Rating Scale. Our view at the time was that any changes, either positive or negative, would cause stress and that high levels of stress, as measured by life change units, would lead to the development of serious physical and psychological problems.	
3. My research on stress led me to postulate a three-stage model to prolonged stress, called the general adaptation syndrome. I believe that the stress response involves the hypothalamus, pituitary gland, adrenal cortex, and release of hormones such as ACTH and corticosteroids.	
4. My view is that what causes us problems in the long run is not so much the major life events, which do cause stress, but the cumulative effect of daily hassles that annoy, irritate, and upset people. I have developed a scale to measure these hassles. The number of daily hassles is a better predictor of physical illness and symptoms than the number of major life events experienced.	
5. In my view, the way people characteristically explain their failures and defeats determines who will persist and who will not. I think there are two basic types of explanatory style, an optimistic explanatory style and a pessimistic explanatory style. Those who use a pessimistic explanatory style experience more stress than those who use an optimistic explanatory style.	

Review of Terms, Concepts, and Names 3

Use the terms in this list to complete the Matching Exercise, then to help you answer the True/False items correctly.

Martin Seligman
optimistic explanatory style
pessimistic explanatory style
Type A behavior pattern
Type B behavior pattern
hostility
social support
stress contagion effect
coping
problem-focused coping
planful problem solving
confrontive coping
emotion-focused coping
escape–avoidance
seeking social support
distancing
denial
positive reappraisal
positive religious coping
negative religious coping
mindfulness meditation

Matching Exercise

Match the appropriate term/name with its definition or description.

1. ________________ Behavioral and cognitive responses used to contend with stressors; involves our efforts to change circumstances, or our interpretation of circumstances, to make them more favorable and less threatening.
2. ________________ Problem-focused coping strategy in which the person relies on aggressive or risky efforts to change the situation.
3. ________________ Psychologist who conducted research on explanatory style and the role it plays in stress, health, and illness.

4. ________________ Emotion-focused coping strategy in which the person shifts his or her attention away from the stressor and toward other activities.
5. ________________ Behavioral and emotional style characterized by a sense of time urgency, hostility, and competitiveness.
6. ________________ The tendency of women to become upset about negative life events that happen to other people whom they care about.
7. ________________ Resources provided by other people in times of need.
8. ________________ Emotion-focused coping strategy that involves turning to friends, relatives, or other people for emotional, tangible, or informational support.
9. ________________ Emotion-focused coping strategy that involves the refusal to acknowledge that the problem exists.
10. ________________ Relaxation technique in which practitioners focus awareness on present experience with acceptance.
11. ________________ A form of coping that involves seeking comfort or reassurance in prayer, a religious community, or believing that your personal experience is spiritually meaningful.

True/False Test

Indicate whether each item is true or false by placing T or F in the space next to each item.

1. ____ An optimistic explanatory style involves accounting for negative events or situations with internal, stable, and global explanations.
2. ____ The Type B behavior pattern is a behavioral and emotional style characterized by a relatively relaxed and laid-back approach to situations and problems.
3. ____ Emotion-focused coping efforts are aimed primarily at relieving or regulating the emotional impact of a stressful situation.
4. ____ The most constructive emotion-focused coping strategy is positive reappraisal, which involves not only minimizing the negative emotional aspects of the situation but also trying to create positive meaning by focusing on personal growth.
5. ____ A pessimistic explanatory style involves accounting for negative events or situations with external, unstable, and specific explanations.
6. ____ An emotion-focused coping strategy in which the individual acknowledges the stressor but attempts to minimize or eliminate its emotional impact is called distancing.
7. ____ Problem-focused coping efforts are aimed primarily at directly changing or managing a threatening or harmful stressor.
8. ____ A problem-focused coping strategy that involves efforts to rationally analyze the situation, identify potential solutions, and then implement them is called planful problem solving.
9. ____ The critical component of the type A behavior pattern that is the strongest predictor of cardiac disease and other health problems is hostility.
10. ____ Individuals who respond to stressful events with negative religious coping become angry, question their religious beliefs, or believe that they are being punished.

Check your answers and review any areas of weakness before going on to the next section.

Something to Think About

It sometimes seems that everyone you meet is stressed out. There are things to be done, deadlines to be met, social and family obligations, financial pressures, work-related problems, and so on. How can people cope with all this stress? Is there anything that can be done? Fortunately, there are several strategies for coping with stress. What advice would you give someone who is experiencing stress?

Check your answers and review any areas of weakness before completing the progress tests.

Progress Test 1

Review the complete chapter (including all boxed inserts), review all your study notes, and then test yourself on the following progress test. Check your answers. If you make a mistake, review your notes, check the appropriate section in the study guide, and, if necessary, go back and read the relevant part of the chapter in your textbook.

1. Natasha experienced a great deal of anxiety when she had three exams on the same day. In this situation, the exams are ________________ and her response is called ________________ .
   (a) stress; stressor
   (b) the biological component; the cognitive component
   (c) stressors; stress
   (d) the social component; the biological component

2. Dr. Turnbull uses the biopsychosocial model to guide his research into how psychological factors influence health, illness, and treatment. In particular his research focuses on the effects of traumatic events and stress on health and well-being. This line of research has shown that
   (a) over 70 percent of those who experience major disasters, such as floods, earthquakes, and hurricanes, develop post-traumatic stress disorder (PTSD).
   (b) most people recover from traumatic events without ever developing post-traumatic stress disorder (PTSD).
   (c) high levels of cumulative adversity are associated with good health and better ability to cope with new misfortunes.
   (d) moderate levels of cumulative adversity are associated with poor health and diminished ability to cope with new misfortunes.

3. Donald scored 300 points on the Social Readjustment Rating Scale. According to the current view of the meaning of scores on the SRRS, which of the following is true?
   (a) It is absolutely certain that Donald will develop physical and psychological problems.
   (b) It is impossible to accurately predict whether Donald will develop physical and psychological problems.
   (c) Donald has probably experienced very few daily hassles during the past year.
   (d) Donald's subjective appraisal of the events in his life during the previous year will have no bearing on his health and well-being.

4. Del got up late and nicked himself three times while shaving. Later, he poured a cup of coffee but he couldn't drink it because there was no cream in the fridge. Then, as he was tying his shoe laces, one of them broke. Richard Lazarus would call these incidents
   (a) major life events.
   (b) daily hassles.
   (c) minor life events.
   (d) life change units.

5. The final exam includes a question asking which researcher identified the endocrine system pathways involved in acute stress and the fight-or-flight response. The correct answer is
   (a) Hans Selye.
   (b) Martin Seligman.
   (c) Walter Cannon.
   (d) Richard Lazarus.

6. Carmen is leaving Bogotá, Colombia, to work and live in the United States and is very excited about the move. When Carmen arrives and starts work in the United States, she is likely to
   (a) be much more relaxed and laid back than she was in Colombia.
   (b) experience increased levels of stress due to the acculturation process.
   (c) become physically and psychologically ill within weeks.
   (d) adapt to the new environment without experiencing any stress whatsoever.

7. When Nibras was chased and attacked by a dog during his regular morning run, he experienced the classic symptoms of the fight-or-flight response. According to Walter Cannon, it is likely that his sympathetic nervous system stimulated his adrenal medulla to secrete hormones called
   (a) catecholamines.
   (b) ACTH.
   (c) corticosteroids.
   (d) lymphocytes.

8. After overcoming the initial shock of having his house broken into and many of his personal possessions stolen, Vincent calls the police for help and starts thinking of ways to help catch the burglar and retrieve his belongings. At this point, Vincent is most likely in the ________ stage of the general adaptation syndrome.
   (a) alarm
   (b) resistance
   (c) exhaustion
   (d) denial

9. When Claudia became ill with a viral infection, the ________ of her immune system kicked into high gear to defend her against the virus.
   (a) lymphocytes
   (b) corticosteroids
   (c) catecholamines
   (d) noradrenaline

10. Dr. Blackman studies the interconnections among psychological processes, the nervous and endocrine systems, and the immune system. Like other specialists in the field of psychoneuroimmunology, Dr. Blackman is aware that researchers have discovered that
    (a) the central nervous system and the immune system are directly linked.
    (b) the surfaces of lymphocytes contain receptor sites for neurotransmitters and hormones, including catecholamines and cortisol.
    (c) lymphocytes themselves produce neurotransmitters and hormones.
    (d) all of these statements are true.

11. When Darcy was taking his statistics exam, he was very anxious and nervous. According to research on stressors that can affect the immune system, the stress of exams
    (a) adversely affects the immune system.
    (b) has no effect on the immune system.
    (c) has a beneficial effect on the immune system.
    (d) is a major cause of post-traumatic stress disorder (PTSD).

12. Whenever anything goes wrong in his life, Dean typically feels that it must be something about him that causes the problem. He also believes that no amount of personal effort will improve his situation. Martin Seligman would say that Dean
    (a) is exhibiting a Type A behavior pattern.
    (b) has an optimistic explanatory style.
    (c) is exhibiting a Type B behavior pattern.
    (d) has a pessimistic explanatory style.

13. After his third month of low sales, Allen is called into the sales manager's office and told that he had better start meeting his quota or he will be laid off. The manager appears to be coping with the problem of low sales by using a(n) ________ strategy called ________ .
    (a) problem-focused; confrontive coping
    (b) emotion-focused; escape–avoidance
    (c) problem-focused; planful problem solving
    (d) emotion-focused; distancing

14. According to In Focus (Gender Differences in Responding to Stress), males tend to adopt the ________ response, and females typically engage in the ________ behavioral pattern of responding.
    (a) fight-or-flight; escape–avoidance
    (b) tend-and-befriend; fight-or-flight
    (c) fight-or-flight; tend-and-befriend
    (d) escape–avoidance; fight-or-flight

15. Critical Thinking (Do Personality Factors Cause Disease?) points out that psychologists and other scientists are cautious in the statements they make about the connection between personality and health. Which of the following reasons is (are) cited for this caution?
    (a) Many studies investigating the role of psychological factors in disease are correlational, which does not indicate causality.
    (b) Personality factors might indirectly lead to disease via poor health habits.
    (c) It may be that the disease influences a person's emotions, rather than the other way around.
    (d) All of these factors are cited as reasons.

Progress Test 2

After you have checked your understanding of the material in Progress Test 1 and have done a complete chapter review with special focus on any areas of weakness, you are ready to assess your knowledge on Progress Test 2. Check your answers. If you make a mistake, review your notes, the relevant section of the study guide, and, if necessary, the appropriate part of your textbook.

1. When Janeen was caught in a traffic jam, she experienced a severe headache. In this case, the traffic jam is to ________________ as her headache is to ________________ .
   (a) fight; flight
   (b) stressor; stress
   (c) flight; fight
   (d) stress; stressor

2. Dr. Porter conducts research involving the functions of bone marrow, the spleen, the thymus, lymph nodes, and in particular lymphocytes, which are manufactured in the bone marrow. This research is concerned with the
   (a) endocrine system.
   (b) immune system.
   (c) sympathetic nervous system.
   (d) general adaptation syndrome.

3. Fifty-five-year-old Maxwell is a very impatient and competitive defense lawyer who feels that he must be the best in his field. He also has a reputation for being hostile toward judges and prosecuting attorneys. Psychologists would probably say that Maxwell
   (a) is exhibiting a Type A behavior pattern.
   (b) has a pessimistic explanatory style.
   (c) is exhibitng a Type B behavior pattern.
   (d) has an optimistic explanatory style.

4. Donald exhibits all the characteristics of a Type A behavior pattern. The component of his behavior that is most likely to contribute to health problems is his
   (a) impatience.
   (b) competitiveness.
   (c) achievement orientation.
   (d) hostility.

5. Heloise is an emergency room nurse. Whenever she has a particularly hectic and stressful shift, she and some other nurses make fun of the patients and the doctors. Heloise is using an emotion-focused coping strategy called
   (a) confrontive coping.
   (b) denial.
   (c) distancing.
   (d) positive reappraisal.

6. Madge wants advice on how to cope with the stress of returning to college after being out of school for a number of years. She would be best advised to approach her classes
   (a) with a sense of personal control and optimism.
   (b) with a realistic but pessimistic attitude.
   (c) using an emotion-focused coping strategy called distancing.
   (d) using an emotion-focused coping strategy called denial.

7. Whenever Beth experiences problems in her relationship with her fiancée, she typically talks to her family about her troubles. Beth is using a(n) ________ strategy called __________ .
   (a) problem-focused; confrontive coping
   (b) emotion-focused; distancing
   (c) problem-focused; planful problem solving
   (d) emotion-focused; seeking social support

8. Dr. Shaw studies stress and its affect on health, and, in particular, the role of telomeres in premature aging. His work on telomeres is likely to show that
   (a) shorter telomeres have been linked with aging, age-related disease, and mortality.
   (b) people under chronic stress have longer telomeres than those with normal stress levels.
   (c) longer telomeres have been linked with aging, age-related disease, and mortality.
   (d) low levels of the stress hormones cortisol and catecholamines are associated with shorter telomeres.

9. After a bank was robbed, the bank tellers and the customers got up off the floor, where they had been held at gunpoint. Because it was such a frightening experience, they are likely to have experienced a rapidly occurring chain of internal physical reactions called
   (a) daily hassles.
   (b) the fight-or-flight response.
   (c) the general adaptation syndrome.
   (d) the stress contagion effect.

10. Following a bank robbery, the customers and tellers who were very frightened probably experienced increased activation of the sympathetic nervous system, stimulation of the adrenal medulla, and the release of hormones called
    (a) lymphocytes.
    (b) catecholamines.
    (c) corticosteroid.
    (d) ACTH.

11. During her final year of medical training, Lissette was under constant pressure; she never seemed to get enough sleep, was anxious and nervous most of the time, and experienced many physical symptoms and disorders. As a result of this prolonged stress, it is likely that her hypothalamus, pituitary gland, and adrenal cortex will work together to release stress-related hormones called
    (a) lymphocytes.
    (b) catecholamines.
    (c) corticosteroids.
    (d) adrenaline and noradrenaline.

12. Gregory was very disappointed when he wasn't accepted to the graduate program at State University. Upon reflection, however, he decided that the preparations he made in putting his application together and the knowledge he gained from the interview were beneficial experiences. Gregory is using a(n) ______________ strategy called ______________ .
    (a) problem-focused; confrontive coping
    (b) emotion-focused; positive reappraisal
    (c) problem-focused; planful problem solving
    (d) emotion-focused; escape–avoidance

13. Focus on Neuroscience (The Mysterious Placebo Effect) discusses a research project in which the experimental group underwent a painful procedure followed by an injection of an actual opioid painkiller. The control group was injected with a saline solution placebo after the procedure. A PET scan revealed that in one participant an area of the brain, called the anterior cingulate cortex, became very active. It is likely that the person, who reported that the injection provided pain relief
    (a) was definitely in the experimental group.
    (b) was definitely in the control group.
    (c) was faking and was, in reality, experiencing extreme pain.
    (d) could have been in either the experimental group or the control group.

14. According to In Focus (Providing Effective Social Support), which of the following is NOT recommended for helping someone in distress?
    (a) Express affection for the person, whether by a warm hug or simply a pat on the arm.
    (b) Be a good listener and show concern and interest.
    (c) Ask questions that encourage the person under stress to express his or her feelings and emotions.
    (d) Give advice the person has not asked for.

15. When Sanjeev went to Britain to attend one of the top universities in the country, he was enthralled by all things English and decided that he would like to live there permanently. He took up cricket, lawn bowling, and polo, preferred to be called Sandy rather than Sanjeev, and enthusiastically embraced the "pub" culture of his adopted home. According to Culture and Human Behavior (The Stress of Adapting to a New Culture), Sanjeev has adopted a pattern of acculturation called ______________ and has probably experienced a ______________ degree of stress as a result of abandoning his old cultural identity.
    (a) integration; low
    (b) separation; high
    (c) assimilation; moderate
    (d) marginalization; high

Progress Test 3

After you have checked your understanding of the material in Progress Tests 1 and 2, and have done a complete chapter review with special focus on any areas of weakness, you are ready to further assess your knowledge with Progress Test 3. Check your answers. If you make a mistake, review your notes, the appropriate parts of the study guide, and, if necessary, the relevant sections of your textbook.

1. Following a bitter divorce and a long-fought custody battle over her two children, Luzmilda is in the exhaustion stage of the general adaptation syndrome. According to Selye, this prolonged stress is likely to activate an endocrine pathway that involves ________________ and the release of ______________ .
    (a) the hypothalamus, the pituitary gland, the adrenal cortex; corticosteroids
    (b) the hypothalamus, the sympathetic nervous system, the adrenal medulla; catecholamines
    (c) the sympathetic nervous system, the adrenal medulla, the immune system; oxytocin
    (d) classical conditioning, the adrenal cortex, the immune system; lymphocytes

2. When Argento encountered a wild cougar on the hiking trail, he experienced acute stress. Which of the following would Walter Cannon consider the correct sequence of Argento's fight-or-flight response?
   (a) pituitary, hypothalamus, ACTH release, sympathetic nervous system
   (b) secretion of corticosteroids, ACTH release, perspiration, cognitive appraisal
   (c) hypothalamus, sympathetic nervous system, adrenal medulla, secretion of catecholamines
   (d) perspiration, ACTH release, respiration, parasympathetic nervous system, secretion of catecholamines

3. If Dr. Penman is like most researchers in the field of psychoneuroimmunology, he probably holds the view that
   (a) prolonged stress activates an endocrine pathway that involves the hypothalamus, the sympathetic nervous system and stimulation of the adrenal medulla to release catecholamines.
   (b) acute stress activates an endocrine pathway that involves the hypothalamus, the pituitary, the release of ACTH, and stimulation of the adrenal cortex to release corticosteroids.
   (c) the endocrine system and the immune system are interconnected, but psychological processes operate independently.
   (d) there are interconnections among psychological processes, nervous and endocrine system functions, and the immune system.

4. Rita and Richard both have a large network of social relationships, including close friends and family members. Compared with Richard, Rita may be potentially vulnerable to some of the problematic aspects of social support because
   (a) women are less likely than men to serve as providers of support.
   (b) women, in general, are more likely than men to suffer from the stress contagion effect.
   (c) women tend to rely on a close personal relationship with their spouse and place less importance on relationships with other people.
   (d) women are less likely than men to become upset about what happens to their friends and relatives.

5. Reena has a successful accounting practice and frequently works 60 hours or more a week. She has to manage her time efficiently to keep up with the demands of her career and family life. Despite all the pressure, Reena loves her job, is always kind and considerate to her employees, and has a cheerful personality. Which of the following is most likely to be true of Reena?
   (a) Because of her stressful lifestyle, she probably has high levels of corticosteroids.
   (b) She is at a high risk for coronary disease and other health problems.
   (c) She is likely to develop coronary disease because of her Type A behavior pattern.
   (d) Because she is low in hostility, her risk of developing coronary disease is no higher than that of anyone else.

6. Forty-year-old Lannie is a widow, lives alone, has very few friends, and rarely interacts with other people except at work. Research suggests that compared with people who have many social contacts and relationships, social isolation such as Lannie's is correlated with
   (a) higher-than-normal levels of catecholamines.
   (b) poor health and higher death rates.
   (c) lower-than-normal levels of corticosteroids.
   (d) good health and lower death rates.

7. Researchers tested the notion in the old saying "whatever doesn't kill you makes you stronger" by measuring health outcomes and cumulative adversity. They are likely to discover that
   (a) very low levels of cumulative adversity are associated with better health and greater resilience.
   (b) there is no association between cumulative adversity, at any level, and resilience or well-being.
   (c) moderate levels of cumulative adversity are associated with better health and greater resilience.
   (d) high levels of cumulative adversity are associated with the development of posttraumatic stress disorder (PTSD) in most people.

8. Kari is a very laid-back, easygoing mail carrier. She loves her job because it allows her to meet people and get daily exercise. Kari would be classified as
   (a) exhibiting a Type A behavior pattern.
   (b) having a high risk of heart disease.
   (c) exhibiting a Type B behavior pattern.
   (d) suffering from stress contagion syndrome.

9. Jacob was naturally disappointed when he didn't get the job he applied for. However, in his usual way, he thought that he would have better luck next time, especially if he took some courses to make himself more qualified for the position. Martin Seligman would say that Jacob
   (a) is exhibiting a Type A behavior pattern.
   (b) has an optimistic explanatory style.
   (c) uses a problem-focused coping style.
   (d) has a pessimistic explanatory style.

10. Hans Selye is to ____________ as Richard Lazarus is to ____________ .
   (a) the fight-or-flight response; psychoneuroimmunology
   (b) the general adaptation syndrome; biopsychosocial model
   (c) fight-or-flight response; explanatory styles
   (d) the general adaptation syndrome; daily hassles

11. Anders, a 52-year-old insurance salesperson, is unexpectedly called into the sales manager's office and told that he is going to be laid off because the company is downsizing. Which stage of the general adaptation syndrome is Anders likely experiencing?
   (a) alarm stage
   (b) resistance stage
   (c) exhaustion stage
   (d) denial stage

12. Dr. Chambers has a very busy clinical practice. To clear his mind of all the problems he faces each day and to cope with the high level of stress, he goes to the gym for a workout four or five times a week. Dr. Chambers is using a(n) ________________ coping strategy called ________________ .
   (a) emotion-focused; escape–avoidance
   (b) problem-focused; denial
   (c) emotion-focused; wishful thinking
   (d) problem-focused; confrontive coping

13. Toward the end of the semester, Reza was under a lot of stress; he had three term papers to write and four final exams to prepare for, and he was called into work much more often than he had anticipated. In contrast, his roommate Erik finished all his term papers and had only two final exams to prepare for. If both people are exposed to the same common cold virus, it is very probable that
   (a) Erik will contract a respiratory infection but Reza will not.
   (b) both Erik and Reza will contract a respiratory infection; exposure to the virus is sufficient, and infection rates are independent of levels of psychological stress.
   (c) neither one will contract a respiratory infection; there is no relationship between psychological stress and rates of respiratory infection.
   (d) Reza will contract a respiratory infection but Erik will not.

14. When Lester was having personal and academic problems in college, he went to see a guidance counselor. The counselor provided some helpful suggestions for improving his study habits and advised him to enroll in a remedial reading course. According to In Focus (Providing Effective Social Support), the type of social support that Lester received is called ________________ support.
   (a) emotional
   (b) tangible
   (c) informational
   (d) confrontive

15. Despite all Chikako's efforts to resolve numerous stressful situations in her life, her problems persist. To minimize the adverse impact of stress on her physical and psychological well-being, which of the following should Chikako AVOID doing (according to Enhancing Well-Being with Psychology: Minimizing the Effects of Stress)?
   (a) Exercise regularly; do a brisk 20-minute walk four or five times a week.
   (b) Use stimulants such as caffeine or nicotine; they will help induce relaxation by lowering blood pressure and heart rate.
   (c) Get sufficient sleep, which promotes resistance to health problems and helps buffer the effects of stress.
   (d) Practice a relaxation technique: try meditation to reduce stress-related symptoms.

Answers

Introduction: Stress and Health Psychology

1. *Stress is defined as* a negative emotional state occurring in response to events that are perceived as taxing or exceeding a person's resources or ability to cope.
2. *The cognitive appraisal model of stress, developed by* Richard Lazarus, *emphasizes* the role of an individual's evaluation (appraisal) of events and situations and of the resources that he or she has to deal with the event or situation.
3. *Health psychologists focus on* how biological, behavioral, and social factors influence health, illness, medical treatment, and health-related behaviors.
4. *The biopsychosocial model is* the belief that physical health and illness are determined by the complex interaction of biological, psychological, and social factors.

Stress and Health Psychology: Sources of Stress

1. *Stressors are* events or situations that are perceived as harmful, threatening, or challenging.
2. *Early stress researchers Thomas Holmes and Richard Rahe believed that* any change, whether positive or negative, that required you to adjust your behavior or lifestyle would cause stress (they developed the Social Readjustment Rating Scale in an attempt to measure the amount of stress people experienced).
3. *Several problems with the life events approach have been pointed out: (a)* The link between scores on the Social Readjustment Rating Scale and the development of physical and psychological problems is relatively weak. Most people don't develop physical or mental problems as a result of major life events. *(b)* The Social Readjustment Rating Scale assumes that a given life event will have the same impact on virtually everyone. *(c)* The life events approach assumes change in itself, whether good or bad, produces stress (research has shown that health is most adversely affected by negative life events, especially when they are unexpected or uncontrollable, whereas positive or desirable events are much less likely to affect health adversely). *However, the Social Readjustment Rating Scale (SRRS) is still a useful tool for quickly measuring exposure to stress, and so* efforts have been made to revise and update the SRRS in an attempt to take into account the influences of gender, age, marital status, and other characteristics, and new scales have been developed for specific groups, such as college students (e.g., the College Student Stress Scale).
4. *Traumatic events are* events or situations that are negative, severe, and far beyond our normal expectations for everyday life or life events. *Post-traumatic stress disorder (PTSD) is* an anxiety disorder that involves intrusive thoughts of the traumatic event, emotional numbness, and physical symptoms of anxiety, such as nervousness, sleep disturbances, and irritability.
5. *Both high and low levels of accumulative adversity are associated with* poor health outcomes. *Moderate levels of cumulative adversity are associated with* better health and a greater ability to cope with recent misfortunes (experiencing some stress is healthier than experiencing no stress at all). *Resilience refers to* the ability to cope with stress and adversity, to adapt to negative or unforeseen circumstances, and to rebound after negative experiences.
6. *Daily hassles are* everyday minor events that annoy and upset people. The frequency of daily hassles is linked to mental and physical illness, unhealthy behaviors, and decreased well-being. *The number of daily hassles people experience is* a better predictor of physical illness and symptoms than is the number of major life events experienced.
7. *Work can affect stress levels because of* concerns about job security, unpleasant working conditions, difficult co-workers and supervisors, unreasonable demands and deadlines. When work stress is prolonged or chronic, it can produce burnout. *Burnout is* an unhealthy condition caused by chronic, or prolonged, work stress. *It is characterized by* exhaustion, cynicism, and a sense of failure and inadequacy. *Factors that produce burnout include* work overload (when the demands of the job exceed the ability to meet them), lack of control (the more control over work conditions the less stress), and lack of community (burnout is less likely when there is a sense of belonging, of teamwork, and of supportive co-workers).
8. *Social factors that are a source of stress include* crowding, crime, poverty, racism and discrimination, and substandard housing (people in the lowest socioeconomic levels of society tend to have the highest levels of psychological distress, illness, and death).

9. *In terms of culture, stress can result when* cultures clash; for refugees, immigrants, and their children, adapting to a new culture can be extremely stress-producing.

Concept Check 1

1. health
2. biopsychosocial
3. high; increased
4. daily hassles
5. microaggressions
6. cognitive appraisals
7. integrated; low
8. Richard Lazarus
9. female; male
10. burnout
11. resilience

Matching Exercise 1

1. Richard Lazarus
2. daily hassles
3. health psychology
4. biopsychosocial model
5. life change units
6. chronic stress
7. burnout
8. resilience
9. post-traumatic stress disorder (PTSD)

True/False Test 1

1. F	4. F	7. T
2. T	5. T	8. T
3. T	6. T	9. T

Physical Effects of Stress: The Mind-Body Connection

1. *Stress can indirectly affect a person's health by* prompting behaviors that jeopardize physical well-being, such as not eating or sleeping properly.
2. *High levels of stress can also interfere with* cognitive abilities, such as attention, concentration, and memory; in turn, such disruptions can increase the likelihood of accidents and injuries.
3. *Stress can directly affect physical health by* altering body functions, leading to symptoms, illness, or disease (for example, stress can cause neck and head muscles to contract and tighten, resulting in stress-induced tension headaches).
4. *The fight-or-flight response refers to* a rapidly occurring chain of internal physical reactions that prepare people to either fight or take flight from an immediate threat (involves both the sympathetic nervous system and the endocrine system).
5. *Catecholamines are* hormones secreted by the adrenal medulla that cause rapid physiological arousal (they include adrenaline and noradrenaline). The hypothalamus and lower brain structures activate the sympathetic nervous system, which stimulates the adrenal medulla to secrete these hormones.
6. *Hans Selye found that prolonged stress activates a* second endocrine pathway that involves the hypothalamus, the pituitary gland, and the adrenal cortex. The hypothalamus signals the pituitary gland to secrete a hormone called adrenocorticotropic hormone (ACTH), which in turn stimulates the adrenal cortex to release stress-related hormones called corticosteroids, the most important of which is cortisol. If a stressor is prolonged, continued high levels of corticosteroids can weaken important body systems, lowering immunity and increasing susceptibility to physical symptoms of illness.
7. *The general adaptation syndrome is* Hans Selye's term for the three-stage progression of physical changes that occur when an organism is exposed to intense and prolonged stress; the three stages are alarm, resistance, and exhaustion.
8. *Telomeres are* repeated, duplicate DNA sequences that are found at the very tips of chromosomes and that protect the chromosomes' genetic data during cell division.
9. *Telomeres may play a role in stress-related aging in a number of ways: (a) with each cell division the string of telomeres* gets shorter and the cell can no longer divide and may die or atrophy, causing tissue damage or loss; *(b) shorter telomeres have been linked with* aging, age-related diseases, and mortality; *(c) chronic stress may lead to* premature aging by shortening the length of telomeres; *and (d) elevated levels of the stress hormones cortisol and the catecholamines have been linked to* shorter telomeres, and people who are under chronic stress tend to have shorter telomeres.
10. *Telomerase is* an enzyme that has the capacity to add DNA to shortened telomeres, rebuilding and extending the length of telomeres. *Acute, short-term stress produces* a positive, adaptive

effect on telomerase activity, *and chronic stress has a* negative, maladaptive effect on telomerase activity.

Physical Effects of Stress: Stress and the Immune System

1. *The immune system consists of* the bone marrow, the spleen, the thymus, and lymph nodes. Most important elements of the immune system are the lymphocytes, which are manufactured in the bone marrow. *The function of this system is* to detect and battle foreign invaders, such as bacteria, viruses, and tumor cells.
2. *Lymphocytes are* specialized white blood cells that protect the body from viruses, bacteria, and tumor cells.
3. *Psychoneuroimmunology* is an interdisciplinary field that studies the interconnections among psychological processes (psycho-), the nervous and endocrine system functions (-neuro-), and the immune system (-immunology).
4. *The three main findings of psychoneuroimmunological research are (a)* The central nervous system and the immune system are directly linked via sympathetic nervous system fibers, which influence the production and functioning of lymphocytes. *(b)* The surfaces of lymphocytes contain receptor sites for neurotransmitters and hormones, including catecholamines and cortisol. *(c)* Lymphocytes themselves produce neurotransmitters and hormones, which, in turn, influence the nervous and endocrine systems.
5. *Extremely stressful events reduce* immune system functioning; chronic stressors that continue for years, such as caring for a family member with Alzheimer's disease, can also diminish immune system functioning.
6. *Subsequent research has shown that immune system functioning was also affected by* common negative life events, such as the end or disruption of important interpersonal relationships, and the commonplace stress of exams. Reduced immune system functioning as a result of stress puts us at greater risk for health problems, with slower recovery times for illnesses and injuries.
7. *Neuroscientists investigating the placebo effect using positron emission tomography (PET) have shown that* both a genuine painkilling drug and a placebo activated the same brain area, the anterior cingulate cortex, which is known to contain many opioid receptors. Although exactly how placebos produce their results is not clear, these researchers concluded that this substantiated the mind–body connection, and that higher mental processes (expectations, learned associations, and emotional responses) can have a profound effect on the perception of pain.

Concept Check 2

1. fight-or-flight
2. adrenal medulla; catecholamines
3. resistance
4. psychoneuroimmunology
5. lymphocytes
6. the same
7. adrenocorticotropic hormone (ACTH); corticosteroids; cortisol
8. faster
9. high levels of stress and chronic stress
10. shorter
11. a positive, adaptive effect; a negative, maladaptive effect

Matching Exercise 2

1. Walter Cannon
2. lymphocytes
3. catecholamines
4. Hans Selye
5. corticosteroids
6. alarm stage
7. immune system
8. cortisol

True/False Test 2

1. T
2. F
3. T
4. T
5. F
6. T
7. T
8. T

Individual Factors That Influence the Response to Stress: Psychological Factors

1. *Psychological factors that influence responses to stressful events include* people's appraisal of the event and their resources for coping with it; whether they have a sense of control over the stressful situation; and whether they are able to take steps to minimize or avoid the stressor. *Feeling a lack of control over events produces* all the hallmarks of the stress response: levels

of catecholamines and corticosteroids increase, and the effectiveness of the immune system functioning decreases.

2. *According to psychologist Martin Seligman, how people characteristically explain* their failures and defeats makes a difference: People who have an optimistic explanatory style tend to use external, unstable, and specific explanations for negative events; people who have a pessimistic explanatory style use internal, stable, and global explanations for negative events.

3. *Explanatory style is related to health consequences in that* explanatory style in early adulthood predicts physical health status decades later; those with optimistic explanatory styles have significantly better health than those with pessimistic explanatory styles and are more likely to cope effectively with stressful situations.

4. *Two effects of chronic negative emotions on health are that* people who are habitually anxious, depressed, angry, or hostile are more likely to develop chronic diseases such as arthritis or heart disease, and people who are tense, angry, and unhappy experience more stress than happier people (they also report more frequent and intense daily hassles and react much more intensely to the stressful events they encounter). *Positive emotions are associated with* increased resistance to infection, decreased illnesses, fewer reports of illness symptoms, less pain, lower risk of developing heart disease, and longer life expectancy.

5. *The Type A behavior pattern refers to* a behavioral and emotional style characterized by a sense of time urgency, hostility, and intense ambition and competitiveness. *The critical component (and strongest predictor of cardiac disease) in the Type A behavior pattern is* hostility, which refers to the tendency to feel anger, annoyance, resentment, and contempt and to hold cynical and negative beliefs about human nature in general. *The Type B behavior pattern is* displayed by people who are relatively relaxed and laid back.

6. *High levels of hostility are associated with* suspiciousness, mistrust, cynicism, and pessimism; increased blood pressure, heart rate, and the production of stress-related hormones; more intense reactions to stressors and a tendency to create more stress; and more severe, negative life events and daily hassles than other people.

Individual Factors That Influence the Response to Stress: Social Factors

1. *Social support refers to* the resources provided by other people in times of need.

2. *Social support may benefit our health and improve our ability to cope with stressors by (a)* modifying our appraisal of a stressor's significance, including the degree to which we perceive it as threatening or harmful (simply knowing that support and assistance are readily available may make the situation seem less threatening); *(b)* decreasing the intensity of physical reactions to a stressor; *(c)* making us less likely to experience negative emotions (in contrast, loneliness and depression are unpleasant emotional states that increase levels of stress hormones and adversely affect immune system functioning); and *(d)* having the most diverse social networks (for example, being married; having close relationships with family members, friends, and neighbors; belonging to political, social, or religious groups), which lowers the incidence of dementia and cognitive loss in old age, decreases the incidence of stroke and cardiovascular disease among women in a high-risk group, and improves resistance to upper respiratory infections (in general, people who have more *different* types of relationships live longest).

3. *Conversely, relationships with others can also be a significant source of stress for four reasons: (a)* Negative interactions with other people are more effective in creating psychological distress than positive interactions are in improving well-being. *(b)* Marital conflict has been shown to have adverse effects on health, especially for women. *(c)* When people are perceived as being judgmental, their presence may increase the individual's physical reaction to a stressor. *(d)* Well-meaning friends or family members may offer unwanted or inappropriate social support.

4. *Some of the main gender differences in social support are (a)* Men tend to have a much smaller social network than women and rely heavily on a close relationship with their spouse, placing less importance on relationships with other people (women, in contrast, are more likely to list close friends along with their spouses as confidants). *(b)* Women are more likely than men to serve as providers of support, which can be a very stressful role. *(c)* Women may be more likely to suffer from the stress contagion effect, becoming upset about negative life events that happen to other people whom they care about.

(d) Men are more likely to be distressed only by negative events that happen to their immediate family—their wives and children.

Coping: How People Deal with Stress

1. *Coping refers to* behavioral and cognitive responses used to deal with stressors; it involves our efforts to change circumstances, or our interpretations of circumstances, to make them more favorable and less threatening. *Adaptive coping is* a dynamic and complex process involving the ability to switch coping strategies as appropriate, evaluate the consequences, and adjust the coping strategies accordingly; adaptive coping often includes developing tolerance for negative life events, maintaining self-esteem, keeping emotions in balance, and preserving important relationships. *Maladaptive coping can involve* thoughts and behaviors that prolong or intensify distress, or that produce self-defeating outcomes.
2. *The two basic types of coping (and their uses) are* problem-focused coping (aimed at managing or changing a threatening or harmful stressor) and emotion-focused coping (aimed at relieving or regulating the emotional impact of the stressful situation).
3. *Problem-focused coping strategies include (a)* planful problem solving (rationally analyzing the situation, identifying potential solutions, and then implementing them), and *(b)* confrontive coping (relying on aggressive or risky efforts to change the situation).
4. *Emotion-focused coping strategies include (a)* escape–avoidance (shifting attention away from the stressor and toward other activities, with the basic goal of escaping or avoiding the stressor and neutralizing distressing emotions), *(b)* seeking social support (turning to friends, relatives, or other people for emotional, tangible, or informational support), *(c)* distancing (acknowledging the stressor while attempting to minimize or eliminate its emotional impact), *(d)* denial (the refusal to acknowledge that the problem even exists), *(e)* positive reappraisal (minimizing the negative emotional aspects of the situation but also trying to create positive meaning by focusing on personal growth), and *(f)* positive religious coping (seeking comfort or reassurance in prayer, a religious community, or believing that your personal experience is spiritually meaningful) or negative religious coping (becoming angry, questioning religious beliefs, or believing that the personal experience is a punishment).
5. *In terms of coping strategies, members of individualistic cultures tend to* emphasize personal autonomy and personal responsibility in dealing with problems (they are less likely to seek social support in stressful situations than are members of collectivistic cultures) and to favor problem-focused strategies, such as confrontive coping and planful problem solving. *Members of collectivistic cultures tend to* be more oriented toward their social group, family, or community and to seek help with their problems; they also place greater emphasis on controlling personal reactions to a stressful situation rather than trying to control the situation itself.

Concept Check 3

1. optimistic
2. Type A
3. hostility
4. chronic negative
5. emotion-focused
6. judgmental; nonjudgmental
7. positive reappraisal
8. tend-and-befriend; oxytocin
9. emotion; escape–avoidance
10. distancing; seeking social support
11. emotion-focused; positive religious

Graphic Organizer 1

1. Walter Cannon
2. Thomas Holmes and Richard Rahe
3. Hans Selye
4. Richard Lazarus
5. Martin Seligman

Matching Exercise 3

1. coping
2. confrontive coping
3. Martin Seligman
4. escape–avoidance
5. Type A behavior pattern
6. stress contagion effect
7. social support
8. seeking social support

9. denial
10. mindfulness meditation
11. positive religious coping

True/False Test 3

1. F	5. F	9. T
2. T	6. T	10. T
3. T	7. T	
4. T	8. T	

Something to Think About

A good place to start in giving advice to someone is to explain what stressors are and what the stress reaction is. Identifying potential sources of stress, from major life events to daily hassles, is useful, and noting how our subjective cognitive appraisal of stressors influences our reactions is also important. It is also helpful to know about physical reactions and psychological and social factors that influence our response to stress.

People vary a great deal in the way they respond to distressing events. Psychologists have identified several different factors that influence an individual's response to stressful events. Having a sense of control reduces the impact of stressors and decreases feelings of anxiety and depression. The type of explanatory style we use—optimistic, pessimistic, or, as in most cases, somewhere in between—can also have an effect on our health. People with a pessimistic explanatory style tend to have poorer physical health, whereas people with an optimistic, confident, and generally positive outlook have better immune system responses and better physical health. Furthermore, chronically grouchy people experience more stress, have more frequent and intense daily hassles, and generally react with far greater distress to stressful events.

Many different strategies can be used to deal with stress, some of which are more adaptive than others. Having good social support is beneficial, but so too are the types of strategies that we adopt to cope with distressing events. Problem-focused and emotion-focused coping strategies are two that the text discusses in detail. In addition, we can minimize the impact of stressors by exercising regularly; avoiding or minimizing stimulants such as coffee, tea, or cigarettes; and regularly practicing a relaxation technique such as mindfulness meditation. Stress is an unavoidable part of life and can influence both our physical and psychological well-being. How we choose to cope with stress can reduce and minimize its destructive effects.

Progress Test 1

1. c	6. b	11. a
2. b	7. a	12. d
3. b	8. b	13. a
4. b	9. a	14. c
5. c	10. d	15. d

Progress Test 2

1. b	6. a	11. c
2. b	7. d	12. b
3. a	8. a	13. d
4. d	9. b	14. d
5. c	10. b	15. c

Progress Test 3

1. a	6. b	11. a
2. c	7. c	12. a
3. d	8. c	13. d
4. b	9. b	14. c
5. d	10. d	15. b

CHAPTER 13

Psychological Disorders

PREVIEW

Reading the section below first will give you a general sense of the chapter's contents and an initial introduction to some of the major concepts and terms. This will prime you for what you are about to read and help you to develop a "cognitive map" that will guide your study of the material in this chapter. Likewise, reading the **preview questions** at the beginning of each major section will improve your ability to understand, learn, and retain the information.

Chapter 13 . . . AT A GLANCE

Chapter 13 begins by addressing the distinction between normal and abnormal behavior, the criteria for diagnosing psychological disorders, according to DSM-IV-TR, and the prevalence of psychological disorders.

Although most people experience anxiety, it is considered a disorder only when it becomes maladaptive. The prevalence, course, and possible causes of anxiety disorders, including generalized anxiety disorder (GAD), panic disorder, phobias, post-traumatic stress disorder (PTSD), and obsessive–compulsive disorder (OCD), are discussed.

Mood disorders involve serious, persistent disturbances in emotions that cause psychological discomfort and/or impair the ability to function. The symptoms of major depression, SAD, dysthymic disorder, bipolar disorder, and cyclothymic disorder are identified, and the course and potential causes of these mood disorders are discussed.

Eating disorders are covered next. The defining characteristic of anorexia nervosa and bulimia nervosa are outlined, and the causes of eating disorders are examined.

Personality disorders are characterized by inflexible and maladaptive personality traits. The symptoms and causes of antisocial and borderline personality disorders are discussed.

Dissociative experiences involve a disruption in awareness, memory, and personal identity. The symptoms and possible causes of dissociative amnesia, dissociative fugue, and dissociative identity disorder (DID) are examined.

The main symptoms and subtypes of schizophrenia are identified, and the prevalence and course of the disorder are presented. Various theories of the causes of schizophrenia are explored, and the conclusion is reached that no single factor has emerged as causing this psychological disorder. Enhancing Well-Being with Psychology suggests ways of helping to prevent suicide.

Introduction: Understanding Psychological Disorders

Preview Questions

Consider the following questions as you study this section of the chapter.

- What is psychopathology, and what characterizes psychological disorders?
- What is DSM-IV-TR, what does it describe, and what has it been criticized for?
- How prevalent are psychological disorders?

Read the section "Introduction: Understanding Psychological Disorders" and ***write*** *your answers to the following:*

1. Psychopathology is ____________________

2. A psychological, or mental, disorder can be defined as ____________________

3. DSM-IV-TR stands for ____________________

   This manual describes ____________________

   It provides mental health professionals with ____________________

   DSM-IV-TR has been criticized for
   (a) ____________________
   (b) ____________________
   (c) ____________________
   (d) ____________________

4. The National Comorbidity Survey Replication (NCS-R) found that one out of four respondents (26 percent) ____________________

   There was also a high degree of comorbidity, which means that ____________________

   In terms of lifetime prevalence of experiencing symptoms of a psychological disorder, the NCS-R found that ____________________

   The lifetime prevalence and names of the four most commonly reported categories of psychological disorders are as follows: ____________________

   The NCS-R found that most people with symptoms of a psychological disorder (59 percent) ____________________

Anxiety Disorders

Preview Questions

Consider the following questions as you study this section of the chapter.

- What is the main symptom of anxiety disorders, and how does pathological anxiety differ from normal anxiety?
- What characterizes generalized anxiety disorder (GAD) and panic disorder, and what causes these disorders?
- How is *phobia* defined, what are specific phobia and social phobia, and how have these phobias been explained?

Read the section "Anxiety Disorders" (up to "Post-Traumatic Stress Disorder") and ***write*** *your answers to the following:*

1. Anxiety is defined as ____________________

   It is often adaptive and normal because ____________________

2. In anxiety disorders, the anxiety is ______________

____

____

3. The three features that distinguish normal anxiety from pathological anxiety are
(a) ______________

____

(b) ______________

____

(c) ______________

____

4. Generalized anxiety disorder (GAD) is characterized by ______________

____

____

Its cause is thought to involve ______________

____

____

5. A panic attack is ______________

____

The most common symptoms are ______________

____

6. A panic disorder is ______________

____

Some panic disorder sufferers go on to develop ______________, which is ______________

____

____

The triple vulnerabilities model states ______________

____

____

The catastrophic cognitions theory proposes

____

____

____

7. A phobia is ______________

____

A specific phobia is ______________

____

Prevalence rates suggest that about ______________

____

A social phobia (or social anxiety disorder) is

____

____

In terms of prevalence, social phobia is

____

____

A Japanese variation, ______________, differs in that ______________

____

8. Some phobias involve various forms of learning, such as ______________

____

____

____

____

____

Anxiety Disorders: Post-Traumatic Stress Disorder and Obsessive–Compulsive Disorder

Preview Questions

Consider the following questions as you study these sections of the chapter.

- How is *post-traumatic stress disorder (PTSD)* defined?
- What are the main characteristics of PTSD, and what causes the disorder?
- What is obsessive–compulsive disorder (OCD), and what causes it?

Read the sections "Post-Traumatic Stress Disorder" and "Obsessive–Compulsive Disorder" and ***write*** *your answers to the following:*

1. Post-traumatic stress disorder (PTSD) is

____

____

It is estimated that in any given year more than ______________

____

2. The three core symptoms that characterize PTSD are
(a) ______________

____

(b) ________________________________

____

(c) ________________________________

____

3. Factors that influence the likelihood of developing post-traumatic stress disorder are
(a) ________________________________

____

(b) ________________________________

____

(c) ________________________________

____

4. Obsessive–compulsive disorder (OCD) is ________________________________

____

Obsessions are ________________________________

____

____

Compulsions are ________________________________

____

____

5. People with obsessive–compulsive disorder commonly experience ________________________________

____

____

6. Two biological factors that seem to be involved in obsessive–compulsive disorder are

____

____

____

After you have carefully studied the preceding sections, complete the following exercises.

Concept Check 1

Read the following and write the correct term in the space provided.

1. By reading the results of the National Comorbidity Study Replication (NCS-R) Jaycee is likely to learn that approximately one out of ________________ respondents (________ percent) reported experiencing the symptoms of a psychological disorder during the previous year.
2. Seventeen-year-old Brad has a shaved head, and he has rings in his nose, ears, and navel. Shortly after purchasing a new pair of jeans, he cut and tore horizontal slits across the thigh and knee areas of each leg. In our present culture, Brad would be classified as ________________.
3. Mr. and Mrs. Jefferson want to hire a new housekeeper. Mr. Jefferson suggests that the best person would be someone who has an excessive dislike and fear of dirt, germs, and insects and who deals with anxiety about contamination by using a very thorough cleaning, washing, and disinfecting routine. Mrs. Jefferson thinks that any person fitting that description might have a problem called ________________________________ disorder.
4. Mr. Alviro suffers from intense anxiety most of the time. He is nervous and worried and is overly concerned about a wide range of life circumstances with little or no justification. Mr. Alviro probably suffers from ________________________ disorder.
5. Maurice is very quiet and introverted. He is painfully shy in the presence of other people and has dropped many college courses simply because they involved oral presentations. He can't get a job because he is intensely afraid and anxious about being interviewed. Maurice would probably be classified as having ________________________.
6. Mr. Shenasi frequently recalls the horrors he and his family experienced in his native Iraq. He suffers from sleep disturbances and is often awakened by terrifying nightmares. Mr. Shenasi is experiencing ________________________ disorder.
7. Ever since the sudden death of her husband, Mrs. Baxter has experienced a number of terrifying and unexpected episodes in which her heart suddenly starts to pound for no apparent

reason; she typically feels a choking sensation, has trouble breathing, and starts to sweat and tremble. Mrs. Baxter is probably experiencing ________________ .

8. Dr. Felkar believes that some phobias can be explained in terms of basic learning principles. For example, Tina's irrational fear of cats may have developed because of ________________ conditioning, ________________ conditioning, or ________________ learning.
9. Thea has been diagnosed with obsessive–compulsive disorder. Although its cause is not fully understood, biological factors such as a deficiency in the neurotransmitters ________________ and ________________ and dysfunctions in brain areas such as those involved in the ________________ response, the ________________ lobes, and the ________________ may all be implicated in obsessive–compulsive disorder.

Graphic Organizer 1

List the main symptoms of each of the following anxiety disorders:

Generalized Anxiety Disorder	Panic Disorder	Phobias

Post-Traumatic Stress Disorder	Obsessive–Compulsive Disorder

Review of Terms and Concepts 1

Use the terms in this list to complete the Matching Exercise, then to help you answer the True/False items correctly.

psychopathology
psychological disorder (mental disorder)
DSM-IV-TR
anxiety
anxiety disorders
generalized anxiety disorder (GAD)
panic attack
panic disorder
agoraphobia
triple vulnerabilities model of panic disorder
catastrophic cognitions theory of panic disorder
ataque de nervios (attack of nerves)
phobia
specific phobia (simple phobia)
social phobia (social anxiety disorder)
taijin kyofusho
post-traumatic stress disorder (PTSD)
obsessive–compulsive disorder (OCD)
obsessions
compulsions
caudate nucleus

Matching Exercise

Match the appropriate term with its definition or description.

1. ________________ The scientific study of the origins, symptoms, and development of psychological disorders.
2. ________________ Abbreviation for the *Diagnostic and Statistical Manual of Mental Disorders,* Fourth Edition, Text Revision, the book published by the American Psychiatric Association that describes the specific symptoms and diagnostic guidelines for different psychological disorders.
3. ________________ Anxiety disorder in which the symptoms of anxiety are triggered by intrusive, repetitive thoughts and urges to perform certain actions.
4. ________________ Unpleasant emotional state characterized by physical arousal and feelings of tension, apprehension, and worry.
5. ________________ Persistent and irrational fear of a specific object, situation, or activity.
6. ________________ Anxiety disorder in which chronic and persistent symptoms of anxiety develop in response to an extreme physical or psychological trauma.
7. ________________ Anxiety disorder involving the extreme and irrational fear of experiencing a panic attack in a public situation and being unable to escape or get help.
8. ________________ Anxiety disorder characterized by an excessive, intense, and irrational fear of a specific object, situation, or activity that is actively avoided or endured with marked anxiety.
9. ________________ Disorder that usually affects young Japanese males and is characterized by extreme social anxiety, avoidance of social situations, and a fear that one's appearance or smell, facial expression, or body language will offend, insult, or embarrass other people.
10. ________________ Theory that people with panic disorder tend to misinterpret the physical signs of arousal as disastrous.
11. ________________ Model that proposes a biological predisposition toward anxiety, a low sense of control over potentially life-threatening events, and an oversensitivity to physical sensations combine to make a person susceptible to panic.

True/False Test

Indicate whether each statement is true or false by placing T or F in the blank space next to each item.

1. ____ Compulsions refer to repeated, intrusive, and uncontrollable irrational thoughts or mental images that cause extreme anxiety and distress.
2. ____ A psychological (or mental) disorder is a pattern of behavioral and psychological symptoms that causes significant personal distress, impairs the ability to function in one or more important areas of daily life, or both.
3. ____ Generalized anxiety disorder (GAD) is characterized by excessive, global, chronic, and persistent symptoms of anxiety; also called free-floating anxiety.
4. ____ Panic disorder is an anxiety disorder in which the person experiences frequent and unexpected panic attacks.
5. ____ Obsessions refer to repetitive behaviors or mental acts that are performed to prevent or reduce anxiety.
6. ____ Social phobia (social anxiety disorder) is an anxiety disorder involving the extreme and irrational fear of being embarrassed, judged, or scrutinized by others in social situations.

7. ____ Anxiety disorders are a category of psychological disorders in which extreme anxiety, the main diagnostic feature, causes significant disruptions in the person's cognitive, behavioral, and interpersonal functioning.

8. ____ A panic attack is a sudden episode of extreme anxiety that rapidly escalates in intensity.

9. ____ In addition to the many symptoms common to panic disorder, the person with *ataque de nervios* (attack of nerves) exhibits such symptoms as hysterical screaming, swearing, striking others, and breaking things.

10. ____ The caudate nucleus, which is involved in regulating movements, is a brain area that has been implicated in obsessive–compulsive disorder.

Check your answers and review any areas of weakness before going on to the next section.

Mood Disorders: Emotions Gone Awry

Preview Questions

Consider the following questions as you study this section of the chapter.

- What are mood (or affective) disorders?
- What characterizes major depression, and what is seasonal affective disorder (SAD)?
- What is dysthymic disorder?
- Why is major depression called "the common cold" of psychological disorders, and how does its prevalence compare with that of bipolar disorder?
- How is *bipolar disorder* defined?
- What characterizes a manic episode, and what is cyclothymic disorder?
- What factors contribute to the development of mood disorders?

*Read the section "Mood Disorders: Emotions Gone Awry" and **write** your answers to the following:*

1. Mood disorders (also called affective disorders) are ______________________________
____
____

2. Major depression is characterized by ______________________________
____
____

3. Seasonal affective disorder is a mood disorder in which ______________________________
____
____

4. Dysthymic disorder is ______________________________
____
____

5. Major depression is called "the common cold" of psychological disorders because ______________________________
____
____
____

6. Bipolar disorder is defined as ______________________________
____
____

   A manic episode is a ______________________________
____
____

7. Cyclothymic disorder is a mood disorder characterized by ______________________________
____

8. The onset of bipolar disorder typically occurs
____
____

9. Multiple factors appear to be involved in the development of mood disorders. These include
____
____
____

Eating Disorders: Anorexia and Bulimia

Preview Questions

Consider the following questions as you study this section of the chapter.

- What is an eating disorder?
- What behaviors and symptoms are associated with anorexia nervosa and bulimia nervosa?
- What factors have been implicated in the development of eating disorders?

Read the section "Eating Disorders: Anorexia and Bulimia" and write your answers to the following:

1. Eating disorders involve ______

2. Anorexia nervosa is an eating disorder characterized by ______

3. Bulimia nervosa is an eating disorder characterized by ______

   Bulimia shares many of the characteristics of anorexia, with the main differences being that ______

4. The main factors implicated in the development of eating disorders are ______

Personality Disorders: Maladaptive Traits

Preview Questions

Consider the following questions as you study this section of the chapter.

- What are the main characteristics of personality disorders, and how are personality disorders categorized into clusters in DSM-IV-TR?
- What is the new approach to classifying personality disorders proposed for DSM-5, and what are the six personality disorders listed?
- What characterizes the behavior of someone with an antisocial or borderline personality disorder?
- What causes borderline personality disorder?

Read the section "Personality Disorders: Maladaptive Traits" and ***write*** *your answers to the following:*

1. Personality disorder is defined as ______

   DSM-IV-TR identified ten distinct personality disorders, which are organized into three basic clusters: ______

2. DSM-5 (scheduled for publication in 2013) has proposed an approach to classifying personality disorders that involves assessing people on two dimensions:

   (a) ______

   (b) ______

   DSM-5 has also proposed reducing the number of personality disorders from ten to six: ______

3. The antisocial personality disorder is characterized by ______

   It is estimated that approximately ______

4. Borderline personality disorder (BPD) is characterized by ______

   In terms of prevalence, BPD is the ______

   It is caused by ______

   and, according to the biosocial developmental theory, ______

The Dissociative Disorders: Fragmentation of the Self

Preview Questions

Consider the following questions as you study this section of the chapter.

- How is a *dissociative experience* defined, and what are dissociative disorders?
- What are dissociative amnesia and dissociative fugue?
- What is dissociative identity disorder (DID), and what is thought to cause it?

Read the section "The Dissociative Disorders: Fragmentation of the Self" and ***write*** *your answers to the following:*

1. The dissociative experience is ______________________________
2. Dissociative disorders are ______________________________
3. Dissociative amnesia is a disorder involving ______________________________

   Dissociative fugue is ______________________________
4. Dissociative identity disorder (DID) involves ______________________________
5. According to one theory, DID is caused by ______________________________

After you have carefully studied the preceding sections, complete the following exercises.

Concept Check 2

Read the following and write the correct term in the space provided.

1. Ursula is generally happy about her move to northern Canada six years ago, but at regular intervals since then she has suffered episodes of depression during the fall and winter months. Ursula is probably suffering from ______________ disorder.
2. Laura suffers from a mood disorder. Her therapist has taken a family history and found that Laura's mother and two sisters also suffer from the same problem. Although her therapist is aware that multiple factors may be involved in her problem, he is most likely to conclude that Laura may have a(n) ______________ predisposition for the disorder.
3. Dr. Markoff takes the position that borderline personality disorder is the outcome of a unique combination of biological, psychological, and environmental factors, and that when a child's innate temperamentally difficult traits and her parents' poor child-rearing practices interact, the child is susceptible to developing the disorder. Dr. Markoff's view is consistent with the ______________ theory of borderline personality disorder.
4. Nedzad has a chronic disorder involving moderate but frequent mood swings that are not severe enough to qualify as bipolar disorder or major depression. He is perceived as being very moody, unpredictable, and inconsistent; taken together, these symptoms may indicate ______________ disorder.
5. Marion Einer, a fifth-grade schoolteacher in Jersey City, disappeared a few days after her husband left her. One year later, she was discovered working as a waitress in a cocktail lounge in San Diego. Calling herself Faye Bartell, she claimed to have no recollection of her past life and insisted that she had never been married. This example illustrates ______________.
6. When Vanessa goes to a movie, she tends to become totally absorbed in the plot and loses all track of time and place; she is also often momentarily disoriented when she leaves the theater. These episodes represent ______________.

7. Although Karlson recently survived an airplane crash with very few injuries, three of his friends were killed in the crash. Karlson is unable to recall any details from the time of the accident until a week later. Karlson has experienced ______________________________ .
8. Dr. Rendell studies people who typically disregard and violate the rights of others and who appear to have no remorse or conscience about their destructive behaviors. Her colleague, Dr. Gideon, studies people who have a personality disorder characterized by instability of interpersonal relationships, self-image, and emotions, and marked impulsivity. Dr. Rendell studies ___________________ personality disorder, and Dr. Gideon studies ___________________ personality disorder.
9. Masayoshi is a young unemployed male who lives in a single room in his parents' house. He spends most of his time alone, preoccupied with video games and surfing the Internet; he refuses all social engagement with the outside world and has very limited interactions with his family. According to Culture and Human Behavior (Culture Bound Syndromes) Masayoshi is likely suffering from a culture specific disorder called ___________________ .
10. Although Claire is of average height, she weighs only 85 pounds and has an irrational fear of gaining weight and a distorted body self-perception. She has lost 30 pounds over the past eight or nine months by eating very little and going to aerobics classes twice a day. Claire probably suffers from _________________________ .

Graphic Organizer 2

List the main symptoms of the mood disorders:

Major Depression	Bipolar Disorder
1. 2. 3. 4. 5. 6.	1. 2. 3.
Dysthymic Disorder 1.	**Cyclothymic Disorder** 1.

Review of Terms and Concepts 2

Use the terms in this list to complete the Matching Exercise, then to help you answer the True/False items correctly.

mood (or affective) disorders
major depression
seasonal affective disorder (SAD)
dysthymic disorder
bipolar disorder
manic episode
flight of ideas
cyclothymic disorder
rapid cycling
lithium
glutamate
eating disorder
anorexia nervosa
lanugo
bulimia nervosa
personality
personality traits
personality disorder
antisocial personality disorder (psychopath or sociopath)
conduct disorder
borderline personality disorder
biosocial developmental theory of borderline personality disorder
dissociative experience
dissociative disorders
dissociative amnesia
dissociative fugue
dissociative identity disorder (DID)
alters (alter egos)

Matching Exercise

Match the appropriate term with its definition or description.

1. ________________ Personality disorder characterized by a pervasive pattern of disregarding and violating the rights of others; such individuals are also referred to as psychopaths or sociopaths.
2. ________________ Once called manic depression, this mood disorder involves periods of incapacitating depression alternating with periods of extreme euphoria and excitement.
3. ________________ Mood disorder in which episodes of depression typically occur during fall and winter and subside during spring and summer.
4. ________________ Mood disorder characterized by extreme and persistent feelings of despondency, worthlessness, and hopelessness, causing impaired emotional, cognitive, behavioral, and physical functioning.
5. ________________ Sudden, rapidly escalating emotional state characterized by extreme euphoria, excitement, physical energy, and rapid thoughts and speech.
6. ________________ Break or disruption in consciousness during which awareness, memory, and personal identity become separated or divided.
7. ________________ Inflexible, maladaptive patterns of thoughts, emotions, behavior, and interpersonal functioning that are stable over time and across situations and deviate from the expectations of the individual's culture.
8. ________________ Consistent and enduring patterns of thinking, feeling, and behaving that characterize a person as an individual.
9. ________________ A dissociative disorder involving extensive memory disruptions along with the presence of two or more distinct identities, or "personalities"; formerly called *multiple personality disorder*.
10. ________________ Medication that helps control bipolar disorder.
11. ________________ Term used to describe the distinct identities or personalities of a person with dissociative identity disorder.
12. ________________ A diagnostic term for a pattern of behavior during childhood and adolescence that draws the attention of authorities, such as being cruel to animals, attacking or harming adults or other children, stealing, setting fires, and destroying property.
13. ________________ A category of psychological disorders characterized by severe disturbances in eating behavior.
14. ________________ The soft, downy, fine body hair that normally occurs during the later stages of human fetal development but can also develop in severe cases of anorexia nervosa or starvation.

True/False Test

Indicate whether each statement is true or false by placing T or F in the blank space next to each item.

1. ____ Mood (or affective) disorders are a category of psychological disorders in which significant and persistent disruptions in mood or emotion cause impaired cognitive, behavioral, and physical functioning.
2. ____ Dissociative fugue involves the partial or total inability to recall important personal information but does not involve sudden, unexpected travel from home.
3. ____ Dissociative amnesia involves sudden and unexpected travel away from home, extensive amnesia, and identity confusion.

4. ____ Cyclothymic disorder involves chronic, low-grade feelings of depression that produce subjective discomfort but do not seriously impair the ability to function and are not severe enough to qualify as major depression.

5. ____ Dissociative disorders are a category of psychological disorders in which extreme and frequent disruptions of awareness, memory, and personal identity impair the ability to function.

6. ____ Borderline personality disorder is characterized by instability of interpersonal relationships, self-image, and emotions, as well as by marked impulsivity.

7. ____ Dysthymic disorder is a mood disorder characterized by moderate but frequent mood swings that are not severe enough to qualify as either bipolar disorder or major depression.

8. ____ Personality traits are relatively stable predispositions to behave or react in certain ways and reflect different dimensions of a person's personality.

9. ____ Flight of ideas refers to thoughts that rapidly and loosely shift from topic to topic during a manic episode when attention is very easily distracted.

10. ____ A small percentage of people with bipolar disorder display *rapid cycling,* experiencing four or more manic or depressive episodes every year.

11. ____ Lithium regulates the availability of the neurotransmitter *glutamate,* which acts as an excitatory neurotransmitter in many brain areas.

12. ____ Anorexia nervosa is an eating disorder characterized by binges of extreme overeating followed by self-induced vomiting or misuse of laxatives or enemas to purge the excessive food and prevent weight gain.

13. ____ Bulimia nervosa is an eating disorder characterized by excessive weight loss, an irrational fear of gaining weight, and distorted body self-perception.

14. ____ The biosocial developmental theory suggests that borderline personality disorder is the outcome of a unique combination of biological, psychological, and environmental factors.

Check your answers and review any areas of weakness before going on to the next section.

Schizophrenia: A Different Reality

Preview Questions

Consider the following questions as you study this section of the chapter.

- How is schizophrenia characterized?
- How do positive and negative symptoms differ?
- What are the main subtypes of schizophrenia?
- What evidence points to the involvement of genetic factors, paternal age, viral infections, abnormal brain structures, and abnormal brain chemistry in the development of schizophrenia?
- How do psychological factors affect the development of schizophrenia?

*Read the section "Schizophrenia: A Different Reality" and **write** your answers to the following:*

1. Schizophrenia is a psychological disorder that involves ______________________________

   ____

   In terms of prevalence, about ______________________________

   ____

2. Positive symptoms include ______________________________

   ____

   ____

   ____

   ____

   Negative symptoms consist of ______________________________

   ____

   ____

3. The three basic subtypes of schizophrenia are

   (a) ______________________________

   ____

   (b) ______________________________

   ____

   (c) ______________________________

   ____

   A fourth label, ______________________________, is used to describe individuals who ______________________________

   ____

   ____

4. Evidence that genetic factors are involved in the development of schizophrenia comes from

   ____

   ____

5. Research on paternal age and the risk of schizophrenia indicates that ____

6. One environmental factor implicated in the development of schizophrenia is ____

7. Neurological evidence from research examining abnormal brain structures indicates that ____

8. The idea that schizophrenia is the result of abnormal brain chemistry is supported largely by two pieces of indirect evidence:
(a) ____
(b) ____

9. Research into psychological factors, such as unhealthy families, has found that ____

After you have carefully studied the preceding section, complete the following exercises.

Concept Check 3

Read the following and write the correct term in the space provided.

1. Franko and Alberto are identical twins. Franko has developed schizophrenia. The probability that Alberto will also develop schizophrenia is almost ______________ percent.
2. Dr. Hansen is conducting research on the viral infection theory. He is likely to find that people born in the winter and spring months, when upper respiratory infections are most common, are ______________ (more/less) likely to suffer from schizophrenia than those born at other times of the year.
3. Derrick hears voices that tell him to be careful because he is being watched by aliens. Kirk believes that he is a famous rock star. Both suffer from the positive symptoms of schizophrenia. Derrick is experiencing ______________, and Kirk is having ______________.
4. Quincy falsely believes that others are plotting against him and are trying to kill him. He believes that these agents are putting poison in the hospital's coffee supply and will attack him if he ever tries to leave the ward. This example illustrates a positive symptom of schizophrenia called ______________________________.
5. Neuroscientists researching changes in the brain structures of normal adolescents and adolescents with schizophrenia took high-resolution brain scans of the participants over a five-year period. Normal teens showed about 1 percent loss of gray matter, while teens with schizophrenia lost more than 5 percent; the amount of loss was directly correlated with clinical symptoms of schizophrenia. More rapid gray matter losses in the temporal lobe were associated with ______________ (positive/negative) symptoms; more rapid losses in the frontal lobes were associated with ______________ (positive/negative) symptoms.
6. Mrs. Perez usually sits passively in a motionless stupor, but if the nurse moves her arms to a new position, she will stay in that position for a very long time. This symptom of catatonic schizophrenia is called ______________.
7. When Darcy was examined by his psychologist, she noted that he displayed some combination of positive and negative symptoms that did not clearly fit the criteria for ______________, ______________, or ______________ types of schizophrenia, so she diagnosed him as having an undifferentiated type of schizophrenia.
8. Mike, who has schizophrenia, had a PET scan while experiencing a schizophrenic hallucination of people shouting at him and telling him to do things. It is very likely that the scan will show activity in the ______________ and ______________ areas of the brain, but not in the ______________, which normally is involved in organizing thought processes.

Graphic Organizer 3

Write the main positive and negative symptoms of schizophrenia in the spaces provided.

Positive Symptoms	Negative Symptoms
1.	1.
2.	2.
3.	3.

Review of Terms and Concepts 3

Use the terms in this list to complete the Matching Exercise, then to help you answer the True/False items correctly.

schizophrenia
positive symptoms
negative symptoms
delusion
delusions of reference
delusions of grandeur
delusions of persecution
delusions of being controlled
hallucination
flat affect
alogia (poverty of speech)
avolition
paranoid type of schizophrenia
catatonic type of schizophrenia
waxy flexibility
disorganized type of schizophrenia (hebephrenic schizophrenia)
undifferentiated type of schizophrenia
ventricles
gray matter
dopamine hypothesis

Matching Exercise

Match the appropriate term with its definition or description.

1. ________________ View that schizophrenia is related to, and may be caused by, excess activity of the neurotransmitter dopamine in the brain.
2. ________________ Psychological disorder in which the ability to function is impaired by severely distorted beliefs, perceptions, and thought processes.
3. ________________ Subtype of schizophrenia that is characterized by the presence of delusions, hallucinations, or both; the person shows virtually no cognitive impairment, disorganized behavior, or negative symptoms; instead, well-organized delusions of persecution or grandeur are operating, and auditory hallucinations are often evident.
4. ________________ Unusual symptom of catatonic schizophrenia in which the person can be molded into any position and will hold that position indefinitely.
5. ________________ Commonly seen negative symptom of schizophrenia in which an individual consistently shows a dramatic reduction in emotional responsiveness and a lack of normal facial expression; few expressive gestures are made, and the person's speech is slow and monotonous, lacking normal vocal inflections.
6. ________________ Falsely held belief that persists despite compelling contradictory evidence.
7. ________________ Delusion in which the person believes that other people are constantly talking about her or that everything that happens is somehow related to her.
8. ________________ False or distorted perception that seems vividly real to the person experiencing it.
9. ________________ Subtype of schizophrenia in which an individual displays some combination of positive and negative symptoms that does not clearly fit the criteria for the paranoid, catatonic, or disorganized type.
10. ________________ Fluid-filled cavities located deep within the brain.

True/False Test

Indicate whether each item is true or false by placing T or F in the space next to each item.

1. ____ In schizophrenia, positive symptoms reflect defects or deficits in normal functioning and include flat affect, alogia, and avolition.

2. ____ Avolition refers to the inability to initiate or persist in even simple forms of goal-directed behaviors, such as dressing, bathing, or engaging in social activities.

3. ____ The catatonic type of schizophrenia is marked by highly disturbed movements or actions and may include bizarre postures or grimaces, waxy flexibility, extremely agitated behavior, complete immobility, echoing words spoken by others, and assuming rigid postures that resist being moved.

4. ____ Alogia, which is also referred to as poverty of speech, is used to describe the symptom in which speech production is greatly reduced.

5. ____ The basic theme of delusions of grandeur is that the person is extremely important, powerful, or wealthy.

6. ____ In schizophrenia, negative symptoms reflect excesses or distortions of normal functioning and include delusions, hallucinations, and disorganized thoughts and behaviors.

7. ____ In delusions of persecution, the basic theme is that others are plotting against or trying to harm the person or someone close to her.

8. ____ The prominent features of the disorganized type of schizophrenia are extremely disorganized behavior, disorganized speech, and flat affect; this subtype is sometimes called hebephrenic schizophrenia.

9. ____ Gray matter is made up of glial cells, neuron cell bodies, and unmyelinated axons that comprise the quarter-inch-thick cerebral cortex.

10. ____ Delusions of being controlled involve the belief that outside forces, such as aliens, the government, or random people, are trying to exert control on the individual.

Check your answers and review any areas of weakness before going on to the next section.

Something to Think About

1. One of the most common misconceptions about mental, or psychological, disorders is that schizophrenia and dissociative identity disorder are the same thing. This myth is fostered by inaccurate portrayals and misinformation in the media. What are the important distinctions between these two disorders, and what would you say to someone who thought they were the same thing?

2. Most people are curious about mental, or psychological, disorders. Students frequently recognize aspects of themselves in the descriptions they read and wonder if they could one day suffer from some form of psychological disorder. What is normal, and what is abnormal? What are the chances of developing symptoms of psychopathology, and what causes psychological disorders?

3. Suppose a friend says that he read somewhere that cigarette smoking causes psychological disorders. Based on what you know from reading the text, how would you respond to this claim?

Check your answers and review any areas of weakness before completing the progress tests.

Progress Test 1

Review the complete chapter (including all boxed inserts), review all your study notes, and then test yourself on the following progress test. Check your answers. If you make a mistake, review your notes, check the appropriate section in the study guide, and, if necessary, go back and read the relevant part of the chapter in your textbook.

1. Phoebe believes that she is the president of the United States and thinks that her indecipherable scribblings are actually top secret memos. Phoebe is most clearly suffering from a(n)
   (a) delusion.
   (b) panic attack.
   (c) hallucination.
   (d) obsession.

2. Shayna has very erratic, unstable relationships, emotions, and self-image. She is extremely impulsive and goes to great lengths to avoid real or imagined abandonment. It is most probable that Shayna has a disorder called
   (a) agoraphobia.
   (b) borderline personality disorder.
   (c) antisocial personality disorder.
   (d) cyclothymic disorder.

3. Dr. Koopman believes that a biological predisposition toward anxiety, a low sense of control over potentially life-threatening events, and an oversensitivity to physical sensations combine to make a person more susceptible to panic disorder. Dr. Koopman adheres to the ________________ of panic disorder.
   (a) triple vulnerabilities model
   (b) biosocial developmental theory
   (c) catastrophic cognitions theory
   (d) abnormal brain structure model

4. Kaila often appears nervous and agitated. She frequently talks in a loud voice and giggles at almost everything she hears. Her behavior is most likely to be diagnosed as a psychological disorder if it
   (a) is not caused by some biological dysfunction.
   (b) is the result of a genetic predisposition.
   (c) represents a significant departure from the prevailing social and cultural norms.
   (d) is caused by drugs or medication.

5. Sidney, a college student, complains that he feels nervous and fearful most of the time but doesn't know why. He worries constantly about everything, and if he manages to deal with one problem, he starts worrying about a dozen others. Sidney most likely suffers from ________________ disorder.
   (a) generalized anxiety
   (b) bipolar
   (c) dissociative
   (d) cyclothymic

6. Imogene, a third-grade teacher, sometimes experiences a pounding heart, rapid breathing, breathlessness, and a choking sensation. She breaks out in a sweat, starts to tremble, and experiences light-headedness and chills. These symptoms last for about 10 minutes and are characteristic of
   (a) post-traumatic stress disorder (PTSD).
   (b) dysthymic disorder.
   (c) cyclothymic disorder.
   (d) panic attack.

7. Paula has been diagnosed with agoraphobia. Her symptoms include which of the following?
   (a) an extreme and irrational fear of experiencing a panic attack in a public place and being unable to escape or get help
   (b) a sudden, rapidly escalating emotional state characterized by extreme euphoria, excitement, physical energy, and rapid thoughts and speech
   (c) partial or total inability to recall important personal information
   (d) all of these symptoms

8. Within the last two years, John has been fired from four different jobs for stealing money and goods from his employers. He feels no remorse and thinks his bosses were stupid for making it so easy to steal from them. John has a long history of problems with the law, which started in his early teens when he was diagnosed with a conduct disorder. It is most likely that John would be diagnosed with
   (a) antisocial personality disorder.
   (b) obsessive–compulsive disorder (OCD).
   (c) paranoid-type schizophrenia.
   (d) dissociative identity disorder (DID).

9. Kevin was working in a building when an explosion occurred; although he escaped with relatively minor injuries, he can't stop thinking about all the dead and seriously injured people he saw. He has frequent nightmares about the event and feels guilty that he survived when many of his co-workers did not. Kevin's symptoms are indicative of
   (a) dissociative fugue.
   (b) dysthymic disorder.
   (c) cyclothymic disorder.
   (d) post-traumatic stress disorder (PTSD).

10. Mrs. Landon has been diagnosed as suffering from major depression. Which of the following symptoms is she most likely to be experiencing?
   (a) feelings of guilt, worthlessness, inadequacy, emptiness, and hopelessness
   (b) awkward and slower-than-usual speech, movement, and gestures and frequent crying spells for no apparent reason
   (c) dull and sluggish thought processes and problems concentrating
   (d) all of these symptoms

11. Karla suffers from a chronic, low-grade depression characterized by many of the symptoms of major depression but less intense; these problems started many years ago when both her parents were killed in a car accident. Karla is likely to be diagnosed as suffering from
   (a) dysthymic disorder.
   (b) agoraphobia.
   (c) cyclothymic disorder.
   (d) dissociative amnesia.

12. About six months ago, 15-year-old Kirsten went on a drastic weight-loss diet that caused her to drop from 115 to 85 pounds. Although she is dangerously underweight and undernourished, she continues to think she looks fat. Kirsten probably suffers from
   (a) *ataque de nervios*.
   (b) anorexia nervosa.
   (c) bulimia nervosa.
   (d) cyclothymic disorder.

13. Twenty-five-year-old Daisuke suffers from a disorder, similar to social phobia, called *taijin kyofusho*. In addition to suffering extreme social anxiety and the need to avoid social situations, Daisuke is likely
   (a) to have a preoccupation with imagined diseases based on his misinterpretation of bodily symptoms or function.
   (b) to be very concerned with being embarrassed in public.
   (c) to worry about being overcome with an irresistible urge to set fire to people and things.
   (d) to fear that his appearance or smell, facial expressions, or body language will offend, insult, or embarrass others.

14. According to Critical Thinking (Are People with Mental Illness as Violent as the Media Portray Them?), which of the following is true?
   (a) People with psychological disorders are generally portrayed with great accuracy in the media.
   (b) Twenty percent of "normal" television characters are murderers, but only 5 percent of "mentally ill" characters are killers.
   (c) The incidence of violent behavior among current or former mental patients is grossly exaggerated in media portrayals.
   (d) Seventy percent of "normal" television characters are violent, but only 40 percent of television characters labeled mentally ill are violent.

15. According to Critical Thinking (Does Smoking Cause Depression and Other Psychological Disorders?), which of the following is true?
   (a) Smoking cigarettes is a major cause of mental illness and psychological disorders.
   (b) Mental illness is a major cause of cigarette smoking behavior in both adolescents and adults.
   (c) Although there is a positive correlation between cigarette smoking and the prevalence of mental illness, the exact causal connection has not been clearly established.
   (d) One of the main active ingredients in cigarettes, nicotine, has no known psychoactive properties, nor does it have any effect on brain structures or on the release of various neurotransmitters.

Progress Test 2

After you have checked your understanding of the material in Progress Test 1 and have done a complete chapter review with special focus on any areas of weakness, you are ready to assess your knowledge on Progress Test 2. Check your answers. If you make a mistake, review your notes, the relevant section of the study guide, and, if necessary, the appropriate part of your textbook.

1. Dr. Moretti believes that schizophrenia is the result of abnormal brain chemistry. Her views are consistent with the
   (a) viral infection theory.
   (b) dopamine hypothesis.
   (c) genetic predisposition theory.
   (d) triple vulnerabilities model.

2. Researchers scan the brains of normal adolescents and adolescents with early-onset schizophrenia. If their results are consistent with the findings of other neuroscientists (Focus on Neuroscience: Schizophrenia: A Wildfire in the Brain), they are likely to discover that
   (a) teenagers with schizophrenia have a severe loss of gray matter (5 percent), compared with normal teens (1 percent).
   (b) the amount of gray matter loss is directly correlated with patients' clinical symptoms; the more gray matter lost the greater the increase in psychotic symptoms.
   (c) more rapid loss of gray matter in the temporal lobes is associated with positive symptoms of schizophrenia, and more rapid loss of gray matter in the frontal lobes is correlated with negative symptoms of schizophrenia.
   (d) all of these statements are true.

3. Dr. Crewe believes that people with panic disorder are not only oversensitive to physical sensations, they also tend to think their experience is a disastrous calamity. This misinterpretation only adds to the problem by causing even more physiological arousal. Eventually, they become conditioned to respond with fear to the physical symptoms of arousal, and repeated panic attacks lead to panic disorder. Dr. Crewe's explanation is most consistent with the ________________ of panic disorder.
   (a) biosocial developmental theory
   (b) abnormal brain structure theory
   (c) catastrophic cognitions theory
   (d) genetic predisposition explanation

4. Nima suffers from a type of schizophrenia that is characterized by hallucinations and delusions of grandeur, but she shows virtually no cognitive impairment, disorganized behavior, or negative symptoms. Nima suffers from ________________-type schizophrenia.
   (a) paranoid
   (b) catatonic
   (c) disorganized
   (d) undifferentiated

5. Tara, a young married woman, has wandered from her home to a distant city where she has completely forgotten her family and her identity. This example illustrates
   (a) undifferentiated-type schizophrenia.
   (b) dissociative fugue.
   (c) disorganized-type schizophrenia.
   (d) dissociative amnesia.

6. Maury repeatedly checks to see if the stove is turned off and frequently turns around on his way to work to return home to double-check the stove. This is an example of a(n)
   (a) delusion.
   (b) obsession.
   (c) hallucination.
   (d) compulsion.

7. Otis turned down a very high-paying job because it meant he would have to fly to the head office in Tokyo two or three times a year. He doesn't know why, but the thought of flying absolutely terrifies him. Otis may be suffering from
   (a) undifferentiated-type schizophrenia.
   (b) a phobia.
   (c) bipolar disorder.
   (d) post-traumatic stress disorder (PTSD).

8. Every semester just before midterm exams, Lilly gets very anxious and worries about how she is going to do. To reduce her apprehension, she studies very hard. Lilly suffers from
   (a) anxiety disorder.
   (b) panic disorder.
   (c) obsessive–compulsive disorder (OCD).
   (d) none of these disorders; her symptoms are quite normal.

9. Jessica rarely leaves her home. She doesn't go shopping because she is frightened of having a panic attack and getting lost or trapped in a crowd. Jessica has symptoms that indicate she may have
   (a) agoraphobia.
   (b) cyclothymic disorder.
   (c) post-traumatic stress disorder (PTSD).
   (d) seasonal affective disorder (SAD).

10. Yvette usually stands motionless and will echo words just spoken to her. She resists directions from others and sometimes assumes a rigid posture to prevent people from moving her. These symptoms suggest that Yvette has a type of ________________ called ________________ type.
   (a) schizophrenia; catatonic
   (b) mood disorder; cyclothymic
   (c) schizophrenia; disorganized
   (d) mood disorder; dysthymic

11. Brandy's doctor prescribed lithium for her symptoms; as long as she keeps taking the medication, she feels fine. It is very likely that Brandy suffers from
   (a) schizophrenia.
   (b) generalized anxiety disorder (GAD).
   (c) bipolar disorder.
   (d) dissociative identity disorder (DID).

12. Regardless of the situation, Philip responds in an emotionally flat manner and consistently shows greatly reduced emotional responsiveness. His speech is slow and monotonous, and he is unable to initiate even simple forms of goal-directed behavior, such as dressing, bathing, or engaging in social activities. Philip is suffering from ________________, and his symptoms are ________________.
   (a) schizophrenia; positive
   (b) anxiety disorder; positive
   (c) schizophrenia; negative
   (d) anxiety disorder; negative

13. Perry has dropped out of college because of the extreme distress that being in social situations causes him. He is unemployed because he is unable to bring himself to go for a job interview. Perry is suffering from
    (a) disorganized-type schizophrenia.
    (b) a dissociative disorder.
    (c) a generalized anxiety disorder (GAD).
    (d) social phobia (social anxiety disorder).

14. Erin has been diagnosed with bulimia nervosa. The main symptoms of her eating disorder are
    (a) binges of extreme overeating and purging by self-induced vomiting and misuse of laxatives or enemas to purge the excessive food and prevent weight gain.
    (b) an increase in brain activity of the neurotransmitter serotonin.
    (c) being 15 to 20 percent below the ideal body weight and having an irrational fear of gaining weight.
    (d) severe food restriction, maladaptive dieting, and the development of lanugo.

15. Akihiro is a young Japanese male who lives with his parents and has been diagnosed with a culture-specific disorder called *hikkomori*. According to Culture and Human Behavior (Culture-Bound Syndromes), his symptoms are likely to include
    (a) an exaggerated concern about and preoccupation with minor or imagined defects in appearance.
    (b) extreme social anxiety because of fear that his appearance or smell, facial expression, or body language will offend, insult, or embarrass other people.
    (c) extreme social withdrawal, a preoccupation with video games and Internet surfing, an inability to work or attend school, and virtually no social interactions with his family or the outside world.
    (d) an extreme and irrational fear of experiencing a panic attack in a public situation and being unable to escape or get help.

Progress Test 3

After you have checked your understanding of the material in Progress Tests 1 and 2, and have done a complete chapter review with special focus on any areas of weakness, you are ready to further assess your knowledge with Progress Test 3. Check your answers. If you make a mistake, review your notes, the appropriate parts of the study guide, and, if necessary, the relevant sections of your textbook.

1. Wendell repeatedly steals small items that he doesn't need and could easily pay for if he wanted to. Harman frequently sets fire to property for no obvious reason other than the pleasure he derives from seeing buildings on fire. According to Table 13.1 (Some Key Diagnostic Categories in DSM-IV-TR), Wendell suffers from ________________, whereas Harman suffers from a disorder called ________________.
    (a) kleptomania; pyromania
    (b) Tourette's disorder; hypochondriasis
    (c) autistic disorder; fetishism
    (d) agoraphobia; pyrophobia

2. Fear of having a panic attack in a public situation is to ________________ as an extreme and irrational fear of being embarrassed, judged, or scrutinized by others in social situations is to ________________.
    (a) social phobia (social anxiety disorder); agoraphobia
    (b) bibliophobia; phonophobia
    (c) agoraphobia; social phobia
    (d) phobophobia; ergophobia

3. Shayne suffers from post-traumatic stress disorder (PTSD). If he is similar to most people who have this disorder, he is likely to exhibit which of the following symptoms?
    (a) frequent, intrusive recollections of a traumatic event, numbing of emotional responsiveness, and avoidance of particular situations
    (b) a preoccupation with imagined diseases based on his misinterpretation of bodily symptoms or functions.
    (c) repetitive behaviors or mental acts that are performed to prevent or reduce anxiety
    (d) the urge to set fires for pleasure, gratification, or relief of tension

4. Mandy is a 45-year-old administrative assistant. Based on the National Comorbidity Survey Replication (NCS-R), the chance that Mandy may have experienced the symptoms of a psychological disorder at some point in her life is about ________________ percent.
    (a) 10
    (b) 46
    (c) 80
    (d) 26

5. Dr. Burstein explains the development of phobias in terms of basic learning principles. Which of the following are likely to be included in his explanation?
   (a) classical conditioning
   (b) operant conditioning
   (c) observational learning
   (d) All of these types of learning may be involved in his explanation.

6. After several weeks of feeling very apathetic and dissatisfied with his life, Elmiro has suddenly become extremely euphoric and full of energy. He talks so rapidly that he is hard to understand, he sleeps very little, and he has gone on a number of very expensive shopping sprees. He gets very irritated when anyone tells him to take it easy and slow down. Elmiro is exhibiting all the signs of
   (a) obsessive–compulsive disorder (OCD).
   (b) catatonic schizophrenia.
   (c) dissociative identity disorder (DID).
   (d) bipolar disorder.

7. Lucille suffers from dissociative identity disorder (DID) and is being treated by a therapist who specializes in dissociative disorders. Her therapist believes that if she is like most people diagnosed with this disorder, she is likely to have experienced
   (a) extreme physical or sexual abuse in childhood.
   (b) episodes when she believed she was the reincarnation of some famous and powerful person.
   (c) exposure to a viral infection during prenatal development or early infancy.
   (d) excess dopamine in her brain during childhood.

8. When Christy was young, she was badly scratched and bitten by a cat she tried to pet. She now has an extreme fear of all cats and has learned to reduce her anxiety by avoiding cats whenever possible. Christy's phobia and avoidance behavior can best be explained by
   (a) the dopamine hypothesis.
   (b) learning theory, specifically classical and operant conditioning.
   (c) the viral infection theory.
   (d) the catatonic hypothesis.

9. Dr. Arnkoff and his colleagues found that people born in the winter and spring months were more likely to suffer from schizophrenia than those born at other times of the year. This correlational research provides support for the ________________ and the influence of ________________ factors.
   (a) viral infection theory; environmental
   (b) dopamine hypothesis; genetic
   (c) paternal age hypothesis; environmental
   (d) unhealthy families theory; genetic

10. Vera has been diagnosed with cyclothymic disorder. Her symptoms are likely to include
   (a) moderate but frequent mood swings for two years or longer.
   (b) chronic low-grade feelings of depression that produce subjective discomfort but do not seriously impair her ability to function.
   (c) partial or total inability to recall important personal information.
   (d) irrational fears of a specific object or situation.

11. Nester's sense of self-esteem is wildly inflated, and he exudes supreme self-confidence. He has delusional, grandiose plans for obtaining wealth, power, and fame and is engaged in a frenzy of goal-directed activities that could cost thousands of dollars. This is an example of a(n)
   (a) manic episode.
   (b) obsession.
   (c) social phobia (social anxiety disorder).
   (d) hallucination.

12. Deidre suffers from frequent and unexpected panic attacks. Despite her apprehension about these episodes, Deidre functions fairly well in her job and has a relatively normal social life. Deidre is likely to be diagnosed with
   (a) panic disorder.
   (b) social phobia (social anxiety disorder).
   (c) bipolar disorder.
   (d) dissociative fugue.

13. Scott repeatedly thinks that he might get a gun and kill all his colleagues at work. These thoughts are very disturbing, intrusive, and uncontrollable and cause Scott great distress and anxiety. Scott is experiencing a(n)
   (a) delusion.
   (b) obsession.
   (c) hallucination.
   (d) compulsion.

14. Konrad has experienced numerous psychiatric and physical symptoms and memory loss, and he has a chaotic personal history. During a session with his therapist, Konrad suddenly began speaking in a very childlike voice and claimed that his name was Arnold and that he was only 10 years old. A short time later he reverted to

his normal adult voice and claimed to have no recollection of the incident. Konrad is likely to be diagnosed as suffering from

(a) paranoid-type schizophrenia.
(b) dissociative identity disorder (DID).
(c) paranoid personality disorder.
(d) post-traumatic stress disorder.

15. According to Enhancing Well-Being with Psychology (Understanding and Helping to Prevent Suicide), the best way to help prevent someone from committing suicide is to
    (a) use some well-known platitudes like "every cloud has a silver lining."
    (b) not let the person talk too much about what is bothering him because it will only make him more depressed.
    (c) suggest that seeking professional help would be a total waste of time and money in the present situation.
    (d) ask the person to delay his decision and encourage him to seek professional help.

Answers

Introduction: Understanding Psychological Disorders

1. *Psychopathology is* the scientific study of the origins, symptoms, and development of psychological disorders.
2. *A psychological, or mental, disorder can be defined as* a pattern of behavioral and psychological symptoms that causes significant personal distress, impairs the ability to function in one or more important areas of daily life, or both. These symptoms must represent a serious departure from prevailing social and cultural norms.
3. *DSM-IV-TR stands for* the *Diagnostic and Statistical Manual of Mental Disorders,* Fourth Edition, Text Revision; it was published by the American Psychiatric Association in 2000 and represents the consensus of a wide range of mental health professionals and organizations. *This manual describes* more than 300 specific psychological disorders (including the symptoms, the exact criteria that must be met to make a diagnosis, and the typical course for each psychological disorder). *It provides mental health professionals with* a common language for labeling psychological disorders and comprehensive guidelines for diagnosing psychological disorders. *DSM-IV-TR has been criticized for (a)* including some conditions that are too "normal" to be considered psychological disorders; *(b)* using arbitrary cutoffs to draw the line between people with and without a particular disorder; *(c)* gender bias; and *(d)* insufficient sensitivity to cultural diversity
4. *The National Comorbidity Survey Replication (NCS-R) found that one out of four respondents (26 percent)* reported experiencing the symptoms of a psychological disorder during the previous year. *There was also a high degree of comorbidity, which means that* people diagnosed with one disorder are also frequently diagnosed with another disorder as well. *In terms of lifetime prevalence of experiencing symptoms of a psychological disorder, the NCS-R found that* almost one out of two adults (46 percent) had experienced symptoms at some point thus far in their life. *The lifetime prevalence and names of the four most commonly reported categories of psychological disorders are as follows:* anxiety disorders, 29 percent; mood disorders, 21 percent; impulse control disorders, 25 percent; substance abuse disorders, 15 percent. *The NCS-R found that most people with symptoms of a psychological disorder (59 percent)* received no treatment during the past year. However, it seems that most people weather the symptoms without becoming completely debilitated.

Anxiety Disorders

1. *Anxiety is defined as* an unpleasant emotional state characterized by physical arousal and feelings of tension, apprehension, and worry that often hits during personal crises and everyday conflicts. *It is often adaptive and normal because* it puts you on physical and mental alert and helps you focus attention on the threatening situation.
2. *In anxiety disorders, the anxiety is* maladaptive, disrupting everyday activities, moods, and thought processes.
3. *The three features that distinguish normal anxiety from pathological anxiety are (a)* Pathological anxiety is irrational (it is provoked by perceived threats that are exaggerated or nonexistent, and the anxiety response is out of proportion to the actual importance of the situation). *(b)* Pathological anxiety is uncontrollable (the person can't shut off the alarm reaction, even when he or she knows it's unrealistic). *(c)* Pathological anxiety is disruptive (it interferes with relationships, job or academic performance, or everyday activities).
4. *Generalized anxiety disorder (GAD) is characterized by* excessive, global, chronic, and

persistent symptoms of anxiety (sometimes called free-floating anxiety). *Its cause is thought to involve* environmental, psychological, and genetic as well as other biological factors (e.g., a brain "wired" for anxiety, problematic relationships, and stressful experiences).

5. *A panic attack is* a sudden episode of extreme anxiety that rapidly escalates in intensity. *The most common symptoms are* a pounding heart, rapid breathing, breathlessness, and a choking sensation, often accompanied by sweating, trembling, light-headedness, chills, or hot flashes.
6. *A panic disorder is* an anxiety disorder in which the person experiences frequent and unexpected panic attacks. *Some panic disorder sufferers go on to develop* agoraphobia, *which is* a fear of having a panic attack in a place from which escape is difficult or impossible. *The triple vulnerabilities model states* that a biological predisposition toward anxiety, a low sense of control over potentially life-threatening events, and an oversensitivity to physical sensations combine to make a person susceptible to panic. *The catastrophic cognitions theory proposes* that not only are people oversensitive to physical sensations, they also tend to catastrophize the meaning of their experience.
7. *A phobia is* a persistent or irrational fear of something, usually a specific object, situation, or activity; as long as the phobia does not interfere with the ability to function in daily life, it would not be considered a psychological disorder. *A specific phobia is* characterized by an excessive, intense, and irrational fear of a specific object or situation that interferes with the ability to function in daily life. *Prevalence rates suggest that about* 13 percent of the population experience a specific phobia at some time in their lives, and more than twice as many women as men suffer from specific phobia. *A social phobia (or social anxiety disorder) is* an anxiety disorder involving the extreme and irrational fear of being embarrassed, judged, or scrutinized by others in social situations. *In terms of prevalence, social phobia is* one of the most common psychological disorders and is more prevalent among women than men. *A Japanese variation,* taijin kyofusho, *differs in that* the person is afraid of embarrassing, insulting, or offending other people.
8. *Some phobias involve various forms of learning, such as* classical conditioning (the feared object is the conditioned stimulus, and the learned fear is the conditioned response, which can generalize to other similar stimuli); operant conditioning, which can also be involved in the avoidance behavior that characterizes phobias (the conditioned response of avoiding the feared object is negatively reinforced by the relief from anxiety and fear that the behavior brings about); observational learning (people can learn to be phobic of certain objects or situations by observing the fearful reactions of someone else who acts as a model in the situation or through seeing media accounts of disasters and catastrophes); and biological preparedness (humans are predisposed through our evolutionary history to acquire fears of certain animals or situations).

Anxiety Disorders: Post-Traumatic Stress Disorder and Obsessive-Compulsive Disorder

1. *Post-traumatic stress disorder (PTSD) is* a long-lasting anxiety disorder in which chronic and persistent symptoms of anxiety develop in response to an extreme physical or psychological trauma (extreme traumas are events that produce intense feelings of horror and helplessness, such as a serious physical injury or threat of injury to yourself or to loved ones). *It is estimated that in any given year more than* 5 million American adults experience PTSD; more than twice as many women as men experience PTSD, and children can also be affected.
2. *The three core symptoms that characterize PTSD are (a)* The person frequently recalls the event, replaying it in his or her mind (it is often unwanted or intrusive and interferes with normal thought processes). *(b)* The person avoids stimuli or situations that tend to trigger memories of the experience and undergoes a general numbing of emotional responsiveness. *(c)* The person experiences the increased physical arousal associated with anxiety (he or she may be easily startled, experience sleep disturbances, have problems concentrating and remembering, and be prone to irritability or angry outbursts).
3. *Factors that influence the likelihood of developing post-traumatic stress disorder are (a)* People with a personal or family history of psychological disorders are more likely to develop PTSD when exposed to extreme trauma. *(b)* The magnitude of the trauma plays an important role—more extreme stressors are more likely to produce PTSD. *(c)* When people undergo multiple traumas, the incidence of PTSD can be quite high.

4. *Obsessive–compulsive disorder (OCD) is* an anxiety disorder in which the symptoms of anxiety are triggered by intrusive, repetitive thoughts and urges to perform certain actions. *Obsessions are* repeated, intrusive, and uncontrollable irrational thoughts or mental images that cause extreme anxiety and distress (they have little or no basis in reality and are often extremely far-fetched). *Compulsions are* repetitive behaviors that are performed to prevent or reduce anxiety and are typically ritual behaviors (overtly physical or covertly mental) that must be carried out in a certain pattern or sequence.
5. *People with obsessive–compulsive disorder commonly experience* both obsessions and compulsions, which are often linked in some way, even if the behaviors bear little logical relationship to the feared consequences (in all cases, people with obsessive–compulsive disorder feel that something terrible will happen if the compulsive action is left undone).
6. *Two biological factors that seem to be involved in obsessive–compulsive disorder are* a deficiency in the neurotransmitters norepinephrine and serotonin (drugs that increase the availability of these substances in the brain decrease symptoms), and dysfunctions in specific brain areas, such as those involved in the fight-or-flight response, the frontal lobes (which play a key role in our ability to think and plan ahead), or the caudate nucleus (which is involved in regulating movements).

Concept Check 1

1. four; 26
2. normal
3. obsessive–compulsive
4. generalized anxiety
5. social phobia (social anxiety disorder)
6. post-traumatic stress
7. panic attacks
8. classical; operant; observational
9. norepinephrine; serotonin; fight-or-flight; frontal; caudate nucleus

Graphic Organizer 1

Generalized Anxiety Disorder
Persistent, chronic, unreasonable worry and anxiety, characterized by general symptoms of anxiety, including persistent physical arousal.

Panic Disorder
Frequent and unexpected panic attacks, with no specific or identifiable trigger, and for some sufferers, agoraphobia (fear of having a panic attack in a public or inescapable situation).

Phobias
A strong or irrational fear of something, usually a specific object, situation, or activity that does not necessarily interfere with the ability to function in daily life. Phobias include specific phobia and social phobia.

Post-Traumatic Stress Disorder
Anxiety triggered by memories of an extreme physical or psychological traumatic experience.

Obsessive–Compulsive Disorder
Anxiety caused by uncontrollable, persistent, recurring, and intrusive thoughts (obsessions) and/or urges to perform certain actions (compulsions).

Matching Exercise 1

1. psychopathology
2. DSM-IV-TR
3. obsessive–compulsive disorder (OCD)
4. anxiety
5. phobia
6. post-traumatic stress disorder (PTSD)
7. agoraphobia
8. specific phobia
9. *taijin kyofusho*
10. catastrophic cognitions theory of panic disorder
11. triple vulnerabilities model of panic disorder

True/False Test 1

1. F	5. F	8. T
2. T	6. T	9. T
3. T	7. T	10. T
4. T		

Mood Disorders: Emotions Gone Awry

1. *Mood disorders (also called affective disorders) are* a category of psychological disorders in which significant and persistent disruptions in mood or emotions cause impaired cognitive, behavioral, and physical functioning.
2. *Major depression is characterized by* extreme and persistent feelings of despondency, worthlessness, and hopelessness, causing impaired emotional, cognitive, behavioral, and physical functioning.

3. *Seasonal affective disorder is a mood disorder in which* episodes of depression typically occur during the fall and winter and subside during the spring and summer.
4. *Dysthymic disorder* is a mood disorder involving chronic, low-grade feelings of depression that produce subjective discomfort but do not seriously impair the ability to function.
5. *Major depression is called "the common cold" of psychological disorders because* it is among the most prevalent disorders, with 7 percent of Americans affected in any given year, and about 15 percent affected at some point in their lives. Women are twice as likely as men to be diagnosed with depression, relapse is common, and with each recurrence symptoms get worse and time between episodes decreases.
6. *Bipolar disorder is defined as* a mood disorder involving periods of incapacitating depression alternating with periods of extreme euphoria and excitement (formerly called manic depression). *A manic episode is a* sudden, rapidly escalating emotional state characterized by extreme euphoria, excitement, physical energy, and rapid thoughts and speech.
7. *Cyclothymic disorder is a mood disorder characterized by* moderate but frequent mood swings that are not severe enough to qualify as bipolar disorder or major depression.
8. *The onset of bipolar disorder typically occurs* in a person's early 20s. This disorder is far less common than major depression, there are no gender differences, it is rarely diagnosed in children, and the lifetime risk of developing bipolar disorder is about 1 percent.
9. *Multiple factors appear to be involved in the development of mood disorders. These include* genetic predispositions, stress, especially traumatic stressful life events, and disruptions in brain chemistry (the neurotransmitters serotonin and norepinephrine have been implicated in depression, and glutamate may be involved in bipolar disorder).

Eating Disorders: Anorexia and Bulimia

1. *Eating disorders involve* serious and maladaptive disturbances in eating behavior and can include extreme reduction of food intake, severe bouts of overeating, and obsessive concerns about body shape and weight.
2. *Anorexia nervosa is an eating disorder characterized by* excessive weight loss, an irrational fear of gaining weight, and distorted body self-perception.
3. *Bulimia nervosa is an eating disorder characterized by* binges of extreme overeating followed by self-induced vomiting and misuse of laxatives or enemas to purge excessive food and prevent weight gain. *Bulimia shares many of the characteristics of anorexia, with the main differences being that* people with bulimia stay within a normal weight range, or may be slightly overweight, and they usually recognize that they have an eating disorder.
4. *The main factors implicated in the development of eating disorders are* decreases in brain activity of serotonin, disrupted brain chemistry (which also contributes to the fact that eating disorders co-occur with other psychiatric disorders), family interaction patterns, and contemporary Western cultural attitudes about thinness and dieting (especially with anorexia) (Note that researchers are now looking at whether eating disorders may be the cause of disruptions in brain chemistry.)

Personality Disorders: Maladaptive Traits

1. *Personality disorder is defined as* inflexible, maladaptive patterns of thought, emotions, behavior, and interpersonal functioning that are stable over time and across situations and deviate from the expectations of the individual's culture (personality disorders usually become evident during adolescence or early adulthood and are evident in about 10 percent of the population). *DSM-IV-TR identified ten distinct personality disorders which are organized into three basic clusters,* the odd, eccentric cluster; the dramatic, emotional, erratic cluster; and the anxious, fearful cluster.
2. *DSM-5 (scheduled for publication in 2013) has proposed an approach to classifying personality disorders that involves assessing people on two dimensions: (a)* a severity scale, which assesses the degree of impairment in personality functioning, and *(b)* a trait scale, which rates the person on pathological personality traits, such as the tendency to be antagonistic, emotionally unstable, impulsive, or manipulative. *DSM-5 has also proposed reducing the number of personality disorders from ten to six:* antisocial, avoidant, borderline, narcissistic, obsessive-compulsive, and schizotypal.
3. *The antisocial personality disorder is characterized by* a pervasive pattern of disregarding and

violating the rights of others (such individuals are often referred to as psychopaths or sociopaths). *It is estimated that approximately* 1 to 4 percent of the population display these characteristics, with men far outnumbering women.

4. *Borderline personality disorder (BPD) is characterized by* instability of interpersonal relationships, self-image, and emotions, and marked impulsivity. *In terms of prevalence, BPD is the* most severe of the personality disorders and the most commonly diagnosed—6 percent of the population—and has the highest prevalence among women, people in lower income groups, and Native American men, with the lowest incidence among women of Asian decent. *It is caused by* multiple factors, such as disruptions in attachment relationships in early childhood, dysfunctional family relationships, *and, according to the biosocial developmental theory,* a unique combination of biological, psychological, and environmental factors (innate biological temperament combined with faulty parenting, modeling and reinforcing patterns of inappropriate intense emotional displays, or possible abuse and neglect).

The Dissociative Disorders: Fragmentation of the Self

1. *The dissociative experience is* a break or disruption in consciousness during which awareness, memory, and personal identity become separated or divided.
2. *Dissociative disorders are* a category of psychological disorders in which extreme and frequent disruptions of awareness, memory, and personal identity impair the ability to function.
3. *Dissociative amnesia is a disorder involving* the partial or total inability to recall important personal information that is not due to a medical condition. *Dissociative fugue is* a disorder involving sudden and unexpected travel away from home, extensive amnesia, and identity confusion.
4. *Dissociative identity disorder (DID) involves* extensive memory disruptions along with the presence of two or more distinct identities, or "personalities" (alters or alter egos); formerly called *multiple personality disorder.*
5. *According to one theory, DID is caused by* trauma in childhood and represents an extreme form of coping through dissociation. Although the dissociative coping theory is accepted by many therapists, it is difficult to test empirically. Another problem is that just the opposite effect occurs to most trauma victims. The scientific debate about the validity of the dissociative disorders is likely to continue.

Concept Check 2

1. seasonal affective
2. genetic
3. biosocial developmental
4. cyclothymic
5. dissociative fugue
6. dissociative experiences
7. dissociative amnesia
8. antisocial; borderline
9. hikkomori
10. anorexia nervosa

Graphic Organizer 2

Major Depression

1. Loss of interest or pleasure in almost all activities
2. Despondent mood, feelings of emptiness or worthlessness, or excessive guilt
3. Preoccupation with death or suicidal thoughts
4. Difficulty sleeping or excessive sleeping
5. Diminished ability to think, concentrate, or make decisions, and often accompanied by the physical symptoms of anxiety
6. Diminished appetite and significant weight loss or excessive eating and weight gain

Bipolar Disorder

1. One or more manic episodes characterized by euphoria, high energy, grandiose ideas, flight of ideas, inappropriate self-confidence, and decreased need for sleep
2. Usually also has one or more episodes of major depression
3. May alternate rapidly between symptoms of mania and major depression

Dysthymic Disorder

1. Chronic, low-grade depressed feelings that are not severe enough to qualify as major depression

Cyclothymic Disorder

1. Moderate, recurring, up-and-down mood swings that are not severe enough to qualify as major depression or bipolar disorder

Matching Exercise 2

1. antisocial personality disorder
2. bipolar disorder
3. seasonal affective disorder (SAD)
4. major depression
5. manic episode
6. dissociative experience
7. personality disorder
8. personality
9. dissociative identity disorder (DID)
10. lithium
11. alters (alter egos)
12. conduct disorder
13. eating disorder
14. lanugo

True/False Test 2

1. T	6. T	11. T
2. F	7. F	12. F
3. F	8. T	13. F
4. F	9. T	14. T
5. T	10. T	

Schizophrenia: A Different Reality

1. *Schizophrenia is a psychological disorder that involves* severely distorted beliefs, perceptions, and thought processes that impair an individual's ability to function. *In terms of prevalence, about* 1 percent of the American population will experience at least one episode at some point in life.
2. *Positive symptoms include* delusions (false beliefs that persist despite compelling contradictory evidence—delusions of reference, grandeur, persecution, or of being controlled), hallucinations (false perceptions that seem vividly real to the person experiencing them), and severely disorganized thought processes, speech, and behavior. *Negative symptoms consist of* marked deficits or decreases in behavioral or emotional functioning, and include flat affect, alogia, and avolition.
3. *The three basic subtypes of schizophrenia are (a)* paranoid type (presence of delusions—of persecution or grandeur—hallucinations, or both, but no cognitive impairment, disorganized behavior, or negative symptoms); *(b)* catatonic type (highly disturbed movements or actions, such as bizarre postures or grimaces, extremely agitated behavior, complete immobility, echoing words spoken by others or imitating their movements); and *(c)* disorganized type (extremely disorganized behavior, disorganized speech, flat affect, and sometimes disorganized delusions and hallucinations; formerly called hebephrenic schizophrenia). *A fourth label,* undifferentiated, *is used to describe individuals who* display some combination of positive and negative symptoms but who do not fit the criteria for the other three types.
4. *Evidence that genetic factors are involved in the development of schizophrenia comes from* family, twin, adoption, and gene studies, but studies of identical twins demonstrate that nongenetic factors play at least an equal role.
5. *Research on paternal age and the risk of schizophrenia indicates that* the risk of schizophrenia is higher in the offspring of older fathers, but older paternal age failed to account for the majority (75%) of cases of schizophrenia in these studies.
6. *One environmental factor implicated in the development of schizophrenia is* exposure to an influenza virus or other viral infection during prenatal development or shortly after birth.
7. *Neurological evidence from research examining abnormal brain structures indicates that* about half the people with schizophrenia show some type of brain structure abnormality, such as enlargement of the fluid-filled ventricles, loss of gray matter in the brain, and lower overall volume of the brain. Note, however, that the evidence is correlational and does not indicate causality. Research continues in this area to determine whether differences in brain structure are the cause or consequence of schizophrenia (or to psychological disorders in general).
8. *The idea that schizophrenia is the result of abnormal brain chemistry is supported largely by two pieces of indirect evidence: (a)* Antipsychotic drugs that reduce or block dopamine activity in the brain reduce schizophrenic symptoms in many people. *(b)* Drugs such as amphetamines or cocaine enhance dopamine activity in the brain (use of these drugs can produce schizophrenia-like symptoms in normal adults or increase symptoms in people who already suffer from schizophrenia). This indirect evidence provides some support for the

dopamine hypothesis. However, a new theory suggests that some parts of the brain (limbic system) may have too much dopamine and other parts (cortex) may have too little. The exact role this neurotransmitter plays in schizophrenia is not clear.

9. *Research into psychological factors, such as unhealthy families, has found that* although there is a complex interaction of genetic and environmental factors involved in the development of schizophrenia, adopted children who are genetically at risk for the disorder benefit from being raised in a healthy psychological environment, and conversely, a psychologically unhealthy family environment can act as a catalyst for the onset of schizophrenia in individuals, especially for those with a genetic history of schizophrenia.

Concept Check 3

1. 50
2. more
3. hallucinations; delusions
4. delusions of persecution
5. positive; negative
6. waxy flexibility
7. paranoid, catatonic; disorganized
8. left auditory; left visual; frontal lobe

Graphic Organizer 3

Positive Symptoms

1. delusions
2. hallucinations
3. disorganized thoughts and behavior

Negative Symptoms

1. flat effect
2. alogia (poverty of speech)
3. avolition

Matching Exercise 3

1. dopamine hypothesis
2. schizophrenia
3. paranoid type of schizophrenia
4. waxy flexibility
5. flat affect (affective flattening)
6. delusion
7. delusions of reference
8. hallucination
9. undifferentiated type of schizophrenia
10. ventricles

True/False Test 3

1. F	4. T	7. T	10. T
2. T	5. T	8. T	
3. T	6. F	9. T	

Something to Think About

1. Dissociative identity disorder (DID), formerly called multiple personality disorder, involves extensive memory disruptions for personal information along with the presence of two or more distinct identities or personalities. Typically, each personality has its own name and each will be experienced as if it has its own personal history and self-image. These alternate personalities, or alters, may be of widely varying ages and of different genders. Typically, the primary personality is unaware of the existence of the alternate personalities. However, the alters may have knowledge of each other's existence and share memories. Sometimes, the experiences of one alter are accessible to another alter but not vice versa. From this description of the disorder, it is clear that symptoms of amnesia and memory problems are a central part of DID. In addition, people with DID have numerous psychiatric and physical symptoms, as well as a chaotic personal history.

   Contrast DID with a description of schizophrenia and the differences between the two disorders become apparent. Schizophrenia is a psychological disorder that involves severely distorted beliefs, perceptions, and thought processes. During a schizophrenic episode, people lose their grip on reality. The positive symptoms of schizophrenia reflect an excess or distortion of normal functioning and include hallucinations, delusions, and severely disorganized thought processes, speech, and behavior. The negative symptoms reflect a restriction or reduction of normal functioning and include flat affect, alogia (poverty of speech), and avolition, or the inability to initiate or persist in even simple forms of goal-directed behavior. There are three different subtypes of schizophrenia: paranoid, catatonic, and disorganized, plus an undifferentiated type, which does not fit any single category. In addition, as noted in the text, the prevalence, course, and cause of schizophrenia are markedly different from those of DID.

2. The first thing to note is that the line that divides normal and abnormal behavior is not clearly defined. In addition, it is affected by

the social and cultural context in which the behavior occurs. Psychopathology is the scientific study of the origins, symptoms, and development of psychological disorders. As you learned in this chapter, DSM-IV-TR describes more than 300 specific disorders, including their symptoms, the exact criteria that must be met to make a diagnosis, and the typical course of each psychological disorder. Categories of psychological disorders include the anxiety disorders, mood disorders, personality disorders, dissociative disorders, and schizophrenia.

According to the text, the chance that someone will experience symptoms of a psychological disorder some time in his or her lifetime is about 50–50. About one in four people will have experienced the symptoms of psychological disorder during the last year. However, about 80 percent of those people will not have sought professional help. The good news is that most people seem to weather the symptoms without becoming completely debilitated and without professional intervention.

Nobody knows for sure what causes psychological disorders. There is no shortage of theories, however. Biological and genetic factors have been implicated, as have abnormalities in brain structure and chemical imbalances. Various environmental and social explanations have also been suggested. Research continues, and someday we may be closer to finding the cause or causes of these abnormalities.

3. The first thing to note about the studies of the relationship between cigarette smoking and the incidence of mental illness is that these studies are correlational in nature. Causality (cause-and-effect relationships) cannot be inferred on the basis of correlations; properly conducted experimental research is required to conclude anything about causality. Although there is a positive correlation between cigarette smoking and the prevalence of psychological disorders, it is not clear what the causal factors are. Does smoking cigarettes cause mental illness, does being mentally ill cause people to smoke more, or are other unknown causal factors at work here? Correlational research does not answer these questions.

   To make the point even clearer, consider the following example. Suppose researchers found that there was a positive correlation between the consumption of chicken soup and the incidence of cold and flu symptoms. Obviously, you would not conclude that chicken soup consumption causes flu or cold symptoms or that having a cold or the flu causes people to consume chicken soup. Other variables, such as cultural factors, traditions, beliefs about natural remedies, and so on could be involved.

   However, correlational research does allow predictions to be made. For example, you could predict that when the prevalence of cold and flu symptoms diminish, the consumption of chicken soup should also decrease, and vice versa.

   Likewise, with cigarette smoking and the level of mental illness. You could predict that if the rate of cigarette smoking declined over a period of a decade or two, then the prevalence of mental illness should also decrease. This, however, has not happened. The level of cigarette smoking has decreased quite dramatically over the last couple of decades but the incidence of mental illness in the population has not. This further illustrates the complex nature of the relationship between these two variables. Further research may shed light on these intriguing correlational research findings.

Progress Test 1

1. a	6. d	11. a
2. b	7. a	12. b
3. a	8. a	13. d
4. c	9. d	14. c
5. a	10. d	15. c

Progress Test 2

1. b	6. d	11. c
2. d	7. b	12. c
3. c	8. d	13. d
4. a	9. a	14. a
5. b	10. a	15. c

Progress Test 3

1. a	6. d	11. a
2. c	7. a	12. a
3. a	8. b	13. b
4. b	9. a	14. b
5. d	10. a	15. d

CHAPTER 14

Therapies

PREVIEW

Reading the section below first will give you a general sense of the chapter's contents and an initial introduction to some of the major concepts and terms. This will prime you for what you are about to read and help you to develop a "cognitive map" that will guide your study of the material in this chapter. Likewise, reading the **preview questions** at the beginning of each major section will improve your ability to understand, learn, and retain the information.

Chapter 14 . . . AT A GLANCE

Chapter 14 discusses the use of psychotherapies and biomedical therapies to treat psychological disorders. Psychoanalysis, which is based on Freud's theory of personality, is described. Contemporary short-term dynamic psychotherapies are based on psychoanalytic theory but differ in that they are typically time-limited and have specific goals, and the therapist's role is active rather than neutral.

Client-centered therapy is discussed as the prime example of the humanistic approach to psychotherapy. An application of humanistic therapy, designed to help people commit to change, is motivational interviewing. Behavior therapy is based on learning principles and assumes that maladaptive behaviors are learned. Techniques based on classical conditioning and operant conditioning are examined. The cognitive therapies, which assume that psychological problems are caused by maladaptive patterns of thinking, are explored next. Cognitive-behavioral therapy combines cognitive and behavioral techniques in an integrated but flexible treatment plan. An emerging approach in cognitive-behavioral therapy, called mindfulness-based therapy, involves the use of mindfulness meditation techniques. The advantages and benefits of group therapy, especially family and couple therapies, are examined.

The effectiveness of psychotherapy is explored. The conclusion is that psychotherapy is generally better than no treatment at all; also, no particular form of psychotherapy is superior to any other. Certain factors contribute to the effectiveness of all forms of therapy, however.

The most common biomedical therapy is psychotropic medication. The discussion includes the nature of these drugs, their effects on the brain, their side effects, and the disorders for which they are prescribed. Electroconvulsive therapy (ECT) is used for treating severe depression. Some new experimental treatments include transcranial magnetic stimulation (TMS), vagus nerve stimulation (VNS), and deep brain stimulation (DBS). Enhancing Well-Being with Psychology provides useful information about what to expect in psychotherapy.

Introduction: Psychotherapy and Biomedical Therapy

Preview Questions

Consider the following questions as you study this section of the chapter.

- What are psychological disorders?
- How is *psychotherapy* defined, and what types of problems are treated using psychotherapy?
- What is the basic assumption common to all forms of psychotherapy?
- What is biomedical therapy, what is its basic assumption, and who can prescribe psychotropic medications?

Read the section "Introduction: Psychotherapy and Biomedical Therapy" and ***write*** *your answers to the following:*

1. Psychological disorders are ______________________

   Not everyone who seeks help is suffering from a psychological disorder. Many people seek help ______________________

2. Psychotherapy refers to ______________________
3. A basic assumption of all psychotherapies is that ______________________
4. Biomedical therapies involve______________________
5. The biomedical therapies are based on the assumption that ______________________
6. Until recently, only licensed physicians ______________________

   However, since the 1990s ______________________

   Psychologists are also urged to adopt a ______________________ approach to treatment.

Psychoanalytic Therapy

Preview Questions

Consider the following questions as you study this section of the chapter.

- What is psychoanalysis, and who developed this form of therapy?
- What techniques are used in psychoanalysis, and what are they designed to accomplish?
- What are short-term dynamic therapies?
- What is interpersonal therapy (IPT), and what four categories of personal problems does it deal with?
- What psychological disorders has IPT been effective in treating?

Read the section "Psychoanalytic Therapy" and ***write*** *your answers to the following:*

1. Psychoanalysis is a ______________________
2. The main psychoanalytic techniques (and their purpose) are

   (a) ______________________

   (b) ______________________

   (c) ______________________

   (d) ______________________

   (e) ______________________
3. Together, these psychoanalytic techniques are designed to ______________________
4. The various forms of short-term dynamic therapies (all based on traditional psychoanalytic notions) have four features in common:

   (a) ______________________

(b) ______________________________
____

(c) ______________________________
____

(d) ______________________________
____

5. Interpersonal therapy (IPT) is ________
____
____

The four categories of personal problems dealt with are

(a) ______________________________
____

(b) ______________________________
____

(c) ______________________________
____

(d) ______________________________
____

6. IPT has been used to treat ________
____
____
____
____
____
____

After you have carefully studied the preceding sections, complete the following exercises.

Concept Check 1

Read the following and write the correct term in the space provided.

1. During a session with her psychoanalyst, Felicity was asked to elaborate on her negative feelings about her husband. She responded by making a few wisecracks about men and then abruptly changed the subject. Her therapist would say she is engaging in

   ________________ .

2. When Felicity's therapist urges her to report all her spontaneous thoughts, mental images, and feelings, he is using the technique called

   ________________ .

3. Felicity's therapist offers a carefully timed explanation of her free associations, hoping to facilitate the recognition of her unconscious conflicts or motivations. This technique is called ________________ .

4. Although her therapist has remained neutral and nonjudgmental throughout their sessions, Felicity is beginning to express toward him the feelings of hostility and anger she once felt for her father. This part of the psychoanalytic process is called ________________ .

5. When Felicity describes a dream she had the previous night, her therapist explores the content and analyzes it for disguised or symbolic wishes and motivations. Her therapist is using

   ________________ .

6. Rabia's therapist uses medication and other medical treatments to deal with the symptoms associated with her psychological disorder. On the other hand, Dean's therapist uses psychological techniques to help him modify his troubling behavior and to encourage him to understand the basis of his emotional problems. This example illustrates the difference between two broad forms of therapy, ________________ and ________________ .

7. Dr. Keller believes that symptoms of depression and other psychological problems are caused and maintained by interpersonal problems; thus, his therapy focuses on the person's current relationships and social interactions rather than on his or her history. Dr. Keller practices a type of psychotherapy called

   ________________ .

8. When Ethan first started therapy, his therapist made a relatively quick assessment and both she and Ethan agreed on specific, concrete, realistic goals. Now, after only a couple of months of sessions that included free associations, interpretations, and active dialogue with the therapist, Ethan is feeling much better. It is probable that Ethan has experienced ____________________ therapy.
9. Vanja is referred to a therapist who uses a short-term dynamic therapy called interpersonal therapy (IPT). Her therapist is likely to try to identify the interpersonal problems that are causing difficulties in her overall psychological functioning. He will be concerned with one or more of four categories of personal problems, which are ____________________ , ____________________ , ____________________ , and ____________________ .

Review of Terms, Concepts, and Names 1

Use the terms in this list to complete the Matching Exercise, then to help you answer the True/False items correctly.

psychological disorder	dream interpretation
psychotherapy	interpretation
biomedical therapies	transference
psychotropic medications	short-term dynamic therapies
psychoanalysis	interpersonal therapy (IPT)
Sigmund Freud	unresolved grief
repressed	role disputes
insight	role transitions
free association	interpersonal deficits
resistance	

Matching Exercise

Match the appropriate term/name with its definition or description.

1. ________________ Term used in interpersonal therapy for absent or faulty social skills that limit the ability to start or maintain healthy relationships with others.
2. ________________ The treatment of emotional, behavioral, and interpersonal problems through the use of psychological techniques designed to encourage understanding of problems and modify troubling feelings, behaviors, or relationships.
3. ________________ Psychoanalytic technique in which the psychoanalyst offers a carefully timed explanation of the patient's dreams, free associations, or behavior to facilitate the recognition of unconscious conflicts or motivations.
4. ________________ Type of psychotherapy originated by Sigmund Freud in which free association, dream interpretation, and analysis of resistance and transference are used to explore repressed or unconscious impulses, anxieties, and internal conflicts.
5. ________________ The use of medications, electroconvulsive therapy, or other medical treatment to treat the symptoms associated with psychological disorders.
6. ________________ Psychotherapies that are based on traditional psychoanalytic notions in which therapeutic contact typically lasts for no more than a few months rather than for years.
7. ________________ Drugs used to treat psychological or mental disorders.
8. ________________ Term used in interpersonal therapy for repetitive conflicts with significant others, such as the person's partner, family members, co-workers, or friends.
9. ________________ Founder of psychoanalysis who theorized that psychological symptoms are the result of unconscious and unresolved conflicts stemming from early childhood.
10. ____ Troubling thoughts, feelings, or behaviors that cause psychological discomfort or interfere with a person's ability to function.

True/False Test

Indicate whether each statement is true or false by placing T or F in the blank space next to each item.

1. ____ Psychoanalysts believe that it is essential to move conflicts from the patient's unconscious to his or her conscious awareness. The process of recognizing and ultimately resolving these long-standing repressed conflicts is called insight.
2. ____ Interpersonal therapy (IPT) is a brief, psychodynamic therapy that focuses on current relationships and assumes that symptoms are caused and maintained by interpersonal problems.

3. ____ In psychoanalysis, the patient's conscious or unconscious attempts to block the revelation of repressed memories and conflicts is called transference.

4. ____ Dream interpretation is a technique used in psychoanalysis in which the content of dreams is analyzed for disguised or symbolic wishes, meanings, and motivations.

5. ____ Free association is a technique used in psychoanalysis in which the patient spontaneously reports all thoughts, feelings, and mental images as they come to mind as a way of revealing unconscious thoughts and emotions.

6. ____ Resistance is the process by which emotions and desires originally associated with a significant person in the patient's life, such as a parent, are unconsciously transferred to the psychoanalyst.

7. ____ In interpersonal therapy, problems dealing with the death of significant others is called unresolved grief.

8. ____ In interpersonal therapy, role transitions refer to problems with major life changes such as going away to college, having children, getting married or divorced, or retiring.

9. ____ When early experiences result in unresolved conflicts and frustrated urges, these emotionally charged memories are *repressed,* or pushed out of conscious awareness.

Check your answers and review any areas of weakness before going on to the next section.

Humanistic Therapy

Preview Questions

Consider the following questions as you study this section of the chapter.

- What does the humanistic perspective emphasize?
- What is the most influential humanistic therapy, and who developed it?
- What therapeutic conditions and techniques are important in client-centered therapy?
- How do client-centered therapy and psychoanalysis differ as insight-oriented therapies?
- What is motivational interviewing (MI)?
- In what areas has the client-centered approach been applied?

Read the section "Humanistic Therapy" and ***write*** *your answers to the following:*

1. The humanistic perspective emphasizes ____________________

2. The most influential humanistic therapy is ____________________ ; it was developed by ____________________ , who deliberately used the word *client* rather than *patient* because ____________________

3. In client-centered therapy, the main conditions are that ____________________

4. Unlike psychoanalysis, humanistic therapy does not offer ____________________

5. Motivational interviewing is designed to ____________________

6. The client-centered approach has been applied to ____________________

Behavior Therapy

Preview Questions

Consider the following questions as you study this section of the chapter.

- What is the goal of behavior therapy?
- What is the basic assumption of behavior therapy?
- How are classical and operant conditioning principles used to treat and modify problem behaviors?
- What two procedures did Mary Cover Jones use?
- What is systematic desensitization, and what are the three steps involved in this technique?

- What is involved in virtual reality therapy and aversive conditioning?
- What is a token economy?
- What problems have behavioral therapies been used to treat?

Read the section "Behavior Therapy" and ***write*** *your answers to the following:*

1. The goal of behavior therapy is to ________________

2. Behavior therapists assume that maladaptive behaviors are ________________

   Therefore, the basic strategy in behavior therapy involves ________________

3. Behavior therapists employ techniques that are based on the learning principles of ________________

4. Mary Cover Jones's procedure, called counterconditioning, involved ________________

5. Along with counterconditioning, Jones used ________________

6. Based on the same premise as counterconditioning, systematic desensitization involves ________________

7. The three basic steps of systematic desensitization are
   (a) ________________
   (b) ________________
   (c) ________________

8. Virtual reality (VR) therapy uses ________________

   VR therapy has been used to treat ________________

9. Aversive conditioning involves ________________

   Aversive conditioning has been applied ________________

   However, mental health professionals ________________

10. B. F. Skinner's operant conditioning model of learning is based on the simple principle that behavior is ________________

    Operant conditioning techniques have been used to treat ________________

11. The token economy is a form of behavior therapy in which ________________

    Token economies have been used in ________________

    A modified version of the token economy is called ________________

    and has been used to treat ________________

After you have carefully studied the preceding sections, complete the following exercises.

Concept Check 2

Read the following and write the correct term in the space provided.

1. Dr. Soos does not analyze or interpret his clients' motives or problems. Instead, he believes that the client is in the best position to discover his or her own ways of effectively dealing with problems and that the role of the therapist is to provide the right conditions that foster self-awareness, psychological growth, and self-directed change. Dr. Soos is obviously a(n) ________________ psychologist who uses ______________________ therapy.
2. In an attempt to help her husband overcome his deep fear of traveling by sea, Mrs. Bowman brings home travel brochures showing exotic destinations reached by cruise ships. She asks her husband to imagine both of them sitting in their deck chairs enjoying the warm sunshine and cool beverages. At the same time, she reassures him that these big ships are totally safe and comfortable and that he has nothing to worry about. Mrs. Bowman's efforts to reduce her husband's fear most closely resemble techniques used in __________________________ .
3. To help Trevor overcome his addiction to nicotine, Dr. Clarke asks him to smoke some cigarettes and at the same time administers electric shock to his arm. Dr. Clarke is using a technique called ________________ conditioning.
4. Children in a group home for the mentally handicapped are given plastic chips for making their beds, brushing their teeth, washing their hands, and being on time for meals. They are allowed to exchange these chips for candy, cookies, or additional TV time. The group home is using a behavioral technique called the ______________________ .
5. Orville is undergoing therapy in which he is learning a new conditioned response that is incompatible with a previously learned response. This therapy is called _________________ and is based on the principles of _________________ . This technique was developed by _________________ .
6. Desiree told her therapist, "I feel so inadequate and useless; I can't seem to cope with even the smallest things in my life. What should I do?" Her therapist answered, "You are feeling very helpless about things in your life, and sometimes you feel unable to cope. Can you think where these feelings come from?" The therapist is using _____________________ therapy and appears to be communicating with __________________________________ .
7. Three-year old Graham cries and screams whenever he is put in his bed at night; he stops only when his parents allow him to sleep in their bed. To deal with this problem, Graham's parents implement a program that involves consistently ignoring the screaming and crying and abundantly praising and encouraging good behaviors. They are using ________________ to decrease undesirable behaviors and ________________ to increase desirable behaviors.
8. Rosalynn, who is in an institution for people with psychological disorders, refuses to leave her room and go to the dining room for her meals. To help her overcome this problem, therapists first give her a reward for leaving her room, then for walking part way down the hallway, then for venturing the whole way, then for going to the staircase, and so on. Eventually, she is rewarded only when she sits at the table. This example illustrates a behavioral technique called ________________ .

Review of Terms, Concepts, and Names 2

Use the terms in this list to complete the Matching Exercise, then to help you answer the True/False items correctly.

humanistic perspective
client- (or person-) centered therapy
Carl Rogers
genuineness
unconditional positive regard
empathic understanding
conditional acceptance
self-actualization
motivational interviewing (MI)
behavior therapy (behavior modification)
Mary Cover Jones
counterconditioning
observational learning
systematic desensitization
progressive relaxation
anxiety hierarchy
control scene
aversive conditioning
Antabuse
shaping
reinforcement (positive and negative)
extinction
baseline rate
token economy
contingency management

Matching Exercise

Match the appropriate term/name with its definition or description.

1. ________________ Psychologist who conducted the first clinical demonstrations of behavior therapy.
2. ________________ Psychological perspective that emphasizes human potential, self-awareness, and freedom of choice.
3. ________________ Form of behavior therapy in which the therapeutic environment is structured to reward desired behaviors with tokens or points that may eventually be exchanged for tangible rewards.
4. ________________ In client-centered therapy, the critical quality of the therapist that involves honestly and openly sharing his or her thoughts and feelings with the client.
5. ________________ Type of psychotherapy that focuses on directly changing maladaptive behavior patterns by using basic learning principles and techniques.
6. ________________ Psychologist who helped found humanistic psychology and developed client-centered therapy.
7. ________________ The first step in systematic desensitization, which involves successively relaxing one muscle group after another until a deep state of relaxation is achieved.
8. ________________ Modified version of the token economy that has been used with outpatients in treatment programs and involves carefully specified behaviors that "earn" the individual concrete rewards.
9. ________________ Type of psychotherapy developed by humanist Carl Rogers in which the therapist is nondirective, and the client directs the focus of each therapy session.
10. ________________ Medication that causes extreme nausea if alcohol is consumed after it is taken; used as a form of aversive conditioning in the treatment of alcohol abuse.
11. ________________ In behavior therapy, the rate of occurrence of a problem behavior before treatment begins; more generally, data or condition used as a reference with which to compare future observations or results.
12. ________________ A technique used to help people overcome fears and phobias by encouraging them to watch others modeling nonfearful behavior while interacting with the feared stimulus.
13. ________________ List of anxiety-provoking images associated with the feared situation, arranged in order from least to most anxiety-producing, that the therapist helps the patient construct as part of systematic desensitization.

True/False Test

Indicate whether each statement is true or false by placing T or F in the blank space next to each item.

1. ___ Aversive conditioning is a behavior therapy technique based on classical conditioning that involves modifying behavior by conditioning a new response that is incompatible with a previously learned response.
2. ___ In client-centered therapy, *empathic understanding* involves active listening and reflecting the content and personal meaning of feelings being experienced by the client.
3. ___ Systematic desensitization is a type of behavior therapy in which phobic responses are reduced by pairing relaxation with a series of mental images or real-life situations that the person finds progressively more fear-provoking; it is based on the principle of counterconditioning.

4. ____ In behavior therapy, when a behavior decreases because it no longer leads to a reinforcer, *extinction* has occurred.
5. ____ In systematic desensitization, the therapist may have the client create a very relaxing scene, unrelated to the hierarchy of anxiety-provoking images, called a *control scene*.
6. ____ In client-centered therapy, unconditional positive regard is created when the therapist values, accepts, and cares for the client, whatever her problems or behaviors.
7. ____ In behavior therapy, the process by which a desired behavior is increased as the result of its consequences is called *reinforcement*.
8. ____ When a person has received acceptance by significant others only if she conforms to their expectations, she is said to have experienced conditional acceptance.
9. ____ Counterconditioning, a relatively ineffective type of behavior therapy, involves repeatedly pairing an aversive stimulus with the occurrence of undesirable behaviors or thoughts.
10. ____ Self-actualization is the realization of a person's unique potential and talents.
11. ____ Shaping involves reinforcing successive approximations of a desired behavior and can be used with extremely impaired patients in whom the desired responses do not normally occur.
12. ____ Motivational interviewing is designed to help clients overcome the mixed feelings or reluctance they might have about committing to change; it is more directive than traditional client-centered therapy, and its main goal is to encourage or strengthen the client's self-motivated statements or "change talk."

Check your answers and review any areas of weakness before going on to the next section.

Cognitive Therapies

Preview Questions

Consider the following questions as you study this section of the chapter.

- On what assumption are cognitive therapies based, and what is the goal of cognitive therapy?
- What is rational-emotive therapy (RET), and who developed it?
- What is Beck's cognitive therapy (CT), and how does it differ from rational-emotive therapy?
- What is cognitive-behavioral therapy (CBT), and what assumption is it based on?
- What is mindfulness, what are mindfulness-based therapies, and what is the goal of these approaches?
- What is Mindfulness-Based Stress Reduction (MBSR), and what is the focus of Mindfulness-Based Cognitive Therapy (MBCT)?
- What problems have the cognitive therapies been used to treat?

Read the section "Cognitive Therapies" and ***write*** *your answers to the following:*

1. Cognitive therapies assume that ____________
____
____
2. The goal of cognitive therapy is to ____________
____
____
3. Rational-emotive therapy (RET) was developed by____________, and it focuses on
____
____
____

   RET has been effective in the treatment of
____
____
____
4. Beck's cognitive therapy (CT) focuses on
____
____
5. Like Ellis, Beck believes that ____________
____
____
____
6. In contrast with Ellis's emphasis on "irrational" thinking, Beck believes that ____________
____
____
____

Cognitive therapy (CT) has been effective in treating ______________________________

7. Cognitive-behavioral therapy (CBT) refers to ______________________________

Cognitive-behavioral therapy is based on the assumption that ______________________________

CBT has been used to treat ______________________________

8. Mindfulness is ______________________________

Mindfulness-based therapies (mindfulness-based interventions or mindfulness and acceptance therapies) involve ______________________________

The goal is ______________________________

9. Mindfulness-Based Stress Reduction (MBSR) involves ______________________________

Mindfulness-Based Cognitive Therapy (MBCT) was developed to treat ______________________________

Mindfulness training has been incorporated as a ______________________________

A meta-analysis has found that MBSR and MBCT are effective treatments for ______________________________

Group and Family Therapy

Preview Questions

Consider the following questions as you study this section of the chapter.

- What is group therapy, and what are some of the advantages of this approach?
- What are family therapy, couple therapy, and behavioral couple therapy?

Read the section "Group and Family Therapy" and ***write*** *your answers to the following:*

1. Group therapy involves ______________________________

2. Some of the key advantages of group therapy are that ______________________________

3. Family therapy is based on the assumption that ______________________________

4. Couple therapy focuses on ______________________________

Behavioral couple therapy is based on the assumption ______________________________

Evaluating the Effectiveness of Psychotherapy

Preview Questions

Consider the following questions as you study this section of the chapter.

- What is meta-analysis, and what has it demonstrated about the general effectiveness of psychotherapy?
- Is one form of psychotherapy superior to another?
- What common factors contribute to effective psychotherapy, and what is eclecticism and integrative psychotherapy?

Read the section "Evaluating the Effectiveness of Psychotherapy" and ***write*** *your answers to the following:*

1. Meta-analysis involves ______________________________

2. When meta-analysis is used to summarize studies, the researchers consistently arrive at the same conclusion: ______________________________

2. Researchers have identified a number of factors that are related to a positive therapy outcome:
(a) ______________________________
(b) ______________________________
(c) ______________________________
(d) ______________________________
(e) ______________________________
(f) ______________________________

4. Eclecticism refers to the ______________________________

Integrative psychotherapy is a technique ______________________________

After you have carefully studied the preceding sections, complete the following exercises.

Concept Check 3

Read the following and write the correct term in the space provided.

1. Dr. McGilvery wants to determine whether psychotherapy is effective for particular psychological disorders. In attempting to analyze the results of numerous published studies on the issue, he should use a statistical technique called ______________ .
2. Mike, a mental health professional, tries to tailor his therapeutic approach to the problems and characteristics of the person seeking help. Mike's pragmatic and integrated use of diverse psychotherapeutic techniques would classify him as a(n) ______________ therapist.
3. Dr. Samson believes that a key aspect of resolving some psychological problems is getting individuals to realize that others have problems similar to their own. To achieve this goal, ______________ therapy would be useful.
4. Jay's therapist attacks and openly criticizes Jay's irrational and self-defeating ways of thinking. Jay's therapist is most likely a ______________ therapist.
5. Dr. Beaven tries to help her clients learn to recognize and monitor the automatic thoughts that occur without conscious effort or control; she then encourages them to test the reality of these thoughts empirically. Dr. Beaven's approach is most consistent with ______________ therapy.

6. Dr. Sidhu believes that in order to understand psychological problems, it is important to investigate interactions among family members within the context of the dynamic family system in which each member plays a unique role. Dr. Sidhu is most likely a ________________ therapist.
7. Ivana's therapist believes that thoughts affect behavior and moods, and that behavior, in turn, can affect cognitions and emotional states. His approach to treating her depression involves a flexible, integrated use of diverse behavioral and cognitive techniques tailored to her unique problem. Ivana's therapist is most likely a ________________ therapist.
8. Draco has been attending Alcoholics Anonymous meetings and learning about their 12-step program ever since he was cited for DUI (driving under the influence) and his driver's license was suspended. Draco is seeking help from a(n) ____________________ .
9. Judd's therapist asks him to focus on the mental image of the traumatic aftermath of the explosion that destroyed his place of work. While Judd is doing this, the therapist moves his finger back and forth in front of Judd's eyes and asks him to visually track the movement. Judd's therapist is using a technique called ____ , a therapeutic approach that is ________________ (significantly better/no better) than other forms of psychotherapy.
10. When Fernando started experiencing a number of psychological problems, he decided that he needed professional help. Before talking with a therapist, however, he discussed his plan with his extended family, including his grandparents and his in-laws, and with some of his closest friends. This tendency of Latinos to stress interdependence over independence and the importance of the extended family network is called ____________________ .
11. Dr. Thorpe is a psychotherapist who treats people suffering from stress-related disorders, emotional problems, or anxiety. His approach involves a structured program of mindfulness meditation, yoga and mindful body practices, and group discussion. Dr. Thorpe is using a cognitive-behavioral therapy called ________________________

Graphic Organizer 1

Fill in each of the following with the correct information. This covers all psychotherapies.

Type of Therapy	Founder	Source of Problems	Treatment Techniques	Goals of Therapy
Psychoanalysis				
Client-Centered Therapy				

Type of Therapy	Founder	Source of Problems	Treatment Techniques	Goals of Therapy
Behavior Therapy				
Rational-Emotive Therapy				
Cognitive Therapy (for depression)				
Cognitive-Behavioral Therapy				

Review of Terms, Concepts, and Names 3

Use the terms in this list to complete the Matching Exercise, then to help you answer the True/False items correctly.

cognitive therapies
Albert Ellis
rational-emotive therapy (RET)
ABC model
Aaron T. Beck
cognitive therapy (CT)
cognitive-behavioral therapy (CBT)
mindfulness-based therapies (mindfulness-based interventions or mindfulness and acceptance therapies)
mindfulness
decentering
Mindfulness-Based Stress Reduction (MBSR)
Mindfulness-Based Cognitive Therapy (MBCT)
group therapy
self-help groups and support groups
family therapy
couple therapy
behavioral couple therapy
spontaneous remission
meta-analysis
empirically supported treatments
eye movement desensitization reprocessing (EMDR)
exposure therapy
eclecticism
integrative psychotherapy

Matching Exercise

Match the appropriate term/name with its definition or description.

1. ________________ Form of psychotherapy that is based on the assumption that the family is a system and that treats the family as a unit.
2. ________________ Group of psychotherapies that are based on the assumption that psychological problems are due to faulty thinking; treatment techniques focus on recognizing and altering these unhealthy thinking patterns.
3. ________________ Type of therapy, developed by psychiatrist Aaron Beck, that focuses on changing the client's unrealistic beliefs.
4. ________________ Form of psychotherapy that involves one or more therapists working simultaneously with a small group of clients.
5. ________________ Type of psychotherapy, developed by psychologist Albert Ellis, that focuses on changing the client's irrational beliefs.
6. ________________ Therapy that integrates cognitive and behavioral techniques and is based on the assumption that thoughts, moods, and behaviors are interrelated.
7. ________________ Therapy technique in which the client holds a vivid mental image of a troubling event or situation while rapidly moving his eyes back and forth in response to the therapist's waving finger, or while the therapist administers some other form of bilateral stimulation such as sounding tones in alternate ears.
8. ________________ A statistical technique that involves pooling or combining the results of many studies into a single analysis that essentially creates one large study that can reveal overall trends in the data.
9. ________________ A form of couple therapy, based on the assumption that couples are satisfied when they experience more reinforcement than punishment in their relationships, that focuses on increasing caring behaviors and teaching couples how to constructively resolve conflict and problems.
10. ________________ A technique related to eclectic psychotherapy that uses multiple approaches that are blended together rather than choosing different approaches for different clients.
11. ________________ Meditation technique that involves present-centered awareness without judgment.
12. ________________ Therapy that involves a structured program of mindfulness meditation, yoga and mindful body practices, and group discussion; developed to treat stress and anxiety disorders.

True/False Test

Indicate whether each item is true or false by placing T or F in the space next to each item.

1. ____ Albert Ellis founded cognitive therapy (CT), a psychotherapy based on the assumption that depression and other psychological problems are caused by biased perceptions, distorted thinking, and inaccurate beliefs.
2. ____ Eclecticism is the pragmatic and integrated use of techniques from different psychotherapies.
3. ____ Spontaneous remission is the phenomenon in which people eventually improve or recover from psychological symptoms simply with the passage of time.
4. ____ Self-help groups and support groups deal with a wide array of psychological, medical, and behavioral problems through group processes and interactions that are typically organized and led by nonprofessionals.

5. ____ Aaron T. Beck founded the cognitive therapy called rational-emotive therapy (RET), which emphasizes recognizing and changing irrational beliefs.

6. ____ Empirically supported treatments are psychotherapies whose effectiveness has been validated by empirical research.

7. ____ A behavioral therapy, used for phobias, panic disorder, post-traumatic stress disorder, or related anxiety disorders, and in which the person is repeatedly exposed to the disturbing object or situation under controlled conditions is called exposure therapy.

8. ____ Couple therapy attempts to improve communication and problem-solving skills as well as increase the intimacy between two people in a committed relationship.

9. ____ According to the ABC model, when an activating event (A) occurs, it is the person's belief (B) about the event that causes emotional consequences (C).

10. ____ Mindfulness-based therapies (mindfulness-based interventions or mindfulness and acceptance therapies) involve the mindfulness meditation technique of present-centered awareness without judgment; they target both thoughts and behaviors without challenging, testing, or replacing the content of thoughts.

11. ____ Mindfulness-Based Cognitive Therapy (MBCT) was developed to treat depression, but it has been expanded to treat other disorders.

12. ____ Decentering is a mindfulness-based technique that teaches individuals to notice, label, and relate to their thoughts and emotions as just "passing events."

Check your answers and review any areas of weakness before going on to the next section.

Biomedical Therapies

Preview Questions

Consider the following questions as you study this section of the chapter.

- What is biomedical therapy?
- What are the most important antipsychotic, atypical antipsychotic, antianxiety, and antidepressant medications; how do they achieve their effects; and what are their advantages?
- What is lithium, and what disorder is it used to treat?
- What does the field of pharmacogenetics study?
- What is electroconvulsive therapy (ECT), what disorder is it used to treat, and what are some new experimental treatments for this disorder?

Read the section "Biomedical Therapies" and ***write*** *your answers to the following:*

1. The biomedical therapies are ______________________________

____

____

2. Antipsychotic medications (neuroleptics) are

____

The most common antipsychotic medications include ______________________________

____

____

Although the early antipsychotics reduced

____

____

____

3. The atypical antipsychotic drugs include

____

____

and they act by ______________________________

____

____

These second-generation antipsychotics cause

____

____

4. Antianxiety medications are ______________________________

____

____

The most common antianxiety medications include ______________________________

____

____

Buspar, a newer antianxiety drug, has fewer side effects and is not a ______________ ; it does not affect ______________________________

____

____

5. Lithium is ______________________________
____
____
____

Depakote, an anticonvulsant, has been used to treat ______________________________
____
____
____
____

6. The antidepressant medications are __________
____
____

The most common antidepressant medications include ______________________________
____
____

New antidepressants, including __________
____

tend to ______________________________
____

The SSRIs are also used to treat __________
______________ .

To help overcome the trial-and-error nature of prescribing antidepressants and other psychotropic drugs, pharmacogenetics, which is
______________________________ ,
has emerged.

7. Electroconvulsive therapy (ECT) is a biomedical therapy used primarily ______________________________
____
____
____

Some of the new experimental treatments (that don't involve seizures) are __________
____
____
____

After you have carefully studied the preceding section, complete the following exercises.

Concept Check 4

Read the following and write the correct term in the space provided.

1. For no apparent reason, Mrs. Bell has constant and persistent feelings of anxiety, nervousness, and apprehension that interfere with her ability to eat, sleep, and perform daily activities. Her psychiatrist is most likely to prescribe a type of psychotropic medication called an ______________ medication.
2. Mr. Millis still experiences intense feelings of despondency, hopelessness, and dejection, and has suicidal thoughts, despite extensive psychotherapy and months of psychotropic medication. Because of this lack of responsiveness, his doctor is likely to consider using ______________ therapy.
3. After being on antipsychotic medications for many years, Florence has developed a number of serious symptoms, such as severe, uncontrollable facial tics and grimaces, chewing movements, and other involuntary movements of the lips, jaw, and tongue. Florence suffers from ______________ .
4. Dwayne has been diagnosed with bipolar disorder. His doctor is most likely to prescribe ______________ .
5. To treat Debra's symptoms of schizophrenia, which included apathy, social withdrawal, and flat emotions, the psychiatrist prescribed a psychotropic medication that selectively affected the levels of the neurotransmitters serotonin and dopamine in her brain. To minimize the potential side effects of the first atypical antipsychotics, he is likely to have prescribed an atypical antipsychotic such as ______________ , ______________ , or ______________ .
6. After 12 weeks of interpersonal therapy (IPT) or 12 weeks of antidepressant medication (Paxil), depressed patients underwent PET scans. It is very likely that there will be ______________ (a higher/a lower/the same) level of normalization of brain activity in the drug group compared with the therapy group.
7. Mari has been given a prescription for the benzodiazepine drug called Xanax. It is very probable that Mari suffers from ______________ .

8. Virgil has been diagnosed with major depression. To avoid the side effects associated with the earlier medications, his doctor prescribes a drug from the third generation of antidepressants, which primarily affect the availability of the neurotransmitter serotonin. These drugs are called ________________, the most popular of which are ________________, ________________, and ________________. If Virgil does experience side effects, his doctor may prescribe one of the new dual-action antidepressants, such as ________________, ________________, or one of the dual-reuptake inhibitors, such as, ________________, ________________ or ________________.

Review of Terms and Concepts 4

Use the terms in this list to complete the Matching Exercise, then to help you answer the True/False items correctly.

psychotropic medications
antipsychotic medications (neuroleptics)
reserpine and chlorpromazine (Thorazine)
tardive dyskinesia
atypical antipsychotic medications
antianxiety medications
benzodiazepines
GABA
Buspar
lithium
glutamate
antidepressant medications
tricyclics and MAO inhibitors
selective serotonin reuptake inhibitors (SSRIs)
dual-action antidepressants
pharmacogenetics
electroconvulsive therapy (ECT)
transcranial magnetic stimulation (TMS)
vagus nerve stimulation (VNS)
deep brain stimulation (DBS)

Matching Exercise

Match the appropriate term with its definition or description.

1. ________________ A naturally occurring substance that is used in the treatment of bipolar disorder.
2. ________________ Drugs that alter mental functions, alleviate psychological symptoms, and are used to treat psychological or mental disorders.
3. ________________ Biomedical therapy used primarily in the treatment of severe depression that involves electrically inducing a brief brain seizure; also called *shock therapy* and *electroshock therapy*.
4. ________________ Prescription drugs used to alleviate the symptoms of anxiety.
5. ________________ Prescription drugs used to reduce the symptoms associated with depression.
6. ________________ Potentially irreversible motor disorder that results from the long-term use of antipsychotic medications and is characterized by severe, uncontrollable facial tics and grimaces, chewing movements, and other involuntary movements of the lips, jaw, and tongue.
7. ________________ New antidepressants (such as Serzone and Remeron) that affect serotonin levels, are as effective as SSRIs but with a somewhat different mechanism, and have different side effects.
8. ________________ A neurotransmitter that inhibits the transmission of nerve impulses in the brain and slows brain activity.
9. ________________ The study of how genes influence an individual's response to drugs.
10. ________________ Biomedical technique that uses electrodes surgically implanted in the brain and a battery-powered neurostimulator implanted in the chest.

True/False Test

Indicate whether each item is true or false by placing T or F in the space next to each item.

1. ____ Antipsychotic medications (also called neuroleptics) are prescription drugs that are used to reduce psychotic symptoms; frequently used in the treatment of schizophrenia.
2. ____ Reserpine and chlorpromazine (Thorazine) are antipsychotic medications that reduce levels of the neurotransmitter dopamine.
3. ____ Benzodiazepines are a group of addictive antianxiety drugs that increase levels of the neurotransmitter GABA throughout the brain.
4. ____ Atypical antipsychotic medications are medications which, in contrast to the early antipsychotic drugs, block dopamine receptors in brain regions associated with psychotic symptoms rather than more globally throughout the brain, resulting in fewer side effects.

5. ___ Selective serotonin reuptake inhibitors (SSRIs) are a class of antidepressant medication, which includes Prozac, Paxil, and Zoloft, that increases the availability of serotonin in the brain and causes fewer side effects than earlier antidepressants.
6. ___ Tricyclics and MAO inhibitors are first-generation antidepressants that affect multiple neurotransmitter pathways and increase the availability of norepinephrine and serotonin.
7. ___ An antianxiety drug that is not a benzodiazepine and does not affect the neurotransmitter GABA but may affect dopamine and serotonin levels is called *Buspar*.
8. ___ Lithium stabilizes the availability of *glutamate,* which is an excitatory neurotransmitter found in many areas of the brain.
9. ___ Vagus nerve stimulation (VNS) involves stimulation of certain regions of the brain with magnetic pulses of various frequencies.
10. ___ Transcranial magnetic stimulation (TMS) involves the surgical implantation of a device about the size of a pacemaker into the left chest wall.

Check your answers and review any areas of weakness before going on to the next section.

Something to Think About

1. Many people become fearful and anxious if they have to take an exam or go to the dentist or doctor or on a job interview, for example. These kinds of fears are normal, and most people manage to cope with such anxiety-provoking situations. Other fears are more serious and may cause the person intense distress and somehow interfere with his or her normal functioning. Imagine a situation in which a friend or family member comes to you seeking help about how to overcome his fear of flying. Based on what you know about the behavior therapy technique of systematic desensitization, what might you say to this person?
2. Many people with psychological problems do not seek help from mental health professionals. There are many reasons for this. One reason may have to do with a lack of understanding about what to expect in psychotherapy. What are some of the important things a person should know about psychotherapy?

Check your answers and review any areas of weakness before completing the progress tests.

Progress Test 1

Review the complete chapter (including all boxed inserts), review all your study notes, and then test yourself on the following progress test. Check your answers. If you make a mistake, review your notes, check the appropriate section in the study guide, and, if necessary, go back and read the relevant part of the chapter in your textbook.

1. Jacqueline's therapist uses dream interpretation and free association to help her become more aware of unresolved conflicts from her childhood. The therapist's techniques and goals best reflect the primary aim of
   (a) psychoanalysis.
   (b) client-centered therapy.
   (c) behavior therapy.
   (d) cognitive therapy.

2. Mrs. Alverz gives her third-grade students a silver sticker every time they get a perfect score on their weekly spelling test. At the end of the term, students can exchange their stickers for prizes. Mrs. Alverz is using a strategy based on ________ conditioning called ________ .
   (a) classical; contingency management
   (b) classical; the token economy
   (c) operant; contingency management
   (d) operant; the token economy

3. Laurel's therapist uses rational-emotive therapy (RET). After identifying Laurel's core irrational beliefs, her therapist is likely to
   (a) help her formulate an anxiety hierarchy.
   (b) encourage her to use free association so that she can get insight into her unconscious motivations and feelings.
   (c) provide her with a warm, supportive atmosphere, unconditional positive regard, and empathic understanding.
   (d) vigorously dispute and challenge her irrational beliefs.

4. Dr. Whorley offers a number of explanations for his patient's dreams and free associations in order to help the patient recognize unconscious conflicts and motivations. Dr. Whorley is using a psychoanalytic technique called
   (a) interpretation. (c) resistance.
   (b) transference. (d) conditional acceptance.

5. Melissa's therapist encourages her to observe and try to change her relationship to her maladaptive thoughts and emotions, explaining that the ability to monitor her thoughts and feelings without judgment can allow her to experience disturbing thoughts and feelings without reacting to them. He teaches her to use the technique of decentering to help her achieve this goal. It is likely that Melissa's therapist is a ___________ who uses an approach called ___________.
   (a) behavior therapist; Mindfulness-Based Stress Reduction (MBSR)
   (b) client-centered therapist; interpersonal therapy (IPT)
   (c) cognitive-behavioral therapist; mindfulness-based therapy
   (d) rational-emotive therapist; mindfulness and acceptance therapy

6. Once a week, Gardner attends a local health clinic, where he attempts to deal with some of his psychological problems by discussing them with five or six other people and two psychologists. Gardner is involved in
   (a) individual therapy.
   (b) group therapy.
   (c) a biomedical treatment program.
   (d) interpersonal therapy (IPT).

7. Mr. Lansdon's intense feelings of despondency and helplessness are periodically interrupted by episodes in which he experiences excessive feelings of personal power and a grandiose optimism that he can change the world to fit his strange ideological beliefs. A biomedical therapist would most likely prescribe
   (a) electroconvulsive therapy.
   (b) lithium.
   (c) antipsychotic medications.
   (d) antidepressant medications.

8. Gabrielle's feelings of unhappiness, despondency, dejection, and hopelessness have become so extreme that she has attempted suicide. Antidepressant drugs and psychotherapy have not helped her. Which of the following treatments is likely to provide her with the quickest relief from her misery?
   (a) systematic desensitization
   (b) Naikan therapy
   (c) integrative psychotherapy
   (d) electroconvulsive therapy (ECT)

9. Because of his persistent psychological problems, Werner has been prescribed a benzodiazepine drug called Valium. It is most likely that Werner suffers from
   (a) bipolar disorder.
   (b) schizophrenia.
   (c) anxiety.
   (d) depression.

10. When Christos was younger, he experienced a very painful tooth extraction. He now has an extreme fear of going to the dentist and has not been for a dental checkup in years. To help Christos overcome his irrational fear, a behavioral therapist is likely to use
    (a) vagus nerve stimulation (VNS).
    (b) systematic desensitization.
    (c) integrative psychotherapy.
    (d) transcranial magnetic stimulation (TMS).

11. Kathleen is on a committee at a community health care facility that has the task of determining which of the major forms of psychotherapy is most effective. After she reviews studies that used meta-analysis to assess the results of treatment outcomes, she is most likely to conclude that
    (a) behavior therapy is the single most effective therapy available.
    (b) client-centered therapy has been consistently more effective than all the other forms of therapy.
    (c) in general, there is little or no difference in the effectiveness of the different forms of psychotherapy.
    (d) psychoanalysis works best for schizophrenia, and cognitive therapy works best for phobias.

12. Tyler has been diagnosed with schizophrenia. His doctor is most likely to prescribe
    (a) electroconvulsive therapy.
    (b) lithium.
    (c) antipsychotic medication.
    (d) antianxiety medication.

13. According to Enhancing Well-Being with Psychology (What to Expect in Psychotherapy), which of the following is true?
    (a) Therapy is a collaborative effort.
    (b) Expect therapy to challenge how you think and act.
    (c) Your therapist will not become a substitute friend and will not make decisions for you.
    (d) All of these statements are true.

14. Mr. Keiko, a middle-aged Japanese American, has been referred to a Western-style psychologist because he is displaying the classic symptoms of anxiety and depression. According to Culture and Human Behavior (Cultural Values and Psychotherapy), Mr. Keiko
    (a) may be reluctant to discuss personal, intimate details of his life with a stranger.
    (b) might try to avoid focusing on upsetting thoughts and resist exploring painful thoughts and feelings that could help resolve his psychological problems.
    (c) may not agree that becoming more assertive, more self-sufficient, less dependent on others, and caring for his own needs first is a good idea.
    (d) might do all of these things.

15. After a session with her therapist, in which she finally expressed all the anger and hostility she felt toward her parents and described the terrible guilt she felt about it, Charlene felt an enormous reduction in and relief from her emotional and physical tension. According to Enhancing Well-Being with Psychology (What to Expect in Psychotherapy), Charlene has probably experienced
    (a) resistance.
    (b) catharsis.
    (c) transference.
    (d) extinction.

Progress Test 2

After you have checked your understanding of the material in Progress Test 1 and have done a complete chapter review with special focus on any areas of weakness, you are ready to assess your knowledge with Progress Test 2. Check your answers. If you make a mistake, review your notes, the relevant section of the study guide, and, if necessary, the appropriate part of your textbook.

1. Dr. Rassmunsen uses medication and other medical procedures, including electroconvulsive therapy, to treat the symptoms of psychological disorders. Dr. Rassmunsen's approach would most likely be classified as
    (a) cognitive therapy.
    (b) behavioral therapy.
    (c) humanistic therapy.
    (d) biomedical therapy.

2. Mr. Damson suffers from auditory hallucinations and falsely believes that his co-workers are not only trying to steal his "secret inventions" but also are plotting to kill him. A biomedical therapist would most likely prescribe
    (a) electroconvulsive therapy.
    (b) lithium.
    (c) antipsychotic medications.
    (d) antidepressant medications.

3. Mervyn's therapist prescribed a medication that is classified as a selective serotonin reuptake inhibitor (SSRI) for his psychological symptoms. It is most likely that Mervyn suffers from
    (a) schizophrenia.
    (b) bipolar disorder.
    (c) anxiety disorder.
    (d) depression.

4. When Freda told her therapist that she wanted his advice on what she should do about her relationship problems, he replied, "It sounds to me like you are experiencing some difficulties with your relationship. Is that right?" The therapist's response reflects the technique of
    (a) transference.
    (b) free association.
    (c) empathic understanding.
    (d) counterconditioning.

5. To help overcome the trial-and-error nature of prescribing antidepressants and other psychotropic drugs, researchers are now studying how genes influence an individual's response to drugs. This relatively new field is called
    (a) deep brain stimulation (DBS).
    (b) integrative therapy.
    (c) interpersonal therapy (IPT).
    (d) pharmacogenetics.

6. When Greta's psychoanalyst asked her to elaborate on certain aspects of her dream, she couldn't think of anything to say. Her lack of responsiveness is likely to be interpreted as
    (a) resistance.
    (b) extinction.
    (c) transference.
    (d) spontaneous remission.

7. Dr. Whelan believes that people can overcome their problems if they learn to recognize and monitor their automatic thoughts and then try to test the reality of those thoughts empirically. Her approach is most consistent with
    (a) behavior therapy.
    (b) biomedical therapy.
    (c) cognitive therapy.
    (d) psychoanalysis.

8. Dr. Lopez is a psychotherapist who utilizes multiple approaches in his practice. He tries to blend these together rather than using different approaches for different clients. Dr. Lopez uses an approach called ________________ in his practice.
   (a) familismo
   (b) family or couple therapy
   (c) group therapy
   (d) integrative psychotherapy

9. For which patient is Dr. Kelly most likely to prescribe the atypical antipsychotic medication olanzapine, which affects both serotonin and dopamine levels in the brain?
   (a) Celia, who smokes three packs of cigarettes a day
   (b) Garth, who irrationally believes that aliens are trying to steal his thoughts
   (c) Manuel, who fluctuates between extreme moods of euphoria and depression
   (d) Rachel, who suffers from nervous apprehension, intense anxiety, and an inability to relax

10. Quentin has an irrational fear of riding in elevators. His therapist first teaches him to relax completely, then he asks him to come up with a list of anxiety-provoking images associated with elevators. Finally, the therapist asks Quentin to close his eyes and imagine very clearly the least fearful scene on the list. Quentin's therapist is a ________________ therapist using ________________ .
    (a) behavior; systematic desensitization
    (b) cognitive; rational-emotive techniques
    (c) humanistic; empathic understanding
    (d) psychoanalytic; free association

11. Jeneen is taking a prescription drug that is a naturally occurring substance called lithium. It is most probable that she is suffering from
    (a) schizophrenia.
    (b) bipolar disorder.
    (c) chronic depression.
    (d) anxiety disorder.

12. Ursula, who lives in a home for children with behavior problems, is able to earn points for getting dressed, maintaining personal hygiene, and engaging in appropriate social interactions. These points can be exchanged for access to desirable items or special privileges. This example illustrates the use of
    (a) aversive conditioning.
    (b) counterconditioning.
    (c) systematic desensitization.
    (d) a token economy.

13. Seven-year-old Niall chews the ends of all his pens and pencils, so his mother paints them with a foul-tasting, but harmless, substance. After a few days of this treatment, Niall stops chewing his pens and pencils. Niall's mother has used a form of
    (a) transference.
    (b) counterconditioning.
    (c) aversive therapy.
    (d) electroconvulsive therapy.

14. To overcome his fear of heights, Gaetan is fitted with special motion-sensitive goggles that expose him to a computer-generated, three-dimensional environment that appears very real. He is progressively exposed to views from different heights as he practices relaxation. According to In Focus (Using Virtual Reality to Conquer Phobias), this approach
    (a) is very likely to make his phobia worse.
    (b) is considered to be a pseudoscience by most psychologists.
    (c) is one form of Naikan therapy.
    (d) is very likely to reduce his fear of heights.

15. According to Critical Thinking (Evaluating New Psychotherapies: The Case of EMDR), eye movement desensitization reprocessing (EMDR)
    (a) has been used to treat post-traumatic stress disorder (PTSD), panic disorder, addiction, substance abuse, sleep disorders, and other psychological disorders.
    (b) is no more effective than standard approaches, such as exposure therapy, in the treatment of anxiety disorders, including PTSD.
    (c) is a pseudoscience, according to some psychologists.
    (d) has all of these characteristics.

Progress Test 3

After you have checked your understanding of the material in Progress Tests 1 and 2, and have done a complete chapter review with special focus on any areas of weakness, you are ready to further assess your knowledge with Progress Test 3. Check your answers. If you make a mistake, review your notes, the appropriate parts of the study guide, and, if necessary, the relevant sections of your textbook.

1. After reviewing the literature on the use of lithium and the mechanism involved in its effectiveness in treating bipolar disorder, Richelle is likely to conclude that lithium
   (a) stabilizes the availability of glutamate, an excitatory neurotransmitter, preventing both abnormal highs and lows.
   (b) boosts the levels of dopamine in the brain.
   (c) selectively inhibits the reuptake of serotonin.
   (d) stabilizes the levels of both dopamine and serotonin in the brain.

2. Aaron Beck is to ________________ as Carl Rogers is to ________________ .
   (a) cognitive therapy; rational-emotive therapy
   (b) behavior therapy; client-centered therapy
   (c) biomedical therapy; psychoanalysis
   (d) cognitive therapy; client-centered therapy

3. Because of Rhian's persistent feelings of hopelessness, dejection, and guilt, and her suicidal thoughts, her doctor prescribes an antidepressant drug. Rhian is most likely to be taking a(n)
   (a) selective serotonin reuptake inhibitor (SSRI) called Prozac.
   (b) benzodiazepine drug called Valium.
   (c) neuroleptic medication called Thorazine.
   (d) anticonvulsant medicine called Depakote.

4. When Clifford decided to pursue a career as an artist instead of complying with his father's wish for him to become a lawyer, both parents were angry, critical, and rejecting. Carl Rogers would say that Clifford's parents are demonstrating
   (a) conditional acceptance.
   (b) empathic understanding.
   (c) unconditional positive regard.
   (d) unconscious motivations and feelings.

5. Mrs. Blonska has been diagnosed with generalized anxiety disorder. Because her doctor is concerned with the long-term treatment of her global and persistent feelings of anxiety, he is likely to prescribe
   (a) Buspar. (c) Depakote.
   (b) Prozac. (d) Thorazine.

6. Mr. MacKaskill has a serious drinking problem. To reduce his intake of alcohol, a behavior therapist might give Mr. MacKaskill a medication called Antabuse, which induces nausea whenever it is taken with alcohol. This behavioral technique is called
   (a) counterconditioning.
   (b) systematic desensitization.
   (c) aversive conditioning.
   (d) the token economy.

7. For no obvious reason, Mr. Henderson has recently begun to express feelings of annoyance, irritability, and anger toward his therapist, who has been consistently patient, concerned, and supportive. Freud would most likely consider Mr. Henderson's hostility toward his therapist an example of
   (a) insight. (c) aversion.
   (b) counterconditioning. (d) transference.

8. Dr. Elson uses a therapeutic technique that involves modifying behavior by conditioning a new response that is incompatible with a previously learned undesired response. Dr. Elson is most likely a ________________ therapist who is using ________________ .
   (a) behavior; counterconditioning
   (b) cognitive; rational-emotive techniques
   (c) psychoanalytic; free association
   (d) biomedical; ECT

9. Nelson's therapist believes that a therapist should be nondirective, providing unconditional positive regard in an open, honest way. Nelson's therapist is most likely a ____________ therapist.
   (a) psychoanalytic (c) cognitive
   (b) behavioral (d) humanistic

10. During a lecture to students interested in graduate work in clinical psychology, Dr. Barton is asked what factors contribute most to effective psychotherapy. He is most likely to respond that
    (a) mutual respect, trust, and hope in the therapeutic situation are important factors.
    (b) therapists who have warmth, sensitivity, sincerity, and genuineness are usually effective.

(c) clients who are motivated, expressive, and actively committed to therapy enhance the success of therapy.
(d) all of these factors contribute to effective psychotherapy.

11. Brian's therapist attempts to tailor her approach to his particular problems and characteristics and, in doing so, uses techniques from different psychotherapies. Brian's therapist would most likely be classified as a(n) ________________ therapist.
   (a) humanistic (c) behavior
   (b) eclectic (d) cognitive

12. Which of the following individuals is most likely to benefit from a psychotropic drug that affects the level of the neurotransmitter dopamine in the brain?
   (a) Herman, who hears imaginary voices telling him that he is going to be abducted by aliens
   (b) Marcel, who is very nervous and anxious all the time
   (c) Carla, who feels sad, despondent, dejected, and worthless most of the time
   (d) Faith, who drinks at least a six-pack of beer every day

13. Harriet has asked her psychology professor whether psychotherapy is more effective than no therapy at all. If her professor is familiar with the meta-analytic studies on the topic, he is most likely to answer that
   (a) psychotherapy is no more effective than talking to a friend.
   (b) it is not possible to measure the effectiveness of psychotherapy.
   (c) psychotherapy harms more people than it helps.
   (d) psychotherapy is significantly more effective than no treatment.

14. According to In Focus (Self-Help Groups), which of the following is true about self-help groups?
   (a) Compared with therapy provided by mental health professionals, self-help groups are generally ineffective for the vast majority of psychological problems.
   (b) All self-help groups are organized and led by nonprofessionals.
   (c) Compared with professional mental health services, self-help groups are much more likely to cause harm to the people involved.
   (d) To operate legally, self-help groups must employ at least one registered professional, such as a clinical psychologist, or a licensed physician, such as a psychiatrist.

15. Masahara goes to a therapist who specializes in a Japanese psychotherapy called Naikan therapy. According to Culture and Human Behavior (Cultural Values and Psychotherapy), it is very probable that he will be advised to
   (a) avoid being self-absorbed and focus on developing a sense of gratitude and obligation toward significant others.
   (b) meditate on how much his parents and others have done for him and how he may have failed to meet their needs.
   (c) reflect on the trouble and problems he may have caused significant others.
   (d) do all of these things.

Answers

Introduction: Psychotherapy and Biomedical Therapy

1. *Psychological disorders are* troubling thoughts, feelings, or behaviors that cause psychological discomfort or interfere with a person's ability to function. *Not everyone who seeks help is suffering from a psychological disorder. Many people seek help* in dealing with troubled relationships (such as parent–child conflicts, an unhappy marriage) or in dealing with life's transitions (such as coping with the death of a loved one, dissolving a marriage, adjusting to retirement); for some, the goal of therapy is to attain greater self-knowledge or personal fulfillment.
2. *Psychotherapy refers to* the treatment of emotional, behavioral, and interpersonal problems through the use of psychological techniques designed to encourage understanding of problems and to modify troubling feelings, behaviors, or relationships.
3. *A basic assumption of all psychotherapies is that* psychological factors play a significant role in a person's troubling feelings, behaviors, or relationships.
4. *Biomedical therapies involve* the use of medications, electroconvulsive therapy, or other medical treatments to treat the symptoms associated with psychological disorders.
5. *The biomedical therapies are based on the assumption that* the symptoms of many psychological disorders involve biological factors, such as abnormal brain chemistry.
6. *Until recently, only licensed physicians* were legally allowed to prescribe psychotropic medi-

cations. *However, since the 1990s* a movement to allow specially trained psychologists to prescribe psychotropic drugs has achieved some success, and two states, Louisiana and New Mexico, have granted prescription-writing privileges to properly trained psychologists (other states may follow soon). In addition, those clinical psychologists who are involved in medication treatment decisions or have clients who are taking psychotropic medications, should follow the new APA (2011) guidelines regarding prescription medications. *Psychologists are also urged to adopt a* biopsychosocial *approach to treatment.*

Psychoanalytic Therapy

1. *Psychoanalysis is a* type of psychotherapy originated by Sigmund Freud in which free association, dream interpretation, and analysis of resistance and transference are used to explore repressed or unconscious impulses, anxieties, and internal conflicts.
2. *The main psychoanalytic techniques (and their purpose) are (a)* free association, in which the patient spontaneously reports all her thoughts, mental images, and feelings while lying on a couch; *(b)* resistance, the patient's conscious and unconscious attempts to block the revelation of repressed memories and conflicts, which is a sign the patient is uncomfortably close to uncovering psychologically threatening material; *(c)* dream interpretation, the analysis of dream content for disguised or symbolic wishes, meanings, and motivations; *(d)* interpretation, in which the psychoanalyst offers a carefully timed explanation of the patient's dreams, free associations, or behavior to facilitate the recognition of unconscious conflicts or motivations; and *(e)* transference, the process by which emotions and desires originally associated with a significant person in the patient's life, such as a parent, are unconsciously transferred to the psychoanalyst.
3. *Together, these psychoanalytic techniques are designed to* help uncover unconscious conflicts so the patient attains insight as to the real source of her problems.
4. *The various forms of short-term dynamic therapies (all based on traditional psychoanalytic notions) have four features in common:* *(a)* Contact lasts for no more than a few months. *(b)* The patient's problems are quickly assessed at the beginning of therapy. *(c)* The therapist and patient agree on specific, concrete, and attainable goals. *(d)* In the actual sessions, most psychodynamic therapists are more directive than traditional psychoanalysts, actively engaging the patient in a dialogue.
5. *Interpersonal therapy (IPT) is* a brief, psychodynamic therapy that focuses on current relationships and social interactions and is based on the assumption that symptoms are caused and maintained by interpersonal problems. *The four categories of personal problems dealt with are (a)* unresolved grief (problems dealing with the death of significant others); *(b)* role disputes (repetitive conflicts with others, such as a person's partner, family members, friends, or co-workers); *(c)* role transitions (problems involving major life changes such as going away to college, becoming a parent, getting married or divorced, or retiring); and *(d)* interpersonal deficits (absent or faulty social skills that limit the ability to start or maintain healthy relationships with others).
6. *IPT has been used to treat* eating disorders, substance abuse, depression, marital conflicts, parenting issues, and conflicts at work. It has been used cross-culturally and has proved valuable in family and group therapy sessions.

Concept Check 1

1. resistance
2. free association
3. interpretation
4. transference
5. dream interpretation
6. biomedical therapies; psychotherapy
7. interpersonal therapy (IPT)
8. short-term dynamic
9. unresolved grief; role disputes; role transitions; interpersonal deficits

Matching Exercise 1

1. interpersonal deficits
2. psychotherapy
3. interpretation
4. psychoanalysis
5. biomedical therapies
6. short-term dynamic therapies
7. psychotropic medications
8. role disputes
9. Sigmund Freud
10. psychological disorder

True/False Test 1

1. T	4. T	7. T
2. T	5. T	8. T
3. F	6. F	9. T

Humanistic Therapy

1. *The humanistic perspective emphasizes* human potential, self-awareness, and freedom of choice.
2. *The most influential humanistic therapy is* client- (or person-) centered therapy; *it was developed by* Carl Rogers *who deliberately used the word* client *rather than* patient *because* he wanted to get away from the idea that the person was sick and was seeking treatment from an all-knowing authority figure. He also wanted to emphasize the client's subjective perception of himself and his environment.
3. *In client-centered therapy, the main conditions are that* the therapist should be nondirective; the client should direct the focus of therapy sessions; and the therapist should be genuine, demonstrate unconditional positive regard, and communicate empathic understanding.
4. *Unlike psychoanalysis, humanistic therapy does not offer* solutions or interpretations about the client's unconscious feelings and motivations; instead, it is nondirective.
5. *Motivational interviewing is designed to* help clients overcome the mixed feelings or reluctance they might have about committing to change; it is more directive than traditional client-centered therapy, and its main goal is to encourage or strengthen the client's self-motivated statements or "change talk."
6. *The client-centered approach has been applied to* marital counseling, parenting, education, business, and even community and international relations.

Behavior Therapy

1. *The goal of behavior therapy is to* modify specific problem behaviors, not to change the entire personality.
2. *Behavior therapists assume that maladaptive behaviors are* learned, just as adaptive behaviors are. *Therefore, the basic strategy in behavior therapy involves* unlearning maladaptive behaviors and learning more adaptive behaviors in their place.
3. *Behavior therapists employ techniques that are based on the learning principles of* classical conditioning, operant conditioning, and observational learning.
4. *Mary Cover Jones's procedure, called counterconditioning, involved* gradually introducing the feared stimulus and pairing it with a pleasant stimulus, such as food, which elicits a positive response that is incompatible with the original conditioned response (this procedure also eliminated fear of objects that were similar to the original feared stimulus).
5. *Along with counterconditioning, Jones used* social imitation, or observational learning, techniques and demonstrated that seeing others acting in a fearless manner encourages the fearful individual to imitate the fearless behavior.
6. *Based on the same premise as counterconditioning, systematic desensitization involves* learning a new conditioned response (relaxation) that is incompatible with or inhibits the old conditioned response (fear and anxiety).
7. *The three basic steps involved in systematic desensitization are (a)* The patient learns progressive relaxation. *(b)* The therapist helps the patient construct a hierarchy of anxiety-provoking images and develop a relaxing control scene. *(c)* The process of desensitization begins by getting the deeply relaxed patient to imagine the least threatening scene in the anxiety hierarchy (over several sessions the patient gradually works his way up the anxiety hierarchy, imagining each scene while maintaining complete relaxation).
8. *Virtual reality (VR) therapy uses* systematic desensitization techniques but exposure is to a computer-generated, three-dimensional environment, which the viewer experiences as if it were real. *VR therapy has been used to treat* phobias and other anxiety disorders., such as social phobia, panic disorder, and post-traumatic stress disorder (PTSD).
9. *Aversive conditioning involves* repeatedly pairing an aversive stimulus with the occurrence of undesirable behaviors or thoughts (a relatively ineffective type of behavior therapy). *Aversive conditioning has been applied to* a wide variety of problems, including addictions such as alcoholism and cigarette smoking. *However, mental health professionals* have concerns about its potential harm or the possibility of its causing discomfort to clients. Also, aversive techniques generally are not very effective.

10. *B. F. Skinner's operant conditioning model of learning is based on the simple principle that behavior is* shaped and maintained by its consequences. This model uses positive reinforcement for desired behaviors and extinction (or nonreinforcement) for undesired behaviors. *Operant conditioning techniques have been used to treat* many different kinds of psychological problems, including habit and weight control problems, helping autistic children learn to speak and behave more adaptively, and modifying the behavior of people who are severely disabled by retardation or mental disorders.
11. *The token economy is a form of behavior therapy in which* the therapeutic environment is structured to reward desired behaviors with tokens or points that may eventually be exchanged for tangible rewards. *Token economies have been used in* classrooms, inpatient psychiatric units, and group homes. *A modified version of the token economy is called* contingency management *and has been used to treat* people who are dependent on heroin, cocaine, alcohol, or multiple drugs.

Concept Check 2

1. humanistic; client-centered
2. behavior therapy (systematic desensitization)
3. aversive
4. token economy
5. counterconditioning; classical conditioning; Mary Cover Jones
6. client-centered; empathic understanding
7. extinction; positive reinforcement
8. shaping

Matching Exercise 2

1. Mary Cover Jones
2. humanistic perspective
3. token economy
4. genuineness
5. behavior therapy (behavior modification)
6. Carl Rogers
7. progressive relaxation
8. contingency management
9. client-centered therapy
10. Antabuse
11. baseline rate
12. observational learning
13. anxiety hierarchy

True/False 2

1. F	4. T	7. T	10. T
2. T	5. T	8. T	11. T
3. T	6. T	9. F	12. T

Cognitive Therapies

1. *Cognitive therapies assume that* most people blame unhappiness and problems on external events and situations, but the real cause of unhappiness is the way the person thinks about the events, not the events themselves.
2. *The goal of cognitive therapy is to* identify the faulty, irrational patterns of thinking and then to change them to more adaptive, healthy patterns.
3. *Rational-emotive therapy (RET) was developed by* Albert Ellis, *and it focuses on* identifying, disputing, and changing the client's irrational beliefs (explained by the ABC model [an *A*ctivating event triggers *B*eliefs about the event that cause emotional *C*onsequences]). *RET has been effective in the treatment of* depression, social phobia, certain anxiety disorders, and in helping people overcome self-defeating behaviors, such as an excessive need for approval, extreme shyness, and chronic procrastination.
4. *Beck's cognitive therapy (CT) focuses on* changing the client's unrealistic and distorted beliefs, and on correcting the cognitive biases that underlie depression and other psychological disorders.
5. *Like Ellis, Beck believes that* what people think creates their moods and emotions; like RET, CT involves helping clients identify faulty thinking and replace unhealthy patterns of thinking with healthier ones.
6. *In contrast with Ellis's emphasis on "irrational" thinking, Beck believes that* depression and other psychological problems are caused by distorted thinking and unrealistic beliefs, and that the task of the cognitive therapist is to encourage the client to empirically test the accuracy of his or her assumptions and beliefs. *Cognitive therapy (CT) has been effective in treating* depression, anxiety disorders, borderline personality disorders, eating disorders, PTSD, relationship problems, and some psychotic symptoms.
7. *Cognitive-behavioral therapy (CBT) refers to* a group of psychotherapies that integrate cognitive and behavioral techniques. *Cognitive-*

behavioral therapy is based on the assumption that thoughts, moods, and behaviors are interrelated; changes in thought patterns affect moods and behaviors, and changes in behavior affect cognitions and emotional states. *CBT has been used to treat* children, adolescents, the elderly, and psychological disorders such as depression, eating problems, substance abuse, anxiety disorders; it has also helped decrease the incidence of delusions and hallucinations and other psychotic symptoms in patients with schizophrenia.

8. *Mindfulness is* a meditation technique that involves present-centered awareness without judgment. *Mindfulness-based therapies (mindfulness-based interventions or mindfulness and acceptance therapies) involve* the mindfulness meditation technique of present-centered awareness without judgment; they target both thoughts and behaviors without challenging, testing, or replacing the **content** of thoughts. *The goal is* to change the **context** in which those thoughts are understood; clients are taught to observe and change their relationship to maladaptive thoughts and emotions (decentering is one technique used to achieve this).
9. *Mindfulness-Based Stress Reduction (MBSR) involves* a structured program of mindfulness meditation, yoga and mindful body practices, and group discussion; it was developed to treat stress and anxiety. *Mindfulness-Based Cognitive Therapy (MBCT) was developed to treat* depression, but it has been expanded to treat other disorders. *Mindfulness training has been incorporated as* a core element in other cognitive-behavioral treatments, including therapies used to treat substance abuse and borderline personality disorder. *A meta-analysis has found that MBSR and MBCT are effective treatments* for mood and anxiety disorders; MBCT has also been found to be effective in preventing relapse after acute depression.

Group and Family Therapy

1. *Group therapy involves* one or more therapists working simultaneously with a small group of clients (the group may be as small as 3 or 4 people, or as large as 10 or more people).
2. *Some of the key advantages of group therapy are that* it is cost-effective; therapists can observe clients interacting with other group members; clients can benefit from the support, encouragement, and practical suggestions provided by other group members; and people can try out new behaviors in a safe, supportive environment.
3. *Family therapy is based on the assumption that* the family is an interdependent system; it focuses on treating the family as a unit, rather than on treating the individual.
4. *Couple therapy focuses on* improving communication, problem-solving skills, and intimacy between members of any couple in a committed relationship. *Behavioral couple therapy is based on the assumption that* couples are satisfied when they experience more reinforcement than punishment in their relationship; it focuses on increasing caring behaviors, teaching couples how to constructively resolve conflicts and problems, improving communication, reducing negative communication, and increasing intimacy between the pair.

Evaluating the Effectiveness of Psychotherapy

1. *Meta-analysis involves* pooling the results of several studies into a single analysis, creating one large study that can reveal overall trends in the data. *When meta-analysis is used to summarize studies, the researchers consistently arrive at the same conclusion:* psychotherapy is significantly more effective than no treatment. In general, there is little or no difference in the effectiveness of different psychotherapies; all the standard psychotherapies have similar success rates, are empirically supported, and some compare favorably with biomedical interventions (see Focus On Neuroscience: Comparing Psychotherapy and Antidepressant Medication).
2. *Researchers have identified a number of factors that are related to a positive therapy outcome: (a)* The most important factors are those associated with the therapeutic relationship, such as mutual respect, trust, and hope; *(b)* certain characteristics of the therapist, such as warmth, sensitivity, responsiveness, being perceived as sincere and genuine, and actively helping people to understand and face their problems; *(c)* client characteristics, such as level of motivation, commitment to therapy, active involvement in the process, along with emotional and social maturity and the ability to express thoughts and feelings; *(d)* external circumstances, such as supportive family members and a stable living situation; *(e)* being sensitive to cultural differences and multicultural issues; and *(f)* for therapy to be optimally effective, the individual should feel comfortable with both the therapist and his or her approach (there should

be a good "match" between the person and the specific psychotherapy techniques used).

3. *Eclecticism refers to the* pragmatic and integrated use of techniques from different psychotherapies (eclectic psychotherapists carefully tailor their approach to the problems and characteristics of the person seeking help). *Integrative psychotherapy is a technique* related to eclectic psychotherapy that uses multiple approaches that are blended together rather than using different approaches for different clients.

Concept Check 3

1. meta-analysis
2. eclectic
3. group
4. rational-emotive
5. cognitive
6. family
7. cognitive-behavioral
8. self-help group
9. eye movement desensitization reprocessing (EMDR); no better
10. familismo
11. Mindfulness-Based Stress Reduction (MBSR)

Graphic Organizer 1

Psychoanalysis:
Founder: Sigmund Freud
Source of Problems: Repressed, unconscious conflicts stemming from early childhood experiences
Treatment Techniques: Free association, analysis of dream content, interpretation, resistance, and transference
Goals of Therapy: To recognize, work through, and resolve long-standing conflicts

Client-Centered Therapy:
Founder: Carl Rogers
Source of Problems: Conditional acceptance and dependence that cause a person to develop a distorted self-concept and worldview
Treatment Techniques: Nondirective therapy, with therapist displaying unconditional positive regard, genuineness, and empathic understanding
Goals of Therapy: To develop self-awareness, self-acceptance, and self-determination

Behavior Therapy:
Founder: Various; derived from the fundamental principles of learning
Source of Problems: Learned maladaptive behavior patterns
Treatment Techniques: Counterconditioning, systematic desensitization, virtual reality therapy, aversive conditioning, shaping, reinforcement and extinction, token economy, and observational learning
Goals of Therapy: To unlearn maladaptive behaviors and learn adaptive behaviors in their place

Rational-Emotive Therapy:
Founder: Albert Ellis
Source of Problems: Irrational beliefs
Treatment Techniques: Very directive therapy: identifying, logically disputing, and challenging irrational beliefs
Goals of Therapy: To surrender irrational beliefs and absolutist demands

Cognitive Therapy (for depression):
Founder: Aaron T. Beck
Source of Problems: Unrealistic, distorted perceptions and interpretations of events due to cognitive biases
Treatment Techniques: Directive collaboration: teaching client to monitor automatic thoughts; testing accuracy of conclusions; correcting distorted thinking and perception
Goals of Therapy: To accurately and realistically perceive self, others, and external events

Cognitive-Behavioral Therapy:
Founder: Various; derived from both cognitive and behavioral traditions
Source of Problems: Cognitions, behaviors, and emotional responses are functionally interrelated; negative thoughts affect moods and behaviors, and maladaptive behaviors affect thoughts and moods
Treatment Techniques: Pragmatic approach that integrates the most appropriate cognitive and behavioral therapeutic approaches for each individual's needs and problems. An emerging approach in cognitive-behavioral therapy involves the use of mindfulness meditation techniques.
Goals of Therapy: To replace maladaptive behaviors and irrational, distorted, unrealistic perceptions and cognitions with more adaptive healthier ones. The goal of the mindfulness-based therapies is to change the context in which thoughts are understood; clients are taught to observe and change their relationship to maladaptive thoughts and emotions.

Matching Exercise 3

1. family therapy
2. cognitive therapies
3. cognitive therapy (CT)

4. group therapy
5. rational-emotive therapy (RET)
6. cognitive-behavioral therapy (CBT)
7. eye movement desensitization reprocessing (EMDR)
8. meta-analysis
9. behavioral couple therapy
10. integrative psychotherapy
11. mindfulness
12. Mindfulness-Based Stress Reduction (MBSR)

True/False Test 3

1. F	4. T	7. T	10. T
2. T	5. F	8. T	11. T
3. T	6. T	9. T	12. T

Biomedical Therapies

1. *The biomedical therapies are* medical treatments for the symptoms of psychological disorders. The most common biomedical therapy is the use of psychotropic medications.
2. *Antipsychotic medications (neuroleptics) are* prescription drugs that are used to reduce psychotic symptoms (they are frequently used in the treatment of schizophrenia). *The most common antipsychotic medications include* reserpine and chlorpromazine (Thorazine), which alter dopamine levels in the brain. *Although the early antipsychotics reduced* the positive symptoms of schizophrenia, they were not very effective in eliminating the negative symptoms. Also, they often produced serious side effects, including tardive dyskinesia, after long-term use.
3. *The atypical antipsychotic medications include* clozapine, risperidone, olanzapine, sertindole, and quetiapine, *and they act by* selectively affecting both serotonin and dopamine levels in the brain (the atypical antipsychotics have several advantages over the older antipsychotics, including that they are less likely to cause movement-related side effects and they are more effective in treating both positive and negative symptoms of schizophrenia). *These second-generation antipsychotics cause* some of the same side effects as the first-generation antipsychotics (weight gain, cardiac problems, and, especially in younger patients, risk of diabetes), and do not produce greater improvements.
4. *Antianxiety medications are* prescription drugs that are used to alleviate the symptoms of anxiety. *The most common antianxiety medications include* the benzodiazepines (such as Valium and Xanax), which are effective in the treatment of anxiety by increasing the level of GABA, but they are potentially addictive and have many side effects. *Buspar, a newer antianxiety drug, has fewer side effects and is not* a benzodiazepine; *it does not affect* the neurotransmitter GABA or cause drowsiness, sedation, or cognitive impairment, and it has a low level of dependency and addiction (however, it does take a few weeks to become effective).
5. *Lithium is* a naturally occurring substance that is used in the treatment of bipolar disorder; it appears to work by stabilizing the availability of glutamate, an excitatory neurotransmitter, preventing both abnormal highs and lows. Because of serious side effects, the patient's blood levels of lithium must be constantly monitored. *Depakote, an anticonvulsant, has been used to treat* those who do not respond to lithium, and those who cycle through bouts of bipolar disorder several times a year.
6. *The antidepressant medications are* prescription drugs that are used to reduce the symptoms associated with depression. *The most common antidepressant medications include* the first-generation tricyclics and MAO inhibitors, and the second-generation antidepressants trazodone and bupropion. *New antidepressants, including* the selective serotonin reuptake inhibitors (SSRIs) Prozac, Paxil, and Zoloft; the dual-action antidepressants Serzone and Remeron; and the dual-reuptake inhibitors Effexor and Cymbalta (which inhibit serotonin and norepinephrine) and Wellbutrin (which is a dopamine-norepinephrine inhibitor) *tend to* produce fewer side effects than the first- and second-generation antidepressants. *The SSRIs are also used to treat* anxiety disorders. *To help overcome the trial-and-error nature of prescribing antidepressants and other psychotropic drugs, pharmacogenetics, which is* the study of how genes influence an individual's response to drugs, *has emerged.*
7. *Electroconvulsive therapy (ECT) is a biomedical therapy used primarily* in the treatment of severe depression; it involves electrically inducing brief brain seizures (also called shock therapy and electroshock therapy). *Some of the new experimental treatments (that don't involve seizures) are* transcranial magnetic stimulation (TMS), vagus nerve stimulation (VNS), and deep brain stimulation (DBS).

Concept Check 4

1. antianxiety
2. electroconvulsive
3. tardive dyskinesia
4. lithium
5. olanzapine; sertindole; quetiapine
6. the same
7. anxiety disorder
8. selective serotonin reuptake inhibitors (SSRIs); Prozac; Zoloft; Paxil; Serzone; Remeron; Effexor; Cymbalta; Wellbutrin

Matching Exercise 4

1. lithium
2. psychotropic medications
3. electroconvulsive therapy (ECT)
4. antianxiety medications
5. antidepressant medications
6. tardive dyskinesia
7. dual-action antidepressants
8. GABA
9. pharmacogenetics
10. deep brain stimulation

True/False Test 4

1. T
2. T
3. T
4. T
5. T
6. T
7. T
8. T
9. F
10. F

Something to Think About

1. The first thing to tell someone with a phobia is that there are many different therapeutic approaches in psychology, such as psychoanalysis, client-centered therapy, cognitive therapy, and behavior therapy. It would be appropriate to briefly explain the differences between each of these approaches and to advise the person to seek professional help if he feels that his problem is severe. Having said that, you can then go on to describe an approach that has been relatively effective in dealing with phobias—systematic desensitization.

   The first step in systematic desensitization is for the person to learn how to relax completely. This is because a state of complete relaxation is incompatible with being tense and anxious. The second step is to have the person generate a hierarchy of feared situations associated with flying. For example, the most feared situation the person can imagine might be sitting on the plane during takeoff and the least fearful might be hearing someone talking about flying. Once the person is totally relaxed, he can start imagining the least fearful situation in the hierarchy. When he can do that for a number of times without tensing up, he can move to the next situation in the hierarchy, and so on. It is also helpful for the person to create an unrelated, relaxing control scene, such as lying on the beach watching the waves roll in, which can be used to help him relax. Over a number of sessions, the person works his way up the hierarchy while relaxing completely, until eventually he can approach the real situation.

   In practice, systematic desensitization is often combined with other techniques, such as counterconditioning (pairing pleasant associations, such as being able to travel to exotic islands, with the feared situation) and observational learning (using the real situation or a video), which involves watching other people being calm and relaxed in the anxiety-provoking situation. A newer technology-based therapy uses systematic desensitization techniques while the person is exposed to a computer-generated, three-dimensional environment, which the viewer experiences as if it were real. Virtual reality therapy has been effective in treating a variety of phobias, including fear of flying.

2. First, people seek help from mental health professionals not only for psychological problems but also for dealing with troubled relationships, coping with transitions in life, and other troubling situations. Second, there should be no stigma attached to getting help when it is needed. The prevalence of psychological disorders and similar types of problems is much higher than most people realize, so we all probably know someone who is or has been in therapy or perhaps needs to be. So, what should we expect from psychotherapy? Enhancing Well-Being with Psychology gives some important guidelines about the therapist–client relationship and the psychotherapy process.

   The cornerstone of psychotherapy is the relationship between the therapist and the person seeking help. This relationship is a collaborative endeavor in which the client is actively involved in the therapeutic process. Therapy requires work not only during the therapy sessions but also outside them. So people should expect to be involved and active. In addition, people should not expect the therapist to make decisions for them. Virtually all forms of therapy are designed to increase a person's sense of responsibility, confidence, and mastery in dealing with life's problems. The therapist is there to help.

A therapist is not a substitute friend. Rather, he or she is more of a consultant, responding objectively and honestly to issues and problems. In addition, ethically and legally, everything that goes on in therapy is totally confidential. And, under no circumstances does therapeutic intimacy include sexual intimacy.

A person should also expect therapy to challenge how he or she thinks and acts, which sometimes can be a painful process. But becoming aware that changes are needed is a necessary step toward developing healthier forms of thinking and behavior. It is important, however, not to confuse insight with change. Just because people gain an understanding of the sources and nature of their psychological problems does not mean that they will automatically resolve these problems. Likewise, the catharsis that often results from therapy is not synonymous with change. With some effort and the help of the therapeutic process, people can move toward changing how they think, behave, and react to other people, but this will not happen overnight.

Progress Test 1

1. a
2. d
3. d
4. a
5. c
6. b
7. b
8. d
9. c
10. b
11. c
12. c
13. d
14. d
15. b

Progress Test 2

1. d
2. c
3. d
4. c
5. d
6. a
7. c
8. d
9. b
10. a
11. b
12. d
13. c
14. d
15. d

Progress Test 3

1. a
2. d
3. a
4. a
5. a
6. c
7. d
8. a
9. d
10. d
11. b
12. a
13. d
14. b
15. d

APPENDIX A

Statistics: Understanding Data

PREVIEW

Reading the section below first will give you a general sense of the appendix's contents and an initial introduction to some of the major concepts and terms. This will prime you for what you are about to read and help you to develop a "cognitive map" that will guide your study of the material in this appendix. Likewise, reading the **preview questions** at the beginning of each major section will improve your ability to understand, learn, and retain the information.

APPENDIX A . . . AT A GLANCE

Appendix A explains how and when various statistical techniques are used. Descriptive statistics are used to organize and summarize data in a meaningful way. Examples discussed include frequency distributions, which can be presented as a table, histogram, or frequency polygon; measures of central tendency (mode, median, and mean); and measures of variability (range and standard deviation). z scores are explained, and the concept of the standard normal distribution is presented.

Correlation, which is introduced in Chapter 1, is described, and how to calculate the correlation coefficient is explained. Both positive and negative correlations are discussed. The relationship between two variables may be presented visually in a scatter diagram. The point is made that correlational research is restricted to prediction and cannot be used to identify cause-and-effect relationships.

Inferential statistics are used to determine whether the outcome of a study can be generalized to a larger population. They provide information about the probability of a particular result if only random factors are operating. An example of an inferential test is the t-test, which can be used to compare the means of two groups to see if any differences are statistically real or simply due to random factors. To compare the means of more than two groups, researchers use the analysis of variance (ANOVA) technique. If the probability of the outcome resulting from chance factors is small, the findings are said to be statistically significant. However, researchers could erroneously conclude that results are significant (a Type I error), or fail to find a significant effect when it really exists (a Type II error). Use of inferential statistics allows researchers to have confidence that the results from a sample are statistically significant.

Descriptive Statistics

Preview Questions

Consider the following questions as you study this section of the appendix.

- What are descriptive statistics, and what are they used for?
- What are frequency distributions and the two types of graphic representations: histograms and frequency polygons?
- What is a skewed distribution, and what is a symmetrical distribution?
- What are the three measures of central tendency?
- What are the two measures of variability?
- What are *z* scores, and how do they relate to the standard normal curve (standard normal distribution)?

*Read the section "Descriptive Statistics" and **write** your answers to the following:*

1. Descriptive statistics are mathematical methods used to ______________________

____

2. A frequency distribution is ______________________

____

____

3. A histogram is______________________

____

____

4. A frequency polygon is ______________________

____

____

5. A skewed distribution is ______________________

____

____

If most people have low scores ______________________

____

If most people have high scores ______________________

____

6. A symmetrical distribution is ______________________

____

____

7. Measures of central tendency are ______________________

____

The mode is ______________________

____

The median is ______________________

____

The mean is ______________________

____

8. Measures of variability are ______________________

____

The range is ______________________

____

The standard deviation is ______________________

____

9. A *z* score is ______________________

____

10. The standard normal curve (standard normal distribution) is ______________________

____

____

A person with a *z* score of +1 on a normal distribution (1 SD above the mean) has

____

A person's z score can tell us______________________

____

____

After you have carefully studied the preceding section, complete the following exercises.

Concept Check 1

Read the following and write the correct term in the space provided.

1. Professor Wilson calculated the mode, median, and mean of the scores from the midterm exam. These descriptive statistics are referred to as ______________________ .
2. Professor Wilson noticed that the most frequently occurring score was 73; this score is called the ______________ .
3. To determine the spread of the scores, Professor Wilson subtracted the lowest score in the distribution from the highest. In this instance, he has calculated a measure of ______________ called the ______________________ .

4. Next, he subtracted the mean from each score in the distribution, squared each of these deviations, added them, divided by the number of scores in the distribution, and took the square root of the number just calculated. Professor Wilson has calculated a measure of ________________ called the ______________________.

5. Finally, Professor Wilson graphically represented the frequency distribution by placing a mark above each score at the point representing its frequency and then connecting these points with straight lines. This type of graph is called a ______________________.

Review of Terms and Concepts 1

Use the terms in this list to complete the Matching Exercise, then to help you answer the True/False items correctly.

statistics	measure of central tendency
descriptive statistics	mode
frequency distribution	median
histogram	mean
frequency polygon	measure of variability
skewed distribution	range
positively skewed distribution	standard deviation
negatively skewed distribution	*z* score
symmetrical distribution	standard normal curve (standard normal distribution)

Matching Exercise

Match the appropriate term with its definition or description.

1. ________________ A number, expressed in standard deviation units, that shows a score's deviation from the mean.
2. ________________ Mathematical methods used to organize and summarize data.
3. ________________ A symmetrical distribution forming a bell-shaped curve in which the mean, median, and mode are all equal and fall in the exact middle.
4. ________________ A summary of how often various scores occur in a sample of scores. Score values are arranged in order of magnitude, and the number of times each score occurs is recorded.
5. ________________ Measure of variability; expressed as the square root of the sum of the squared deviations around the mean divided by the number of scores in the distribution.
6. ________________ An asymmetrical distribution; more scores pile up on one side of the distribution than on the other.
7. ________________ A single number that presents information about the spread of scores in a frequency distribution.
8. ________________ Distribution in which the scores fall equally on both sides of the graph. The normal curve is an example.
9. ________________ Measure of variability; the highest score in a distribution minus the lowest score.

True/False Test

Indicate whether each statement is true or false by placing T or F in the blank space next to each item.

1. ____ In a positively skewed distribution, most people have high scores.
2. ____ The mode is the most frequently occurring score in a distribution.
3. ____ A measure of central tendency is a single number that presents some information about the "center" of a frequency distribution.
4. ____ In a negatively skewed distribution, most people have low scores.
5. ____ A histogram is a way of graphically representing a frequency distribution where frequency is marked above each score category on the graph's horizontal axis and the marks are connected by straight lines.
6. ____ The mean is the sum of a set of scores in a distribution divided by the number of scores; it is usually the most representative measure of central tendency.
7. ____ A frequency polygon is a way of graphically representing a frequency distribution and is a type of bar chart using vertical bars that touch.
8. ____ The median is the score that divides a frequency distribution exactly in half, so that the same number of scores lies on each side of it.
9. ____ The branch of mathematics used by researchers to organize, summarize, and interpret data is called statistics.

Correlation and Inferential Statistics

Preview Questions

Consider the following questions as you study these sections of the appendix.

- How is *correlation* defined, and what is the correlation coefficient?
- What is the difference between a positive and a negative correlation?
- How are correlations depicted graphically?
- What are inferential statistics?
- What are *t*-tests and the analysis of variance (ANOVA) technique used for?
- What is meant by statistical significance?
- What are Type I and Type II errors, and how can researchers deal with the problem of these errors?
- What is meant by the terms *population* and *sample*?

Read the sections "Correlation" and "Inferential Statistics" and ***write*** *your answers to the following:*

1. Correlation is the ____________________
2. The correlation coefficient is a numerical indication of ____________________
3. A positive correlation is a finding that ____________________
4. A negative correlation is a finding that ____________________
5. A correlation coefficient close to 1.00 (whether positive or negative) indicates ____________________

   while a number close to zero indicates ____________________
6. Correlations are depicted graphically ____________________

   A positive correlation is indicated by ____________________

   A negative correlation is indicated by ____________________
7. Inferential statistics are ____________________
8. A *t*-test is used to ____________________

   Analysis of variance (ANOVA) is used to ____________________
9. Statistical significance refers to the fact that if the results of a study are ____________________
10. A Type I error occurs when ____________________

    A Type II error occurs when ____________________

    Because of the possibility of a Type I error, it is important that ____________________

    One way to avoid a Type II error is to ____________________
11. A population is ____________________

    Because the entire population of interest usually cannot be studied, researchers use ____________________

After you have carefully studied the preceding section, complete the following exercises.

Concept Check 2

Read the following and write the correct term in the space provided.

1. Dr. Jabul discovers that the more education people have, the more money they tend to earn. Dr. Jabul has discovered a ____________________ correlation.

2. Based on his research, Dr. Jabul can use one variable to ________________ the other, but he cannot say that one variable ________________ the other.
3. When Professor Alphonse plotted his data on a scatter diagram (scatter plot), he noticed that they clustered in a pattern that extends from the upper left of the graph to the lower right. This pattern suggests that the two variables are ________________ correlated.
4. When Kayla analyzed the correlational data for her psychology project, the correlation coefficient was +.07. Kayla can conclude that the two variables ________________ (are/are not) correlated.
5. When researchers analyzed the data from their experiment, they found large differences between the control group and the experimental group that were not due to chance. They can conclude that the results are ________________________________ .
6. To discover how people feel about the level of service provided, ABC Company asks a randomly selected subset of their customers to fill out a brief questionnaire. ABC's customers represent the ________________ , and the subset surveyed is a ________________ .
7. The means of the two groups being studied were different. To increase confidence that this difference was not simply due to chance alone the researchers should use a test called a ________________ .
8. In her research, Dr. Quinn compared the means from four different groups to determine if the observed differences between the means were statistically significant. Dr. Quinn has used an inferential technique called ________________________________ .
9. After the data had been collected and analyzed, the researchers erroneously concluded that the study results were significant, a mistake called a ________________ .
10. Dr. Kaslo was disappointed that the results of his study failed to reach statistical significance, so he replicated the study using a better research design and twice as many participants. Dr. Kaslo has increased the ____________ of the study in an attempt to avoid a ________________ .

Review of Terms and Concepts 2

Use the terms in this list to complete the Matching Exercise, then to help you answer the True/False items correctly.

correlation
correlation coefficient
positive correlation
negative correlation
scatter diagram (scatter plot)
experimental method
inferential statistics
t-test
analysis of variance (ANOVA)
statistically significant
Type I error
Type II error
power
population
sample

Matching Exercise

Match the appropriate term with its definition or description.

1. ________________ Graph that represents the relationship between two variables.
2. ________________ Numerical indication of the magnitude and direction of the relationship (the correlation) between two variables.
3. ________________ Mathematical methods used to determine how likely it is that a study's outcome is due to chance and whether the outcome can be legitimately generalized to a larger population.
4. ________________ A complete set of something —people, nonhuman animals, objects, or events.
5. ________________ The relationship between two variables.
6. ________________ Test used to establish whether the means of two groups are statistically different from each other.
7. ________________ A mistake that occurs when researchers erroneously conclude that the results of the study are significant.
8. ________________ A technique used in inferential statistics to compare the means of more than two groups for statistical significance.

True/False Test

Indicate whether each statement is true or false by placing T or F in the blank space next to each item.

1. ____ Results can be considered statistically significant when the probability of obtaining them, if chance, or random, factors alone are operating, is less than .05 (5 chances out of 100).
2. ____ A positive correlation is a finding that two factors vary systematically in opposite directions, one increasing in size as the other decreases.
3. ____ A sample is a subset of a population.
4. ____ A negative correlation is a finding that two factors vary systematically in the same direction, increasing or decreasing in size together.
5. ____ The experimental method is the only research method that can provide scientific evidence of a cause-and-effect relationship between two or more variables.
6. ____ A Type II error occurs when researchers fail to find a significant effect that does, in fact, exist.
7. ____ Higher *power* can be achieved in a study by improving the research design and measuring instruments, or by increasing the number of participants or subjects being studied.

Check your answers and review any areas of weakness before completing the progress tests.

Progress Test 1

Review the complete appendix, review all your study notes, and then test yourself on the following progress test. Check your answers. If you make a mistake, review your notes, review the relevant section of the study guide, and, if necessary, go back and read the appropriate part of your textbook.

1. Professor Admunson used a scatter diagram to depict the relationship between her students' high school GPA and their first-year grade point average (GPA) in college. She noticed that the data points clustered in a pattern that extends from the lower left corner of the graph to the upper right corner. This pattern suggests that the two variables
   (a) are negatively correlated.
   (b) have no relationship.
   (c) are positively correlated.
   (d) have a cause-and-effect relationship.

2. A measure of variability is to ________________ as a measure of central tendency is to ________________ .
   (a) mode; median
   (b) correlation; scatter plot
   (c) standard deviation; mean
   (d) histogram; frequency polygon

3. One student in the class got an extremely low score of 10 out of 100 on a test. Which measure of central tendency is most affected by this low score?
   (a) mode
   (b) mean
   (c) median
   (d) range

4. Following the final exam, Professor Farrar calculated a number of statistics and noticed that the standard deviation was extremely small. This indicates that
   (a) the scores on the exam were clustered around the mean and not spread out.
   (b) the distribution was skewed.
   (c) the scores had a great deal of variability and were not clustered around the mean.
   (d) there were very few students in her class.

5. Mrs. Kodiak has seven children aged 3, 5, 8, 9, 12, 15, and 15. The median age of her children is
   (a) 9.
   (b) 15.
   (c) 12.
   (d) 67.

6. Researchers decided that the most appropriate inferential statistic to use in analyzing their data was a technique called analysis of variance (ANOVA). It is very probable that
   (a) the resulting correlation coefficient will be greater than + 1.0.
   (b) they were comparing the means of only two groups.
   (c) the resulting *z* scores for each group will be statistically significant.
   (d) they were comparing the means of more than two groups.

7. For his class presentation, Liam prepared a graph that depicted a frequency distribution with vertical bars that touched each other. Liam has constructed a
   (a) scatter diagram.
   (b) frequency polygon.
   (c) histogram.
   (d) standard deviation.

8. Liam's graph is a symmetrical distribution with an equal number of scores on each side of the graph. It is very likely that the
   (a) mean is larger than the median.
   (b) mode is larger than the mean.
   (c) mean, mode, and median have the same value.
   (d) median is larger than the mode.

9. When researchers calculated the correlation coefficients for two different sets of data, they discovered that set A had a negative correlation of –.85 and set B had a positive correlation of +.62. They can conclude that
   (a) set A has a stronger correlation than set B.
   (b) either a Type I or Type II error has occurred.
   (c) set B has a stronger correlation than set A.
   (d) a calculation error has been made because a correlation coefficient cannot have values between +1.0 and –1.0.

10. Students in a methodology class conducted individual experiments. After completing his statistical analysis, Peter failed to find a significant effect even though a significant effect actually existed. On the other hand, Tanya erroneously concluded that her results were significant. Peter's conclusion reflects a ____________ and Tanya's conclusion reflects a ____________.
   (a) failure to use the correct inferential statistic; failure to use the correct descriptive statistic
   (b) Type II error; Type I error
   (c) failure to replicate his findings; lack of power in her study
   (d) Type I error; Type II error

Progress Test 2

After you have checked your understanding of the material in Progress Test 1 and have done a complete appendix review with special focus on any areas of weakness, you are ready to assess your knowledge on Progress Test 2. Check your answers. If you make a mistake, review your notes, the relevant section of the study guide, and, if necessary, the appropriate part of your textbook.

1. In addition to calculating the range, Matthew also calculated the standard deviation for his frequency distribution of scores. Matthew is using
   (a) measures of variability.
   (b) inferential statistics.
   (c) measures of central tendency.
   (d) correlational statistics.

2. When Professor Kitahara finished marking the final exams, he plotted the results on a graph by marking the frequency above each score category on the horizontal axis and then connecting the marks using straight lines. Professor Kitahara has constructed a
   (a) frequency distribution.
   (b) histogram.
   (c) frequency polygon.
   (d) scatter diagram.

3. Professor Kitahara observed that the graph was a symmetrical distribution that resembled a bell-shaped curve and that the mean, median, and mode were all equal. A student who scored better than 84 percent of the other students in this distribution would have a *z* score of
   (a) +1.
   (b) –1.
   (c) +.84.
   (d) –.84.

4. Hanna has a grade point average of 3.5. Which measure of central tendency was used to calculate this statistic?
   (a) median
   (b) standard deviation
   (c) mode
   (d) mean

5. In her research, Dr. Simiak found that the more credit cards people have, the less money they have in their savings accounts. Dr. Simiak has found a ________________ correlation between the number of credit cards owned and savings.
   (a) positive
   (b) zero
   (c) negative
   (d) skewed

6. Range is to mode as ________________ is to ________________.
   (a) correlation; scatter diagram
   (b) median; mode
   (c) correlation coefficient; *z* score
   (d) variability; central tendency

7. In comparing two frequency distributions, Fydor noticed that in the first distribution most people had low scores and in the second distribution most people had high scores. The first distribution is ________________, and the second distribution is ________________.
   (a) positively skewed; negatively skewed
   (b) symmetrical; normal
   (c) negatively skewed; positively skewed
   (d) a polygon; a histogram

8. When Tyborg calculated the mean and standard deviation for a set of scores, he found that the mean was 55 out of 100, and the standard deviation was 15. If the scores are normally distributed, Tyborg can conclude that approximately 68 percent of the scores are between
   (a) 40 and 70.
   (b) 25 and 85.
   (c) 55 and 70.
   (d) 40 and 55.

9. Dr. Hadley found a difference in the means between his experimental group and control group. He then used a *t*-test to establish whether the difference was statistically significant. Dr. Hadley is using
   (a) descriptive statistics.
   (b) inferential statistics
   (c) correlational statistics.
   (d) the analysis of variance (ANOVA) technique.

10. During the past month Karianne read 8 books, Kyle read 2 books, Phyllis read 4 books, and Philip read 6 books. The mean number of books read by this group is
   (a) 5.
   (b) 20.
   (c) 8.
   (d) 6.

Progress Test 3

After you have checked your understanding of the material in Progress Tests 1 and 2, and have done a complete review with special focus on any areas of weakness, you are ready to further assess your knowledge with Progress Test 3. Check your answers. If you make a mistake, review your notes, the appropriate parts of the study guide, and, if necessary, the relevant sections of your textbook.

1. A complete set of something (people, objects, events, etc.) is to a ________________ as a representative subset is to a ________________ .
   (a) descriptive statistics; inferential statistics
   (b) sample; population
   (c) inferential statistics; descriptive statistics
   (d) population; sample

2. Dr. Soryun carried out the appropriate calculations on her data and noticed that results were more extreme than would be expected by chance. She concluded that the probability of obtaining these results if random factors alone were operating was less than 1 chance out of 100. Dr. Soryun has used ________ statistics, and the results can be called ____________ .
   (a) descriptive statistics; statistically significant
   (b) inferential statistics; positively skewed
   (c) descriptive statistics; positively skewed
   (d) inferential statistics; statistically significant

3. Organizing and summarizing data is to ________________ as making inferences and drawing conclusions is to ________________ .
   (a) descriptive statistics; inferential statistics
   (b) correlational research; experimental research
   (c) inferential statistics; descriptive statistics
   (d) experimental research; correlational research

4. Researchers at State University are interested in determining the extent to which personality variables such as impatience, aggressiveness, and hostility could be used to predict the risk of cardiovascular disease. These researchers are most likely to use ________________ in their research.
   (a) a measure of variability
   (b) the correlation coefficient
   (c) the standard normal distribution
   (d) the standard deviation

5. After analyzing his data, Jamie decided to depict his results in a graph. He noticed that the data points clustered in a pattern that extended from the upper left to the lower right on his graph. Jamie has constructed a ________________ that shows a ________________ .
   (a) polygon; skewed distribution
   (b) scatter diagram; positive correlation
   (c) histogram; symmetrical distribution
   (d) scatter diagram; negative correlation

6. Unfortunately for Yvette, her colleagues discovered that she had made a Type II error in her research project. This means that
   (a) she failed to find a significant effect that did, in fact, exist.
   (b) her correlation coefficient exceeded 1.0.
   (c) she erroneously concluded that her study results were significant.
   (d) she used a *t*-test instead of the more appropriate analysis of variance (ANOVA).

7. When Harpinder plotted his data, his graph closely resembled the normal curve and had a mean of 50 and a standard deviation of 5. Harpinder can be confident that approximately 68 percent of the scores are between
   (a) +1 and –1 SDs.
   (b) +2 and –2 SDs.
   (c) +3 and –3 SDs.
   (d) correlation coefficients of +1.00 and –1.00.

8. Raphael's *z*-score on the midterm was +1. If the class scores are normally distributed, Raphael has
   (a) scored better than 34.13 percent of the class.
   (b) scored worse than 34.13 percent of the class.
   (c) scored better than 84 percent of the class.
   (d) scored worse than 84 percent of the class.

9. When Professor Exman compared the statistics from her two introductory biology classes, she noticed that the standard deviation was 8.24 in class A and 3.76 in class B. She can conclude that
   (a) the students in class A studied much harder than those in class B.
   (b) the scores in class A had much more variability than those in class B.
   (c) the range for both classes is likely to be identical.
   (d) one very extreme score probably distorted the standard deviation for class A.

10. As a first step in analyzing her data, Tracianne calculated the mean, the mode, and the median. Tracianne has
   (a) used inferential statistics.
   (b) determined the statistical significance of her results.
   (c) used descriptive statistics.
   (d) calculated measures of variability.

Answers

Descriptive Statistics

1. *Descriptive statistics are mathematical methods used to* organize and summarize data.
2. *A frequency distribution is* a summary of how often various scores occur in a sample of scores. Score values are arranged in order of magnitude, and the number of times each score occurs is recorded.
3. *A histogram is* a way of graphically representing a frequency distribution. It is like a bar chart with two special features: the bars are always vertical, and they always touch.
4. *A frequency polygon is* another way of graphically representing a frequency distribution. In contrast to a histogram, a frequency polygon involves a mark above each category at the point representing its frequency; these marks are then connected by straight lines.
5. *A skewed distribution is* an asymmetrical distribution with more scores piled up on one side of the distribution than on the other. *If most people have low scores,* the distribution is positively skewed. *If most people have high scores,* the distribution is negatively skewed.
6. *A symmetrical distribution is* a distribution in which scores fall equally on both halves of the graph (an example of a symmetrical distribution is the normal curve).
7. *Measures of central tendency are* single numbers that present some information about the "center" of a frequency distribution. *The mode is* the score or category that occurs most frequently in a set of raw scores or in a frequency distribution. *The median is* the score that divides a frequency distribution exactly in half, so that the same number of scores lie on each side of it. *The mean is* the sum of a set of scores in a distribution divided by the number of scores; it is usually the most representative measure of central tendency.
8. *Measures of variability are* single numbers that present information about the spread of scores in a distribution. *The range is* the highest score in a distribution minus the lowest score. *The standard deviation is* expressed as the square root of the sum of the squared deviations around the mean divided by the number of scores in the distribution.
9. *A* z *score is* a number, expressed in standard deviation units, that shows a score's deviation from the mean.
10. *The standard normal curve (standard normal distribution) is* a symmetrical distribution forming a bell-shaped curve in which the mean, median, and mode are all equal and fall in the exact middle. *A person with a* z *score of +1 on a normal distribution (1 SD above the mean) has* scored better than 84 percent of the other people in the distribution (34.13 percent between 0 and +1, plus the 50 percent that falls below 0). *A person's* z *score can tell us* exactly where the person stands relative to everyone else in the distribution.

Concept Check 1

1. measures of central tendency
2. mode
3. variability; range
4. variability; standard deviation
5. frequency polygon

Matching Exercise 1

1. *z* score
2. descriptive statistics
3. standard normal curve (standard normal distribution)
4. frequency distribution
5. standard deviation
6. skewed distribution
7. measure of variability
8. symmetrical distribution
9. range

True/False Test 1

1. F	4. F	7. F
2. T	5. F	8. T
3. T	6. T	9. T

Correlation and Inferential Statistics

1. *Correlation is the* relationship between two variables; it does not indicate causality between the two variables.
2. *The correlation coefficient is a numerical indication of* the magnitude and direction of the relationship (the correlation) between two variables.
3. *A positive correlation is a finding that* two factors vary systematically in the same direction, increasing or decreasing in size together.
4. *A negative correlation is a finding that* two factors vary systematically in opposite directions, one increasing in size as the other decreases.
5. *A correlation coefficient close to 1.00 (whether positive or negative) indicates* a strong relationship, *while a number close to zero indicates* a weak relationship.
6. *Correlations are depicted graphically* on a scatter diagram (scatter plot), which is a graph that represents the relationship between two variables. *A positive correlation is indicated by* the upward-sloping pattern of dots, from lower left to upper right (when one variable is high, the other also tends to be high, and vice versa). *A negative correlation is indicated by* the downward-sloping pattern of dots, from upper left to lower right (when one variable is high, the other tends to be low, and vice versa).
7. *Inferential statistics are* mathematical methods used to determine how likely it is that a study's outcome is due to chance and whether the outcome can be legitimately generalized to a larger population.
8. *A* t*-test is used to* establish whether the means of two groups are statistically different from each other. *Analysis of variance (ANOVA) is used to* compare the means of more than two groups for statistical significance.
9. *Statistical significance refers to the fact that if the results of a study are* more extreme than would be expected by chance alone, we reject the idea that no real effect has occurred and conclude that the manipulation of the independent variable is the reason for the obtained results. When this happens, the results are statistically significant, and the probability of getting these results, if random factors alone are operating, is less than .05 (5 chances in 100) or .01 (1 chance in 100).
10. *A Type I error occurs when* researchers erroneously conclude that the results of the study are significant. *A Type II error occurs when* they fail to find a significant effect that does, in fact, exist. *Because of the possibility of a Type I error, it is important that* the study be repeated, or replicated. If the same results are found, it can be assumed that a Type I error was not likely to have occurred, and we can have more confidence that the results were, in fact, statistically significant. *One way to avoid a Type II error is to* increase the power of a study by improving the research design and measuring instruments, or by increasing the number of participants or subjects in the study.
11. *A population is* a complete set of something—people, nonhuman animals, objects, or events. *Because the entire population of interest usually cannot be studied, researchers use* a sample, which is a subset of a population.

Concept Check 2

1. positive
2. predict; causes
3. negatively
4. are not

5. statistically significant
6. population; sample
7. t-test
8. analysis of variance (ANOVA)
9. Type I error
10. power; Type II error

Matching Exercise 2

1. scatter diagram (scatter plot)
2. correlation coefficient
3. inferential statistics
4. population
5. correlation
6. t-test
7. Type I error
8. analysis of variance (ANOVA)

True/False Test 2

1. T
2. F
3. T
4. F
5. T
6. T
7. T

Progress Test 1

1. c
2. c
3. b
4. a
5. a
6. d
7. c
8. c
9. a
10. b

Progress Test 2

1. a
2. c
3. a
4. d
5. c
6. d
7. a
8. a
9. b
10. a

Progress Test 3

1. d
2. d
3. a
4. b
5. d
6. a
7. a
8. c
9. b
10. c

Industrial/Organizational Psychology

PREVIEW

Reading the section below first will give you a general sense of the appendix's contents and an initial introduction to some of the major concepts and terms. This will prime you for what you are about to read and help you to develop a "cognitive map" that will guide your study of the material in this appendix. Likewise, reading the **preview questions** at the beginning of each major section will improve your ability to understand, learn, and retain the information.

APPENDIX B . . . AT A GLANCE

Appendix B first identifies and briefly describes the nine content areas of industrial/organizational (I/O) psychology. Next, a brief history of I/O psychology is provided, and the two main specialty areas of I/O are identified and explored in depth. Personnel psychology is the "I," or industrial, side of I/O psychology and organizational behavior is the "O," or organizational, side of I/O psychology.

Job analysis, personnel selection, effective job training programs, and accurate evaluation of job performance are all part of the work carried out in personnel psychology. Personnel psychologists use many devices to help with the goal of selecting the best applicants for jobs and are concerned with the validity of these selection devices.

The discussion of organizational behavior begins with the topic of job satisfaction. Researchers have tried to explain different levels of job satisfaction by using the discrepancy hypothesis, which focuses on gaps between what a person wants from a job and what he or she actually experiences. A number of approaches used to explain leader effectiveness are explored, including the trait, the behavioral, and the situational, or contingency, theories of leader effectiveness. Blake and Mouton's Managerial Grid identifies five different leadership styles. The leader–member exchange model examines how supervisors and subordinates interact and identifies two types of relationships that can develop (positive leader–member and negative leader–member). A discussion of narcissistic leaders and servant leaders is included in this section. Finally, workplace trends and issues within I/O psychology are presented, and for those interested in pursuing a career in I/O psychology, information on work settings, type of training, earnings, and employment outlook is provided.

What Is Industrial/Organizational Psychology?

Preview Questions

Consider the following questions as you study this section of the appendix.

- What is industrial/organizational psychology?
- What are the nine content areas of industrial/organizational psychology, and what is the focus of each?
- What two psychologists played a role in the development of I/O psychology, and what were their contributions?

*Read the section "What Is Industrial / Organizational Psychology?" and **write** your answers to the following:*

1. Industrial/organizational psychology is ______________________________

   ____

   The "I" side of I/O psychology is called ______________________________ and is concerned with ______________________________

   ____

   It helps companies ______________________________

   ____

   The "O" side of I/O psychology is called ______________________________ and is concerned with ______________________________

   ____

   It helps companies ______________________________

   ____

2. The nine content areas of I/O psychology (and the focus of each) are

   (a) ______________________________

   (b) ______________________________

   (c) ______________________________

   (d) ______________________________

   (e) ______________________________

   (f) ______________________________

   (g) ______________________________

   (h) ______________________________

   (i) ______________________________

3. Wundt's first research assistant was ______________________________, and his contributions to I/O psychology were ______________________________

   ____

   Another one of Wundt's students was ______________________________, and he is considered by many to be ______________________________

   ____

   His book, ______________________________

   ____

Industrial (Personnel) Psychology

Preview Questions

Consider the following questions as you study this section of the appendix.

- What are the three major goals of personnel psychology?
- What is job analysis, and how is it important for designing training programs and performance appraisal systems?
- What is selection device validity?
- What are the most common types of psychological tests and personnel selection devices used in personnel psychology?

*Read the section "Industrial (Personnel) Psychology" and **write** your answers to the following:*

1. The three major goals of personnel psychologists are
(a) ______
(b) ______
(c) ______
2. Job analysis is a technique in which ______
______
______
It is also important for designing ______
______
______
Finally, job analysis is useful in designing ______
______
______
3. Selection device validity refers to ______
______
______
4. The six most common psychological tests are
(a) ______
(b) ______
(c) ______
(d) ______
(e) ______
(f) ______
Assessment of abnormal personality characteristics might be appropriate for ______
______
More common for the selection of employees are
______
______
5. Two other types of personnel selection devices are
(a) work samples, which are typically used for
______
______
(b) situational exercises, which are typically used for ______
______
6. Unstructured selection interviews are
______
Structured behavioral interviews are
______
The structured behavioral interview should be based on ______
______
______

Organizational Behavior

Preview Questions

Consider the following questions as you study these sections of the appendix.

- What is the focus of organizational behavior (OB)?
- How is the *discrepancy hypothesis* defined, what three ideas does it consist of, and what other factors have been identified as contributing to job satisfaction?
- What is leadership, and how do the trait, behavioral, and situational (or contingency) theories explain leader effectiveness?
- What is the Blake and Mouton Managerial Grid, and what five leadership styles does it identify?
- What is the leader–member exchange model and what are the consequences of positive versus negative leader–member relationships?
- What other topics are the focus of recent leadership research?

*Read the section "Organizational Behavior" and **write** your answers to the following:*

1. Organizational behavior focuses on ______
______
______
2. The discrepancy hypothesis consists of three ideas:
(a) ______
______
(b) ______
______
(c) ______
______

3. Other factors that have been identified as contributing to job satisfaction are ______________

4. The trait approach to leader effectiveness is based on ______________

5. Behavioral theories of leader effectiveness focus on ______________

   Blake and Mouton's Managerial Grid has two dimensions: ______________

   This grid identifies five different leadership styles:
   (a) ______________
   (b) ______________
   (c) ______________
   (d) ______________
   (e) ______________

6. Situational (contingency) theories of leader effectiveness focus on ______________

7. The leader–member exchange model of leadership suggests ______________

   Positive leader–member relationships are characterized by ______________

   They have many benefits, including ______________

   Negative leader–member relationships show ______________

   They lead to ______________

8. More recently, leadership research has focused on topics such as ______________

Workplace Trends and Issues

Preview Questions

Consider the following questions as you study this section of the appendix.

- What are the six major challenges that companies face, and what does the workforce of the future need to focus on?
- How are companies addressing four of these issues?
- What role will I/O psychologists play in the future?

Read the section "Workplace Trends and Issues" and ***write*** *your answers to the following:*

1. The Society for Human Resource Management (SHRM, 2007) has identified six challenges facing companies today:
   (a) ______________
   (b) ______________
   (c) ______________
   (d) ______________
   (e) ______________
   (f) ______________

2. To face these challenges, the workplace of the future is expected to become ______________

3. The four challenges discussed in detail (and how they are being met) are
   (a) ______________

(b) ______________________________
____
____

(c) ______________________________
____
____

(d) ______________________________
____
____

4. In the future, I/O psychologists will ______
____
____

Employment Settings, Type of Training, Earnings, and Employment Outlook

Preview Questions

Consider the following questions as you study this section of the appendix.

- What are the requirements for working in the field of I/O psychology, and what are the principal employment settings of I/O psychologists?
- What jobs and careers are open to people with bachelor's degrees, and what are the earnings potential for those with master's and doctorate degrees?

*Read the section "Work Settings, Type of Training, Earnings, and Employment Outlook" and **write** your answers to the following:*

1. The principal employment settings for I/O psychologists are ______________
   (a) ______________________________
   (b) ______________________________
   (c) ______________________________
   (d) ______________________________
2. To work in the field of I/O psychology requires
   ____
   ____
   ____
   ____
3. In terms of qualifications, the majority of SIOP (Society for Industrial and Organizational Psychologists) members hold ______________
   ____
4. To obtain a doctorate degree requires ______
   ____
   ____

   It qualifies you for ______________
   ____
   ____
5. Most master's degree programs require______
   ____

   A master's degree qualifies you to ______
   ____
   ____
   ____
6. People with bachelor's degrees may find work as ______________________________
   ____
   ____
7. The 2006 SIOP survey indicated that the median salary for I/O psychologists with doctorate degrees was ______________ ; for those with master's degrees the median salary was ______________ .

After you have carefully studied the preceding sections, complete the following exercises.

Concept Check

Read the following and write the correct term in the space provided.

1. Dr. Lomburg works in an area of industrial/organizational psychology that is primarily concerned with the "I" side of I/O. This side of I/O psychology is often called ______________ .
2. Rather than focusing on the impact of leaders on followers, Dr. Hagan's research is concerned with the interaction between supervisors and subordinates and in particular with the unique relationships between leaders and their followers. Dr. Hagan is interested in the ______________ of leader effectiveness.

3. Gertrude has just graduated with a Ph.D. in I/O psychology and is seeking employment. According to text Figure B.5 (Work Settings of I/O Psychologists), if she is like most I/O psychologists, she will work ________________ .
4. When Laleet applied for a job as a mechanic, he was given a test in which he had to take apart the car's gearbox and locate and fix an engine problem. Laleet was given a ________________ personnel selection test.
5. The management style of Snape Corporation was assessed by an independent I/O psychology consulting firm. The report indicated that the company leaders were low on both the x and y dimensions of the Managerial Grid (1,1). The management style of Snape Corporation would therefore be ________________ .
6. Ursula's job at ABC Company is to determine the duties of particular positions and the personal characteristics that best match those duties. As part of her job, she interviews employees, observes them at work, and asks them to complete surveys regarding major job duties and tasks. Ursula is most likely employed as a ________________ .
7. While studying the history of I/O psychology, Pete discovered that ________________ is considered by many to be the founding father of I/O psychology and that his book, *Psychology of Industrial Efficiency* (1913), was the field's first textbook.
8. To deal with some of the challenges facing companies today, Extra Dimension Electronics Company hired an industrial/organizational psychologist. One aspect of his job is to focus on factors that contribute to a productive and healthy workforce such as perk-packages and employee-centered policies. This content area of I/O psychology is called ________________ .
9. In his consulting practice, Dr. Moreno specializes in finding the most appropriate candidates for sensitive jobs, such as nuclear plant operators and airline pilots. The selection device most likely to be used for this purpose is a ________________ test, which is designed to measure ________________ .
10. Dr. Harrison is an I/O psychologist who conducts research on job satisfaction. He believes that job satisfaction results from the difference between what a person desires from a job and how that person evaluates what is actually experienced. Dr. Harrison's view of job satisfaction is most consistent with the ________________________ .

Review of Terms and Concepts

Use the terms in this list to complete the Matching Exercise, then to help you answer the True/False items correctly.

industrial/organizational (I/O) psychology
personnel psychology
organizational behavior
job analysis
selection and placement
training and development
performance management and evaluation
organizational development
leadership development
team building
quality of work life
ergonomics
selection device validity
integrity tests
cognitive ability tests
mechanical ability tests
motor ability tests
sensory ability tests
personality tests
structured behavioral interviews
discrepancy hypothesis
trait approach to leader effectiveness
behavioral theories of leader effectiveness
situational (contingency) theories of leadership
leader–member exchange model
work–life balance (work–family conflict)

Matching Exercise

Match the appropriate term with its definition or description.

1. ________________ Technique that identifies the major responsibilities of a job and the human characteristics needed to fill it.

2. ________________ Content area of I/O psychology that focuses on bringing about positive change in an organization, through the assessment of the organizational social environment and culture.
3. ________________ Model of leadership emphasizing that the quality of the interactions between supervisors and subordinates varies depending on the unique characteristics of both.
4. ________________ Branch of psychology that focuses on the study of human behavior in the workplace.
5. ________________ Leadership theories claiming that various situational factors influence a leader's effectiveness.
6. ________________ Approach to explaining job satisfaction that focuses on the discrepancy, if any, between what a person wants from a job and how that person evaluates what is actually experienced at work.
7. ________________ Tests that measure fine dexterity in fingers and hands, accuracy and speed of arm and hand movement, as well as eye–hand coordination.
8. ________________ Content area of I/O psychology that strives to identify the traits, behaviors, and skills that great leaders have in common.
9. ________________ Tests that measure visual acuity, color vision, and hearing.
10. ________________ Content area of I/O psychology that focuses on the development of assessment techniques to help select job applicants most likely to be successful in a given job or organization.
11. ________________ Tests that measure mechanical reasoning and that may be used to predict job performance for engineering, carpentry, and assembly work.
12. ________________ Content area of I/O psychology that focuses on designing customized training programs and evaluating the effectiveness of these programs.
13. ________________ Content area of I/O psychology that is concerned with ways to improve companies' performance evaluation systems; it includes teaching managers how to collect evaluation data, how to avoid evaluation errors, and how to communicate the results.

True/False Test

Indicate whether each statement is true or false by placing T or F in the blank space next to each item.

1. ____ Personality tests are designed to measure either abnormal or normal personality traits and characteristics.
2. ____ Personnel psychology is a subarea of I/O psychology that focuses on the workplace culture and its influence on employee behavior.
3. ____ Behavioral theories of leader effectiveness focus on differences in the behaviors of effective and ineffective leaders.
4. ____ Ergonomics is a content area of I/O psychology that focuses on the design of equipment and the development of work procedures in accordance with human capabilities and limitations.
5. ____ Selection device validity is the extent to which a personnel selection device is successful in distinguishing between those who will become high performers at a certain job and those who will not.
6. ____ Quality of work life, one content area of I/O psychology, focuses on factors that contribute to a productive and healthy workforce, such as perk packages and employee-centered policies.
7. ____ An approach to determining what makes an effective leader that focuses on the personal characteristics displayed by successful leaders is called the trait approach to leader effectiveness.
8. ____ Organizational behavior is a subarea of I/O psychology that focuses on matching people's characteristics to job requirements, accurately measuring job performance, and assessing employee training needs.
9. ____ Work–life balance is a challenge facing companies today and refers to the struggle of trying to juggle the demands of a career with the demands of one's family (also called work–family conflict).
10. ____ Team building is a content area of I/O psychology that focuses on team membership and successful team design.
11. ____ Integrity tests attempt to assess an applicant's level of honesty.

12. ____ Cognitive ability tests measure general intelligence or specific cognitive skills, such as mathematical or verbal ability.

13. ____ The structured behavioral interview is based on job analysis, prepared in advance, standardized for all applicants, and evaluated by a panel of interviewers trained to record and rate the applicant's responses using a numeric scale.

Check your answers and review any areas of weakness before completing the progress tests.

Progress Test 1

Review the complete appendix, review all your study notes, and then test yourself on the following progress test. Check your answers. If you make a mistake, review your notes, review the relevant section of the study guide, and, if necessary, go back and read the appropriate part of your textbook.

1. Dr. Garcia is an I/O psychologist who is concerned with developing assessment techniques to help select from a pool of job applicants those who are most likely to be successful in a given job or organization. Dr. Darton, on the other hand, focuses on identifying criteria or standards that determine the degree to which employees are performing their jobs well, accurately measuring their job performance, and honestly conveying performance results to these employees. Dr. Garcia works in the content area called ________________ , and Dr. Darton works in ________________ .
   (a) training and development; quality of work life
   (b) selection and placement; performance management and evaluation
   (c) ergonomics; organizational development
   (d) performance management and evaluation; ergonomics

2. Dr. Foggerty focuses on the design of equipment and the development of work procedures in accordance with human capabilities and limitations. Dr. Foggerty's area of interest is called
   (a) ergonomics.
   (b) personnel psychology.
   (c) performance management and evaluation.
   (d) organizational behavior.

3. When Kamala goes to graduate school, she plans to specialize in matching people's characteristics to job requirements, accurately measuring job performance, and assessing employee training needs. Kamala is interested in
   (a) personnel psychology.
   (b) organizational psychology.
   (c) organizational development.
   (d) ergonomics.

4. Helmut has a bachelor's degree and is interested in working in the field of I/O psychology. Which of the following statements about Helmut's prospects is true?
   (a) It will be very easy for him to find employment as an I/O psychologist, either at a university or as a consultant.
   (b) Some areas related to I/O, such as personnel, training, and labor relations specialists, are open to him.
   (c) There are no employment opportunities for people with bachelor's degrees in the field of I/O psychology.
   (d) His earning potential for work within the field of I/O psychology is $72,000 to $98,000.

5. Olivia's research focuses on how the organization and the social environment in which people work affect their attitudes and behaviors. Olivia works in a subarea of I/O psychology called
   (a) personnel psychology.
   (b) selection and placement.
   (c) ergonomics.
   (d) organizational behavior.

6. Gulbinder is the chief personnel officer for a large corporation. She is very concerned that the methods and techniques used in personnel selection are successful in distinguishing between applicants who will become high performers and those who will not. Gulbinder's concerns are related to
   (a) quality of work life.
   (b) ergonomics.
   (c) selection device validity.
   (d) organizational development.

7. Bradford believes that leaders are born, not made, and he cites many examples of people who possess certain qualities or characteristics that make them natural leaders. Bradford's views are most consistent with the
   (a) situational (or contingency) theories of leader effectiveness.
   (b) behavioral theories of leader effectiveness.
   (c) leader–member exchange model of leadership.
   (d) trait approach to leader effectiveness.

8. Surveys have shown that although most Americans report that they are satisfied with their jobs, they appear less satisfied with some aspects than with others. To explain differences in job satisfaction, researchers are likely to use an approach based on the
   (a) managerial grid concept of job satisfaction.
   (b) behavioral theory of job satisfaction.
   (c) contingency hypothesis of job satisfaction
   (d) discrepancy hypothesis of job satisfaction.

9. Mrs. Afyia's task is to determine the major responsibilities of a job and the personal characteristics needed to fill it. Her goal is to select appropriate people for a particular position. Mrs. Afyia's task is concerned with
   (a) ergonomics.
   (b) job analysis.
   (c) selection device validity.
   (d) the managerial grid approach.

10. In Focus (Servant Leadership: When It's Not All About You) notes that some leaders take an employee-centered approach. They recognize and encourage emerging employee leaders and create organizational support for them to reach their potential. According to In Focus, this style of leadership exemplifies the ________ leader.
   (a) servant
   (b) team
   (c) transactional
   (d) charismatic

Progress Test 2

After you have checked your understanding of the material in Progress Test 1 and have done a complete appendix review with special focus on any areas of weakness, you are ready to assess your knowledge on Progress Test 2. Check your answers. If you make a mistake, review your notes, the relevant section of the study guide, and, if necessary, the appropriate part of your textbook.

1. Dr. Daviduk has just completed a report identifying major workplace trends and issues and how the challenges identified by the Society for Human Resource Management (SHRM, 2007) are being met. Which of the following is NOT likely to appear in her report?
   (a) telecommuting or telework and Internet recruiting
   (b) the issue of selection device validity
   (c) workforce diversity
   (d) the issue of work–life balance

2. Before building their new factory, XYZ Manufacturing Company hired an I/O psychologist to help in the design of new equipment, work procedures, and safety standards. This consultant is involved in which content area of I/O psychology?
   (a) quality of work life
   (b) ergonomics
   (c) organizational development
   (d) performance management and evaluation

3. In his research on leader effectiveness, Dr. Grether focuses on differences in the actions of effective and ineffective leaders. Dr. Grether's work is most consistent with the ________________ of leader effectiveness.
   (a) trait theories
   (b) behavioral theories
   (c) situational theories
   (d) leader–member exchange model

4. Lance wants to become an I/O psychologist but he is not sure what the future holds for this profession. Research on this topic is likely to reveal that
   (a) I/O psychologists will continue to have a significant impact on the workplace.
   (b) most I/O psychologists will become redundant in the near future due to technological advances.
   (c) increased diversity of the workforce, technological advances, and a global economy will mean a gradual decline in the need for I/O psychologists.
   (d) it will be extremely difficult for people with bachelor's degrees to find employment in the field of I/O psychology.

5. Mr. Wentworth wants to bring about positive change in his organization through assessment of the organizational social environment and culture. The content area of I/O psychology most concerned with this issue is
   (a) personnel psychology.
   (b) ergonomics.
   (c) organizational development.
   (d) performance management and evaluation.

6. Gladys believes that job satisfaction results from the difference between what a person wants from a job and how that person evaluates what is experienced. Gladys's view supports the hypothesis of job satisfaction.
   (a) trait
   (b) behavioral
   (c) discrepancy
   (d) contingency

7. At a party, Justina was asked what she does for a living. She replied that she focuses on the study of human behavior in the workforce. Justina is most likely a(n)
   (a) behavioral psychologist.
   (b) social psychologist.
   (c) industrial/organizational psychologist.
   (d) clinical psychologist.

8. When asked to elaborate on the type of work she does as an I/O psychologist, Stacey said that she is primarily interested in research on factors that contribute to a productive and healthy workforce, such as perk packages and employee-centered policies. Stacey works in the content area of I/O psychology called
   (a) quality of work life.
   (b) training and development.
   (c) selection and placement.
   (d) performance management and evaluation.

9. In her work, Dr. Tahler uses a variety of psychological tests that measure cognitive ability, mechanical aptitude, motor and sensory ability, and normal and abnormal personality traits. It is most likely that Dr. Tahler is a(n)
   (a) behavioral psychologist.
   (b) personnel psychologist.
   (c) organizational psychologist.
   (d) ergonomics psychologist.

10. In Focus (Name, Title, Generation) discusses the way different generations of workers respond to feedback. Which one of the following people is most likely to respond to the issue of feedback with the statement "Once a year, with lots of documentation"?
   (a) Kerri who was born in 1985
   (b) Dwayne who was born in 1950
   (c) Polly who was born in 1944
   (d) Quentin who was born in 1970

Progress Test 3

After you have checked your understanding of the material in Progress Tests 1 and 2, and have done a complete review with special focus on any areas of weakness, you are ready to further assess your knowledge with Progress Test 3. Check your answers. If you make a mistake, review your notes, the appropriate parts of the study guide, and, if necessary, the relevant sections of your textbook.

1. The employees of a small but very successful company are committed people with a "common stake" in the company's goals. The owner, Harvey, encourages interdependence and is well respected and trusted by those who work for him. According to Blake and Mouton's managerial grid concept, which of the following leadership styles best describes Harvey?
   (a) country-club management
   (b) impoverished management
   (c) team management
   (d) organization man management

2. Researchers interested in leader effectiveness believe that the quality of the interactions among supervisors and subordinates varies depending on the unique characteristics of both. Their approach to the topic of leadership is most consistent with
   (a) the trait approach to leader effectiveness.
   (b) the leader–member exchange model.
   (c) the behavioral theories of leader effectiveness.
   (d) the situational (contingency) theories of leadership.

3. Gregory believes that a leader's effectiveness most likely results from a particular combination of personality characteristics, rather than from situational factors. Gregory's views are most consistent with ______________ theories of leader effectiveness.
   (a) behavioral
   (b) contingency
   (c) team management
   (d) trait

4. Professor Kress focuses on the design of equipment and the development of work procedures in light of human capabilities and limitations. Professor Fergus focuses on bringing about positive change in organizations through the assessment of the organizational social environment and culture. Professor Kress works in an area of I/O called ________________ , and Professor Fergus works in ________________ .
   (a) ergonomics; organizational development
   (b) training and development; performance management
   (c) organizational development; ergonomics
   (d) performance management and evaluation; selection and placement

5. The personnel psychologist at El Gourdo Corporation uses a number of different psychological tests for employee selection purposes. Which of the following is he NOT likely to use in the selection process?
   (a) personality tests
   (b) cognitive ability tests
   (c) the polygraph test
   (d) mechanical, motor, and sensory ability tests

6. Zander Corporation is concerned about selecting the appropriate person for the job of production manager. Mrs. Juarez, the personnel manager, assesses and records the position's responsibilities and the personal characteristics required by the job. Mrs. Juarez is conducting a(n)
   (a) quality of work analysis.
   (b) job analysis.
   (c) ergonomic analysis.
   (d) discrepancy analysis.

7. In a report for the personnel department of Utopia Corporation, Dr. Raimundo makes recommendations regarding the validity and reliability of the company's various selection devices. Which of the following is Dr. Raimundo likely to suggest has the lowest validity?
   (a) work samples
   (b) unstructured selection interviews
   (c) psychological testing
   (d) situational exercises

8. The job application process as we know it today was influenced by advances in the field of mental testing and, in particular, by the contributions of ________________ , who founded the Psychological Corporation, one of the largest publishers of psychological tests.
   (a) Michael Scott
   (b) Robert Blake and Jane Mouton
   (c) Hugo Münsterberg
   (d) James McKeen Cattell

9. Hannalee is interested in improving the performance evaluation systems in her rapidly expanding company. She would like her managers to learn how to collect evaluation data, to avoid evaluation errors, and to effectively communicate the results. Hannalee should probably consult an I/O psychologist who specializes in a subarea called
   (a) leadership development.
   (b) ergonomics.
   (c) job analysis.
   (d) performance management and evaluation.

10. Mrs. Addersly is considered by most of her employees to be a servant leader. According to In Focus (When It's Not All About You), her most prominent trait is likely to be her
    (a) conscientiousness.
    (b) humility.
    (c) efficiency.
    (d) sense of humor.

Answers

What Is Industrial/Organizational Psychology?

1. *Industrial/organizational psychology is* the branch of psychology that focuses on the study of human behavior in the workplace. *The "I" side of I/O psychology is called* personnel psychology *and is concerned with* matching human characteristics to job requirements, accurately measuring job performance, and assessing employee training needs. *It helps companies* attract, recruit, select, and train the best employees for the organization. *The "O" side of I/O psychology is called* organizational behavior (OB) *and is concerned with* the workplace culture and its influence on employee behavior. *It helps companies* develop a culture that fulfills organizational goals while addressing employee needs and applies psychological findings to areas such as leadership development, team building, motivation, ethics training, and wellness planning.

2. *The nine content areas of I/O psychology (and the focus of each) are (a)* Job analysis, which focuses on matching personal characteristics with the duties of a particular position. *(b)* Selection and placement, which focuses on the development of assessment techniques to help select job applicants most likely to be

successful in a given job or organization. *(c)* Training and development, which focuses on designing and evaluating customized training programs. *(d)* Performance management and evaluation is concerned with ways to improve a company's performance evaluation system. *(e)* Organizational development, whose goal is to bring about positive change in an organization. *(f)* Leadership development, which strives to identify the traits, behaviors, and skills of great leaders. *(g)* Team building, which focuses on team membership and successful team design. *(h)* Quality of work life, which focuses on factors that contribute to a productive and healthy workforce. *(i)* Ergonomics, which focuses on the design of equipment and the development of work procedures based on human capabilities and limitations.

3. *Wundt's first research assistant was* James McKeen Cattell *and his contributions to I/O psychology were* the concept of mental testing, which influenced the job application process as we know it today, and founding the Psychological Corporation, one of the largest publishers of psychological tests. *Another one of Wundt's students was* Hugo Münsterberg, *and he is considered by many to be* the founding father of I/O psychology. *His book, Psychology of Industrial Efficiency* (1913), was the field's first textbook.

Industrial (Personnel) Psychology

1. *The three major goals of personnel psychologists are (a)* selecting the best applicants for jobs, *(b)* training employees so that they perform their jobs effectively, and *(c)* accurately evaluating employee performance.
2. *Job analysis is a technique in which* the major responsibilities of a job, along with the human characteristics needed to fill it, are determined. Information about the job is usually collected from employees who currently hold the job or from their supervisors; this may be done through interviews, observations, or surveys. *It is also important for designing* effective training programs that integrate job analysis data with organizational goals. To maximize success, modern training programs should include collaborative and on-demand delivery methods, such as e-learning, virtual classrooms, and podcasts, and training objectives that are **OK?** linked to performance measures for best results. *Finally, job analysis is useful in designing* performance appraisal systems, in which job competencies are defined and clarified so that performance appraisal instruments can be developed and training results assessed. This process helps managers make their expectations and ratings clear and easier for the employees to understand.
3. *Selection device validity refers to* the extent to which a selection device is successful in distinguishing between those applicants who will become high performers at a certain job and those who will not.
4. *The six most common psychological tests are*
   (a) integrity tests
   (b) cognitive ability tests
   (c) mechanical ability tests
   (d) motor ability tests
   (e) sensory ability tests
   (f) personality tests.
   Assessment of abnormal personality characteristics might be appropriate for selecting people for sensitive jobs, such as nuclear plant operator, police officer, and airline pilot. *More common for the selection of employees* are tests designed to measure the Big Five personality traits.
5. *Two other types of personnel selection devices are (a) work samples, which are typically used for* positions involving the manipulation of objects, and *(b) situational exercises, which are typically used for* jobs involving managerial or professional skills.
6. *Unstructured selection interviews are* subjective, outdated, and non-research based; nevertheless, they continue to be used (40 percent of companies responding to the SHRM survey used them). *Structured behavioral interviews are* adequate predictors of job performance if they are developed and conducted properly. *The structured behavioral interview should be based on* a job analysis, prepared in advance, standardized for all applicants, and evaluated by a panel of interviewers trained to record and rate the applicant's responses using a numeric scale.

Organizational Behavior

1. *Organizational behavior focuses on* how the organization and the social environment in which people work affect their attitudes (especially regarding job satisfaction) and behaviors.
2. *The discrepancy hypothesis consists of three ideas: (a)* that people differ in what they want from a job; *(b)* that people differ in how they evaluate what they experience at work; and *(c)* that job satisfaction is based on the differ-

ence between what is desired and what is experienced.

3. *Other factors that have been identified as contributing to job satisfaction are* compensation, benefits, job security, work–life balance, and communication between employees and senior management.

4. *The trait approach to leader effectiveness is based on* the idea that leaders are born, not made, and focuses on the personal characteristics displayed by successful leaders.

5. *Behavioral theories of leader effectiveness focus on* differences in the behaviors of effective and ineffective leaders. *Blake and Mouton's Managerial Grid has two dimensions:* concern for production (x-axis) and concern for people (y-axis), each having a 1 (low) to 9 (high) scale. *The grid identifies five different leadership styles: (a)* country-club management (1,9), *(b)* impoverished management (1,1), *(c)* team management (9,9), *(d)* authority obedience (9,1), and *(e)* organization man management (5,5).

6. *Situational (contingency) theories of leader effectiveness focus on* how a particular situation influences a leader's effectiveness.

7. *The leader–member exchange model of leadership suggests* that the quality of the interactions between supervisors and subordinates varies depending on the unique characteristics of both. *Positive leader–member relationships are characterized by* mutual trust, respect, and liking. *They have many benefits, including* higher job satisfaction, goal commitment, improved work climate, and lower turnover rates. *Negative leader–member relationships show* a lack of trust, respect, and liking. *They lead to* decreased job satisfaction and job performance, among other consequences.

8. *More recently, leadership research has focused on topics such as* transformational versus transactional leadership, charismatic leadership, shared leadership, and servant leadership.

Workplace Trends and Issues

1. *The Society for Human Resource Management (SHRM, 2007) has identified six challenges facing companies today: (a)* succession planning (replacement of retiring leaders); *(b)* recruitment and selection of talented employees; *(c)* engaging and retaining talented employees *(d)* providing leaders with the skills to be successful; *(e)* rising health care costs; *(f)* creating/maintaining a performance-based culture (rewarding exceptional job performance)

2. *To face these challenges, the workplace of the future is expected to become* more dynamic, diversified, flexible, and responsive, with a need for organizations and employees to adapt to the ever-changing world of work, complete with resource limitations and technological innovations.

3. *The four challenges discussed in detail (and how they are being met) are*
(a) The challenge of workforce diversity (recruiting and retaining diverse talent) has been addressed by creating perk-packages, offering telecommuting, and other benefits, such as compressed workweeks, on-site gyms, job sharing, and on-site child care. *(b)* The challenge of telework and telecommuting is being met by companies offering more telework options to employees (up from 30 percent in 2007 to 42 percent in 2008). Research has shown that telecommuting has predominately positive effects for both employees and employers, including higher job satisfaction, employee morale, autonomy, and improved supervisor/ employee relations. *(c)* Internet recruiting (using the Web to recruit top talent) has changed the way in which employees are recruited: Research has found that 73 percent of job seekers used the Internet to find information about prospective employers, to post resumes on job boards, and to gain career advice. This has posed new challenges for employers, such as compliance with new legal requirements for online applicant tracking, or simply how to narrow down the large number of resume submissions.
(d) The work/life balance (engaging and retaining employees with families) challenge is not been met very successfully; paid maternity leave, paid sick days, alternative work schedules, and other family-friendly polices are lacking in many U.S. companies. More employers must begin to adopt family-friendly policies and build pro-family cultures to attract and retain this large sector of the workforce.

4. *In the future, I/O psychologists will continue* to have a significant role in the workplace. To keep pace with the changing needs of employees and rapid technological advances, I/O psychologists will constantly need to adjust the focus of their research and its applications to improve the experiences of people at work.

Employment Settings, Type of Training, Earnings, and Employment Outlook

1. *The principal employment settings for I/O psychologists are (a)* academic settings, primarily universities and colleges; *(b)* consultants to organizations; (c) private organizations; and *(d)* public organizations.
2. *To work in the field of I/O psychology requires* a master's degree (M.A.) or a doctorate (Ph.D.) (some areas that are closely related to I/O are open to those with bachelor's degrees).
3. *In terms of qualifications, the majority of SIOP (Society for Industrial and Organizational Psychologists) members hold* doctorate degrees (87 percent) as opposed to master's degrees (13 percent).
4. *To obtain a doctorate degree requires* attending graduate school full time for 5 to 6 years, conducting a detailed research project, and writing a dissertation. *It qualifies you for* I/O positions at major corporations, research and teaching positions at universities and colleges, and it provides the most credibility to conduct consulting work.
5. *Most master's degree programs require* 2 to 3 years of graduate coursework and the completion of a research project. *A master's degree qualifies you to* work as an I/O psychologist carrying out I/O duties for private or public organizations, teach at two-year colleges, and take on consulting work.
6. *People with bachelor's degrees may find work as* personnel, training, and labor-relations specialists, and as managers and employment interviewers.
7. *The 2006 SIOP survey indicated that the median salary for I/O psychologists with doctorate degrees was* $98,500; *for those with master's degrees the median salary was* $72,000.

Concept Check 1

1. personnel psychology
2. leader–member exchange model
3. in an academic setting (college or university)
4. work sample
5. impoverished management
6. job analyst
7. Hugo Münsterberg
8. quality of work life
9. personality; either abnormal or normal personality characteristics
10. discrepancy hypothesis

Matching Exercise

1. job analysis
2. organizational development
3. leader–member exchange model
4. industrial/organizational (I/O) psychology
5. situational (or contingency) theories of leader effectiveness
6. discrepancy hypothesis
7. motor ability tests
8. leadership development
9. sensory ability tests
10. selection and placement
11. mechanical ability tests
12. training and development
13. performance management and evaluation

True/False Test

1. T	6. T	11. T
2. F	7. T	12. T
3. T	8. F	13. T
4. T	9. T	
5. T	10. T	

Progress Test 1

1. b	5. d	9. b
2. a	6. c	10. a
3. a	7. d	
4. b	8. d	

Progress Test 2

1. b	5. c	9. b
2. b	6. c	10. b
3. b	7. c	
4. a	8. a	

Progress Test 3

1. c	5. c	9. d
2. b	6. b	10. b
3. d	7. b	
4. a	8. d